I0293000

THE COVENANT OF BAHÁ'U'LLÁH

By the same author

TRUSTEES OF THE MERCIFUL
(Bahá'í Publishing Trust, London, 1972)

THE REVELATION OF BAHÁ'U'LLÁH
1. Baghdád 1853–63
2. Adrianople 1863–68
3. 'Akká, The Early Years 1868–77
4. Mazra'ih and Bahjí 1877–92

Tablet in Bahá'u'lláh's handwriting addressed to 'Abdu'l-Bahá
Translated by Shoghi Effendi as follows:

O Thou Who art the apple of Mine eye! My glory, the ocean of My loving-kindness, the sun of My bounty, the heaven of My mercy rest upon Thee. We pray God to illumine the world through Thy knowledge and wisdom, to ordain for Thee that which will gladden Thine heart and impart consolation to Thine eyes. The glory of God rest upon Thee, and upon whatsoever serveth Thee and circleth around Thee.

THE COVENANT OF BAHÁ'U'LLÁH

by

ADIB TAHERZADEH

GEORGE RONALD
OXFORD

George Ronald, *Publisher*
Oxford
www.grbooks.com

Reprinted 1995, 2000, 2009

British Library Cataloguing in Publication Data

Taherzadeh, Adib
The Covenant of Baha'u'llah
I. Title
297.892

ISBN 978-0-85398-344-6

Contents

List of Illustrations ix
Notes & Acknowledgements x
Foreword xi
Introduction 1
Prologue: The Covenant and the Human Soul 5

PART ONE
THE GREATER COVENANT
'Him Whom God shall make manifest'

1 The Covenant of the Báb 31
2 The Fulfilment of the Covenant of the Báb 52
3 Mírzá Yaḥyá, The Nominee of the Báb 60
4 The Breaking of the Báb's Covenant 65
5 The Triumph of the Covenant of the Báb 89

PART TWO
THE LESSER COVENANT
1. The Ministry of 'Abdu'l-Bahá

6 'Abdu'l-Bahá, the Centre of the Covenant 99
7 The Family of Bahá'u'lláh 111
8 The Arch-breaker of Bahá'u'lláh's Covenant 125
9 The Relationship of Bahá'u'lláh and 'Abdu'l-Bahá 135
10 The Appointment of 'Abdu'l-Bahá 141
11 The Breaking of Bahá'u'lláh's Covenant 148
12 'The Day that Shall Not Be Followed by Night' 155
13 Principal Covenant-breakers during the Ministry of 'Abdu'l'Bahá 164
14 Clandestine Opposition to the Covenant 170

15 Mírzá Áqá Ján 181
16 Discrediting the Centre of the Covenant 193
17 'Abdu'l-Bahá in Action 201
18 Covenant-breaking in Persia 208
19 Building the Shrine of the Báb 223
20 Years of Incarceration 231
21 Covenant-breaking in the West 245
22 The Bahá'í Attitude to Covenant-breaking 253
23 Fostering Steadfastness in the Covenant 261

PART THREE
THE LESSER COVENANT
2. The Formative Age

24 The Close of the Heroic Age 273
25 Shoghi Effendi, Guardian of the Faith 280
26 Building the Foundations of the Administrative Order 292
27 The Expounder of the Revelation of Bahá'u'lláh 307
28 The Administrative Order in Action 314
29 Vital Developments at the World Centre 322
30 Rebellion in the East against the Guardian 332
31 Rebellion in the West 343
32 The Faithless Relatives of Shoghi Effendi 351
33 The Onward March of the Faith 370
34 The Chief Stewards 377
35 The Universal House of Justice 394
36 The Unfoldment of the Covenant 408

Appendices
1 The Will and Testament of 'Abdu'l-Bahá 416
2 Letter from the Hands of the Cause in the Holy Land to all National Spiritual Assemblies, 15 October 1960 429
3 The Guardianship and the Universal House of Justice: Letters from the Universal House of Justice 433

Bibliography 442
References 445
Index 454

LIST OF ILLUSTRATIONS

Frontispiece

Tablet of Bahá'u'lláh in His handwriting, addressed to 'Abdu'l-Bahá

Between pages 252 and 253

'Abdu'l-Bahá, the Centre of the Covenant
'Abdu'l-Bahá as a young man
Bahíyyih Khánum, the Greatest Holy Leaf
'Abdu'l-Bahá and the Purest Branch
Áqáy-i-Kalím, faithful brother of Bahá'u'lláh
Ustád Muḥammad-'Alíy-i-Salmaní
Ḥájí Mírzá Ḥaydar-'Alí
Dr Yunis Khán-i-Afrukhtih
Dr Habíb Mu'ayyad
Ḥáji 'Alí Yazdí
The House of 'Abdu'lláh Páshá
The House of 'Abdu'l-Bahá in Haifa
The Shrine of the Báb built by 'Abdu'l-Bahá
The superstructure of the Shrine of the Báb

Between pages 412 and 413

Shoghi Effendi, Guardian of the Cause of God
The Shrine of Bahá'u'lláh and the Mansion of Bahjí surrounded by the residences of the Covenant-breakers
The Pilgrim House at Bahjí
Views of the Mansion of Bahjí in ruins
The Mansion of Bahjí restored to its original condition
A view of the formal gardens surrounding the Shrine of Bahá'u'lláh
The Shrine of Bahá'u'lláh
The Mansion of Mazra'ih
The International Archives Building
The resting-places of the Purest Branch and Navváb
The Hands of the Cause of God
The resting-place of the Greatest Holy Leaf, with a view of the Seat of the Universal House of Justice

NOTES AND ACKNOWLEDGEMENTS

THE extracts from the Writings of the Báb and Bahá'u'lláh quoted in this book are from the matchless translations by Shoghi Effendi, the Guardian of the Bahá'i Faith, and those carried out under the auspices of the Universal House of Justice. Published sources are acknowledged in the References and Bibliography. There are many other quotations from Persian manuscripts and publications, and these I have translated, unless otherwise indicated. Most quotations had to be edited prior to translation. The footnotes to these quotations, however, are mostly mine, and this is indicated explicitly where confusion may arise. Persian and Arabic names are transliterated in accordance with the system adopted for books on the Bahá'í Faith, but quotations are reproduced in their original form.

I am deeply indebted to the Audio-Visual Department of the Bahá'í World Centre for supplying the photographs printed in this book.

I wish to extend my warmest appreciation to Dr May Hofman Ballerio for her excellent and skilful editorial work on this book. Her advice and expert assistance on many issues have been of great value to me. I am truly indebted to my dear wife Lesley for her selfless and loving support which she has extended to me in the course of my writing this book.

My special grateful thanks to Mr Thomas Howe for reading the manuscript in its early stages and offering valuable suggestions to improve its syntax.

I wish to extend my warmest thanks and gratitude to Miss Carol Clyde, Miss Corinne Logue and Miss Johanna Merritt for their excellent typing of the manuscript from my scribbled and often illegible notes. I am grateful to Dr Wendi Momen for the skilful production of the index and many helpful suggestions.

FOREWORD

THIS book is an attempt to provide some basic material, however limited in scope, for the study of the Covenant of Bahá'u'lláh – the unique and priceless heritage He has bestowed upon His followers. The enormous potentialities latent within so mighty an institution, unprecedented in past Dispensations, will need to be manifested in the course of time stretching far into the future, unfolding thereby the glory and the perfection of Bahá'u'lláh's new world order destined to usher in the Golden Age of His Faith on this planet.

This peerless Covenant revolves around its Centre, 'Abdu'l-Bahá, extolled by Shoghi Effendi as Bahá'u'lláh's 'most exalted handiwork, the stainless Mirror of His light, the perfect Exemplar of His teachings, the unerring Interpreter of His word, the embodiment of every Bahá'í ideal, the incarnation of every Bahá'í virtue, the Most Mighty Branch sprung from the Ancient Root, the Limb of the Law of God, the Being round whom all names revolve, the Mainspring of the Oneness of Humanity, the Ensign of the Most Great Peace, the Moon of the Central Orb of this Most Holy Dispensation'.

The Will and Testament of 'Abdu'l-Bahá, the child of this Covenant, provides its extension through the establishment of the Administrative Order, supported by the two mighty pillars of the Guardianship and the Universal House of Justice and perpetuating into the future the manifold functions with which the author of the Faith has endowed the institutions of His world-embracing order. These include the protection of the revealed Word from human interference, the preservation of the integrity of the Faith and of the purity of its teachings, principles and laws, the safeguarding of the unity of the Bahá'í community, the promotion of an ever-advancing civilization, the provision of means for the spiritualization of the human race, and the development of the necessary agencies needed to establish the Bahá'í World Commonwealth as envisaged in the Holy Writings.

In order to grasp the mysteries of the Covenant, and to apprehend its immeasurable potentialities for the unification of humanity and the establishment of the Kingdom of God on earth, the followers of

Bahá'u'lláh are duty bound to study this important feature of their Faith.

The *Kitáb-i-'Ahd* (The Book of the Covenant) and the *Will and Testament of 'Abdu'l-Bahá*, the two major documents upon which the Covenant of Bahá'u'lláh is based, are quoted in full in this volume; it is the hope of the present author that the study of this book might help the reader to appreciate the significance of their contents as well as details of many historical episodes recorded therein.

This appreciation depends also upon the individual's endeavour to deepen his knowledge of the verities of the Faith of Bahá'u'lláh, and to meditate, in a prayerful attitude, on His Writings and those of 'Abdu'l-Bahá and Shoghi Effendi in order to discover for himself 'the pearls of wisdom' hidden within the ocean of Bahá'u'lláh's Revelation and thereby perceive, to the extent of his capacity, the preponderating role of Bahá'u'lláh's mighty Covenant as well as the mysteries it enshrines.

That this book, however inadequate, may even to a small extent assist those who embrace the Faith of Bahá'u'lláh in the study of His Covenant, is the ardent hope of the present author.

INTRODUCTION

PHYSICAL life in the world around us is governed by the laws of nature. The sun pours its energy upon all living things on this planet, the earth supplies the food, while every creature responds to the dictates of nature. The mineral, vegetable and animal kingdoms are all under its control and cannot deviate a hair's breadth from the course which the Creator has set for them. For instance, the bee is created to make its hive only in the form of a hexagon; it cannot choose to build it in a different form. The fish must live in the water, and the beast inhabit the land. Each living organism and, indeed, the whole universe involuntarily obeys the laws of nature.

Man is the only exception. God has endowed him with two opposite natures, the animal or physical, and the spiritual. Man's physical being is subject to the laws of nature; but his soul, his spiritual nature, is not. The soul emanates from the spiritual worlds of God and cannot be bound by material ties. Because of his spiritual qualities man has been endowed by the Creator with the special faculty of free will, a faculty which is absent in the rest of His creation on earth. Furthermore, God has created man in His own image, meaning that He has conferred all His attributes upon man, attributes that are latent within him.

In order to enable the soul to progress and attain spiritual qualities and so reveal these latent attributes, God has made a Covenant with man and has required him to abide by its provisions. We note therefore that whereas the body of man is bound by the laws of nature, his soul is governed by the laws of the Covenant of God. A covenant is a contract between two sides, each of whom has obligations to fulfil. It follows that a meaningful covenant between God and man must require freedom of choice on both sides, and that man must exercise his free will in choosing his response to his Creator.

The relationship of God with man in this Covenant is somewhat similar to the relationship between the principal of a school and the child. As soon as a child goes to school for the first time, he enters into a covenant with the school principal, although often without really knowing it. In this contract the principal provides the means for the education of the child. He appoints teachers to teach him, draws up the educational programme and ensures the child's well-being and development in every way. The child's part in this covenant is to follow the instructions of the teacher and learn every lesson he is taught. It is through this process that the child acquires knowledge, develops his capacity, and becomes endowed with intellectual and spiritual powers. As the child grows in learning and maturity, the principal will appoint other teachers to contribute to his education. In this covenant, the responsibilities of the two parties are fundamentally different. They cannot be confused and are not interchangeable.

Another feature of this covenant is that the two parties are not of the same calibre. One side, the school principal, is knowledgeable, wise and strong. The other, the child, is unlearned, weak and immature. The terms of this covenant are drawn up entirely by the strong party and the child has no say in them. Usually, the weaker party is the loser when a contract is drawn up solely by the strong. Not so in this case, for the motive of the principal in making all the arrangements is his love for the child and concern for its education. His greatest ambition is to see the child attain wisdom and knowledge. He longs to see his pupil become a mature person.

The same is true of God. He is the Creator, the Almighty, the Author of the Covenant, whose terms He Himself has stipulated unilaterally without the help of man. As in the above example, God's part in this Covenant is different from man's. God's part is to release the vivifying forces of life and of Revelation, and man's is to receive these voluntarily and obey His commandments wholeheartedly.

We learn from the study of religions that it is the act of creation itself that brings about this Covenant of God with man. God's part in the Covenant is to confer life upon the individual, to provide him, on the one hand, with his physical needs by placing at his disposal all the resources of this earth and, on the other, to bestow upon his soul the bounty of His Revelation by sending His Messengers to guide his steps toward his everlasting abode.

Bahá'u'lláh tells us that everything in the physical world is created for the well-being and development of humanity. Addressing man in *Hidden Words*, He affirms:

> *O Son of Bounty!*
> Out of the wastes of nothingness, with the clay of My command I made thee to appear, and have ordained for thy training every atom in existence and the essence of all created things. Thus, ere thou didst issue from thy mother's womb, I destined for thee two founts of gleaming milk, eyes to watch over thee, and hearts to love thee. Out of My loving kindness,

'neath the shade of My mercy I nurtured thee, and guarded thee, by the essence of My grace and favour . . .[1]

This and many similar passages in the Writings of Bahá'u'lláh indicate that God has created the mineral, the vegetable and the animal worlds for man's benefit and for his use. There is a delicate relationship between all levels of creation in which the lower kingdom serves the higher kingdom while the higher kingdom lives in harmony with the lower. Indeed, the world of nature is placed at man's disposal to enrich the quality of his life while on this earth, while man is duty bound to respect and preserve his environment.

God provides not only for man's physical well-being, but He also reveals Himself to him through His Messengers in order to develop his spiritual life. Through the influence of these Messengers humanity has passed through the stages of infancy, childhood, and adolescence, and today, as a result of the Revelation of Bahá'u'lláh, is destined to come of age. The Messengers are similar to the teachers in the above analogy. They reveal progressively the teachings of God in accordance with the capacity of the people of their own age.

As the recipient of God's spiritual bounties, mankind has progressed in each age to the extent that it has been able to carry out the teachings of His Messengers and Prophets. As in the analogy where a child's progress depends on his willingness to obey the teacher and carry out his instructions, the spiritual advancement of the human soul is, to a great extent, dependent upon the receptivity of the individual and his readiness to obey his Lord. Should he submit to the will of God, be willing to obey the teaching of His Messengers, and open his heart to receive the outpouring of God's Revelation for the age he lives in, then he has been faithful to the Covenant of God. But if he fails to turn to God's Messengers and His Manifestation, he will become spiritually impoverished. This is true both for individuals and for society as a whole.

This eternal Covenant of God with man encompasses several distinguishable forms. The Bahá'í scholar George Townshend, for instance, has identified seven types of covenant as being subsidiaries of the eternal Covenant. He outlines them as follows:

1. The . . . Covenant, beginning with Adam and closing with Bahá'u'lláh, between God and the whole human race.
2. Between God and each Messenger, assigning His Mission.
3. Between a Messenger and the faithful: Covenant of the next (or of a later) Manifestation.
4. Between the Messenger and the faithful: Ethical Covenant of faith and obedience.
5. Between the Messenger and the faithful: Covenant of immediate Successor.

6. Between the Messenger and a disciple.
7. Between the immediate Successor (e.g. the Centre of the Covenant) and the faithful:
   i. Covenant of continuing succession
   ii. Ethical Covenant[2]

The question of successorship (nos. 3, 5 and 7 in Townshend's analysis) is of prime importance in the history of religion. A lack of consensus among the faithful has been one of the major causes of schism and disunity within religions and is one of the reasons why each Manifestation of God has been persecuted. This question can be divided into two aspects: the Greater Covenant and the Lesser Covenant. The Greater Covenant is that which a Manifestation of God makes with His followers concerning the next Manifestation. The Lesser Covenant is the one which a Manifestation of God makes concerning His immediate successor.

In this book we will discuss mainly three forms of the Covenant which are of great significance to the followers of Bahá'u'lláh:

1. The Covenant of the Bab concerning the Revelation of Bahá'u'lláh described as 'Him Whom God shall make manifest': the Greater Covenant in the Dispensation of the Báb.

2. The Covenant of Bahá'u'lláh concerning the appointment of 'Abdu'l-Bahá as His successor; part of the Lesser Covenant.

3. The Covenant made by 'Abdu'l-Bahá concerning Shoghi Effendi and the Universal House of Justice: also part of the Lesser Covenant.

These three themes correspond to the three main parts of this book.

In the great scheme of the Covenant of God, divine bounties reach humanity through the agency of the human soul. Thus, at this early stage of the book we will focus our attention on the nature of the soul, in an attempt to gain a deeper understanding of this essential agent in the divine plan of the will of God for this age.

PROLOGUE

The Covenant and the Human Soul

THE basic principle which governs the operation of the Covenant of God with man may be said to have been revealed by Bahá'u'lláh in the following passage in *Hidden Words*:

> Love Me that I may love thee. If thou lovest Me not, My love can in no wise reach thee. Know this, O Servant.[1]

It is clear from the above statement that there is a love relationship between God and man. But to receive the bounties of God's love, man must take the first steps. It is like opening a channel, and needs to be done by the individual in the first place.

The soul is a spiritual entity. It has no physical existence; one cannot observe or understand it through scientific or other material means. Its essence, its reality, are beyond the understanding and comprehension of man.

In a Tablet revealed in Baghdád and addressed to Mullá Hádíy-i-Qazvíní,* a Letter of the Living who later became a follower of Mírzá Yaḥyá, Bahá'u'lláh refers to the human soul as a 'divinely ordained and subtle mystery' and the 'sign of the revelation of the All-Abiding, All-Glorious God'. He affirms that no one will ever know the essence of the soul:

> Wert thou to ponder in thine heart, from now until the end that hath no end, and with all the concentrated intelligence and understanding which the greatest minds have attained in the past or will attain in the future, this divinely ordained and subtle Reality, this Sign of the revelation of the All-Abiding, All-Glorious God, thou wilt fail to comprehend its mystery or to appraise its virtue.[2]

Although it is impossible for man, at least in this world, to discover the essence of his own soul, he can observe its powers and witness the expression of its attributes within himself. Belief in the soul, and knowledge of its existence and attributes, come to us

* Concerning this Tablet, see *The Revelation of Bahá'u'lláh*, vol. 2, pp. 144–5.

originally through the words of the Manifestations of God. It is they who primarily impart to mankind the vision of spiritual realities.

In past dispensations humanity had not acquired the capacity to understand the spiritual realms of God. Christ confirmed this fact when He stated:

> I have yet many things to say unto you, but ye cannot bear them now. Howbeit when he, the Spirit of truth, is come, he will guide you unto all truth . . .[3]

This is why the Manifestations of old spoke about the soul but did not explain its nature or reveal any of its mysteries. Muḥammad, the Prophet of Islám, who was the last Messenger of God in the Prophetic Cycle and whose Revelation was the latest of all the older Dispensations, referred to the soul only in one short sentence in the *Qur'án*:

> They ask thee concerning the spirit. Say: The spirit (was created) at the command of my Lord. But you have no knowledge given unto you except a little.[4]

In this Dispensation, however, Bahá'u'lláh and 'Abdu'l-Bahá shed much light on the subject. In many Tablets they testify to the existence of the soul, describe it as an unknowable spiritual reality, acknowledge its exalted station, refer to it as a 'mighty sign of God', and reveal a great deal about its qualities and attributes, its immortality, its condition and its progress in the afterlife. So vast is the range of these Writings that a large volume could be compiled of all their utterances on the subject. Indeed, Bahá'u'lláh's explanations of the human soul are among the great contributions that He has made to religious knowledge, revealed in proportion to the capacity of the people of this age.

These explanations are limited to the description of the characteristics of the soul; in no way do they reveal the reality of the soul itself. Since it is a spiritual entity, the soul emanates from the spiritual worlds of God, and it is therefore impossible to describe its innermost essence in words; it cannot be understood by human intellect or other physical senses. Bahá'u'lláh confirms this in a Tablet addressed to a certain believer known as 'Abdu'r-Razzáq:

> Know, verily, that the soul is a sign of God, a heavenly gem whose reality the most learned of men hath failed to grasp, and whose mystery no mind, however acute, can ever hope to unravel . . .
>
> Verily I say, the human soul is, in its essence, one of the signs of God, a mystery among His mysteries. It is one of the mighty signs of the Almighty, the harbinger that proclaimeth the reality of all the worlds of

God. Within it lieth concealed that which the world is now utterly incapable of apprehending.[5]

Nevertheless, a study of Bahá'u'lláh's Writings is enlightening. We learn from the Writings that the soul, being an emanation from the spiritual worlds of God, comes into existence at the time of conception, when it becomes associated with the body. The belief that the soul exists before conception is therefore contrary to the teachings of Bahá'u'lláh. Shoghi Effendi, the Guardian of the Faith, states, 'the soul or spirit of the individual comes into being with the conception of his physical body'.[6] The soul, being exalted above entry or exit, ascent or descent, cannot be physically placed inside a body or have any connection with material things.

Bahá'u'lláh declares in the same Tablet to 'Abdu'r-Razzáq:

> Verily I say, the human soul is exalted above all egress and regress. It is still, and yet it soareth; it moveth, and yet it is still. It is, in itself, a testimony that beareth witness to the existence of a world that is contingent, as well as to the reality of a world that hath neither beginning nor end.[7]

The association of the soul and the body is similar to the association of light and the mirror. The light is not inside the mirror, but reflected on it from a different source. When the mirror breaks, the light remains unaffected.

When the soul becomes associated with the body, a human being with a unique identity is created. This creation has a beginning at the time of conception, but has no end. 'Abdu'l-Bahá states: 'The spirit of man has a beginning, but it has no end; it continues eternally.'[8] The soul is thus immortal and will progress in the spiritual worlds of God for all eternity. Such a concept of everlasting life is truly a most uplifting vision for the human race. This thought of immortality can evoke in the heart of every believer the feelings of utmost joy and gratitude for having been endowed with eternal life by Almighty God. Another feature of this bounty is that God has bestowed an everlasting privilege upon the parents who become aware of, and rejoice in, being instrumental in bringing into this world children whose souls are destined to progress in the worlds of God throughout eternity.

To understand any spiritual reality, one needs to read the Holy Writings and meditate upon them. Another source from which the individual may learn is nature itself, through an examination of the principles of nature, provided he can relate his findings to the truths enshrined in the Holy Writings. The combination of the two can enable him to grasp a measure of the reality of any spiritual subject, including the human soul. A word of warning is needed, however, in that whereas the Holy Writings are self-sufficient sources for the understanding of spiritual truth, the study of the laws of nature will have to be harmonized with the Writings. Otherwise, by merely employing some principles of nature in one's study of spiritual life, the result could be misleading indeed.

A deeper understanding of religious truth may be realized when the individual recognizes the fact that God's creation is one entity. The spiritual and physical worlds are not separate entities, but parts of one realm of being. The laws and principles governing the world of nature are similar to those which operate in the spiritual worlds of God, in the world of religion and in the world of man. To give an example: we note a great similarity between the laws governing the life of a tree and those which motivate the life of man, both physically and spiritually. We note that the tree thrusts its roots deep into the soil and draws on the minerals in the earth for its food. The soil is inferior to the tree; the tree is nevertheless dependent upon it for its existence. In spite of this dependence, the tree grows in the opposite direction, away from the soil. As if disliking the soil, it raises up its branches high towards the sky. This is similar to man and his state of detachment from the material world when his soul aspires to spiritual things and renounces earthly desires.

By growing upwards, away from the soil, the tree becomes the recipient of the rays of the sun, the most precious thing in this physical world. As a result of the outpouring of energies released by the sun, the tree becomes verdant and produces beautiful blossoms and fruit. Of course, the growth of the tree is involuntary. But let us suppose that it had a choice and, because it loves the earth and is dependent on the soil, inclined its branches downwards and buried itself in the ground. Then it could no longer receive the rays of the sun; in the end, it would rot away.

The same principles apply to a human being who has to live in this world and work to earn a living, and who depends upon material things for his existence. God, however, has destined in His Covenant with man that the soul of man should become detached from the things of this world and aspire towards spiritual realms. But unlike the tree, which has no choice, man has free will. If he chooses to disregard the provisions of the Covenant and to fall in love with the world, its vanities and its material attractions, then he becomes a bondslave of earthly things and his soul, deprived of the power of faith, becomes impoverished.

On the other hand, when the individual aspires to spiritual things, turns to the Manifestation of God, and does not direct all his affections towards this mortal world, then his soul becomes illumined with the rays of the Sun of Truth and will fulfil the purpose for which it has been created. The above example showing the similarity between tree and man demonstrates that the physical and the spiritual worlds of God are related to each other by similar laws. It is therefore possible to discover some spiritual principles by examining physical laws. Similarly, the basic laws and teachings of a religion can be seen as the laws of nature in a higher realm. The difference is that as the laws of a lower kingdom are applied to a higher kingdom, certain features are added which are absent in the lower one. This fact was noted in the above example; the added feature is that man exercises his free will to decide his own destiny, while the tree grows involuntarily, the element of choice being absent in the vegetable kingdom.

In one of His Tablets[9] Bahá'u'lláh states that every created thing in this physical world has some counterpart in the worlds of God. In order to identify these, we can turn to the words and utterances of the Manifestations of God and be guided by their explanations. For example, the study of the Writings of Bahá'u'lláh and 'Abdu'l-Bahá leads us to believe that a counterpart of the Manifestation of God in this physical kingdom is the sun. As the sun pours out its energies upon this earth and is the cause of life, so is the Manifestation of God in relation to humanity. The study of some of the characteristics of the sun could help us to appreciate some of the powers and attributes of the Manifestation of God, to the extent of our human limitations.

We may ask what the physical counterpart of the soul is in this world. It seems from the study of the Writings that it is the embryo growing in the womb of a mother. From a study of the latter, we can deduce some attributes and characteristics of the former. We can observe striking similarities between the two; for example, we note that the embryo begins its life as one cell. There are no limbs and organs at first, but the cell has the capacity to multiply, and in the fullness of time become transformed into a perfect human body. Similarly the soul when it is first created is a 'heavenly gem'. It is without experience and its qualities and powers are latent within it, but it is capable of acquiring these latent qualities progressively in the course of a lifetime. God has decreed that the embryo develop limbs and organs while shielded within the womb. Similarly, He has ordained that the soul develop spiritual qualities in the course of its association with the body. It is in this life, this womb-world, that the soul can acquire divine virtues and perfections. If it so chooses, it can become the repository of knowledge, of wisdom, of love and all the other attributes of God.

The growth of limbs and organs in the embryonic life, and the development of spiritual qualities by the soul, are governed by the same principles. But there is a major difference. The growth of the embryo is involuntary and dictated by nature, while the soul has freedom of choice. This is an added dimension granted to the soul which does not exist in the physical world of nature.

In a Tablet revealed in honour of Ḥájí Muḥammad-Ibráhím-i-Khalíl,* a believer of note from Qazvín, Bahá'u'lláh states:

> And now, concerning thy question regarding the creation of man. Know thou that all men have been created in the nature made by God, the Guardian, the Self-Subsisting. Unto each one hath been prescribed a pre-ordained measure, as decreed in God's mighty and guarded Tablets. All that which ye potentially possess can, however, be manifested only as a result of your own volition.[10]

Another similarity between the soul and the embryo is that the latter grows within the womb for only a short period of time. It is a transitory stage, not designed as a place to live in for ever. This world is also of limited duration for the soul. It is not a place of eternal residence; every human being will inevitably have to depart from it. The goal of life for every child is to die to the womb and be born into this world, its next world. So is the goal for the soul, whose ultimate destiny is to depart from this world and enter into the spiritual worlds of God.

Another similarity between the soul and the embryo is that the child must develop his limbs and organs in the womb of his mother. If he is born without some of these, he will be handicapped, for he is unable to acquire them in this life. The soul too must develop spiritual qualities in this world. The acquisition of wisdom, knowledge, love, humility and all other divine attributes is possible only in this earthly kingdom. We note that some limbs or organs seem to be useless in the womb-world. For instance, eyes are incapable of seeing there, but when the child is born, the light will bring vision to his eyes. The combination of the two – eyes acquired in the womb, and the rays of light existing in this world – endow a human being with vision. Similarly, the virtues and perfections which the soul has acquired in this world, combined with the conditions of the spiritual worlds which are unknown to us while on this mortal plane, will cause the soul to progress in the next life.

As long as a human being lives in this world, the soul and the body are associated with each other. When death takes place, this association comes to an end; the body will return to its origin, which is the earth. The soul also returns to its origin which is the spiritual worlds of God. The embryo begins its life as one cell, but ends up as a perfect human body by the time of its birth. The soul is the same. When it first emanates from the spiritual worlds of God, it has no

* For further information about him, see *The Revelation of Bahá'u'lláh*, vol. 2, pp. 259–261.

powers. But if it has grown properly, lived a good life on this earth, and acquired spiritual qualities, then it returns in a state of might and glory to its own original habitation. Manifesting the signs of God and possessing divine attributes, it retains its own individuality and identity, and as Bahá'u'lláh promises, it will associate with God's Messengers and Chosen Ones in the realms above.

In the Tablet to 'Abdu'r-Razzáq, Bahá'u'lláh discloses the grandeur of the soul after its separation from the body, a soul which has walked in the path of its Lord in this life:

> When it [the soul] leaveth the body, however, it will evince such ascendancy, and reveal such influence as no force on earth can equal. Every pure, every refined and sanctified soul will be endowed with tremendous power, and shall rejoice with exceeding gladness.[11]

Here we see a vast contrast between the soul at the beginning, when it is first associated with the body at the time of conception, and at its consummation, when it returns to its origin in the spiritual worlds of God. At first devoid of all power, at the end it is the possessor of many attributes and spiritual qualities. The condition of the soul in the next world is, therefore, dependent on the acquisition of spiritual attributes, in the same way that the condition of the child born into this world depends on his healthy development in the world of the womb.

We learn from the Holy Writings and by looking at nature that God's creation is not finite: it is infinite in every respect. This is true of the physical universe, which is limitless in size. It is also true of the spiritual worlds of God. Bahá'u'lláh and 'Abdu'l-Bahá have in many of their Tablets revealed that the soul of man will continually progress in the spiritual worlds which are countless in number and infinite in range. In one of His Tablets[12] Bahá'u'lláh states that all the spiritual worlds of God revolve around this world, and that in every world a particular condition has been decreed by God for each soul.

One of the fascinating mysteries of creation is the whereabouts of the next world, the spiritual domain which is mentioned in all the heavenly Books. The study of the Writings of Bahá'u'lláh and a look at nature will resolve this question. One of the principles of nature is that higher forms of life revolve around, and depend upon, the lowest. In this physical world we observe that all living things derive their sustenance from the mineral world, which is the lower kingdom. This earth, although the lowest form of life, gives birth to higher forms and may be regarded as a pivot round which the kingdoms of the vegetable, the animal and man revolve. Similarly, the spiritual worlds of God, as testified by Bahá'u'lláh in His Tablets, revolve around this world, the world of man. This means that the next world is not divorced from life in this world, but rather encompasses it. We notice in nature that while the child grows in the womb, he is, in reality, in this world. Only a small barrier separates the womb-world from this one. It is like a chicken inside an egg: before the egg breaks open, a thin shell acts as a barrier, but both the egg and the chicken are in this world from the beginning.

The child in the womb of the mother is unable to discover that the world into which he is destined to be born is amazingly close to him. This principle applies in the spiritual realms also. As long as man dwells in the physical world he is unable to apprehend the features of the next world, which embraces the human world and all that it contains. Nor is he capable of visualising the grandeur and the splendour of heavenly kingdoms. It is only after its separation from the body that the soul will appreciate how close the spiritual world has been, and how it encompasses this physical world. Then it will realize that, as Bahá'u'lláh testifies in one of His Tablets, 'the world beyond is as different from this world as this world is different from that of the child while still in the womb of its mother'.[13]

God has not granted to the unborn child the ability to discover the smallness of its temporary abode, or the vastness and the beauty of this world. Similarly, He has not endowed the human being, while on this earth, with the ability to perceive even to an infinitesimal measure the conditions of the spiritual worlds of God. If He had, the stability as well as the purpose of this life would have been completely undermined. Bahá'u'lláh states in one of His Tablets that should the station destined for a true believer in the world beyond be revealed to the extent of a needle's eye, every soul would expire in ecstasy. The story of Siyyid Ismá'íl of Zavárih, surnamed Dhabíḥ (Sacrifice) who attained the presence of Bahá'u'lláh in Baghdád, is an example. Bahá'u'lláh complied with his plea and revealed to him a glimmer of the unknowable worlds of God. As a result of this experience, Dhabíḥ could no longer bear to live in this world and took his own life.*

Those who have passed into the next life abide in a realm which enfolds and embraces this life. The influence which pure and enlightened souls in the spiritual kingdom exert upon the world of humanity is the main cause of its progress, according to the teachings of Bahá'u'lláh. This truth may be appreciated if one looks at nature and examines the relationship of the unborn child to those who care for him in this world. There are a host of people who are deeply interested in the welfare of the unborn. First, there is the mother who bears the child, loves it, and is even willing to risk her life for its

* See *The Revelation of Bahá'u'lláh*, vol. 1, pp. 101–103.

health and protection. Then, there is the father and many other people who are directly or indirectly involved in its welfare. But the child, so long as it is going through the embryonic stage of growth, is unaware of the love and care which are directed towards it. Similarly, those souls in the next world who are possessed of spiritual qualities are the instruments of man's welfare, development and growth on this earth. In many of His Writings Bahá'u'lláh has attributed man's progress in this world to the influence of the 'Concourse on high', the gathering of the Prophets and God's holy and chosen souls. He also indicates that when the believers in this Dispensation have shown extraordinary heroism and self-sacrifice in the path of God, these acts have caused great jubilation and rejoicing among the Concourse on high.*

In the same Tablet to 'Abdu'r-Razzáq, Bahá'u'lláh describes the influence of pure and holy souls upon mankind. These are His assuring words:

> Thou hadst, moreover, asked Me concerning the state of the soul after its separation from the body. Know thou, of a truth, that if the soul of man hath walked in the ways of God, it will, assuredly, return and be gathered to the glory of the Beloved. By the righteousness of God! It shall attain a station such as no pen can depict, or tongue describe. The soul that hath remained faithful to the Cause of God, and stood unwaveringly firm in His Path shall, after his ascension, be possessed of such power that all the worlds which the Almighty hath created can benefit through him. Such a soul provideth, at the bidding of the Ideal King and Divine Educator, the pure leaven that leaveneth the world of being, and furnisheth the power through which the arts and wonders of the world are made manifest. Consider how meal needeth leaven to be leavened with. Those souls that are the symbols of detachment are the leaven of the world. Meditate on this, and be of the thankful.[14]

The influence which these holy souls exert upon humanity can only be for the good of mankind. 'Abdu'l-Bahá states, 'God has never created an evil spirit . . .'[15] There can be no such thing as evil influences from the next world affecting anyone in this world. This is because the soul, when ascending to the next world, cannot carry with it 'bad' qualities. And since there is no evil in that realm, there can be no evil effects which could reach this world.

The soul carries with it divine attributes and spiritual qualities to the next world, but cannot take with it bad qualities for badness has no existence of its own; it is only the lack of goodness. In order to clarify this point further, let us look at the following examples. We may note that darkness has no real existence; it is the absence of light.

* For an example, see the story of Badí', *The Revelation of Bahá'u'lláh*, vol. 3, ch. 9.

It is the same with poverty; a poor man cannot claim that he carries his poverty around with him. What he has is very little money. There is no standard for measuring poverty; it can only be defined as lack of riches, and is measured by the standard of wealth. A bad person may be described as one who has very few good qualities. His soul is impoverished and therefore he can take only a very small measure of goodness with him to the spiritual worlds of God.

The degree of the progress of one's soul in the spiritual worlds of God depends upon the extent to which the individual has adorned his being with the 'ornaments of goodly character and praiseworthy virtues'. This is the main reason that God has sent His Manifestations, so that they can cast light upon man's path in this life and show him how to acquire spiritual qualities and heavenly attributes. We have seen that these attributes, which may be likened to spiritual limbs and organs, are needed in the next world for the continued progress of one's soul. Obedience to the teachings of God will endow the soul with divine attributes, otherwise the soul will return to the spiritual realms of God in a state of loss and impoverishment. In one of His Tablets Bahá'u'lláh reveals these weighty utterances:

> If it [the soul] be faithful to God, it will reflect His light, and will, eventually, return unto Him. If it fail, however, in its allegiance to its Creator, it will become a victim to self and passion, and will, in the end, sink in their depths . . . Every soul that walketh humbly with its God, in this Day, and cleaveth unto Him, shall find itself invested with the honour and glory of all goodly names and stations.[16]

From the study of the Writings we gather that as in this world where there are degrees of existence such as the mineral, the vegetable, the animal and man – and within each kingdom there are many divisions – the soul will also progress in the spiritual worlds of God on different levels, depending on the qualities it has acquired in this life. The level in which the soul can abide in the next world is determined by its closeness to God and the spiritual attributes that it takes with it after its separation from the body. However, there is another determining factor, and that is the bounty of God. Through this the soul may be elevated, and its outpouring is beyond the comprehension of man.*

It is stated in the Writings of Bahá'u'lláh that the souls on a higher level will encompass those on a lower one, while the latter will not be able to comprehend the powers and realities of the former. In fact, the grading of human souls and their different stations is similar to the variety of creatures which God has created on this earth. We note that in this physical world also the lower kingdom is blind to the

* For an example of this, see *The Revelation of Bahá'u'lláh*, vol. 2, p. 401.

qualities of a higher one. For instance, while the three kingdoms are so closely linked together, breathing the same air and receiving the same sunshine, the vegetable does not understand the animal and the animal is incapable of really knowing the human being. Conversely, based on the same principles, we note that the higher kingdom dominates the lower ones. The animal has ascendancy over the vegetable, while man rules over the entire world of nature.

In a Tablet revealed in honour of one of His apostles, Zayn'ul-Muqarrabín,* Bahá'u'lláh reveals these thought-provoking words:

> And now concerning thy question whether human souls continue to be conscious one of another after their separation from the body . . .
>
> The people of Bahá, who are the inmates of the Ark of God, are one and all well aware of one another's state and condition, and are united in the bonds of intimacy and fellowship. Such a state, however, must depend upon their faith and their conduct. They that are of the same grade and station are fully aware of one another's capacity, character, accomplishments and merits. They that are of a lower grade, however, are incapable of comprehending adequately the station, or of estimating the merits, of those that rank above them. Each shall receive his share from thy Lord. Blessed is the man that hath turned his face towards God, and walked steadfastly in His love, until his soul hath winged its flight unto God, the Sovereign Lord of all, the Most Powerful, the Ever-Forgiving, the All-Merciful.
>
> The souls of the infidels, however, shall – and to this I bear witness – when breathing their last be made aware of the good things that have escaped them, and shall bemoan their plight, and shall humble themselves before God. They shall continue doing so after the separation of their souls from their bodies.
>
> It is clear and evident that all men shall, after their physical death, estimate the worth of their deeds, and realize all that their hands have wrought. I swear by the Day Star that shineth above the horizon of Divine power! They that are the followers of the one true God shall, the moment they depart out of this life, experience such joy and gladness as would be impossible to describe, while they that live in error shall be seized with such fear and trembling, and shall be filled with such consternation, as nothing can exceed. Well is it with him that hath quaffed the choice and incorruptible wine of faith through the gracious favour and the manifold bounties of Him Who is the Lord of all Faiths. . . .[17]

The knowledge that souls will be divided in the next world, and that each one in accordance with its capacity will progress on its own level, can exert a considerable influence upon the individual to mend his ways in this life, to turn to God and consciously adorn his soul with the 'ornament of pure deeds and goodly character'.

* For a short reference to his life, see *The Revelation of Bahá'u'lláh*, vol. 1, pp. 25–6.

'Abdu'l-Bahá has shed further light on this subject. Speaking to His guests at His dinner table in 'Akká, he said:

> As the divine bounties are endless, so human perfections are endless. If it were possible to reach a limit of perfection, then one of the realities of the beings might reach the condition of being independent of God, and the contingent might attain to the condition of the absolute. But for every being there is a point which it cannot overpass; that is to say, he who is in the condition of servitude, however far he may progress in gaining limitless perfections, will never reach the condition of Deity. It is the same with the other beings: a mineral, however far it may progress in the mineral kingdom, cannot gain the vegetable power; also in a flower, however far it may progress in the vegetable kingdom, no power of the senses will appear. So this silver mineral cannot gain hearing or sight; it can only improve in its own condition, and become a perfect mineral, but it cannot acquire the power of growth, or the power of sensation, or attain to life; it can only progress in its own condition.
>
> For example, Peter cannot become Christ. All that he can do is, in the condition of servitude, to attain endless perfections; for every existing reality is capable of making progress.[18]

From the above words we may conclude that the soul will continue to progress in the spiritual worlds of God on its own level, and that this progress is due to the bounty of God. The soul may also progress by means of prayers for the departed offered by those still in this life. Bahá'u'lláh and 'Abdu'l-Bahá have revealed many prayers for this occasion. It is also stated in the Bahá'í Writings that acts of charity in memory of the departed will uplift the condition of the soul. It is for this reason that individual Bahá'ís customarily commemorate the passing of their loved ones by holding a meeting of prayer and remembrance.

It is interesting to note that the early believers in the East during the days of Bahá'u'lláh and 'Abdu'l-Bahá never celebrated their own birthdays. They considered that such an act would imply self-glorification, a means of boosting one's ego. It never crossed their minds that a certain day was their birthday. So real and genuine was this attitude that a great many individuals did not know the exact date of their birth. In the absence of birth certificates, some parents would record the date of the birth of their children in a certain book, much as Westerners used the family Bible for the same purpose. Even then an individual would be deeply insulted if someone wanted to celebrate his birthday,* for the only persons whose birthday merited celebration were the Prophets and Chosen Ones of God. Instead of celebrating birthdays, however, these people held regular

* It must be noted that there is nothing in the Bahá'í writings either to condemn the celebration of one's birthday or to encourage it.

annual memorial meetings, inviting their friends to join in remembering one of their loved ones who had passed away. In such a meeting, they prayed for the progress of his soul, recounted his services to the Cause, described his qualities, recited Tablets revealed in his honour, if any, and offered charitable donations on his behalf. This practice of annual remembrance of the departed, which is not a binding obligation in the Bahá'í Faith, is now followed by many Bahá'í families. The organisation of such meetings is not usually the responsibility of the institutions of the Faith. They are arranged by individuals on the anniversaries of the passing of their loved ones.

The following are the words of 'Abdu'l-Bahá as He spoke to His guests at His dinner table in 'Akká:

> Also a father and mother endure the greatest troubles and hardships for their children; and often when the children have reached the age of maturity, the parents pass on to the other world. Rarely does it happen that a father and mother in this world see the reward of the care and trouble they have undergone for their children. Therefore, children, in return for this care and trouble, must show forth charity and beneficence, and must implore pardon and forgiveness for their parents. So you ought, in return for the love and kindness shown you by your father, to give to the poor for his sake, with greatest submission and humility implore pardon and remission of sins, and ask for the supreme mercy.
>
> It is even possible that the condition of those who have died in sin and unbelief may become changed – that is to say, they may become the object of pardon through the bounty of God, not through His justice – for bounty is giving without desert, and justice is giving what is deserved. As we have power to pray for these souls here, so likewise we shall possess the same power in the other world, which is the Kingdom of God. Are not all the people in that world the creatures of God? Therefore, in that world also they can make progress. As here they can receive light by their supplications, there also they can plead for forgiveness and receive light through entreaties and supplications. Thus as souls in this world, through the help of the supplications, the entreaties and the prayers of the holy ones, can acquire development, so is it the same after death. Through their own prayers and supplications they can also progress, more especially when they are the object of the intercession of the Holy Manifestations.[19]

The spiritual qualities acquired by the soul in the course of a lifetime – qualities such as knowledge, wisdom, humility, love and other virtues – are acquired gradually. The individual grows in maturity with the passage of time. The spiritual growth of the soul is similar to the organic growth of living creatures. To return to the metaphor of the tree, whose life begins with the planting of a seed: it grows gradually, bringing forth branches, leaves, shoots and offshoots one after another, until the time comes when it produces its fruit. The stage of fruition may be said to constitute the crowning achievement of the tree; it is that stage in which the tree has fulfilled the purpose for which it was created. But the tree cannot produce its fruit by itself. It acts as a female and has to be pollinated by a male element which fertilizes its ovules. Other living creatures which produce their young also go through the same process of intercourse with their male counterparts.

The same is true of the soul. It comes into being at the time of conception, it gradually acquires divine qualities, but there comes a time when it has to produce its fruit. Not until the soul reaches this point can it be said to have fulfilled its destiny. This can happen when, following the above principle of male and female interaction, the soul assumes the function of the female and establishes a spiritual intercourse with another agency. If it chooses the material world as a partner, then the child born of that union will be a materialistic way of life which deprives the soul of its spiritual heritage. A great many people in the world allow themselves to fall in love with material things; consequently the soul is impoverished and although it is a spiritual entity, it becomes sullied with worldly affections and gives birth to materialism, an offspring unworthy of its high station. But the Covenant of God enjoins upon man to recognize His Manifestation and turn to Him. These are the words of Bahá'u'lláh as revealed in a prayer stating the purpose of creation:

> I bear witness, O my God, that Thou has created me to know Thee and to worship Thee . . .[20]

By turning with devotion to Bahá'u'lláh, the Manifestation of God in this day, by submitting to His Will and becoming enamoured of Him, the soul becomes a fertile instrument and a worthy recipient for the outpouring of His Revelation. Through the establishment of a spiritual intercourse with the energizing forces of this Revelation, the soul becomes fertilized and will give birth to a noble offspring – the spirit of faith. This is the ultimate and most glorious destiny for the soul, the purpose for which it is created.

In each Dispensation the Manifestations of God have bestowed the gift of faith on their followers. Christ referred to it as the 'second birth'. In this day the child of faith is conceived in the soul when a person's heart is touched by the love of Bahá'u'lláh and he becomes assured of the truth of His Revelation. And when it becomes evident that the individual has been illumined by the 'spirit of faith', he will need to take spiritual nourishment so that his new-born faith may be enabled to grow. This spiritual food is the Word of God, revealed in this day by Bahá'u'lláh. By reciting His Words regularly every day and every night, as He has ordained, and through obedience to His teachings, the spirit of faith will grow step by step and the believer will become steadfast in faith and assured and happy in his life. If he neglects this vital necessity, his faith will diminish in strength and he may even lose it altogether.

In many of His Tablets Bahá'u'lláh has extolled the station of a soul who has been endowed with the spirit of faith and confirms that if 'that station were to be unveiled to mankind, every beholder would be consumed away in his longing to attain it'.[21]

Referring to the station of a soul who has truly recognized Him, Bahá'u'lláh, in a Tablet, reveals these words:

> We dare not, in this Day, lift the veil that concealeth the exalted station which every true believer can attain, for the joy which such a revelation must provoke might well cause a few to faint away and die . . .
>
> By the righteousness of the one true God! The very breath of these souls is in itself richer than all the treasures of the earth. Happy is the man that hath attained thereunto, and woe betide the heedless.[22]

So precious is the soul of a true believer in the estimation of God that Bahá'u'lláh states, in one of His Tablets[23] revealed in honour of one of the Afnáns, that it is for the sake of His loved ones that God has created the heavens and the earth and all that is therein.

There are numerous Tablets* in which Bahá'u'lláh has disclosed the nature of the soul and described its main features. Notable among these is a Tablet revealed in 'Akká in honour of 'Abdu'l-Vahháb, a believer from Qú<u>ch</u>án in the Province of <u>Kh</u>urásán. We cite part of this Tablet in these pages:

> And now concerning thy question regarding the soul of man and its survival after death. Know thou of a truth that the soul, after its separation from the body, will continue to progress until it attaineth the presence of God, in a state and condition which neither the revolution of ages and centuries, nor the changes and chances of this world, can alter. It will endure as long as the Kingdom of God, His sovereignty, His dominion and power will endure. It will manifest the signs of God and His attributes, and will reveal His loving kindness and bounty. The movement of My Pen is stilled when it attempteth to befittingly describe the loftiness and glory of so exalted a station. The honour with which the Hand of Mercy will invest the soul is such as no tongue can adequately reveal, nor any other earthly agency describe. Blessed is the soul which, at the hour of its separation from the body, is sanctified from the vain imaginings of the peoples of the world. Such a soul liveth and moveth in accordance with the Will of its Creator, and entereth the all-highest

* Parts of these Tablets are translated by Shoghi Effendi and published in *Gleanings from the Writings of Bahá'u'lláh*, nos. LXXVII, LXXVIII and LXXX (both parts of the same Tablet), LXXIX, LXXXI, LXXXII, LXXXIII and LXXXVI.

Paradise. The Maids of Heaven, inmates of the loftiest mansions, will circle around it, and the Prophets of God and His chosen ones will seek its companionship. With them that soul will freely converse, and will recount unto them that which it hath been made to endure in the path of God, the Lord of all worlds. If any man be told that which hath been ordained for such a soul in the worlds of God, the Lord of the throne on high and of earth below, his whole being will instantly blaze out in his great longing to attain that most exalted, that sanctified and resplendent station. . . . The nature of the soul after death can never be described, nor is it meet and permissible to reveal its whole character to the eyes of men. The prophets and Messengers of God have been sent down for the sole purpose of guiding mankind to the straight Path of Truth. The purpose underlying their revelation hath been to educate all men, that they may, at the hour of death, ascend, in the utmost purity and sanctity and with absolute detachment, to the throne of the Most High. The light which these souls radiate is responsible for the progress of the world and the advancement of its peoples. They are like unto leaven which leaveneth the world of being, and constitute the animating force through which the arts and wonders of the world are made manifest. Through them the clouds rain their bounty upon men, and the earth bringeth forth its fruits. All things must needs have a cause, a motive power, an animating principle. These souls and symbols of detachment have provided, and will continue to provide, the supreme moving impulse in the world of being. The world beyond is as different from this world as this world is different from that of the child while still in the womb of its mother. When the soul attaineth the Presence of God, it will assume the form that best befitteth its immortality and is worthy of its celestial habitation. Such an existence is a contingent and not an absolute existence, inasmuch as the former is preceded by a cause, whilst the latter is independent thereof. Absolute existence is strictly confined to God, exalted be His glory. Well is it with them that apprehend this truth.[24]

God loves to attract a soul to Himself, but there are many barriers interposed between man and his Creator. These are all in the nature of attachment to material, intellectual and spiritual things which prevent man from drawing near to his God.* These formidable barriers must be removed before man can draw near to God; it is for this purpose that God has sent His Messengers throughout the ages.

In one of His Tablets[25] Bahá'u'lláh states that there are three barriers between man and God. He exhorts the believers to pass beyond these so that they may attain His Presence. The first barrier is attachment to the things of this world, the second is attachment to the rewards of the next world, and the third is attachment to the Kingdom of Names.

* Nearness to the Essence and Reality of God is impossible. By 'God' is meant God revealed to man, i.e. His Manifestation.

A believer becomes attached to the things of this world when he allows his material, intellectual and selfish interests to take precedence over the interests of the Cause of God. This does not mean that he has to forego his personal interests, but rather to use them in promoting his spiritual pursuits, and not to allow earthly things to come between him and God.

Since attachment to this world is a great barrier which prevents man from fulfilling his part in the Covenant of God, Bahá'u'lláh and 'Abdu'l-Bahá have exhorted their followers in many of their Tablets to become detached from earthly desires, to turn instead to God and obey His commandments.

> O My servants! Could ye apprehend with what wonders of My munificence and bounty I have willed to entrust your souls, ye would of a truth, rid yourselves of attachment to all created things, and would gain a true knowledge of your own selves – a knowledge which is the same as the comprehension of Mine own Being. Ye would find yourselves independent of all else but Me, and would perceive, with your inner and outer eye, and as manifest as the revelation of My effulgent name, the seas of My loving-kindness and bounty moving within you. Suffer not your idle fancies, your evil passions, your insincerity and blindness of heart to dim the lustre, or stain the sanctity, of so lofty a station. Ye are even as the bird which soareth, with the full force of its mighty wings and with complete and joyous confidence, through the immensity of the heavens, until, impelled to satisfy its hunger, it turneth longingly to the water and clay of the earth below it, and, having been entrapped in the mesh of its desire, findeth itself impotent to resume its flight to the realms whence it came. Powerless to shake off the burden weighing on its sullied wings, that bird, hitherto an inmate of the heavens, is now forced to seek a dwelling-place upon the dust. Wherefore, O My servants, defile not your wings with the clay of waywardness and vain desires, and suffer them not to be stained with the dust of envy and hate, that ye may not be hindered from soaring in the heavens of My divine knowledge.[26]

This concept of detachment from material things is often misunderstood and is taken to mean renouncing the world. Many people think that the way to detachment is to shut oneself away in a monastery, lead an ascetic life, or live as a mendicant, careless of one's personal affairs and responsibilities.

None of these practices conform with the teachings of Bahá'u'lláh. In His second Tablet* to Napoleon III, Bahá'u'lláh, addressing the Christian monks, admonishes them in these words:

> O concourse of monks! Seclude not yourselves in churches and cloisters. Come forth by My leave, and occupy yourselves with that which will profit your souls and the souls of men. Thus biddeth you the

* See *The Revelation of Bahá'u'lláh*, vol. 3.

King of the Day of Reckoning. Seclude yourselves in the stronghold of My love. This, verily, is a befitting seclusion, were ye of them that perceive it. He that shutteth himself up in a house is indeed as one dead. It behoveth man to show forth that which will profit all created things, and he that bringeth forth no fruit is fit for fire. Thus counselleth you your Lord, and He, verily, is the Almighty, the All-Bounteous. Enter ye into wedlock, that after you someone may fill your place. We have forbidden you perfidious acts, and not that which will demonstrate fidelity.[27]

Attachment to this world may be described as anything which becomes a barrier between God and man, depriving the individual from drawing near to his Maker. It is clear from the Writings of Bahá'u'lláh that God has created this world for man alone. For instance, in *The Hidden Words*, Bahá'u'lláh declares:

O Son of Dust! all that is in heaven and on earth I have ordained for thee except the human heart . . .[28]

This means that the world and all that is therein is created for man. God wants him to benefit from its wealth, to exploit its resources wisely and in harmony with nature, to work and possess all the good things he can earn, and to enjoy all the legitimate pleasures that life bestows upon him. But at no time must he allow the things of this world to possess him and rule over his heart and soul.

Indeed, in this Dispensation Bahá'u'lláh has ordained work rendered in the spirit of service to mankind as worship of God. He enjoins upon man the duty of working for the betterment of the world and the building of a new world order on this planet. In one of His Tablets Bahá'u'lláh has revealed these exalted words:

Should a man wish to adorn himself with the ornaments of the earth, to wear its apparels, or partake of the benefits it can bestow, no harm can befall him, if he alloweth nothing whatever to intervene between him and God, for God hath ordained every good thing, whether created in the heavens or in the earth, for such of His servants as truly believe in Him. Eat ye, O people, of the good things which God hath allowed you, and deprive not yourselves from His wondrous bounties. Render thanks and praise unto Him, and be of them that are truly thankful.[29]

One may be wealthy, yet detached from material things. Man can achieve this if he lives his life in accordance with the teachings of God. In one of His Tablets[30] Bahá'u'lláh states that the good things of this world and its beautiful products are all the manifestations of the attributes of God. To possess them will not become the cause of attachment to material things, provided the individual does not fix his affections upon them, nor allow himself to be possessed by them, because this world and all that is therein are like unto a passing shadow and transitory. He further explains that one meaning of attachment to this world is attachment to those who have denied Him and repudiated His Cause.

To appreciate the true meaning of detachment, let us examine the nature of a human being. We note that the animal nature in man makes him selfish. The instinct for survival drives him to find food, clothing and shelter for himself. He pursues comfort, wealth and well-being, and has an insatiable appetite for collecting any beautiful and pleasurable object that comes his way. All these, as well as his emotional, spiritual and intellectual pursuits are aimed at benefitting his own self. He is the master of his own life, a pivot around which circle all his material possessions as well as his intellectual pursuits. One day he finds the Cause of God, recognizes its truth, falls in love with it, and then he adds it, like his other possessions, to his collection. He remains the master figure in the centre and all his possessions, including the Faith, revolve around him and serve his interests. Such a person is attached to the things of this world, for he allows his own interests to take precedence over the interests of the Cause, and his own ego to rule over his spiritual side. He puts his religion on a par with his other pursuits and selfishly expects to benefit from it just as he benefits from his other possessions.

On the other hand, genuine detachment from earthly things is achieved when the individual makes the Cause of God the pivot of his life, so that all his personal and material interests may revolve around his Faith. In this case, he can benefit from his material possessions without being attached to them. And since the Cause of God is the prime motivating influence in his life, he will never act against the teachings of his Faith. Every step he takes in his daily activities will be in harmony with the commandments of God. When a person reaches this exalted position, the interests of the Faith take precedence over his personal interests. And when he arises to serve the Cause of God, he will be ready to meet the challenge whatever the cost. Such a person has reached the summit of detachment.

Becoming detached from the things of this world is often a painful process and involves sacrifice. But when the believer gives up something dear to him for the sake of the Cause of God, mysterious forces will be released which will cause the Faith to grow. To offer up one's time, to labour for the establishment of the Faith in a locality, to give up the comforts of home and to go as a pioneer to foreign lands, to offer up one's substance for the promotion of the Cause, to be persecuted for one's faith, and even to give one's life at the end – all these sacrifices are meritorious in the sight of God and will undoubtedly bring victory to His Cause, provided one's motives are pure and sincere. That is the essential condition of loyalty and steadfastness in the Covenant of God – purity of motive. Without it one's deeds are not acceptable by God. Bahá'u'lláh testifies to this truth in these words:

> *O Children of Adam!*
> Holy words and pure and goodly deeds ascend unto the heaven of celestial glory. Strive that your deeds may be cleansed from the dust of self and hypocrisy and find favour at the court of glory; for ere long the assayers of mankind shall, in the holy presence of the Adored one, accept naught but absolute virtue and deeds of stainless purity. This is the day-star of wisdom and of divine mystery that hath shone above the horizon of the divine will. Blessed are they that turn thereunto.[31]

As to the second barrier: we note in the Holy Writings that the purpose of the creation of man is that he may know God. One of the traditions of Islám states that in the beginning God was a 'Hidden Treasure', but desired to be discovered and recognized. He created man for this purpose. And now man has found God and turned to Him. Returning to the Short Obligatory Prayer which Bahá'u'lláh revealed for His followers to recite each day, we read: 'I bear witness, O my God, that Thou hast created me to know Thee and to worship Thee . . .'

Man, therefore, is created to serve his Lord and worship him with a pure heart, hoping to attain His good pleasure. The purpose is not that he receive reward for his actions. Man's deeds are thus praiseworthy in the sight of God when they are performed solely for His love and for no other reason. To this Bahá'u'lláh testifies in the *Kitáb-i-Aqdas*: 'Observe My commandments, for the love of My beauty.'[32] In fact, when a believer turns to the Manifestation of God with true love, he cannot help but leave aside his personal interests. His attraction to the Manifestation is such that he will offer up everything to his Lord and will seek no benefits for himself.

If a man's actions are motivated by the thought that he may reap a reward for himself in the next world, then this is attachment, and a barrier between himself and God. To be detached means to do everything for the sake of God and to seek no recompense.

As to the third barrier: There are many references in the Writings of Bahá'u'lláh to the 'Kingdom of Names'. God, in His own essence, is exalted above attributes. However, in all His dominions and within each of His worlds, both spiritual and physical, He reveals the kingdom of His attributes. Every created thing manifests the names and attributes of God. In the spiritual world, these attributes are manifest with such intensity that man will never be able to comprehend them in this life. In the human world, however, these attributes appear within the 'Kingdom of Names' and man often becomes attached to these names.

In many of His Tablets Bahá'u'lláh exhorts His followers not to become the bond-slaves of the Kingdom of Names. The well-known Islamic saying, 'The Names come down from heaven', has many meanings. In this world every one of God's attributes is clad with a name, and every such name reveals the characteristics of that attribute. For instance, generosity is an attribute of God, and it manifests itself in human beings. However, a person who has this attribute often becomes proud of it and loves to be referred to as generous. When his generosity is acknowledged by other people, he becomes happy, and when it is ignored, he is unhappy. This is one form of attachment to the Kingdom of Names. Although this example concerns the name 'generosity', the same is true of all the names and attributes of God manifested within the individual. Usually man ascribes these attributes to his own person rather than to God and employs them to boost his own ego. For instance, a learned man uses the attribute of knowledge to become famous and feels gratified and uplifted when his name is publicized far and wide. Or there is the individual whose heart leaps with feelings of pride and satisfaction when he hears his name mentioned and finds himself admired. These are examples of attachment to the Kingdom of Names.

Human society at present exerts a pernicious influence upon the soul of man. Instead of allowing him to live a life of service and sacrifice, it is highly competitive and teaches him to pride himself on his accomplishments. From early childhood he is trained to develop his ego and to seek to exalt himself above others, in the ultimate aim of achieving self-importance, success and power.

The Revelation of Bahá'u'lláh aims to reverse this process. The soul of man needs to be adorned with the virtues of humility and self-effacement so that it may become detached from the Kingdom of Names.

'Abdu'l-Bahá, the true Exemplar of the teachings of Bahá'u'lláh, demonstrated this form of detachment by His actions. He never in the course of His life wished to exalt His name, nor did He seek publicity for Himself. For instance, He had an immense dislike of being photographed. He said, '. . . to have a picture of oneself is to emphasize the personality . . .'. During the first few days of His visit to London, He refused to be photographed. However, as a result of much pressure by the newspaper reporters, and persistent pleas by the friends to be allowed to take His photograph, 'Abdu'l-Bahá acquiesced in order to make them happy.

The exalted titles conferred upon Him by Bahá'u'lláh are indicative of 'Abdu'l-Bahá's lofty station. Yet 'Abdu'l-Bahá never applied them to Himself. Instead, after the Ascension of Bahá'u'lláh, He took the title of 'Abdu'l-Bahá (Servant of Bahá) and urged the believers to call Him only by this name. True servitude at the threshold of Bahá'u'lláh was all He prized. These are some of His words as He describes with utter self-effacement the reality of His station:

> My name is 'Abdu'l-Bahá. My qualification is 'Abdu'l-Bahá. My reality is 'Abdu'l-Bahá. My praise is 'Abdu'l-Bahá. Thraldom to the Blessed Perfection* is my glorious and refulgent diadem, and servitude to all the human race my perpetual religion . . . No name, no title, no mention, no commendation have I, nor will ever have, except 'Abdu'l-Bahá. This is my longing. This is my greatest yearning. This is my eternal life. This is my everlasting glory.[33]

One of the distinguishing features of Bahá'u'lláh's embryonic world order is that it does not harbour egotistical personalities. Bahá'u'lláh has conferred authority on its institutions, whether local, national or international, but the individuals who are privileged to serve on them are devoid of any authority. Unlike men who wield power in the world today and seek to acquire fame and popularity, members of Bahá'í institutions cannot but manifest humility and self-effacement if they are to remain faithful to Bahá'u'lláh. Those who do not succeed, through immaturity or lack of faith, in living up to these standards are indeed attached to the Kingdom of Names and become deprived of the bounties of God in this age.

To sever oneself from the Kingdom of Names may prove to be the most difficult task for a Bahá'í, and the struggle may indeed last a lifetime. If a man can only realize that his virtues are not intrinsically his own, but rather are manifestations of the attributes of God, then he is freed from the Kingdom of Names and becomes truly humble. Such a man will bestow divine perfections upon the world of humanity. This is the loftiest station that God has destined for man. To the extent that a believer succeeds in severing himself from these three forms of attachment, will he be fulfilling his part in the Covenant of God.

To achieve this exalted goal man needs to recognize the station of Bahá'u'lláh as the Manifestation of God for this age and then observe His commandments with clear vision, mature reflection and a prayerful attitude. This can be achieved through deepening one's knowledge of the Faith and in serving His Cause. It is then that the heart will become the recipient of the knowledge of God, and will attain certitude in its faith. It is then that obedience to the teachings of

* Bahá'u'lláh.

the Faith becomes wholehearted, as the individual grasps the significance of God's commandments, and comes to understand their wisdom, their excellence and their necessity. It is then that his thoughts, his vision, his aspirations, his words, and his deeds will all be in harmony with the Covenant of God. And it is then that his soul will acquire spiritual qualities and virtues. This is the ultimate outcome of obedience to the Covenant, which will enable the soul to progress in the spiritual worlds of God.

PART I

THE GREATER COVENANT

'Him Whom God shall make manifest'

CHAPTER ONE

The Covenant of the Báb

The Báb was an independent Manifestation of God Who inaugurated the Bábí Dispensation. In several of his writings Shoghi Effendi, the Guardian of the Bahá'í Faith, extols the station of the Báb and describes at length the uniqueness of His Mission. The following is a brief extract from *God Passes By*:

> The Báb, acclaimed by Bahá'u'lláh as the '*Essence of Essences*', the '*Sea of Seas*', the '*Point round Whom the realities of the Prophets and Messengers revolve*', '*from Whom God hath caused to proceed the knowledge of all that was and shall be*', Whose '*rank excelleth that of all the Prophets*', and Whose '*Revelation transcendeth the comprehension and understanding of all their chosen ones*', had delivered His Message and discharged His mission. He Who was, in the words of 'Abdu'l-Bahá, the '*Morn of Truth*' and '*Harbinger of the Most Great Light*', Whose advent at once signalized the termination of the '*Prophetic Cycle*', and the inception of the '*Cycle of Fulfilment*', had simultaneously through His Revelation banished the shades of night that had descended upon His country, and proclaimed the impending rise of that Incomparable Orb Whose radiance was to envelope the whole of mankind. He, as affirmed by Himself, '*the Primal Point from which have been generated all created things*', '*one of the sustaining pillars of the Primal Word of God*', the '*Mystic Fane*', the '*Great Announcement*', the '*Flame of that supernal Light that glowed upon Sinai*', the '*Remembrance of God*', concerning Whom '*a separate Covenant hath been established with each and every Prophet*', had, through His advent, at once fulfilled the promise of all ages and ushered in the consummation of all Revelations.[1]

The Báb wielded the sceptre of an independent Manifestation of God. With a stroke of His pen He abrogated the laws of Islám, which were regarded as the most sacred and unassailable heritage bequeathed by the Prophet Muḥammad to His followers. No one except a Manifestation of God has the authority to abrogate the laws of a former Dispensation, and this the Báb did. In their place He formulated new laws which were destined to be short-lived, and designed to be overtaken by the laws of Bahá'u'lláh. He thus founded an independent religion which spread throughout Persia so rapidly and with such dynamism as to revolutionize the lives of many a person in that land.

But the Báb's Mission was two-fold. He was also the harbinger of the Supreme Manifestation of God Whom He designated as 'Him Whom God shall make manifest'. However, we must bear in mind the following comment by Shoghi Effendi.

> Indeed the greatness of the Báb consists primarily, not in His being the divinely-appointed Forerunner of so transcendent a Revelation, but rather in His having been invested with the powers inherent in the inaugurator of a separate religious Dispensation, and in His wielding, to a degree unrivalled by the Messengers gone before Him, the sceptre of independent Prophethood.[2]

Indeed, the Mission of the Báb was unique. Never in the history of religion do we find two independent Revelations appearing in such rapid succession. Only nine years separated the birth of these two Revelations. The two Manifestations were contemporaries; the Báb was two years* younger than Bahá'u'lláh. They were natives of the same country, spoke the same language, practised the same religion, followed the same social customs but lived about five hundred miles apart and never met each other in person. In fact there is a Tablet of Bahá'u'lláh addressed to Varqá,† one of His great apostles, written in the words‡ of His amanuensis Mírzá Áqá Ján, in which it is stated that the Báb had attained the presence of Bahá'u'lláh in person.[3] But 'Abdu'l-Bahá has stated that they never met. As He is the authorized Interpreter of Bahá'u'lláh's Writings, we accept 'Abdu'l-Bahá's statement that the Báb did not attain the presence of Bahá'u'lláh in person.

In a Tablet addressed to Shaykh Káẓim-i-Samandar[4]§ Bahá'u'lláh states that at one time He revealed certain words addressed to the Báb, words which illumined all the Holy Books of God. Upon reading these words, the Báb was so carried away by the breezes of divine revelation that with His whole being He soared in the heaven of nearness to Bahá'u'lláh, and decided to present Himself before the face of His Lord. The revealed words exhilarated Him in such wise that no pen can record or tongue explain. Bahá'u'lláh asserts that for the protection of the Faith, this episode was not made public.

The Báb's unique Mission in the history of religion is that He stood in between two religious cycles. With his advent He closed, on the one hand, the 'Prophetic Cycle', which began with Adam as the

* There is a tradition attributed to Imám 'Alí in which he is reported to have said: 'I am two years younger than my Lord.' This is especially applicable to the Báb, whose name was 'Alí-Muḥammad.

† For a story of his illustrious life, see *The Revelation of Bahá'u'lláh*, vol. 4, ch. 4.

‡ Some Tablets of Bahá'u'lláh are composed in such a way that the whole or part of the Tablet is in the words of His amanuensis, but was in fact dictated by Bahá'u'lláh to appear as if composed by the amanuensis. Every word of these Tablets, from beginning to end, is from Bahá'u'lláh Himself. For more information see *The Revelation of Bahá'u'lláh*, vol. 1, pp. 40–42.

§ For an account of his life, see *The Revelation of Bahá'u'lláh*, vol. 3.

first Manifestation of God in recorded history and ended with the Dispensation of Islám and, on the other, He opened the 'Cycle of Fulfilment' whose duration, according to the Writings of Bahá'u'lláh and 'Abdu'l-Bahá, will be at least five thousand centuries.

It is important to note that the mission of all the Manifestations of God in the prophetic cycle, up to and including Muḥammad, was to prophesy the advent of the Day of God. Hence they are included in the 'Prophetic Cycle'. Muḥammad was the last one among them and is therefore designated 'Seal of the Prophets'. Bahá'u'lláh's claim, on the other hand, makes it clear that He is not a Prophet in the category of those who prophesy, but His station is that of the Supreme Manifestation of God who inaugurates the 'Cycle of Fulfilment' and ushers in the Day of God whose advent had been so clearly foretold by all the Prophets gone before Him.

As we survey the Ministry of the Báb, which lasted a little over six years, we note that the most significant part of His Writings was devoted to establishing a mighty covenant with His followers concerning the Revelation of 'Him Whom God shall make manifest' – Bahá'u'lláh. Indeed, no Manifestation of God before Him has devoted so much of His Revelation to the subject of the Covenant. When we carefully study the *Bayán** we note that on practically every page of that Book there is a mention of 'Him Whom God shall make manifest', stating some aspect of His Revelation, but always extolling His station and mentioning His Name with a reverence which staggers the imagination. The Báb has mentioned 'Him Whom God shall make manifest' in the *Persian Bayán* more than three hundred times, and in the *Arabic Bayán* more than seventy. There are also references to Him without mentioning this designation. In several instances He identifies 'Him Whom God shall make manifest' with the designation 'Bahá'u'lláh'.

The announcement of the Revelation of 'Him Whom God shall make manifest' is not limited to the *Bayán*. In the great majority of His Writings the Báb has directed the attention of the Bábís to that great Revelation which was to follow Him, established a firm covenant with them and directed all the forces of His Revelation towards the spiritual enrichment of the Bábí community in order to rear a new race of men worthy to attain the presence of 'Him Whom God shall make manifest', recognize His station and embrace His Cause.

The laws He promulgated, some very severe, were designed to shake up the lethargic people of Persia in general and to inflame His own followers with the zeal and fervour of a new and dynamic Faith

* The 'Mother-Book' of the Bábí Dispensation.

in particular. In past Dispensations, the energies latent within God's Revelation have taken about a thousand years to be fully released and diffused gradually within human society. In the Dispensation of the Báb, however, the energies of a mighty Revelation had to be released within a very short period of time. Therefore, everything associated with His Faith, His laws, His teachings, His own public appearances, His Ministry, His personal life and His martyrdom were all characterized by a dynamism and forcefulness unparalleled in the annals of past religions, and which exerted a most potent and electrifying influence upon friend and foe alike.

The laws of the *Bayán* were promulgated for the sake of 'Him Whom God shall make manifest'. The aim of the Báb in revealing the laws of His Dispensation was to edify the souls of His followers and mould their conduct in such wise that they could be worthy to embrace the Cause of Bahá'u'lláh. In the *Kitáb-i-Asmá'*, one of His celebrated Writings, He reveals these thought-provoking words.

> But for the sole reason of His* being present amongst this people, We would have neither prescribed any law nor laid down any prohibition. It is only for the glorification of His Name and the exaltation of His Cause that We have enunciated certain laws at Our behest, or forbidden the acts to which We are averse, so that at the hour of His manifestation ye may attain through Him the good-pleasure of God and abstain from the things that are abhorrent unto Him.[5]

The Covenant that the Báb made with His followers concerning 'Him Whom God shall make manifest' was firm and irrevocable. His advent was unquestionable, assured as the mid-day sun. It was in the early days of His Revelation in Shíráz that He despatched Mullá Ḥusayn, the first to believe in the Báb, to Ṭihrán for the sole purpose of searching for and establishing contact with 'Him Whom God shall make manifest', the One Who was the Source of the Revelation of the Báb, the object of His adoration, and the One in Whose path He longed to lay down His life. Nabíl-i-A'ẓam, the well-known Bahá'í historian, relates the following account:

> To Mullá Ḥusayn, as the hour of his departure approached, the Báb addressed these words: 'Grieve not that you have not been chosen to accompany Me on My pilgrimage to Ḥijáz. I shall, instead, direct your steps to that city which enshrines a Mystery of such transcendent holiness as neither Ḥijáz† nor Shíráz‡ can hope to rival.'[6]

The story of Mullá Ḥusayn as he tries to find a trace of His Beloved in Ṭihrán is fascinating. The hand of providence brought

* 'Him Whom God shall make manifest'.
† Signifies the Islamic Faith. (A.T.)
‡ Signifies the Bábí Faith. (A.T.)

him into close contact with a certain Mullá Muḥammad who became immensely attracted to Mullá Ḥusayn and the Message of the Báb. The story, recorded in the words of this Mullá Muḥammad in *The Dawn-Breakers*, is as follows:

'What is your name, and which city is your home?' 'My name,' I replied, 'is Mullá Muḥammad, and my surname Mu'allim. My home is Núr, in the province of Mázindarán.' 'Tell me,' further enquired Mullá Ḥusayn, 'is there to-day among the family of the late Mírzá Buzurg-i-Núrí, who was so renowned for his character, his charm, and artistic and intellectual attainments, anyone who has proved himself capable of maintaining the high traditions of that illustrious house?' 'Yea,' I replied, 'among his sons now living, one has distinguished Himself by the very traits which characterised His father. By His virtuous life, His high attainments, His loving-kindness and liberality, He has proved Himself a noble descendant of a noble father.' 'What is His occupation?' he asked me. 'He cheers the disconsolate and feeds the hungry,' I replied. 'What of His rank and position?' 'He has none,' I said, 'apart from befriending the poor and the stranger.' 'What is His name?' 'Ḥusayn-'Alí.' 'In which of the scripts of His father does He excel?' 'His favourite script is shikastih-nasta'líq.' 'How does He spend His time?' 'He roams the woods and delights in the beauties of the countryside.' 'What is His age?' 'Eight and twenty.' The eagerness with which Mullá Ḥusayn questioned me, and the sense of delight with which he welcomed every particular I gave him, greatly surprised me. Turning to me, with his face beaming with satisfaction and joy, he once more enquired: 'I presume you often meet Him?' 'I frequently visit His home,' I replied. 'Will you,' he said, 'deliver into His hands a trust from me?' 'Most assuredly,' was my reply. He then gave me a scroll wrapped in a piece of cloth, and requested me to hand it to Him the next day at the hour of dawn. 'Should He deign to answer me,' he added, 'will you be kind enough to acquaint me with His reply?' I received the scroll from him and, at break of day, arose to carry out his desire.

As I approached the house of Bahá'u'lláh, I recognised His brother Mírzá Músá, who was standing at the gate, and to whom I communicated the object of my visit. He went into the house and soon reappeared bearing a message of welcome. I was ushered into His presence, and presented the scroll to Mírzá Músá, who laid it before Bahá'u'lláh. He bade us both be seated. Unfolding the scroll, He glanced at its contents and began to read aloud to us certain of its passages. I sat enraptured as I listened to the sound of His voice and the sweetness of its melody. He had read a page of the scroll when, turning to His brother, He said: 'Músá, what have you to say? Verily I say, whoso believes in the Qur'án and recognises its Divine origin, and yet hesitates, though it be for a moment, to admit that these soul-stirring words are endowed with the same regenerating power, has most assuredly erred in his judgment and has strayed far from the path of justice.' He spoke no more. Dismissing me from His presence, He charged me to take to Mullá Ḥusayn, as a gift from Him, a loaf of Russian sugar and a package of tea,* and to convey to him the expression of His appreciation and love.

I arose, and, filled with joy, hastened back to Mullá Ḥusayn, and delivered to him the gift and message of Bahá'u'lláh. With what joy and exultation he received them from me! Words fail me to describe the intensity of his emotion. He started to his feet, received with bowed head the gift from my hand, and fervently kissed it. He then took me in his arms, kissed my eyes, and said: 'My dearly beloved friend! I pray that even as you have rejoiced my heart, God may grant you eternal felicity and fill your heart with imperishable gladness.' I was amazed at the behaviour of Mullá Ḥusayn. What could be, I thought to myself, the nature of the bond that unites these two souls? What could have kindled so fervid a fellowship in their hearts? Why should Mullá Ḥusayn, in whose sight the pomp and circumstance of royalty were the merest trifle, have evinced such gladness at the sight of so inconsiderable a gift from the hands of Bahá'u'lláh? I was puzzled by this thought and could not unravel its mystery.

A few days later, Mullá Ḥusayn left for Khurásán. As he bade me farewell, he said: 'Breathe not to anyone what you have heard and witnessed. Let this be a secret hidden within your breast. Divulge not His name, for they who envy His position will arise to harm Him. In your moments of meditation, pray that the Almighty may protect Him, that, through Him, He may exalt the downtrodden, enrich the poor, and redeem the fallen. The secret of things is concealed from our eyes. Ours is the duty to raise the call of the New Day and to proclaim this Divine Message unto all people. Many a soul will, in this city, shed his blood in this path. That blood will water the Tree of God, will cause it to flourish, and to overshadow all mankind.'[7]

The Báb had directed Mullá Ḥusayn to send Him a letter and inform Him of that great Mystery which he was to discover in Ṭihrán. That letter arrived on the night preceding 10 October 1844 when Quddús was present, with whom the Báb shared a number of its passages. Nabíl-i-A'ẓam continues the story in these words:

He sent his letter by way of Yazd, through the trustworthy partners of the Báb's maternal uncle who were at that time residing in Ṭabas. That letter reached the Báb on the night preceding the twenty-seventh day of Ramaḍán,† a night held in great reverence by all the sects of Islám and regarded by many as rivalling in sacredness the Laylatu'l-Qadr itself, the night which, in the words of the Qur'án, 'excelleth a thousand months'.‡ The only companion of the Báb, when that letter reached Him that night, was Quddús, with whom He shared a number of its passages.

* Tea and that variety of sugar being extremely rare in Persia at that time, both were used as gifts among the higher classes of the population. (A.T.)

† Corresponding with the night preceding the 10th October 1844 A.D.

‡ The Laylatu'l-Qadr, meaning literally 'Night of Power', is one of the last ten nights of Ramaḍán, and, as is commonly believed, the seventh of those nights reckoning backward.

I have heard Mírzá Aḥmad* relate the following: 'The Báb's maternal uncle himself described to me the circumstances attending the receipt of Mullá Ḥusayn's letter by the Báb: "That night I saw such evidences of joy and gladness on the faces of the Báb and of Quddús as I am unable to describe. I often heard the Báb, in those days, exultingly repeat the words, 'How marvellous, how exceedingly marvellous, is that which has occurred between the months of Jamádí and Rajab!' As He was reading the communication addressed to Him by Mullá Ḥusayn, He turned to Quddús and, showing him certain passages of that letter, explained the reason for His joyous expressions of surprise. I, for my part, remained completely unaware of the nature of that explanation." '

Mírzá Aḥmad, upon whom the account of this incident had produced a profound impression, was determined to fathom its mystery. 'Not until I met Mullá Ḥusayn in Shíráz,' he told me, 'was I able to satisfy my curiosity. When I repeated to him the account described to me by the Báb's uncle, he smiled and said how well he remembered that between the months of Jamádí and Rajab he chanced to be in Ṭihrán. He gave no further explanation, and contented himself with this brief remark. This was sufficient, however, to convince me that in the city of Ṭihrán there lay hidden a Mystery which, when revealed to the world, would bring unspeakable joy to the hearts of both the Báb and Quddús.'[8]

The story of Bahá'u'lláh's immediate acknowledgement of the truth of the Message of the Báb, when He read a few lines of the Báb's newly-revealed Writings, may lead some to an erroneous conclusion that Bahá'u'lláh had no prior knowledge of the Báb's Revelation and that He was converted through reading a page of that historic scroll. Such a belief is contrary to many statements of the Báb and Bahá'u'lláh themselves. For the Báb has made it very clear in His Writings that every word revealed by Him had originated from 'Him Whom God shall make manifest', Whose station was exalted beyond any description. The spiritual link of divine revelation existed between the two. The only link which needed to be established was a physical one, and this was achieved by the visit of Mullá Ḥusayn. In the *Persian Bayán*, the Báb states:

> And know thou of a certainty that every letter revealed in the Bayán is solely intended to evoke submission unto Him Whom God shall make manifest, for it is He Who hath revealed the Bayán prior to His Own manifestation.[9]

There are many passages in the Writings of the Báb similar to the above. Bahá'u'lláh also refers to the Revelation of the Báb as 'My Own previous Revelation'. The perusal of the Writings of the Báb will make it abundantly clear that His relationship with Bahá'u'lláh,

* 'The first to embrace the Faith in Khurásán was Mírzá Aḥmad-i-Azghandí, the most learned, the wisest, and the most eminent among the 'ulamás of that province.' (*The Dawn-Breakers*, p. 125)

Whom He designated as 'Him Whom God shall make manifest', was similar to that of Christ with the 'Heavenly Father' Who is reported in the Gospels as the Source of Christ's Revelation.

The station of Bahá'u'lláh is that of the Supreme Manifestation of God, the inaugurator of a universal cycle.* His Revelation is that of the Heavenly Father Himself. In order to appreciate this truth one could turn to the many references in the Holy Writings stating that God in His Essence is unknowable and exalted above any relationship with His creation. Bahá'u'lláh states that even the Prophets of God have no knowledge of His inner reality, His Essence. Speaking of God, Bahá'u'lláh explains:

> From time immemorial, He, the Divine Being, hath been veiled in the ineffable sanctity of His exalted Self, and will everlastingly continue to be wrapt in the impenetrable mystery of His unknowable Essence . . . Ten thousand Prophets, each a Moses, are thunderstruck upon the Sinai of their search at God's forbidding voice, 'Thou shalt never behold Me!'; whilst a myriad Messengers, each as great as Jesus, stand dismayed upon their heavenly thrones by the interdiction 'Mine Essence thou shalt never apprehend!'[10]

And further, in His communion with God, Bahá'u'lláh proclaims:

> How bewildering to me, insignificant as I am, is the attempt to fathom the sacred depths of Thy knowledge! How futile my efforts to visualize the magnitude of the power inherent in Thine handiwork – the revelation of Thy creative power![11]

In another prayer Bahá'u'lláh clearly testifies to His inability to know the Essence of God or have any access to it.

> I swear by Thy Beauty, O King of eternity Who sittest on Thy most glorious Throne! He [Bahá'u'lláh] Who is the Day-Spring of Thy signs and the Revealer of Thy clear tokens hath, notwithstanding the immensity of His wisdom and the loftiness of His knowledge, confessed His powerlessness to comprehend the least of Thine utterances, in their relation to Thy most exalted Pen – how much more is He incapable of apprehending the nature of Thine all-glorious Self and of Thy most august Essence![12]

Although God in His Essence is inaccessible to His Prophets, He reveals Himself to Them through the instrumentality of His Kingdom of Revelation, or His Most Great Spirit. It is this 'Most Great Spirit' which has been described as the Holy Spirit in previous Dispensations that has animated all the Manifestations of God. This has

* For more information on this topic see *The Revelation of Bahá'u'lláh*, vol. 1, pp. 309–14.

been eloquently described by Shoghi Effendi in this passage about Bahá'u'lláh's experience in the Síyáh-Chál:

> It was in such dramatic circumstances, recalling the experience of Moses when face to face with the Burning Bush in the wilderness of Sinai, the successive visions of Zoroaster, the opening of the heavens and the descent of the Dove upon Christ in the Jordan, the cry of Gabriel heard by Muḥammad in the Cave of Hira, and the dream of the Báb, in which the blood of the Imám Ḥusayn touched and sanctified his lips, that Bahá'u'lláh, He 'around Whom the Point of the Bayán hath revolved', and the Vehicle of the greatest Revelation the world has yet seen, received the first intimation of His sublime Mission, and that a ministry which, alike in its duration and fecundity, is unsurpassed in the religious history of mankind, was inaugurated. It was on that occasion that the 'Most Great Spirit', as designated by Bahá'u'lláh Himself, revealed itself to Him, in the form of a 'Maiden', and bade Him 'lift up' His 'voice between earth and heaven'—that the same Spirit which, in the Zoroastrian, the Mosaic, the Christian, and Muḥammadan Dispensations, had been respectively symbolized by the 'Sacred Fire', the 'Burning Bush', the 'Dove', and the 'Angel Gabriel'.[13]

Concerning the 'Most Great Spirit', Bahá'u'lláh has revealed these words in the Súriy-i-Haykal:

> The Holy Spirit Itself hath been generated through the agency of a single letter revealed by this Most Great Spirit, if ye be of them that comprehend.[14]

In his elucidation of the above passage Shoghi Effendi writes:

> As to your question concerning the Holy Spirit and its relation to Bahá'u'lláh: the Holy Spirit may well be compared to the rays of the sun, and Bahá'u'lláh to a perfect mirror reflecting these rays which radiate from the sun. Briefly stated the comparison is this: God is the sun; the Holy Spirit is the rays of the sun; and Bahá'u'lláh is the mirror reflecting the rays of the sun. In the passage you have quoted from the 'Súriy-i-Haykal' Bahá'u'lláh refers to His station of identity with God, to His reality which is Divine. In this passage it is really God speaking through Bahá'u'lláh. Bahá'u'lláh is not the intermediary between God and the other Manifestations, although these are under His shadow, for the simple reason that the Messengers of God are all inherently one; it is their Message that differs. Bahá'u'lláh appearing at a time when the world has attained maturity, His message must necessarily surpass the message of all previous prophets. Not only so, but His message is potentially greater than any message which later prophets within His own cycle may reveal. This is because the stage of maturity is the most momentous stage in the evolution of mankind . . .[15]

It is important to realize that every word that Bahá'u'lláh uttered and every action He took originated not from His human personality, but were all manifestations of that Great Spirit. It is for this reason that any reference to Bahá'u'lláh is not a reference to a human being, but rather to the 'Most Great Spirit of God' which was manifested through Him. On the other hand, His human temple was so integrated with the forces of His Revelation that one cannot discard His human side altogether. The human and the spiritual were so thoroughly interwoven as to enable Him to communicate His great Revelation to mankind.

Whenever the individual comes to realize that the 'Most Great Spirit of God' has manifested itself to man through Bahá'u'lláh, he will then be able to appreciate some of the significance of the following utterances revealed by Him extolling the greatness of His Revelation:

> Verily I say! No one hath apprehended the root of this Cause. It is incumbent upon every one, in this day, to perceive with the eye of God, and to hearken with His ear. Whoso beholdeth Me with an eye besides Mine own will never be able to know Me. None among the Manifestations of old, except to a prescribed degree, hath ever completely apprehended the nature of this Revelation.[16]

> The purpose underlying all creation is the revelation of this most sublime, this most holy Day, the Day known as the Day of God, in His Books and Scriptures – the Day which all the Prophets, and the Chosen Ones, and the holy ones, have wished to witness.[17]

> Every Prophet hath announced the coming of this Day, and every Messenger hath groaned in His yearning for this Revelation – a revelation which, no sooner had it been revealed than all created things cried out saying, 'The earth is God's, the Most Exalted, the Most Great!'[18]

> The soul of every Prophet of God, of every Divine Messenger, hath thirsted for this wondrous Day. All the divers kindreds of the earth have, likewise, yearned to attain it.[19]

> Be fair, ye peoples of the world; is it meet and seemly for you to question the authority of one Whose presence 'He Who conversed with God' (Moses) hath longed to attain, the beauty of Whose countenance 'God's Well-beloved' (Muḥammad) had yearned to behold, through the potency of Whose love the 'Spirit of God' (Jesus) ascended to heaven, for Whose sake the 'Primal Point' (the Báb) offered up His life?[20]

> He it is Who in the Old Testament hath been named Jehovah, Who in the Gospel hath been designated as the Spirit of Truth, and in the Qur'án acclaimed as the Great Announcement . . . But for Him no Divine Messenger would have been invested with the robe of prophethood, nor would any of the sacred scriptures have been revealed.[21]

Naught is seen in My temple but the Temple of God, and in My beauty but His Beauty, and in My being but His Being, and in My self but His Self, and in My movement but His Movement, and in My acquiescence but His Acquiescence, and in My pen but His Pen, the Mighty, the All-Praised. There hath not been in My soul but the Truth, and in Myself naught could be seen but God . . . The Holy Spirit Itself hath been generated through the agency of a single letter revealed by this Most Great Spirit, if ye be of them that comprehend.[22]

It is important to note that the Manifestations of God have two sides, the human and the divine. All these attributes and designations refer not to the human side of Bahá'u'lláh, but to His divine side, the Spirit of God which motivated Him and of which He was a Mouthpiece.

It is not possible for man with his limited capacity to fathom the mysteries of Divine Revelation. Even those who have embraced the Cause of Bahá'u'lláh are bewildered at the immensity of His Mission and the exalted nature of His Revelation. Only the Chosen Ones of God who are endowed with divine power can claim to understand the awe-inspiring station of Bahá'u'lláh. Let us, therefore, turn to the Writings of the Báb, Himself a Manifestation of God, to get a true glimpse of the greatness of Bahá'u'lláh's Revelation:

Of all the tributes I have paid to Him Who is to come after Me, the greatest is this, My written confession, that no words of Mine can adequately describe Him, nor can any reference to Him in My Book, the Bayán, do justice to His Cause.[23]

The Báb has clearly stated to His followers that His Revelation was entirely dependent upon 'Him Whom God shall make manifest' and that He was only a servant at His threshold. In His *Qayyúmu'l-Asmá'*, the first emanations of His Pen, the Báb communes with Bahá'u'lláh in these words:

Out of utter nothingness, O great and omnipotent Master, Thou hast, through the celestial potency of Thy might, brought me forth and raised me up to proclaim this Revelation. I have made none other but Thee my trust; I have clung to no will but Thy will.[24]

And in the same Book, He craves for martyrdom in the path of Bahá'u'lláh, Whom He addresses as the 'Remnant of God'.

. . . O Thou Remnant of God! I have sacrificed myself wholly for Thee; I have accepted curses for Thy sake, and have yearned for naught but martyrdom in the path of Thy love. Sufficient witness unto me is God, the Exalted, the Protector, the Ancient of Days.[25]

In a Tablet which the Báb addressed to 'Him Whom God shall make manifest', He writes:

This is an epistle from this lowly servant to the All-Glorious Lord – He Who hath been aforetime and will be hereafter made manifest. Verily He is the Most Manifest, the Almighty.[26]

There are many passages in the Writings of the Báb in which He states that He will be the first to acknowledge the Cause of 'Him Whom God shall make manifest' and bow before Him as a lowly servant. We cite a few examples:

Were He to appear this very moment, I would be the first to adore Him, and the first to bow down before Him.[27]

'I, verily, am a believer in Him, and in His Faith, and in His Book, and in His Testimonies, and in His Ways, and in all that proceedeth from Him concerning them. I glory in My kinship with Him, and pride Myself on My belief in Him'. And likewise, He saith: 'O congregation of the Bayán and all who are therein! Recognize ye the limits imposed upon you, for such a One as the Point of the Bayán Himself hath believed in Him Whom God shall make manifest, before all things were created. Therein, verily, do I glory before all who are in the kingdom of heaven and earth.'[28]

'The whole of the Bayán is only a leaf amongst the leaves of His Paradise.' And likewise, He saith: 'I am the first to adore Him, and pride Myself on My kinship with Him.'[29]

As we survey the Writings of the Báb, we come across innumerable passages in which He glorifies the station of 'Him Whom God shall make manifest' in such wise that one becomes awe-struck at the sublimity of His words when He identifies Him as God personified. Before proceeding to quote a few such passages, it is important to recall the explanations given in previous pages concerning the station of Bahá'u'lláh, lest one may be misled to identify Him as the Inner Reality, the Essence of God. To come to such a conclusion would amount to blasphemy. Shoghi Effendi has clarified this point when he writes:

Let no one meditating, in the light of the afore-quoted passages, on the nature of the Revelation of Bahá'u'lláh, mistake its character or misconstrue the intent of its Author. The divinity attributed to so great a Being and the complete incarnation of the names and attributes of God in so exalted a Person should, under no circumstances, be misconceived or misinterpreted. The human temple that has been made the vehicle of so overpowering a Revelation must, if we be faithful to the tenets of our Faith, ever remain entirely distinguished from that 'innermost Spirit of Spirits' and 'eternal Essence of Essences' – that invisible yet rational God Who, however much we extol the divinity of His Manifestations on earth, can in no wise incarnate His infinite, His unknowable, His incorruptible and all-embracing Reality in the concrete and limited frame of a mortal being. Indeed, the God Who could so incarnate His own reality would, in the light of the teachings of Bahá'u'lláh, cease immediately to be God.[30]

The following are utterances of the Báb gleaned from His various Writings as He extols the person of 'Him Whom God shall make manifest'. In the *Persian Bayán*, the Báb states that 'He Whom God shall make manifest' as the Mouthpiece of God will proclaim:

> Verily, verily, I am God, no God is there but Me; in truth all others except Me are My creatures. Say, O My creatures! Me alone, therefore, should ye fear.[31]

and again:

> He, verily, is the One Who, under all conditions, proclaimeth: 'I, in very truth, am God.'[32]

> The glory of Him Whom God shall make manifest is immeasurably above every other glory, and His majesty is far above every other majesty. His beauty excelleth every other embodiment of beauty, and His grandeur immensely exceedeth every other manifestation of grandeur. Every light paleth before the radiance of His light, and every other exponent of mercy falleth short before the tokens of His mercy. Every other perfection is as naught in face of His consummate perfection, and every other display of might is as nothing before His absolute might. His names are superior to all other names. His good-pleasure taketh precedence over any other expression of good-pleasure. His pre-eminent exaltation is far above the reach of every other symbol of exaltation. The splendour of His appearance far surpasseth that of any other appearance. His divine concealment is far more profound than any other concealment. His loftiness is immeasurably above every other loftiness. His gracious favour is unequalled by any other evidence of favour. His power transcendeth every power. His sovereignty is invincible in the face of every other sovereignty. His celestial dominion is exalted far above every other dominion. His knowledge pervadeth all created things, and His consummate power extendeth over all beings.[33]

The Báb further testifies:

> I swear by the sanctified Essence of God that every true praise and deed offered unto God is naught but praise and deed offered unto Him Whom God shall make manifest.
>
> Deceive not your own selves that you are being virtuous for the sake of God when you are not. For should ye truly do your works for God, ye would be performing them for Him Whom God shall make manifest and would be magnifying His Name.[34]

and again:

'Were He to make of every one on earth a Prophet, all would, in very truth, be accounted as Prophets in the sight of God.' And likewise, He saith: 'In the day of the revelation of Him Whom God shall make manifest all that dwell on earth will be equal in His estimation. Whomsoever He ordaineth as a Prophet, he, verily, hath been a Prophet from the beginning that hath no beginning, and will thus remain until the end that hath no end, inasmuch as this is an act of God. And whosoever is made a Viceregent by Him, shall be a Viceregent in all the worlds, for this is an act of God. For the will of God can in no wise be revealed except through His will, nor His wish be manifested save through His wish.'[35]

It has been stated in the above pages that man, and even the Prophets of God, have no access to the Inner Reality of God – His Essence. From eternity all Revelations and His creation have come into being through the instrumentality of His 'Most Great Spirit' which was manifested on this planet for the first time through Bahá'u'lláh as 'Him Whom God shall make manifest'. The Báb, in the following pages, confirms that man in his effort to praise and adore God can only reach out to 'Him Whom God shall make manifest', the embodiment of that 'Most Great Spirit'.

Say, He Whom God shall make manifest is indeed the Primal Veil of God. Above this Veil ye can find nothing other than God, while beneath it ye can discern all things emanating from God. He is the Unseen, the Inaccessible, the Most Exalted, the Best Beloved.

If ye seek God, it behooveth you to seek Him Whom God shall make manifest . . .[36]

and similarly He states:

From the beginning that hath no beginning all men have bowed in adoration before Him Whom God shall make manifest and will continue to do so until the end that hath no end. How strange then that at the time of His appearance ye should pay homage by day and night unto that which the Point of the Bayán hath enjoined upon you and yet fail to worship Him Whom God shall make manifest.[37]

In the *Persian Bayán* the Báb states[38] that attaining unto the presence of God as promised in the Holy Books would be none other than attaining the presence of 'Him Whom God shall make manifest', for man has no access to the Essence of God.

In another passage[39] He mentions Bahá'u'lláh by name and categorically states that He is the 'Primal Will' of God. In several other instances the Báb refers to Bahá'u'lláh by name. In a celebrated passage in the *Persian Bayán* He states:

Well is it with him who fixeth his gaze upon the Order of Bahá'u'lláh,

> and rendereth thanks unto his Lord. For He will assuredly be made manifest. God hath indeed irrevocably ordained it in the Bayán.[40]

In the *Kitáb-i-Panj-Sha'n* the Báb clearly identifies Bahá'u'lláh as 'Him Whom God shall make manifest'. He enquires, 'Do ye know Bahá'u'lláh or not? For He is the glory of Him Whom God shall make manifest.'[41]

It is known that Bahá'u'lláh assumed this title of 'Bahá' at the Conference of Badasht,* a title which was confirmed by the Báb later. This title was exclusive to Him and no one else among the followers of the Báb was known by it. It is highly significant that prior to this conference the Báb had already revealed the *Persian Bayán* and in it He had identified Bahá'u'lláh by name as 'Him Whom God shall make manifest'.

The Báb considered His own Revelation to be as a gift to 'Him Whom God shall make manifest'. These are some of His utterances concerning the *Bayán*, the Mother Book of the Bábí Dispensation.

> Suffer not yourselves to be shut out as by a veil from God after He hath revealed Himself. For all that hath been exalted in the Bayán is but as a ring upon My hand, and I Myself am, verily, but a ring upon the hand of Him Whom God shall make manifest – glorified be His mention! He turneth it as He pleaseth, for whatsoever He pleaseth, and through whatsoever He pleaseth. He, verily, is the Help in Peril, the Most High.[42]

> The whole of the Bayán is only a leaf amongst the leaves of His Paradise.[43]

> The Bayán is from beginning to end the repository of all of His attributes, and the treasury of both His fire and His light.[44]

> I swear by the most holy Essence of God – exalted and glorified be He – that in the Day of the appearance of Him Whom God shall make manifest a thousand perusals of the Bayán cannot equal the perusal of a single verse to be revealed by Him Whom God shall make manifest.[45]

> I swear by the most sacred Essence of God that but one line of the Words uttered by Him is more sublime than the words uttered by all that dwell on earth. Nay, I beg forgiveness for making this comparison. How could the reflections of the sun in the mirror compare with the wondrous rays of the sun in the visible heaven?[46]

> The year-old germ that holdeth within itself the potentialities of the Revelation that is to come is endowed with a potency superior to the combined forces of the whole of the Bayán.[47]

The Báb has clearly stated that the *Bayán* revolves around the

* See *The Dawn-Breakers*.

words of 'Him Whom God shall make manifest'. In another passage in the same chapter[48] He warns His followers that the *Bayán* will not be pleased with them unless they bear allegiance to 'Him Whom God shall make manifest', Who is the Revealer of the *Bayán* and all the heavenly Books. The Báb also forbids the interpretation of the *Bayán* and states that only 'He Whom God shall make manifest' or those whom He endows with His knowledge can interpret the Words of God.

Knowing that the duration of His Dispensation was very short and the Revelation of Bahá'u'lláh was at hand, the Báb did not fix the Qiblih (Point of Adoration). He instead ordained that the Qiblih is 'Him Whom God shall make manifest' and that the faithful should turn to Him wherever He might be.

There are innumerable passages in the Báb's Writings exhorting His followers to be watchful, and as soon as the Supreme Manifestation of God reveals Himself, to recognize and follow Him immediately. He counsels them to allow no doubt to enter their minds when informed of the appearance of 'Him Whom God shall make manifest'. He warns them repeatedly to beware lest anything in the world, including the *Bayán* or any other of the Báb's Writings, should become a barrier between them and 'Him Whom God shall make manifest'. The following utterances of the Báb, urging and pleading with His followers to be faithful to 'Him Whom God shall make manifest', are but a few quotations gleaned from among many.

> At the time of the manifestation of Him Whom God shall make manifest everyone should be well trained in the teachings of the Bayán, so that none of the followers may outwardly cling to the Bayán and thus forfeit their allegiance unto Him. If anyone does so, the verdict of 'disbeliever in God' shall be passed upon him.[49]

The Báb enjoined on His followers to read once every nineteen days Chapter VI:8 of the *Bayán* so that they might prepare themselves for the Revelation of 'Him Whom God shall make manifest'.

> Once every nineteen days this Chapter should be read, that haply they may not be veiled, in the time of the revelation of Him Whom God shall make manifest. . . .[50]

> Beware, beware lest, in the days of His Revelation, the Váḥid of the Bayán (eighteen Letters of the Living) shut thee not out as by a veil from Him, inasmuch as this Váḥid is but a creature in His sight. And beware, beware that the words sent down in the Bayán shut thee not out as by a veil from Him.[51]

> O ye who are invested with the Bayán! Be ye watchful on the Day of Resurrection, for on that Day ye will firmly believe in the Váḥid of the

Bayán, though this, even as your past religion which proved of no avail, can in no wise benefit you, unless ye embrace the Cause of Him Whom God shall make manifest and believe in that which He ordaineth. Therefore take ye good heed lest ye shut yourselves out from Him Who is the Fountain-head of all Messengers and Scriptures, while ye hold fast to parts of the teachings which have emanated from these sources.[52]

Whenever ye learn that a new Cause hath appeared, ye must seek the presence of its author and must delve into his writings that haply ye may not be debarred from attaining unto Him Whom God shall make manifest at the hour of His manifestation.[53]

Recognize Him by His verses. The greater your neglect in seeking to know Him, the more grievously will ye be veiled in fire.[54]

Let not names shut you out as by a veil from Him Who is their Lord, even the name of Prophet, for such a name is but a creation of His utterance.[55]

Say, God shall of a truth cause your hearts to be given to perversity if ye fail to recognize Him Whom God shall make manifest; but if ye do recognize Him God shall banish perversity from your hearts . . .[56]

The Báb repeatedly gave the year nine as the date of the appearance of 'Him Whom God shall make manifest'. The declaration of the Báb took place in the year 1260 AH (AD 1844). The year nine is 1269 AH, which began about the middle of October 1852 when Bahá'u'lláh had already been imprisoned for about two months in the Síyáh-Chál of Ṭihrán, the scene of the birth of His Revelation.

The following are a few passages concerning the year nine.

'In the year nine ye will attain unto all good.' On another occasion He saith: 'In the year nine ye will attain unto the Presence of God.'[57]

Ere nine will have elapsed from the inception of this Cause, the realities of the created things will not be made manifest. All that thou hast as yet seen is but the stage from the moist germ until We clothed it with flesh. Be patient, until thou beholdest a new creation. Say: 'Blessed, therefore, be God, the most excellent of Makers!'[58]

To 'Aẓím, a noted disciple, the Báb states:

Wait thou until nine will have elapsed from the time of the Bayán. Then exclaim: 'Blessed, therefore, be God, the most excellent of Makers!'[59]

In a Tablet to Mullá Báqir, a Letter of the Living, the Báb in the following passage intimates that he will attain the presence of God in eight years time. The Báb has stated categorically that by attaining the presence of God is meant attaining the presence of 'Him Whom

God shall make manifest'. Mullá Báqir attained the presence of Bahá'u'lláh in Baghdád.

> Haply thou mayest in eight years, in the day of His Revelation, attain unto His Presence.[60]

It is in this same letter that the Báb testifies, in these words, to the exalted character of the Revelation of Him Whom God shall make manifest.

> I have written down in My mention of Him* these gem-like words: 'No allusion of Mine can allude unto Him, neither anything mentioned in the Bayán' . . . 'Exalted and glorified is He above the power of any one to reveal Him except Himself, or the description of any of His creatures. I Myself am but the first servant to believe in Him and in His signs, and to partake of the sweet savours of His words from the first-fruits of the Paradise of His knowledge. Yea, by His glory! He is the Truth. There is none other God but Him. All have risen at His bidding.'[61]

The Báb has also referred to the year nineteen for the Revelation of 'Him Whom God shall make manifest'. This is a reference to the public declaration of Bahá'u'lláh in the Garden of Riḍván in Baghdád which occurred nineteen years after the inception of the Bahá'í Era in 1844.

> The Lord of the Day of Reckoning will be manifested at the end of Váḥid and the beginning of eighty.[62]

Each váḥid is nineteen, and eighty is a reference to 1280 AH (1863). There is a remarkable statement by the Báb in His second Tablet to 'Him Whom God shall make manifest' in which He describes His utter submissiveness to Bahá'u'lláh and pleads with Him not to appear before nineteen years have elapsed from the inception of His Faith. These are His words:

> . . . the Bayán and such as bear allegiance to it are but a present from me unto Thee and to express my undoubting faith that there is no God but Thee, that the kingdoms of Creation and Revelation are Thine, that no one can attain anything save by Thy power and that He Whom Thou hast raised up is but Thy servant and Thy Testimony. I, indeed, beg to address Him Whom God shall make manifest, by Thy leave in these words: 'Shouldst Thou dismiss the entire company of the followers of the Bayán in the Day of the Latter Resurrection† by a mere sign of Thy finger even while still a suckling babe, Thou wouldst indeed be praised in

* Him Whom God shall make manifest.

† In the Writings of the Báb, the 'Day of Resurrection' is a reference to the day of appearance of 'Him Whom God shall make manifest'.

Thy indication. And though no doubt is there about it, do Thou grant a respite of nineteen years as a token of Thy favour so that those who have embraced this Cause may be graciously rewarded by Thee. Thou art verily the Lord of grace abounding.[63]

Although the Báb has made several references to the years nine and nineteen, nevertheless He makes it abundantly clear that the time of the advent of 'Him Whom God shall make manifest' is entirely in His Own hands. Whenever He appears, all must follow Him. He warns His followers not to let any statement made in the *Bayán* or His other Writings become a cause of denying Him at the time of His Revelation.

Were He to appear this very moment, I would be the first to adore Him, and the first to bow down before Him.[64]

The Báb exhorted His followers to adorn themselves with divine virtues and characters so as to be a cause of pleasure to 'Him Whom God shall make manifest'. For example, He writes:

O ye that are invested with the Bayán! Ye should perform such deeds as would please God, your Lord, earning thereby the good-pleasure of Him Whom God shall make manifest. Turn not your religion into a means of material gain, spending your life on vanities, and inheriting thereby on the Day of Resurrection* that which would displease Him Whom God shall make manifest, while ye deem that what ye do is right. If, however, ye observe piety in your Faith, God will surely nourish you from the treasuries of His heavenly grace.

Be ye sincere in your allegiance to Him Whom God shall make manifest, for the sake of God, your Lord, that perchance ye may, through devotion to His Faith, be redeemed on the Day of Resurrection.[65]

Anxious to ensure that none among His followers would act in such a way as to bring displeasure to Bahá'u'lláh, the Báb advised His followers not only to purify their hearts from attachment to the things of this world, but in addition, should be clean and tidy in their appearance and clothing so as not to offend Him in case they should meet Him in public. He also forbade the Bábís to engage in heated arguments or disputes as practised in Islamic circles. The Muslim clergy in their seminars, while discussing religious subjects, would often enter into heated controversy which usually resulted in physical fighting. The Báb had warned His followers not to follow that example, because they might come in contact with 'Him Whom God shall make manifest' and their behaviour would displease Him. He exhorted them to be chaste in their writings and conversation, and always to be courteous in their manners. He admonishes them in the *Bayán* in these words:

> . . . ye have been forbidden in the Bayán to enter into idle disputation and controversy, that perchance on the Day of Resurrection ye may not engage in argumentation, and dispute with Him Whom God shall make manifest.[66]

> In the Bayán God hath forbidden everyone to pronounce judgement against any soul, lest he may pass sentence upon God, his Lord, while regarding himself to be of the righteous, inasmuch as no one knoweth how the Cause of God will begin or end.[67]

The Báb testifies in the *Bayán* that the greatest proof of 'Him Whom God shall make manifest' is the revelation of His Words. He further states that should anyone claim this station falsely, he will not be able to sustain it, as he will be powerless to adduce any proof. Nevertheless, for the sake of honouring the station of 'Him Whom God shall make manifest', and in order to prevent anyone from mistakenly opposing His person the Báb warned His followers not to oppose anyone who might claim that station. He has clearly stated:

> Should any one make a statement, and fail to support it by any proof, reject him not.[68]

and again:

> O ye who are invested with the Bayán! Should ye be apprised of a person laying claim to a Cause and revealing verses which to outward seeming are unlikely to have been revealed by anyone else save God, the Help in Peril, the Self-Subsisting, do not pass sentence against him, lest ye may inadvertently pass sentence against Him Whom God shall make manifest. Say, He Whom God shall make manifest is but one of you; He will make Himself known unto you on the Day of Resurrection. Ye shall know God when the Manifestation of His Own Self is made known unto you, that perchance ye may not stray far from His Path.[69]

As a token of respect for 'Him Whom God shall make manifest', Whose station is regarded in the *Bayán* as being far exalted above the comprehension of the believers, the Báb has forbidden His followers to ask any questions of Bahá'u'lláh, except those which are worthy of His station. He reveals in the *Bayán*:

> It is not permissible to ask questions from Him Whom God will make manifest, except that which well beseemeth Him. For His station is that of the Essence of divine Revelation . . . Should anyone desire to ask questions, he is allowed to do so only in writing, that he may derive ample understanding from His written reply and that it may serve as a

sign from his Beloved. However, let no one ask aught that may prove unworthy of His lofty station. For instance, were a person to inquire the price of straw from a merchant of rubies, how ignorant would he be and how unacceptable. Similarly unacceptable would be the questions of the highest-ranking people of the world in His presence, except such words as He Himself would utter about Himself in the Day of His manifestation.[70]

In another instance He writes:

When the Day-Star of Bahá will shine resplendent above the horizon of eternity it is incumbent upon you to present yourselves before His Throne. Beware lest ye be seated in His presence or ask questions without His leave. Fear ye God, O concourse of the Mirrors.

Beg ye of Him the wondrous tokens of His favour that He may graciously reveal for you whatever He willeth and desireth, inasmuch as on that Day all the revelations of divine bounty shall circle around the Seat of His glory and emanate from His presence, could ye but understand it.

It behooveth you to remain silent before His Throne, for indeed of all the things which have been created between heaven and earth nothing on that Day will be deemed more fitting than the observance of silence.[71]

However, Bahá'u'lláh annulled this prohibition of the Báb. In the *Kitáb-i-Aqdas* He stated that the believers were free to ask any question from Him.

The station of Bahá'u'lláh is so exalted in the sight of the Báb that He has directed His followers, as a sign of respect, to arise from their places when they hear the words 'Him Whom God shall make manifest'. He also ordains in the *Persian Bayán* that in every meeting the Bábís should leave a seat of honour vacant for Him.

In the same Book, the Báb makes a statement which reveals His sense of humour. He says that 'He Whom God shall make manifest' will also leave a seat of honour vacant in His own home, because the believers will not recognize Him! He will be inwardly amused by those who venerate His name while remaining veiled from Him at the time of His Revelation.

Innumerable are passages in the Writings of the Báb in which He extols the station of Him Whom God shall make manifest, portrays His person as majestic, awe-inspiring, incomparable and infinitely glorious, describes the inconceivable greatness of His Revelation, regards Himself as the lowliest servant at His threshold, recognizes Him as the Source of His own Revelation and the object of His adoration, and cherishes the desire to lay down His life in His path. Indeed, no Manifestation of God has ever made such a mighty Covenant with His followers regarding the Manifestation Who was to follow.

CHAPTER TWO

The Fulfilment of the Covenant of the Báb

THE promise of the Báb, so unequivocally proclaimed concerning the appearance of 'Him Whom God shall make manifest', was indeed fulfilled in the year nine (1852–53) with the birth of the Revelation of Bahá'u'lláh in the Síyáh-Chál of Ṭihrán. Within that darksome dungeon, the Most Great Spirit of God descended upon the radiant soul of Bahá'u'lláh as He breathed the foul air of a filthy and pestilential underground pit, chained and fettered in the most appalling conditions and surrounded by criminals and assassins.* That the light of this mighty Revelation should break upon the world in that gloomy place and in such dramatic circumstances is a mystery that continues to baffle our imagination.

The Dispensation of the Báb had now come to its end, and His Covenant was fulfilled. For the believers who learned of it later on, the first glimmerings of this still newer Revelation appeared in the form of a sublime ode known by the Persian believers as *Rashḥ-i-'Amá*, revealed by the Tongue of Grandeur in that dungeon. The verses revealed in this soul-stirring poem announce, in joyous terms, the advent of the Day of God. Although only nineteen lines long, this ode is indeed a mighty book revealing the character, the potentialities, the power and the glory of a Revelation identified with God Himself and destined to usher in that Day of Days so emphatically prophesied by the Báb and foretold by former Manifestations of God.

Written in allusive language, the poem clearly proclaims the joy of Bahá'u'lláh's divine experience. It announces the glad-tidings of that release of spiritual energies of which He was the vehicle, and clearly identifies His Revelation with the Day foretold in Islám when the well-known saying 'I am He' would be fulfilled. 'I' signifies the Person of Bahá'u'lláh and 'He' is the designation of God Himself. This identity with God, as already discussed, is in the realm of His attributes and not of His Essence which is beyond the reach of His Manifestations.

* See *God Passes By*.

The revelation of this joyful and wondrous poem at a time when Bahá'u'lláh was afflicted with unbearable and torturous sufferings is an indication of the power and glory with which, from its very inception, the Cause of Bahá'u'lláh had been endowed. For the first time in the recorded history of mankind a Revelation was born which was the culmination of all Revelations before it. The Supreme Manifestation of God, Bahá'u'lláh, now ushered in the Day of God and inaugurated a universal cycle* whose duration, according to His own testimony, was to be five thousand centuries.

To enable us to grasp a small measure of Bahá'u'lláh's awe-inspiring station, and to review the statements and prophecies which the prophets of old have left to posterity, we can do no better than to quote the following passages from Shoghi Effendi concerning the Revelation of Bahá'u'lláh:

> He Who in such dramatic circumstances was made to sustain the overpowering weight of so glorious a Mission was none other than the One Whom posterity will acclaim, and Whom innumerable followers already recognize, as the Judge, the Lawgiver and Redeemer of all mankind, as the Organizer of the entire planet, as the Unifier of the children of men, as the Inaugurator of the long-awaited millennium, as the Originator of a new 'Universal Cycle', as the Establisher of the Most Great Peace, as the Fountain of the Most Great Justice, as the Proclaimer of the coming of age of the entire human race, as the Creator of a new World Order, and as the Inspirer and Founder of a world civilization.
>
> To Israel He was neither more nor less than the incarnation of the 'Everlasting Father', the 'Lord of Hosts' come down 'with ten thousands of saints'; to Christendom Christ returned 'in the glory of the Father', to Shí'ah Islám the return of the Imám Ḥusayn; to Sunní Islám the descent of the 'Spirit of God' (Jesus Christ); to the Zoroastrians the promised Sháh-Bahrám; to the Hindus the reincarnation of Krishna; to the Buddhists the fifth Buddha.
>
> In the name He bore He combined those of the Imám Ḥusayn, the most illustrious of the successors of the Apostle of God – the brightest 'star' shining in the 'crown' mentioned in the Revelation of St. John – and of the Imám 'Alí, the Commander of the Faithful, the second of the two 'witnesses' extolled in that same Book. He was formally designated Bahá'u'lláh, an appellation specifically recorded in the Persian Bayán, signifying at once the glory, the light and the splendour of God, and was styled the 'Lord of Lords', the 'Most Great Name', the 'Ancient Beauty', the 'Pen of the Most High', the 'Hidden Name', the 'Preserved Treasure', 'He Whom God will make manifest', the 'Most Great Light', the 'All-Highest Horizon', the 'Most Great Ocean', the 'Supreme Heaven', the 'Pre-Existent Root', the 'Self-Subsistent', the 'Day-Star of

* For more information, see *The Revelation of Bahá'u'lláh*, vol. 1, pp. 309–11.

the Universe', the 'Great Announcement', the 'Speaker on Sinai', the 'Sifter of Men', the 'Wronged One of the World', the 'Desire of the Nations', the 'Lord of the Covenant', the 'Tree beyond which there is no passing'. He derived His descent, on the one hand, from Abraham (the Father of the Faithful) through his wife Katurah, and on the other from Zoroaster, as well as from Yazdigird, the last king of the Sásáníyán dynasty. He was moreover a descendant of Jesse, and belonged, through His father, Mírzá 'Abbás, better known as Mírzá Buzurg – a nobleman closely associated with the ministerial circles of the Court of Fatḥ-'Alí Sháh – to one of the most ancient and renowned families of Mázindarán.

To Him Isaiah, the greatest of the Jewish prophets, had alluded as the '*Glory of the Lord*', the '*Everlasting Father*', the '*Prince of Peace*', the '*Wonderful*', the '*Counsellor*', the '*Rod come forth out of the stem of Jesse*' and the '*Branch grown out of His roots*', Who '*shall be established upon the throne of David*', Who '*will come with strong hands*', Who '*shall judge among the nations*', Who '*shall smite the earth with the rod of His mouth, and with the breath of His lips slay the wicked*', and Who '*shall assemble the outcasts of Israel, and gather together the dispersed of Judah from the four corners of the earth*'. Of Him David had sung in his Psalms, acclaiming Him as the '*Lord of Hosts*' and the '*King of Glory*' . . .

He alone is meant by the prophecy attributed to Gautama Buddha Himself, that '*a Buddha named Maitreye, the Buddha of universal fellowship*' should, in the fullness of time, arise and reveal '*His boundless glory*'. To Him the Bhagavad-Gita of the Hindus had referred as the '*Most Great Spirit*', the '*Tenth Avatar*', the '*Immaculate Manifestation of Krishna*'.

To Him Jesus Christ had referred as the '*Prince of this world*', as the '*Comforter*' Who will '*reprove the world of sin, and of righteousness, and of judgment*', as the '*Spirit of Truth*' Who '*will guide you into all truth*', Who '*shall not speak of Himself, but whatsoever He shall hear, that shall He speak*', as the '*Lord of the Vineyard*', and as the '*Son of Man*' Who '*shall come in the glory of His Father*' '*in the clouds of heaven with power and great glory*', with '*all the holy angels*' about Him, and '*all nations*' gathered before His throne. To Him the Author of the Apocalypse had alluded as the '*Glory of God*', as '*Alpha and Omega*', '*the Beginning and the End*', '*the First and the Last*'. Identifying His Revelation with the '*third woe*', he, moreover, had extolled His Law as '*a new heaven and a new earth*', as the '*Tabernacle of God*', as the '*Holy City*', as the '*New Jerusalem, coming down from God out of heaven, prepared as a bride adorned for her husband*', To His Day Jesus Christ Himself had referred as '*the regeneration when the Son of Man shall sit in the throne of His glory*' . . .

To Him Muḥammad, the Apostle of God, had alluded in His Book as the '*Great Announcement*', and declared His Day to be the Day whereon '*God*' will '*come down*' '*overshadowed with clouds*', the Day whereon '*thy Lord shall come and the angels rank on rank*', and '*The Spirit shall arise and the angels shall be ranged in order*' . . .

The Báb had no less significantly extolled Him as the '*Essence of Being*', as the '*Remnant of God*', as the '*Omnipotent Master*', as the '*Crimson, all-*

encompassiung Light', as '*Lord of the visible and invisible*', as the '*sole Object of all previous Revelations, including the Revelation of the Qá'im Himself*. He had formally designated Him as '*He Whom God shall make manifest*', had alluded to Him as the '*Abhá Horizon*' wherein He Himself lived and dwelt, had specifically recorded His title, and eulogized His '*Order*' in His best-known work, the Persian Bayán, had disclosed His name through His allusion to the '*Son of 'Alí, a true and undoubted Leader of men*', had, repeatedly, orally and in writing, fixed, beyond the shadow of a doubt, the time of His Revelation, and warned His followers lest '*the Bayán and all that hath been revealed therein*' should '*shut them out as by a veil*' from Him . . .

'*He around Whom the Point of the Bayán* (Báb) *hath revolved is come*' is Bahá'u'lláh's confirmatory testimony to the inconceivable greatness and preeminent character of His own Revelation. '*If all who are in heaven and on earth*', He moreover affirms, '*be invested in this day with the powers and attributes destined for the Letters of the Bayán, whose station is ten thousand times more glorious than that of the Letters of the Qur'ánic Dispensation, and if they one and all should, swift as the twinkling of an eye, hesitate to recognize My Revelation, they shall be accounted, in the sight of God, of those that have gone astray, and regarded as "Letters of Negation"*.' '*Powerful is He, the King of Divine might*', He, alluding to Himself in the Kitáb-i-Íqán, asserts, '*to extinguish with one letter of His wondrous words, the breath of life in the whole of the Bayán and the people thereof, and with one letter bestow upon them a new and everlasting life, and cause them to arise and speed out of the sepulchres of their vain and selfish desires.*' '*This*', He furthermore declares, '*is the king of days*', the '*Day of God Himself*, the '*Day which shall never be followed by night*', the '*Springtime which autumn will never overtake*', '*the eye to past ages and centuries*', for which '*the soul of every Prophet of God, of every Divine Messenger, hath thirsted*', for which '*all the divers kindreds of the earth have yearned*', through which '*God hath proved the hearts of the entire company of His Messengers and Prophets, and beyond them those that stand guard over His sacred and inviolable Sanctuary, the inmates of the Celestial Pavilion and dwellers of the Tabernacle of Glory*' . . .

And last but not least is 'Abdu'l-Bahá's own tribute to the transcendent character of the Revelation identified with His Father: '*Centuries, nay ages, must pass away, ere the Day-Star of Truth shineth again in its mid-summer splendour, or appeareth once more in the radiance of its vernal glory.*' '*The mere contemplation of the Dispensation inaugurated by the Blessed Beauty*', He furthermore affirms, '*would have sufficed to overwhelm the saints of bygone ages – saints who longed to partake for one moment of its great glory.*'[1]

By the time Bahá'u'lláh was released from the Síyáh-Chál, He had been already stripped of His vast possessions, His health impaired by the ill-treatment and hardships of life in the dungeon, His neck badly injured and His back bent by the weight of heavy chains; but His soul was in the utmost joy. He did not intimate to anyone His experience of Divine Revelation. Only 'Abdu'l-Bahá, then nine years of age, intuitively recognized the spiritual transformation of His Father into a Manifestation of the Divine Being. The Greatest Holy Leaf, that noble and illustrious daughter of Bahá'u'lláh, has described her feelings after the release of her Father in these words:

> Jamál-i-Mubárak* had a marvellous divine experience whilst in that prison.
>
> We saw a new radiance seeming to enfold him like a shining vesture, its significance we were to learn years later. At that time we were only aware of the wonder of it, without understanding, or even being told the details of the sacred event.[2]

It is important to note that although Bahá'u'lláh did not intimate His station to the Bábís, several souls among them recognized Him as 'Him Whom God shall make manifest' during the Ministry of the Báb, long before Bahá'u'lláh's imprisonment in the Síyáh-Chál. Mullá Ḥusayn, the one who first made contact with Him, was aware of His station. Likewise Quddús and Ṭáhirih had discovered that He, and no one else, was the Promised One of the Bayán. Indeed, when we study the events that took place at the Conference of Badasht,† it becomes clear that these two outstanding disciples of the Báb had full knowledge of the station of Bahá'u'lláh. Some of those who took part in that conference were surprised to witness the expressions of utmost lowliness and humility by Quddús and Ṭáhirih towards Bahá'u'lláh. The reverence which they showed to Him at Badasht by far exceeded the homage they paid to the Báb. Indeed, Ṭáhirih has composed and left to posterity some beautiful poems in adoration of Bahá'u'lláh Whom she refers to by name, and regards Him as her Lord.[3] Similarly Quddús, at that same conference, mentioned Bahá'u'lláh by name in a treatise and paid tribute to His exalted station.

Bahá'u'lláh Himself was fully aware of His station from childhood. In one of His Tablets[4] He describes that when He was very young He was overcome by a condition which completely affected His manners, His thoughts and His words.

A transfiguration took place, the ocean of utterance‡ began to surge within Him, and this condition, Bahá'u'lláh testifies, continued throughout His life.§ Some may find this statement contrary to the belief that Bahá'u'lláh received the intimation of His station in the Síyáh-Chál of Ṭihrán. 'Abdu'l-Bahá has explained in His Writings

* Literally, Blessed Beauty, Bahá'u'lláh.
† See *The Dawn-Breakers*.
‡ Bahá'u'lláh has often referred to the outpouring of His Revelation as the surging of the ocean of His utterance.
§ For a further discussion of this subject, see *The Revelation of Bahá'u'lláh*, vol. 2, pp. 346–9.

that a Manifestation of God is always a Manifestation. Even from childhood, long before He receives the call of Prophethood, He has all the powers of the Manifestation latent within Him. He describes this state as a lamp which is hidden under a bushel, its lights hidden from the eyes of men. He also likens Him to a man who is asleep and does not reveal His powers until the hour strikes for the birth of His Mission.

It is not possible for man to fully understand the mysteries of divine Revelation and to appreciate the nature and the workings of the Manifestations of God. In the case of Bahá'u'lláh, however, we can discover from the records of His life and from His conduct that prior to the birth of His Revelation, He was fully aware of His exalted station. To cite one example:

One of the devoted disciples of the Báb was the celebrated Shaykh Ḥasan-i-Zunúzí.* The Báb had intimated to him that he would attain the presence of the Promised Ḥusayn† in the city of Karbilá where Shaykh Ḥasan used to live. Bahá'u'lláh visited Karbilá in 1851, about one year before His imprisonment in the Síyáh-Chál. In that city He met Shaykh Ḥasan and, as prophesied by the Báb, he intimated to him His exalted station. Nabíl-i-A'ẓam tells the story as recounted to him by Shaykh Ḥasan.

> Sixteen lunar months, less twenty and two days, had elapsed since the day of the martyrdom of the Báb, when, on the day of 'Arafih,‡ in the year 1267 A.H.,§ while I was passing by the gate of the inner courtyard of the shrine of the Imám Ḥusayn, my eyes, for the first time, fell upon Bahá'u'lláh. What shall I recount regarding the countenance which I beheld! The beauty of that face, those exquisite features which no pen or brush dare describe, His penetrating glance, His kindly face, the majesty of His bearing, the sweetness of His smile, the luxuriance of His jet-black flowing locks, left an indelible impression upon my soul. I was then an old man, bowed with age. How lovingly He advanced towards me! He took me by the hand and, in a tone which at once betrayed power and beauty, addressed me in these words: 'This very day I have purposed to make you known as a Bábí throughout Karbilá.' Still holding my hand in His, He continued to converse with me. He walked with me all along the market-street, and in the end He said: 'Praise be to God that you have remained in Karbilá, and have beheld with your own eyes the countenance of the promised Ḥusayn.' I recalled instantly the promise which had been given me by the Báb. His words, which I had regarded as referring

* See *The Dawn-Breakers*.
† It is believed in Islám that two Revelations will succeed one another. Shí'ah Islám expects that after the appearance of the Qá'im, the Promised Ḥusayn will manifest Himself. It is noteworthy that Bahá'u'lláh's name was Ḥusayn -'Alí.
‡ The ninth day of the month of Dhi'l-Ḥijjih.
§ October 5, 1851.

> to a remote future, I had not shared with anyone. These words of Bahá'u'lláh moved me to the depths of my being. I felt impelled to proclaim to a heedless people, at that very moment and with all my soul and power, the advent of the promised Ḥusayn. He bade me, however, repress my feelings and conceal my emotions. 'Not yet', He breathed into my ears; 'the appointed Hour is approaching. It has not yet struck. Rest assured and be patient.' From that moment all my sorrows vanished. My soul was flooded with joy.[5]

On that occasion, Bahá'u'lláh actually imparted to Shaykh Ḥasan the glad-tidings that the unveiling of His Revelation would take place in Baghdád.*

Although a few of the disciples of the Báb had the spiritual capacity to recognize Bahá'u'lláh as the Promised One of the *Bayán*, both before and after the birth of His Revelation in the Síyáh-Chál, the believers in general were completely unaware of it. The Bábí community was at that time experiencing the most harrowing persecution and sufferings. By the time of Bahá'u'lláh's imprisonment in the Síyáh-Chál, over two years had passed since the Martyrdom of the Báb. Many of His outstanding followers had been mown down by an inveterate enemy. Every hope which the Bábís entertained for the ascendancy and triumph of His Cause was dashed, and they were dispirited and dismayed. Bahá'u'lláh, the only leader Who inspired them with confidence and assurance, had, soon after the Martyrdom of the Báb, been advised to retire for a period of time to Karbilá in 'Iráq. His sojourn lasted a little under a year and soon after His return He had been cast into the Síyáh-Chál of Ṭihrán in the most humiliating circumstances. And finally, He had been exiled to 'Iráq. When we consider the lack of a proper system of communication in Persia in those days, we can appreciate how the followers of the Báb were cut off and did not know where to turn for guidance.

The only leader they had been told to turn to was Mírzá Yaḥyá, but he spent most of this time in hiding. He was a fugitive, frightened and roaming around the countryside in disguise so that no one could contact him. When Bahá'u'lláh was imprisoned in the Síyáh-Chál, a bloodbath of unprecedented ferocity was unleashed on the Bábís. Anyone who had any connection with the Faith of the Báb was executed in the most cruel circumstances. Those who escaped the net were driven underground. They lived their lives confused and leaderless.

In order to appreciate the history of this particular time and the two decades which followed, we can do no better than to study

* See *The Dawn-Breakers*, p. 593.

closely the provisions which were made by the Báb during His lifetime concerning the leadership of the Bábí community after His martyrdom until the appearance of 'Him Whom God shall make manifest'. This is where Mírzá Yaḥyá, entitled Subḥ-i-Azal (Morn of Eternity) plays a major rôle.

CHAPTER THREE

Mírzá Yaḥyá, the Nominee of the Báb

Mírzá Yaḥyá was a paternal half-brother of Bahá'u'lláh. He was about fourteen years younger, and when their father died he was only a boy of eight. He thus grew up under the care and protection of Bahá'u'lláh, Who paid special attention to his education and upbringing. When the Báb declared His Mission in 1844, Mírzá Yaḥyá was thirteen years old. When the Message of the Báb reached Bahá'u'lláh, He helped Mírzá Yaḥyá to recognize the station of the Báb and to embrace the newly-born Faith, and encouraged him to read the Writings of the Báb and become familiar with their style of composition.

A few months before the Báb was martyred in 1850, Sayyáḥ, one of His distinguished disciples, attained the presence of Bahá'u'lláh in Ṭihrán. On this occasion Bahá'u'lláh sent a communication to the Báb through Sayyáḥ. Nabíl-i-A'ẓam records this account:

> Ere the departure of Sayyáḥ from Ṭihrán, Bahá'u'lláh entrusted him with an epistle, the text of which He had dictated to Mírzá Yaḥyá, and sent it in his name. Shortly after, a reply, penned in the Báb's own handwriting, in which He commits Mírzá Yaḥyá to the care of Bahá'u'lláh and urges that attention be paid to his education and training, was received.[1]

Thus Mírzá Yaḥyá grew up under the guidance of Bahá'u'lláh and became conversant with the Writings of the Báb.

In those days the believers who were educated used to make handwritten copies of the holy Words. In order to deepen his understanding of the Writings of the Báb, Bahá'u'lláh especially assigned Mírzá Yaḥyá the task of transcribing them. Consequently Mírzá Yaḥyá learnt not only the style of the composition of the Báb's Writings, but was also able to write in the same fashion and imitate the Báb's handwriting – an art which served him well some years later when he rebelled against Bahá'u'lláh, and by forging the Báb's handwriting interpolated his own words into the Báb's Writings to produce texts in his own favour.

The appointment by the Báb of Mírzá Yaḥyá as the leader of the Bábí community took place on the advice of Bahá'u'lláh. 'Abdu'l-

Bahá states that some time after the death of Muḥammad Sh̲áh it became evident that Bahá'u'lláh's fame had spread far and wide in Persia and it was essential to divert public attention away from His Person. To achieve this aim Bahá'u'lláh advised the Báb to nominate Mírzá Yaḥyá. This advice was communicated through the medium of a trusted believer, Mullá 'Abdu'l-Karím of Qazvín, otherwise known as Mírzá Aḥmad, who was able to make contact with the Báb. The appointment of Mírzá Yaḥyá, who was then in his late teens, had the obvious advantage of enabling Bahá'u'lláh to direct the affairs of the community behind the scenes through the instrumentality of Mírzá Yaḥyá, who, in reality, was merely the ostensible head until the advent of 'Him Whom God shall make manifest'.

The Bábí community was not informed of the reasons behind this appointment. It must have come as a surprise to many when they realized that the appointee of the Báb was a youth in his teens, and those who knew his personality were aware of his shallowness and vanity. Apart from Mullá 'Abdu'l-Karím, the only other person who was privy to this secret arrangement was Bahá'u'lláh's faithful brother, Mírzá Musá, entitled Áqáy-i-Kalím. It must be stated here that the Báb in all His Writings urged the believers to be ready for the manifestation of 'Him Whom God shall make manifest' and no one else. So emphatic was His advent and so close was the timing of His Revelation that the Báb never contemplated the appointment of a successor to Himself. Indeed, He confirms this in the *Bayán*, saying that in His Dispensation there was to be no mention of successorship. Yet Mírzá Yaḥyá, as we shall see later, broke the Covenant of the Báb and claimed to be His successor.

Mírzá Yaḥyá was devoid of outstanding qualities. He was easily influenced by people, ambitious and, above all, very timid by nature. At the age of nineteen he married his cousin and for some time they lived in the village of Tákur in the province of Núr. The Bábí community of Tákur was one of the most thriving communities in Persia at the time. The reason for this was that as soon as the news of the Declaration of the Báb reached Bahá'u'lláh, He arose to teach the Faith to the members of His family and others in Núr. Many relatives and friends in that area embraced the Faith and through the influence of Bahá'u'lláh became staunch believers.

When the news of the Martyrdom of the Báb reached Mírzá Yaḥyá, he was so frightened for his own life that he disguised himself in the garb of a dervish and, leaving his wife and child behind, fled into the mountains of Mázindarán. Soon after, Bahá'u'lláh left Persia for 'Iráq and Mírzá Yaḥyá could no longer avail himself of His protection and guidance. Thus he roamed the countryside in fear and trepidation. This behaviour, especially at a time when Bahá'u'lláh was absent from Persia, had a deadly effect upon the believers in the province of Núr. Through Mírzá Yaḥyá's cowardly behaviour and lack of faith in the religion of the Báb, many believers were disappointed in him as a leader, became disenchanted and left the Faith altogether.

This tragic situation brought great sorrow to Bahá'u'lláh. Some years later in 'Akká, He uttered these words on the subject as recounted by Nabíl:

> God knows that at no time did We attempt to conceal Ourself or hide the Cause which We have been bidden to proclaim. Though not wearing the garb of the people of learning, We have again and again faced and reasoned with men of great scholarship in both Núr and Mázindarán, and have succeeded in persuading them of the truth of this Revelation. We never flinched in Our determination; We never hesitated to accept the challenge from whatever direction it came. To whomsoever We spoke in those days, We found him receptive to our Call and ready to identify himself with its precepts. But for the shameful behaviour of the people of Bayán, who sullied by their deeds the work We had accomplished, Núr and Mázindarán would have been entirely won to this Cause and would have been accounted by this time among its leading strongholds.[2]

When the attempt was made on the life of Náṣiri'd-Dín Sháh by a few mentally disturbed Bábís in 1852, hell broke loose upon the Bábí community. Many of the followers of the Báb were martyred in the most cruel circumstances and Bahá'u'lláh, along with others, was imprisoned in the Síyáh-Chál. The Sháh ordered his Prime Minister, Mírzá Áqá Khán,* who was a native of Núr himself, to send troops to Núr and arrest all the followers of the Báb in that area. The troops carried out their orders; some believers were killed and some were taken to the Síyáh-Chál, their houses demolished and their properties confiscated. The house of Bahá'u'lláh, which was royally furnished, was turned into ruins. Its roof was destroyed and all items of exquisite furnishings confiscated. So terrified was Mírzá Yaḥyá as a result of these persecutions that he fled to Gílán in disguise and then to Kirmánsháh in the west of Persia. There he decided to engage himself in a profession so that no one could identify him. He took work as a salesman with a certain 'Abdu'lláh-i-Qazvíní who was a maker of shrouds.

Some months later Bahá'u'lláh and His family passed through Kirmánsháh on their way to Baghdád. In Kirmánsháh several people of rank and position came to visit Bahá'u'lláh and pay their respects, but Mírzá Yaḥyá was afraid to contact Him. Such was his state of mind that when Áqáy-i-Kalím, Bahá'u'lláh's faithful brother, called

* He was related to Bahá'u'lláh through the marriage of his niece to Mírzá Muḥammad-Ḥasan, an elder half-brother of Bahá'u'lláh.

on him, Mírzá Yaḥyá was apprehensive lest some one should recognize his true identity. After some persuasion by Áqáy-i-Kalím, he went and visited Bahá'u'lláh, knowing that Bahá'u'lláh would extend to him His protection and guidance. Feeling secure in His presence, he expressed the desire to go to Baghdád and live alone, incognito, in a house close to Bahá'u'lláh's and engage in a trade there. Bahá'u'lláh gave him a small sum of money and he bought a few bales of cotton, disguised himself as an Arab and soon after Bahá'u'lláh's arrival in Baghdád, found his way to that city.

Being a master in the art of disguise, he arrived at Bahá'u'lláh's doorstep dressed as a dervish, kashkúl (alms box) in hand. So well was he disguised that Áqáy-i-Kalím, who answered the door, did not recognize him at first. He stayed for a few days in the house of Bahá'u'lláh, but asked that neither his identity nor his arrival in the city be divulged to the believers in 'Iráq. He was helped to secure a residence in the Arab quarter of the city where no Persians resided. There he spent his time in hiding during the day, emerging only at night when he would go to the house of Bahá'u'lláh, meet with Áqáy-i-Kalím, and then return home in the late hours. He even had threatened that if anyone insisted on visiting him and revealing his identity, he would excommunicate him from the Bábí community.

It must be noted that from the early days when the Báb announced him as the leader of the Bábí community, Mírzá Yaḥyá, who was also a highly ambitious person, had entertained the thought of one day bypassing Bahá'u'lláh (who used to direct his activities) and independently asserting himself as the successor of the Báb. In those days before his rebellion, it was Bahá'u'lláh's practice to call Mírzá Yaḥyá into His presence to take down Bahá'u'lláh's words and communicate His message to the Bábís in his own name as the leader of the Bábí community.* But it is a well-known fact that whenever he entered into the presence of Bahá'u'lláh and came face to face with His majestic Person, he was unable to put forward his thoughts and became utterly speechless. Some individuals who were close to him have testified to this. Mírzá Áqá Ján, Bahá'u'lláh's amanuensis, was at first surprised to find Mírzá Yaḥyá so helpless and mute in the presence of Bahá'u'lláh, until later he realized that Mírzá Yaḥyá was like anyone else in His presence.

Many Bábís, through their devotion to the Faith, were eager to meet Mírzá Yaḥyá since he had been nominated by the Báb, but very few succeeded and these were utterly disappointed after meeting him. To cite an example: Shaykh Salmán,† honoured by Bahá'u'lláh

* In one of His Tablets Bahá'u'lláh describes this period of the Faith. See *The Revelation of Bahá'u'lláh*, vol. 2, pp. 241–3.

† For an account of his services, see *The Revelation of Bahá'u'lláh*, vols. 1 and 2.

as the 'Messenger of the Merciful' and one of the outstanding believers who for almost forty years carried Tablets and messages from Bahá'u'lláh and 'Abdu'l-Bahá to the believers, was very eager to meet Mírzá Yaḥyá in the early days of Bahá'u'lláh's arrival in Baghdád. After much pleading by Shaykh Salmán, Mírzá Yaḥyá agreed to meet him outside the city on a hilltop. When the interview took place, Mírzá Yaḥyá had nothing to say except trivialities. He was interested in the telegraph poles (a novelty in those days) and wanted Shaykh Salmán to guess the distance between two poles for him! There were a few others who succeeded in meeting Mírzá Yaḥyá in Baghdád and they too recognized his ignorance and shallow-mindedness. Those few – and there were not many – who met him face to face knew that Mírzá Yaḥyá was merely the ostensible head appointed by the Báb for convenience.

But the Bábí community as a whole was not aware of the true situation. Many, in the earlier part of Baha'u'llah's sojourn in Baghdád, were attracted to him. But this attraction was only to a name, for he was inaccessible to everybody. Gradually, as the followers of the Báb turned to Bahá'u'lláh, the truth of the Faith began to dawn on them. Many travelled to Baghdád, attained His presence and were vivified by the majesty and the glory of His Person. Some of them recognized Him as the Promised One of the *Bayán* but were not allowed to divulge their belief to others. But soon after Bahá'u'lláh's arrival, great tests surrounded the Bábí community. A severe crisis assailed the infant Faith of God from within and shook it to its very foundations for almost two decades.

CHAPTER FOUR

The Breaking of the Báb's Covenant

SHORTLY after Mírzá Yaḥyá had settled in Baghdád, he decided to engage in a profession so as to hide his identity. At first he changed his headgear, adopting a large turban and assuming the name of Ḥájí 'Alíy-i-Lás-Furúsh.* He then took a shop in a dilapidated part of the city in a bazaar and started working. In the meantime, a man of great evil described by Bahá'u'lláh as 'the embodiment of wickedness and impiety', 'the prime mover of mischief' and 'one accursed of God', entered the scene to influence Mírzá Yaḥyá. He was the notorious Siyyid Muḥammad-i-Iṣfahání, known as the 'Antichrist of the Bahá'í Revelation'. In the early days of the Faith this man was a student at a theological school in Iṣfahán, but was expelled for reprehensible conduct. He embraced the Faith during the early part of the Ministry of the Báb and later went to Karbilá where he joined the ranks of the believers. In the *Kitáb-i-Íqán* Bahá'u'lláh alludes to him as that 'one-eyed man, who . . . is arising with the utmost malevolence against us'. Of him Shoghi Effendi writes:

> The black-hearted scoundrel who befooled and manipulated this vain and flaccid man† with consummate skill and unyielding persistence was a certain Siyyid Muḥammad, a native of Iṣfáhán, notorious for his inordinate ambition, his blind obstinacy and uncontrollable jealousy. To him Bahá'u'lláh had later referred in the Kitáb-i-Aqdas as the one who had '*led astray*' Mírzá Yaḥyá, and stigmatized him, in one of His Tablets, as the '*source of envy and the quintessence of mischief*', while 'Abdu'l-Bahá had described the relationship existing between these two as that of '*the sucking child*' to the '*much-prized breast*' of its mother.[1]

Siyyid Muḥammad was in Karbilá when Bahá'u'lláh visited that city in 1851. As soon as he met Bahá'u'lláh, Whom he considered merely as another Bábí, he was struck by His authority and majesty, and when he saw the marks of honour and reverence shown to Him by others he was filled with an uncontrollable envy which never left him till the end of his tragic life.

* 'Lás Furúsh' means a dealer in silk. It is interesting that Mírzá Yaḥyá was known in official circles as Ḥájí 'Alí until the end of his life.
† Mírzá Yaḥyá.

Ḥájí Siyyid Javád-i-Karbilá'í,* an outstanding follower of the Báb, one of the Mirrors† of the Bábí Dispensation who recognized the station of Bahá'u'lláh from the early days and became an ardent Bahá'í, was in Karbilá and also met Bahá'u'lláh there for the first time in 1851. The following is his spoken chronicle as he describes his meeting with Him at a gathering where Siyyid Muḥammad was also present.

> . . . I was in Karbilá when the news of the arrival of Bahá'u'lláh in that city reached me. The first person who gave me this information was Ḥájí Siyyid Muḥammad-i-Iṣfahání.
>
> Before I attained His presence, I expected to find Him a youth of noble lineage, the son of a vizier, but not one endowed with immense knowledge or wisdom. Together with some friends I went to meet Bahá'u'lláh. As was their custom, my friends would not enter the room before me; so I went in first and occupied the seat of honour in that gathering.
>
> After we had exchanged greetings Bahá'u'lláh turned to those present and asked them what subjects they, the disciples of the late Siyyid,‡ usually discussed when they gathered in a meeting. Did they discuss the topics of religion as was current among men? What would they do if God manifested Himself to man, rolled up the old doctrines and philosophies, revealed a new set of teachings and opened up a new page in divine knowledge? What then would be their position? Bahá'u'lláh spoke for some time in this vein. It was not long before I realized that we, known as men of learning and knowledge, dwelt in the depths of ignorance, whereas He, Whom we considered to be only a youth, the son of a vizier, stood upon the highest pinnacle of understanding, knowledge and wisdom. After this experience, whenever I entered His presence, I would sit at His feet in absolute humility and refrain from speaking. I always listened attentively to Him in order to benefit from His knowledge and understanding. This attitude of mine, however, used to annoy my friend Siyyid Muḥammad. Once he rebuked me, saying: 'Assuming that all agree that Jináb-i-Bahá is of the same calibre as ourselves, why do you sit in silence and show so much humility towards Him?'
>
> I pleaded with my friend not to be angry with me. I told him that I could neither specify a station for Him nor, God forbid, consider Him as one of us. I regarded Him as incomparable and unique.[2]

The high esteem in which Bahá'u'lláh was held by the Bábís and the Shaykhís served to arouse in Siyyid Muḥammad feelings of jealousy and inner animosity as well as a determination to counteract His supremacy and exalted position in the Bábí community.

When Bahá'u'lláh was exiled to 'Iráq in 1853, the Bábís were in great disarray. They were frightened and helpless people who since

* See *The Revelation of Bahá'u'lláh*, vols. 1, 2 and 3.
† The Báb had exalted certain individuals to this rank.
‡ Siyyid Káẓim-i-Rashtí (A.T.)

the martyrdom of the Báb had been driven underground. They did not dare associate with each other in public for fear of being persecuted. When Bahá'u'lláh arrived in 'Iráq, He inspired them to come out into the open and gradually through His wise and loving leadership the Bábí community acquired a new lease of life. The ascendancy of Bahá'u'lláh in public and His rising prestige intensified the fire of jealousy which was now burning fiercely in Siyyid Muḥammad's heart.

Describing the circumstances in which some of the followers of the Báb in Baghdád recognised the station of Bahá'u'lláh and turned to Him in adoration, Shoghi Effendi recounts the reaction shown by Siyyid Muḥammad in these words:

> To these evidences of an ever deepening veneration for Bahá'u'lláh and of a passionate attachment to His person were now being added further grounds for the outbreak of the pent-up jealousies which His mounting prestige evoked in the breasts of His ill-wishers and enemies. The steady extension of the circle of His acquaintances and admirers; His friendly intercourse with officials including the governor of the city; the unfeigned homage offered Him, on so many occasions and so spontaneously, by men who had once been distinguished companions of Siyyid Káẓim; the disillusionment which the persistent concealment of Mírzá Yaḥyá, and the unflattering reports circulated regarding his character and abilities, had engendered; the signs of increasing independence, of innate sagacity and inherent superiority and capacity for leadership unmistakably exhibited by Bahá'u'lláh Himself – all combined to widen the breach which the infamous and crafty Siyyid Muḥammad had sedulously contrived to create.[3]

Knowing Mírzá Yaḥyá's weaknesses and fully aware of his ambitions, this scheming Siyyid allied himself closely with him. His influence upon Mírzá Yaḥyá was as effective as it was satanic. As a result of this close association, Mírzá Yaḥyá began to sow the seeds of doubt in the minds of those who had become Bahá'u'lláh's ardent admirers and were attracted to His Person. By various means, sometimes openly and sometimes in a subtle way, he began to try to discredit Bahá'u'lláh and misrepresent His motives in reviving the declining fortunes of the Bábí community.

While in hiding, Mírzá Yaḥyá employed a Persian merchant named Abu'l-Qásim as an intermediary between himself and the believers. As the nominee of the Báb, he began, with the help of Siyyid Muḥammad and through Abu'l-Qásim, to disseminate his baneful and misguided directives to all the Bábís in Baghdád. As this campaign of misrepresentation gathered momentum , the fortunes of the Faith began to decline, and many Bábís became confused and disenchanted.

It was during these days, too, that Siyyid Muḥammad and Mírzá Yaḥyá found a way to legitimize their own foul conduct in the community. This they did by abusing the proclamation which had been made at Badasht concerning the abrogation of the laws of Islám.* They claimed that the Bábí Dispensation had lifted the bounds (Kasr-i-Ḥudúd) which the laws of God had imposed upon the faithful. This refers to the annulment of the laws of Islám which had indeed been swept away through the Dispensation of the Báb, and not to the bounds of human decency and morality. Mírzá Yaḥyá misinterpreted this 'lifting of the bounds' to mean the abrogation of moral principles as well. Thus he began to commit many reprehensible acts. For instance, he ordered his servant to assassinate several outstanding individuals among the Bábís, as we shall see.

Bahá'u'lláh is referring to this misleading concept when He thus admonishes the believers in the *Kitáb-i-Aqdas*:

> We verily have commanded you to refuse the dictates of your evil passions and corrupt desires and not to transgress the bounds which the Pen of the Most High hath fixed . . .[4]

Although only a few years had elapsed since the birth of their Faith, the Bábís in Persia were bitterly divided among themselves, mainly for theological reasons. In Qazvín, the home of Ṭáhirih, where a large number of Bábís resided, there were four sects, each bearing a name. One was identified with Quddús, another with Ṭáhirih, another with Mírzá Yaḥyá, and one known as Bayánís, the followers of the Book of the *Bayán*.

In the meantime the situation in 'Iráq grew worse. Encouraged by Siyyid Muḥammad, Mírzá Yaḥyá made the preposterous claim of being the successor of the Báb – a position never contemplated by Him. Indeed, He categorically states in the *Persian Bayán*[5] that He appoints no successor to Himself. As a result of such harmful propaganda and acts of treachery and deceit, which kindled dissension among the believers, 'the fire of the Cause of God', as testified by Nabíl, 'had been well-nigh quenched in every place'.[6]

It is important to recognise that every religion has had its beginnings characterized by the onrushing forces of divine Revelation vivifying the souls of men as in a spring season. But at the end of the Dispensation winter sets in and the spiritual energies die down. This process, in older Dispensations, lasted several centuries. For example, the springtime of Christianity, which lasted about three years during the Ministry of Jesus, was followed by the summer season a few centuries later when the Christian religion flourished. But with the advent of Muḥammad, it lost its vitality and spiritual

* See *God Passes By*, p. 403, and *The Dawn-Breakers*, pp. 293–8.

potency. The advent of a new Dispensation brings about the close of the older one.* All past religions have gone through this cycle of spring, summer and winter, and the Dispensation of the Báb is no exception. The only difference is that whereas this cycle in older religions lasted several centuries, in the case of the Báb's it took only a decade for the spiritual winter to set in. Shoghi Effendi describes eloquently the rise and fall of the Bábí religion:

> In sheer dramatic power, in the rapidity with which events of momentous importance succeeded each other, in the holocaust which baptized its birth, in the miraculous circumstances attending the martyrdom of the One Who had ushered it in, in the potentialities with which it had been from the outset so thoroughly impregnated, in the forces to which it eventually gave birth, this nine-year period may well rank as unique in the whole range of man's religious experience. We behold, as we survey the episodes of this first act of a sublime drama, the figure of its Master Hero, the Báb, arise meteor-like above the horizon of Shíráz, traverse the sombre sky of Persia, from south to north, decline with tragic swiftness, and perish in a blaze of glory. We see His satellites, a galaxy of God-intoxicated heroes, mount above that same horizon, irradiate that same incandescent light, burn themselves out with that self-same swiftness, and impart in their turn an added impetus to the steadily gathering momentum of God's nascent Faith.[7]

Bahá'u'lláh, in some Tablets revealed in that period, foreshadows the appearance of severe tests and trials as a result of the machinations of Mírzá Yaḥyá and Siyyid Muḥammad. In one Tablet He utters these words of warning:

> The days of tests are now come. Oceans of dissension and tribulation are surging, and the Banners of Doubt are, in every nook and corner, occupied in stirring up mischief and in leading men to perdition . . .[8]

In the *Tablet of Qullu'ṭ-Ṭa'ám*, Bahá'u'lláh alludes to His intention to depart from Baghdád;† this He did when tests and tribulations reached a climax. Without informing anyone, including the members of His family, He left Baghdád for the mountains of Kurdistán. This was in April 1854.‡ In the *Kitáb-i-Íqán* He writes these thought-provoking words:

> In the early days of Our arrival in this land, when We discerned the signs of impending events, We decided, ere they happened, to retire . . . By the righteousness of God! Our withdrawal contemplated no return, and Our separation hoped for no reunion. The one object of Our retirement was to avoid becoming a subject of discord among the faithful, a source of disturbance unto Our companions, the means of injury to any soul, or

* See the *Kitáb-i-Íqán*.
† For a more detailed study, see *The Revelation of Bahá'u'lláh*, vol. 1, p. 55.
‡ For details of Bahá'u'lláh's withdrawal to the mountains of Kurdistán, see *God Passes By*.

the cause of sorrow to any heart. Beyond these, We cherished no other intention, and apart from them, We had no end in view.[9]

The absence of Bahá'u'lláh for about two years resulted in the swift decline and near extinction of the Bábí community. Under the leadership of Siyyid Muḥammad and Mírzá Yaḥyá, it had degenerated completely. Unlike the glorious days of a decade earlier, when its heroes and martyrs had demonstrated the vitality of their faith and the purity of their motives, the so-called followers of the Báb in 'Iráq during Bahá'u'lláh's retirement had sunk to the lowest depths of degradation and perversity. They were known to be in the forefront for thievery, highway robbery and murder for hire.

Mírzá Yaḥyá, disguised as a shopkeeper and sometimes hidden in a house, emboldened by the absence of Bahá'u'lláh and directed by Siyyid Muḥammad, embarked upon some of his cowardly activities, both within and outside the Bábí community. As we shall see later, the atrocities which were committed in his name and on his orders constitute some of the most shameful events in the history of the Faith, events which helped to bring about the near extinction of the Bábí religion.

It must be noted that in order to preserve the integrity of the Faith, Bahá'u'lláh for several years neither questioned the validity of Mírzá Yaḥyá's appointment as the leader of the Bábí community, nor announced the nullification of his leadership to that community. Indeed, when He departed for the mountains of Kurdistán, He directed the members of His own family to treat Mírzá Yaḥyá with consideration and to obey him. The following account by the Greatest Holy Leaf, depicting the hardships and difficulties suffered by the Holy Family during Bahá'u'lláh's absence, throws light on their relationship with this unfaithful brother of Bahá'u'lláh, and reveals some of his reprehensible conduct.

> At length my father decided to leave Ba<u>gh</u>dád for a time. During his absence, Ṣubḥ-i-Azal* could convince himself whether or not the Bábís desired to turn their faces to him as their leader, as he, in the petty conceit of a small mind and undisciplined nature, asserted, would, if given an opportunity, prove to be the case.
>
> Before my father left for his retreat into the wilderness, he commanded the friends to treat Ṣubḥ-i-Azal with consideration. He offered him and his family the shelter and hospitality of our house.
>
> He asked Mírzá Músá, my mother and me, to care for them and to do everything in our power to make them comfortable. Our grief was intense when my father left us. He told none of us either where he was going or when he would return. He took no luggage, only a little rice, and some coarse bread.

* Mírzá Yaḥyá.

So we, my mother, my brother 'Abbás and I, clung together in our sorrow and anxiety.

Ṣubḥ-i-Azal rejoiced, hoping to gain his ends, now that Jamál-i-Mubárak was no longer present.

Meanwhile, he was a guest in our house. He gave us much trouble, complaining of the food. Though all the best and most dainty things were invariably given to him.

He became at this time more than ever terrified lest he should one day be arrested. He hid himself, keeping the door of our house locked, and stormed at anybody who opened it.

As for me, I led a very lonely life, and would have liked sometimes to make friends with other children. But Ṣubḥ-i-Azal would not permit any little friends to come to the house, neither would he let me go out!

Two little girls about my own age lived in the next house. I used to peep at them; but our guest always came and shouted at me for opening the door, which he promptly locked. He was always in fear of being arrested, and cared for nothing but his own safety.

We led a very difficult life at this time as well as a lonely one. He would not even allow us to go to the Hammám to take our baths. Nobody was permitted to come to the house to help us, and the work therefore was very hard.

For hours every day I had to stand drawing water from a deep well in the house; the ropes were hard and rough, and the bucket was heavy. My dear mother used to help, but she was not very strong, and my arms were rather weak. Our guest never helped.

My father having told us to respect and obey this tyrannical person, we tried to do so, but this respect was not easy, as our lives were made so unhappy by him.

During this time the darling baby brother, born after our arrival in Baghdád, became seriously ill. Our guest would not allow a doctor, or even any neighbour to come to our help.

My mother was heart-broken when the little one died; even then we were not allowed to have anybody to prepare him for burial.

The sweet body of our beautiful baby was given to a man, who took it away, and we never knew even where he was laid. I remember so clearly the sorrow of those days.

A little while after this, we moved into a larger house – fortunately Ṣubḥ-i-Azal was too terrified of being seen, if he came with us – so he preferred to occupy a little house behind ours. We still sent his food to him, also provided for his family, now increased, as he had married another wife, a girl from a neighbouring village.

His presence was thus happily removed from our daily life; we were relieved and much happier.[10]

During Bahá'u'lláh's absence, the news reached Baghdád of the martyrdom of a certain believer of Najaf-Ábád, near Iṣfahán. Mírzá Yaḥyá was highly alarmed, fearing that an outbreak of persecution could lead the enemies of the Faith to him, the nominee of the Báb, and take his life. With these thoughts in mind, he decided to change his residence. With the help of a certain Mírzá 'Alíy-i-Tabrízí, he bought a consignment of shoes, disguised himself as a Jew and went to Basra where he remained for some time and occupied himself in his newly-found profession of shoe merchant. Later, when he realized that there was no need for alarm, he returned to Baghdád.

It was during this period under the leadership of Mírzá Yaḥyá, inspired by his wicked advisor Siyyid Muḥammad, that some of the most heinous atrocities were committed. Mírzá Asadu'lláh of Khúy, surnamed Dayyán by the Báb and one of His outstanding followers, was murdered on Mírzá Yaḥyá's orders. Another victim was Mírzá 'Alí-Akbar, a paternal cousin of the Báb.

Dayyán was referred to by the Báb as the repository of the trust of God, and the treasury of His knowledge. He was also promised to be the third person to believe in 'Him Whom God shall make manifest'. When Mírzá Yaḥyá claimed to be the successor of the Báb, Dayyán wrote an epistle in which he refuted his claims, quoting many passages from the Writings of the Báb in support of his argument. This bold and truthful epistle angered Mírzá Yaḥyá, who replied by writing his inflammatory book known as *Mustayqiẓ* (Sleeper Awakened). In it he severely condemns Dayyán, whom he refers to as the 'father of calamities'. He also rebukes another believer of note, a certain Siyyid Ibráhim, who was an admirer of Dayyán and whom he stigmatizes as 'the father of iniquities'. He also calls on the Bábís to take the lives of these two. Not satisfied with this condemnation, Mírzá Yaḥyá despatched his servant Mírzá Muḥammad-i-Mázindarání to Adhirbáyján with explicit orders to murder Dayyán. In the meantime Dayyán had left for Baghdád, and Mírzá Yaḥyá's servant had to return.

Upon his arrival in Baghdád, Dayyán was confronted with great antagonism by the Bábís who were spurred on by Mírzá Yaḥyá's denunciation of him. This was during the time when Bahá'u'lláh was in Baghdád. Knowing that the life of Dayyán was in danger, Bahá'u'lláh called the believers to His house one by one and rebuked them for their behaviour toward Dayyán. In the meantime Dayyán attained the presence of Bahá'u'lláh, and as the Báb had promised, recognized His Person as 'Him Whom God shall make manifest'. A few days later, Dayyán was murdered by that same servant of Mírzá Yaḥyá. This tragic crime brought great sorrow to the heart of Bahá'u'lláh. It is significant that on that day, a sandstorm of exceptional severity swept over the city of Baghdád and obscured the light of the sun for some hours.

Not satisfied with this iniquitous crime, Mírzá Yaḥyá turned his attention to the admirers of Dayyán and issued instructions to kill them also. The next victim was Mírzá 'Alí-Akbar, the cousin of the Báb, who was murdered by the same Mírzá Muḥammad. Bahá'u'lláh pays tribute to Dayyán in the *Epistle to the Son of the Wolf* and describes this tragic episode in some detail.*

These criminal activities by Mírzá Yaḥyá were matched only by certain acts of infamy which he committed, bringing dishonour to the Cause of the Báb. He betrayed the honour of the Báb while Bahá'u'lláh was in Kurdistán by marrying Fáṭimih, the Báb's second wife,† and after a few days giving her in marriage to Siyyid Muḥammad. When Bahá'u'lláh learnt of this shameful act, His grief knew no bounds. In several Tablets He has severely condemned this outrageous betrayal by one who professed to be the nominee of the Báb. In the *Epistle to the Son of the Wolf*, He states:

> Reflect a while upon the dishonour inflicted upon the Primal Point. Consider what hath happened. When this Wronged One, after a retirement of two years during which He wandered through the deserts and mountains, returned to Baghdád, as a result of the intervention of a few, who for a long time had sought Him in the wilderness, a certain Mírzá Muḥammad-'Alí of Rasht came to see Him, and related, before a large gathering of people, that which had been done, affecting the honour of the Báb, which hath truly overwhelmed all lands with sorrow. Great God! How could they have countenanced this most grievous betrayal? Briefly, We beseech God to aid the perpetrator of this deed to repent, and return unto Him. He, verily, is the Helper, the All-Wise.[11]

Those who were in close contact with Mírzá Yaḥyá were fully aware of his immoderate sexual appetites.

In the *Epistle of the Son of the Wolf*, Bahá'u'lláh alludes to this when He addresses Hádíy-i-Dawlat-Ábádí‡ in these words.

> Regardest thou as one wronged he who in this world was never dealt a single blow, and who was continually surrounded by five of the handmaidens of God? And imputest thou unto the True One, Who, from His earliest years until the present day, hath been in the hands of His enemies, and been tormented with the worst afflictions in the world, such charges as the Jews did not ascribe unto Christ? Hearken unto the voice of this Wronged One, and be not of them that are in utter loss.[12]

'Abdu'l-Bahá mentions that one of Mírzá Yaḥyá's preoccupations was to marry one wife after another. He mentions eleven wives. But some historians have accounted for three more.

When Bahá'u'lláh was in the mountains of Kurdistán, Mírzá Yaḥyá was driven by an insatiable appetite to satisfy his base and carnal desires. In one of His Tablets Bahá'u'lláh describes an episode

* See *Epistle to the Son of the Wolf*, p. 174–6.
† See *The Revelation of Bahá'u'lláh*, vol. 2, p. 262.
‡ Successor of Mírzá Yaḥyá. For details see *The Revelation of Bahá'u'lláh*, vol. 4.

which brings further shame to his already shameful career. Mírzá Yaḥyá sent a message to a certain believer, Áqá Muḥammad-Karím, asking for the hand of his daughter in marriage. The parents of the girl refused to comply, and instead gave their daughter in marriage to a certain Abu'l-Qásim who had been in the service of Mírzá Yaḥyá for some years. No sooner had this happened than Mírzá Yaḥyá ordered the elimination of Abu'l-Qásim, and he was never seen again.

As a result of such atrocities, which were committed in the name of religion, the Bábí community was utterly degraded in the eyes of the public. When Bahá'u'lláh returned from the mountains of Kurdistán the Bábís were dispirited and spiritually as dead. Once again Bahá'u'lláh took the reins of the Cause in His hands. He breathed new life into the dying community of the Báb, and through His loving advice and exhortations, both verbally and in writing, He raised the morale of the believers in Baghdád and the neighbouring towns. Bahá'u'lláh Himself testified to these words:

> After Our arrival, We revealed, as a copious rain, by the aid of God and His Divine Grace and mercy, Our verses, and sent them to various parts of the world. We exhorted all men, and particularly this people, through Our wise counsels and loving admonitions, and forbade them to engage in sedition, quarrels, disputes and conflict. As a result of this, and by the grace of God, waywardness and folly were changed into piety and understanding, and weapons converted into instruments of peace.[13]

'Abdu'l-Bahá also states:

> Bahá'u'lláh after His return (from Sulaymáníyyih) made such strenuous efforts in educating and training this community, in reforming its manners, in regulating its affairs and in rehabilitating its fortunes, that in a short while all these troubles and mischiefs were quenched, and the utmost peace and tranquillity reigned in men's hearts.[14]

This transformation of spirit and the ascendancy of the community in 'Iráq and Persia, in spite of Mírzá Yaḥyá, continued until the end of Bahá'u'lláh's stay in that country.

The outpouring of the Revelation of Bahá'u'lláh in Baghdád began to vivify the community of the Báb not only in Iraq, but also in Persia where thousands of Bábís had been left leaderless. The many Tablets and Epistles which flowed from the Pen of the Most High, especially the *Kitáb-i-Íqán* and *Hidden Words*, inspired the believers and breathed a new spirit into their souls. At the same time, the evidences of ascendancy and grandeur which were increasingly manifested by Bahá'u'lláh served to inflame the fire of jealousy which was smouldering in the heart of Mírzá Yaḥyá. Since he could never find the courage to utter a word of opposition to Bahá'u'lláh whenever he came into His presence, he sowed the seeds of doubt in the minds of believers and spread false rumours concerning Bahá'u'lláh among the community in Persia.

The person who conceived and carried out these misguided plans aimed at discrediting Bahá'u'lláh was Siyyid Muḥammad. To cite one example, soon after the *Kitáb-i-Íqán* was revealed in honour of Ḥájí Siyyid Muḥammad, the uncle of the Báb, several copies were made and circulated among the believers. This book came as a shattering blow to Mírzá Yaḥyá, who could see the overpowering influence of this outstanding work among the friends. Siyyid Muḥammad circulated rumours that the *Kitáb-i-Íqán* was the work of Mírzá Yaḥyá which had been published in Bahá'u'lláh's name. The following is an interesting account by Ḥájí Mírzá Ḥaydar-'Alí,* who was then one of the followers of the Báb in Persia.

> Although I was persecuted several times in Iṣfahán and suffered great hardships and ill-treatment, I was happy, on fire with the Faith, attracted and in love with the Writings and Tablets of the Báb, especially the Persian Bayán. I made two copies of this Book. The more I read it the more eager I became to read further. In those days everyone was convinced that the coming of 'Him Whom God shall make manifest' was at hand. I often used to say . . . that if the Dispensation of the Báb . . . were not followed immediately by the Dispensation of 'Him Whom God shall make manifest', then all the Writings, Tablets and testimonies of the Báb would remain unfulfilled and were useless. I did not have a heartfelt regard for Azal.† I used to remark, 'What is the difference between the hidden Azal and the Hidden Qá'im? . . .'‡ Furthermore, I regarded his writings to be truly nonsensical, except of course his quotations from the Writings of the Báb which were exalted words. However, I used to be condemned by my own conscience for these thoughts, as I had imagined my own understanding to be above that of other people. Then two holy Tablets from the Blessed Beauty . . . arrived in honour of Zaynu'l-Muqarrabín§ and Áqá Muḥammad-'Alíy-i-Tambákú-Furúsh+ from Iṣfahán. These Tablets captivated me and I became enamoured of the utterances of Bahá'u'lláh.
>
> Later . . . Ḥájí Siyyid Muḥammad, the uncle of the Báb . . . came for a visit to Iṣfahán and brought with him the *Kitáb-i-Íqán*, revealed in answer to his own questions. As a result of reading the *Kitáb-i-Íqán*, I became a thousand times more enchanted with the blessed utterances of the Ancient Beauty. I used to mention quite openly that I regarded Bahá'u'lláh's magnanimity, His unique and incomparable reality, the power of

* See *The Revelation of Bahá'u'lláh*, vol. 2.

† Mírzá Yaḥyá.

‡ Shí'ah Islám believes that the Qá'im, the Promised One, is living in a hidden city where no one can have access to Him, and that He will manifest Himself at the appointed hour. (A.T.)

§ See *The Revelation of Bahá'u'lláh*, vol. 1, p. 25. (A.T.)

\+ See *The Revelation of Bahá'u'lláh*, vol. 2, pp. 370–73. (A.T.)

His utterance, the sway of His pen and the persuasiveness of His proofs to be supernatural and the greatest and foremost miracle of all.

But some people were not pleased with my views and would intimate to me that the *Kitáb-i-Íqán* had been written by Azal.

Even Mír Muḥammad-'Alíy-i-'Aṭṭár, one of the early believers, called on me and told me in confidence that 'since the Báb had always given the glad tidings of the coming of "Him Whom God shall make manifest", has not laid down any conditions or specified any time for His advent, has enjoined upon all to accept and acknowledge Him as soon as He reveals Himself, has prohibited investigation, caution or delay [in accepting His Message], has condemned to hell-fire [those who do not recognize Him], has strictly forbidden the seeking of proofs from Him, and has regarded Himself as the servant and forerunner of "Him Whom God shall make manifest", all these have prompted Jináb-i-Bahá* to claim this position for Himself. He has imprisoned Azal and sometimes has whipped him to make him answer His questions. These answers are recorded by Jináb-i-Bahá and published in His own name. Siyyid Muḥammad has journeyed twice from Baghdád to Iṣfahán on behalf of Azal and has confidentially told the faithful about his loneliness and the wrongs he has suffered!'

My amazement at hearing this knew no bounds. I stated that it was impossible and I had never heard such nonsense and vain assertions. The words and passages in the *Kitáb-i-Íqán* were of a style easy to apprehend yet impossible to imitate. The words of Azal were neither weighty nor eloquent . . .[15]

Ḥájí Mírzá Ḥaydar-'Alí describes his observations and experiences as he travelled around Persia soon after the revelation of the *Kitáb-i-Íqán*. The following is a summary of his words:

I was watchful for the advent of the Supreme Manifestation of God, 'Him Whom God shall make manifest'. The hypocrisy, lies and machinations of Mír Muḥammad-'Alí and Siyyid Muḥammad were as clear as the sun to me. Therefore I decided to leave Iṣfahán.

Although I was most eager to attain the presence of the Day-Star of Revelation,† I was apprehensive lest my coming in contact with the two hypocrites Siyyid Muḥammad and Mullá Rajab-'Alí,‡ who were in Karbilá and Baghdád, might somehow affect my soul and conscience. Therefore for a period of five or six years I travelled around Persia . . . With great difficulties and hardship I visited many places, sometimes on foot, sometimes riding, but I was in the utmost joy. I spoke everywhere about the Revelation of the Báb and gave the glad-tidings that the advent of 'Him Whom God shall make manifest' was at hand. In many towns I was persecuted, beaten and imprisoned . . .

In Shíráz I met Ḥájí Siyyid Muḥammad, the uncle of the Báb, and some other believers . . . They were filled with love for Him and were

* Bahá'u'lláh.
† Bahá'u'lláh.
‡ A brother of the second wife of the Báb. He became a follower of Mírzá Yaḥyá.

joyously awaiting the Revelation of 'Him Whom God shall make manifest'. There was no mention of Azal . . . The late Áqá Siyyid 'Abdu'r-Raḥím-i-Iṣfahání had made certain extracts from the *Bayán* and other books of the Báb through which he used to prove that Bahá'u'lláh, exalted be His glory, was the Promised One of the *Bayán*, that Azal was only a name without a reality, like a body without a soul. As a result of such pronouncements Áqá Siyyid 'Abdu'r-Raḥím was denounced by some. He used to give us the following account.

'After the martyrdom of the Báb when Azal had become famous, I travelled from Iṣfahán to Ṭihrán with the express purpose of meeting him. In the bazaar I met Bahá'u'lláh, the Day-Star of Revelation, the Speaker on Sinai . . . the mention of whose name has adorned the Books and Tablets of the Báb. I attained His presence at a time when His glory was hidden behind a myriad veils of light. He asked me if I had come to meet Azal? I answered in the affirmative. I had actually attained the presence of Bahá'u'lláh before this at Badas͟ht. I had recognized His glory and greatness, His uniqueness and magnanimity by the manner in which Quddús and Ṭáhirih used to bow before Him. I also knew the deeds and actions of Azal; nevertheless since he was known as the nominee of the Báb I considered meeting with him as a means of nearness to God. I went, in the company of Bahá'u'lláh, to His house. He asked for tea to be served. Thereupon Azal brought the samovar and served the tea. He was standing in the presence of Bahá'u'lláh, from Whose tongue were flowing the rivers of wisdom and knowledge. After drinking tea, Bahá'u'lláh rose, and turning to Azal said, "He has come to see you", and then went into the inner court of the house. Azal sat down, I bowed and expressed my devotion to him, but he had nothing to say to me.'[16]

The news of Bahá'u'lláh's imminent departure from Bag͟hdád to Istanbul disturbed and frightened Mírzá Yaḥyá. He who had hidden himself from the public eye in Bag͟hdád over the years and who, in spite of his iniquitous deeds, relied heavily on Bahá'u'lláh's protection and loving kindness, found himself suddenly plunged into a grievous situation. The thought of remaining alone in Bag͟hdád was deeply distressing to him. Bahá'u'lláh advised him that since he was free to travel, he should proceed to Persia, and there disseminate the Writings of the Báb among the believers. It is to be noted that through Bahá'u'lláh's directive these Writings had been transcribed by Mírzá Yaḥyá some years before and were ready to be taken to Persia. But he had no interest in teaching the Cause of the Báb or disseminating its Holy Scriptures. He refused to comply with Bahá'u'lláh's advice on the grounds that the authorities in Persia were ruthlessly persecuting the Bábís and therefore his life would be in great danger if he went there.

At one point Mírzá Yaḥyá decided to flee to India, or Abyssinia (Ethiopia), where he thought he would be left alone, free of persecution. But soon he changed his mind and resigned himself to remaining in 'Iráq. He asked Bahá'u'lláh to arrange the building of a secure hiding place for him. He wanted a cottage to be built in a garden situated in Huvaydar in the vicinity of Ba<u>gh</u>dád, which was owned by <u>Sh</u>ay<u>kh</u> Sulṭán. Bahá'u'lláh acceded to his request and asked <u>Sh</u>ay<u>kh</u> Sulṭán, who was one of His devoted Arab followers, to build the cottage for him. But as the building work proceeded Mírzá Yaḥyá felt increasingly insecure, and eventually cancelled his plans in favour of going to Istanbul incognito. However, he made it clear that he did not intend to travel with Bahá'u'lláh, for he was very suspicious of the intention of the authorities in inviting Bahá'u'lláh to Istanbul. He feared that Bahá'u'lláh and His companions might be either handed over to Persian officials or killed on the way.

To go on this long journey he needed a passport. Not wishing to identify himself to the authorities, he sent a certain Ḥájí Muḥammad-Káẓim, who resembled him, to the government house to procure a passport for him in his newly-assumed name of Mírzá 'Alíy-i-Kirmán<u>sh</u>áhi. He then proceeded to Mosul in disguise accompanied by an Arab servant, and reached there before Bahá'u'lláh's caravan arrived in that city.

It is noteworthy that Bahá'u'lláh had allowed Siyyid Muḥammad-i-Iṣfahání to be included in the party which accompanied Him to Istanbul. It appears that whenever possible Bahá'u'lláh ensured that the trouble-makers and those who were not inwardly faithful to Him were not left at large among the believers. He often kept such people close to His own Person so as to be able to check their mischief. Although Siyyid Muḥammad was a treacherous individual causing untold difficulties for Bahá'u'lláh and His devoted companions, he was never barred, while in Ba<u>gh</u>dád, from attaining His presence or taking part in the gatherings of the believers. By allowing him to accompany Him in His exile, Bahá'u'lláh protected the believers in 'Iráq and elsewhere from his satanic influence. Of course the faithful companions of Bahá'u'lláh, both those who travelled with Him and those who remained behind, were fully aware of the iniquitous deeds of that evil and hypocritical individual who used to pretend, whenever he came into their gatherings, to be a loyal believer himself.

Mírzá Yaḥyá waited in Mosul until Bahá'u'lláh's caravan arrived. There he sent his servant to inform Áqáy-i-Kalím (Bahá'u'lláh's most faithful brother, known also as Mírzá Músá) of his whereabouts in the city. 'Abdu'l-Bahá in one of His Tablets tells the story in these words:

When we reached Mosul, and a camp was set up on the bank of the Tigris, where the notables of the town flocked group after group to come into His blessed presence [Bahá'u'lláh's], on a midnight that aforementioned Arab, Ẓáhir, came to say that his Honour [Mírzá Yaḥyá] was staying at an inn outside the city, and wished to meet someone. 'My uncle, Mírzá Músá, went there at midnight and met him. Mírzá Yaḥyá asked about his family, and was told that they were there and had their own tent and he could visit them. He said that he did not at all consider it advisable to do so, but he would accompany the caravan with which his family too would be travelling. Thus he continued to Diyárbakr, a black cord around his head, and a begging-bowl in his hand, consorting only with the Arabs and the Turks in the caravan. At Diyárbakr, he sent word that he would visit his family at night and join the main body of the caravan in the morning. That was done. Since Ḥájí Siyyid Muḥammad knew him, he gave out that he was a Persian dervish, an acquaintance of his, and visited him, but other friends because they had never seen him [Mírzá Yaḥyá], did not recognize him.[17]

Mírzá Yaḥyá, who was now introducing himself as Ḥájí 'Alí, pretended that he did not know anybody in the party, including Bahá'u'lláh, and claimed to be returning from Mecca. He was not recognized by most of the companions because he had been living in disguise and hiding himself from the believers while in 'Iráq. The crafty Siyyid Muḥammad had the nerve to introduce Mírzá Yaḥyá as a dervish friend of his to Bahá'u'lláh's companions, but these soon discovered his real identity as they approached their destination. Thus Mírzá Yaḥyá, whose wives were among the female group travelling with Bahá'u'lláh, accompanied them until they reached the shores of Istanbul. There his identity was disclosed and everyone knew who he was. But during his stay in Istanbul, Mírzá Yaḥyá did not dare to reveal his true identity to the authorities. To Shamsí Big, who was appointed by the government to act as host to Bahá'u'lláh, he introduced himself as a servant in His household, and sometimes used to sleep in the servants' quarters to prove his case.

When Bahá'u'lláh was exiled to Adrianople, Mírzá Yaḥya and Siyyid Muḥammad went with him. Bahá'u'lláh, in the *Epistle to the Son of the Wolf*, mentions that Mírzá Yaḥyá followed Him from place to place:

> Wherever this Wronged One went Mírzá Yaḥyá followed Him . . . The Siyyid of Iṣfahán, however, surreptitiously duped him. They committed that which caused the greatest consternation.[18]

Soon after his arrival in Adrianople, Mírzá Yaḥyá realized that there was no longer any danger to his life, because within a short period of time Bahá'u'lláh had won the respect and admiration of the dignitaries, including the Governor of Adrianople. The inhabitants of the city showed such a spirit of friendliness and co-operation toward the exiled community that Bahá'u'lláh instructed the believers to engage in some work or profession and integrate themselves into the community. Since there was no apparent reason for persecution of the Bahá'ís, Mírzá Yaḥyá, emboldened by Siyyid Muḥammad, decided to emerge from his self-imposed seclusion.

Through his constant association with Siyyid Muḥammad and a certain Ḥájí Mírzá Aḥmad-i-Káshání, an infamous mischief-maker notorious for his vulgar conduct and foul language, Mírzá Yaḥyá began to openly sound his rebellion against Bahá'u'lláh. He who always felt so insignificant when he came face to face with Bahá'u-'lláh and fell speechless in His presence, was now, prompted by his wicked lieutenant, to rise up against Him and attempt to wrest the leadership of the community from His hands.

To achieve this long-cherished ambition, Mírzá Yaḥyá embarked upon a plan which involved him in further acts of crime. He decided that the only way to accomplish his goal was to take Bahá'u'lláh's life, for he knew that he had neither the courage nor the personality to confront Him. Indeed, it was not unthinkable for a man who had already masterminded the assassination of several believers in Baghdád, including the Báb's own cousin, to contemplate ways and means of taking Bahá'u'lláh's life.

The first attempt on the life of Bahá'u'lláh was carried out by Mírzá Yaḥyá's own hands when he poisoned Him with a deadly substance. Shoghi Effendi describes this shameful episode in these words:

> Desperate designs to poison Bahá'u'lláh and His companions, and thereby reanimate his own defunct leadership, began, approximately a year after their arrival in Adrianople, to agitate his mind. Well aware of the erudition of his half-brother, Áqáy-i-Kalím, in matters pertaining to medicine, he, under various pretexts, sought enlightenment from him regarding the effects of certain herbs and poisons, and then began, contrary to his wont, to invite Bahá'u'lláh to his home, where, one day, having smeared His tea-cup with a substance he had concocted, he succeeded in poisoning Him sufficiently to produce a serious illness which lasted no less than a month, and which was accompanied by severe pains and high fever, the aftermath of which left Bahá'u'lláh with a shaking hand till the end of His life. So grave was His condition that a foreign doctor, named Shíshmán, was called in to attend Him. The doctor was so appalled by His livid hue that he deemed His case hopeless, and, after having fallen at His feet, retired from His presence without prescribing a remedy. A few days later that doctor fell ill and died. Prior to his death Bahá'u'lláh had intimated that doctor Shíshmán had sacrificed his life for Him. To Mírzá Áqá Ján, sent by Bahá'u'lláh to visit him, the doctor had stated that God had answered his prayers, and that after his death a certain Dr. Chúpán, whom he knew to be reliable, should, whenever necessary, be called in his stead.[19]

Despite this heinous crime, Bahá'u'lláh advised His followers not to spread the news of the poisoning. But Mírzá Yaḥyá lost his nerve and shamefully accused Bahá'u'lláh of trying to poison *him*, and as a result, the story had to be told. The believers and those who were in close contact with them then became aware that the poison administered by Mírzá Yaḥyá had been the cause of Bahá'u'lláh's serious illness. Here we can see the contrast between light and darkness, between truth and falsehood, Bahá'u'lláh's sin-covering eye and Mírzá Yaḥyá's corruption and wickedness.

This episode created deep turmoil and agitation within the community. Some time passed and the situation was beginning to simmer down when another serious attempt by Mírzá Yaḥyá to assassinate Bahá'u'lláh brought about an unprecedented commotion within the community, resulting in the final parting of the ways between Bahá'u'lláh and His unfaithful half-brother.

This time Mírzá Yaḥyá made plans to carry out his sinister designs in the public bath* frequented by Bahá'u'lláh. For some time he began to show favours to Ustád Muḥammad-'Alíy-i-Salmání,† a barber who served in the household of Bahá'u'lláh and was His bath attendant. Eventually he intimated to Salmání in a subtle way that he could render a great service to the Cause if he were to assassinate Bahá'u'lláh while attending Him in the bath.

The following is a summary translation of Salmání's memoirs describing this shameful incident:

> One day I went to the bath and awaited the arrival of the Blessed Beauty. Azal‡ arrived first. I attended to him and applied henna. He began to talk to me. For some time he had been trying hard to make me his follower, but he was doing this in a secret way. He said to me: 'Last night I dreamt that someone had a sweeping brush in his hand and was sweeping the area around me.'§ He gave me to understand that this person was the Blessed Beauty. From the tone of his conversation, I knew that he wanted me to do something for him, but he did not tell me anything and soon left the bath . . .

* Public baths, known in the West as Turkish baths, were the only type available to people in those days because houses had no baths built in them. These baths, with their warm and steamy atmosphere, were used by people as a place to wash and relax for hours. This meant that a public bath was a place for social occasions where people gathered, exchanged news and discussed many topics. In these baths people were not fully naked and wore loin-cloths. Often, friends used to go to the bath on the same day in order to spend time together. The baths provided customers with attendants who washed them and performed other services such as the applying of henna, shaving and massaging. Important people usually had their own bath attendants.

† For a story of his life and services, see *The Revelation of Bahá'u'lláh*, vol. 2, p. 155. Salmání should not be confused with Shaykh Salmán.

‡ Mírzá Yaḥyá.

§ The connotation of these words in Persian is that Bahá'u'lláh was a humble servant of Mírzá Yaḥyá.

I was deep in my thoughts concerning the words of Azal. I did not understand his purpose in implying that the Blessed Beauty was sweeping the floor around him. However, it was quite clear that he wanted me to carry out a special task for him. At the same time I noted that Ḥájí Mírzá Aḥmad was trying to convert me to follow Azal. During the course of several days he persisted in trying to win me over.[20]

As we have mentioned above, Ḥájí Mírzá Aḥmad was a close associate of Siyyid Muḥammad. Salmání stood firm and forcefully rejected Ḥájí Mírzá Aḥmad's persuasive arguments in support of Mírzá Yaḥyá. In the end Salmání became very angry and verbally attacked Ḥájí Mírzá Aḥmad, using harsh and unspeakably offensive language. This confrontation was reported to Bahá'u'lláh who revealed a Tablet* addressed to Ḥájí Mírzá Aḥmad and instructed His amanuensis, Mírzá Áqá Ján, to read it aloud in the gathering of the believers. Salmání continues the story of Mírzá Yaḥyá's treachery in his memoirs:

He said, 'A certain Mírzá Na'ím, the former Governor of Nayríz, killed many believers and perpetrated many crimes against the Cause.' He then praised courage and bravery in glowing terms. He said that some were brave by nature and at the right time they would manifest that quality in their actions. He then continued the story of Mírzá Na'ím. 'From the persecuted family of the believers there remained a young boy aged ten or eleven. One day, when Mírzá Na'ím went into the bath, this boy went in with a knife. As he was coming out of the water, the boy stabbed him and ripped his belly open. Mírzá Na'ím screamed and his servants who were in the ante-room rushed in. They went for the boy, attacked and beat him. Then they went to see how their master was. The boy, although wounded, rose up and stabbed him again.' Azal praised courage again and said, 'How wonderful it is for a man to be brave. Now, see what they are doing to the Cause of God. Everybody harms it, everyone has arisen against me, even my brother. I have no comfort whatsoever and am in a wretched state.' His tone implied that he, the nominee of the Báb, was the wronged one, and his Brother (I take refuge in God!) was the usurper and aggressor. Then he once more praised courage and said that the Cause of God needed help. In all this talk, the tone of his remarks, the story of Mírzá Na'ím, the praise of courage and his encouragement to me, he was in fact telling me to kill Bahá'u'lláh.

The effect of all this upon me was so disturbing that in all my life I had never felt so shattered. It was as if the whole building was falling upon my head. I was frightened; without uttering a word I went out to the ante-room. My mind was in a state of the utmost agitation. I thought to myself that I would go inside and cut Azal's head off regardless of consequences. Then I thought, to kill him is easy, but perhaps I would

* Part of the *Tablet of Aḥmad* in Persian (not to be confused with the celebrated *Tablet of Aḥmad* in Arabic) is translated by Shoghi Effendi and published in *Gleanings from the Writings of Bahá'u'lláh*, CLII and CLIII. For details see *The Revelation of Bahá'u'lláh*, vol. 2, ch. 6.

offend the Blessed Beauty. One thing which prevented me from carrying out my intention was the thought that if I killed him and then went into the presence of the Blessed Beauty, and He asked me why I had killed him, what answer could I give?

I returned to the bath and being extremely angry, I shouted at him 'Go and get lost, clear off!' He whimpered and trembled and asked me to pour water over him. I complied. Washed or unwashed he went out in a state of great trepidation, and I have never seen him since.

My state of mind, however, was such that nothing could calm me. As it happened, that day the Blessed Beauty did not come to the bath, but Áqá Mírzá Músáy-i-Kalím [Bahá'u'lláh's faithful brother] came. I told him that Azal had set me on fire with his sinister suggestion. Áqá Mírzá Músá said: 'He has been thinking of this for years, this man has always been thinking in this way. Do not pay any attention to him.' He counselled me to disregard the whole thing and went inside the bath.

However, when my work was finished in the bath, I went to the Master* and reported to Him what Mírzá Yaḥyá had told me, and how I was filled with rage and wanted to kill him . . . the Master said, 'This is something that you alone know. Do not mention it to anyone, it is better that it remain hidden.' I then went to Mírzá Áqá Ján, reported the details of the incident, and asked him to tell Bahá'u'lláh. He returned and said 'Bahá'u'lláh says to tell Ustád Muḥammad-'Alí not to mention this to anyone.'

That night I collected all the writings of Azal and went to the tea-room† of Bahá'u'lláh's house and burnt them all in the brazier. Before doing so, I showed them to seven or eight of the believers who were present. They all saw that they were the writings of Azal. They all protested to me and asked me the reason for doing this. I said, 'Until today I esteemed Azal highly, but now he is less than a dog in my sight.'‡[21]

It must be remembered that because of Bahá'u'lláh's sin-covering eye and His loving kindness toward Mírzá Yaḥyá, and because he was His half-brother, the faithful believers treated him with respect and consideration. But after these vicious attacks on Bahá'u'lláh, it was natural for them to turn their backs on him. After Salmání failed to keep the details of the incident to himself, the news spread and created a great upheaval in the community.

It was at this point that Bahá'u'lláh decided to formally declare to Mírzá Yaḥyá, as the nominee of the Báb, His claim to be the Author of a new Revelation, the Person of 'Him Whom God shall make manifest' foretold by the Báb. Of course, Mírzá Yaḥyá was well aware of Bahá'u'lláh's declaration in the Garden of Riḍván and the

* 'Abdu'l-Bahá.
† Reception room of Bahá'u'lláh where the believers usually gathered.
‡ In Persian, this designation is much more insulting than it sounds in English.

Tablets which had been subsequently revealed by Him. But now the time had come for the Supreme Manifestation of God to formally announce His station to the one who was nominated by the Báb to be the leader of His followers until the advent of 'Him Whom God shall make manifest'.

In order to communicate this message to Mírzá Yaḥyá, Bahá'u'lláh revealed the *Súriy-i-Amr* (Súrih of Command) in His own handwriting* and instructed His amanuensis Mírzá Áqá Ján to take the Tablet to Mírzá Yaḥyá, read it aloud, and demand a conclusive reply from him. On becoming apprised of the contents of the Tablet and the claims of Bahá'u'lláh, Mírzá Yaḥyá indicated that he needed some time during which to meditate on the subject. The following day he sent a message to Bahá'u'lláh that he himself had become the recipient of divine Revelation and it was incumbent upon all to obey and follow him.

Such a claim maintained by so perfidious a person evoked the wrath of God, and brought about the eventual split between Bahá'u'lláh and Mírzá Yaḥyá. It must be remembered that the majority of the believers in Adrianople were faithful to Bahá'u'lláh and up till then had been used to associate freely with Mírzá Yaḥyá and a small number of his henchmen; now the situation changed.

Mírzá Yaḥyá's response to the *Súriy-i-Amr* was a clear signal for parting of the ways. Bahá'u'lláh, who was then residing in the House of Amru'lláh, changed His residence to the House of Riḍá Big. This was on 10 March 1866. Only the members of His own family and one servant moved to this house and He allowed no one else to attain his presence. As a result, the community of exiles was cut off from His Blessed Person and left entirely on its own. This withdrawal, similar to His withdrawal to the mountains of Kurdistán a few years earlier, plunged the community into a grievous state and created severe tests and trials for the believers. On the other hand, it afforded each one of the exiles the opportunity to choose between Bahá'u'lláh and His unfaithful brother.

Bahá'u'lláh's faithful followers, those lovers of His beauty, became dispirited. The light had departed from their midst and they were enveloped in a darkness which obscured their vision and left them helpless and disconsolate. Áqáy-i-Kalím, Bahá'u'lláh's faithful brother who carried the weight of responsibility during Bahá'u'lláh's retirement in the House of Riḍá Big, has recounted to Nabíl these words:

* The facsimile of the first page of this Tablet in the handwriting of Bahá'u'lláh appears as the frontispiece of *The Revelation of Bahá'u'lláh*, vol. 2. A mere glance at this page will indicate that the hand of Bahá'u'lláh was terribly shaky soon after His being poisoned by Mírzá Yaḥyá.

> That day witnessed a most great commotion. All the companions lamented in their separation from the Blessed Beauty.[22]

Another witness to those grievous days has recorded:

> Those days were marked by tumult and confusion. We were sore-perplexed and greatly feared lest we be permanently deprived of the bounty of His presence.[23]

Even those who were unfaithful to Him felt disturbed by His withdrawal, as they knew only too well that it was through His guiding influence that they were living in relative safety and security. These men were now left to their own devices and soon were engulfed in a most troublesome situation created by their own hands.

The retirement of Bahá'u'lláh to the House of Riḍá Big and His refusal to meet with any of the exiles created a situation in which everyone was left by himself to decide his own spiritual destiny. Those few who were inclined towards Mírzá Yaḥyá congregated together and began to launch their attacks on the faithful ones, while the rest occupied their time mostly in prayer and devotions, supplicating God to relieve them of their grievous plight of separation from their Lord.

Before taking up residence in the House of Riḍá Big, Bahá'u'lláh ordered His brother Áqáy-i-Kalím to send half of all the furniture, bedding and utensils to the house of Mírzá Yaḥyá. He also sent him certain historic relics such as the rings of the Báb, His seals and manuscripts. These were the items which the Báb had sent to Bahá'u'lláh prior to His martyrdom and which were coveted by Mírzá Yaḥyá. Bahá'u'lláh also asked Darvísh Ṣidq-'Alí, one of His faithful followers, to act as a servant in the household of Mírzá Yaḥyá. Although loathe to serve the one who was in his sight the embodiment of deceit and falsehood, this devoted soul wholeheartedly obeyed Bahá'u'lláh and engaged himself in Mírzá Yaḥyá's service. Soon other circumstances relieved him of this most unpleasant task. As already mentioned, those few individuals who were weak and vacillating in their faith joined Mírzá Yaḥyá and, emboldened by the absence of Bahá'u'lláh, began their contemptible activities against the Faith of God.

Mírzá Yaḥyá and Siyyid Muḥammad started a vigorous letter-writing campaign to discredit Bahá'u'lláh in the eyes of the believers and the authorities. They loaded their letters with lies and disgraceful calumnies, accusing Bahá'u'lláh of those very crimes which they themselves had committed, and disseminated them far and wide among the believers in Persia and 'Iráq. These slanderous letters disturbed the Bábí community and confused many. Some weaker believers lost their faith altogether; a small number were inclined toward Mírzá Yaḥyá. A few wrote to Bahá'u'lláh for clarification as a result of which several Tablets were revealed in this period describing the true state of affairs. However, the majority of the believers remained faithful to the Cause of Bahá'u'lláh. These souls arose with determination and dedication to vindicate the truth of the Cause of God. Many of them, such as Nabíl-i-A'ẓam, Muníb* and Aḥmad-i-Yazdí* travelled throughout Persia, championed the Cause of Bahá'u'lláh and defended it notably against the onslaught of the unfaithful.

It was through Mírzá Yaḥyá's own actions that the news of his infidelity to the Cause of God was effectively communicated to the community in Persia and signalized the permanent rupture between him and his illustrious Brother. While Bahá'u'lláh had withdrawn Himself from the community in Adrianople, Siyyid Muḥammad and Mírzá Yaḥyá were actively engaged in damaging His reputation in government circles. The latter sent a petition to the Governor Khurshíd Páshá and his assistant, 'Azíz Páshá. It was couched in obsequious language, contained false statements about Bahá'u'lláh, and was aimed at discrediting Him in the eyes of the Governor who was one of His ardent admirers.

Later, the Governor shared this letter with Bahá'u'lláh and its contents became known to the believers. Ḥájí Mírzá Ḥaydar-'Alí, who arrived in Adrianople a few months after this shameful episode, writes concerning Mírzá Yaḥyá's petition to the authorities in these words:

> When Azal arose in hostility with his satanic spirit to oppose and challenge the Blessed Beauty, through calumnies and false accusations, he wrote a letter to the Governor of Adrianople. We all saw this letter. It opened with these words: 'May my soul and body be a sacrifice to thee.' It went on to say: 'O thou 'Azíz,† we come to you in destitution, grant us some corn.' He continues falsely to accuse the Ancient Beauty of having cut off his livelihood.
>
> The opening sentence of his letter, the statement of his needs, and the complaints all demonstrate that God cannot be confused with man, and that there is no likeness between the two. We see the contrast, for instance, in these words of the Ancient Beauty as He addressed the late Sulṭán 'Abdu'l-'Azíz:‡ 'O thou Ra'ís [Chief], hearken to the voice of God, the Supreme Ruler, the Help in Peril, the Self-Subsisting. He verily calleth between earth and heaven and summoneth mankind to the scene of effulgent glory.'
>
> In this blessed Tablet, He prophesies that the Sulṭán would lose his throne and the country would pass out of his hands . . . To return to our

* See *The Revelation of Bahá'u'lláh*, vol. 2 for accounts of these two.
† 'Aziz Páshá
‡ This Tablet is actually addressed to 'Álí Páshá, the Grand Vizir of the Sultan.

> subject: Bahá'u'lláh had, through an intermediary, proved to the Governor that these allegations [by Mírzá Yaḥyá] were false and, in a message, explained to him that these calumnies were designed to hurt and humiliate Him.[24]

Concerning these distasteful events, Shoghi Effendi writes:

> . . . He [Bahá'u'lláh] was soon after informed that this same brother [Mírzá Yaḥyá] had despatched one of his wives to the government house to complain that her husband had been cheated of his rights, and that her children were on the verge of starvation – an accusation that spread far and wide and, reaching Constantinople, became, to Bahá'u'lláh's profound distress, the subject of excited discussion and injurious comment in circles that had previously been greatly impressed by the high standard which His noble and dignified behaviour had set in that city.[25]

Some time later in a Tablet* to Shaykh Salmán, Bahá'u'lláh reveals the agony of His heart during this period, and recounts the calumnies of Mírzá Yaḥyá concerning his share of the government allowance which was always divided equitably between the exiles. In this Tablet He explains that had it not been for the sake of His companions in exile, He would have never accepted any allowance from the authorities. Indeed, soon after these heart-rending events, Bahá'u'lláh refused to draw this allowance, and sometimes had to sell some of His belongings in order to provide for His daily needs.

As a result of the many calumnies which were circulating in Adrianople and were extremely hurtful to Him and His loved ones, Bahá'u'lláh ended His retirement which had lasted about two months and came forward to check the misdeeds of His wicked opponents. It was at this time that Siyyid Muḥammad-i-Iṣfahání was finally and effectively expelled from the community and the parting between Bahá'u'lláh and Mírzá Yaḥyá became official; it was referred to as 'the Most Great Separation'. The two-month withdrawal of Bahá'u'lláh was an act of Providence in that it identified the unfaithful. When Bahá'u'lláh emerged from His withdrawal every one of the exiles knew to which side he belonged. The few who gathered around Mírzá Yaḥyá intensified their evil activities and spread their shameful calumnies further to the heart of the Ottoman Empire, poisoning the minds of the Grand Vizir and the Sultan against Bahá'u'lláh.

The announcement by Bahá'u'lláh of 'the Most Great Separation' had an electrifying effect on the community of believers in Persia. The great majority of the followers of the Báb, estimated by Ḥájí Mírzá Ḥaydar-'Alí in his immortal *Bihjatu'ṣ-Ṣudúr* to be about

* See *The Revelation of Bahá'u'lláh*, vol. 2, ch. 13, and vol. 1, pp. 109–13.

ninety-nine percent, embraced the Cause of Bahá'u'lláh. From that time onward those who followed Mírzá Yaḥyá were identified as the breakers of the Covenant of the Báb and became known as Azalís. At the same time the followers of Bahá'u'lláh were designated as the people of Bahá, the Bahá'ís.

CHAPTER FIVE

The Triumph of the Covenant of the Báb

THE separation between Bahá'u'lláh and Mírzá Yaḥyá was a clear signal for the followers of Bahá'u'lláh to dissociate themselves from Mírzá Yaḥyá and those who had gathered around him. Mírzá Yaḥyá was now living with his family in a separate house and Siyyid Muḥammad among the Muslims. For about eighteen months these two continued to devise ways and means of discrediting Bahá'u'lláh and His faithful companions. They spread calumnies and falsehoods among the citizens of Adrianople and the authorities in Istanbul, all aimed at undermining the foundations of the Cause of God and tarnishing the good reputation and honour of its Author. In Persia too, Mírzá Yaḥyá distributed among the believers his letters loaded with untrue stories. The confusion created by his venomous statements gave rise to much conflict and disturbance in that community.

About one-and-a-half years passed and Mírzá Yaḥyá's intrigues and machinations had reached their climax when suddenly the hand of God struck him down, brought about his doom and degraded him in the eyes of his supporters and the authorities in Adrianople. The incident which precipitated this downfall was entirely of his own making.

Siyyid Muḥammad was heavily engaged in his activities aimed at discrediting Bahá'u'lláh in public. In the course of his plottings he came up with the idea of arranging a public confrontation between Bahá'u'lláh and Mírzá Yaḥyá. In advocating this confrontation, Siyyid Muḥammad was confident that Bahá'u'lláh would never accept such a challenge, because he had observed over the years that Bahá'u'lláh usually did not seek to appear in public. He also knew of His forbearance and sin-covering attitude whenever He was confronted with those who opposed Him. For these reasons he apprised his Muslim associates of his plans.

This type of public confrontation, known in Islám as Mubáhilih, goes back to the days of Muḥammad when a deputation of the unbelievers of Najrán in Medina challenged the Prophet to a confrontation. It is a challenge between truth and falsehood. The two parties come together face to face and it is believed that in such a confrontation the power of truth will destroy the ungodly.

Siyyid Muḥammad confidently asserted to the Muslim community that whereas Mírzá Yaḥyá was ready and willing to take part in a public confrontation, Bahá'u'lláh was not.

While these wild statements were circulating in Adrianople, the believers in Persia were in a state of agitation because of Mírzá Yaḥyá's false propaganda. One of the believers from Shíráz, a certain Mír Muḥammad-i-Mukárí (driver of beasts of burden) came to Adrianople. This believer had accompanied the Báb from Baghdád as a caravan-driver to Mecca and later Bahá'u'lláh from Baghdád to Istanbul.

Mír Muḥammad was of the opinion that a public confrontation would help to clarify the situation. He urged Siyyid Muḥammad to induce Mírzá Yaḥyá to meet Bahá'u'lláh in a public place for all to see. And he himself promised to invite Bahá'u'lláh to accept the challenge. This he did and Bahá'u'lláh responded positively to his request.

Shoghi Effendi describes this episode in these words.

> Foolishly assuming that his illustrious Brother would never countenance such a proposition, Mírzá Yaḥyá appointed the mosque of Sulṭán Salím as the place for their encounter. No sooner had Bahá'u'lláh been informed of this arrangement than He set forth, on foot, in the heat of midday, and accompanied by this same Mír Muḥammad, for the aforementioned mosque, which was situated in a distant part of the city, reciting, as He walked, through the streets and markets, verses, in a voice and in a manner that greatly astonished those who saw and heard Him.
>
> '*O Muḥammad!*', are some of the words He uttered on that memorable occasion, as testified by Himself in a Tablet, '*He Who is the Spirit hath, verily, issued from His habitation, and with Him have come forth the souls of God's chosen ones and the realities of His Messengers. Behold, then, the dwellers of the realms on high above Mine head, and all the testimonies of the Prophets in My grasp. Say: Were all the divines, all the wise men, all the kings and rulers on earth to gather together, I, in very truth, would confront them, and would proclaim the verses of God, the Sovereign, the Almighty, the All-Wise. I am He Who feareth no one, though all who are in heaven and all who are on earth rise up against Me. . . . This is Mine hand which God hath turned white for all the worlds to behold. This is My staff; were We to cast it down, it would, of a truth, swallow up all created things.*' Mír Muḥammad, who had been sent ahead to announce Bahá'u'lláh's arrival, soon returned, and informed Him that he who had challenged His authority wished, owing to unforeseen circumstances, to postpone for a day or two the interview. Upon His return to His house Bahá'u'lláh revealed a Tablet, wherein He recounted what had happened, fixed the time for the postponed interview, sealed the Tablet with His seal, entrusted it to Nabíl, and instructed him to

deliver it to one of the new believers, Mullá Muḥammad-i-Tabrízí, for the information of Siyyid Muḥammad, who was in the habit of frequenting that believer's shop. It was arranged to demand from Siyyid Muḥammad, ere the delivery of that Tablet, a sealed note pledging Mírzá Yaḥyá, in the event of failing to appear at the trysting-place, to affirm in writing that his claims were false. Siyyid Muḥammad promised that he would produce the next day the document required, and though Nabíl, for three successive days, waited in that shop for the reply, neither did the Siyyid appear, nor was such a note sent by him. That undelivered Tablet, Nabíl, recording twenty-three years later this historic episode in his chronicle, affirms was still in his possession, 'as fresh as the day on which the Most Great Branch had penned it, and the seal of the Ancient Beauty had sealed and adorned it', a tangible and irrefutable testimony to Bahá'u'lláh's established ascendancy over a routed opponent.[1]

Ḥají Mírzá Ḥaydar-'Alí, the celebrated Bahá'í teacher, was in Adrianople at the time and recounts the events as he witnessed them on that memorable day. The following is a summary translation of his memoirs:

The meeting was to be on Friday at the mosque of Sulṭán Salím at the time of the congregational prayer when the Muslims gather inside in great numbers . . . Mír Muḥammad-i-Mukárí from Shíráz who was a Bábí . . . could not imagine that Azal had broken the Covenant. So he begged the Blessed Beauty to enlighten him. Bahá'u'lláh said to him that if ever Azal came face to face with Him at a meeting-place, then he could consider Azal's claims to be true. Mír Muḥammad accepted this statement as a criterion for distinguishing between truth and falsehood, and he endeavoured to bring this meeting about.

The news and date of the confrontation became known among the peoples of the Muslim, Christian and Jewish religions in the city. All of them had heard of the miracles of Moses and the story of His confrontation with Pharaoh. And now they were expecting the meeting face to face in the mosque between His Holiness the Shaykh Effendi [a designation by which the people called Bahá'u'lláh to express their reverence for Him] and Mírzá 'Alí who had denied Him. [For fear of being recognized, Azal had called himself by this name.] Therefore, from the morning of Friday until noon, a large multitude drawn from the followers of these three religions had thronged the area between the house of Amru'lláh . . . and the entrance to the mosque. The crowd was so large that it was difficult to move about. Bahá'u'lláh, the Day-Star of Glory, emerged from His home . . . and as He passed through the crowd, people showed such reverence as is difficult to describe. They greeted Him with salutations, bowed and opened the way for Him to pass. Many of them prostrated themselves at His feet and kissed them. Bahá'u'lláh, the countenance of majesty and omnipotence, in acknowledgement greeted the crowd by raising His hands (as was customary among the Ottomans), and expressed His good wishes. This continued all the way to the mosque. As soon as He entered the mosque, the preacher, who was delivering his discourse, became speechless or perhaps he forgot his words. Bahá'u'lláh went forward, seated Himself and then gave permission for the preacher to continue. Eventually the preaching and prayers came to an end. But Azal did not turn up. We heard that he had feigned illness and asked to be excused.

In every city in the Ottoman Empire there are Mawlavís, who are dervishes and follower of Mawlaví [Jaláli'd-Dín-i-Rúmí], the author of *Mathnaví*. Every Friday they hold their services in their takyihs [centres of congregation] when they whirl around their master and chant certain words in unison. Inside its chambers some play music and sing delightful melodies. When Bahá'u'lláh was about to leave the mosque He said: 'We owe a visit to the Mawlavís. We had better go to their takyih.' As He rose to go, the Governor of Adrianople and other dignitaries, together with the divines, availed themselves of the opportunity to be in His presence and so they accompanied Him. As a token of their humility and courtesy, the Governor, the Shaykhu'l-Islám,* the 'ulamá [divines and men of learning] and other dignitaries walked four or five steps behind Bahá'u-'lláh while the stream of His utterance was flowing.† Sometimes, through His grace and loving-kindness, Bahá'u'lláh would stop and beckon the Governor and the others to walk in front. But they would refuse to do so. In this way, with majesty and glory born of God, Bahá'u'lláh arrived in the takyih. At that time the Shaykh of the Mawlavís was standing in the centre and the dervishes were circling around and chanting. As soon as their eyes beheld Him, they all stopped their service without any reason. They bowed and showed their respect for Him and became absolutely silent. Bahá'u'lláh then seated Himself and permitted others who were with Him to be seated. He then gave permission to the Shaykh to resume his service again.

The news was widely circulated in Adrianople that when Shaykh Effendi‡ had entered the mosque the preacher was unable to deliver his sermon and when he went to the takyih, the dervishes and their leader forgot their words and stopped their service. The following evening some believers attained His presence and I was among them . . . Bahá'u'lláh made these remarks: 'When We entered the crowded mosque, the preacher forgot the words of his sermon, and when We arrived inside the takyih, the dervishes were suddenly filled with such awe and wonder that they became speechless and silent. However, since people are brought up in vain imaginings, they foolishly consider such events as supernatural acts and regard them as miracles!'§[2]

* The head of the Muslim ecclesiastical institution in the city. (A.T.)

† When an important person walked it was considered discourteous if his subordinates walked in front of, or abreast of him except at night when someone carried a lantern before him. In order to show their humility they always walked a few steps behind. This is how, for example, the oriental believers conducted themselves when they were walking with Bahá'u'lláh, 'Abdu'l-Bahá or Shoghi Effendi. (A.T.)

‡ Bahá'u'lláh (A.T.)

§ These are not the exact words of Bahá'u'lláh, but convey their import. (A.T.)

Mírzá Yaḥyá was now discredited in the eyes of many in Adrianople. In Persia the news of this episode spread among the believers. A Tablet known as *Lawḥ-i-Mubáhilih*, addressed to Mullá Ṣádiq-i-Khurásání and describing this event, reached the Bahá'í community in that land and caused some wavering souls among the friends to recognize the power and majesty of Bahá'u'lláh in breaking up, once and for all, this great 'idol' of the Bábí community.

This dramatic downfall of Mírzá Yaḥyá was, as testified by Shoghi Effendi, clearly foretold by St Paul in the following passage.

> Let no man deceive you by any means; for that day shall not come, except there come a falling away first, and that man of sin be revealed, the son of perdition; who opposeth and exalteth himself above all that is called God, or that is worshipped; so that he as God sitteth in the temple of God, showing himself that he is God . . .
>
> And then shall that Wicked be revealed, whom the Lord shall consume with the spirit of His mouth, and shall destroy with the brightness of His coming . . .[3]

The tragic downfall of this perfidious figure who betrayed his Lord and rose up against Him coincided with an unprecedented outpouring from the Supreme Pen. The verses of God were sent down in great profusion and resulted, soon afterwards, in the proclamation of His Message to the kings and rulers of the world.

In the following passages Shoghi Effendi describes this prodigious outpouring of divine verses.

> The '*Most Great Idol*' had at the bidding and through the power of Him Who is the Fountain-head of the Most Great Justice been cast out of the community of the Most Great Name, confounded, abhorred and broken. Cleansed from this pollution, delivered from this horrible possession, God's infant Faith could now forge ahead, and, despite the turmoil that had convulsed it, demonstrate its capacity to fight further battles, capture loftier heights, and win mightier victories.
>
> A temporary breach had admittedly been made in the ranks of its supporters. Its glory had been eclipsed, and its annals stained forever. Its name, however, could not be obliterated, its spirit was far from broken, nor could this so-called schism tear its fabric asunder. The Covenant of the Báb, to which reference has already been made, with its immutable truths, incontrovertible prophecies, and repeated warnings, stood guard over that Faith, insuring its integrity, demonstrating its incorruptibility, and perpetuating its influence.
>
> Though He Himself was bent with sorrow, and still suffered from the effects of the attempt on His life, and though He was well aware a further banishment was probably impending, yet, undaunted by the blow which His Cause had sustained, and the perils with which it was encompassed,

Bahá'u'lláh arose with matchless power, even before the ordeal was overpast, to proclaim the Mission with which He had been entrusted to those who, in East and West, had the reins of supreme temporal authority in their grasp. The day-star of His Revelation was, through this very Proclamation, destined to shine in its meridian glory, and His Faith manifest the plenitude of its divine power.

A period of prodigious activity ensued which in its repercussions outshone the vernal years of Bahá'u'lláh's ministry. 'Day and night', an eye-witness has written, 'the Divine verses were raining down in such number that it was impossible to record them. Mírzá Áqá Ján wrote them as they were dictated, while the Most Great Branch was continually occupied in transcribing them. There was not a moment to spare.' 'A number of secretaries', Nabíl has testified, 'were busy day and night and yet they were unable to cope with the task. Among them was Mírzá Báqir-i-Shírází. . . . He alone transcribed no less than two thousand verses every day. He laboured during six or seven months. Every month the equivalent of several volumes would be transcribed by him and sent to Persia. About twenty volumes, in his fine penmanship, he left behind as a remembrance for Mírzá Áqá Ján.' Bahá'u'lláh, Himself, referring to the verses revealed by Him, has written: '*Such are the outpourings . . . from the clouds of Divine Bounty that within the space of an hour the equivalent of a thousand verses hath been revealed.*' '*So great is the grace vouchsafed in this day that in a single day and night, were an amanuensis capable of accomplishing it to be found, the equivalent of the Persian Bayán would be sent down from the heaven of Divine holiness.*' '*I swear by God!*' He, in another connection has affirmed, '*In those days the equivalent of all that hath been sent down aforetime unto the Prophets hath been revealed.*' '*That which hath already been revealed in this land* (Adrianople),' He, furthermore, referring to the copiousness of His writings, has declared, '*secretaries are incapable of transcribing. It has, therefore, remained for the most part untranscribed.*'[4]

The story of Mírzá Yaḥyá's tragic career would not be complete without referring, however briefly, to his writings. He wrote several books and epistles which are the greatest testimony to the shallowness of his knowledge and understanding. They consist of a series of nonsensical words which baffle the imagination of any reader. One may read a few pages without following the subject matter, as in most cases there is none; instead the reader will find vain repetitions and absurdities. Fortunately, some of his writings are kept in famous museums available for anyone to read and discover the depth of the author's ignorance and foolishness.

The casting out of Mírzá Yaḥyá and his followers from the community of the Most Great Name brought about the gradual downfall of this perfidious figure and his ultimate extinction in later years. In the summer of 1868 the Edict of Sulṭán 'Abdu'l-'Azíz condemned Bahá'u'lláh to life-long imprisonment in the fortress-city of 'Akká in the Holy Land and Mírzá Yaḥyá to the island of Cyprus.

Mírzá Áqá Ján, Bahá'u'lláh's amanuensis, has written in a Tablet[5] an interesting episode relating to the island of Cyprus, known to the ancient Turks as the Isle of Satan. He states that he received a letter in 'Akká from a friend who was of foreign nationality. In this letter his correspondent had quoted two traditions which were translated into Arabic from an ancient Greek book, which he does not identify. The following is a summary translation of these two. The first tradition:

> Soon will the Satan appear in the Isle of Q [Qibris, i.e. Cyprus] and will prevent people from attaining to the presence of the Lord. When that time comes turn ye towards the Holy Land wherefrom the sweet savours of God will be wafting.

The second:

> The Satan will appear in the island related to him. He is short in stature, heavily bearded. He has a small countenance, a narrow chest, and greenish-yellow eyes. The hair on his back resembles that of a camel and on his chest is similar to that of a goat. When he should come, turn toward Carmel, the holy vale, the gathering place of mankind, this snow-white spot.

It is affirmed in this Tablet that all these physical features were clearly evident in Mírzá Yaḥyá.

It is significant that through the operation of the divine Will, Bahá'u'lláh's enemies became instrumental in fulfilling the age-old prophecies concerning the advent of the Lord in the Holy Land. Shoghi Effendi describes the exile of Bahá'u'lláh in these words.

> Within the confines of this holy and enviable country, '*the nest of all the Prophets of God*', '*the Vale of God's unsearchable Decree, the snow-white Spot, the Land of unfading splendour*', was the Exile of Baghdád, of Constantinople and Adrianople condemned to spend no less than a third of the allotted span of His life, and over half of the total period of His Mission. '*It is difficult*', declares 'Abdu'l-Bahá, '*to understand how Bahá'u'lláh could have been obliged to leave Persia, and to pitch His tent in this Holy Land, but for the persecution of His enemies, His banishment and exile.*'
>
> Indeed such a consummation, He assures us, had been actually prophesied '*through the tongue of the Prophets two or three thousand years before*'. God, '*faithful to His promise*', had, '*to some of the Prophets*' '*revealed and given the good news that the "Lord of Hosts should be manifested in the Holy Land"*'. Isaiah had, in this connection, announced in his Book: '*Get thee up into the high mountain, O Zion that bringest good tidings; lift up thy voice with strength, O Jerusalem, that bringest good tidings. Lift it up, be not afraid; say unto the cities of Judah: "Behold your God! Behold the Lord God will come with strong hand, and His arm shall rule for Him."*' David, in his Psalms, had predicted: '*Lift up your heads, O ye gates; even lift them up, ye everlasting doors; and the King of Glory shall come in. Who is this King of Glory? The Lord of Hosts, He is the King of Glory.*' '*Out of Zion, the perfection of beauty,*

God hath shined. Our God shall come, and shall not keep silence.' Amos had, likewise, foretold His coming: '*The Lord will roar from Zion, and utter His voice from Jerusalem; and the habitations of the shepherds shall mourn, and the top of Carmel shall wither.*'[6]

Mírzá Yaḥyá was confined in the city of Famagusta until 1878 when the island passed out of Turkish rule and came under the British. He then decided to remain in Cyprus and receive a pension from the British Government. This he did and lived freely on that island until his death in 1912. During this time he achieved nothing significant in his life. 'Abdu'l-Bahá, in one of His talks,[7] describes how in all these years Mírzá Yaḥyá did not succeed in converting a single soul on that island to his cause. Instead he spent his life in the company of his many wives and was father to several ill-bred children of low intelligence and capacity. Shoghi Effendi describes Mírzá Yaḥyá's fate in these words:

> Nor can this subject be dismissed without special reference being made to the Arch-Breaker of the Covenant of the Báb, Mírzá Yaḥyá, who lived long enough to witness, while eking out a miserable existence in Cyprus, termed by the Turks 'the Island of Satan', every hope he had so maliciously conceived reduced to naught. A pensioner first of the Turkish and later of the British Government, he was subjected to the further humiliation of having his application for British citizenship refused. Eleven of the eighteen 'Witnesses' he had appointed forsook him and turned in repentance to Bahá'u'lláh. He himself became involved in a scandal which besmirched his reputation and that of his eldest son, deprived that son and his descendants of the successorship with which he had previously invested him, and appointed, in his stead, the perfidious Mírzá Hádíy-i-Dawlat-Ábádí, a notorious Azalí, who, on the occasion of the martyrdom of the aforementioned Mírzá Ashraf, was seized with such fear that during four consecutive days he proclaimed from the pulpit-top, and in a most vituperative language, his complete repudiation of the Bábí Faith, as well as of Mírzá Yaḥyá, his benefactor, who had reposed in him such implicit confidence. It was this same eldest son who, through the workings of a strange destiny, sought years after, together with his nephew and niece, the presence of 'Abdu'l-Bahá, the appointed Successor of Bahá'u'lláh and Centre of His Covenant, expressed repentance, prayed for forgiveness, was graciously accepted by Him, and remained, till the hour of his death, a loyal follower of the Faith which his father had so foolishly, so shamelessly and so pitifully striven to extinguish.[8]

PART II

THE LESSER COVENANT

1. *The Ministry of 'Abdu'l-Bahá*

CHAPTER SIX

'Abdu'l-Bahá, the Centre of the Covenant

THE Covenant made by the Manifestation of God with His followers concerning His immediate successor is known as the Lesser Covenant. In the *Kitáb-i-Aqdas* and later in His Will and Testament known as the *Kitáb-i-'Ahd*, Bahá'u'lláh made such a covenant with His followers. Through these writings Bahá'u'lláh established a mighty and irrefutable covenant unprecedented in the annals of past religions. Never before has a Manifestation of God left behind an authoritative statement in which He has explicitly directed His people to turn to someone as His successor, or follow a defined system of administration for governing the religious affairs of the community.

The Gospels are silent on the question of successorship. Only a vague and inconclusive statement, '. . . thou art Peter, and upon this rock I will build my church', has led some to consider Peter as Christ's successor. Such a claim, which is not upheld by a clear and unequivocal declaration in the Gospels, has resulted in bitter conflicts throughout the checkered history of Christianity. As a result the religion founded by Christ has been divided into major sects from the early centuries, and these have multiplied in the course of time.

A similar situation arose in Islám. The story of Muḥammad and the references He is reported to have made to 'Alí, His cousin and son-in-law, at Ghadír-i-Khumm is recounted by both the Shí'ah and Sunní sects of Islám, and each interprets it differently. The story is as follows:

Having completed the rites of pilgrimage to Mecca in the last year of His life, Muḥammad, on His way back to Medina, ordered the large concourse of His followers to stop at a place known as Ghadír-i-Khumm. In that vast plain a number of saddles were stacked up, making an improvised pulpit from which Muḥammad delivered an important address to the congregation. There, He is reported to have taken 'Alí by the hand and said, 'Whoever considers Me as his Lord, then 'Alí is also his Lord.'

This is only a verbal statement, but the Shí'ah sect considers it to be authoritative and an indication that 'Alí is the lawful successor to the Prophet. But the majority of the Islamic people, the Sunnís, reject this view. The followers of Muḥammad were divided into these two major sects almost immediately after His passing. The dire conflicts and fierce turmoils which have engulfed the nation of Islám ever since were, as testified by 'Abdu'l-Bahá, the consequence of the bitter division which occurred after the death of the Prophet.

One of the distinguishing features of the Revelation of Bahá'u'lláh, then, is that its Author has established a mighty covenant with His followers concerning His successor, a covenant whose characteristics are delineated by Bahá'u'lláh Himself, a covenant written in His own hand, unequivocal in the provisions it has made for the future of His Cause, and acknowledged as an authentic document even by those who violated it. It is through this divinely ordained instrument alone that the unity of the Bahá'í community is preserved, the purity of its teachings safeguarded, and the incorruptibility of its institutions guaranteed. 'This is a Day that shall not be followed by night,' is Bahá'u'lláh's own testimony in this regard.

When God reveals Himself to man through the Prophet, the Words which the Prophet utters are supremely creative and a source of essential life to human souls. Revelation of the Word of God by His Manifestation resembles the downpouring of rain. In the same way that showers in the spring season vivify the world of nature, the Word of God penetrates the hearts of men and imparts to them the spirit of faith. This process goes on as long as the Revelation of the Prophet lasts, and ceases with His passing.

During the rainy season the green pastures are refreshed directly, and when the rain stops, one can be revived by the waters of a pool which that rain has created. Likewise, when the Manifestation of God is no longer with man, the Words He has left behind become the source of spiritual life for the believers. Thus the *Gospels* for the Christians and the *Qur'án* for the Muslims have acted as the spiritual reservoir of the water of life and the repository of God's teachings for them. We observe, however, that if people have free access to a reservoir, and are allowed to use it without limitation or to immerse themselves in it, the purity of the water will be lost and after some time it will be fully adulterated.

In older Dispensations, the Manifestations of God left their words to posterity, and in most cases the gist of these words were recorded and compiled, so constituting the Holy Books of the major religions. But since there was no provision made for further guidance, the followers were left free to interpret the utterances as they pleased. History shows that as a result of this freedom, people disagreed in their understanding of the teachings. The followers grossly interfered with the Word of God; they compromised the laws and precepts which were promulgated by the Prophet. Man-made dogmas and rituals were added, human innovations and practices were introduced and, as in the analogy of the reservoir, the purity of the teachings was lost.

It was because of this freedom to interpret the words of the Prophet and the freedom to interfere in His teachings that differences appeared among the followers. Schisms took place and sects and denominations were created within a religion. The unity and love which had existed among the followers during the lifetime of the Founder of the religion disappeared after Him and in the course of time were replaced by enmity and contention.

In this Dispensation the Revelation of the Word of God has taken a different form altogether. Whereas in former times the words of the Prophets, in most cases, were recorded years after their revelation, the words of Bahá'u'lláh were taken down by His amanuensis the moment they were uttered. In some cases even He Himself inscribed the verses revealed to Him. These writings, usually referred to as Sacred Text, or Tablets, are preserved and safeguarded and their authenticity assured.

One distinguishing feature is the vastness of this Revelation of Bahá'u'lláh. The words have been revealed with such profusion that – as Bahá'u'lláh Himself testifies – were His Writings to be compiled, they would produce no less than one hundred volumes of Holy Scripture for mankind in this age. The analogy of the pool is no longer apt. More appropriate would be the analogy of an ocean created when the Words of God were sent down as copious rain.

The *Qur'án* consists of over six thousand verses and was revealed by Muḥammad in twenty-three years. The speed of the Revelation of the words of Bahá'u'lláh* was about one thousand verses in an hour! For example, the *Kitáb-i-Íqán* (Book of Certitude), one of the most important of Bahá'u'lláh's Writings, was revealed in the course of just a few hours. During the forty-year Ministry of Bahá'u'lláh the world of humanity was immersed in an ocean of Divine Revelation whose latent energies are destined to revitalize the whole of mankind.

Another distinguishing feature of the Revelation of Bahá'u'lláh is that the Word of God, sent down for the spiritualization and guidance of man, has not been simply handed over to him freely, as in past Dispensations. To no one is given the right to interpret His words, to add even a dot, or to take one away. Bahá'u'lláh has sealed off the ocean of His Revelation from all intruders. On the one hand,

* For more information on the manner of revelation of Tablets, see *The Revelation of Bahá'u'lláh*, vol. 1, pp. 23–4.

He has revealed the Word of God for the benefit of all mankind; on the other, He does not allow anyone to interfere with it. The manner in which He has resolved these two contrasting features is through the institution of the Covenant.

God has in this day vouchsafed to humanity two priceless gifts. One is the Revelation itself, supreme over all things; the other is an instrument to shield the Revelation. The one is manifested through Bahá'u'lláh, the other fulfilled through 'Abdu'l-Bahá. To revert to the analogy: Bahá'u'lláh has brought the water of life and created the ocean, while 'Abdu'l-Bahá acts as a mighty wall around it.

This wall – the Covenant – prevents any intruder from polluting the waters of the Revelation and thus preserves its purity and vitality. Hence, the appointment of 'Abdu'l-Bahá as the sole authoritative Interpreter of the Writings of Bahá'u'lláh provides the guarantee for the incorruptibility of the revealed Word.

Instead of allowing man to interpret His Writings and act upon them as he likes, Bahá'u'lláh has released the outpourings of His Revelation within the person of 'Abdu'l-Bahá who received them on behalf of all mankind. He became the recipient of the Revelation of Bahá'u'lláh and the authorized interpreter of His words. His soul embraced every virtue and power which that Revelation conferred upon Him, virtues and powers which, through the operation of the institution of the Covenant, are to be vouchsafed progressively to humanity in the course of this Dispensation, and which are the cause of the social, the intellectual and spiritual development of man on this planet until the advent of the next Manifestation of God.

'Abdu'l-Bahá acts in this analogy as a receptacle. Before a receptacle is filled, it must first be empty. If it contains anything, even a minute quantity of any substance, that substance will pollute the pure water which is poured into it. One of the most glorious aspects of the Cause of Bahá'u'lláh is that the person of 'Abdu'l-Bahá had so surrendered His will to that of Bahá'u'lláh that He was utterly empty of self. He had nothing to express or manifest in His being except self-effacement and absolute servitude.

When 'Abdu'l-Bahá was a child in Baghdád, Bahá'u'lláh intimated to Him His own Station and unfolded the Mission with which God had entrusted Him. On hearing such a declaration, 'Abdu'l-Bahá, who had already felt intuitively the glory and the radiance which emanated from His Father, instantly acknowledged the truth of His Cause, prostrated Himself at His feet and in humility and earnestness begged Bahá'u'lláh to grant Him the privilege of laying down His life in His path.

The Person of 'Abdu'l-Bahá and His servitude to Bahá'u'lláh, His Lord, are inseparable. A true servant abides in the depths of lowliness and humility, and not in the heights of glory. The greater the measure of servitude, the lower will be the position of the individual. By virtue of His station, 'Abdu'l-Bahá occupies the lowest plane of servitude, a plane to which no other human being can ever descend. Bahá'u'lláh is the Manifestation of glory and is at the summit of majesty. 'Abdu'l-Bahá is at the opposite pole of servitude and utter selflessness. Bahá'u'lláh may be likened to the peak of a mountain, 'Abdu'l-Bahá as the lowest valley. When water pours down from the mountain top it will all accumulate in the deepest valley. In like manner, the Word of God, sent down from the Heaven of Divine Utterance, so permeated the person of 'Abdu'l-Bahá that He became a worthy carrier of the energies latent within the Revelation of Bahá'u'lláh. His whole being became the incarnation of every goodly virtue, a stainless mirror reflecting the light of glory cast upon Him by Bahá'u'lláh.

'Abdu'l-Bahá states that there are three stations in this vast creation: the station of God, which is unapproachable, the station of the Manifestations of God, which is equally inaccessible, and the station of man. The only station befitting man is that of servitude. To the extent that the individual believer abides on the plane of servitude, he will grow closer to God and become the recipient of His power, grace and bounties. 'Abdu'l-Bahá reached the lowest depths of servitude, hence He became the embodiment of all divine qualities and attributes. Although He genuinely considered Himself a servant of the servants of Bahá'u'lláh, He manifested a majesty and grandeur which no other human being could ever hope to possess. 'Abdu'l-Bahá was not a Manifestation of God, but by virtue of being the Repository of Bahá'u'lláh's Revelation, He had all the powers of the Manifestation conferred upon Him. He knew the secrets of the hearts of men and His words were creative.

The Most Great Infallibility mentioned by Bahá'u'lláh is inherent in the Manifestation of God and no one can share in it.* 'Abdu'l-Bahá did not possess this, but Bahá'u'lláh conferred upon Him infallibility. The Manifestation of God is like a sun which generates its own heat and light; it does not receive them from an outside source. But the moon does not possess its own light; it receives it from the sun and reflects it on the earth. Similarly, Bahá'u'lláh acts as the Sun of Truth and 'Abdu'l-Bahá as the Moon of this Dispensation.

It would be a mistake to consider 'Abdu'l-Bahá as an ordinary human being who persevered in His efforts until He emptied Himself of selfish desire and consequently was appointed by Bahá'u'lláh as His Successor. Such a concept is contrary to the belief of those

* See *The Revelation of Bahá'u'lláh*, vol. 4, pp. 143, 145, 149–53.

who have embraced the Faith of Bahá'u'lláh. 'Abdu'l-Bahá was created by God for the sole purpose of becoming the recipient of God's Revelation in this age. We shall never know His real station, because He was the 'Mystery of God', a title conferred upon Him by Bahá'u'lláh. He was the priceless gift of Bahá'u'lláh to mankind.

In the *Súriy-i-Ghuṣn* Bahá'u'lláh testifies to this truth:

> We have sent Him* down in the form of a human temple. Blest and sanctified be God Who createth whatsoever He willeth through His inviolable, His infallible decree. They who deprive themselves of the shadow of the Branch, are lost in the wilderness of error, are consumed by the heat of worldly desires, and are of those who will assuredly perish.[1]

When 'Abdu'l-Bahá was in His early teens in Baghdád, Bahá'u'lláh designated Him as 'the Master'. Other titles conferred upon Him in His youth are all indicative of a mysterious Being who is the Centre of Bahá'u'lláh's Covenant.

In elucidation of 'Abdu'l-Bahá's station, Shoghi Effendi writes:

> That 'Abdu'l-Bahá is not a Manifestation of God, that He gets His light, His inspiration and sustenance direct from the Fountain-head of the Bahá'í Revelation; that He reflects even as a clear and perfect Mirror the rays of Bahá'u'lláh's glory, and does not inherently possess that indefinable yet all-pervading reality the exclusive possession of which is the hallmark of Prophethood; that His words are not equal in rank, though they possess an equal validity with the utterances of Bahá'u'lláh; that He is not to be acclaimed as the return of Jesus Christ, the Son Who will come 'in the glory of the Father' – these truths find added justification, and are further reinforced, by the following statement of 'Abdu'l-Bahá, addressed to some believers in America. . . . '*You have written that there is a difference among the believers concerning the "Second Coming of Christ". Gracious God! Time and again this question hath arisen, and its answer hath emanated in a clear and irrefutable statement from the pen of 'Abdu'l-Bahá, that what is meant in the prophecies by the "Lord of Hosts" and the "Promised Christ" is the Blessed Perfection* (Bahá'u'lláh) *and His holiness the Exalted One* (the Báb). *My name is 'Abdu'l-Bahá. My qualification is 'Abdu'l-Bahá. My reality is 'Abdu'l-Bahá. My praise is 'Abdu'l-Bahá. Thraldom to the Blessed Perfection is my glorious and refulgent diadem, and servitude to all the human race my perpetual religion . . . No name, no title, no mention, no commendation have I, nor will ever have, except 'Abdu'l-Bahá. This is my longing. This is my greatest yearning. This is my eternal life. This is my everlasting glory.*'[2]

It is beyond the scope of this book to describe 'Abdu'l-Bahá's divine attributes or to recount the numerous stories left behind by a host of believers, admirers, and even some of His adversaries, all of whom have paid unmistakable tribute to His superhuman powers,

* 'Abdu'l-Bahá

His unfailing love, His selflessness, His servitude, His magnanimity and all the other virtues which He manifested throughout His life. Numerous books have been written extolling 'Abdu'l-Bahá's Christ-like example. A few excerpts will suffice to inform those who are not as yet aware of His vibrant and magnetic personality.

Shaykh Aḥmad-i-Rúḥí,* a follower of Mírzá Yaḥyá and an inveterate enemy of the Faith, was stigmatized by Bahá'u'lláh as a 'foreboder of evil'. He was notorious for acting treacherously to tarnish the honour and good name of the Blessed Beauty. Notwithstanding, this same Shaykh Aḥmad once announced from the pulpit that if there was one proof by which Bahá'u'lláh could substantiate His claims to Prophethood, it would be that He reared a Son such as 'Abbás Effendi.†

Professor Edward G. Browne of Cambridge, the noted Victorian orientalist, has left to posterity the following account of his meeting the Master for the first time in 'Akká in 1890.

> Seldom have I seen one whose appearance impressed me more. A tall strongly-built man holding himself straight as an arrow, with white turban and raiment, long black locks reaching almost to the shoulder, broad powerful forehead indicating a strong intellect combined with an unswerving will, eyes keen as a hawk's, and strongly-marked but pleasing features – such was my first impression of 'Abbás Efendí, 'the master' (*Áḳá*) as he *par excellence* is called by the Bábís. Subsequent conversation with him served only to heighten the respect with which his appearance had from the first inspired me. One more eloquent of speech, more ready of argument, more apt of illustration, more intimately acquainted with the sacred books of the Jews, the Christians, and the Muhammadans, could, I should think, scarcely be found even amongst the eloquent, ready, and subtle race to which he belongs. These qualities, combined with a bearing at once majestic and genial, made me cease to wonder at the influence and esteem which he enjoyed even beyond the circle of his father's followers. About the greatness of this man and his power no one who had seen him could entertain a doubt.[3]

'Abdu'l-Bahá's knowledge and eloquence, mentioned by Professor Browne, were not acquired at schools. They were conferred upon Him by Bahá'u'lláh. The history of 'Abdu'l-Bahá's life clearly demonstrates that apart from going to an old-fashioned preparatory school for about one year in Ṭihrán when he was approximately seven years of age, He had no opportunity to attend school. At the age of eight, when Bahá'u'lláh was imprisoned in the Síyáh-Chál and His wealth was confiscated, the family was completely stripped of its

* For some details of his iniquitous activities in Istanbul, see *The Revelation of Bahá'u'lláh*, vol. 4, pp. 399–402.

† 'Abdu'l-Bahá

possessions, deprived of its comfort and robbed of all its privileges. In those circumstances there was no way that 'Abdu'l-Bahá could have continued His schooling. Soon afterwards, when He was hardly nine years of age, He accompanied His Father into exile. From then on 'Abdu'l-Bahá was engulfed by tribulations and sufferings making it impossible for Him to continue His formal education.

In spite of this, 'Abdu'l-Bahá surpassed the most learned of His times. Men of consummate knowledge and culture, both Persian and Arab, have testified to 'Abdu'l-Bahá's superb erudition and learning. In the West too, He manifested such loving-kindness and wisdom in every field of human activity that a great many people were drawn to Him. In His contact with philosophers, scientists, ecclesiastics and others in Europe and America, 'Abdu'l-Bahá showed a profound understanding of the most complex issues, and often made authoritative statements which evoked the admiration and sometimes the amazement of those concerned.

When 'Abdu'l-Bahá was in His early teens in Baghdád, many notables and divines recognized His unusual insight and wisdom and became His admirers. To cite an example of His innate knowledge, once He attended a gathering of some learned divines in that city. When the origin of a certain word was being questioned, everyone agreed that it was Persian except 'Abdu'l-Bahá, who, although He was not educated in the Arabic tongue, declared it to be Arabic, and suggested it be looked up in the dictionary. To everyone's amazement, they, who were all well-versed in the Arabic language, discovered that 'Abdu'l-Bahá was right.

'Alí Shawkat Páshá was one of the high-ranking dignitaries of 'Iráq. He made a request to Bahá'u'lláh for the elucidation of the inner significance of a certain tradition of Islám which describes the purpose of God in creating man. The voice of God proclaims in this tradition: 'I was a hidden Treasure, I loved to be known, hence I created man to know Me.'

Bahá'u'lláh instructed 'Abdu'l-Bahá, who was in His adolescence, to write a commentary on this tradition. In obedience to His Father, 'Abdu'l-Bahá wrote a lengthy, profound and illuminating treatise which astounded the Páshá and aroused his admiration and respect for this youthful person. But Shawkat Páshá was not the only one who recognized the greatness of 'Abdu'l-Bahá. There were many who became aware of His extraordinary knowledge and wisdom, and some, including the renowned Ḥájí Siyyid Javád-i-Karbilá'í,* concluded that one of the unmistakable proofs of the truth of the Mission of Bahá'u'lláh was that His son 'Abdu'l-Bahá had written

* See *The Revelation of Bahá'u'lláh*, vols. 1 and 2.

such a profound and significant treatise, shedding new light on this important tradition.

From a literary point of view the Writings of 'Abdu'l-Bahá, both in Arabic and Persian, are considered by scholars to be of the highest standard. The beauty of His style, the eloquence of His words, the flow and lucidity of His composition and the profundity of His utterances move the reader and uplift the soul.

There are innumerable stories left behind by Westerners who came into contact with 'Abdu'l-Bahá, either in the Holy Land or in Europe and America.

Major Wellesley Tudor-Pole, a British officer who met 'Abdu'l-Bahá in Palestine on many occasions, has written a great deal about the Master. The following is a brief excerpt:

> Although of a little less than medium height, Abdu'l Baha made an impression on all who met him by his dignity, friendliness, and his aura of spiritual authority. His blue-grey eyes radiated a luminosity of their own and his hands were beautiful in their grace and healing magnetism. Even his movements were infused with a kind of radiance . . .
>
> The most abiding impression I received from intimate contact with him was his immense breadth of outlook, permeated with the spirit of deep and loving kindness. Whatever the topic under discussion – ranging from religion to the weather, from sunsets to the flowers, from ethics to personal behaviour, Abdu'l Baha always struck the universal note, the note of Oneness as between the Creator and all His creation, great or small . . .
>
> He was a man of great spiritual stature and prophetic vision and I shall always cherish the affection he bestowed upon me and the inspiration that his life and example have given to me ever since he first came into my life in 1908.[4]

Horace Holley, an American Bahá'í later appointed as one of the Hands of the Cause of God, met 'Abdu'l-Bahá for the first time in the summer of 1911. He described his memorable meeting with the Master in these words:

> He displayed a beauty of stature, an inevitable harmony of attitude and dress I had never seen nor thought of in men. Without having ever visualized the Master, I knew that this was he. My whole body underwent a shock. My heart leaped, my knees weakened, a thrill of acute, receptive feeling flowed from head to foot. I seemed to have turned into some most sensitive sense-organ, as if eyes and ears were not enough for this sublime impression. In every part of me I stood aware of Abdul Baha's presence. From sheer happiness I wanted to cry – it seemed the most suitable form of self-expression at my command. While my own personality was flowing away, even whilst I exhibited a state of complete humility, a new being, not my own, assumed its place. A

glory, as it were, from the summits of human nature poured into me, and I was conscious of a most intense impulse to admire. In Abdul Baha I felt the awful presence of Baha'o'llah, and, as my thoughts returned to activity, I realized that I had thus drawn as near as man now may to pure spirit and pure being . . .

During our two days' visit, we were given unusual opportunity of questioning the Master, but I soon realized that such was not the highest or most productive plane on which I could meet him . . . I yielded to a feeling of reverence which contained more than the solution of intellectual or moral problems. To look upon so wonderful a human being, to respond utterly to the charm of his presence – this brought me continual happiness. I had no fear that its effects would pass away and leave me unchanged . . . Patriarchal, majestic, strong, yet infinitely kind, he appeared like some just king that very moment descended from his throne to mingle with a devoted people . . .[5]

Howard Colby Ives, a Unitarian Minister who later embraced the Bahá'í Faith, went to see 'Abdu'l-Bahá when He was in New York. A number of friends also had gathered in a hotel room for the same purpose. This is the account he wrote of that first memorable meeting with the Master.

So I was somewhat withdrawn from the others when my attention was attracted by a rustling throughout the room. A door was opening far across from me and a group was emerging and 'Abdu'l-Bahá appeared saying farewell. None had any eyes save for Him. Again I had the impression of a unique dignity and courtesy and love. The morning sunlight flooded the room to center on His robe. His fez was slightly tilted and as I gazed, His hand, with a gesture evidently characteristic, raised and, touching, restored it to its proper place. His eyes met mine as my fascinated glance was on Him. He smiled and, with a gesture which no word but 'lordly' can describe, He beckoned me. Startled gives no hint of my sensations. Something incredible had happened. Why to me, a stranger unknown, unheard of, should He raise that friendly hand? I glanced around. Surely it was to someone else that gesture was addressed, those eyes were smiling! But there was no one near and again I looked and again He beckoned and such understanding love enveloped me that even at that distance and with a heart still cold a thrill ran through me as if a breeze from a divine morning had touched my brow!

Slowly I obeyed that imperative command and, as I approached the door where still He stood, He motioned others away and stretched His hand to me as if He had always known me. And, as our right hands met, with His left He indicated that all should leave the room, and He drew me in and closed the door. I remember how surprised the interpreter looked when he too was included in this general dismissal. But I had little thought then for anything but this incredible happening. I was absolutely alone with 'Abdu'l-Bahá. The halting desire expressed weeks ago was fulfilled the very moment that our eyes first met.

Still holding my hand 'Abdu'l-Bahá walked across the room towards where, in the window, two chairs were waiting. Even then the majesty of His tread impressed me and I felt like a child led by His father, a more than earthly father, to a comforting conference. His hand still held mine and frequently His grasp tightened and held more closely. And then, for the first time, He spoke, and in my own tongue. Softly came the assurance that I was His very dear son.

What there was in these simple words that carried such conviction to my heart I cannot say. Or was it the tone of voice and the atmosphere pervading the room, filled with spiritual vibrations beyond anything I had ever known, that melted my heart almost to tears? I only know that a sense of *verity* invaded me. Here at last *was* my Father. What earthly paternal relationship could equal this? A new and exquisite emotion all but mastered me. My throat swelled. My eyes filled. I could not have spoken had life depended on a word. I followed those masterly feet like a little child.

Then we sat in the two chairs by the window: knee to knee, eye to eye. At last He looked right into me. It was the first time since our eyes had met with His first beckoning gesture that this had happened. And now nothing intervened between us and He looked at me. *He looked at me!* It seemed as though never before had anyone really seen *me*. I felt a sense of gladness that I at last was at home, and that one who knew me utterly, my Father, in truth, was alone with me.

As He looked such play of thought found reflection in His face, that if He had talked an hour not nearly so much could have been said. A little surprise, perhaps, followed swiftly by such sympathy, such understanding, such overwhelming love – it was as if His very being opened to receive me. With that the heart within me melted and the tears flowed. I did not weep, in any ordinary sense. There was no breaking up of feature. It was as if a long-pent stream was at last undammed. Unheeded, as I looked at Him, they flowed.

He put His two thumbs to my eyes while He wiped the tears from my face; admonishing me not to cry, that one must always be happy. And He laughed. Such a ringing, boyish laugh. It was as though He had discovered the most delightful joke imaginable: a divine joke which only He could appreciate.

I could not speak. We both sat perfectly silent for what seemed a long while, and gradually a great peace came to me. Then 'Abdu'l-Bahá placed His hand upon my breast saying that it was the heart that speaks. Again silence: a long, heart-enthralling silence. No word further was spoken, and all the time I was with Him not one single sound came from me. But no word was necessary from me to Him. I knew that, even then, and how I thanked God it was so.

Suddenly He leaped from His chair with another laugh as though consumed with a heavenly joy. Turning, He took me under the elbows and lifted me to my feet and swept me into his arms. Such a hug! No mere embrace! My very ribs cracked. He kissed me on both cheeks, laid His arm across my shoulders and led me to the door.

That is all. But life has never been quite the same since.[6]

These few personal impressions give us glimpses of the noble life of the One Who was appointed by Bahá'u'lláh as the Centre of His Covenant. Not only did 'Abdu'l-Bahá direct the affairs of the Cause as the successor of the Manifestation of God, but also He was the most effective influence during Bahá'u'lláh's ministry in promoting and safeguarding the vital interests of an infant and struggling Faith. It is significant that the birth of Bahá'u'lláh's Revelation did not take place until the Person of 'Abdu'l-Bahá, that Vehicle designed to receive and contain its energising forces, was present in the world as a child.

The Báb states[7] that the advent of a Manifestation of God depends upon the existence of a person – the first believer – who has the capacity to understand and embrace His Cause. Should such an individual be found among mankind God will immediately reveal Himself and will not postpone His Revelation, even for a fraction of a minute. The Báb gives the example of His own Revelation and states that since the appearance of Muḥammad God had been watching for a person to appear and become the recipient of His Message and that it took 1260 lunar years until Mullá Ḥusayn acquired the capacity to know Him. The Báb further asserts that had Mullá Ḥusayn been ready to acknowledge the truth of His Cause one moment earlier than he did, He would have correspondingly revealed Himself to him that much sooner.

The birth of Bahá'u'lláh's Revelation occurred at a time when 'Abdu'l-Bahá, though a mere child, was able to perceive intuitively the glorious Mission with which His Father was invested. It seems also providential that 'Abdu'l-Bahá was born on the same day that the Báb declared His Mission to Mullá Ḥusayn. It is significant indeed that as the Declaration of the Báb, the Herald of Bahá'u'lláh, took place on that memorable evening, so did the birth of the Person who was destined to become the recipient of His great Revelation.

As 'Abdu'l-Bahá grew up, the scope of His activities increased. Innumerable were the outstanding services He rendered His Father in Baghdád, Adrianople and 'Akká. He represented Bahá'u'lláh on many occasions as His deputy, defending the interests of the Faith before the public and acting as a mighty shield to protect Him from His enemies.

CHAPTER SEVEN

The Family of Bahá'u'lláh

At the passing of Bahá'u'lláh in 1892 the Bahá'í community was plunged into such a state of grief and consternation as it had never experienced before. The light of divine Revelation, which had shone forth for forty years, was now withdrawn, and the believers tasted the bitter agony of separation from their Lord. Their only source of consolation was the Person of 'Abdu'l-Bahá who, as the Centre of Bahá'u'lláh's Covenant, succeeded in imparting new life and vigour to the body of the Cause of God and who called on the believers to arise and spread the healing message of Bahá'u'lláh to the people of the East and the West. Within a short period of time the fringes of the five continents of the globe were illumined with the splendours of the light of the Faith.

Stupendous as was this progress of the Cause during the Ministry of the Master, the onslaught of the unfaithful from within the community and especially the fierce opposition of most of the members of Bahá'u'lláh's family to the Centre of the Covenant, created an unprecedented tempest. This raged furiously within the community for several decades and threatened to disrupt its unity and shake its divinely ordained but young and vulnerable institutions. The fierce onslaught of the Covenant-breakers upon the Cause of God on the one hand, and their eventual extinction on the other, constitute the most dramatic episodes in the ministries of 'Abdu'l-Bahá and Shoghi Effendi. These are some of the darkest pages in the history of the Faith, and yet they cast light upon the mysterious forces operating within the Cause of God, forces that tear down every obstacle in the onward march of the Cause toward its ultimate victory. They clearly demonstrate the vitality and the indestructibility of the Faith and serve to delineate the pattern of crisis and victory which characterises its future growth and development throughout the world.

In order to study the Covenant of Bahá'u'lláh and grasp its significance, it is necessary to examine the manner in which Bahá'u'lláh conducted His personal life and the way He communicated His Message to mankind. A common feature of the Manifestations of God is that they appear among people without making a great display of their divine power, knowledge or glory. They seem to be ordinary people with all the human characteristics. Inwardly they are invested with divine knowledge and power, but it is against the law of God for them to reveal these qualities to the generality of mankind, for if they do, all human beings will witness their awesome glory, will bow before their majesty and submit their will entirely to God's Viceregent on earth. Should this happen, man would become a puppet of God and lose his free will; everyone would follow the path of truth not by his own volition, but by capitulating to the irresistible power of the Manifestation of God. By the force of God's command, all would obey His Teachings and would live a goodly life; no one could have the choice to be different and there would be no wickedness. If this were to happen, man would become devoid of the power of creativity, and turn into a creature whose actions were controlled from a higher realm. Then the principles of justice, of reward and punishment would become inoperative and meaningless in society. This is one of the reasons why a Manifestation of God conceals His glory and powers behind the veil of His human characteristics. Only those who have spiritual eyes can see a glimpse of His radiant Light and recognize His station; the great majority of the people fail to discover His inner spiritual reality. In this way man can exercise his free will to accept or to reject the Message of God, to live in accordance with His teachings or to disobey Him.

We therefore observe that a Manifestation of God has two sides: human and divine. It is the human side which veils the splendours of the divine light that shine within His Person. A Manifestation of God is subject to all human characteristics. He has to eat, sleep, and carry on His life like any other person. These limitations of human nature become barriers for people in recognizing Him as the Manifestation of God. One of these barriers is the question of marriage. This is an especially great obstacle for many of Christian background, who have been brought up to believe that celibacy befits a holy person and that marriage is inappropriate for a Manifestation of God. Perhaps this attitude stems from the fact that Christ did not seem to have been married when He declared His Mission. However, Christ Himself did not speak against marriage. On the other hand, should one attribute a lack of sexual urge to a holy person, this would amount to a physical deficiency rather than a virtue, for the Manifestations of God are perfect in body as in spirit. That Christ did not marry is probably because His Ministry was short and that for most of it He was homeless, going from place to place until He was crucified.

Since the Manifestations of God share with the people all characteristics of human nature, it follows that they may live a normal life, engage in a profession, have a home, marry and raise a family. They also possess all the human sentiments and emotions. They are sensitive beings with feelings of joy and sadness, of pain and comfort, of likes and dislikes. What distinguishes them from the rest of mankind is that their spiritual side completely dominates their physical nature, and they are absolutely detached from the material world.

Another feature of the life of a Manifestation of God is that He lives in accordance with the laws and conventions of the society to which He belongs. He eats the same type of food, wears the same type of clothes, and carries out the same customs as the rest of the people of his culture and background. He does not live His life in the pattern of a future society which will emerge centuries later as a result of His teachings and about which He has full knowledge. For example, during the Ministry of Jesus two thousand years ago. Christ lived in a manner similar to the Israelites of the time. He did not project Himself out of that society and did not live a different pattern of life from that of the age He lived in.

By following the customs of the people of His own land, the Manifestation of God does not appear conspicuously different from the rest of the people, and this is how His glory is hidden behind His human façade. In this way, His contemporaries look upon Him as an ordinary man.

Bahá'u'lláh belonged to a noble family of Ṭihrán. His father, Mírzá 'Abbás-i-Núrí, known as Mírzá Buzurg, held a very important ministerial position in the court of the Sháh, and was regarded in high esteem by the dignitaries of the realm. Circumstances of family life in Islamic countries were totally different from those of present-day Western society. The law of Islám concerning polygamy was in force, allowing men to have a maximum of four wives at the same time. Mírzá Buzurg married four wives and had three concubines and fifteen children – five daughters and ten sons. Bahá'u'lláh was born on 12 November 1817 in Ṭihrán. His mother, Khadíjih Khánum, the second wife of Mírzá Buzurg, had a son and two daughters from a previous marriage. As a result Bahá'u'lláh had ten brothers and seven sisters.* Some of them became steadfast believers, some followed Mírzá Yaḥyá, while others remained indifferent or died before Bahá'u'lláh's declaration in the Garden of Riḍván.

Bahá'u'lláh received an elementary education in His childhood in Ṭihrán. The nobility of those days usually employed the services of a teacher at home to tutor their children. The main subjects were calligraphy, the study of the *Qur'án* and the works of the Persian

* For more details, see Balyuzi, *Bahá'u'lláh, The King of Glory*, pp. 13–14.

poets. This type of schooling ended after only a few years when the child was in his early teens. Bahá'u'lláh's education did not go further than this: He Himself testifies in His Tablet to Náṣiri'd-Dín Shāh that He did not attend any school in His life:

> O king! I was but a man like others, asleep upon My couch, when lo, the breezes of the All-Glorious were wafted over Me, and taught Me the knowledge of all that hath been. This thing is not from Me, but from One Who is Almighty and All-Knowing. And He bade Me lift up My voice between earth and heaven, and for this there befell Me what hath caused the tears of every man of understanding to flow. The learning current amongst men I studied not; their schools I entered not. Ask of the city wherein I dwelt, that thou mayest be well assured that I am not of them who speak falsely. This is but a leaf which the winds of the will of thy Lord, the Almighty, the All-Praised, have stirred. Can it be still when the tempestuous winds are blowing? Nay, by Him Who is the Lord of all Names and Attributes! They move it as they list.[1]

It is beyond the scope of this book to dwell on Bahá'u'lláh's eventful life during the years of His youth. Some of these stories are already published.[2] For the purpose of studying the Covenant, however, it is necessary to become informed of Bahá'u'lláh's marriages and His children. Bahá'u'lláh had married three wives before the declaration of His Mission in 1863. As has already been stated, the Manifestation of God conducts His personal life according to the customs of the time. Polygamy was a normal practice in those days; indeed, it would have been abnormal for a man who belonged to the nobility to be monogamous in that society.

In order to appreciate this subject, it is essential to become familiar with the Islamic world of the nineteenth century. Among the Muslim communities of the Middle East, women lived entirely under the domination of men and were not allowed to take part in public affairs. Girls grew up in the home of their parents, lived most of their time indoors and had no contact with the public. When they were given in marriage to their husbands (an event over which they had no control) they moved into a different house and spent most of their time in complete seclusion until they died. No man, except a very close relative, was ever allowed to see the face of a woman. She had to wear a chadur* and veil her face. When a male guest arrived at a home, all the women had to retire into the inner apartment, their sanctuary where no strange man would ever be admitted. It was considered a sin for a woman to show her face to any man.

Another restriction was that women, especially unmarried girls, were not supposed to talk to men. Neither would they be permitted

* A large piece of cloth which covers the entire body from top to toe and is wrapped around one's clothes.

to go out for shopping or other services; these were the exclusive function of men. Such an act would have necessitated women taking part in public affairs and coming into contact with men. So strict was this practice that if ever a woman was seen talking to a strange man she would receive very severe punishment from her parents or husband. The stigma attached to this behaviour was so repugnant that sometimes the poor victim would commit suicide.

Some Muslim clergy in Persia are known to have inflicted torturous chastisements upon a man who was accused of talking to a woman. Usually a much more severe punishment awaited a non-Muslim man if he was ever found speaking to a Muslim woman.

Women in those days had no status in the community. They were treated as if they were part of the furniture. Some members of the clergy went as far as to claim that women had no souls, much as Christian theologians had done seven hundred years earlier. Within such a society a woman's life was spent almost entirely within the four walls of a house, caring for her family and all the menfolk who lived there. It was very rare for a young girl to receive any education. The great majority of women were illiterate and were therefore left out of the mainstream of human progress and civilization.

Even the few who received some education were circumscribed in their activities. For instance, the renowned Ṭáhirih, the heroine of the Bábí Dispensation, usually sat behind a curtain in order to take part in the seminars conducted by her teacher Siyyid Káẓim, for it was considered unchaste for a women to sit among men. How revolutionary, then, was her act of proclamation at the Conference of Badasht when she appeared in the gathering of men unveiled and seated herself beside Quddús. It is hardly surprising that as a result of her action several Bábís present at the conference left the Faith of the Báb altogether. One person went so far as to cut his own throat after observing Ṭáhirih breaking, even momentarily, one of the most cherished Islamic practices of segregation between the sexes. The following account by Nabíl-i-A'ẓam vividly portrays the scenes of alarm among the participants,

> . . . when suddenly the figure of Ṭáhirih, adorned and unveiled, appeared before the eyes of the assembled companions. Consternation immediately seized the entire gathering. All stood aghast before this sudden and most unexpected apparition. To behold her face unveiled was to them inconceivable. Even to gaze at her shadow was a thing which they deemed improper, inasmuch as they regarded her as the very incarnation of Fáṭimih,* the noblest emblem of chastity in their eyes.

* The daughter of the Prophet Muḥammad, she is considered to be the holiest woman in Islam.

> Quietly, silently, and with the utmost dignity, Ṭáhirih stepped forward and, advancing towards Quddús, seated herself on his right-hand side. Her unruffled serenity sharply contrasted with the affrighted countenances of those who were gazing upon her face. Fear, anger, and bewilderment stirred the depths of their souls. That sudden revelation seemed to have stunned their faculties. 'Abdu'l-Kháliq-i-Iṣfáhání was so gravely shaken that he cut his throat with his own hands. Covered with blood and shrieking with excitement, he fled away from the face of Ṭáhirih. A few, following his example, abandoned their companions and forsook their Faith. A number were seen standing speechless before her, confounded with wonder.[3]

It was the parents' responsibilities to arrange marriages for their children. Usually the parties most concerned had no say in the arrangement; it was customary to betrothe boy and girl soon after they were born. When the boy reached his late teens, he had to marry; the couple had no choice in the matter. There was no question of the partners loving each other before their marriage; the boy was not even allowed to see the face of his bride until after the wedding. If the two parties were not betrothed so young, the parents would usually seek a bride for their son once he was in his teens. This was done by a female member of the family, such as a mother or a sister. Once the choice was made, by them , the marriage could take place. All the young man knew about his future wife was a figure wrapped in a chadur and heavily veiled. Perhaps his female relatives had described to him what his bride really looked like!

The parents were also responsible for providing their son with his livelihood, his home and all his needs – including a wife, who would be given to him as a matter of routine!

In the western world today, a couple meet and get to know one another, fall in love and get married. But in the time of Bahá'u'lláh this was not the case in the East, and often not in the West either. 'Love' took second place to family duty, appropriate social ties and questions of inheritance.

But although a couple were not in a position to choose their partners in marriage and had no possibility of knowing and loving each other, the reader must not believe that all marriages were devoid of love and unity. It is not difficult to visualize the case of a couple unacquainted with each other initially, who develop a bond of friendship, love and harmony after marriage. Yet within such an atmosphere, the domineering position of the husband was noticeably upheld as he exercised unquestioned authority over his wife.

In these circumstances all the responsibility of running the home – which entailed hard labour in those days – was left to the wife, who would be lucky if there were other female members of the family to help her in her duties. It was considered improper to employ a maid to assist in the work, since only a woman who was a close relative could be admitted into the household. However, since polygamy was commonly practised, a man could usually marry up to four wives, and they were expected to assist each other in managing the family home. This often became a necessity where the husband was a wealthy and influential person and had to maintain a large household and conduct a life-style befitting his station in society. Usually it was the first wife who would seek out, or give her consent for, the person who was to become the second wife.

It is clear that marriage customs in Persia during the nineteenth century were not by any stretch of the imagination comparable to those of the present-day in most parts of the world. The mere mention of polygamy today will raise in people's minds such things as sex, lustfulness, corruption and unchastity. But this was not true in the case of people who contracted marriages according to Islamic law over a hundred years ago. Men practiced polygamy not necessarily because of lust but because they were conducting their lives within a society which had established certain customs and conventions to which all had to conform. Thus, a young man happily submitted his will to that of his parents and carried out their wish in marrying someone of their choosing; thereafter he contracted further marriages as a routine matter.

Bahá'u'lláh married Ásíyih Khánum in Ṭihrán in 1251 AH (1835) when He was over eighteen years of age. Ásíyih Khánum, later surnamed Navváb by Bahá'u'lláh, was a daughter of a nobleman, Mírzá Ismá'il-i-Vazír. Her date of birth is not known. She was a most noble and faithful follower of Bahá'u'lláh who served her Lord till the end of her life in 1886. There were seven children of the marriage, four of whom died in childhood. The other three were 'Abbás, entitled the 'Most Great Branch', 'Abdu'l-Bahá'; Fáṭimih, entitled Bahíyyih Khánum, the Greatest Holy Leaf; and Mihdí, entitled 'the Purest Branch'.

The second wife of Bahá'u'lláh, whom He married in Ṭihrán in 1849, was Fáṭimih Khánum, usually referred to as Mahd-i-'Ulyá. She was a cousin of Bahá'u'lláh, and gave birth to six children of whom four survived. They were one daughter, Ṣamadíyyih, and three sons, Muḥammad-Áli, Ḍíyá'u'lláh and Badí'u'lláh. These four, along with their mother, violated the Covenant of Bahá'u'lláh. Mahd-i-'Ulyá died in 1904.

The third wife, Gawhar Khánum, was not known by any other title. Her dates of birth, marriage and death are not known. Her marriage took place some time in Baghdád before the declaration of Bahá'u'lláh's Mission. While Navváb and Mahd-i-'Ulyá travelled with Him in all His exiles, Gawhar Khánum remained in Baghdád with her brother, Mírzá Mihdíy-i-Káshání.* For some years she was among the Bahá'í refugees in Mosul,† and later went to 'Akká at Bahá'u'lláh's instruction. She gave birth to one daughter, Furúghíyyih; mother and daughter both became Covenant-breakers after the passing of Bahá'u'lláh.

It is appropriate at this juncture to clarify a point which has puzzled the minds of many, namely the lack of detailed information about the wives of Bahá'u'lláh. Here again, one has to consider the social circumstances of the time. As has already been stated, women in those days took no part in public affairs; their entire lives were spent at home in private life. To enquire into the life of a woman was considered to be unethical, even insulting. It was discourteous to ask even the name of someone's wife. She would be usually referred to as the 'person in the house', or, if she had a son, she could be called 'mother of . . .'. Within such a society historians (always male) usually did not, and could not, invade the privacy of women by delving into their lives. Otherwise, they could highly offend the men folk!

Although one would not find such practices in Bahá'u'lláh's household, and those believers who were close to Him had come in contact with the female members of His family, nevertheless, owing to the customs of the time and the privacy to which women in general were entitled, very little has been recorded about their lives by oriental historians of the Faith.

Navváb, honoured by Bahá'u'lláh by the designation 'The Most Exalted Leaf', was truly an embodiment of nobility. She was utterly detached from the things of the world and most faithful to the Cause of God. Navváb's deep attachment to the Cause of Bahá'u'lláh was one of her great distinguishing features. She had a compassionate and loving nature, was patient, humble and utterly resigned to the will of Bahá'u'lláh. She suffered a great deal at the hands of those in the family who later broke the Covenant. Her faith in Bahá'u'lláh, whom she knew as the Supreme Manifestation of God, was resolute and unshakeable. She served her Lord with exemplary devotion and complete self-effacement. Her daughter, the Greatest Holy Leaf, has described her in these words:

> I wish you could have seen her as I first remember her, tall, slender, graceful, eyes of dark blue – a pearl, a flower amongst women.
>
> I have been told that even when very young, her wisdom and intelligence were remarkable. I always think of her in those earliest days of my

* See 'Abdu'l-Bahá, *Memorials of the Faithful*, p. 95.

† See *The Revelation of Bahá'u'lláh*, vol. 2.

memory as queenly in her dignity and loveliness, full of consideration for everybody, gentle, of a marvellous unselfishness, no action of hers ever failed to show the loving-kindness of her pure heart; her very presence seemed to make an atmosphere of love and happiness wherever she came, enfolding all comers in the fragrance of gentle courtesy.[4]

In one of His Tablets Bahá'u'lláh bestows upon Navváb the unique distinction of being His perpetual consort in all the worlds of God. The following passages gleaned from the Writings of Bahá'u-'lláh clearly demonstrate the glory with which He invested her:

The first Spirit through which all spirits were revealed, and the first Light by which all lights shone forth, rest upon thee, O Most Exalted Leaf, thou who hast been mentioned in the Crimson Book! Thou art the one whom God created to arise and serve His own Self, and the Manifestation of His Cause, and the Day-Spring of His Revelation, and the Dawning-Place of His signs, and the Source of His commandments; and Who so aided thee that thou didst turn with thy whole being unto Him, at a time when His servants and handmaidens had turned away from His Face. . . . Happy art thou, O My handmaiden, and My Leaf, and the one mentioned in My Book, and inscribed by My Pen of Glory in My Scrolls and Tablets. . . . Rejoice thou, at this moment, in the most exalted Station and the All-highest Paradise, and the Abhá Horizon, inasmuch as He Who is the Lord of Names hath remembered thee. We bear witness that thou didst attain unto all good, and that God hath so exalted thee, that all honour and glory circled around thee.

O Navváb! O Leaf that hath sprung from My Tree, and been My companion! My glory be upon thee, and My loving-kindness, and My mercy that hath surpassed all beings. We announce unto thee that which will gladden thine eye, and assure thy soul, and rejoice thine heart. Verily, thy Lord is the Compassionate, the All-Bountiful. God hath been and will be pleased with thee, and hath singled thee out for His own Self, and chosen thee from among His handmaidens to serve Him, and hath made thee the companion of His Person in the day-time and in the night-season.

Hear thou Me once again . . . God is well-pleased with thee, as a token of His grace and a sign of His mercy. He hath made thee to be His companion in every one of His worlds, and hath nourished thee with His meeting and presence, so long as His Name, and His Remembrance, and His Kingdom, and His Empire shall endure. Happy is the handmaid that hath mentioned thee, and sought thy good-pleasure, and humbled herself before thee, and held fast unto the cord of thy love. Woe betide him that denieth thy exalted station, and the things ordained for thee from God, the Lord of all names, and him that hath turned away from thee, and rejected thy station before God, the Lord of the mighty throne.

O faithful ones! Should ye visit the resting-place of the Most Exalted Leaf, who hath ascended unto the Glorious Companion, stand ye and say: 'Salutation and blessing and glory upon thee, O Holy Leaf that hath sprung from the Divine Lote-Tree! I bear witness that thou hast believed in God and in His signs, and answered His Call, and turned unto Him, and held fast unto His cord, and clung to the hem of His grace, and fled thy home in His path, and chosen to live as a stranger, out of love for His presence and in thy longing to serve Him. May God have mercy upon him that draweth nigh unto thee, and remembereth thee through the things which My Pen hath voiced in this, the most great station. We pray God that He may forgive us, and forgive them that have turned unto thee, and grant their desires, and bestow upon them, through His wondrous grace, whatever be their wish. He, verily, is the Bountiful, the Generous. Praise be to God, He Who is the Desire of all worlds; and the Beloved of all who recognize Him.

'Abdu'l-Bahá in a Tablet states that the 54th chapter of Isaiah refers to Navváb, the Most Exalted Leaf, whose 'seed shall inherit the Gentiles', and whose husband is the 'Lord of Hosts'. 'Abdu'l-Bahá also refers to the verse, 'For more are the children of the desolate, than the children of the married wife', and states that this refers to Navváb. This is part of the 54th chapter:

Sing, O barren, thou that didst not bear; break forth into singing, and cry aloud, thou that didst not travail with child: for more are the children of the desolate than the children of the married wife, saith the Lord.

Enlarge the place of thy tent, and let them stretch forth the curtains of thine habitations: spare not, lengthen thy cords, and strengthen thy stakes;

For thou shalt break forth on the right hand and on the left; and thy seed shall inherit the Gentiles, and make the desolate cities to be inhabited.

Fear not; for thou shalt not be ashamed: neither be thou confounded; for thou shalt not be put to shame: for thou shalt forget the shame of thy youth . . .

For thy Maker is thine husband; the Lord of Hosts is his name; and thy Redeemer the Holy One of Israel; The God of the whole earth shall he be called.

For the Lord hath called thee as a woman forsaken and grieved in spirit . . .

For a small moment have I forsaken thee; but with great mercies will I gather thee . . .

For the mountains shall depart, and the hills be removed; but my kindness shall not depart from thee, neither shall the covenant of my peace be removed, saith the Lord that hath mercy on thee.

O thou afflicted, tossed with tempest, and not comforted, behold, I will lay thy stones with fair colours, and lay thy foundations with sapphires.

And I will make thy windows of agates, and thy gates of carbuncles, and all thy borders of pleasant stones.

And all thy children shall be taught of the Lord; and great shall be the peace of thy children . . . whosoever shall gather together against thee shall fall for thy sake.

'Abdu'l-Bahá goes on to bear witness to the sufferings of Navváb and extol her wonderful qualities:

And truly the humiliation and reproach which she suffered in the path of God is a fact which no one can refute. For the calamities and afflictions mentioned in the whole chapter are such afflictions which she suffered in the path of God, all of which she endured with patience and thanked God therefor and praised Him, because He had enabled her to endure afflictions for the sake of Bahá. During all this time, the men and women (Covenant-breakers) persecuted her in an incomparable manner, while she was patient, God-fearing, calm, humble and contented through the favour of Her Lord and by the bounty of her Creator.[7]

The three members of the family of Navváb occupy the highest rank in the Faith. 'Abdu'l-Bahá is of course the Centre of the Covenant of Bahá'u'lláh, the Perfect Exemplar and the embodiment of all divine virtues. His sister, the Greatest Holy Leaf, is regarded as the noblest woman in this Dispensation and its outstanding heroine.

Even a brief outline of her life is outside the scope of this book; the following passages must suffice. They allow us a few glimpses of her saintly life* – a life laden with unbearable sufferings in the path of Bahá'u'lláh and dedicated to the service of His Cause. These are the words of Bahá'u'lláh as He showers His loving bounties upon His Greatest Holy Leaf.

Let these exalted words be thy love-song on the tree of Bahá, O thou most holy and resplendent Leaf: 'God, besides Whom is none other God, the Lord of this world and the next!' Verily, We have elevated thee to the rank of one of the most distinguished among thy sex, and granted thee, in My court, a station such as none other woman hath surpassed. Thus have We preferred thee and raised thee above the rest, as a sign of grace from Him Who is the Lord of the throne on high and earth below. We have created thine eyes to behold the light of My countenance, thine ears to hearken unto the melody of My words, thy body to pay homage before My throne. Do thou render thanks unto God, thy Lord, the Lord of all the world.

How high is the testimony of the Sadratu'l-Muntahá for its leaf; how exalted the witness of the Tree of Life unto its fruit! Through My remembrance of her a fragrance laden with the perfume of musk hath been diffused; well is it with him that hath inhaled it and exclaimed: 'All praise be to Thee, O God, my Lord the most glorious!' How sweet thy

* For a more detailed study of her life see *Bahíyyih Khánum, The Greatest Holy Leaf* (Bahá'í World Centre, 1982).

presence before Me; how sweet to gaze upon thy face, to bestow upon thee My loving-kindness, to favour thee with My tender care, to make mention of thee in this, My Tablet – a Tablet which I have ordained as a token of My hidden and manifest grace unto thee.[8]

In another Tablet He testifies to her faithfulness and devotion to His Cause.

O My Leaf! Hearken thou unto My Voice: Verily there is none other God but Me, the Almighty, the All-Wise. I can well inhale from thee the fragrance of My love and the sweet-smelling savour wafting from the raiment of My Name, the Most Holy, the Most Luminous. Be astir upon God's Tree in conformity with thy pleasure and unloose thy tongue in praise of thy Lord amidst all mankind. Let not the things of the world grieve thee. Cling fast unto this divine Lote-Tree from which God hath graciously caused thee to spring forth. I swear by My life! It behoveth the lover to be closely joined to the loved one, and here indeed is the Best-Beloved of the world.[9]

In many Tablets 'Abdu'l-Bahá too pays tribute to the purity and nobility of her soul. For example, He writes to her in these words:

O thou my affectionate sister! In the day-time and in the night-season my thoughts ever turn to thee. Not for one moment do I cease to remember thee. My sorrow and regret concern not myself; they centre around thee. Whenever I recall thine afflictions, tears that I cannot repress rain down from mine eyes . . .[10]

On the occasion of her ascension to the Kingdom on high in 1932, Shoghi Effendi, grief-stricken at the loss of that noble heroine of the Faith, wrote a most moving eulogy. The following are a few excerpts from his celebrated letter to the Bahá'ís of the world.

It would take me too long to make even a brief allusion to those incidents of her life, each of which eloquently proclaims her as a daughter, worthy to inherit that priceless heritage bequeathed to her by Bahá'u'lláh. A purity of life that reflected itself in even the minutest details of her daily occupations and activities; a tenderness of heart that obliterated every distinction of creed, class and colour; a resignation and serenity that evoked to the mind the calm and heroic fortitude of the Báb; a natural fondness of flowers and children that was so characteristic of Bahá'u'lláh; an unaffected simplicity of manners; an extreme sociability which made her accessible to all; a generosity, a love, at once disinterested and undiscriminating, that reflected so clearly the attributes of 'Abdu'l-Bahá's character; a sweetness of temper; a cheerfulness that no amount of sorrow could becloud; a quiet and unassuming disposition that served to enhance a thousandfold the prestige of her exalted rank; a forgiving nature that instantly disarmed the most unyielding enemy – these rank among the outstanding attributes of a saintly life which history will acknowledge as having been endowed with a celestial potency that few of the heroes of the past possessed . . .

Dearly-beloved Greatest Holy Leaf! Through the mist of tears that fill my eyes I can clearly see, as I pen these lines, thy noble figure before me, and can recognize the serenity of thy kindly face. I can still gaze, though the shadows of the grave separate us, into thy blue, love-deep eyes, and can feel in its calm intensity, the immense love thou didst bear for the Cause of thine Almighty Father, the attachment that bound thee to the most lowly and insignificant among its followers, the warm affection thou didst cherish for me in thine heart. The memory of the ineffable beauty of thy smile shall ever continue to cheer and hearten me in the thorny path I am destined to pursue. The remembrance of the touch of thine hand shall spur me on to follow steadfastly in thy way. The sweet magic of thy voice shall remind me, when the hour of adversity is at its darkest, to hold fast to the rope thou didst seize so firmly all the days of thy life . . .

Whatever betide us, however distressing the vicissitudes which the nascent Faith of God may yet experience, we pledge ourselves, before the mercy-seat of thy glorious Father, to hand on, unimpaired and undivided, to generations yet unborn, the glory of that tradition of which thou has been its most brilliant exemplar.

In the innermost recesses of our hearts, O thou exalted Leaf of the Abhá Paradise, we have reared for thee a shining mansion that the hand of time can never undermine, a shrine which shall frame eternally the matchless beauty of thy countenance, an altar whereon the fire of thy consuming love shall burn for ever.[11]

The third child of Navváb was her noble and long-suffering son, the Purest Branch. He was the one who, in the prime of youth, offered up his life in the path of his Lord.* In a prayer revealed after his martyrdom Bahá'u'lláh makes the following statement which Shoghi Effendi describes as astounding:

I have, O my Lord, offered up that which Thou has given Me, that Thy servants may be quickened and all that dwell on earth be united.[12]

It is at once significant and mysterious that the unity of mankind, the pivot around which all the teachings of Bahá'u'lláh revolve, would come into being as a result of the sacrifice of the Purest Branch. Here are Bahá'u'lláh's words after that tragic event:

At this very moment, My son is being washed before My face, after Our having sacrificed him in the Most Great Prison. Thereat have the dwellers of the Abhá Tabernacle wept with a great weeping, and such as have suffered imprisonment with this Youth in the path of God, the Lord of the promised Day, lamented. Under such conditions My Pen hath not been prevented from remembering its Lord, the Lord of all nations. It summoneth the people unto God, the Almighty, the All-Bountiful. This is the day whereon he that was created by the light of Bahá has suffered

* For a more detailed study of his life, see *The Revelation of Bahá'u'lláh*, vol. 3.

martyrdom, at a time when he lay imprisoned at the hands of his enemies.

Upon thee, O Branch of God! be the remembrance of God and His praise, and the praise of all that dwell in the Realm of Immortality, and of all the denizens of the Kingdom of Names. Happy art thou in that thou hast been faithful to the Covenant of God and His Testament, until Thou didst sacrifice thyself before the face of thy Lord, the Almighty, the Unconstrained. Thou, in truth, hast been wronged, and to this testifieth the Beauty of Him, the Self-Subsisting. Thou didst, in the first days of thy life, bear that which hath caused all things to groan; and made every pillar to tremble. Happy is the one that remembereth thee, and draweth nigh, through thee, unto God, the Creator of the Morn.

Glorified art Thou, O Lord, my God! Thou seest me in the hands of Mine enemies, and My son blood-stained before Thy face, O Thou in Whose hands is the kingdom of all names. I have, O my Lord, offered up that which Thou hast given Me, that Thy servants may be quickened and all that dwell on earth be united. Blessed art thou, and blessed he that turneth unto thee, and visiteth thy grave, and draweth nigh, through thee, unto God, the Lord of all that was and shall be . . . I testify that thou didst return in meekness unto thine abode. Great is thy blessedness and the blessedness of them that hold fast unto the hem of thy outspread robe . . . Thou art, verily, the trust of God and His treasure in this land. Erelong will God reveal through thee that which He hath desired. He, verily, is the Truth, the Knower of things unseen. When thou wast laid to rest in the earth, the earth itself trembled in its longing to meet thee. Thus hath it been decreed, and yet the people perceive not. . . . Were We to recount the mysteries of thine ascension, they that are asleep would waken, and all beings would be set ablaze with the fire of the remembrance of My Name, the Mighty, the Loving.[13]

Indeed, the prophecy of Isaiah concerning Navváb, whose 'husband' is 'the Lord of Hosts', has been fulfilled.

And all thy children shall be taught of the Lord; and great shall be the peace of thy children.

CHAPTER EIGHT

The Arch-breaker of Bahá'u'lláh's Covenant

THE history of Bahá'u'lláh's family has two contrasting features: one of glory and faithfulness, the other of dishonour and treachery. Navváb, her two sons 'Abdu'l-Bahá and the Purest Branch, and her daughter the Greatest Holy Leaf, shine brilliantly above the horizon of Bahá'u'lláh's Revelation and occupy immeasurably exalted positions within His Cause. The rest of the family including Mahd-i-'Ulyá, Gawhar Khánum and their sons and daughters, all became darkened and perished spiritually; they sank miserably into ignominy and oblivion. This contrast of light and darkness, of good and evil in Bahá'u'lláh's own family is one of the most thought-provoking and mysterious features of His Ministry. His eldest Son was made the perfect Mirror reflecting His light, and the Centre of His mighty Covenant, while at the same time another son turned into the 'centre of sedition' and the arch-breaker of that same Covenant. Some thoughts on this mystery are offered elsewhere in this book.*

This arch-breaker of the Covenant of Bahá'u'lláh is Mírzá Muḥammad-'Alí, the eldest son of Bahá'u'lláh's second wife Mahd-i-'Ulyá. He was born in Baghdád in the first year of Bahá'u'lláh's arrival there. From the early days of his youth, he found that he could not rise to the level of 'Abdu'l-Bahá, who was nine years his senior. He lacked those spiritual qualities which distinguished his eldest brother, who became known as the Master from the early days in Baghdád.

The most essential prerequisites for the spiritual survival of all those who were close to Bahá'u'lláh were humility, self-effacement and utter nothingness in His presence. If these qualities were missing in an individual, he would be in great danger of spiritual downfall and eventual extinction.

While 'Abdu'l-Bahá, the Greatest Holy Leaf, the Purest Branch, and their illustrious mother were all embodiments of servitude and selflessness, Muḥammad-'Alí, his brothers and sister, together with their mother, were the opposite. Although the latter group were all

* See below, pp. 130–34.

sheltered beneath Bahá'u'lláh's protection, and flourished through the outpouring of His favours, in reality they were the victims of selfish desires and worldly ambitions. During Bahá'u'lláh's lifetime they were subdued by His authority and kept under control through His admonitions. At the same time, Mírzá Muḥammad-'Alí and his brothers were the recipients of a great many favours from the believers who, because of their love for Bahá'u'lláh, honoured and revered them too. Thus these three sons acquired an undeserved prestige and basked in the sunshine of their Father's glory and majesty.

Inwardly, Mírzá Muḥammad-'Alí was a faithless person, and he led his two younger brothers in the same direction. But outwardly he utilized the power of the Faith and the resources of the community to bolster up his own image in the eyes of the followers of Bahá'u'lláh. He emerged as an important person in the service of his Father by transcribing some of His Tablets and by the use of calligraphy of which he was a master. From the days of his youth he entertained the ambition to occupy a position of eminence within the Faith, a position similar to that of 'Abdu'l-Bahá, who, from early on, had distinguished Himself among the entire family.

In Muḥammad-'Alí's childhood Bahá'u'lláh conferred upon him the power of utterance, and this became obvious as he grew up. But instead of utilizing this gift to promote the Cause of God, he embarked on a career which hastened his downfall. When he was in his early teens in Adrianople, he composed a series of passages in Arabic and without Bahá'u'lláh's permission disseminated them among some of the Persian Bahá'ís, introducing them as verses of God which, he claimed, were revealed to him. He intimated to the believers that he was a partner with Bahá'u'lláh in divine Revelation. Several believers in Qazvín were influenced by him and drawn to him. This created a great controversy in Qazvín, and resulted in disunity among some of the believers there. The city of Qazvín was already notorious for its different factions among the Bábís, and there were some followers of Mírzá Yaḥyá actively disseminating false propaganda against the followers of Bahá'u'lláh.

Now, in the midst of these conflicting groups, Mírzá Muḥammad-'Alí's claim to be the revealer of the verses of God[1] brought about an added confusion among the followers of Bahá'u'lláh. In his writings, which are of considerable length, the teen-age Muḥammad-'Alí refers to himself, among other things, as 'the King of the spirit', calls on the believers to 'hear the voice of him who has been manifested to man', admonishes those who deny his verses revealed in his childhood, declares his revelation to be 'the greatest of God's revelations', asserts that 'all have been created through a word from him', considers himself to be 'the greatest divine luminary before whose radiance all other suns pale into insignificance', and proclaims himself to be 'the sovereign ruler of all who are in heaven and on earth'.

Such preposterous claims, such a display of personal ambition, evoked the wrath of Bahá'u'lláh, who rebuked him vehemently and chastised him with His own hands. The controversy in Qazvín continued for some time. Three believers in particular fell under the spell of Muḥammad-'Alí; they were Mírzá 'Abdu'lláh, Ḥájí Ḥasan and his brother, Áqá 'Alí. These three and a few others, who considered their youthful candidate to be a partner with Bahá'u'lláh and of equal station to His, entered into argument with several believers who refuted their claims. Shaykh Káẓim-i-Samandar,* a tower of strength for the Bahá'ís of Qazvín, emphatically rejected the claims of Muḥammad-'Alí and declared that his writings amounted to no more than a string of Arabic sentences which in no way could be the Word of God.

This controversy prompted Ḥájí Muḥammad-Ibráhím, entitled Khalíl, to write a letter to Bahá'u'lláh begging Him to clarify His own station and the station of His sons. Ḥájí Khalíl was already confused about the claims of Mírzá Yaḥyá and wished to be enlightened and find the truth. In his petition he also asked other questions. Bahá'u'lláh responded by revealing a Tablet in his honour, known as the *Lawḥ-i-Khalíl* (*Tablet of Khalíl*).† In it He declares His own station and states that as long as His sons observe the commandments of God, persevere in edifying their souls, testify to what has been revealed by God, believe in Him Whom God shall make manifest, do not create divisions in His Cause and do not deviate from His revealed laws, they can be considered as the leaves and branches of His Tree of holiness and members of His family. Through them will the light of God be diffused and the signs of His bounty be made manifest.

Mírzá Muḥammad-'Alí did not live up to these standards. Apart from his shameful claim of equality with Bahá'u'lláh, he became a source of sedition in the community, inflicted severe injuries upon the Cause of God, and after Bahá'u'lláh's ascension, broke His Covenant and rose up to extinguish the light of His Faith.

In the *Tablet of Khalíl* Bahá'u'lláh alludes to 'Abdu'l-Bahá in terms which immensely exalt Him above the others. He refers to Him as One among His sons 'from Whose tongue God will cause the signs

* See *The Revelation of Bahá'u'lláh*, vol. 3, pp. 88–91.

† Parts of this Tablet are translated by Shoghi Effendi in *Gleanings from the Writings of Bahá'u'lláh*, XXXIII, XXXVIII, LXXVII, and CXXVII.

of His power to stream forth', and as the One Whom 'God hath specially chosen for His Cause'.[2]

In another Tablet revealed at this time[3] when a few believers had been influenced by Mírzá Muḥammad-'Alí's claim, Bahá'u'lláh asserts that when Muḥammad-'Alí was a child of tender years He conferred upon him the power of utterance, so that people might witness His might and glory. He grieves in this Tablet at the state of some of His foolish followers who have thought to recognize a partner with Him in Revelation, and who have made great mischief in the land. He expresses astonishment at the behaviour of some who have attained His presence and witnessed the outpouring of His Revelation and yet have spread such shameful rumours among the believers. Referring to Muḥammad-'Alí in this Tablet, He further states:

> He, verily, is but one of My servants . . . should he for a moment pass out from under the shadow of the Cause, he surely shall be brought to naught.[4]

In this Tablet He further confirms that all beings are created through a word from Him and that no one can claim equality, likeness, or partnership with Him. He and He alone is the possessor of the Most Great Infallibility which is the prerogative of every Manifestation of God.

Concerning the three believers in Qazvín who were misled by Muḥammad-'Alí's claim, Bahá'u'lláh invited Ḥájí Ḥasan and his brother to come to Adrianople. Here they attained His presence and fully recognized their folly.

In distinct contrast to Mírzá Muḥammad-'Alí's claim was 'Abdu'l-Bahá's utter self-effacement. Many believers during Bahá'u'lláh's Ministry used to write letters to 'Abdu'l-Bahá, but He would not respond to them. For instance, Mírzá 'Alí-Muḥammad-i-Varqá,* who was later martyred, wrote a great many letters to Him. To none of these did 'Abdu'l-Bahá send a reply. At the end Varqá wrote to Mírzá Áqá Ján, Bahá'u'lláh's amanuensis, and complained. When Bahá'u'lláh was informed about this He summoned 'Abdu'l-Bahá to His presence, and directed Him to send a reply to Varqá. 'Abdu'l-Bahá wrote a brief letter to him saying that when the Pen of the Most High is moving upon His Tablets, how could 'Abdu'l-Bahá be expected to write? Indeed, whatever 'Abdu'l-Bahá wrote during the lifetime of Bahá'u'lláh was directed by Him and received His sanction. This episode alone demonstrates the vast difference between the two: 'Abdu'l-Bahá, a true servant, humble and lowly

* See *The Revelation of Bahá'u'lláh*, vol. 4.

before His Lord; Mírzá Muḥammad-'Alí, ambitious, vain and faithless.

Mírzá Muḥammad-'Alí's claim was not the only sign pointing to his ambitious nature, craving for leadership from this early age. His daily behaviour, even during Bahá'u'lláh's lifetime, gave clear indications of his lack of spirituality and purity of motive, and his jealousy of 'Abdu'l-Bahá was apparent to those who were close to him. As Mírzá Muḥammad-'Alí grew older, he acquired greater prestige among the believers. He thrived on the special consideration shown him by Bahá'u'lláh's followers in order to honour his Father. But many of Bahá'u'lláh's disciples who had spiritual eyes soon discovered his real nature and found him devoid of those divine virtues and spiritual qualities which characterize a true believer. Long before he broke the Covenant they were able to detect in him an air of superiority and self-glorification, and a craving for leadership and power. For instance, Ḥájí Muḥammad Ṭáhir-i-Málmírí* has described in his memoirs his first meeting with Mírzá Muḥammad-'Alí a day after he arrived in 'Akká to attain the presence of Bahá'u'lláh in 1878.

When we arrived in Haifa . . . we were taken to the home of Áqá Muḥammad-Ibráhím-i-Káshání. He had been directed by Bahá'u'lláh to make his residence in Haifa, to handle the distribution of letters and to give assistance and hospitality to Bahá'í pilgrims. When Bahá'u'lláh was informed that the three of us had arrived, He advised, through Mírzá Áqá Ján . . . that in 'Akká I should stay with my brother Ḥájí 'Alí.† We were driven from Haifa to 'Akká in 'Abdu'l-Bahá's carriage. I was taken to Ḥájí 'Alí's residence, which was situated in the Khán-i-Súq-i-Abiyaḍ (White Market), in close proximity to the residence of Mírzá Músá, Bahá'u'lláh's brother, and several other Bahá'ís such as Nabíl-i-A'ẓam . . . That day I was most happy. Joy and ecstasy filled my soul. The next day, Mírzá Muḥammad-'Alí, accompanied by his two brothers, Mírzá Ḍíyá'u'lláh and Mírzá Badí'u'lláh, came to Nabíl-i-A'ẓam's quarters to meet me. Very eagerly my brother and I went there to meet them. But no sooner had I met Mírzá Muḥammad-'Alí and Mírzá Badí'u'lláh than I became depressed and all the joy in my heart was transformed into sadness and grief. I was distressed . . . and bitterly disappointed with myself. I was wondering what had happened so suddenly that, in spite of all the eagerness and excitement which had filled my being on arrival in 'Akká, I had become so utterly gloomy and dispirited. I was convinced at that time that I had been rejected by God . . .

I was plunged into such a state of distress and anguish that I wanted to leave that gathering forthwith, but did not dare to do so. In my heart I was communing with God . . . anxiously awaiting for the visitors to

* The father of the present author. See *The Revelation of Bahá'u'lláh*, vol. I.

† See *The Bahá'í World*, vol. IX, pp. 624–5, article on Ḥájí 'Alí Yazdí. (A.T.)

leave so that I could go out and try to find a solution for my sad condition. I noticed that whereas my brother and Nabíl-i-A'ẓam were enjoying themselves talking most happily with these sons of Bahá'u'lláh, I was in a state of mental turmoil and agony throughout the meeting . . . After about an hour, when the visitors were leaving, my brother thanked them most warmly and joyfully.

In the evening he informed me that we were to go and attain the presence of the Master in His reception room. Although depressed and grief-stricken as a result of meeting Muḥammad-'Alí, I went with him. As soon as I came into the presence of the Most Great Branch, a new life was breathed into me. My whole being was filled with such joy and felicity that all the agonies and disturbances of the past vanished in an instant.

A few days later my brother invited me to go with him to meet Mírzá Muḥammad-'Alí again, but in spite of much persuasion on his part I refused to go . . . During the period that I stayed in 'Akká, Mírzá Muḥammad-'Alí came several times to the residence of Nabíl-i-A'ẓam, but I always found some excuse not to go there.

Among Mírzá Muḥammad-'Alí's misdeeds during the lifetime of Bahá'u'lláh was his altering the text of the Holy Writings. Since he was highly skilled in the art of calligraphy, Bahá'u'lláh sent him from 'Akká on a mission to India to help print a book containing a selected compilation of His Writings. This compilation, known as the *Kitáb-i-Mubín*, contains some of His most important Tablets, including the *Súriy-i-Haykal.** The book was printed in the handwriting of Mírzá Muḥammad-'Alí by the printing firm of Náṣirí, which was part of a business organisation established in Bombay by a few members of the Afnán family. Mírzá Muḥammad-'Alí took advantage of this opportunity and betrayed Bahá'u'lláh by changing a certain passage in which He refers to the One who will come after Him. Thinking the passage alluded to 'Abdu'l-Bahá, he altered the text and changed the subject totally. Of course, this treacherous act of interpolation was soon exposed by comparing these passages with the authentic Writings of Bahá'u'lláh.

And yet, the Blessed Beauty, in spite of Muḥammad-'Alí's reprehensible conduct, conferred upon him a rank next to that of 'Abdu'l-Bahá. These are the words of Bahá'u'lláh in the *Kitáb-i-'Ahd*, His Will and Testament:

> Verily God hath ordained the station of the Greater Branch [Muḥammad-'Alí] to be beneath that of the Most Great Branch ['Abdu'l-Bahá]. He is in truth, the Ordainer, the All-Wise. We have chosen 'The Greater' after 'The Most Great,' as decreed by Him Who is the All-Knowing, the All-Informed.[5]

* See *The Revelation of Bahá'u'lláh*, vol. 3.

His grace, who abide by His bidding. This Covenant necessitates an interaction between the two parties. As in the analogy of the landlord and the tenant, if the followers of Bahá'u'lláh, the recipients of His grace, had faithfully carried out what was expected of them in this Covenant, then every provision of the *Kitáb-i-'Ahd* would have been fulfilled and the plan of God, as ordained by Bahá'u'lláh, would have materialized. But they did not. The Covenant was broken by no less a person than Mírzá Muḥammad-'Alí himself, who rose up against the Centre of the Cause. Consequently, the plan of God as envisaged by Bahá'u'lláh was changed, and Shoghi Effendi, the eldest grandson of 'Abdu'l-Bahá, was appointed as Guardian of the Faith to succeed Him. The same argument may hold for the *Will and Testament of 'Abdu'l-Bahá* in which the question of a successor to Shoghi Effendi did not materialize.*

The other question, concerning the appointment of such a disloyal person to so exalted a position, may be resolved by a careful examination of another essential feature of the Covenant of Bahá'u-'lláh; namely, the non-interference of each party in the functions of the other. The two parties to this Covenant are not of equal station. After all, the station of Bahá'u'lláh is awe-inspiring and the believers are but humble servants. However, God in His justice gives His creatures the opportunity to carry out their duties without His interference; they are given free will to behave as they please. Of course, He has full knowledge of how each individual will behave in discharging the obligations which the Covenant of Bahá'u'lláh has placed on him, but He leaves the person free to play his part, and He does not judge him before he commits an error. This is similar to the relationship between a teacher and pupil. In the course of teaching his students the teacher will usually come to know the ability and capacity of each one. Suppose that he finds one of his pupils to be inattentive to his work and negligent in his school duties. He may be certain that his pupil is going to fail his examinations, but foreknowledge of that failure does not entitle the teacher to prevent the student from taking part in them. It is the student's prerogative to sit for examinations and no one has the right to deprive him of that privilege.

This analogy helps to clarify the statement about Mírzá Muḥammad-'Alí in the *Kitáb-i-'Ahd*. Bahá'u'lláh was fully aware of Mírzá Muḥammad-'Alí's shortcomings, yet, as the second surviving son of Bahá'u'lláh, it was his birthright to occupy a station next to that of 'Abdu'l-Bahá. God did not pronounce judgement on him before his rebellion against the Cause. Mírzá Muḥammad-'Alí was given the

* See Appendix 1.

chance to mend his ways and take his rightful position within the Faith but he failed, as in a test, and thus perished spiritually.

Had Mírzá Muḥammad-'Alí remained a true and steadfast believer, had he lived a life of humility and self-effacement, had he devoted all his efforts to the promotion of the Cause and detached himself from earthly things, and had he followed in the footsteps of the Master and emulated the One who was the supreme Exemplar of the teachings of Bahá'u'lláh, then who could have been more suited than he, a son of Bahá'u'lláh, to take over the reins of the Cause of God after 'Abdu'l-Bahá? But he did not fulfil any of these conditions, and deprived himself of the bounties which could have been vouchsafed to him by Bahá'u'lláh.

Through his intense jealousy of 'Abdu'l-Bahá and his lack of spiritual qualities, Mírzá Muḥammad-'Alí sought throughout his life to undermine the position of 'Abdu'l-Bahá and usurp His God-given station as the Centre of the Covenant. During the lifetime of Bahá'u'lláh he was impotent to achieve the evil promptings of his heart, because the overshadowing power of Bahá'u'lláh and His overwhelming authority frustrated his ambitions. But as we shall see later, he rebelled against the Covenant immediately after the passing of Bahá'u'lláh and arose in opposition to 'Abdu'l-Bahá, its Centre.

CHAPTER NINE

The Relationship of Bahá'u'lláh and 'Abdu'l-Bahá

DURING His Ministry Bahá'u'lláh showered His unfailing bounties upon 'Abdu'l-Bahá, that Being Whom He had created to be the Centre of His Covenant and the Interpreter of His Word.

It must be remembered that the relationship of Bahá'u'lláh and the members of His family who remained faithful to the Cause was not like the relationship which exists between members of ordinary families. Normally, a father and a son at home have a very intimate and informal attitude towards each other. But in the case of Bahá'u'lláh and His faithful children, it was very different indeed, although that intimate relationship of father and son did exist. However, the station of Bahá'u'lláh as the Manifestation of God completely overshadowed His position as a physical father. 'Abdu'l-Bahá, the Greatest Holy Leaf and the Purest Branch looked upon Bahá'u'lláh not merely as their father, but as their Lord, and because they had truly recognized His station, they acted at all times as most humble servants at His threshold. 'Abdu'l-Bahá always entered the presence of Bahá'u'lláh with such genuine humility and reverence that no one among His followers could express the spirit of lowliness and utter self-effacement as He did. The humility of 'Abdu'l-Bahá as He bowed before His Father, or prostrated Himself at His feet, demonstrated the unique relationship which existed between this Father and His faithful sons and daughter.

When Bahá'u'lláh moved to the Mansions of Mazra'ih and Bahjí, 'Abdu'l-Bahá stayed in 'Akká. Whenever He went to attain the presence of His Father, He dismounted from His steed when He approached the Mansion, because he considered it disrespectful for a servant to be riding when he visited his lord.

While 'Abdu'l-Bahá showed such lowliness and humility, the outpouring of love and admiration by Bahá'u'lláh for His Son knew no bounds. His pleasure and joy when 'Abdu'l-Bahá visited Him at the Mansion were evident. So eager was He to receive 'Abdu'l-Bahá with marks of honour that He would despatch a contingent of the believers, including His sons, to distant fields outside the Mansion as a welcoming party, while He Himself would be standing on the balcony to watch Him arrive.

One of the reasons that 'Abdu'l-Bahá stayed in 'Akká and did not move with the Blessed Beauty to the Mansions of Mazra'ih and Bahjí was that His half-brother Mírzá Muḥammad-'Alí, and Mahd-i-'Ulyá his mother, were so jealous of Him. By staying away from Bahá'u'lláh, who cherished His eldest Son and extolled His station in glowing terms, 'Abdu'l-Bahá hoped to somewhat dampen their fires of jealousy. This separation from Bahá'u'lláh was painful to 'Abdu'l-Bahá, who nevertheless voluntarily deprived Himself of the bounty of the presence of His Lord in order to pacify His unfaithful brothers. There were also times when Bahá'u'lláh missed His Most Great Branch. On several occasions He even wrote in His own handwriting asking Him in tender and loving language to come and visit Him. No pen can describe the true relationship which existed between these two. The outpouring of infinite love and admiration by Bahá'u'lláh, and the manifestation of absolute humility and utter nothingness by 'Abdu'l-Bahá are beyond the experience and understanding of ordinary men.

In many of His Tablets Bahá'u'lláh writes in glowing terms of the station of 'Abdu'l-Bahá. The following passages are gleaned from a wide range of His Writings, some of which are written in His own hand.

In the *Súriy-i-Ghuṣn* (Súrih of the Branch),* He exalts the station of 'Abdu'l-Bahá in these words:

> There hath branched from the Sadratu'l-Muntahá this sacred and glorious Being, this Branch of Holiness; well is it with him that hath sought His shelter and abideth beneath His shadow. Verily the Limb of the Law of God hath sprung forth from this Root which God hath firmly implanted in the Ground of His Will, and Whose Branch hath been so uplifted as to encompass the whole of creation. Magnified be He, therefore, for this sublime, this blessed, this mighty, this exalted Handiwork! . . . Render thanks unto God, O people, for His appearance; for verily He is the most great Favour unto you, the most perfect bounty upon you; and through Him every mouldering bone is quickened. Whoso turneth towards Him hath turned towards God, and whoso turneth away from Him hath turned away from My Beauty, hath repudiated My Proof, and transgressed against Me. He is the Trust of God amongst you, His charge within you, His manifestation unto you and His appearance among His favoured servants . . .[1]

In another Tablet in His own handwriting, Bahá'u'lláh thus addresses 'Abdu'l-Bahá:

* See *The Revelation of Bahá'u'lláh*, vol. 2.

O Thou Who art the apple of Mine eye! My glory, the ocean of My loving-kindness, the sun of My bounty, the heaven of My mercy rest upon Thee. We pray God to illumine the world through Thy knowledge and wisdom, to ordain for Thee that which will gladden Thine heart and impart consolation to Thine eyes.[2]

In yet another Tablet, these verses have been revealed by Him:

The glory of God rest upon Thee, and upon whosoever serveth Thee and circleth around Thee. Woe, great woe, betide him that opposeth and injureth Thee. Well is it with him that sweareth fealty to Thee; the fire of hell torment him who is Thine enemy.[3]

And again:

We have made Thee a shelter for all mankind, a shield unto all who are in heaven and on earth, a stronghold for whosoever hath believed in God, the Incomparable, the All-Knowing. God grant that through Thee He may protect them, may enrich and sustain them, that He may inspire Thee with that which shall be a wellspring of wealth unto all created things, an ocean of bounty unto all men, and the dayspring of mercy unto all peoples.[4]

When 'Abdu'l-Bahá was on a visit to Beirut, Bahá'u'lláh expressed sorrow because of separation from Him in these words:

Praise be to Him Who hath honoured the Land of Bá (Beirut) through the presence of Him round Whom all names revolve. All the atoms of the earth have announced unto all created things that from behind the gate of the Prison-city there hath appeared and above its horizon there hath shone forth the Orb of the beauty of the great, the Most Mighty Branch of God – His ancient and immutable Mystery – proceeding on its way to another land. Sorrow, thereby, hath enveloped this Prison-city, whilst another land rejoiceth . . . Blessed, doubly blessed, is the ground which His footsteps have trodden, the eye that hath been cheered by the beauty of His countenance, the ear that hath been honoured by hearkening to His call, the heart that hath tasted the sweetness of His love, the breast that hath dilated through His remembrance, the pen that hath voiced His praise, the scroll that hath borne the testimony of His writings.[5]

The bounties which Bahá'u'lláh showered upon 'Abdu'l-Bahá were not confined to these and the other Tablets which streamed from His Pen. Innumerable were the occasions both public and private in which He poured out His praise upon 'Abdu'l-Bahá, described His divine attributes in glowing terms, and paid tribute to His noble deeds among the people. Ḥájí Mírzá Ḥaydar-'Ali,* that spiritual giant immortalized by the title 'The Angel of Carmel', has recorded the following reminiscences of one of his memorable audiences when Bahá'u'lláh spoke about the important role 'Abdu'l-

* For his story see *The Revelation of Bahá'u'lláh*, vol. 2. These are not to be taken as the exact words of Bahá'u'lláh; they are only recollections of His utterances by Ḥají Mírzá Ḥaydar-'Alí.

Bahá played in shielding Him from the pressures of the outside world.

> During the days of Baghdád We ourself used to visit the coffee house* and meet with everyone. We associated with people whether they were in the community or outside, whether acquaintances or strangers, whether they came from far or near.
>
> We considered those who were distant from us to be near, and the strangers as acquaintances. We served the Cause of God, supported His Word, and exalted His Name. The Most Great Branch ['Abdu'l-Bahá] carried out all these services, withstood all the difficulties, and endured the sufferings and calamities to a great extent in Adrianople, and now to a far greater extent in 'Akká. Because while in Baghdád, to all appearances We were not a prisoner, and the Cause of God had hardly enjoyed a fame it does today. Those who opposed it and the enemies who fought against it were comparatively few and far between.
>
> In Adrianople We used to meet with some of the people and gave permission to some to attain Our presence. But while in the Most Great Prison We did not meet with anyone† and have completely closed the door of association with the people. Now the Master has taken upon Himself this arduous task for Our comfort. He is a mighty shield facing the world and its peoples, and so He has relieved Us [from every care]. At first He secured the Mansion of Mazra'ih for Us and We stayed there, then the Mansion of Bahjí. He is so occupied in the service of the Cause that for weeks He does not find the opportunity to come to Bahjí. We are engaged in meeting with the believers and revealing the verses of God, while He labours hard and faces every ordeal and suffering. Because to deal and associate with these people is the most arduous task of all.[6]

Mírzá Maḥmúd-i-Káshání,‡ a trusted follower of Bahá'u'lláh who was in His service from the days of Baghdád and accompanied Him to Adrianople and 'Akká, has recounted in his memoirs his recollection of the words of Bahá'u'lláh as He spoke to a number of believers about the exalted station of 'Abdu'l-Bahá. Following is a summary translation of his notes:

> . . . The word Áqá (The Master) was a designation given to 'Abdu'l-Bahá. I recall that one day when Bahá'u'lláh was in the Garden of Vashshásh which was a delightful place situated outside Baghdád, which He occasionally used to visit, someone referred to certain individuals as the Áqá.§ On hearing this Bahá'u'lláh was heard to say with a commanding voice: 'Who is the Áqá? There is only one Áqá, and He is the Most Great Branch.'

* See *The Revelation of Bahá'u'lláh*, vol. 3, pp. 250–51. (A.T.)
† Non-Bahá'ís (A.T.)
‡ See *The Revelation of Bahá'u'lláh*, vol. 1, p. 288.
§ As a common noun the word 'Áqá' in the Persian language is used as a title before a name. It is similar to 'Mr' in English. But if it is used on its own as a proper noun it signifies the exalted position of a person.

Bahá'u'lláh said the same thing again in the Garden of Riḍván in 'Akká . . . On that occasion, someone addressed Mírzá Muḥammad-'Alí as Áqá, whereupon Bahá'u'lláh admonished him saying: 'There is one and only one Áqá and He is the Most Great Branch, others should be addressed by their names' . . .

Many a time I was in the presence of Bahá'u'lláh when the Master was also present. Because of His presence Bahá'u'lláh would be filled with the utmost joy and gladness. One could see His blessed countenance beaming with delight and exultation so lovingly that no words can adequately describe it. Repeatedly He would laud and glorify the Master, and the mere mention of His name would suffice to evoke an indescribable feeling of ecstasy in the Person of the Blessed Beauty. No pen is capable of fully describing this. In many of His Tablets Bahá'u'lláh has extolled the station of 'Abdu'l-Bahá . . .

Ḥájí Mírzá Ḥabíbu'lláh-i-Afnán, a younger son of Áqá Mírzá Áqá entitled Núru'd-Dín,* one of the distinguished members of the Afnán family, has written in his memoirs some interesting stories of his pilgrimage in 1891. The following is an extract from his notes summarized and translated:

One evening we were informed that the Beloved of the World [Baha'u'lláh] intended to visit the Garden of Junaynih† and had directed that all the pilgrims and resident Bahá'ís accompany Him in the morning. That night we could not sleep because we were so excited . . . that we should have the bounty of being in His holy presence for several hours the next day. At the hour of dawn we faced His blessed room and engaged in prayers and devotions. Before sunrise we all assembled outside the gate of the Mansion. It took about one hour until His Blessed Person came downstairs and mounted a white donkey . . . All the believers followed Him on foot to the garden. One of the local believers, Ḥájí Khávar, was a tall man. He walked alongside Bahá'u'lláh and held an umbrella over His head as a protection against the heat of the sun. The air was refreshing as we arrived in the garden . . . His Blessed Person was extremely happy that day and each one of the friends received his share of the bounties from His presence. We had lunch in the garden, then we assembled together and attained His presence.

It was at that time that 'Abdu'l-Bahá arrived from 'Akká. The Blessed Beauty said, 'The Master is coming, hasten to attend Him' . . . On those days Bahá'u'lláh used to sow the seeds of loyalty and servitude toward 'Him Whom God hath purposed' ['Abdu'l-Bahá] in the hearts of the believers and explained the lofty station and hidden reality of the Master to all.

Attended by everyone, 'Abdu'l-Bahá came with great humility into the presence of the Blessed Beauty. Then the Tongue of Grandeur uttered words to this effect, 'From morning until now this garden was not pleas-

* For a detailed account of his life and services see *The Revelation of Bahá'u'lláh*, vol. 4.

† A garden situated in the north of 'Akká, near the Mansion of Mazra'ih.

ant, but now with the presence of the Master it has become truly most delightful.' Then, turning to the Master, He remarked, 'You should have come in the morning.' 'Abdu'l-Bahá responded, 'The Governor of 'Akká and some residents had requested to meet with Me. Therefore I had to receive and entertain them.' Bahá'u'lláh, with a smiling face, said, 'The Master is our shield. Everybody here lives in the utmost comfort and peace. Association with the outside people such as these is very, very difficult. It is the Master who stands up to everything, and prepares the means of comfort for all the friends. May God protect Him from the evil of the envious and the hostile.'*

* These are not to be taken as the exact words of Bahá'u'lláh or 'Abdu'l-Bahá. (A.T.)

CHAPTER TEN

The Appointment of 'Abdu'l-Bahá

INNUMERABLE are the occasions on which Bahá'u'lláh has extolled the station of 'Abdu'l-Bahá and praised His outstanding qualities. But at no time during His Ministry did Bahá'u'lláh disclose to His followers the position of 'Abdu'l-Bahá as His Successor and the Centre of His Covenant. He kept this a well-guarded secret, and to no one did He intimate that 'Abdu'l-Bahá would be ministering the affairs of the Cause after Him. The only two references in His Writings on the question of successorship may be found in the *Kitáb-i-Aqdas* (The Most Holy Book). In these passages He alludes in language meaningful, profound and eloquent to the One who will become the Centre of the Cause after Him, but does not explicitly mention His name; only indicates that He has issued from Him.

> When the ocean of My presence hath ebbed and the Book of My Revelation is ended, turn your faces toward Him Whom God hath purposed, Who hath branched from this Ancient Root.[1]

> When the Mystic Dove will have winged its flight from its Sanctuary of Praise and sought its far-off goal, its hidden habitation, refer ye whatsoever ye understand not in the Book to Him Who hath branched from this mighty Stock.[2]

It is known that 'Alí-Muḥammad Varqá, the renowned Apostle of Bahá'u'lláh, asked Him about the identity of the person alluded to in the above verses. In a Tablet[3] addressed to Varqá, Bahá'u'lláh indicated that the intended person was the Most Great Branch, and after Him the Greater Branch. But this disclosure was not shared with the Bahá'í community.

These words were revealed in the *Kitáb-i-Aqdas* nineteen years before the Ascension of Bahá'u'lláh. During these years, no one who read these passages had any doubt as to the identity of the One 'Whom God had purposed, Who had branched from this Ancient Root'. It was obvious to all, especially to every member of Bahá'u'lláh's family, that this was a reference to 'Abdu'l-Bahá and no one else.

The only document which explicitly announced 'Abdu'l-Bahá as the Centre of the Covenant of Bahá'u'lláh and the One to Whom all must turn after His Ascension was the *Kitáb-i-'Ahdí* (The Book of My Covenant) which was published among the believers only after His passing. This historic document was probably written at least one year before the Ascension of Bahá'u'lláh, for it is alluded to in the *Epistle to the Son of the Wolf* as the 'Crimson Book'. Bahá'u'lláh kept His *Will and Testament* secret, retained it in His own possession and did not share its contents with anyone during His lifetime. But there is evidence to suggest that He had intimated its contents to 'Abdu'l-Bahá.

Bahá'u'lláh entrusted the *Kitáb-i-'Ahd* to 'Abdu'l-Bahá during His last illness before His Ascension and informed the members of His family a few days before He departed from this world that in a document entrusted by Him to 'Abdu'l-Bahá, He had commended them all to His care. The first time the *Kitáb-i-'Ahd* was read aloud in the presence of a number of friends was on the ninth day after the Ascension of Bahá'u'lláh, and soon afterwards its text was released to the believers.

Since it is so essential to the study of the Covenant of Bahá'u'lláh, the text of the *Kitáb-i-'Ahd* is given here.

> Although the Realm of Glory hath none of the vanities of the world, yet within the treasury of trust and resignation we have bequeathed to Our heirs an excellent and priceless heritage. Earthly treasures We have not bequeathed, nor have We added such cares as they entail. By God! In earthly riches fear is hidden and peril is concealed. Consider ye and call to mind that which the All-Merciful hath revealed in the Qur'án: 'Woe betide every slanderer and defamer, him that layeth up riches and counteth them.'* Fleeting are the riches of the world; all that perisheth and changeth is not, and hath never been, worthy of attention, except to a recognized measure.
>
> The aim of this Wronged One in sustaining woes and tribulations, in revealing the Holy Verses and in demonstrating proofs hath been naught but to quench the flame of hate and enmity, that the horizon of the hearts of men may be illumined with the light of concord and attain real peace and tranquillity. From the dawning-place of the divine Tablet the day-star of this utterance shineth resplendent, and it behoveth everyone to fix his gaze upon it: We exhort you, O peoples of the world, to observe that which will elevate your station. Hold fast to the fear of God and firmly adhere to what is right. Verily I say, the tongue is for mentioning what is good, defile it not with unseemly talk. God hath forgiven what is past. Henceforward everyone should utter that which is meet and seemly, and should refrain from slander, abuse and whatever causeth sadness in men. Lofty is the station of man! Not long ago this exalted Word streamed

* *Qur'án* 104:1–2.

forth from the treasury of Our Pen of Glory: Great and blessed is this Day – the Day in which all that lay latent in man hath been and will be made manifest. Lofty is the station of man, were he to hold fast to righteousness and truth and to remain firm and steadfast in the Cause. In the eyes of the All-Merciful a true man appeareth even as a firmament; its sun and moon are his sight and hearing, and his shining and resplendent character its stars. His is the loftiest station, and his influence educateth the world of being.

Every receptive soul who hath in this Day inhaled the fragrance of His garment and hath, with a pure heart, set his face towards the all-glorious Horizon is reckoned among the people of Bahá in the Crimson Book. Grasp ye, in My Name, the chalice of My loving-kindness, drink then your fill in My glorious and wondrous remembrance.

O ye that dwell on earth! The religion of God is for love and unity; make it not the cause of enmity or dissension. In the eyes of men of insight and the beholders of the Most Sublime Vision, whatsoever are the effective means for safeguarding and promoting the happiness and welfare of the children of men hath already been revealed by the Pen of Glory. But the foolish ones of the earth, being nurtured in evil passions and desires, have remained heedless of the consummate wisdom of Him Who is, in truth, the All-Wise, while their words and deeds are prompted by idle fancies and vain imaginings.

O ye the loved ones and the trustees of God! Kings are the manifestation of the power, and the daysprings of the might and riches, of God. Pray ye on their behalf. He hath invested them with the rulership of the earth and hath singled out the hearts of men as His Own domain.

Conflict and contention are categorically forbidden in His Book. This is a decree of God in this Most Great Revelation. It is divinely preserved from annulment and is invested by Him with the splendour of His confirmation. Verily He is the All-Knowing, the All-Wise.

It is incumbent upon everyone to aid those daysprings of authority and sources of command who are adorned with the ornament of equity and justice. Blessed are the rulers and the learned among the people of Bahá. They are My trustees among My servants and the manifestations of My commandments amidst My people. Upon them rest My glory, My blessings and My grace which have pervaded the world of being. In this connection the utterances revealed in the *Kitáb-i-Aqdas* are such that from the horizon of their words the light of divine grace shineth luminous and resplendent.

O ye My Branches! A mighty force, a consummate power lieth concealed in the world of being. Fix your gaze upon it and upon its unifying influence, and not upon the differences which appear from it.

The Will of the divine Testator is this: It is incumbent upon the Aghsán, the Afnán and My kindred to turn, one and all, their faces towards the Most Mighty Branch. Consider that which We have revealed in Our Most Holy Book: 'When the ocean of My presence hath ebbed and the Book of My Revelation is ended, turn your faces toward Him Whom God hath purposed, Who hath branched from this Ancient

Root.' The object of this sacred Verse is none other except the Most Mighty Branch ['Abdu'l-Bahá]. Thus have We graciously revealed unto you our potent Will, and I am verily the Gracious, the All-Powerful. Verily God hath ordained the station of the Greater Branch [Muḥammad-'Alí] to be beneath that of the Most Great Branch ['Abdu'l-Bahá]. He is in truth the Ordainer, the All-Wise. We have chosen 'the Greater' after 'the Most Great', as decreed by Him Who is the All-Knowing, the All Informed.

It is enjoined upon everyone to manifest love towards the Aghsán, but God hath not granted them any right to the property of others.

O ye My Aghsán, My Afnán and My Kindred! We exhort you to fear God, to perform praiseworthy deeds and to do that which is meet and seemly and serveth to exalt your station. Verily I say, fear of God is the greatest commander that can render the Cause of God victorious, and the hosts which best befit this commander have ever been and are an upright character and pure and goodly deeds.

Say: O servants! Let not the means of order be made the cause of confusion and the instrument of union an occasion for discord. We fain would hope that the people of Bahá may be guided by the blessed words: 'Say: all things are of God.' This exalted utterance is like unto water for quenching the fire of hate and enmity which smouldereth within the hearts and breasts of men. By this single utterance contending peoples and kindreds will attain the light of true unity. Verily He speaketh the truth and leadeth the way. He is the All-Powerful, the Exalted, the Gracious.

It is incumbent upon everyone to show courtesy to, and have regard for the Aghsán, that thereby the Cause of God may be glorified and His Word exalted. This injunction hath time and again been mentioned and recorded in the Holy Writ. Well is it with him who is enabled to achieve that which the Ordainer, the Ancient of Days hath prescribed for him. Ye are bidden moreover to respect the members of the Holy Household, the Afnán and the kindred. We further admonish you to serve all nations and to strive for the betterment of the world.

That which is conducive to the regeneration of the world and the salvation of the peoples and kindreds of the earth hath been sent down from the heaven of the utterance of Him Who is the Desire of the world. Give ye a hearing ear to the counsels of the Pen of Glory. Better is this for you than all that is on the earth. Unto this beareth witness My glorious and wondrous Book.[4]

Those who are unfamiliar with the history and origins of the Cause of Bahá'u'lláh, or who have a superficial understanding of His Faith, may find it strange that whereas Bahá'u'lláh explained every subject to His followers and clarified every question which they raised, He did not specifically name His successor during His lifetime. It is customary, and indeed essential, for a monarch to nominate his heir to the throne. In this way his subjects will have every opportunity to become familiar with their future head of state and orientate themselves towards him. What were the reasons that prevented Bahá'u'lláh from doing that? Could He not have announced to the entire Bahá'í community the appointment of 'Abdu'l-Bahá as the Centre of His Covenant during His own days? Looking at it purely from a human point of view, it appears that had Bahá'u'lláh made such an appointment during His lifetime, all the differences which arose after His Ascension could have been avoided. He, as the Manifestation of God, had the wisdom and authority to settle every misunderstanding, to suppress any opposition, to establish the position of 'Abdu'l-Bahá in the minds and hearts of the believers on a firm foundation, and to ensure the loyal support of all the members of His family towards His successor.

But Bahá'u'lláh did none of these things. He did not disclose the identity of the person who was to succeed Him, but kept it a well-guarded secret that had to be divulged only after His passing. As we shall see later, 'Abdu'l-Bahá also did the same thing in relation to His successor. He did not reveal the identity of Shoghi Effendi as Guardian of the Cause of God during His own lifetime. That also was a well-guarded secret which was disclosed only when His Will and Testament was read. It is true that 'Abdu'l-Bahá intimated to one or two individuals the identity of His successor, but the generality of the Bahá'í community remained unaware of this.

That the identity of the Centre of the Covenant was kept secret and revealed only after the ascension of Bahá'u'lláh constitutes one of the most important features of the Covenant. A deeper understanding of this Covenant depends upon the individual appreciating the manifold wisdoms hidden in this act of Bahá'u'lláh. Not until one grasps the purpose and significance of such secrecy in the appointment of the successor, be he 'Abdu'l-Bahá, Shoghi Effendi, or the Universal House of Justice, will the believer be able to acquire a true comprehension of the Covenant of Bahá'u'lláh in all its aspects.

Although such an understanding must come about primarily through the believer himself meditating upon the Holy Writings, studying the history of the Covenant, its genesis, and its workings, and praying that his heart may become the recipient of divine knowledge, yet the following explanation may throw some light on this important subject.

The main function of the Manifestation of God is to reveal the teachings of God for the age in which He appears. In so doing, He is ready to explain to His followers the meaning and purpose of His Revelation and to solve any difficult questions for them. Both in His association with the believers and in His Tablets, Bahá'u'lláh was always ready to explain the significances which were enshrined in His Writings. Many of His Tablets were revealed in response to the various questions which were asked by His followers and, at times, by others. These questions ranged from weighty religious and spiritual matters to unimportant minor problems which affected the lives and activities of the friends. To all these questions Bahá'u'lláh responded by expounding His teachings, interpreting the Scriptures of the past, clarifying many of their abstruse passages and statements, revealing the mysteries surrounding some of His profound utterances, delineating the features of His New World Order, giving details of the application of His laws and ordinances, and explaining, in simple terms, the verities of His Faith to those who requested further elucidation.

However, on one subject Bahá'u'lláh remained silent: designating the person who was to succeed Him. There are many wisdoms in this. Let us return yet again to the analogy of the teacher. It is the teacher's duty to impart knowledge to his pupils and help them in their work, and he is always ready to explain the various subjects to his pupils and answer their questions. But on one occasion he must remain silent and refrain from helping them or answering their questions: namely, on the examination day. On that day the students are left on their own and will have to find the answers by themselves. Only those who pass the examinations are elevated to a higher class, and those who fail are not.

The history of the Faith demonstrates that the Covenant has always provided great tests for the believers. The Báb gave the glad-tidings of the coming of 'Him Whom God shall make manifest' but did not reveal specifically His identity. Bahá'u'lláh kept the appointment of 'Abdu'l-Bahá a secret, and so the *Kitáb-i-'Ahd* became, in the terms of the above analogy, the examination paper for the believers. The winds of tests began to blow immediately once the contents of that historic document were published. As we shall see later, the community of the Most Great Name was engulfed in a tempest of unprecedented severity. Many souls who were unfaithful and ambitious broke the Covenant and arose with all their might to wrest the leadership of the Cause from the hand of 'Abdu'l-Bahá, persisting in their ignoble activities for years until, by their own deeds, they brought about their own extinction.

These tests* associated with so mighty an institution as the Covenant are inevitable and constitute an inseparable feature of the Cause of Bahá'u'lláh for all time. Similar tests appeared when the

* For a fuller discussion of tests in this life see *The Revelation of Bahá'u'lláh*, vol. 3. See also below pp. 364–5.

contents of the *Will and Testament of 'Abdu'l-Bahá* were made public. Some ambitious people, among them most of the members of 'Abdu'l-Bahá's own family, who sought leadership and proved to be insincere in their faith, broke the Covenant and rose up against Shoghi Effendi. Here again, the *Will and Testament of 'Abdu'l-Bahá* became an examination paper for the believers.

After the passing of Shoghi Effendi, too, the winds of tests blew and some misguided and egotistical personalities broke away and were cast out of the community of the Most Great Name. This time the non-existence of a will and testament by Shoghi Effendi became the examination paper.

The Covenant of Bahá'u'lláh will continue to provide the testing ground for the followers of Bahá'u'lláh. Those few who may succumb to the dictates of their own selfish desires and arise in opposition to the divinely-ordained institutions of the Faith will cut themselves off the tree of the Cause of God and will wither and perish in time. Indeed, one of the distinguishing features of the Faith of Bahá'u'lláh is that although many of its outstanding followers rebelled against the Covenant and tried with all their might to undermine its foundations, they did not succeed in creating schisms and breaking the unity of the community.

CHAPTER ELEVEN

The Breaking of Bahá'u'lláh's Covenant

THE passing of Bahá'u'lláh on 28 May 1892 in the Mansion of Bahjí marks the beginning of the most turbulent epoch within the Bahá'í community, an epoch which witnessed the onslaught of the unfaithful against the Cause on a far greater scale than any so far encountered in the course of its eventful history, including the rebellion of Mírzá Yaḥyá. The blessed remains of Bahá'u'lláh were not yet laid to rest when Mírzá Muḥammad-'Alí revealed his true self. Up till then he had given the appearance of being loyal to his Father and to 'Abdu'l-Bahá, but now he launched his ignoble plans to undermine the foundation of the Covenant and overthrow 'Abdu'l-Bahá, its Centre.

In a celebrated Tablet, the *Lawḥ-i-Hizár Baytí* (Tablet of One Thousand Verses) 'Abdu'l-Bahá describes the grievous events which occurred immediately before and just after the ascension of Bahá'u-'lláh. He states that during the days of Bahá'u'lláh's illness, He, 'Abdu'l-Bahá, was in attendance on His blessed Person by day and by night, most of the time in a state of deep sorrow and depression. One day as He lay in His sick-bed, Bahá'u'lláh ordered 'Abdu'l-Bahá to gather all those of His papers which were in the room and place them in two special cases. It was Bahá'u'lláh's practice that whenever He left the Mansion for 'Akká or elsewhere, He used to put all His papers in these large cases. Aware of the implications of this command, 'Abdu'l-Bahá was shaken to the very depths of his being. As He hesitated to comply, Bahá'u'lláh reiterated His orders. With trembling hands and tearful eyes, 'Abdu'l-Bahá was beginning to gather the papers when Majdu'd-Dín entered the room.

Majdu'd-Dín was a son of Bahá'u'lláh's faithful brother Áqáy-i-Kalím, but he was utterly different from his father. The most treacherous among the family, he was the most formidable enemy of 'Abdu'l-Bahá. Indeed, as we shall see later, he was the backbone, if not the principal instigator, of Mírzá Muḥammad-'Alí, the arch-breaker of the Covenant of Bahá'u'lláh.

In this Tablet, 'Abdu'l-Bahá further describes the agony of His heart as He forced Himself to gather Bahá'u'lláh's papers. Seeing

Majdu'd-Dín, 'Abdu'l-Bahá asked for his assistance, so that this task, so extremely painful to Him, might be soon finished. When all the papers, the seals and other items had been locked into the cases, Bahá'u'lláh said to 'Abdu'l-Bahá, 'These two now belong to you.' These words, implying the approach of the final hours of Bahá'u-'lláh's earthly life, pierced 'Abdu'l-Bahá's heart like an arrow.

When the ascension took place, 'Abdu'l-Bahá's grief knew no bounds. The shock He sustained as a result of this calamitous event was so intense that He found it difficult to describe it. He says that in the morning, along with His brother, He began the task of preparing the remains for burial. When they were about to wash Bahá'u'lláh's blessed body, Mírzá Muḥammad-'Alí suggested to 'Abdu'l-Bahá that since the floor would become wet, it would be better to take the two cases out of the room into Badí'u'lláh's* room. 'Abdu'l-Bahá was at that point in such a state of shock and grief that He was almost unconscious of His surroundings. He never thought that behind this suggestion could be a treacherous plot designed to rob Him of that precious trust.

He agreed, and the two cases were taken out and that was the last He saw of them.

The sacred remains were laid to rest that same day. 'Abdu'l-Bahá was disconsolate and heartbroken. He says that for three consecutive days and nights He could not rest a single moment. He wept for hours and was in a state of unbearable grief. The Light of the World had disappeared from His sight and all around Him had been plunged into darkness. On the fourth night after the ascension, He arose from His bed around midnight and walked a few steps hoping that it might help to bring a measure of tranquillity to His agonized heart. As He began to pace the room, He saw through the window a scene His eyes could scarcely believe. His unfaithful brothers had opened the cases and were looking through Bahá'u'lláh's papers, those papers which had been entrusted to Him!

'Abdu'l-Bahá was deeply disturbed by the treachery of His brothers so soon after the ascension of their Father. This act of unfaithfulness committed so dishonourably against the most sacred trust of God, inflicted further pain and suffering upon His sorrow-laden heart. He returned to His bed immediately after this incident, for He did not wish His brothers to know He had seen them interfering with the contents of the cases. At this point 'Abdu'l-Bahá thought to Himself that since His brothers had not seen the *Will and Testament* of Bahá'u'lláh, which was in 'Abdu'l-Bahá's possession, they were trying to find some document among His Writings with

* The youngest brother of Mírzá Muḥammad-'Alí.

which to justify their intended action of undermining the foundation of the Cause of God and creating a division within the ranks of its avowed supporters. However, 'Abdu'l-Bahá hoped, when they saw the *Will and Testament*, their efforts would be frustrated and they would then return His trust to Him.

But alas, this did not happen! The *Kitáb-i-'Ahd* was read by Áqá Riḍáy-i-Qannád* on the ninth day after the ascension of Bahá'u'lláh in the presence of nine witnesses chosen from among Bahá'u'lláh's companions and members of Bahá'u'lláh's family, including Mírzá Muḥammad-'Alí. On the afternoon of the same day it was read by Majdu'd-Dín in the Shrine of Bahá'u'lláh before a large company of the friends, consisting of the Aghsán, the Afnán, the pilgrims and resident believers. 'Abdu'l-Bahá says that after the *Kitáb-i-'Ahd* was read and its contents noted, some rejoiced with exceeding gladness and some grieved with great sorrow. The faces of the faithful were illumined with the light of joy, and those of the falsehearted were covered in the dust of despondency and gloom. 'Abdu'l-Bahá states that on that day the foundations of Covenant-breaking were laid, the ocean of vain imagining began to surge, and the fire of dissension and strife was lit, its flame burning more fiercely with the passage of time and consuming the hearts and souls of the faithful in its tormenting heat.

Soon after that historic day when the *Kitáb-i-'Ahd* was read, one of the Afnán asked 'Abdu'l-Bahá to use one of Bahá'u'lláh's blessed seals to seal a Tablet which had been revealed by Bahá'u'lláh in his honour. When 'Abdu'l-Bahá asked His brothers to give Him the seals of Bahá'u'lláh which had been placed in the cases, they pleaded ignorance, saying they did not know anything about the two cases! Bewildered and perplexed by such a remark, 'Abdu'l-Bahá was plunged further into sorrow and grief. He describes how His whole being began to tremble when He heard such a response from His brothers, and knew that great tests and trials lay ahead.

Indeed the *Kitáb-i-'Ahd* had the same effect on the believers as an examination paper does on the pupils: divided into two categories, those who pass and those who fail. As soon as the contents of the *Kitáb-i-'Ahd* were made public the community was divided into two. Those who remained faithful to its sacred provisions rose to exalted realms of certitude and entered the ark of salvation. Those who violated the provisions were spiritually cast out of the community and returned to the deadly abodes of their own self and passions.

Although the violation of the Covenant of Bahá'u'lláh began in earnest immediately after His ascension, 'Abdu'l-Bahá did not

* For a brief account of his life, see *The Revelation of Bahá'u'lláh*, vol. 2.

disclose the rebellion of Mírzá Muḥammad-'Alí, and a host of others who followed him in the Holy Land, to the believers in the East or the West. He tried, as He put it, to stop the foul odour of Covenant-breaking from spreading. He endured in silence for about four years all the suffering and humiliation that they heaped upon Him, as well as their onslaught against the Cause of which He was the only Centre. During these years He endeavoured to His utmost to guide these wayward people, who were intent upon destroying the Edifice of the Cause of God, to the path of truth and to infuse into their dying souls the breath of life. But they were haughty and vainglorious, and His loving counsels and admonitions did not penetrate the hardness of their hearts. At the end it was they themselves who disseminated their evil suggestions and vain imaginings among the believers.

The whole story of the violation of the Covenant by Mírzá Muḥammad-'Alí was initially made public by himself. Soon the disease spread through Persia and later in the West, and the plague of Covenant-breaking encompassed the community of the Most Great Name everywhere. Consequently 'Abdu'l-Bahá wrote innumerable Tablets in which He told the story of Covenant-breaking, unmasked the ugly face of this misguided rebellion, named the violators of the Covenant, demonstrated their unfaithfulness and their evil designs and expatiated on His own sufferings at their hands. He elucidated in great detail the basic principles of the Covenant, its origins, its power and its indestructibility. He also urged the believers to remain steadfast in the Covenant, and inspired them to scale loftier heights in service to His Cause.

It is appropriate here to define the term Covenant-breaker. A believer who recognizes Bahá'u'lláh as the Manifestation of God for this age will wholeheartedly obey His teachings and commandments. One of these commandments is to turn to 'Abdu'l-Bahá as the Centre of His Covenant, to be submissive to Him and abide by His bidding. The same is true in relation to Shoghi Effendi and the Universal House of Justice. A true believer, therefore, is one who believes in Bahá'u'lláh and follows those upon whom He has placed the mantle of authority. A Covenant-breaker is one who while professing to believe in Bahá'u'lláh arises in active opposition to Him; or to the Centre of the Covenant, 'Abdu'l-Bahá; or to Shoghi Effendi; or today to the Universal House of Justice.

Bahá'u'lláh has described those who break the Covenant as 'birds of night'. This description is very apt because these birds dislike the rays of the sun; if there is light somewhere they flee from it, preferring the darkness. This is the nature of a Covenant-breaker. He perceives the spiritual power and ascendancy of the Centre of the

Cause, but cannot bring himself to submit to His authority. Instead he rises in opposition against the One whom he knows to be invested with the potency of Bahá'u'lláh's Revelation.

In the days of Bahá'u'lláh, the authority to expel Covenant-breakers was vested in Himself; later it devolved upon 'Abdu'l-Bahá as the Centre of the Covenant, and then upon Shoghi Effendi as the Guardian of the Cause. At present, should anyone break the Covenant, his expulsion would be by decision of the Hands of the Cause of God residing in the Holy Land, subject to the approval of the Universal House of Justice.

It is interesting at this juncture to refer briefly to Mírzá Badí'u'lláh, the youngest son of Bahá'u'lláh who joined hands with his older brother Mírzá Muḥammad-'Alí, violated the Covenant and rose up in opposition to 'Abdu'l-Bahá. Some years passed and he, for reasons of his own, went to 'Abdu'l-Bahá, repented his wrongdoings and begged 'Abdu'l-Bahá to forgive him. With that loving-kindness characteristic of the Master, he was forgiven. On that occasion he wrote and published an epistle addressed to the Bahá'í world, in which he described some of the iniquitous activities of Mírzá Muḥammad-'Alí. However, Mírzá Badí'u'lláh's change of heart lasted for only a short time. He allied himself again with Mírzá Muḥammad-'Alí and resumed his nefarious activities against the Centre of the Covenant. This son of Bahá'u'lláh, who survived his commander-in-chief Mírzá Muḥammad-'Alí by many years, inflicted much pain and suffering upon both 'Abdu'l-Bahá and Shoghi Effendi.

In his 'epistle of repentance' Mírzá Badí'u'lláh reveals among other things some of the ignoble works perpetrated by Mírzá Muḥammad-'Alí immediately after the Ascension of Bahá'u'lláh. The following is a summary translation of this episode.

> During His last illness, Bahá'u'lláh directed 'Abdu'l-Bahá to place His papers and Tablets in two special large cases . . . These were entrusted by Him to 'Abdu'l-Bahá. . . . When the time came to wash the sacred body of Bahá'u'lláh, they brought water in the room. Mírzá Muḥammad-'Alí said to 'Abdu'l-Bahá that since water would be poured around the room, it would be better to remove the two cases to another room so that they would not get wet. 'Abdu'l-Bahá assented and Mírzá Muḥammad-'Alí asked Majdu'd-Dín to move them to my room. This was done and the cases were placed in a special cabinet and locked.
>
> Three days after the ascension of Bahá'u'lláh, Mírzá Muḥammad-'Alí asked me to give him the keys so that he might open the cases. He said: 'Bahá'u'lláh has placed a certain document in these cases which needs to be studied.' He took the keys from me. The next thing I noticed was that with the help of Majdu'd-Dín, Alí Riḍá, his sister, and the mother of

Shu'á'u'lláh* the cases were taken out of the window onto the balcony of the mansion and from there into the room of Mírzá Muḥammad-'Alí. He took out all the Tablets of Bahá'u'lláh which were addressed to individual believers. When I protested at his action, he explained, among other things, that the responsibility of the protection of the Holy Writings had been given to him by Bahá'u'lláh, and that he had a Tablet to this effect. However, he did not show me any such Tablet . . . He also indicated to me in a subtle way that the Most Great Branch† was against the Cause of Bahá'u'lláh and if these Holy Writings were to fall into His hands, he would destroy them and would obliterate the name and every trace of the Blessed Beauty from this world!

Another violation by Mírzá Muḥammad-'Alí was the interpolation of the Holy Writings. For a long time . . . he used to say that he possessed a Tablet from the Supreme Pen concerning the person of 'Abdu'l-Bahá and that if he were to publish it, the credibility of 'Abdu'l-Bahá would be finished and His name effaced forever. He spoke of this on numerous occasions to members of the family. Some time elapsed, during which a few individuals questioned me concerning the Tablet in question. I, therefore, asked Mírzá Muḥammad-'Alí to show it to us, but every time I mentioned it to him, he offered me an excuse and sought a pretext to avoid it. Until, one day, he took out of the case a blessed Tablet which was revealed before Bahá'u'lláh's imprisonment in the Most Great Prison and gave it to me to read. In it Bahá'u'lláh condemns the iniquities and wicked deeds perpetrated by His brother Mírzá Yaḥyá, whom He addresses as 'My brother'. I said to Mírzá Muḥammad-'Alí that this Tablet had no relevance to the present situation. He said: 'I have permission from Bahá'u'lláh to use my pen and interpolate His Writings for the protection of the Cause. Now since some individuals have exaggerated the station of 'Abdu'l-Bahá, and the Master claims to be the embodiment of Divinity, I will erase the words "My brother" and insert in its place "My Greatest Branch". This I will show to some people in order to check His influence.'

. . . After a few minutes, he carried out this interpolation in front of my eyes. Successfully, he changed the words 'My brother' to 'My Greatest Branch'. I pointed out to him that this action amounted to the betrayal of God's trust and constituted a sin. I warned him that if he showed the Tablet in this form to anyone, I would divulge the whole event and report the act of interpolation. . . . On hearing these words he became disturbed and promised that he would not show the Tablet to anyone. He also requested me not to reveal the matter.[1]

In his 'epistle of repentance', Mírzá Badí'u'lláh discloses further acts of interpolation of the Holy Tablets. He states that Mírzá Muḥammad-'Alí interpolated some of the Tablets which were addressed to the Bábís who had rebelled against Bahá'u'lláh. These

* He was a son of Mírzá Muḥammad-'Alí; see below pp. 277 and 419.
† 'Abdu'l-Bahá.

Tablets were condemnatory in tone, and he interpolated them in such a way as to make them appear to condemn the person of 'Abdu'l-Bahá.

Thus the Covenant-breakers began their shameful careers with acts of deceit, falsehood and corruption of the Text. As the years went by, they intensified their nefarious activities against the Cause of God and its divinely appointed Centre. They created a temporary breach in the ranks of the believers, and caused heart-rending sufferings for 'Abdu'l-Bahá and His loved ones. But in the end they were overwhelmed by the power of the Covenant, and the only traces they left behind are the stains of their unfaithfulness imprinted upon the pages of the history of the Cause.

CHAPTER TWELVE

'The Day that Shall Not Be Followed by Night'

THE *Kitáb-i-'Ahd* has been the most vital and momentous instrument for safeguarding and strengthening the foundations of the Cause of Bahá'u'lláh. On the one hand it tested the faithfulness of the believers, separating the good from the evil; on the other, it provided the means for protecting the unity and ensuring the wholesomeness of the community. It has been and will continue to be the guarantor of the invincibility of the institutions of the Faith and the means of the fulfilment of the words of Bahá'u'lláh that 'this is the day that shall not be followed by night'.

Shoghi Effendi describes the *Kitáb-i-'Ahd* in these words:

> To direct and canalize these forces let loose by this Heaven-sent process, and to insure their harmonious and continuous operation after His ascension, an instrument divinely ordained, invested with indisputable authority, organically linked with the Author of the Revelation Himself, was clearly indispensable. That instrument Bahá'u'lláh had expressly provided through the institution of the Covenant, an institution which He had firmly established prior to His ascension. This same Covenant He had anticipated in His Kitáb-i-Aqdas, had alluded to it as He bade His last farewell to the members of His family, who had been summoned to His bed-side, in the days immediately preceding His ascension, and had incorporated it in a special document which He designated as 'the Book of My Covenant', and which He entrusted, during His last illness, to His eldest son 'Abdu'l-Bahá.
>
> Written entirely in His own hand; unsealed on the ninth day after His ascension in the presence of nine witnesses chosen from amongst His companions and members of His Family; read subsequently, on the afternoon of that same day, before a large company assembled in His Most Holy Tomb, including His sons, some of the Báb's kinsmen, pilgrims and resident believers, this unique and epoch-making Document, designated by Bahá'u'lláh as His 'Most Great Tablet', and alluded to by Him as the 'Crimson Book' in His 'Epistle to the Son of the Wolf', can find no parallel in the Scriptures of any previous Dispensation, not excluding that of the Báb Himself. For nowhere in the books pertaining

to any of the world's religious systems, not even among the writings of the Author of the Bábí Revelation, do we find any single document establishing a Covenant endowed with an authority comparable to the Covenant which Bahá'u'lláh had Himself instituted.[1]

By this momentous document the station of 'Abdu'l-Bahá as the Centre of the Covenant of Bahá'u'lláh was announced to the believers. What was only implicit in the *Kitáb-i-Aqdas* was now made explicit in the *Kitáb-i-'Ahd*. The passage, 'Turn your faces towards Him Whom God hast purposed, Who hath branched from this Ancient Root', revealed in the former Book, was now clearly stated to mean 'Abdu'l-Bahá. Bahá'u'lláh unequivocally affirms:

> The object of this sacred Verse is none other except the Most Mighty Branch.*

This clear appointment of 'Abdu'l-Bahá as the Centre of Covenant safeguards the unity of the Bahá'í community and protects it against schism and all manner of division. No other religious dispensation, including that of the Báb, has brought into being an instrument designed to so ensure the unity of its community. Through the institution of the Covenant, the mighty stronghold of the Cause of God has become invincible in spite of the powerful assaults launched against it over a long period of time by the Covenant-breakers. As we shall see later in this book, Mírzá Muḥammad-'Alí and his supporters viciously attacked the Cause of God with such ferocity that the opposition made against the faithful in previous Dispensations fades into insignificance compared to it. In spite of this, the Covenant-breakers failed miserably and the Covenant of Bahá'u'lláh triumphed.

It was not so in past religions. For instance, as we look back upon the history of Islám we note that after the Prophet passed away, His followers almost immediately became divided into the two major sects of Sunní and Shí'ah. It has been stated already in this book that Muḥammad had made a verbal statement appointing 'Alí-Ibn-i-Abú Ṭálib, known as Imám 'Alí, as His Successor. But this appointment became a controversial subject as Muḥammad left behind no document to support it.

There is an episode widely spoken of, especially among the Shí'ahs, concerning the last days of Muḥammad's earthly life. It is claimed that as He lay in His death-bed, four of His outstanding followers were sitting at His bedside. They were Abú Bakr, 'Umar, 'Uthmán, and 'Alí. Abú Bakr was the father-in-law of the Prophet,

* One of 'Abdu'l-Bahá's titles given to Him by Bahá'u'lláh was 'The Most Mighty Branch'. After the ascension of Bahá'u'lláh, however, 'Abdu'l-Bahá chose the title of 'Abdu'l-Bahá (Servant of Bahá'u'lláh) and asked the believers to refer to Him only by this name.

and 'Alí was His cousin and son-in-law. Muḥammad is reported to have called for writing materials, wishing to leave some guidance for His followers. But the scheming 'Umar, a shrewd tactician, did not allow the wish of the Prophet to be realized. He said that the Prophet, so near the time of His death, was not of sound mind and therefore no writing material should be given to Him. The Sh̲i'ahs, who follow Imám 'Alí, claim that had the Prophet been allowed to write His will he would have confirmed the verbal statement He had made at G̲h̲adír-i-K̲h̲umm concerning the appointment of 'Alí as His Successor.

When Muḥammad passed away, 'Umar rallied the majority of the followers around the old and ailing Abú Bakr who enjoyed a great deal of prestige among the people. He became the first K̲h̲alíf (Caliph) of Islám. Two years later when Abú Bakr died, 'Umar became the second K̲h̲alíf and soon under his direction the military conquests of the Muslims began. Through the influence exerted by 'Umar the great majority of the followers of Muḥammad, the Sunnis, rejected the claims of Imám 'Alí to successorship.

It is a fundamental belief of the Bahá'ís that Imám 'Alí was the lawful successor of the Prophet of Islám. After him his lineal male descendants known as the 'holy Imáms' led the Sh̲i'ah community until the year 260 AH. Bahá'u'lláh regarded the Imáms as the legitimate successors of the Prophet, acknowledged the value of their work in the elucidation of the Qur'án, confirmed many of their sayings as recorded in the books of 'Aḥádít̲h̲' (traditions), quoted several of these in His Writings, interpreted their words, extolled their station (especially that of Ḥusayn, the third Imám) in glowing terms, and referred to them as 'those unquenchable lights of divine guidance'[2] and 'those lamps of certitude'.[3]

Through his misguided opposition to 'Alí, 'Umar frustrated the intentions of Muḥammad as to His successorship and the direction of the affairs of Islám. Imám 'Alí attempted to assert his position as Muḥammad's verbally designated successor and the expounder of the Words of God as revealed in the Qur'án. But the response of 'Umar to this claim was his fateful remark: 'The Book of God is sufficient unto us.' This short statement has echoed through the centuries and ages until 'Abdu'l-Bahá, in His celebrated Tablet, the Lawḥ-i-Hizár Baytí (Tablet of One Thousand Verses), described its woeful consequences. 'Abdu'l-Bahá states that it was this very statement which caused the foundation of the religion of God in the Islamic Dispensation to be shattered and the ignoble worshippers of self and passion to rule over the righteous souls. It became a deadly weapon with which the Imám 'Alí himself was martyred, which caused great divisions within the nation of Islám, and which changed the loving spirit of that nation to that of warriors armed with sword and weapons. As a result of this statement, the head of Imám Ḥusayn, the most illustrious of the Imáms, was decapitated on the plain of Karbilá, the other holy Imáms were inflicted with great sufferings, imprisonment and death, and the blood of countless innocent souls was shed for wellnigh twelve hundred years.

'Abdu'l-Bahá further affirms that this statement uttered by 'Umar was transformed into the hundreds of bullets centuries later which pierced the breast of the Báb in Tabríz, that this statement became the chains which were placed around the blessed neck of Bahá'u'lláh, and brought about the untold sufferings inflicted upon Him in the course of His successive exiles.

All these and many more atrocities committed during the Islamic dispensation 'Abdu'l-Bahá attributes to the influence of the simple statement 'The Book of God is sufficient unto us'. It deprived the greater part of the Islamic nation from the wealth of spiritual knowledge which the holy Imáms imparted to their followers through their interpretation and elucidation of the many abstruse passages in the *Qur'án*, as well as their illuminating prophecies concerning the advent of the Qá'im, the Promised One of Islám.

The course of history itself changed as a result of 'Umar's opposition to Imám 'Alí. The successful breaking of the Covenant of Muḥammad by 'Umar through his refusal to submit to Imám 'Alí as the lawful successor of the Prophet and the interpreter of His words, brought about, according to 'Abdu'l-Bahá, the direst of consequences for many nations and peoples. Who knows in what manner the Faith of Islám would have spread and its community developed had all the followers remained faithful to the wishes of Muḥammad and followed Imám 'Alí as His lawful successor? 'Abdu'l-Bahá implies in the above Tablet that if the nation of Islám had been faithful to 'Alí, many of the atrocities and cruelties committed since the passing of Muḥammad could have been mitigated or avoided.

'Abdu'l-Bahá wrote the Tablet of *Hizár Baytí* to Jalíl-i-Khú'í,* a believer who was being drawn into the Covenant-breakers' net in the province of Ádhirbáyján. The reason why 'Abdu'l-Bahá dwells at length in this Tablet on the episode of 'Umar and explains the dire results of his action in leading the people away from the lawful successor of Muḥammad is in order to demonstrate the evils of Covenant-breaking and the tragic consequences of the violation of the *Kitáb-i-'Ahd*, Bahá'u'lláh's Will and Testament.

In past Dispensations the Prophets did not establish a firm and unequivocal Covenant with their followers concerning their successors,

* See below, p. 166.

nor did they leave behind clear guidance as to how to conduct the affairs of the community after their departure from this world. Consequently, religions became divided into many sects resulting in conflicts and disunity among the followers. But the non-existence of a clear Covenant and lack of guidance should not be construed as a failure on the part of the Founders of religions. To attribute to the Manifestations of God a lack of understanding, of vision and knowledge, is tantamount to attributing shortcomings and imperfections to God Himself. That the Manifestations of God are possessed of divine knowledge and are infallible in their actions constitutes the bedrock of faith and belief in God.

We may ask ourselves, then, why did the Founders of the past religions leave no clear guidance for their followers and what were the reasons which prevented them from making a Covenant in writing as did Bahá'u'lláh?

A careful study of the history of religions will enable us to realize that the Manifestations of old, those embodiments of God's attributes, did not make an unequivocal written Covenant with their followers because of the immaturity of the people of the age, who could not have sustained the rigours, the tests and the strict discipline which the observance of such a Covenant would inevitably have required. Mankind has gone through the stages of infancy, childhood and adolescence. This is the day of the coming of age of humanity. For the Manifestations of God in past ages to establish a written Covenant with their followers would have been like giving a child new clothes and expecting him to keep them clean and tidy forever. It is obvious that he will not be able to comply. A child may roll in mud and stain his clothes, but that is normal for his age: he cannot realistically be assigned a responsibility that he will be unable to undertake. One cannot ask a child to be accountable beyond his stage of development. Only when he comes of age will he become accountable for his actions according to adult expectations.

Some of the qualities which are essential for remaining faithful to the Covenant are humility and self-abnegation, steadfastness in one's faith and unquestioned loyalty to the Centre of the Cause, the Successor to the Prophet. The acquiring of these spiritual qualities and the living in accordance with them place great responsibilities on the believers. God therefore relieved the followers of past religions of this burden, knowing that it was beyond their capacity at that time to be held responsible for observing the terms of the Covenant. However, now that mankind is destined to come of age in this day, God has for the first time established a mighty and irrefutable Covenant, and required His servants to obey His commandments and be answerable for their deeds.

In spite of the many divisions, schisms and sects formed in past religions, and the great conflicts which ensued as a result, each division flourished and gained strength with the passage of time. For instance, Christians divided themselves into several denominations, and these multiplied as the years went by. Yet the tree of Christianity blossomed even after acquiring several more branches, and each one remained verdant and flourishing. The denominations have survived centuries of conflict and bloodshed. This turmoil and discord within the communities were the growing pains of humanity characteristic of the period of childhood, through which it was passing, and Christ in His all-encompassing wisdom did not impose upon His followers a Covenant whose terms would have been beyond their capacity.

Islám experienced similar conflicts in its turbulent history. Although it is the most recent of the older religions, yet Muḥammad's followers were not sufficiently mature to be given a firm Covenant, similar to that established by Bahá'u'lláh, requiring them to obey strictly the Prophet's commandments and above all, not to create divisions within their ranks.

There was another feature in Islám which it is important to understand. Since Muḥammad had made a verbal declaration concerning the station of Imám 'Alí implying that he was to be His successor, as we have already stated, the majority of the Muslims violated the wishes of their Prophet, rejected 'Alí, and for centuries dominated over those who had followed him. Bahá'u'lláh explains in the *Tablet of Salmán** that the domination of the unfaithful over the faithful in the Islamic Dispensation was a pre-destined phenomenon which was foreshadowed in a verse of the Qur'án: 'There is none other God but God.' This phrase contains the most fundamental truth upon which the religion of Islám is based. It is the cardinal statement of faith which every Muslim must make in order to declare his belief in Islam. Bahá'u'lláh states that there is a mystery hidden in this verse which no one had been able to discover until He revealed it in this Day.

In this Tablet, Bahá'u'lláh affirms that God, through His wisdom, so worded this phrase that the letter of negation in it ('none') precedes that of affirmation. He thus attributes the domination of the unfaithful over the faithful in the Dispensation of Islám to the mysterious influence of this sacred phrase, which appears repeatedly in the *Qur'án*. Therefore, as a result of the creative influence of this phrase ever since it was revealed by Muḥammad, the violators of His unwritten Covenant – those who rejected 'Alí and represented by the letters of negation – ruled over His faithful followers. All the

* See *The Revelation of Bahá'u'lláh*, vol. 2, ch. 13.

suffering which the hands of the unfaithful – those who disregarded Muḥammad's wishes and opposed His intended successor – inflicted upon the steadfast Muslims was indeed the fulfilment of the hidden significance of this utterance of Muḥammad. He must have known, through the mystery enshrined in the verse, 'There is none other God but God', that His followers would be incapable of maintaining their unity after Him. God had, through His wisdom, so destined that the froward and the insincere took precedence over the obedient and the faithful.

Referring to this phrase, Bahá'u'lláh in the same Tablet proclaims in majestic and powerful language that in this day He has removed the letter of negation which had been placed before that of affirmation. This phrase, which the Prophet of Islám regarded as the cornerstone of His Faith, is now in the Dispensation of Bahá'u'lláh symbolically replaced by the affirmative phrase 'He is God'. This signifies that the Author of this Faith holds within His own hands the reins of authority, and, unlike the Dispensations of the past, no one will have the power to wrest it from Him. Hence the assurance in His Writings that this is 'the Day which shall not be followed by night'.

In another of His Tablets He reveals these reassuring words:

> The Hand of Omnipotence hath established His Revelation upon an unassailable, an enduring foundation. Storms of human strife are powerless to undermine its basis, nor will men's fanciful theories succeed in damaging its structure.[4]

There is yet another mystery in the *Tablet of Salmán*: while effecting the removal of the letter of negation and replacing it with that of affirmation, Bahá'u'lláh indicates that He will be issuing the command for this change and communicating it to the believers at a later time. After the ascension of Bahá'u'lláh, the believers who were steadfast in the Covenant were convinced that the command for removing the letter of negation as described in the *Tablet of Salmán* was none other than the *Kitáb-i-'Ahd*, the Will and Testament of Bahá'u'lláh.

Through this mighty document the Covenant of Bahá'u'lláh was established and its Centre appointed. The proof that the letter of negation has been removed is that in this Dispensation the Covenant-breakers have never been, nor will they ever be, able to undermine the unity of the followers of Bahá'u'lláh or to seize the reins of authority from the divinely ordained institutions which are charged by Bahá'u'lláh to direct the affairs of His Cause. History has so far confirmed this, and it is one of the distinguishing features of this Dispensation. There have been many powerful attacks launched against the Centre of the Cause from within. Those who rebelled against 'Abdu'l-Bahá were not ignorant or senseless people. On the contrary, most of them were intelligent and capable; some were highly knowledgeable teachers, immensely respected by the Bahá'í community in Persia. In the Holy Land too, some members of the family of Bahá'u'lláh were knowledgeable and powerful men. Mírzá Muḥammad-'Alí, who so prided himself on his talents, was a master of calligraphy, which in those days carried great prestige in the community. He also exerted great influence over people. The ceaseless efforts of the Covenant-breakers at the time of 'Abdu'l-Bahá to destroy the edifice of the Cause of God appeared to many to be successful at first, but as we have seen, all of them, together with their misguided notions and theories, were thrown into the abyss of extinction and perished miserably.

The *Kitáb-i-'Ahd* has been referred to by Bahá'u'lláh as the Crimson Book.* He used this term in alluding to it about a year before His ascension, in His *Epistle to the Son of the Wolf.* This designation is not used exclusively to refer to the *Kitáb-i-'Ahd*, but that Tablet is certainly a document which became instrumental in testing the faith of every believer, resulting in separation between the pure in heart and the insincere. Everything revealed in this mighty document may be summarized in one short phrase: 'Turn toward'.

> When the ocean of My presence has ebbed and the Book of My Revelation is ended, turn your faces toward Him Whom God hath purposed, Who hath branched from this Ancient Root.[5]

The spiritual forces released by the Revelation of Bahá'u'lláh for forty years were thus vouchsafed to 'Abdu'l-Bahá. His words, although not of the same rank, have the same validity as the Words of Bahá'u'lláh. Everything that Bahá'u'lláh had brought to mankind was deposited within the soul of 'Abdu'l-Bahá and to receive these the believers had to 'turn toward' Him. This act of 'turning' is the pivot round which the Covenant of Bahá'u'lláh revolves for all time, and steadfastness in the Covenant will be determined by the extent to which a believer readily turns to the Centre of the Cause.

To recognize the station of Bahá'u'lláh and believe in Him as the Supreme Manifestation of God is the first and the most essential step for man in his journey to his spiritual abode. But belief in Bahá'u'lláh will not be acceptable to God unless the believer turns to the Centre of the Covenant, is submissive to Him and wholeheartedly carries out His commandments. Moreover, this magical phrase 'turn toward' is not limited to the Ministry of 'Abdu'l-Bahá only. It is applicable

* 'Crimson' implies, among other things, tests and sacrifice.

for all time. After the passing of 'Abdu'l-Bahá, the believers had again to 'turn toward' Shoghi Effendi, and today toward the Universal House of Justice.

To emphasize this important feature of the Covenant the following analogy may be helpful. An aircraft flies in the air because its engines create a special condition which enables the machine to fly; without them the craft will not move. Similarly, belief in Bahá'u'lláh as the Supreme Manifestation of God in this age uplifts the soul and enables it to soar into the spiritual realms. A believer's faith in Bahá'u'lláh thus acts like the engine in the above analogy. But a powerful engine, however needed, cannot ensure the safety of an aircraft or its smooth landing at its destination. There is a need for the navigational signals which a modern aircraft receives from the control tower to determine its direction, height and speed, and the pilot obeys these instructions almost blindly until the machine lands safely. Without navigational aids and the readiness of the pilot to follow these signals, there is every likelihood that a disaster will take place.

Similarly, faith in Bahá'u'lláh is not completely sufficient unto itself. The believer has to faithfully obey the guidance he receives from the Centre of the Cause. During the Ministry of Bahá'u'lláh, it was to Him that the believers turned for guidance. Later it was 'Abdu'l-Bahá who became the Centre for this guidance, after Him Shoghi Effendi, the Guardian of the Faith, and today the Universal House of Justice. If someone reaches the pinnacle of faith and certitude in the Revelation of Bahá'u'lláh, but refuses to follow the guidance of 'Abdu'l-Bahá, of Shoghi Effendi, or the House of Justice, he cannot be considered a true believer. Those who regarded themselves to be followers of Bahá'u'lláh but arose actively in opposition to 'Abdu'l-Bahá or Shoghi Effendi were pronounced as Covenant-breakers and cast out of the Community of the Most Great Name.

It is the same today. Those who claim to be believers, accepting the station of 'Abdu'l-Bahá and Shoghi Effendi, but who oppose the Universal House of Justice, are treated in the same way. The imperative necessity of removing such people from the community will become clear as we continue the story.

CHAPTER THIRTEEN

Principal Covenant-Breakers during the Ministry of 'Abdu'l-Bahá

When the *Kitáb-i-'Ahd* was read no one among the family of Bahá'u'lláh or the believers questioned its authenticity. Even Mírzá Muḥammad-'Alí, the chief violator of its provisions, accepted the fact that the Will and Testament was in the handwriting of Bahá'u'lláh Himself. Nevertheless, as has already been stated, this unfaithful brother tried very hard through interpolation and corruption of the writings of Bahá'u'lláh and by forging documents, to discredit the person of 'Abdu'l-Bahá. At the same time he began to sow seeds of doubt concerning 'Abdu'l-Bahá in the minds of the believers in the Holy Land through misrepresentation. At first this rebellion was covert, but it gathered momentum during the first few years of 'Abdu'l-Bahá's Ministry until it turned into a most vicious campaign of open hostility and opposition towards Him, creating the most serious crisis in the history of the Faith since the ascension of Bahá'u'lláh.

In order to survey, however briefly, the nefarious activities of the Covenant-breakers during 'Abdu'l-Bahá's Ministry, it is necessary to mention a few individuals who were the props and mainstay of Mírzá Muḥammad-'Alí in his activities. Foremost among them in the Holy Land was Majdu'd-Dín, the son of Áqáy-i-Kalím, the noble brother of Bahá'u'lláh. He was the backbone, the motivating force behind Mírzá Muḥammad-'Alí. He had married Ṣamadíyyih, Mírzá Muḥammad-'Alí's sister, and was a bitter enemy of 'Abdu'l-Bahá. 'Abdu'l-Bahá prophesied that Majdu'd-Dín would live a long life to see the triumph of the Cause and the frustration of his evil plots. This prophecy was fulfilled: he lived to be over a hundred years old and saw the birth of the Administrative Order, the child of the Covenant, and the strengthening of its foundations by Shoghi Effendi. Majdu'd-Dín died in 1955, two years after the Ten Year Crusade was launched by the Guardian, having witnessed the indisputable ascendancy of the Covenant and the extinction of his hopes and evil designs.

Another ally and close companion of Mírzá Muḥammad-'Alí was his youngest brother Mírzá Badí'u'lláh. We have already described the story of his short-lived repentance.* His shameful activities against the Centre of the Covenant, and his opposition at a later date to Shoghi Effendi will be referred to in the following pages. It is interesting to note that Mírzá Badí'u'lláh also lived a long life and died at an advanced age.

Bahá'u'lláh's other son, Mírzá Ḍíyá'u'lláh, was a vacillating person who wavered in his allegiance to the Centre of the Covenant; he was easily manipulated and became a willing tool in the hands of Mírzá Muḥammad-'Alí. He lived in the Mansion of Bahjí along with the rest of the family, all of whom were affected by the spirit of Covenant-breaking. Mírzá Ḍíyá'u'lláh died in 1898 not very long after the passing of Bahá'u'lláh. He did not live to take an effective part in all the hostile activities which his brother was conducting against 'Abdu'l-Bahá. After his death 'Abdu'l-Bahá said that He had forgiven him.

Apart from these members of Bahá'u'lláh's family who rose up against 'Abdu'l-Bahá, there were others in the Holy Land who joined hands with them. Notorious among them was Mírzá Áqá Ján, Bahá'u'lláh's amanuensis, who had fallen from grace during the last months of Bahá'u'lláh's Ministry.† His rebellion against the Centre of the Covenant wiped out his forty-year record of service to Bahá'u'lláh and stained the annals of the Faith.

Another opponent of the Covenant was Muḥammad-Javád-i-Qazvíní. He first attained the presence of Bahá'u'lláh in Baghdád; some years later he went to Adrianople and remained in the service of Bahá'u'lláh there. He was among those who accompanied Him to 'Akká, was the recipient of His boundless favours, transcribed His Writings, and was entitled 'Ismu'lláhu'l-Javád' (The Name of God Javád) by Him. Muḥammad-Javád was an arrogant man who after the ascension of Bahá'u'lláh betrayed his Lord and became one of the adversaries of 'Abdu'l-Bahá in spite of 'Abdu'l-Bahá's efforts to protect him from Mírzá Muḥammad-'Alí's wicked designs. Although he was devoid of knowledge and learning, he attacked the Centre of the Covenant in his venomous writings which contain many inaccuracies, falsehoods and calumnies.

At the same time as the believers in the Holy Land were being tested by the disease of Covenant-breaking, a number of outstanding teachers of the Faith in Persia who were ambitious for the leadership of that community also defected and rose up in opposition against the Centre of the Covenant. The main source of rebellion was the

* See above, pp. 152–3.

† See *The Revelation of Bahá'u'lláh*, vol. 1, pp. 41–42.

proud and egotistical Jamál-i-Burújirdí. For many years during Bahá'u'lláh's Ministry this ambitious and deceitful man was foremost among the teachers of the Faith and his fame had spread throughout the community. Bahá'u'lláh concealed his faults, revealed many Tablets in his name, entitled him 'Ismu'lláhu'l-Jamál' (The Name of God Jamál), exhorted him to faithfulness and purity of motive, at times admonished him for those of his actions which were harmful to the Faith, and overlooked his shortcomings with forbearance and magnanimity. However, his hypocrisy was known to those who were close to him. Before embracing the Faith of Bahá'u'lláh, Jamál had been a learned mujtahid from the town of Burújird. Many Bahá'ís in Persia who could not see his deceitful and egotistical nature looked upon him as a man of God and treated him with great respect. It was after the passing of Bahá'u'lláh that Jamál showed his true colours, rejected the Covenant and rebelled against its Centre.

There were other teachers of the Faith in Persia who were also proud and ambitious. Notorious among them was Siyyid Mihdíy-i-Dahají entitled by Bahá'u'lláh 'Ismu'lláhu'l-Mihdí' (The Name of God Mihdí). He too was treated with loving kindness and forbearance by Bahá'u'lláh, was an eloquent teacher of the Cause and highly esteemed by the believers. Jalíl-i-Khú'í was another well-known believer, for whom Bahá'u'lláh revealed the *Tablet of Ishráqát*. These men and several others who were engaged in the service of the Cause during Bahá'u'lláh's Ministry but who in their hearts lusted for glory and leadership of the community, were tested through the institution of the Covenant. They failed to comply with the provisions of the *Kitáb-i-'Ahd*, broke the Covenant and were expelled from the community.

Those who are unfamiliar with the workings of the Faith of Bahá'u'lláh may find it difficult to understand the reasons why these hypocritical, proud and ambitious men were not cast out of the community by Bahá'u'lláh Himself during His lifetime since He was well aware of their corruption and deceit. To appreciate this important point, one must remember that although the Manifestation of God continually urges the believers to purify their motives in the service of the Cause and exhorts them to remove every trace of hypocrisy from their hearts, He does not question those motives. Rather He looks upon them with a sin-covering eye and instead of examining their hearts to find their faults and shortcomings, He calls upon them to serve His Cause and praises them when they do so. Through the outpouring of loving kindness and encouragement He seeks to improve the character of those who have embraced His Cause. Only if a believer arises to actively oppose the Centre of the Cause will he then need to be cast out of the community.

Jamál, and others like him who later became Covenant-breakers, were assiduously serving the Cause during Bahá'u'lláh's Ministry. They did not rise up to oppose His Cause or His Person. Consequently, they received His blessings and favours continually. However, when the provisions of the *Kitáb-i-'Ahd* were announced and the faithful were separated from the unfaithful, they cut themselves off from the body of the Cause of God.

One of the main factors which turns a believer into a Covenant-breaker is ambition to become prominent in the community, to rise to a high station within the Faith. This is the common objective of most Covenant-breakers. Such individuals have not realized that the only station which God has destined for man is that of servitude – servitude to God and servitude to his fellow-man. Bahá'u'lláh has abolished priesthood and to no one has He given any authority to rule over others. There are no individual leaders in the Bahá'í community, and the Faith does not harbour egotistical personalities. Of course there are learned Bahá'ís, outstanding teachers, administrators and pioneers, but none of these people, however outstanding, can exert authority over the community. Their greatness is in their humility, servitude and self-effacement. Those who rebelled against the Covenant did not understand or pay attention to this principle, of such importance to the Covenant of God with man.

In this life we note that opposites attract each other like the poles of a magnet. God and man may be said to be positioned on the two opposite poles. God is the Sovereign Lord of all, and man a humble servant, hence there is a force of attraction between the two. 'I loved thy creation, hence I created thee', is the voice of God addressing His servants. God is the possessor of all divine attributes. But by reason of His Sovereignty, He cannot be humble. The best gift, then, which man can offer to God is the only one which He does not already possess, namely, humility and servitude. These are the most befitting attributes for man. The lordship of God and the servitude of man are opposites bound together by the force of love. On the other hand, we note in the analogy of the magnet that similar poles repel each other. Therefore, should an individual, having recognized a Manifestation of God, aspire to reach His station or attempt to appear equal with Him, such an act will provoke the wrath of God and there will be a force of repulsion between the two parties. This is Covenant-breaking.

In the *Tablet of the Holy Mariner*,* whose main theme is the Covenant, Bahá'u'lláh confirms that should man be desirous to rise to that level which is beyond him and which is solely ordained for

* The full text of this Tablet, with an explanation of its significance, is given in *The Revelation of Bahá'u'lláh*, vol. 1, ch. 14.

God's Chosen Ones, he will be cast out from the realms on high. These are His words:

> . . . They have desired to ascend unto that state which the Lord hath ordained to be above their stations.
>
> Whereupon the burning meteor cast them out from them that abide in the Kingdom of His Presence,
>
> And they heard the Voice of Grandeur raised from behind the unseen pavilion upon the Height of Glory:
>
> 'O guardian angels! Return them to their abode in the world below,
>
> 'Inasmuch as they have purposed to rise to that sphere which the wings of the celestial dove have never attained . . .'

Mírzá Yaḥyá through his actions proved to be the fulfilment of these words, for he longed to take the place of Bahá'u'lláh and, indeed, when formally apprised in Adrianople of Bahá'u'lláh's claim he made his counterclaim and announced himself as the bearer of a new Revelation.

Mírzá Muḥammad-'Alí was the same. He knew the station of 'Abdu'l-Bahá as the Centre of the Covenant, the One to whom all believers must turn. Yet he wanted to be a partner with 'Abdu'l-Bahá. The fact that Mírzá Muḥammad-'Alí rose up with all his power to oppose 'Abdu'l-Bahá is a clear sign that he considered himself equal to the Master.

A child will never challenge a giant to a fight, because he knows that he is no match for the giant. But a man who chooses to fight with another, must of necessity regard himself to be possessed of at least the same strength as his opponent. The very act of opposition by one party is in itself an indication that it considers itself to be on a par with the other. All those who became Covenant-breakers were in this category. They rose up in opposition against the Centre of the Cause, but in reality their opposition amounted to exalting themselves to a position from which they were able to encounter 'Abdu'l-Bahá and challenge His authority. Consequently, as in the analogy of the poles of the magnet, they were rejected and cast out of the community of the Most Great Name.

Another feature of these episodes of Covenant-breaking which has puzzled many people is the fact that almost the entire family of Bahá'u'lláh defected. Why is it that those who were nearest to Him, who were members of His household, His sons and daughters, should be foremost among the violators of His Covenant? In normal circumstances when a person attains a prominent position in the community, it is often the family members who rally around him and lend their whole-hearted support. But in the case of Bahá'u'lláh, it was the reverse, and as we shall see, a similar situation was created within the family of 'Abdu'l-Bahá after His passing. To appreciate the reasons for this, we observe once again that the proper attitude of a believer towards the Manifestation of God should be a true demonstration of servitude, self-effacement and complete obedience. Whenever these qualities are absent, a barrier will be created between man and God. In such a case the believer may be associating with the Manifestation of God in person, yet because of this barrier, he will not be able to appreciate His glory or become enchanted with His Revelation.

One might, by way of analogy, compare such believers to those who, with no knowledge of mathematics, go to hear an eminent mathematician expounding his theories. Obviously, they are not able to understand him or appreciate his brilliant work. They can see him in no other light than that of an ordinary human being whose words are incomprehensible to them. So they begin to judge the scientist by their own standards and consequently remain unmoved by his intellectual powers. The closer they are to him, the better they can see his personal and human nature, which acts as a barrier and hides his greatness from them. Only those who understand mathematics can appreciate the real genius of the scientist. In their view, his scientific knowledge outweighs his human characteristics, and therefore they do not focus their attention on his outward appearance and human limitations.

This analogy sheds light on the Covenant-breaking by most members of Bahá'u'lláh's family and on the reasons for their unfaithfulness to Him. Mírzá Muḥammad-'Alí and his kinfolk who followed him did not possess that spiritual quality which makes a man humble and enables him to recognize the splendours of God's Revelation in this day. Because of their ambitious nature and their lack of spirituality and self-effacement, their inner eyes were blinded – unable to discern Bahá'u'lláh's spiritual powers. They could see Him only with their outward eyes, and because they were closest to Him, they saw Him as an ordinary human being. They found Him to be, in their estimation, just a great man and nothing more. In reality they had not recognized Bahá'u'lláh as a Manifestation of God. As long as Bahá'u'lláh was among them, they were subdued by His authority and at the same time basked in the sunshine of His favours and were accorded honours and privileges by His followers. But after His ascension, these same members of His family turned their backs on Him and broke His Covenant.

CHAPTER FOURTEEN

Clandestine Opposition to the Covenant

That 'Abdu'l-Bahá did not disclose the rebellion of Mírzá Muḥammad-'Alí, or of those who followed him, to the Bahá'ís outside the Holy Land for about four years was made possible because the rebellion was at first covert and only those who were close to the Holy Family were aware of it. As the years went by Mírzá Muḥammad-'Alí became more vociferous in his opposition and the news of his dissension gradually leaked out. During these four years 'Abdu'l-Bahá instructed that all letters written by the believers in the Holy Land addressed to the friends in Persia had to be submitted to Him for approval. He usually placed His seal on the letters if the contents met with His approval. Even most of the dissidents used to comply. In this way 'Abdu'l-Bahá tried to contain this deadly disease of Covenant-breaking within the Holy Land. During this four-year period He made every effort to guide these misguided souls to the straight path of truth. He even intimated to Mírzá Muḥammad-'Alí that since Bahá'u'lláh had appointed him to succeed 'Abdu'l-Bahá* he could achieve his heart's desire at a later time. But Mírzá Muḥammad-'Alí is reported to have responded: 'How can I be sure that I shall survive you?'

Unfortunately, the more 'Abdu'l-Bahá showered loving counsel upon the Covenant-breakers, the more haughty and rebellious they became. At last it was they themselves who announced their rebellion by distributing their messages of calumny and falsehood to the believers in the East. They made subtle remarks in their letters to Persia designed to undermine the faith of the believers in the person of 'Abdu'l-Bahá. The following is a summary translation of an account given by Ḥájí Mírzá Ḥaydar-'Alí, that renowned teacher of the Faith of Bahá'u'lláh, of a letter he received in Persia from Muḥammad-Javád-i-Qazvíní, one of the Covenant-breakers resident in the Holy Land.

* For the significance and the far-reaching consequences of this appointment by Bahá'u'lláh, see above, pp. 131–4.

Since the days of Bahá'u'lláh in Adrianople I had a close relationship with Muḥammad-Javád-i-Qazvíní. He was my correspondent through whom I used to dispatch my letters to His Holy Presence. I received a confidential letter from Javád [during the early years of 'Abdu'l-Bahá's ministry] in which he advised me that in my letters to the friends, I should not write the usual words, 'May my life be a sacrifice for you', nor begin my letters [to 'Abdu'l-Bahá] with words of praise or supplication to Him. Neither should I address them to any single Ghuṣn (Branch),* instead they should be addressed to the Aghṣán (Branches).

The perusal of this letter indicated to me that some form of secret opposition to the Centre of the Covenant was taking place and that Muḥammad-Javád himself was one of the dissidents . . .

In reply I wrote him a letter in which I rejected his proposals and stated that unless 'Abdu'l-Bahá made such a demand, I would not pay any attention to such advice. I also told him not to write to me again. Since Muḥammad-Javád did not respond to my letter I was assured that the birds of darkness were on the move and the clamour of the foreboders of evil would be heard soon. I felt certain that Javád and Jamál-i-Burújirdí were both secretly involved, so with all my heart and soul I used to pray on their behalf so that they might return to the path of truth. I kept this matter confidential, but it never occurred to me that the source of sedition was Mírzá Muḥammad-'Alí along with other members of Bahá'u'lláh's family, because I did not think they were so foolish and egotistical.[1]

Soon after these developments, Ḥájí Mírzá Ḥaydar-'Alí, with 'Abdu'l-Bahá's permission, proceeded to the Holy Land. En route he visited the believers in many towns and villages including 'Ishqábád, Bákú, Nakhjaván, Ganjih and Tiflís (Tbilisi). Everywhere he found the believers steadfast in the Covenant, enchanted by the utterances of 'Abdu'l-Bahá in His Tablets, and serving the Faith with enthusiasm and devotion. Being assured in his heart that severe tests and trials were about to engulf the community, Ḥájí in his contact with the believers encouraged them to turn with heart and soul to no one but the Master, to regard His words and utterances to be as valid as the words of Bahá'u'lláh Himself, and to refrain from any action which ran counter to His good-pleasure. The loving counsels of Ḥájí were warmly welcomed everywhere, and the believers vowed to remain steadfast in the Covenant, come what may.

When Ḥájí arrived in Beirut he stayed with a devoted believer, Áqá Muḥammad-Muṣṭafáy-i-Baghdádí, who intimated to him the opposition and rebellion of Mírzá Muḥammad-'Alí and a few others, contained so far by 'Abdu'l-Bahá within the family and a small circle of friends. Immediately upon his arrival at the pilgrim house in 'Akká, Ḥájí wrote a letter to the Master. He talks about his letter,

* A designation by which a male descendant of Bahá'u'lláh is known. Aghṣan is the plural.

tells the story of attaining the presence of 'Abdu'l-Bahá and of other events associated with his pilgrimage during those turbulent months. This is a summary translation of his reminiscences:

> . . . In this letter I stated that I do not turn to anybody except the Master, and I do not wish to meet with any believer except those whom the Beloved wishes me to meet. Even praying at the Holy Shrine of Bahá'u'lláh and circumambulating that exalted spot around which circle in adoration the Concourse on High, are dependent on the will of the Master. Praise and thanksgiving be to God that on the day of my arrival I was given the privilege of praying at and circumambulating the Shrine in the presence of 'Abdu'l-Bahá who chanted the Tablet of Visitation Himself. In what a radiant condition I found myself, and to what heights of spirituality I was carried as a result of this experience, are impossible for me to describe. With my inner eyes I saw the Heavenly Kingdom, witnessed the Blessed Beauty, exalted be His glory, seated upon the Throne of His Majesty and Authority, and was assured of the penetration of His Holy Word in the hearts of men . . .
>
> Through the flattery and empty compliments of some hypocrites, Mírzá Muḥammad-'Alí, in the prime of his youth, entertained the thought of rebellion, cherished the inordinate ambition of becoming great, and lusted for leadership. He therefore put together some absurd passages and referred to them as Revelations from God and secretly despatched them far and wide.* And, when his mischievous deeds and the corrupt intentions hidden in his heart were disclosed, the Pen of Glory revealed a Tablet stating that He had conferred upon Mírzá Muḥammad-'Alí the power of utterance, that he was only as a leaf of the divine lote-tree, and that if the holy breezes of His Revelation were to cease to waft over him he would, as a dry leaf, fall upon the earth and perish. In reality he was already spiritually cut off in those days [in Adrianople], but it was hidden from the eyes because He Who conceals the faults of men had covered it up.
>
> It was obvious that Mírzá Muḥammad-'Alí had not truly repented after committing these misdeeds. On the contrary, he and a few others were watering the tree of his rebelliousness. They were secretly engaged in intrigues and satanic ambitions. Some believers were aware of their condition, but for the sake of God they did not reveal it. This situation continued until the last years of the Ministry of the Day-Star of the World [Bahá'u'lláh], when Muḥammad-Javád-i-Qazvíní and Jamál-i-Burújirdí secretly united with Mírzá Muḥammad-'Alí in their plots to create discord and dissension within the community. They succeeded in enlisting a few others within their fold. These two men convinced Mírzá Muḥammad-'Alí that since the bulk of the believers in Persia were looking up to them, he would become the one to whom all would turn and he could present himself as the Centre of the Cause. Their deceit-

* This relates to his activities in Adrianople, see above, pp. 126–7, and also *The Revelation of Bahá'u'lláh*, vol. 2, pp. 259–61.

fulness and hypocrisy were fully disclosed through their misdeeds after the setting of the Sun of Truth.

As the Day-Star of the Incomparable Beauty hid itself from the eyes of men, and began to shed its light from the Realm of Glory upon the peoples of the world, and His confirmations and assistance were showered upon the Centre of His Covenant, these unfaithful ones began to promote their designs. When they came in contact with the believers, whether residents or pilgrims, they opened the subject of the oneness of God saying that God is one, there is no partner with Him, and the Most Great Infallibility belongs to Him, exalted be His Glory.* The believers were surprised and bewildered at such statements. They could not understand to whom they were imputing their strange suggestions, for no one had claimed to be a partner with God or be a possessor of the Most Great Infallibility.

These insinuations continued until the believers noticed that 'Abdu'l-Bahá treated Mírzá Muḥammad-'Alí with much greater respect than at the time of Bahá'u'lláh. On the other hand, the Arch-breaker of the Covenant and his entourage had considerably lessened the measure of honour and respect that they humbly used to show the Master in the days of the Blessed Beauty. Added to this treatment, the Covenant-breakers through their words and deeds and by subtle hints were attempting to belittle the Master and to dishonour Him. When the believers realized this, they kept away from the unfaithful and as far as possible did not seek to associate with them in private.

Two devoted believers, Áqá Muḥammad-Riḍáy-i-Shírází† and Mírzá Maḥmúd-i-Kasháni, went together to meet Mírzá Muḥammad-'Alí. They showed the utmost respect to him, and in a spirit of humility and loving kindness counselled him with genuine concern. By giving some hints or relating certain stories, they conveyed to him the dire consequences of his rebellion. But instead of taking to heart their admonitions, and heeding their loving advice to change his ways, he was hurt that they counselled him in this manner.

The Master continued to overlook Mírzá Muḥammad-'Alí's wrongdoings and treated him with the utmost love and kindness in spite of his rebellion. Whereas in the days of the Blessed Beauty Mírzá Muḥammad-'Alí showed so much respect to 'Abdu'l-Bahá that he would not take a seat in His presence without His permission, now it was different; it was the Master who as a sign of loving respect would arise from His seat when he or his associates arrived in a gathering. At first 'Abdu'l-Bahá's counsels were given to them in private, through hints and suggestions which pointed the way to their everlasting salvation and glory. But since through their rebellion they gradually tore apart the veil which had until then concealed their wrongdoings, the Master began to counsel them

* One of the shameful accusations which the Covenant-breakers spread around was that 'Abdu'l-Bahá had claimed to be a Manifestation of God. They even went further and accused Him of claiming the station of divinity for Himself. This was the reason why they were talking about partnership with God.

† See *The Revelation of Bahá'u'lláh*, vol. 1, pp. 288–9.

publicly in words such as these: 'Do not by your actions quench the fire and extinguish the light of God. Take not a step that would lead to degradation of the Word of God. Do not behave in such a way as to cause the enemies to rejoice and the loved ones to lament.'* 'Abdu'l-Bahá warned them lovingly and repeatedly about the dire consequences of their evil doings, but all these counsels fell on deaf ears and they followed the path of pride, hate and rebellion.

About three months after my arrival in the Holy Land, the Master sent me to Egypt. Since 'Abdu'l-Bahá had warned the friends not to discuss the rebellion of Mírzá Muḥammad-'Alí, I addressed a letter to him when I was in Egypt, the gist of which was as follows: 'The people of Bahá expected that after the setting of the Sun of Truth, you would show the same measure of humility, submissiveness and obedience to the Centre of the Covenant that you demonstrated in the Holy Presence of Bahá'u'lláh. We have all observed that in the days of the Blessed Beauty, you would not have taken your seat in the presence of the Master without His permission. Each time that He came to Bahjí to attain the presence of His beloved Father, you along with others, as commanded by Bahá'u'lláh, went as a welcoming party as far as the Garden of Jammál† to greet Him. Now we see that when any one of you arrives in the room, it is the Master who as a token of respect for you arises from His seat and will not sit down until the person takes his seat.

We have also noticed that when His blessed Person arrives at Bahjí after having walked‡ all the way from 'Akká as a token of His utter humility to the sacred Threshold, not only do you refuse to go out to welcome Him, but after He enters the Sacred Shrine, those who are in your company come down the steps of the Mansion slowly one by one and go towards the Shrine, and you yourself are the last one to appear. Again, when He has come out of the Shrine and is about to depart for 'Akká, you walk away towards the Mansion before being dismissed from His presence.§ Indeed, you are back inside the Mansion before He leaves. Now that you do not go to welcome Him at the entrance of the Garden of Jammál, you could at least ask permission to leave His presence, or wait outside the Shrine until He departs.

In the past you always addressed Him as 'the Master', but now refer to Him as 'my brother'. We are surprised and do not know the reason for all this humiliating treatment to which you have subjected His blessed Person. Is your contemptuousness because of all the services that He has rendered to the Cause and to the Person of the Blessed Beauty? Or is it because He was the One who brought about your exaltation and honour

* These are not the exact words of 'Abdu'l-Bahá, but convey the gist of what He said on that occasion.

† Properties lying at the south entrance to the Mansion.

‡ It is an expression of humility and self-effacement for a servant to walk to his master and not to go to him riding.

§ It was considered highly discourteous for a man to take his seat in the presence of an eminent person without his permission. Similarly it was discourteous to leave his presence before being dismissed. The believers always observed the utmost courtesy when they came into the presence of Bahá'u'lláh, 'Abdu'l-Bahá and Shoghi Effendi.

among the people, and enabled you to live in the utmost comfort and luxury? While you enjoyed a life of pleasure, and engaged in pastimes such as hunting and other recreations, His blessed Person did not have a moment to rest. Do you behave toward Him in a disdainful manner because it was He who, from the early days of the rising of the Day-Star of the World [Bahá'u'lláh] from the horizon of Ṭihrán and 'Iráq, was the Master and the leader of all the people of Bahá? Or is your behaviour towards Him due to all the sufferings and hardships that were, and are, being inflicted upon His blessed Person from every quarter? He has stood up with the utmost firmness and strength in resisting the onslaught of the enemy and has, singly and alone, exerted every effort in the promotion of the word of God and the diffusion of its fragrances, while you are conducting a life of luxury and spending your time in riding and sightseeing. Does the particular text of the *Kitáb-i-Aqdas* which was later confirmed in the *Kitáb-i-'Ahd*, that all the Aghṣán must turn to Him, and gird up their loins in His obedience, provide justification for you to belittle His exalted station?

Besides all this, when this servant and other believers notice the extraordinary loving kindness and humility the Centre of the Covenant shows to you, while you appear proud and haughty before His peerless and incomparable Person, what conclusion do we reach? In the light of all this, whom should we regard as a true believer in the Blessed Beauty, and whom should we consider steadfast in His Covenant?

The believers have endured all manner of oppression. They have suffered imprisonment and exile and been inflicted with hardship and persecution. These souls will not deviate from the straight path. They will cling fast to the Covenant of Bahá'u'lláh and its Centre, He 'who hath branched from this Ancient Root'. They will not loosen their hold on that 'excellent and priceless heritage' which Bahá'u'lláh has bequeathed to His heirs . . .[2]

Some time later, Ḥájí Mírzá Ḥaydar-'Alí returned to 'Akká and from there was directed by 'Abdu'l-Bahá to proceed to Persia via Bombay. The day before his departure, 'Abdu'l-Bahá asked him to pay a visit to the Mansion of Bahjí for the purpose of saying farewell to the family of Bahá'u'lláh.

At this juncture we recall that 'Abdu'l-Bahá and His family did not live in the Mansion of Bahjí but that the rest of Bahá'u'lláh's family resided there. Only some rooms on the ground floor were reserved for 'Abdu'l-Bahá's use whenever He visited the Mansion. Even these were taken over by the Covenant-breakers once their opposition to Him was intensified and became public. It was then that 'Abdu'l-Bahá took over a few rooms known as the pilgrim house, in the vicinity of the Shrine of Bahá'u'lláh, for His own use. Here He rested after the fatigue of the journey from 'Akká. He also received the believers in that house. The Mansion was occupied by the Covenant-breakers for several decades after the Master's passing and it was

Shoghi Effendi who succeeded in driving them out and cleansing that hallowed spot from their pollution.

'Abdu'l-Bahá intimated to Ḥájí Mírzá Ḥaydar-'Alí that when he visited the Mansion to say farewell, he would be invited by Mírzá Muḥammad-'Alí to meet with him in private. 'Abdu'l-Bahá advised the Ḥájí that should he receive such an invitation, he should accept and with great humility say whatever his heart and conscience dictated to him. This is how the Ḥájí records the story of the interview.

> It was late at night that Mírzá Muḥammad-'Alí summoned me to his room. He asked his son Shu'á'u'lláh, who was present, to leave, because he wanted to talk to me confidentially. After much conversation, he said: 'I wish to ask you a question in confidence. Don't you think that I could have also inherited what my brother ['Abdu'l-Bahá] has inherited from the Blessed Beauty?'
>
> I said to him: 'In all His references to 'Abdu'l-Bahá, the Blessed Beauty has assigned to Him all the exalted names and praiseworthy attributes. He enjoined on us all to show forth, for the exaltation of His Cause, the utmost love and humility toward His Person. In the *Kitáb-i-'Ahd*, He has clearly stated: 'It is incumbent upon the Aghṣan, the Afnán and My kindred to turn, one and all, their faces toward the Most Mighty Branch.' Therefore to the extent that you show forth humility, self-effacement and utter nothingness to His blessed Person ['Abdu'l-Bahá], you will accordingly acquire the exalted qualities you wish to have. Based on the same principle, you will lose these qualities to the extent that you lessen the measure of your humility and submissiveness toward Him. The reason for this is that all the praise and honour which are bestowed upon you by Bahá'u'lláh are dependent upon certain conditions. Certain verses of the *Kitáb-i-Aqdas* and their further elucidation in the *Kitáb-i-'Ahd* are as unequivocal and clear as the sun in mid-sky. God forbid, if for one moment in your heart you might think the passage in the *Kitáb-i-'Ahd* ought to have directed the Aghṣan, the Afnán and others to turn their faces to Ghuṣn-i-Akbar [The Greater Branch, i.e. Mírzá Muḥammad-'Alí). It is clear that you do not possess what the Master possesses. God, exalted be He, does not act hypocritically, nor does He create means of division among people. It is impossible for the One True God to entrust the guardianship of His Cause to two individuals at the same time . . . Apart from all this, who is it in this world of being that can claim to rival the Master on any level?'
>
> I was talking on these lines when he arose from his seat saying it was time to go to bed, so I left him.[3]

The campaign of opposition to 'Abdu'l-Bahá led by Mírzá Muḥammad-'Alí acquired greater momentum as the years went by. Soon after the passing of Bahá'u'lláh, Mırzá Muḥammad-'Alí, who had already won the support of most members of Bahá'u'lláh's family, began secretly to undermine the faith of the believers in 'Akká, to weaken their love and loyalty toward the Master and eventually win them over to his own camp. He and his associates knew those who were steadfast in the Covenant and those who were weak, simple-hearted, or proud and ambitious. They by-passed the former and concentrated on sowing the seeds of doubt in the hearts of the latter, adopting different methods to achieve their purpose. In all these they hid themselves under the cloak of hypocrisy and did their best to pose as the most devoted, the most pious and the most humble Bahá'ís in the land. For example, one way of misleading a simple-hearted Bahá'í was for a few agents of Mírzá Muḥammad-'Alí to get close to him individually, and establish bonds of friendship with him. Each one of them posed as the most humble followers of 'Abdu'l-Bahá, and in the course of conversation they praised the Master with unusual exaggeration. For instance they would say that He was a Manifestation of God, that His station was equal to Bahá'u'lláh's, that He was the embodiment of divinity Himself and that in their prayers they turn to Him instead of turning to God. One after the other would convey to the individual such preposterous thoughts and assure him falsely that 'Abdu'l-Bahá had claimed such a station for Himself. When they were sure that the loyal Bahá'í was beginning to have doubts about 'Abdu'l-Bahá's station, they would then despatch other persons to him who would disprove and strongly criticize those fabricated claims which they had slanderously attributed to 'Abdu'l-Bahá. In this way through deceit and falsehood, they would weaken the faith of the believer to a point where he would be invited to join a group of dissidents.

Another trick played by Mírzá Muḥammad-'Alí was to shower praise upon an outstanding teacher of the Faith who was steadfast in the Covenant. Consequently, some believers would conclude that the famous Bahá'í teacher must have joined the ranks of the Covenant-breakers. This could result in the defection of some weak and uninformed believers. Once, Mírzá Muḥammad-'Alí's associates published a paper in which they paid great tribute to the famous Bahá'í scholar Mírzá Abu'l-Faḍl, and extolled him in superlative terms. No sooner was Mírzá Abu'l-Faḍl informed of this than he wrote an open letter saying that they had no right to praise him and that this action alone had exposed their hypocrisy, for he was abhorred in their sight. If any praise was due to him, it ought to come from the friends of 'Abdu'l-Bahá. He handed this letter to the Master who directed that it be read aloud at a meeting of the friends.

There were other ways through which the Covenant-breakers succeeded by deceitful practices in gathering a number of the Bahá'ís around themselves. At the same time, Mírzá Muḥammad-'Alí had established secret links with Jamál-i-Burújirdí and a few others in Persia. Together they had designed a strategy to make their rebellion public and divide the community of the Most Great Name at a propitious time.

As we have stated before, for four years 'Abdu'l-Bahá had done everything in His power to guide these people to the straight path, and He did not reveal their breaking of the Covenant to the Bahá'ís outside the Holy Land. However, after four years of strengthening their position, Mírzá Muḥammad-'Alí and his party felt that it was time to unmask themselves. They did this by printing letters loaded with falsehoods, misleading statements, and calumnies against the Centre of the Covenant, posing themselves as the voice of truth trying to purify the Cause which they shamelessly claimed to have been polluted by those who were faithful to 'Abdu'l-Bahá. In his propaganda, Mírzá Muḥammad-'Alí did not contest the authenticity of the *Kitáb-i-'Ahd*, rather he expressed his grievance that he had been barred from partnership with 'Abdu'l-Bahá in directing the affairs of the Cause. He wanted to share with Him the station of the Centre of the Covenant.

It was as a result of these letters by Mírzá Muḥammad-'Alí that 'Abdu'l-Bahá in His Tablets began openly to refer to the breaking of the Covenant by His unfaithful brother; from then on, right up to the end of His life, He explained in innumerable Tablets the significance of the Covenant and urged the friends to remain steadfast in the Cause of God.

Concerning the dispatch for the first time of Mírzá Muḥammad-'Alí's letters to Persia, Dr Yúnis Khán-i-Afrúkhtih, one of the faithful secretaries of the Master, relates the following story.

> 'Abdu'l-Bahá often used to say: 'One day Mírzá Ḍíyá'u'lláh* came to see Me. I noticed he was looking at his fingers which were stained with ink and was expecting Me to comment on them. I did not say anything, so he himself volunteered the information, saying, "Last night until the early hours of the morning we were engaged in writing letters and gelatine printing, consequently my fingers have been stained. My brother [Mírzá Muḥammad-'Alí] had written a letter of which we printed several copies and sent them away this morning." I asked him: Did you really write and dispatch them? And when he answered in the affirmative, I said: I swear by the Righteousness of God, a day shall come when Mírzá Muḥammad-'Alí would wish that his fingers had been cut off so that he could not have taken the pen to announce his breaking of the Covenant. For four years I have concealed this matter so that the beloved of God might not learn of your unfaithfulness to the Covenant. It is now beyond my power to conceal it any longer. You have announced yourselves to the believers.[4]

* The younger brother of Mírzá Muḥammad-'Alí.

The family of Bahá'u'lláh, those who became Covenant-breakers, were leading a very comfortable life in the Mansion of Bahjí. During Bahá'u'lláh's lifetime, His three sons and His amanuensis Mírzá Áqá Ján had hoarded a great many valuable gifts which the believers had presented to Bahá'u'lláh. These gifts Bahá'u'lláh had declined to accept for Himself. He was detached from all earthly possessions, and so were 'Abdu'l-Bahá, His mother and His sister, the Greatest Holy Leaf. Mírzá Áqá Ján coveted these gifts, and so did Mírzá Muḥammad-'Alí. Consequently these individuals had amassed considerable wealth. Indeed, as we shall see later in this book, Mírzá Muḥammad-'Alí and his brothers at one time plotted to take Mírzá Áqá Ján's life in order to take over his possessions.

After the passing of Bahá'u'lláh, the family lived prosperously. 'Abdu'l-Bahá continued for many years to send funds and large supplies of food to the inhabitants of the Mansion; He sent them everything they needed to make them comfortable. The three brothers, their families and close relatives all enjoyed a life of luxury and leisure. The following is a summary translation of Ḥájí Mírzá Ḥaydar-'Alí's remarks on the above subject.

> All the gifts that the Master received, as well as the funds relating to the Ḥuqúqu'lláh, He used to send to the Mansion for the upkeep of the family. Also He had bought for them a number of horses of the best breed which were kept in the stables at the Mansion. The Covenant-breakers often spent their time riding and hunting. When they went to 'Akká, they rode horses* flanked on each side by ten or twelve armed horsemen as guards. In this way they impressed everyone. They entered the city with a pomp and grandeur usually reserved for the governor and the chiefs. In contrast to this, the Master often used to walk and occasionally rode a donkey as He went alone to the Shrine of Bahá'u'lláh. Thus they considered themselves victorious when they reflected on their outward pomp and glory, while they regarded 'Abdu'l-Bahá's lowliness and simplicity as a sign of His weakness and defeat . . .
>
> The Master had instructed Áqá Faraju'lláh, who was His caterer, to send to the Mansion any amount of food and other supplies which the Covenant-breakers requested. But they used to demand five or six times more than their needs. They were determined to take excessive funds from the Master so as to make Him helpless and force upon Him the humiliation of borrowing money from the people. In spite of all this, 'Abdu'l-Bahá ensured that they received large supplies of food, clothing, and other necessities of life. Moreover, every gift which was sent to Him 'Abdu'l-Bahá would dispatch to the Mansion, and many of the funds which He received as Ḥuqúqu'lláh were given to them. These manifestations of generosity and compassion which 'Abdu'l-Bahá showered upon

* In those days important people rode horses and this was a sign of their eminence in the community. Ordinary people either walked or rode donkeys.

them in spite of their malevolence were interpreted by them as fear and helplessness. Consequently the more they received His gracious gifts and favours, the more haughty they became, and progressively intensified their opposition to His blessed Person.[5]

During the early years of their rebellion, the Covenant-breakers, noticing on the one hand their own prosperity and apparent success in converting a considerable number to their side, and 'Abdu'l-Bahá's humility and loving generosity on the other, were convinced that theirs would be a victorious outcome. Dr Yúnis Khán recounts:

> I heard several times from the Master saying: 'Once I was counselling Majdu'd-Dín* and trying to guide him in a spirit of love and compassion. I admonished him to abandon the path of error, and warned him of the remorseful consequences of his deeds. But I spoke to him with such fervour that tears came to My eyes. Then I noticed that upon seeing my emotions, Majdu'd-Dín was scornfully smiling at Me, thinking in his heart how well I had been defeated! Thereupon I raised my voice at him saying "O wretched one! My tears were shed when, out of pity, I reflected upon your miserable state, and not for myself. Did you think I had become helpless and impotent because of my pleading to you?" '[6]

'Abdu'l-Bahá's patience and loving kindness, demonstrated in the above story, were thus interpreted by the Covenant-breakers as weakness. This misconception, coupled with the notion that theirs was a life of prosperity and honour, while 'Abdu'l-Bahá and His family were living an austere life burdened by having to supply the exorbitant expenses they demanded, emboldened the Covenant-breakers to step up their campaign of misrepresentation against 'Abdu'l-Bahá. In this, they received encouragement from the enemies of the Faith, as well as from the aides and deputies of Mírzá Muḥammad-'Alí in Persia.

* See above, p. 164.

CHAPTER FIFTEEN

Mírzá Áqá Ján

On the fifth anniversary of the Ascension of Bahá'u'lláh, Mírzá Áqá Ján, Bahá'u'lláh's amanuensis, threw in his lot with the Covenant-breakers and became one of Mírzá Muḥammad-'Alí's most powerful tools. He created a great disturbance among the believers which brought suffering and anguish to the heart of 'Abdu'l-Bahá for some time.

Mírzá Áqá Ján had been the first person to believe in Bahá'u'lláh as 'Him Whom God shall make manifest'. He did not belong to the learned class, having only an elementary education. In his youth he used to make soap and sell it for a living. Soapmaking was a humble trade in those days, and it was often carried out in the home by people who were not well educated. Mírzá Áqá Ján went to 'Iráq soon after the arrival of Bahá'u'lláh in that country, and his first meeting with Him took place in the house of a friend in Karbilá.

There in the presence of Bahá'u'lláh he sensed a great spiritual power emanating from Him, a power that transformed his whole being. He was the first one to whom Bahá'u'lláh gave an intimation of the as yet unrevealed glory of His station. He also chose him as His personal servant and gave him the title of K͟hádim (servant), and later K͟hádimu'lláh (servant of God).

At the same time that Mírzá Áqá Ján was the 'servant in attendance', he was empowered by Bahá'u'lláh to act as His amanuensis in spite of his inadequate education. This he did till the end of the Ministry of Bahá'u'lláh. This man indeed served Bahá'u'lláh assiduously for years in the triple functions of secretary, servant and companion. In the whole range of Bahá'u'lláh's companions, there was nobody so close to Him as Mírzá Áqá Ján. He was for years a channel of communication between Bahá'u'lláh and the believers. It was a common practice for the believers to send their petitions or letters to Mírzá Áqá Ján who would then present them to Bahá'u'lláh.

During Bahá'u'lláh's retirement to the mountains of Kurdistán, Mírzá Áqá Ján was engaged for some time in the service of Mírzá

Yaḥyá who wanted him to go to Ṭihrán on a secret mission to assassinate Náṣiri'd-Dín Sháh. Mírzá Áqá Ján accepted this criminal mission, and soon after his arrival in Ṭihrán managed to obtain access to the court of the Sháh in the guise of a labourer. However, having failed to carry out his sinister intention and realizing the extent of his folly, he returned to Baghdád. When Bahá'u'lláh came back from His solitary retirement in the mountains of Kurdistán, Mírzá Áqá Ján begged Bahá'u'lláh's forgiveness for his part in Mírzá Yaḥyá's evil scheme and was then permitted to resume his services to Bahá'u'lláh.

As we have seen, being very close to the Manifestation of God can be spiritually fatal to anyone who is not detached from the things of this world. Only those who are humble, utterly self-effacing and without any trace of ambition, yearning only for His good-pleasure, can survive in His presence. Mírzá Áqá Ján did not have these qualities. In the course of his service to Bahá'u'lláh, and as the years went by, he became proud of himself and at times caused displeasure to Bahá'u'lláh through his misconduct. At such times, 'Abdu'l-Bahá used to rebuke him and plead with Bahá'u'lláh to forgive his wrongdoings. There were even occasions when 'Abdu'l-Bahá chastised him with His own hand because of the serious nature of his conduct toward Bahá'u'lláh.

In spite of all these shortcomings, Mírzá Áqá Ján worked very hard and for years was engaged day and night in taking down the words which were revealed by Bahá'u'lláh. His 'revelation writings'* are a testimony to the onrushing forces of the Revelation of the words of God, which were sent down with a rapidity and profusion unprecedented in the history of religion. It was close to the end of His earthly life that, deeply displeased with Mírzá Áqá Ján's unbefitting behaviour at the time, Bahá'u'lláh dispensed with his services and dismissed him from His presence.

It is interesting that God establishes His Faith in the world with the help of the most unsuitable people. Mírzá Áqá Ján was neither a learned person capable of assuming the awesome responsibility of an amanuensis to the Manifestation of God, nor did he have those qualities which are essential for serving Him. 'Abdu'l-Bahá also had some individuals who worked very closely with Him; among them were a few who proved to be both unfaithful and incompetent servants. Indeed, Bahá'u'lláh and 'Abdu'l-Bahá were both surrounded by a number of close companions who later became Covenant-breakers. Yet, in spite of this serious handicap of working with incompetent, unfaithful, and sometimes dangerous individuals, God promotes His Faith, and thereby demonstrates His power and

* See *The Revelation of Bahá'u'lláh*, vol. 1, ch. 3.

omnipotence to His servants. The Revealers of the Word of God in past Dispensations have testified to this. In the Gospels we read:

Blessed are the meek, for they shall inherit the earth.[1]

And in the *Qur'án*:

We wished to favour those who were weak in the land and make them leaders and heirs.[2]

Even today, when almost one hundred and fifty years have passed since the birth of the Faith, the Bahá'í community – in spite of its inadequate resources as compared with mankind's enormous resources in every field – is growing all over the world. The institutions of the Faith are established in many parts of the globe and the foundations of its Administrative Order, destined in the fullness of time to emerge as a world order for the unification of the human race, are being laid everywhere by men and women who in most cases are devoid of fame, social standing, power or authority.

During his years of service to Bahá'u'lláh, Mírzá Áqá Ján had accumulated some wealth by requesting Bahá'u'lláh to let him have some of the gifts which the believers had sent to Him. As we have seen, Bahá'u'lláh mostly gave away these offerings to individuals. Mírzá Áqá Ján had also acquired some properties with the cooperation of the three sons of Bahá'u'lláh who were highly attached to material things.

Soon after the ascension of Bahá'u'lláh, the Covenant-breakers led by Mírzá Muḥammad-'Alí plotted to take Mírzá Áqá Ján's life in order to gain possession of his properties. Their pretext was that because of his unfaithfulness to Bahá'u'lláh towards the end of His earthly life, he had to be put to death. Dr Yúnis Khán-i-Afrúkhtih, a devoted believer who served 'Abdu'l-Bahá as a secretary for nine years in 'Akká, and was acclaimed by Shoghi Effendi as a 'herald of the Covenant', and 'trusted secretary' of the Master, has left to posterity a most interesting account concerning Mírzá Áqá Ján's later years in 'Akká around 1897. The following is a summary translation of some extracts from his memoirs describing his first meeting with Mírzá Áqá Ján and of the events which took place on the fifth anniversary of the ascension of Bahá'u'lláh, when a great tragedy was quietly and effectively diverted:

At the time of the passing of Bahá'u'lláh, Mírzá Áqá Ján, who had fallen from grace, was living an ignominious life. However, as a result of Bahá'u'lláh's generosity, he had a reasonable income. The Covenant-breakers had secretly resolved to take his life. Probably the reason for this was either to seize his properties or because Bahá'u'lláh had not been pleased with his conduct towards the end of His life. Mírzá Áqá Ján discovered their plot and went immediately to 'Abdu'l-Bahá, begged forgiveness for his misdeeds and took refuge in His house . . .

. . . On most occasions when we were summoned to the presence of 'Abdu'l-Bahá in His reception room, I noticed that an old man, short in stature, with a white beard and brown complexion, arrived in the room after everyone else. First he would prostrate himself at the threshold of the room ['Abdu'l-Bahá's], then he would enter, bow to the waist and, when 'Abdu'l-Bahá acknowledged him, sit at the threshold. I was curious to know who this person was and several times it occurred to me that when I left the room I should inquire of the resident believers as to his identity. For some time, however, I forgot to ask. This was due to the fact that we were so intoxicated by the wine of the Master's bounteous utterances that when we left Him we were not in a mood to talk to each other.

One day I was sitting [in the presence of 'Abdu'l-Bahá] very close to the entrance of the room. I saw the old man arriving. At first he prostrated himself at the entrance to the corridor, then approached the room and again prostrated himself at the threshold. He then entered, bowed low before 'Abdu'l-Bahá and stood there until 'Abdu'l-Bahá indicated to him to be seated, whereupon he sat with downcast eyes near the door . . . By this time I was very curious to know who this person was, and why I had not seen him among the believers in the town.

When we all left the presence of the Master, I noticed that this man went into the inner section of the house. I asked someone about him and was told that he was Mírzá Áqá Ján . . . I questioned my friends further, asking what Mírzá Áqá Ján was doing here. Is he not, I asked, the person who was rejected by Bahá'u'lláh and whom the Covenant-breakers were intent upon murdering? They told me that he had now taken refuge in the house of the Master. In those days I often thought about Mírzá Áqá Ján, who had fallen from grace, and wondered what would happen to him in the end. How little did I know then that, in a fortnight's time, he would play an important and unforgettable role in the arena of the Cause and that I myself would be one of the spectators . . .[3]

Ḥájí 'Alíy-i-Yazdí,* also a resident in 'Akká since the early days of Bahá'u'lláh's arrival in that city, was fully informed about Mírzá Áqá Ján's involvement with the Covenant-breakers. In his memoirs, he has recorded his story. The following is a summary translation of his account:

Some time after Mírzá Áqá Ján was permitted by 'Abdu'l-Bahá to take refuge in His house, the ill-fated standard of Covenant-breaking was upraised. The Aghṣán† began to regret the departure of Mírzá Áqá Ján from their midst. They thought that if he were present among them, with his cooperation they could influence more believers to join the

* The paternal uncle of the author. For his life story, see *The Bahá'í World*, vol. IX, p. 625.
† In this context, it means 'Abdu'l-Bahá's unfaithful brothers.

Covenant-breakers. They deplored his absence among them, and tried over a long period of time to devise a plan for arranging his return to the Mansion of Bahjí where he had been originally living. After some time, through careful planning, Muḥammad-Javád-i-Qazvíní* managed to meet Mírzá Áqá Ján when the latter was shopping at a certain bakery. He conversed with him there for a considerable period of time and urged him to leave the house of the Master and return to Bahjí. But he did not succeed in winning him over.

At this point the Aghṣán and a few others including Majdu'd-Dín and Javád-i-Qazvíní consulted together and decided to address a letter to Mírzá Áqá Ján purported to be on behalf of all the Bahá'ís of Persia. The gist of the letter was as follows: 'O Khádem!† how long will you remain silent? For how long should we tarry in the wilderness of error? All of us look for your guidance and turn to you to hear your counsel. This is because you are aware of all things, you were the amanuensis of Bahá'u'lláh. Everyone is now awaiting to hear from you. We know that the Aghṣán are not as informed as you are. You are responsible for all the wrongs that the believers go through because you remain silent. The differences which have arisen after the Ascension of Bahá'u'lláh have made all the Bahá'ís of Persia bewildered and perplexed. Because of your silence you are responsible for this distressing situation. All our eyes are turned to you and our ears are waiting to hear from you.'

The Aghṣán sent the above draft to Mullá Ḥusayn-i-Jahrumí‡ who was residing in Bombay, India, and instructed him to copy it in his own handwriting and post it to Mírzá Áqá Ján, care of the Archbreaker of the Covenant. This he did and when the letter arrived, they decided that he should receive it personally. They arranged to hand the letter to him in the Shrine of Bahá'u'lláh. Usually when Mírzá Áqá Ján went to the Shrine, he would sit down for about an hour, close his eyes and raise his hands upwards saying prayers. One day when he was seated in this manner, the daughter of Samandar§ inconspicuously placed the letter in his hands. Later, he opened his eyes and saw the letter, but did not know who had placed it there.

He took the letter with him to 'Akká. We can guess what kind of thoughts must have come to him when he read it. He imagined that as soon as he made a statement, all the believers in Persia would respond positively to him. The fire of pride and rebellion began to burn within his heart. He then intimated to Muḥammad-Javád-i-Qazvíní his intention to give a feast on the anniversary of the Ascension of Bahá'u'lláh, invite all the believers to it, and there release some important news and announce to them certain vital matters.

* See above, pp. 165, 170–71.

† Literally 'servant', the appellation by which Mírzá Áqá Ján was called.

‡ A notorious Covenant-breaker.

§ She was the wife of Mírzá Ḍíyá'u'lláh, son of Bahá'u'lláh. Her father was Shaykh Káẓim-i-Samandar, one of the Apostles of Bahá'u'lláh. After the death of Ḍíyá'u'lláh, the Covenant-breakers kept his widow against her will at Bahjí, and when her father went to take her home with him, he was viciously attacked and badly beaten by order of Mírzá Muḥammad-'Alí and was thrown out of Bahjí. 'Abdu'l-Bahá advised Samandar not to pursue the matter.

Some time passed and the anniversary of the Ascension drew near. He made all the arrangements for the feast. When the time arrived, and the believers had assembled, he stood up and began his talk. He explained that when he was utterly oblivious of himself and his surroundings at the Shrine, a letter came down from heaven and landed in his hands. He then started reading it when some believers stopped him, saying that his story was nothing but vain imaginings, and that everyone must turn to the Centre of the Covenant. Through his action, he was about to create a great upheaval, when suddenly the Master arrived at the scene and quenched this fire which was about to engulf everyone.

Dr Yúnis Khán elaborates the story. The following is a summary translation of his words:

As we were approaching the anniversary of the Ascension of Bahá'u-'lláh, the friends seemed depressed with heavy hearts. Their usual enthusiasm and joy was not evident any more. There appeared to be some dark event on the horizon. The tone of the Master's utterances was also different. The friends attributed all this to the approaching anniversary of the Ascension. We were informed that on that anniversary the believers would commemorate the passing of Bahá'u'lláh by keeping vigil and staying awake the whole night, that before the dawn, they would all go to the Shrine of Bahá'u'lláh, and that on the following day a feast would be given in the name of Mírzá Áqá Ján.

On the evening of the anniversary, all the believers resident in Haifa and 'Akká who were able to take part attended a special commemoration meeting which was held in the Pilgrim House [at 'Akká]. Prayers and Tablets were chanted in the presence of the Master . . . Before the dawn we were summoned by the Master who gave to each one of us a glass containing rose-water and a lighted candle. In this way we all walked in an orderly manner in a procession towards the gate of the city on our way to the Shrine of Bahá'u'lláh. We were all in a state of grief and sorrow. The Master was walking along with us. He ordered two or three believers who had melodious voices to take turns and chant some prayers and poems of Bahá'u'lláh on the way. Our souls were truly carried away to the realms beyond as we walked with tearful eyes towards the Holy Shrine.

We all entered the Shrine, and as directed by the Master, we poured the rose-water on the flowerbed in the small garden and pushed the lighted candles into the soil. Grief-stricken and with the utmost humility we stood as the Master chanted the Tablet of Visitation. As He chanted, as always tears flowed from His eyes. We all wept aloud with Him and when He retired to another room, we could not control our weeping . . . After He had gone we kept on praying in the Shrine.

In the morning, we went to the pilgrim house situated on the ground floor of the Mansion,* had our own morning tea and rested for some time . . . Once again we went to the Shrine and prayed. Then we came

* This was before the Covenant-breakers took over these rooms. See p. 175 above.

out, had lunch and rested for a while. We all felt spiritually tired, our hearts were heavy and our thoughts agitated. We noticed the Covenant-breakers were actively moving around with a few non-Bahá'ís. It did not take long before we discovered their evil conspiracy designed to create a great upheaval for us.[4]

In order to appreciate the seriousness of the events which would have disrupted the affairs of the community and placed 'Abdu'l-Bahá's life in danger had the Covenant-breakers' plans materialized, we should note that when the Covenant-breakers realized that they were no longer in a position to take Mírzá Áqá Ján's life, as he had sought asylum in the house of 'Abdu'l-Bahá, they decided to exploit him instead for their own purposes. While he was living in the house of 'Abdu'l-Bahá, the Covenant-breakers secretly established contact with him and together they made a plan of action against 'Abdu'l-Bahá. Dr Yúnis Khán writes the story:

> . . . The Covenant-breakers decided to take advantage of Mírzá Áqá Ján's situation to create trouble and mischief [for 'Abdu'l-Bahá] . . . They succeeded in establishing a secret link with him and urged him to help them in stirring up sedition among believers. They maintained communication with him, and, over a long period, devised a plan to create discord and disturbance within the community. Since Mírzá Áqá Ján had been Bahá'u'lláh's amanuensis and had recorded the words of God as they were revealed, he was induced to arise and himself lay claim to divine revelation.
>
> As a result of their promptings, Mírzá Áqá Ján, this ill-fated man, worked for a long time to prepare some writings. In these he claimed that in a dream he had attained the presence of Bahá'u'lláh and had become the recipient of divine revelation and inspiration. These writings contained passages which invoked the wrath of God upon certain believers and were intended to be delivered to them.
>
> Mírzá Áqá Ján even claimed that he had received a Tablet from heaven written in green ink, in which he was commanded to save the Faith from the hands of infidels. The false accusations and calumnies with which he charged 'Abdu'l-Bahá, the Centre of the Covenant, were much worse than those which Covenant-breakers had already brought against Him. It was arranged that on a certain day, which should be the time of revolt, Mírzá Áqá Ján would hand all these papers written in the same style as his 'Revelation writings' to the Covenant-breakers who would then have them transcribed, as in the days of Bahá'u'lláh, in the handwriting of Mírzá Majdu'd-Dín*, and disseminated among the Bahá'ís.[5]

Dr Yúnis Khán in his memoirs goes on to explain that the Covenant-breakers had decided to put their plans into operation on the day of the anniversary of the Ascension of Bahá'u'lláh. They

* See above, pp. 164, 180.

knew that all the believers would then be assembled outside the Shrine of Bahá'u'lláh, and so they planned with Mírzá Áqá Ján that he should speak openly against 'Abdu'l-Bahá in that gathering, in order to create tension and unrest. At the same time the Covenant-breakers made arrangements for a certain Yaḥyá Ṭábúr Áqásí to be present on that day. He was a high-ranking government official hostile to 'Abdu'l-Bahá; he was heavily bribed by the Covenant-breakers and was very friendly towards them. His function was to remain out of sight until the expected disturbances had broken out, when he and his men would appear on the scene and take action against the believers. He would then send a report against 'Abdu'l-Bahá to the government authorities in Constantinople and request His banishment from the Holy Land. That would also give the Covenant-breakers the opportunity to take possession of the Shrine of Bahá'u'lláh which was in 'Abdu'l-Bahá's custody.

We turn again to the memoirs of Dr Yúnis K͟hán who describes the sequence of events which took place in the afternoon of that day:

> Having had afternoon tea, everyone was on the point of going to the Shrine of Bahá'u'lláh, when we heard that Mírzá Áqá Ján wished to speak and that there were chairs placed for us in front of the Mansion.
>
> This old man who was always prostrating himself at the feet of 'Abdu'l-Bahá was now standing on a stool so that he might be seen by all . . . As he spoke I noticed that he was far from coherent and I waited to catch the import of his words, but eventually became frustrated . . . I could see that he was filled with fear and was trembling, but I could hear only a few words now and then, such as: 'As I prostrated myself, I fell asleep . . .' 'The Blessed Beauty told me . . .' 'This letter in green ink was handed to me . . .' 'Why are you sitting idle?' 'Why, why?' Having abstained from sleep the night before, and having now to listen to such ridiculous talk, I became impatient and left. Mírzá Maḥmúd-i-Kás͟hání, a resident believer, protested to Mírzá Áqá Ján and soon there was an uproar.[6]

Dr Yúnis K͟hán adds that just then, Mírzá 'Alí-Akbar, son of Mis͟hkín-Qalam and a steadfast believer, hurriedly ran to 'Abdu'l-Bahá's room and informed Him of the incident. As soon as 'Abdu'l-Bahá arrived with an angry countenance, Mírzá Áqá Ján ran towards the Shrine and entered it shouting abuse, followed by the same Mírzá 'Alí-Akbar who confronted him inside. In the course of some struggle which ensued between the two, a few bundles of paper consisting of Mírzá Áqá Ján's writings, which had been tied around his waist and hidden inside his cloak, fell to the ground. By this time 'Abdu'l-Bahá had entered the Shrine and ordered Mírzá 'Alí-Akbar to take possession of the papers. These were written in Mírzá Áqá Ján's hand, imitating the style of Bahá'u'lláh's writings in a wrathful tone.

Addressed to many believers, they contained passages highly condemnatory of 'Abdu'l-Bahá, attacking Him in most shameful language.

As a result of 'Abdu'l-Bahá's presence, and as He went toward the Shrine, the believers followed Him and in absolute calm and with a sense of profound reverence stood outside. The hostile government officials headed by Yaḥyá Ṭábúr Áqásí, who were viewing these events from behind the windows of the room of Mírzá Muḥammad-'Alí and waiting for a struggle to ensue between the Bahá'ís and the Covenant-breakers so that they could charge the former with disturbance of the peace, were disappointed, as were their fellow-conspirators.

After this event Mírzá Áqá Ján openly threw in his lot with the Covenant-breakers and became one of their ablest supporters. Some time later, they arranged for him to reside in the very building of the Shrine of Bahá'u'lláh. He lived there till his death in 1901. As a result of this reprehensible action enabling such a perfidious figure as Mírzá Áqá Ján to live within the confines of the holiest spot on this earth, 'Abdu'l-Bahá did not permit the faithful believers to enter the Shrine during this period. He Himself used to pray outside the Holy Precincts.

One of the most beautiful scenes depicting 'Abdu'l-Bahá's profound humility, reverence and utter nothingness as He approached the Shrine of Bahá'u'lláh is described by Dr Yúnis Khán in his memoirs. He recounts details of 'Abdu'l-Bahá's visits to the Shrine of Bahá'u'lláh during the first few years after the Ascension of His beloved Father. 'Abdu'l-Bahá had directed the believers to visit the Holy Shrine in the afternoons of Fridays and Sundays and He Himself often joined them. Arrangements were made for them to be taken from 'Akká to Bahjí, usually in 'Abdu'l-Bahá's two carriages* which made several journeys to transport the entire community. The Master Himself often used to walk the entire distance. When the believers had all assembled, they would be summoned by 'Abdu'l-Bahá to enter the Shrine. One by one, with absolute devotion and in complete silence, they entered, while 'Abdu'l-Bahá filled the palm of the hand of each person with rose-water, with which they refreshed themselves. When everyone had entered, 'Abdu'l-Bahá would chant the Tablet of Visitation with such fervour and devotion that all hearts were uplifted and souls exhilarated.

Dr Yúnis Khán further describes that the visit to the Shrine of Bahá'u'lláh on Holy Days was much more ceremonious and was

* One larger carriage known as the 'American Carriage' could take up to nine, the other, only four.

conducted with such dignity and spirituality that the inhabitants of 'Akká and the neighbouring towns were deeply touched by the devotion of the Bahá'ís. The government officials, judges and other dignitaries were so impressed with the spirit which animated the believers as they walked together toward the Shrine of Bahá'u'lláh, that they longed to join their procession and partake of the spiritual bounties which were conferred upon them by 'Abdu'l-Bahá.

The following is a summary translation of Dr Yúnis Khán's account:

> On the day of the Bahá'í festivals, a large quantity of pots filled with flowers intended for the Shrine of Bahá'u'lláh were brought to the outer apartment of the house of 'Abdu'l-Bahá. All the pilgrims and resident believers dressed in their best clothes would assemble outside the house at a certain time (usually about two hours before sunset, or at other times when the heat of the sun was not unbearable). The procession to the Shrine would then start. The believers walked two by two, each person carrying a flower-pot on his shoulder. In later years, because of the opposition of the Covenant-breakers, the procession would start outside the gate of the city of 'Akká where the flower-pots were also placed.
>
> While carrying a flower-pot on His shoulders, the Blessed Person of 'Abdu'l-Bahá, like the commander of an army, walked sometimes in the front and sometimes beside the procession and issued various instructions on the way. Usually two or three people who had melodious voices were directed by Him to chant, one after the other, some poems of Bahá'u'lláh or other suitable verses related to a particular Bahá'í festival which famous Bahá'í poets had written. In this way, solemnly and with great dignity, they would walk slowly towards the Shrine of Bahá'u'lláh.
>
> As soon as that Holy Place became visible to the eye, all would halt at the behest of the Master . . . while someone would chant a prayer. To what spiritual worlds one would be carried at this time is impossible for me to describe . . . As the believers approached the Shrine, the flower-pots were handed in, and another prayer chanted. Then all would retire to a room where refreshments would be served. When all had rested and refreshed themselves, they would be summoned by 'Abdu'l-Bahá to enter the Shrine. The Tablet of Visitation would be chanted as usual by 'Abdu'l-Bahá. Then the believers were allowed to sit down to chant prayers and Tablets . . .[7]

Dr Yúnis Khán mentions that it was when the Covenant-breakers intensified their attacks against the Cause that they took possession of the room on the ground floor of the Mansion where the believers usually assembled. As a result, the believers moved to a house (pilgrim house) near the Mansion where the same facilities were provided for them. He recounts that as time went on, the Master obtained about one hundred large copper vessels for carrying water. Thus the believers were enabled to take water from a nearby spring and carry the vessels on their shoulders to water the flower-beds which 'Abdu'l-Bahá had made around the Shrine. He considered this service to be so meritorious that He Himself used to accompany the friends to the spring and carry a water-vessel on His own shoulder.

Ḥájí Mírzá Ḥaydar-'Alí recalls many scenes in which 'Abdu'l-Bahá was seen to be carrying heavy vessels of water on His shoulder for watering the flowers and shrubs in the garden around the Shrine. So strenuous was this task for the Master that sweat could be seen pouring from His face as He carried this heavy burden. The same chronicler has recounted that on several occasions, He was seen gathering soil, placing it inside His cloak and carrying the load on His shoulders to where He was making some flower-beds in the small garden He had created with His own hands in order to beautify the approaches to the Holy Shrine.

Dr Ḥabíb Mu'ayyad, another faithful secretary of 'Abdu'l-Bahá, writes in his memoirs that when a few years later a mechanical pump was installed in the garden near the Shrine, 'Abdu'l-Bahá used to pump water from the well with His own hands. Dr Mu'ayyad recalls that on a certain day in 1914, 'Abdu'l-Bahá, who was then seventy years of age, moved the handle of the pump for 19 minutes non-stop and stored a great deal of water for later use in the gardens!

Returning to the story of Mírzá Áqá Ján, we have noted that as long as he used the building of the Shrine of Bahá'u'lláh as his residence, the Master did not allow the believers to enter it. Instead of praying inside the Shrine, 'Abdu'l-Bahá, accompanied by the believers, would stand outside in the small garden and chant the Tablet of Visitation, following which 'Abdu'l-Bahá and the believers would sit on the ground near the Shrine and recite prayers. But Mírzá Áqá Ján, who was a very vulgar man, often caused a disturbance for those who had assembled to pray. Ḥájí Mírzá Ḥaydar-'Alí, recalling one of those occasions when 'Abdu'l-Bahá together with a large number of believers, including Ḥájí himself, had gone to pray at the Shrine of Bahá'u'lláh, recounts the following story:

> After saying the Tablet of Visitation and circumambulating the Holy Shrine, the Master, in great humility and self-effacement sat on the ground outside, and the friends sat in rows behind Him. As Mírzá Maḥmúd-i-Ká<u>sh</u>ání* began to chant a prayer, Mírzá Áqá Ján, wearing a white shroud, ran out of the Shrine bare-headed and bare-foot muttering some words and like a drunkard staggering to the right and to the left, came toward us. As he walked in the middle of the rows where we were sitting, one of the Covenant-breakers came by the order of the Centre of Sedition [Mírzá Muḥammad-'Alí] and took him away. When he left him,

* An old and faithful companion of 'Abdu'l-Bahá.

> Mírzá Áqá Ján came back again. The same person took him away for the second time. These comings and goings were repeated five or six times. At the end, the order was issued from the same Source of Sedition to hold him in front of the Shrine. Thereupon, Mírzá Áqá Ján, turning his face toward the assembled friends, began to hurl unspeakable insults at them in loud and offensive language.[8]

In his memoirs, Ḥájí Mírzá Ḥaydar-'Alí quotes some of the words which this notorious man had shouted at the top of his voice in the presence of 'Abdu'l-Bahá, words which were not only vulgar and offensive but which were blasphemous in relation to Bahá'u'lláh whom He had served for almost forty years. Such a man was honoured and respected by the Covenant-breakers and was regarded as one of their best agents for fomenting discord and spreading sedition within the community.

CHAPTER SIXTEEN

Discrediting the Centre of the Covenant

As Mírzá Muḥammad-'Alí's campaign of discrediting 'Abdu'l-Bahá in the eyes of the Bahá'ís gathered momentum, he began to direct his attention to the non-Bahá'í public, fertile ground for spreading false accusations against Him. It was much easier to poison the minds of those who, although they knew the Master, were not spiritually close to Him. The Covenant-breakers invented several stories of different kinds and began to propagate them among influential people, those who held important positions in 'Akká and neighbouring towns. Thus they completely disregarded the interests of the Faith they claimed to believe in, and acted in a manner that clearly demonstrated their disbelief in Bahá'u'lláh and their denunciation of His Cause.

One of the most shameful pieces of propaganda was their accusation that 'Abdu'l-Bahá had cut off their livelihood by withholding funds and provisions to which they were entitled. Nothing could have been further from the truth. As has been stated before, 'Abdu'l-Bahá used to send to Mírzá Muḥammad-'Alí a great part of the funds which He received from the believers in Persia. He also had made ample arrangements for all members of Bahá'u'lláh's family to receive food and other provisions, amounting to many times more than their needs. Whereas the Master and His family lived a life of austerity, His unfaithful brothers and the rest of Bahá'u'lláh's family lived luxuriously in the Mansion of Bahjí. Despite all this, Mírzá Muḥammad-'Alí and his younger brothers used to complain to people that they were destitute and their families on the verge of starvation.

It must be remembered that in all the years that 'Abdu'l-Bahá lived in 'Akká no one except a few enemies had ever doubted His exalted character, His magnanimity, His loving kindness and generosity towards the inhabitants of the Holy Land in general and 'Akká in particular. He was a compassionate father to all, a refuge for the poor, a true guide for the rich and a wise counsellor for the rulers of the land. But now because of the falsehoods invented by the

Covenant-breakers, people who were hitherto great admirers of 'Abdu'l-Bahá became at first confused and in the course of time when similar accusations were repeated, became disillusioned and lost their faith and confidence in Him altogether.

In order to deceive people into believing that he had become destitute, Mírzá Muḥammad-'Alí used to send his sons, dressed in rags, to the homes of important people where they begged for money. They pretended that they did not have even a loaf of bread in their home and that the whole family was on the verge of starvation. In spite of the fact that they were living a life of luxury due to the care and protection of 'Abdu'l-Bahá, they were yet accusing Him of withholding their source of livelihood. Dr Yúnis Khán tells an interesting story, summarised below:

> One of the deceitful schemes contrived by Covenant-breakers after the ascension of Bahá'u'lláh was that, on the one hand, they placed a great financial burden on 'Abdu'l-Bahá by receiving exorbitant sums of money from Him, and on the other, claimed poverty, destitution and hunger. At the same time they spread false rumours among the believers (in Persia) that some of 'Abdu'l-Bahá's companions had stolen His seals, with which they were issuing receipts for Ḥuququ'lláh* and pocketing the proceeds. The Master often told us that the Covenant-breakers had done this so that the believers might stop sending funds and cause financial hardships for Him.
>
> Their claims of poverty however, became so serious . . . that eventually they began to beg. They continued in carrying out this shameful practice of begging from people both high and low, and consequently they brought about great degradation for the Cause of God . . . Whenever they received a gift of money from the Master they would intensify their begging operation. When the news of such activities reached 'Abdu'l-Bahá, He would usually be overcome with grief and sorrow. To cite an example:
>
> One afternoon, when a number of visitors and resident believers had assembled in the Bírúní [outer apartment] of the house of 'Abdu'l-Bahá, a certain respectable Shaykh (his name I do not recall) arrived. He was well known to the Master and trusted by Him. He was held in high esteem by the people of Syria and Palestine and was a successful merchant in these regions. Since he was a pious man, he had been appointed by the Ottoman government as the Mufti of 'Akká, and was a centre of attention to all the people. He sat next to the Master and after a brief exchange of greetings he began to convey some information to 'Abdu'l-Bahá by whispering into His ear.
>
> At this time everyone was silently gazing upon the face of the Master. His countenance displayed various modes of expression – anger, astonishment and a mild smile. When the whispering came to an end, 'Abdu'l-Bahá . . . asked the Shaykh to recount his story to the assembled friends

* For information about Ḥuqúqu'lláh, see *The Revelation of Bahá'u'lláh*, vol. 4.

. . . which he did in these words: 'A certain honoured person [one of the dignitaries known to the Master] came to see me in my office this morning . . . I noticed he was very sad and depressed . . . After much persuasion on my part he said: "A person ['Abdu'l-Bahá] whom up to now I considered to be equal to a Prophet of God is, today, in my sight . . ." He did not finish the sentence.

'After much insistence on my part, promising that I should keep his story confidential, he continued: "Today I met Mírzá Muḥammad-'Alí. He complained bitterly about his brother, Abbás Effendi.* He told me many stories which deeply surprised and saddened me . . . This poor man is now destitute . . . He is in need of daily bread. Mírzá Muḥammad-'Alí told me that his children were today crying for a piece of bread and he could not provide for them . . . I was so shaken and upset hearing Mírzá Muḥammad-'Alí's story that I was about to give him some money, but decided instead to send him some wheat . . ."

'When his story was finished, not wishing to disclose to my friend that Mírzá Muḥammad-'Alí had a credit account with me, and that I keep his money for him in my bank, I said to him, "There is no need for you to send wheat or other provisions. Please go and tell Mírzá Muḥammad-'Alí that he can come to me for funds up to a thousand Liras." My friend, who did not understand me, said, "Mírzá Muḥammad-'Alí is a respectable person, he will never beg for money."

"Realizing that my friend could not see that Mírzá Muḥammad-'Alí had been lying to him, I decided to disclose to him the true situation. I said to him, "Please go to Mírzá Muḥammad-'Alí and tell him that the Shaykh says that he should take a fraction of the sixty Liras he received the other day from his office and purchase some bread for his children." My friend still could not understand, he said, "If Mírzá Muḥammad-'Alí had even a piece of bread to eat, he would not have come to me in such a state of degradation and humility." At this point I opened my safe and showed him a cheque which bore Mírzá Muḥammad-'Alí's signature and which I had cashed for him only the day before. I said, "Now that you have seen the cheque with his signature go and tell Mírzá Muḥammad-'Alí that he should be ashamed of himself feigning poverty and resorting to beggary. Tell him that no one will be deceived by his imposture."

'Upon seeing the cheque, my friend was stunned. He was overcome by an inner agitation which showed itself outwardly in his face. He was so highly disturbed that for a few minutes he remained speechless. Then, with tears flowing down his face, he said, "What a fool I have been. I was deceived by this Satan, and uttered some disparaging remarks about my Lord. Now how can I atone for this transgression." He then asked me to come here and beg forgiveness for him, saying "I will go myself later to the presence of 'Abdu'l-Bahá and will kiss the hem of His garment." '†

Before leaving us, the Shaykh said to 'Abdu'l-Bahá: 'My Lord, in this world you have no enemy except Your own brother.'

* 'Abdu'l-Bahá.

† This action signifies the expression of the utmost humility toward a person.

When the Shaykh departed, the Master spoke about the Covenant-breakers and said that they had girded up their loins for the extinction of the Cause of God. He spoke in this vein for a short time and when He saw that the friends were all becoming sad, He changed the subject and with His soul-stirring utterances, He gave us the glad tidings of the ascendency of the Cause of God in the future. He categorically stated that ere long these dark clouds would be dispersed, the domain of the Covenant-breakers would be rolled up, and assured us that the Cause of God would not become the plaything of children. He told us to ponder upon the activities of the Covenant-breakers. Because of their enmity toward Him, they go through so much degradation and abasement, appear in the guise of beggars, and solicit alms for themselves. Yet, they have achieved nothing except to bring upon themselves further humiliation and dishonour.[1]

There are innumerable accounts left by 'Abdu'l-Bahá's friends describing similar activities by the Covenant-breakers. Ḥájí 'Alí Yazdí* who was one of the resident Bahá'ís in 'Akká during the days of Bahá'u'lláh and 'Abdu'l-Bahá and lived long to serve the Cause of God during Shoghi Effendi's ministry, recounts a similar story. He writes:

One day when the Master received from 'Adasíyyih a large quantity of wheat, the annual income from a certain property, He sent it all to the Mansion of Bahjí, but Mírzá Muḥammad-'Alí returned it to Him. At the same time, he sent a petition to the local government complaining that 'Abdu'l-Bahá owed him his share of the annual income of that same property which he had earlier refused to accept, and pleaded with the authorities to intervene so that he could remedy a serious shortage of food in his household.

This ignoble action was so manifestly provocative that even some of his supporters warned him that government intervention would harm the Cause. He is reported to have said, 'Which harm is greater, this one or 'Abdu'l-Bahá's claim that He is a Manifestation of God, that Bahá'u-'lláh and the Báb are His forerunners, and that He is determined to eliminate the Cause of Bahá'u'lláh and establish instead His own Cause and new teachings?'

This petition was sent purely to humiliate the Master. The officer in charge sent for 'Abdu'l-Bahá and acquainted Him of His brother's claim. Whereupon, 'Abdu'l-Bahá summoned Áqá Riḍá Qannád who was in charge of His domestic affairs and who in the presence of the officer produced the books and determined the full annual income, which amounted to five hundred and twenty Liras. It was further determined that Mírzá Muḥammad-'Alí's share was only eighty Liras. But 'Abdu'l-Bahá informed the officer that upon getting a receipt from Mírzá Muḥammad-'Alí, He would be glad to pay him the full amount of five

* See above, p. 184.

hundred and twenty Liras to be transferred to him through the government officer. A messenger was sent by the officer to inform Mírzá Muḥammad-'Alí of the offer and to ask him to sign the document.

A day later, 'Abdu'l-Bahá was again invited to the government office and handed a receipt, which, although it was issued by Mírzá Muḥammad-'Alí, bore a signature which had no resemblance to his. 'Abdu'l-Bahá refused to accept it and the officer in charge rebuked the messenger and ordered him to return to Mírzá Muḥammad-'Alí and get a genuine signature this time. When the document arrived a second time 'Abdu'l-Bahá was again invited to the office. Again it was the same story. The signature was not genuine. This time the officer became very angry because of Mírzá Muḥammad-'Alí's deceitful action. He apologized to 'Abdu'l-Bahá and offered to sign the receipt himself and send the money to its recipient – an offer which was accepted by Him.

All these things were done to inflict humiliation upon the Master and to hurt Him as much as possible. For many years the Covenant-breakers carried out this type of campaign to discredit 'Abdu'l-Bahá, not knowing that falsehood can never survive and that the power of truth will prevail in the end. Of course, the Cause of God became victorious through the potency of the Covenant, and the Covenant-breakers by their actions extinguished their own spiritual life. But in the meantime, until they finally became impotent, they created a great disturbance within the community. Not satisfied with sowing the seeds of disunity among the Bahá'ís, not content with spreading falsehood among the inhabitants of 'Akká and the neighbouring lands, they took their tales of woe to foreign nationals too. Disguised as paupers, they claimed to have been treated cruelly by 'Abdu'l-Bahá.

One such person in whom the Covenant-breakers confided was Rosamond Dale Owen, the wife of Laurence Oliphant, the Victorian traveller and writer who lived several years in the Holy Land. Mrs Oliphant, a staunch Christian committed to the defence of the Christian religion, became alarmed at the progress of the Faith, as can be seen from her book *My Perilous Life in Palestine*. Mírzá Badí'u'lláh deceitfully complained to her that 'Abdu'l-Bahá had usurped his rights and those of his brothers and that consequently he was in dire financial need. He and Mírzá Muḥammad-'Alí made other preposterous claims, all designed to discredit 'Abdu'l-Bahá. These brothers knew only too well that Mrs Oliphant was very unhappy about the growth of the Faith and its spread among Christians in the West; they hoped that their slanderous remarks about 'Abdu'l-Bahá might serve as ammunition in her opposition to the Faith and to the Master as its Head. And this is exactly the way it happened.

The following few passages gleaned from Mrs Oliphant's book show the extent to which the calumnies and falsehoods which Mírzá Badí'u'lláh had uttered played into the hands of its author, who used them to discredit the Cause of Bahá'u'lláh.

> He [Mírzá Badí'u'lláh] was a political prisoner in St. Jean d'Acre for a number of years, and I found that he and his family of seven persons were about to starve . . .
>
> Abbas Effendi and his family live comfortably, whereas Bedi-Allah [sic] and his family would almost have starved had I not come to the rescue . . .
>
> I understand that Mohammed Ali [sic] the second son, is as great a sufferer, having been saved from extreme poverty only by the exertions of some relatives in America . . .
>
> If the numerous Christian followers of Abbas Effendi, in England and America, consider this a noble course of action, their ideas of brotherly love, must be, so it seems to me, somewhat peculiar . . .
>
> I understand that there are at least three million Christians who are followers and admirers of Abbas Effendi. This scarcely seems possible, but if it be true, then it is for these people to determine whether a man of the character of Abbas Effendi, letting his brother almost starve while he lived comfortably, is fitted to teach Christians a more Christ-like mode of life.[2]

Much has happened since these uncomplimentary remarks were written about the Master. It is evident today that the darkness of falsehood has been vanquished by the light of truth. The Christ-like Person of 'Abdu'l-Bahá, the perfect Exemplar of the teachings of Bahá'u'lláh and a stainless Mirror reflecting His light, established a noble example for man to follow in this Dispensation. These disparaging remarks about the Master, whose virtuous life of service to humanity has been acclaimed by friends and foe alike, would have brought great satisfaction to the Covenant-breakers, had it not been for the fact that by the time Mrs Oliphant's book was published they had become powerless and were on the verge of extinction.

Another act of treachery which that prime mover of mischief Mírzá Muḥammad-'Alí perpetrated soon after the defection of Mírzá Áqá Ján was the drawing up of an official indictment against 'Abdu'l-Bahá replete with preposterous accusations. This he did with the help of Ṭábúr Áqásí,* the chief of police whom he had bribed heavily. The case was taken to a court in 'Akká; there were five main complaints which the sons of Bahá'u'lláh lodged against 'Abdu'l-Bahá. They claimed that:

1. Bahá'u'lláh was only a holy man who did not claim to be a prophet. He spent His time in seclusion, prayer and meditation,

* See above pp. 188–9.

whereas 'Abdu'l-Bahá for political ends had exalted the station of His Father to that of a Supreme Manifestation of God, and of the Essence of Divinity.

2. 'Abdu'l-Bahá did not deal with them in accordance with the provisions of Bahá'u'lláh's Will and Testament.
3. They had been deprived of their right to inherit a vast estate left behind by their Father, Bahá'u'lláh.
4. None of the gifts or funds which were sent in the name of Bahá'u'lláh were given to them.
5. 'Abdu'l-Bahá had caused thousands of their friends in Persia and India to turn against them and shun their company.

Such reckless action by members of Bahá'u'lláh's family against the Cause which they privately claimed to uphold, whose Author they knew was not just a 'holy man', but One who had proclaimed His mission to the kings and rulers of the world as the Promised One of all ages, exposes the hypocrisy of the Covenant-breakers, their treachery and their utter faithlessness in the Cause of God. These characteristics are true of the Covenant-breakers of the past, present and future. They are cut off from the tree of the Cause and as such are devoid of faith and spiritual life. They never shirk from employing any means, however degrading and nefarious, to undermine the foundations of the Cause and rob the believers of their faith.

In taking his case to court, Mírzá Muḥammad-'Alí never imagined that in defence of the Cause 'Abdu'l-Bahá would go so far as to read aloud the contents of the *Kitáb-i-'Ahd*, Bahá'u'lláh's Will and Testament, in the courtroom. By reading parts of this momentous document, 'Abdu'l-Bahá made it clear that the station of Bahá'u'lláh was not merely that of a 'holy man' who spent His time in prayer and meditation. Rather, he was the Lord of all men calling the peoples of the world to carry out His teachings and exhorting them to unity and fellowship.

It is reported that in the presence of the officials 'Abdu'l-Bahá openly declared His own position as the Centre of the Covenant of Bahá'u'lláh, the Promoter of His Cause and the Interpreter of His teachings, the One to whom the Aghṣán, the Afnán, the kindred of Bahá'u'lláh and all the believers must turn. He explained that since the Covenant-breakers had arisen against Him they had violated the provisions of Bahá'u'lláh's Will, and consequently the believers had cut off their relationship with them. He is reported to have told the officials that for four years He had not disclosed their rebellion to the believers, but that the Covenant-breakers themselves had announced to the Bahá'í world their opposition to Him and had thereby cut themselves off from the Bahá'í community.

He refuted the other claims of His brothers just as forcefully. Quoting the *Kitáb-i-'Ahd*, He demonstrated that they were not entitled to receive any of the Funds of the Faith which were donated by the believers, for Bahá'u'lláh in that document states: '. . . God hath not granted them any right to the property of others'. On the question of inheritance, 'Abdu'l-Bahá stated that Bahá'u'lláh had lived a life of austerity and had left no estate for anyone to inherit. He is reported to have quoted the celebrated passage from the *Kitáb-i-'Ahd*, 'Earthly treasures We have not bequeathed, nor have We added such cares as they entail. By God! in earthly riches fear is hidden and peril is concealed.'

However, 'Abdu'l-Bahá confirmed that there were two priceless items in Bahá'u'lláh's possession – one a rare copy of the *Qur'án* and the other a set of prayer beads – and that both these items of inestimable value had been seen by a few dignitaries of 'Akká. These two unique possessions of Bahá'u'lláh had been taken by Mírzá Muḥammad-'Alí and were kept by him. These and other personal effects of Bahá'u'lláh such as His garments were distributed by him to various officials to serve as chattels of bribery and at the same time provide a means of humiliating 'Abdu'l-Bahá. For Mírzá Muḥammad-'Alí knew that the Master considered Bahá'u'lláh's personal belongings to be sacred and that they should be preserved with reverence. Therefore, in order to hurt 'Abdu'l-Bahá, he gave Bahá'u'lláh's prayer beads to one of the enemies of the Faith and persuaded him to try to show them to Him. It is reported that one day this man showed the beads to 'Abdu'l-Bahá and asked Him if He could put a price on them, to which He responded that their value depended on who was using them.

On another occasion Mírzá Muḥammad-'Alí gave Bahá'u'lláh's cloak and a pair of His spectacles to the Deputy Governor of Haifa as a bribe and urged him to wear them when he visited the Master. This he did, and appeared before 'Abdu'l-Bahá brazenly spectacled and wearing Bahá'u'lláh's cloak. Soon afterwards however, this man was dismissed from his post and met with some misfortune. He then went to 'Abdu'l-Bahá, begged forgiveness for his shameful behaviour and confessed that he had been urged by Mírzá Muḥammad-'Alí to act as he did. 'Abdu'l-Bahá showered His kindness and generosity upon him, and helped him to resolve his difficulties. This was always 'Abdu'l-Bahá's way – to extend a helping hand with all His love to those enemies who had wronged Him and inflicted sufferings upon Him. The above episode of the court case was widely publicized and once again the Covenant-breakers were frustrated in their actions and failed to humiliate the Master.

CHAPTER SEVENTEEN

'Abdu'l-Bahá in Action

WHILE all these calumnies were circulating in 'Akká and the neighbouring areas, 'Abdu'l-Bahá, through His exemplary life, dispelled the gloom resulting from the falsehoods which had been surrounding the community of the Most Great Name. During this time, when He Himself was the target of dire afflictions and sufferings, He cast upon everyone around Him the light of truth, of divine virtues and spiritual teachings.

Although we can never understand the reality of Bahá'u'lláh, the Manifestation of God, or of 'Abdu'l-Bahá, the Most Great Mystery of God and the Centre of His Covenant, we can observe some of their superhuman characteristics. Unlike a human being whose mind can only deal with one subject at a time, 'Abdu'l-Bahá, who had all the powers of Bahá'u'lláh conferred upon Him, was free from this limitation. Usually a person becomes overwhelmed when afflicted by sufferings or faced with insurmountable obstacles. Under such circumstances even men of outstanding ability show their weakness and reveal their human frailty. They try to cope with one problem at a time, and they often seek the help of experts and advisors to help them make a decision.

Not so with 'Abdu'l-Bahá. In the first place He acted independently, for no individual was qualified to advise or assist Him in His manifold activities. His soul was not bound by the limitations of the world of humanity, and His mind was not overwhelmed when faced with a host of problems simultaneously. In the midst of calamities, when the ablest of men would have succumbed to pressure, He remained detached, while directing His attention to whatever He desired. This is one of the distinguishing characteristics of the Manifestation of God and His Chosen Ones. Bahá'u'lláh has explained this in the *Kitáb-i-Íqán*, quoting the celebrated Islamic passage: 'Nothing whatsoever keepeth Him from being occupied with any other thing.'*

* See *The Revelation of Bahá'u'lláh*, vol. I, pp. 262–3 and below, p. 206.

Although the Manifestations of God and these specially chosen ones such as 'Abdu'l-Bahá feel the agony of sufferings inflicted on them by their enemies, and their human nature experiences pain both mental and physical, their souls are not affected by any man-made affliction. They abide in a realm far beyond the ken of mortal men, and wield the spiritual sceptre of authority and power with which they rule over humanity. These powers are at first hidden from the eyes of most people, but with the passage of time humanity observes the influence of their word and the spread of their Faith.

Thus we observe that at a time when 'Abdu'l-Bahá was suffering grievously at the hands of the Covenant-breakers and was continually confronted by the implacable enmity of his unfaithful brothers, He was occupied day and night with the promotion of the Cause throughout the world. Unaffected by the onslaught of the Covenant-breakers, His love and encouragement continued to be showered in great profusion upon the believers in both the East and the West. No amount of opposition was capable of deterring Him from His purpose. At a time when He was being attacked on every side by the Covenant-breakers, and the believers were dispirited and disconsolate, He cheered the friends, strengthened their faith, assured them of the invincibility of the Covenant and widened their vision to see the greatness of the Cause and its ultimate victory.

'Abdu'l-Bahá's trusted secretary and confidant Dr Yúnis Khán has left to posterity his reminiscences of the Master during this most turbulent period of His Ministry. The following is a summary translation of his celebrated memoirs.

> In those days when the showers of sedition and conspiracy were raining down, and the storms of tests and trials were blowing with fury, a fierce hurricane was raging around the Ark of the Cause of God. But it was the Centre of the Covenant who was at the helm. Through the potency of His words and the authority of His directives, He was navigating the Sacred Ark toward the shores of salvation. The sway of His pen and the influence of His utterances were both means whereby He was guiding the people to the highway of blissfulness and prosperity. In the same way that the traces of His pen are imprinted for all time upon the pages of His Tablets, His blessed words were engraved upon the hearts of those who were privileged to hear Him and their recollections were transmitted from heart to heart. His utterances in those days were as varied as His Writings.
>
> In His talks He often used to share with us many glad tidings of the future progress of the Cause of God. He likened our days of anguish and sadness to the early days of Christianity and Islám which had also been very turbulent; but these religions were later exalted in the land. Similarly, He assured us in clear terms of the ascendancy and victory of

the Cause of Bahá'u'lláh . . . His utterances on the future of the Cause were delivered with eloquence and effectiveness and were imbued with a power and authority born of the heavenly realms such that they penetrated the depths of our hearts. Our souls were so assured and uplifted that we, His hearers, did not have to imagine forthcoming events. Rather, we found ourselves experiencing all the bountiful happenings of the future. The eternal glory and ultimate successes of the Cause of God were so vividly portrayed by Him that the passage of time was irrelevant, for we saw the past, present and the future at the same time. All of this was because the promises of the Master concerning the ascendancy of the Cause were absolutely clear, explicit and irrevocable . . . Now [after a few decades] many of the prophecies of 'Abdu'l-Bahá have already been fulfilled, for instance who could ever have imagined that the small village of Haifa would become, within so short a period, as foreshadowed by 'Abdu'l-Bahá, a great city and an important port . . .[1]

Dr Yúnis Khán describes how 'Abdu'l-Bahá, in the midst of intense suffering at the hand of the Covenant-breakers, earnestly prayed that yet more suffering and hardship might descend upon Him. As tribulations increased, His desire to bear them increased correspondingly. He often used to speak about illustrious martyrs such as Varqá, and then, in a joyous and excited tone, He would express His heartfelt desire to lay down His life in the path of Bahá'u'lláh. So moving were His words that all His loved ones who heard Him were overcome with emotion, their souls uplifted and their hearts filled with a new spirit of sacrifice in their readiness to follow in the footsteps of their Beloved.

Another of 'Abdu'l-Bahá's exhortations, according to Dr Yúnis Khán, concerned the ordinance of teaching the Faith versus steadfastness in the Covenant. Of course, teaching the Cause of God is the most meritorious of all deeds and is described by Him as 'the head corner-stone of the foundation itself'. Teaching the Cause is the primary and the most vital duty of a believer. Yet during those perilous times when the Covenant-breakers were actively engaged in spreading their venomous propaganda within the community, and were trying with all their power to break up the unity of the Bahá'ís, the Master advised the believers that deepening the friends in the subject of the Covenant and assisting them to remain firm in their faith took precedence over teaching. He explained that Bahá'u'lláh had ordained that when serving the Faith one must act with wisdom, taking into consideration the particular circumstances existing at a given time.

He likened the work of the friends in those days to that of building a house while the Covenant-breakers were trying to raze it to the ground. In such circumstances, instead of adding another storey to the house, all efforts must be directed to the protection of the structure itself. He assured those who were privileged to hear Him of the advent of a day when the foundation of the Cause of God would be secure and safe, and promised that when that time came He would direct the believers to engage once again in actively teaching the Cause of God.

During those turbulent years when the Covenant-breakers were engaged in making mischief in the Holy Land, the believers' only refuge was the shelter of 'Abdu'l-Bahá's presence. He could be likened to a vast ocean at whose shores His loved ones gathered in order to receive a portion of its life-giving waters. Each believer received his share in accordance with his capacity. Some who had come empty-handed merely enjoyed seeing that vast and fathomless ocean. Others who had more capacity had come with a vessel in hand, and each one received a draught of the water of life. Still others, yet unsatisfied, immersed themselves in that ocean and found some of the inestimable pearls of wisdom and knowledge which lay concealed in its depths.

That ocean – the person of 'Abdu'l-Bahá – appeared in various forms on different occasions. At times it was calm, at others surging with mighty waves. When it was calm, every beholder would find himself in a state of joy and tranquillity. When its billowing waves surged, it cast gems of inestimable value upon the shores. At such times, the utterances of 'Abdu'l-Bahá captivated the hearts of His loved ones, who were carried away into spiritual realms utterly oblivious of their own selves and wholly devoted to Him. The effect of the presence of 'Abdu'l-Bahá upon the believers cannot be adequately explained by the above analogy. Suffice it to say that the pure in heart who attained His presence were transformed into a new creation; they became spiritual giants who championed the Cause of the Covenant and defended it with heroism and sacrifice.

Dr Yúnis Khán in his memoirs asserts that the mere glance of 'Abdu'l-Bahá upon a believer released mysterious forces which at times were capable of transforming the life of the individual. This is a summary of his observations as he describes the various effects of the Master's glances:

> One glance, which thankfully did not appear except on rare occasions, was that of wrath and anger. It reflected the wrath of God from which one had to flee for refuge to Him . . .
>
> There was a glance of love and compassion which was evident at all times. It conferred life and brought joy to everyone . . .
>
> Another glance was that which enchanted the hearts and attracted the souls. I observed many a time in the narrow and dark streets of 'Akká, that with one look, the strangers were so attracted to 'Abdu'l-Bahá as to

follow Him until He dismissed them. This particular glance has many aspects which I am not in a position to describe . . .

There was a glance by which He expressed His satisfaction and pleasure to a person, as if to say, 'I am pleased with you.' This glance was shown to both the obedient and the rebellious.

Another glance was one which released great spiritual potency. If ever He cast such a glance upon a person, that person's greatest wish would have been granted, if he so desired. But who is it that in such an atmosphere could have any desire other than to seek the good-pleasure of His Lord? I myself have seen this type of a glance many a time. In this mood, one longs for sufferings in the path of God. And, some like Varqá have, under the influence of this glance, gone to the field of martyrdom.*

There was a glance through which a person realized that all that was hidden in his heart, whether of the past or of the future, was known to the Master.

Above all, there was a glance which, if ever it was directed to an individual, caused that individual to become the recipient of knowledge and understanding. At one time we all saw two believers who were enchanted by this glance and became the possessors of divine knowledge. One was Fáḍil-i-Shírází,† the other Shaykh 'Alí-Akbar-i-Qúchání . . .‡[2]

It can be seen from these reminiscences that the person of 'Abdu'l-Bahá strengthened the faith of His loved ones who attained His presence through the spiritual powers conferred upon Him by Bahá'u'lláh, and thus enabled them to withstand the onslaught of the Covenant-breakers. This privilege was the experience of those believers who were resident in the Holy Land and the pilgrims who arrived from time to time. But the great majority of the friends who were living in other parts of the world received their spiritual sustenance from the Master through the innumerable Tablets which flowed from His pen.

Again we turn to Dr Yúnis Khán's memoirs for a glimpse of the manner in which 'Abdu'l-Bahá wrote Tablets or dictated them in the presence of the believers.

There are various accounts by Bahá'í pilgrims and visitors concerning the revelation of Tablets by 'Abdu'l-Bahá. Some have said that at the time of revelation their souls were transported into realms of the spirit while their whole beings were shaking with excitement. Others have testified that they saw with their own eyes that while the Master was entertaining believers and non-believers and speaking to them in Turkish he was, at the same time, dictating His Tablets in Arabic and the secretary was taking down His words. Some have said that they saw the Master Himself writing Tablets in Arabic while speaking in Turkish to the

* For a story of his life see *The Revelation of Bahá'u'lláh*, vol. 4.
† An outstanding teacher of the Faith.
‡ He was martyred during 'Abdu'l-Bahá's Ministry.

friends. Others have seen Him writing a Tablet in His own hand in Persian, while at the same time dictating one to His secretary in Arabic. Some speak of the unusual speed of His writing as well as the majesty of His utterances. There are no exaggerations in the above statements. Each person has described his observations in accordance with his own understanding . . .

The revelation of Tablets had a greater effect on the believers than other experiences in the presence of 'Abdu'l-Bahá. His Tablets were written in the following manner. Whenever 'Abdu'l-Bahá was freed from His various daily engagements, He summoned Mírzá Núru'd-Dín, His secretary, and began dictating to him. At times He would simultaneously review the Tablets previously revealed, inscribed and ready for His signature. It was on such occasions that He wrote and dictated at the same time. He was truly the embodiment of the verse: 'Nothing whatsoever keepeth Him from being occupied with any other thing.' There was no thought or action which could distract Him.

As the revelation of Tablets continued, the believers, who were usually gathered in the room below, or in the Pilgrim House, or walking in the streets of 'Akká, were all eager to attain the presence of the Master and hear His words as He dictated to His secretary in answer to letters He had received. When summoned, they would arrive and be seated. After greeting them lovingly, the revelation of Tablets would begin. Sometimes He would dictate in a loud, clear voice, sometimes He would chant His dictation in the same melodious voice as He chanted the Tablet of Visitation at the Shrine of Bahá'u'lláh. As a result of this marvellous experience, those present were immersed in the sea of astonishment. Some would find that their questions were answered, and some learned a lesson from this heavenly experience. As the revelation of the Tablets continued, all became exhilarated and turned their hearts and souls to the Kingdom on high.

But alas, such meetings of fellowship and love would often be interrupted by visiting strangers. The house of the Master was open to all. There being no guards posted at the gate, people would come in. If the new arrivals were not antagonistic toward the Faith and were worthy to listen to the exalted words of the Master, then after welcoming them and showing His loving kindness to each one, He would resume dictating His words to His secretary. But if they were not worthy, or if they overcrowded the room, the Master dismissed the believers and dealt with the situation as He deemed proper. This was how 'Abdu'l-Bahá dictated to His secretary.

But most of the time He wrote the Tablets with His own hand in the circumstances described above. Whenever He was free, He would take the pen and begin to write. But as He did not wish the believers who were assembled in the room to become tired or bored, He would talk to them while He was writing . . . As others arrived, He would welcome each and shower upon all His loving kindness, and yet His pen was moving. Occasionally he would read aloud what He was writing. There were also periods of silence. The Master, as He continued to write, often broke the silence saying: 'Talk among yourselves, I will be able to hear you.' However, the believers were so carried away by His peerless Beauty that they would remain silent.

Only the new arrivals, those who had not been invited, such as some Arab Shaykh, or an Ottoman dignitary, would break the silence. After the usual greetings and words of welcome which befitted the guests, the pen of 'Abdu'l-Bahá would begin to move while He conversed with them. Whenever there was silence, He would ask the newly arrived guest to broach a subject and discuss it together. Then He Himself entered the conversation . . . Sometimes the guests conducted heated arguments and yet throughout the noise and clamour they created, the Master's Pen kept on moving on His Tablets . . .

My purpose in describing the revelation of the Tablets in detail is to enable the people to appreciate the manner in which these Tablets, which uplift the souls and exhilarate the hearts, were written under such difficult and trying circumstances. Another amazing aspect of these Tablets is that it was not only the believers, who heard the Master reciting them, who were inspired, but also the deniers and mischief-makers, who were deeply moved and humbled by this experience.[3]

CHAPTER EIGHTEEN

Covenant-breaking in Persia

SOON after the ascension of Bahá'u'lláh, when Mírzá Muḥammad-'Alí's rebellion became known in private circles within the family, secret contacts were established between him and a number of eminent teachers of the Faith in Persia, those who were corrupt and ambitious individuals and who lusted for leadership in the community. Thus, from the very start, the Arch-breaker of the Covenant sowed the seeds of dissension in the hearts of those who were egotistical by nature and were disposed to disloyalty and faithlessness. Some among these misguided people played their part very well in that for a number of years they did not disclose to anyone their true intentions. They mingled with the faithful believers and posed as loyal defenders of the Covenant.

Notorious among them was Jamál-i-Burújirdí, the most prominent among the Covenant-breakers in Persia. It will be helpful for the study of the spread of Covenant-breaking in Persia to dwell at some length on the infamous life of this man who considered himself the chief representative of Mírzá Muḥammad-'Alí in that country.*

Before embracing the Faith during the Ministry of Bahá'u'lláh, Jamál was an accomplished Muslim clergyman. He was knowledgeable, a notable orator. When he accepted the Faith, he did not relinquish those practices which were characteristic of the Muslim clergy. For instance, he continued to wear cleric's robes, and never gave up the trait of superiority and pride which had been ingrained upon his character in his former days. He continued his customary Islamic practice of making his hands available for those believers who would wish to kiss them. He used to explain that although Bahá'u'lláh had forbidden the kissing of hands in this Dispensation, Jamál had decided that in the circumstances prevailing at the time, such a practice would be conducive to the exaltation of the Cause! Yet, in spite of all this, when he entered the Faith, the believers in

* We have already told the stories of Jamál-i-Burújirdí and Siyyid Mihdíy-i-Dahají in *The Revelation of Bahá'u'lláh*, vol. 2; a certain amount of repetition is inevitable here.

Persia gathered around him, for he was a man of learning and knowledge.

It must be understood that in those days the people of Persia – most of whom were illiterate – were brought up to follow the clergy. In Islamic countries, men of learning were highly revered by the masses. There is no clergy in the Faith of Bahá'u'lláh, but He has exhorted His followers to honour the truly learned in the Cause, those whose knowledge and learning have not become the cause of pride and self-glorification.

No doubt it is concerning such people that Bahá'u'lláh has revealed in the *Kitáb-i-Aqdas*:

> Happy are ye, O ye the learned ones in Bahá. By the Lord! Ye are the billows of the Most Mighty Ocean, the stars of the firmament of Glory, the standards of triumph waving betwixt earth and heaven. Ye are the manifestations of steadfastness amidst men and the daysprings of Divine Utterance to all that dwell on earth. Well is it with him that turneth unto you and woe betide the froward.[1]

A person who is truly learned in the Faith is one who reaches such heights of detachment that he sincerely regards his learning as utter nothingness compared with the truths of the Cause of God. He becomes the embodiment of humility and self-effacement. Unfortunately Jamál did not fall into this category of 'the learned ones in Bahá'; he was a deceitful and hypocritical man who longed for glory. Yet the great majority of the believers did not realize this; they considered him a man of God and treated him with great respect.

Till the end of His earthly life Bahá'u'lláh showered His bounties upon Jamál. He concealed his faults and shortcomings and instead exhorted him to righteousness and piety. In one of His Tablets,[2] Bahá'u'lláh explains that through His attribute 'the Concealer', He has concealed the faults and shortcomings of many deceitful men, who, as a result, have thought that the Manifestation of God was ignorant of their evil deeds. These men did not realize that, through the knowledge of God, Bahá'u'lláh was fully aware of their wrongdoings. The sin-covering eye of God did not disclose their iniquities, and only when they were about to rise up against the Centre of the Cause and involve themselves in activities which harmed the Faith, did Bahá'u'lláh expel them from the community of the Most Great Name.

In a Tablet to a certain Muḥammad-'Alí, Bahá'u'lláh reveals these exalted words:

> I swear by the beauty of the Well-Beloved! This is the Mercy that hath encompassed the entire creation, the Day whereon the grace of God hath permeated and pervaded all things. The living waters of My mercy, O

'Alí, are fast pouring down, and Mine heart is melting with the heat of My tenderness and love. At no time have I been able to reconcile Myself to the afflictions befalling My loved ones, or to any trouble that could becloud the joy of their hearts.

Every time My name 'the All-Merciful' was told that one of My lovers hath breathed a word that runneth counter to My wish, it repaired, grief-stricken and disconsolate to its abode; and whenever My name 'the Concealer' discovered that one of My followers had inflicted any shame or humiliation on his neighbour, it, likewise, turned back chagrined and sorrowful to its retreats of glory, and there wept and mourned with a sore lamentation. And whenever My name 'the Ever-Forgiving' perceived that any one of My friends had committed any transgression, it cried out in its great distress, and, overcome with anguish, fell upon the dust, and was borne away by a company of the invisible angels to its habitation in the realms above.

By Myself, the True One, O 'Alí! The fire that hath inflamed the heart of Bahá is fiercer than the fire that gloweth in thine heart, and His lamentation louder than thy lamentation. Every time the sin committed by any one amongst them was breathed in the Court of His Presence, the Ancient Beauty would be so filled with shame as to wish He could hide the glory of His countenance from the eyes of all men, for He hath, at all times, fixed His gaze on their fidelity, and observed its essential requisites.[3]

Because of his knowledge and learning, Jamál emerged as one of the most famous teachers of the Faith during the Ministry of Bahá'u'lláh, Who overlooked his shortcomings, revealed many Tablets in his honour, and entitled him Ismu'lláhu'l-Jamál (The Name of God Beauty). His fame spread throughout the community, and the believers flocked to the meetings in which he was present.

Jamál displayed much pride in his association with the believers. He was a vain and conceited person who sacrificed everything to his own fame and popularity. In one of His talks[4] to the friends in Haifa, 'Abdu'l-Bahá is reported to have said that Jamál was so proud that he did not allow the believers to sit in his presence. In order to show their respect, they had to stand to hear him speak. Once, an old man who was not a believer had come to one of his meetings to investigate the Faith. When he saw everyone was standing, he had to obtain special permission from Jamál to sit down, for he was an old person and could not stand on his feet for long. 'Abdu'l-Bahá said that it was a good thing that Jamál was finally expelled, as he was like unto a poison to the Bahá'í community. He said that the Cause of God was like an ocean which cleanses itself by casting upon its shores the dead bodies and loathsome objects which are no use to it.

It is a well-known story among the believers who knew him closely, that when he went to visit his friends, after knocking on the door, when the owner of the house asked 'Who is it?', he used to respond: 'This is Jamál-i-Mubárak' (The Blessed Beauty), a title which is exclusively used to designate Bahá'u'lláh.

In his writings he used to refer to himself in such superlative terms that if the reader were unaware of the identity of the writer, he could easily mistake the author for Bahá'u'lláh glorifying His divine station in exalted terms. For example, his name being Jamál (Beauty), he prefaced one of his letters in these words:

> Verily, Jamálu'l-'Ilm (Beauty of Knowledge) has manifested himself with the power of truth.

and he closed this letter with these words:

> Verily, God has opened to my face the door of all knowledge. It is fitting that you seek my advice in all things . . . For in truth I am the most learned of the divines on this earth . . .

These preposterous claims were made by this man during the time that he was regarded as one of the outstanding teachers of the Faith. Bahá'u'lláh often exhorted him to moderation, chastity and piety.

Although most believers were unable at first to see through the hypocrisy of Jamál, or tolerated him because Bahá'u'lláh through His sin-covering eye concealed his shortcomings, there were some who recognized his true nature at first sight. There were even some who found him so unbearable that they confronted him in different ways. One such a person was Ustád Muḥammad-'Alíy-i-Salmání, that devoted believer who for many years acted as a servant in the household of Bahá'u'lláh, serving Him as a barber and bath-attendant and who had not been able to keep silent about Mírzá Yaḥya's faithlessness.* Although uneducated, he has left behind verses of poetry written in adoration of Bahá'u'lláh of which critics have acknowledged the beauty, lucidity and profundity. Believers who recite them become uplifted and inspired. His words, deep and full of significance, move the soul and open before one's eyes vistas of love and adoration for Bahá'u'lláh.

There was another side to Salmání's personality. He was a brave and outspoken person who could at times use rough and offensive language. He was also very perceptive of people's motives and character. The following is a story from Salmání's memoirs which describes his immediate reaction upon meeting Jamál-i-Burújirdí for the first time. This meeting took place in the outer apartment of the house of Bahá'u'lláh in Adrianople where Jamál was seated in anticipation of being ushered into His presence.

* See above, pp. 81–3.

> One day I brought water into the outer apartment of the house of Bahá'u'lláh where I learnt that Áqá Jamál-i-Burújirdí had arrived. I went into the reception room and found him seated in a corner, clad in an 'abá [cloak] and wearing a large turban.* He held his hands in such a way that if anyone was so inclined he could kiss them!† He had not yet attained the presence of Bahá'u'lláh. That creature was a peculiar looking priest.
>
> I used to consider myself to be a schemer and a man of cunning. So I walked in, uttered a casual greeting of 'Alláh-u-Abhá', and without paying any attention to him sat at the other end of the room. Then I lay down on the floor and after some time arose and sat down again. I did all this to hurt his vanity for he was a pompous man who was seated in the reception room of the Blessed Beauty with an air of superiority and a greatly inflated ego. After having treated him disrespectfully in this manner, I looked at him for a while and then said, 'How are you?' He merely shook his head at me. I then left him there and went about my own duties until the afternoon when they brought the news that he was summoned to the presence of Bahá'u'lláh. I went in and called him to follow me. I took him to the inner apartments of the house; we went up the stairs into Bahá'u'lláh's room. The Purest Branch‡ was standing in the presence of the Blessed Beauty.
>
> I stood at the entrance to the room. Jamál went in pretending to be trembling all over and then fell on the ground; this was a mere act. The Blessed Beauty was seated; the Purest Branch went forward to help Jamál to his feet. But Bahá'u'lláh stopped him, saying 'Leave him alone, he will get up himself.' After a while he arose; he sat at first and then stood up. Bahá'u'lláh afterwards dismissed him from His presence and did not say anything. Jamál . . . stayed for a few days, then Bahá'u'lláh sent him back to Persia. This man was corrupt from the beginning, his aim was nothing but leadership . . .[5]

Jamál was one of those who read the text of the *Kitáb-i-Aqdas* soon after it was revealed. Bahá'u'lláh permitted him to copy some excerpts and share them with the believers. According to his own testimony, he asked Bahá'u'lláh to make him exempt from obedience to the laws of the *Kitáb-i-Aqdas*. Bahá'u'lláh granted him his wish and conveyed to him that he was free and did not have to obey the laws of that book. It is interesting to note that on one occasion when he was boasting about the freedom which Bahá'u'lláh had granted him, someone recited these words of the *Kitáb-i-Aqdas* to him: 'Know ye that the embodiment of liberty and its symbol is the animal.'

* Muslim priests wore turbans; the greater the turban, the more important the priest. Jamál during his Bahá'í career did not discard his turban and priestly attire. (A.T.)

† Muslims showed great respect towards the priests who used to display their hands for the public to kiss. Bahá'u'lláh has forbidden the kissing of hands. (A.T.)

‡ Mírzá Mihdí, the youngest brother of 'Abdu'l-Bahá who later died in 'Akká. His death is regarded by Bahá'u'lláh as His own sacrifice. For further details see *The Revelation of Bahá'u'lláh*, vol. 3. (A.T.)

Since Jamál considered himself superior to others, he rose up against several outstanding teachers of the Faith during the lifetime of Bahá'u'lláh. He opposed the Hands of the Cause who were appointed by Bahá'u'lláh, was highly jealous of Mírzá 'Alí-Muḥammad Varqá, one of the illustrious Apostles of Bahá'u'lláh, and, since he considered himself an authority in the Faith, he worked very hard until he prevented Varqá from settling in Ṭihrán where Jamál resided at the time.

The lust for leadership had so possessed him that he rose up against any of the teachers of the Faith who became successful in service to the community. For example, on one occasion, two outstanding believers, Ḥájí Mírzá Ḥaydar-'Alí and Ibn-i-Aṣdaq (who was later appointed by Bahá'u'lláh as a Hand of His Cause), were on their way to the province of Khurásán to meet the believers and teach the Cause. Jamál became highly jealous of these two men. Secretly he warned the friends to keep away from them and introduced them with a vulgar term as two 'foreboders of evil'. This action evoked the wrath of Bahá'u'lláh. The veil of concealment which for years had protected Jamál in the hope that he would repent was now rent asunder. The sin-covering eye of God which through loving-kindness had watched over him for so long was withdrawn. In a wrathful Tablet Bahá'u'lláh condemned the actions of Jamál and severely rebuked him for his behaviour. Jamál, however, survived this great blow, which for a time, shattered his prestige and reputation among the friends. He was a master of hypocrisy and soon managed to regain his position as one of the renowned teachers of the Faith in the community.

When the ascension of Bahá'u'lláh took place Jamál became very tense and agitated. When he saw the first message which 'Abdu'l-Bahá sent to the Bahá'ís of the East, he dismissed it by saying, 'The Aghṣán* are young and immature.' This remark was a reference to 'Abdu'l-Bahá. Jamál was the first among the Bahá'ís of Persia to travel to the Holy Land, very soon after the ascension. He went there without seeking permission from 'Abdu'l-Bahá, met with Mírzá Muḥammad-'Alí, stayed there for a few months, and returned to Persia. From that time onwards, his attitude and feelings disturbed the hearts of those who came in close contact with him. The words and counsels of 'Abdu'l-Bahá exhorting him to servitude and detachment went unheeded. The poison of Covenant-breaking had been effectively injected into his whole being by Mírzá Muḥammad-'Alí, and, although outwardly he professed loyalty to 'Abdu'l-Bahá, inwardly he was preparing himself for the day when he would

* The male descendants of Bahá'u'lláh.

become the head of the Faith in Persia. To this end, he influenced certain individuals in each province to act as his representatives. This was not difficult for him to achieve, since several teachers of the Faith in different parts of the country were his supporters, and, as the rebellion of Mírzá Muḥammad-'Alí was kept a secret for a few years, Jamál had no choice but to continue his activities within the Bahá'í Community.

During the early years of the Ministry of 'Abdu'l-Bahá, the Hands of the Cause and Ḥájí Mírzá Ḥaydar-'Alí had come to the conclusion that Jamál was disloyal to the Covenant, and they used to confront him in different ways, but 'Abdu'l-Bahá tried His utmost to keep him within the fold so as to protect the faithful from his satanic influence. Some time before the election of the first Spiritual Assembly of Ṭihrán* 'Abdu'l-Bahá asked the four Hands of the Cause to establish a consultative council consisting of themselves and a few prominent teachers of the Faith. When the Hands did not include Jamál in their meetings he became indignant and openly attacked the Hands in such unspeakably offensive language that the believers became deeply disturbed and were apprehensive of the consequences of such open confrontations.

At this juncture, through the mediation of certain believers including Ḥájí Mírzá Ḥaydar-'Alí, the Hands decided to include Jamál in their consultative meetings for the sake of the unity of the Cause. However, when invited to take part, he made his acceptance conditional upon his becoming the chairman of the Consultative Council, and he demanded that, similar to the Hands, he should have the right of casting two votes. In order to pacify this egotistical man, the Hands accepted his terms, and Jamál thrived as chairman of the Council for a period.

Over the course of several decades Jamál had captured the attention of many admirers. For example, many believers in the city of Qazvín were his staunch supporters and he considered that city to be his stronghold and refuge in time of need. He was also very popular among the believers in the province of Mázindarán. His position as the chairman of the Council boosted his standing in the Faith and the believers in these communities rallied around him in every way possible.

In the meantime, 'Abdu'l-Bahá continued to exhort Jamál to steadfastness in the Covenant, and to purity of motive. The Tablets addressed to him during this period are indicative of His loving concern for Jamál's spiritual survival. But, alas, in the end Jamál lost

* For more details about the formation of this first Spiritual Assembly in the Bahá'í world, see *The Revelation of Bahá'u'lláh*, vol. 4, pp. 290–293.

this battle. When the rebellion of Mírzá Muḥammad-'Alí became public knowledge and his circular letters misrepresenting the station of 'Abdu'l-Bahá reached the Bahá'ís of Persia, Jamál threw in his lot with the Arch-breaker of the Covenant. By transferring his loyalty to Mírzá Muḥammad-'Alí, Jamál expected to become the indisputable head of the Faith in Persia, a position which had been promised him by Mírzá Muḥammad-'Alí himself, but after Jamál became involved in activities against the Covenant, he was expelled from the Faith by 'Abdu'l-Bahá. No sooner did the believers become informed of this than the entire Bahá'í community in Persia, with the exception of a handful of people, shunned his company. Those very few individuals who joined him in his odious activities were likewise cast out of the community and also isolated.

The manner in which the believers swiftly cut their association with Jamál came as a surprise to many an observer. For example, he was rejected by almost the entire community in Qazvín, where he had his most ardent admirers. The same thing happened in Mázindarán. While the believers had previously given him respect and veneration, after his defection he was shunned so effectively that he could not find even one family to offer him hospitality in that province. In some places, for example in Á<u>dh</u>irbáyján, he found a few individuals who harboured him, but he and his dwindling associates swiftly sank into oblivion.

At the height of Jamál's popularity and success, 'Abdu'l-Bahá wrote him a Tablet in which He emphasized the importance of steadfastness in the Covenant. In this Tablet He states[6] that in this day the confirmations of Bahá'u'lláh will reach only those who are firm in the Covenant. He affirms that even should the embodiment of the Holy Spirit fail to turn to the Centre of the Covenant, it will become a dead body, whereas a child who remains steadfast in the Covenant will be assisted by the hosts of the Supreme Concourse. Ironically, this Tablet of 'Abdu'l-Bahá found its fulfilment in Jamál and his few assistants, who withered away spiritually.

Notorious among Jamál's lieutenants was Jalíl-i-<u>Kh</u>ú'í, who acted for some time as his agent in Á<u>dh</u>irbáyján. The *Tablet of I<u>sh</u>ráqát* was revealed by Bahá'u'lláh in honour of Jalíl. It was to him that 'Abdu'l-Bahá wrote the celebrated Tablet known as *Lawḥ-i-Hizár Baytí (Tablet of One Thousand Verses)** in order to protect Jalíl from the venomous influence of Mírzá Muḥammad-'Alí. In this Tablet 'Abdu'l-Bahá explains the basis of the Covenant, describes its vital role in preserving the unity of the Faith, relates the causes of disunity among the followers of older religions, and lays great emphasis on

* See above, pp. 148–9, 157–8, 229.

the importance of firmness in the Covenant in order to preserve unity in this dispensation.

In this Tablet 'Abdu'l-Bahá recounts the following story. A certain King of Syria wrote a letter ordering the Governor of Aleppo to count the Jews in his town. By the time the letter reached the Governor a fly had deposited a dot on the word 'Iḥṣú' (count), and it read 'Ikhṣú' (castrate). Consequently, because of the adding of a dot, a tragic injustice was committed and all the males of the Jewish community in that city were castrated. 'Abdu'l-Bahá uses this story to illustrate the importance of adhering to the sacred Text, not to add man-made interpretations to it, neither adding a dot or taking one away. He thus refers to the treachery of Mírzá Muḥammad-'Alí who was at the time busy corrupting the Writings of Bahá'u'lláh.

The *Lawḥ-i-Hizár Baytí** is one of the most momentous Tablets of 'Abdu'l-Bahá concerning the Covenant and its significance in this Dispensation. It was revealed by the Master in the year 1315 AH (1897–8), a time of great agitation in the Holy Land when the Covenant-breakers were actively looking for any material with which to criticize the Master. Since 'Abdu'l-Bahá in this Tablet had equated the activities of Mírzá Muḥammad-'Alí to that of 'Umar, the second Caliph of Islám, he knew that if the Tablet fell into the hands of the Covenant-breakers, it would add fuel to the fire. Therefore He sent a trusted servant of the Cause, Mírzá Maḥmúd-i-Zarghání to Tabríz, the capital of Ádhirbáyján, with instructions to read aloud the full contents of the Tablet to Jalíl, but not to hand him a copy. Jalíl heard this highly enlightening Tablet in full but, alas, the lust of leadership had blinded his eyes and stopped his ears. He continued with his rebellion, but soon witnessed the futility of his efforts and died in ignominy.

There were a few other teachers who also rebelled against the Covenant in Persia. Siyyid Mihdíy-i-Dahají was one. Like Jamál he was also a learned man and a very capable teacher of the Faith. Bahá'u'lláh had conferred upon him the title of Ismu'lláhu'l-Mihdí (The Name of God Mihdí) and revealed many Tablets in his honour. Siyyid Mihdí was a native of Dahaj in the province of Yazd. He attained the presence of Bahá'u'lláh in Baghdád, Adrianople and 'Akká and received His unfailing bounties. Like Jamál, he travelled widely throughout Persia and was much honoured by the believers. Yet people who were endowed with discernment found him to be insincere, egotistical and deeply attached to the things of this world. Notable among those who have written their impressions of him is Ḥájí Mírzá Ḥaydar-'Alí, who also wrote about Jamál-i-Burújirdí. A

* This Tablet has not yet been translated into English.

perusal of his narratives makes it clear that these two men had at least one thing in common, namely their insatiable lust for leadership. For example, Siyyid Mihdí always entered Bahá'í gatherings with an air of superiority. He loved to have a retinue of the faithful walk behind him, and at night he was preceded by a number of believers who carried lanterns for him. As there was no public lighting in those days, people carried lanterns at night. Important men had their servants carry a lantern in front of them. This made a spectacular scene in those days; for normally only one servant or friend with a lantern accompanied a prominent person at night. In Siyyid Mihdí's case some believers even vied with each other to perform this service, and Ḥájí Mírzá Ḥaydar-'Alí recalls an evening when no less than fourteen men, with lanterns in hand, escorted him to a meeting!

Men such as these always fall. The Faith of Bahá'u'lláh does not harbour people who are egotistical and seek to glorify themselves. Its hallmark is servitude, and the standard it demands is sincerity and purity of motive. It is not therefore surprising that, like Jamál, Siyyid Mihdí was toppled to the ground when the winds of tests began to blow. He ultimately broke the Covenant of Bahá'u'lláh, and, in the hope of becoming one of the undisputed leaders of the Faith in Persia, joined hands with Mírzá Muḥammad-'Alí and rebelled against the appointed Centre of the Cause of God. When this became known in Persia, the believers left him to his own devices, and soon his glory was turned into abasement. In response he at first made a great deal of clamour and noise within the community, which agitated the minds of many, but the power of the Covenant finally swept him into the abyss of ignominy and cleansed the Faith from his pollution.

Seldom in the history of the Cause do we find an occasion when the power of the Covenant manifested itself with such intensity and effectiveness as it did in Persia after the expulsion from the Faith of those who rebelled against the Centre of the Covenant. The speed with which the pollution of Covenant-breaking was removed from the community of the Most Great Name in the Cradle of the Faith was truly spectacular. The reaction of the believers in that country to the news of the defection of some of the great teachers of the Faith such as Jamál and others was to shun them almost immediately. No less significant was the fact that the entire Bahá'í community of Persia, with the exception of a very few individuals, remained loyal to the Centre of the Covenant of Bahá'u'lláh. The efforts of the Covenant-breakers in misleading the believers were so ineffective that towards the end of 'Abdu'l-Bahá's Ministry there was hardly a soul anywhere in that vast community who could be labelled as a Covenant-breaker.

This magnificent achievement was due primarily to the devotion and attachment of the believers to the Cause, and further, to the untiring activities of some of the most loyal and learned teachers of the Faith who deepened the believers in the subject of the Covenant. These holy souls, 'the learned ones in Bahá' whom He describes as 'the billows of the most Mighty Ocean', and 'the stars of the firmament of Glory', were the Hands of the Cause of God as well as some outstanding teachers like Ḥájí Abu'l-Ḥasan-i-Amín, Ḥájí Mírzá Ḥaydar-'Alí, Mírzá Abu'l-Faḍl and several others. Soon after the ascension of Bahá'u'lláh these souls travelled extensively throughout Persia and met with the entire community. In spite of the lack of modern transport facilities these steadfast souls travelled by donkey to every town and village, and met with every believer either individually or in gatherings. They explained the verities of the Faith to them in great detail, helped them to study many of the Tablets of Bahá'u'lláh and 'Abdu'l-Bahá, discussed the significances enshrined in the *Kitáb-i-Aqdas* and the *Kitáb-i-'Ahd*, and convincingly clarified any questions which they raised. These devoted teachers of the Cause were so imbued with the love of Bahá'u'lláh and 'Abdu'l-Bahá, that wherever they went they imparted that same love to the believers. They were truly 'a river of life eternal' to the loved ones of God and were instrumental in strengthening the faith of the believers and confirming them in the Covenant of Bahá'u'lláh.

Although Covenant-breaking did not become an issue in Persia itself, the believers in that country were aware of the perfidy of the Arch-breaker of the Covenant and his associates in conducting their disgraceful intrigues against 'Abdu'l-Bahá in the Holy Land. These ignoble activities became instrumental in increasing the love that the Bahá'ís entertained in their hearts for the Master. The more the Covenant-breakers inflicted sufferings upon Him, the more intense became this love, and as the Bahá'ís turned with more devotion to 'Abdu'l-Bahá they became more successful in their teaching activities, and consequently the community expanded considerably during those days.

Another outcome of this love for the Master was the manner in which the believers in Persia referred to Him in glowing terms and praised His station in laudatory language. Whereas He considered Himself a servant of Bahá'u'lláh, the believers called Him by those exalted designations which the Pen of Bahá'u'lláh had conferred upon Him, designations such as 'The Master', 'The Most Great Mystery of God', 'The Most Mighty Branch', 'The Limb of the Law of God', the Being 'round Whom all names revolve', and several others. This made 'Abdu'l-Bahá very unhappy. Indeed, 'Abdu'l-Bahá always emphasized His station as one of servitude to the

Blessed Beauty. In his memoirs Dr Yúnis K͟hán reports 'Abdu'l-Bahá as saying that He does not claim a station for Himself, but that Bahá'u'lláh had conferred upon Him a special bounty, that His words became creative and that whatever He says will come to pass.

Soon after the ascension of Bahá'u'lláh there were differences among the believers concerning the station of 'Abdu'l-Bahá. Some regarded Him as having the same identity as Bahá'u'lláh – a belief which runs counter to the basic verities enshrined within the Faith – and in several Tablets 'Abdu'l-Bahá clarified His own position. He explained that although He was the Centre of the Covenant of Bahá'u'lláh and the Interpreter of His words, He was nevertheless a lowly servant at the threshold of Bahá'u'lláh. In one of His Tablets 'Abdu'l-Bahá writes:

> This is my firm, my unshakable conviction, the essence of my unconcealed and explicit belief – a conviction and belief which the denizens of the Abhá Kingdom fully share: The Blessed Beauty is the Sun of Truth, and His light the light of truth. The Báb is likewise the Sun of Truth, and His light the light of truth . . . My station is the station of servitude – a servitude which is complete, pure and real, firmly established, enduring, obvious, explicitly revealed and subject to no interpretation whatever . . . I am the Interpreter of the Word of God; such is my interpretation.[7]

At one time Ḥájí Mírzá Ḥaydar-'Alí, to whom we have referred previously, wrote a letter to 'Abdu'l-Bahá and asked Him to explain the significance of Bahá'u'lláh's utterances in the *Súriy-i-G͟huṣn* and other Tablets including certain verses in the *Mat͟hnaví* concerning the exalted station of the Branch. In reply, 'Abdu'l-Bahá wrote a Tablet in which He announced His station of servitude most eloquently and besought the Almighty to immerse Him in the ocean of servitude. He then made the following statement:

> I am according to the explicit texts of the Kitáb-i-Aqdas and the Kitáb-i-'Ahd the manifest Interpreter of the Word of God . . . Whoso deviates from my interpretation is a victim of his own fancy . . . I affirm that the true meaning, the real significance, the innermost secret of these verses, of these very words, is my own servitude to the sacred Threshold of the Abhá Beauty, my complete self-effacement, my utter nothingness before Him. This is my resplendent crown, my most precious adorning. On this I pride myself in the kingdom of earth and heaven. Therein I glory among the company of the well-favoured![8]

The following is a summary translation of Dr Yúnis K͟hán's recollections concerning 'Abdu'l-Bahá's station of servitude.

> As the Covenant-breakers intensified their campaign of troublemaking for the Master and went on belittling His station, many of the steadfast believers, due to their enormous love for Him, exaggerated His

station. Eventually all this resulted in a situation that if a believer was moved, for instance, to compose a poem about 'Abdu'l-Bahá's servitude, he would assuredly become the recipient of the Master's unbounded favours and bounties. But if, on the contrary, he would sing His praises and exalt His name, He would be displeased, and even ask the writer to repent and beg forgiveness.

The only station that He retained for Himself was that of the appointed Interpreter of the Writings of Bahá'u'lláh. And this He did so that if a person ever sought to glorify His station by referring to the many exalted titles by which Bahá'u'lláh had designated Him, he then would merely say, 'I am the Interpreter of the Words of God and my interpretation of all these designations is 'Abdu'l-Bahá (Servant of Bahá'u'lláh)' . . . At one stage He wrote many Tablets and prayers concerning His own station of servitude. Among them was a prayer which is now used as a Prayer of Visitation for 'Abdu'l-Bahá. Concerning this prayer He wrote, 'Whoso reciteth this prayer with lowliness and fervour will bring gladness and joy to the heart of this servant; it will be even as meeting Him face to face.'

In this prayer He describes His station of servitude in such lowly terms: 'Lord! Give me to drink from the chalice of selflessness; with its robe clothe me, and in its ocean immerse me. Make me as dust in the pathway of Thy loved ones, and grant that I may offer up my soul for the earth ennobled by the footsteps of Thy Chosen ones in Thy path, O Lord of Glory in the Highest.'

O dear reader! Most of the believers know this prayer by heart and are in the habit of reciting it every morning, this is why this servant has not quoted its full text here. My appeal to you now is to recite this prayer* first and then read the following which is entitled:

The Story of a Bitter-Sweet Experience

In those days when the friends in Persia were aflame with the fire of love, and at the same time, they were, with a spirit of forbearance, burning in that fire of envy and hatred, of calumny and slander created by the people of malice and the Covenant-breakers, Bahá'í poets and people of letters in that country used to write poems in praise and glorification of 'Abdu'l-Bahá. In laudatory and most eloquent language they used to acclaim His exalted station.

But we, the resident Bahá'ís of 'Akká, the spot round which the Concourse on High circle in adoration, were very careful not to breathe a word about the station of sovereignty and lordship of the blessed Person of 'Abdu'l-Bahá. We knew well that He had often advised the poets that instead of singing His praise they ought to exalt His station of servitude and utter self-effacement.

During this time, one day I received a letter from one of the handmaidens of God . . . This letter, composed in verse, and laudatory in its tone, was addressed to 'Abdu'l-Bahá in the form of a supplication to the holy presence of God. I handed the poem to the Master as He was

* *Tablet of Visitation* revealed by 'Abdu'l-Bahá, in most Bahá'í prayer books.

coming down the steps of the house in front of the sea. I thought it was the right moment to give it to Him. He had hardly read one or two lines when He suddenly turned His face towards me and with the utmost sadness and a deep sense of grief said: 'Now even you hand me letters such as this! Don't you know the measure of pain and sorrow which overtakes me when I hear people addressing me with such exalted titles? Even you have not recognized me! If you have not appreciated this, then what can be expected of others? Don't you see all that I do day and night, and everything I write in my letters . . . I swear by Almighty God that I consider myself lowlier than each and every one of the loved ones of the Blessed Beauty. This is my firm conviction . . . Tell me if I am wrong. This is my greatest wish. I don't even wish to make this claim, because I dislike every claim. He then turned towards the Qiblíh and said, 'O Blessed Beauty, grant me this station' . . .

'Abdu'l-Bahá spoke angrily in this vein with such vigour that my heart almost stopped. I had a sensation of choking, my whole body became numb. Truly, I felt that life was going out of me. Not only was the power of speech taken from me, but energy for breathing seemed to have gone also. I wished the earth would open and swallow me up so that I might never again see my Lord so grief-stricken as this. Truly for a moment I was not present in this world. Only when the Master resumed His walking down the stairs, the sound of His shoes jolted me. I quickly followed Him. I heard Him say: 'I told the Covenant-breakers that the more they hurt me, the more will the believers exalt my station to the point of exaggeration . . .'

Now that the blame was removed from the believers and placed on the Covenant-breakers, I somewhat regained consciousness and a little life. I listened carefully to His words, but my thoughts were elsewhere. I now understood that it was the iniquities and transgressions perpetrated by these ruthless Covenant-breakers which had produced a strong reaction among the believers who could not control their feelings and sentiments.

This bitter experience of mine was ended now. The Master was pacing up and down the hall and speaking more about the machinations of the Covenant-breakers. But I was not in a position to think properly or meditate deeply. I was very perturbed that I had brought such grief upon the Master, and I did not know what to do. Then I heard Him say: 'This is in no way the fault of the friends. They say these things because of their steadfastness, their love and devotion . . .' Again my thoughts were directed to His words. Then I heard Him say to me: 'You are very dear to Me, etc . . .* From these utterances I realized that it was always the Master's way never ever to allow a soul to be hurt. And now this was a time for giving me comfort and encouragement. The pressure in my heart was now released. All the anguish pent up in me was gone. I burst into tears which flowed in great profusion upon my cheeks and I listened more carefully. I heard His utterances as He showered His bounties upon

* It is obvious that through his modesty and humility Dr Yúnis Khán does not wish to reveal all the praise and encouragement which the Master had showered upon him.

me in such heartwarming and affectionate terms that they went far beyond the normal limits of encouragement. So much loving kindness and favour He bestowed upon me that when I considered my limited capacity and worth, I could not bear to hear Him; therefore I never allowed those words to enter into my memory. Nevertheless, I was filled with such an indescribable joy and ecstasy that I wished the doors of heaven would open and I could ascend to the Kingdom on high.

When He dismissed me from His presence I went towards the Pilgrim House in such a state of intoxication and excitement that I walked all around the streets of 'Akká, not knowing where I was going!

And now, my dear reader, you can see how a bitter experience turned into a sweet one, and how it all ended. The earth did not open up to swallow me, neither did the heavens open to let me go up! And, so I can write down the stories of those days and in memory of His radiant countenance may say to you: 'Allah'u'Abhá!'[9]

CHAPTER NINETEEN

Building the Shrine of the Báb

In the early part of the year 1900 'Abdu'l-Bahá began to build the foundations of the Shrine of the Báb and consequently Haifa became the focal point of His attention. The Master rented three houses in Haifa. One was for Himself and the occasional visit by members of His family. Another was a four-roomed house for Eastern pilgrims. One room in this house was set aside for the Master Himself, one for the office of Ḥájí Siyyid Taqíy-i-Man<u>sh</u>ádí,* and the other two for the use of pilgrims. A third house with four rooms was suitably furnished for the increasing number of Western pilgrims who had begun to visit 'Abdu'l-Bahá from late 1898. Up to the year 1900 there were several pilgrims who stayed in these houses, but once 'Abdu'l-Bahá began to build the Shrine on Mount Carmel, He discouraged Bahá'ís from coming on pilgrimage† and so the houses remained for the most part untenanted. Dr Yúnis <u>Kh</u>án describes the state of affairs in Haifa just after the turn of the century. The following is a summary translation from his fascinating memoirs:

> The work of building the foundation of the Shrine of the Báb was proceeding well. The Blessed Master used to come to Haifa frequently for supervision of the construction work. He would stay a few days during which the Bahá'ís and non-Bahá'ís attained His presence . . .
>
> Certain changes had taken place during the three or four years preceding the year 1900.
>
> 1. Mírzá Áqá Ján . . . had passed away.
> 2. Mírzá Díyá'u'lláh, the vacillating son of Bahá'u'lláh . . . had also passed away.
> 3. The room on the ground floor of the Mansion of Bahjí which was used by the believers had been taken over by the Covenant-breakers . . .
> 4. The Covenant-breakers had given up their earlier practice of demanding payment of their expenses from the Master; consequently, the

* This believer served Bahá'u'lláh and the Master in the Holy Land for many years. See *Memorials of the Faithful*, p. 54.

† See below, p. 233.

hardships in His own household resulting from the shortage of funds in previous years, had somewhat eased. However, from time to time, He would find some reason to send funds to His unfaithful brothers.

5. The activities of the chief of police of 'Akká, Yaḥyá Ṭábúr Áqásí, against the Cause of God, had produced the opposite effect. He himself was dismissed from his post and later when he became destitute, he went to the Master and received help from Him.
6. During the past three years, groups of pilgrims from both the East and the West had visited regularly. The town of Haifa had become a centre for the believers where meetings and festive gatherings were often held, but in obedience to the advice of the Master, these gatherings are not so frequent these days.
7. The Covenant-breakers, who had not succeeded in their previous intrigues against 'Abdu'l-Bahá, began to create fresh trouble by causing alarm among the mischievous elements of the population. They misrepresented 'Abdu'l-Bahá's plans for the construction of the mausoleum of the Báb.
8. Two of the Covenant-breakers made attempts on the life of 'Abdu'l-Bahá. One had, on two different occasions, placed poison in a jug of drinking water used by Him. This was discovered in time. The other one carried a dagger hidden under his clothes with the intention of taking His life, but did not succeed in his attempt. Later both men regretted their actions. 'Abdu'l-Bahá forgave one and turned a blind eye to the other.[1]

The construction of the Shrine of the Báb was the greatest undertaking during the opening years of the twentieth century. This was a sacred task which Bahá'u'lláh during the last years of His life had specifically asked 'Abdu'l-Bahá to accomplish. The purchase of the site for the Shrine took a long time, for under the influence of the Covenant-breakers the owner at first refused to sell. After many difficulties, when negotiations for the sale of the land were completed and ownership passed to 'Abdu'l-Bahá, it became necessary to purchase another piece of land situated on the south side to provide access to the building site. At the instigation of the Covenant-breakers, the owner demanded an exorbitant price for this land, and even when 'Abdu'l-Bahá offered to pay a very large sum for it, the owner was determined not to sell. 'Abdu'l-Bahá was heard to make the following remark concerning this episode:

> Every stone of that building, every stone of the road leading to it, I have with infinite tears and at tremendous cost, raised and placed in position. One night I was so hemmed in by My anxieties that I had no other recourse than to recite and repeat over and over again a prayer of the Báb which I had in My possession, the recital of which greatly calmed Me. The next morning the owner of the plot himself came to Me, apologized and begged Me to purchase the property.[2]

Dr Yúnis Khán heard 'Abdu'l-Bahá say that when the owner offered his land, he begged the Master to forgive him, saying that His brothers had urged him not to sell and had promised to pay twice as much as 'Abdu'l-Bahá. The Master at first declined to purchase the property, the owner insisted and at the end prostrated himself at the feet of 'Abdu'l-Bahá and begged Him to take the land free of charge. Thereupon 'Abdu'l-Bahá summoned Áqá Riḍáy-i-Qannád, who was in charge of His financial affairs, and directed him to make the necessary arrangements for the purchase of the plot at a fair price.

As soon as He purchased the site which had been blessed by the footsteps of the Ancient Beauty, 'Abdu'l-Bahá focused all His attention on the building work. So deeply was He committed to erecting a worthy mausoleum for the Martyr-Prophet of the Faith, that according to the testimony of some of His loved ones He used to speak enthusiastically about it every day. His frequent visits to Haifa were for the sole purpose of supervising the work, and the believers resident in Haifa used to assemble on Mount Carmel to attain His presence. At that time, when there was nothing on the site but heaps of stones and mud, the Master often spoke to them joyously about the future of that blessed spot. He prophesied that the Shrine and the gardens around it would become the most beautiful and majestic spectacle on the mountain. So emphatic and clear were His words about the future of the Shrine that the believers who heard Him speak were able to visualize its grandeur and beauty with their mind's eye.

Some years later, 'Abdu'l-Bahá is reported by Dr Ḥabíb Mu'ayyad to have spoken the following words at a time when Mount Carmel was still a largely uninhabited heap of rocks, and the Shrine consisted of only six rooms built of stone. Today much of His vision has been fulfilled:

> On one occasion when 'Abdu'l-Bahá was strolling in the gardens [near the Shrine of the Báb] His eyes were focused upon the sea and the city of 'Akká for some time. After a few moments of silence, He said, 'I have seen many places abroad, but nowhere has the fresh air and the beautiful scenery of the Shrine of the Báb. Ere long this mountain will become habitable. Many fine buildings will be built on it. The Shrine of the Báb will be constructed in the most exquisite fashion and will appear with the utmost beauty and magnificence. Terraces will be built from the bottom of the mountain to the top. Nine terraces from the bottom to the Shrine and nine terraces from the Shrine to the summit. Gardens with colourful flowers will be laid down on all these terraces. A single street lined with flower beds will link the seafront to the Shrine. Pilgrims who arrive by ship will be able to see the dome of the Shrine from a long distance out at sea. The kings of the earth, bare-headed, and the queens, will walk up the

street of the Shrine carrying bouquets of flowers. With bowed heads they will arrive as pilgrims, and prostrate themselves at the sacred threshold . . .*[3]

The same chronicler has recounted that on another occasion 'Abdu'l-Bahá spoke on the same subject to a number of believers in the Holy Land:

> . . . The future of Mount Carmel is very bright. I can see it now covered all over with a blanket of light. I can see many ships anchored at the Port of Haifa. I can see the kings of the earth with vases of flowers in their hands walking solemnly toward the Shrine of Bahá'u'lláh and the Báb with absolute devotion and in a state of prayer and supplication. At the time that they put a crown of thorns on His head, Christ could see the kings of the earth bowing before Him, but others could not see this.
>
> And now I can see not only powerful lamps which will floodlight this mountain brightly, but I can also see Houses of Worship, hospitals, schools, homes for the handicapped, orphanages and all the other humanitarian institutions erected on Mount Carmel.*[4]

As the building work on Mount Carmel proceeded the believers were overjoyed at the prospect of the interment of the remains of the Báb in that holy spot. But the Covenant-breakers, who were being continually frustrated in their devious activities and forced to witness the ascendancy of the Covenant, particularly the arrival of pilgrims from the West, were aroused to inflict yet another blow upon the Master.

It was in the year 1901 that 'Abdu'l-Bahá, in the course of His talks with the believers, foresaw the approach of some impending tribulation which would be caused by the Covenant-breakers. He is reported to have intimated to the friends that the Covenant-breakers would create great trouble for Him, but that they themselves would be the first to be trapped in the mesh of their own devising and that only later would He Himself become a target of their schemes. 'Abdu'l-Bahá often spoke in this vein to His companions during those days. He intimated to them that whereas He welcomed afflictions in the path of God, His brothers would be the ones who would suffer. The believers were concerned about such predictions and did not know what kind of problems would be created for the Master. Their only prayer was that God might intervene and avert any ordeal which might be in store for Him.

By August 1901 the building work on Mount Carmel had reached an advanced stage, and 'Abdu'l-Bahá was visiting Haifa frequently, when suddenly a great upheaval occurred in 'Akká. On 20 August

* These are not the exact words of 'Abdu'l-Bahá, but they are very close to what He said. (A.T.)

1901 the believers celebrated the anniversary of the Declaration of the Báb (according to the lunar calendar) at the Shrine of Bahá'u'lláh at Bahjí. On His return to 'Akká, 'Abdu'l-Bahá was informed that His brothers had been escorted by soldiers from Bahjí and brought to 'Akká in great humiliation. Majdu'd-Dín had also been brought from Tiberias. The Master immediately went to the authorities to enquire about the reason for their arrest. It was then that the Governor informed 'Abdu'l-Bahá of the contents of an order from the Sultan that He and His brothers were to be confined within the walls of the city of 'Akká, and that the same restrictions which had been imposed upon Bahá'u'lláh and His companions in the Most Great Prison were to be re-introduced. Furthermore, none of the believers themselves were to be allowed to leave the city and all their activities had to be monitored by the authorities.

Although in the early days of Bahá'u'lláh's arrival in 'Akká such restrictions were enforceable, now, after so many years, when the Master had become the object of the love and adoration of the people, it was impossible to enforce this edict fully. Indeed, the Governor himself, who was a great admirer of 'Abdu'l-Bahá, had been so embarrassed by the order that he had delayed its implementation for some time.

This re-incarceration was the direct result of Mírzá Muḥammad-'Alí's misrepresentations to Náẓim Pá<u>sh</u>á, the Governor of the Province of Syria. The circumstances of this episode are described by Mírzá Badí'u'lláh in his 'letter of confession'* written a few years after this incident. He states that Mírzá Muḥammad-'Alí sent Mírzá Majdu'd-Dín to Damascus to present a petition to the Governor complaining about the activities of 'Abdu'l-Bahá. The main purpose of this treacherous act was to alarm the authorities by misrepresenting the purpose of the building on Mount Carmel as a fortress designed to raise rebellion, and informing them of large gatherings in 'Akká, and the comings and goings of Americans whom he described as military advisers.

It is known that Majdu'd-Dín took expensive gifts for the Governor as a bribe, and asked his help in bringing about 'Abdu'l-Bahá's deportation. Indeed, at other times and in the course of their several appeals to the government authorities in Syria, the Covenant-breakers had had to raise large sums of money to bribe various officials. Having used up the entire estate of Mírzá Áqá Ján for this purpose, they sold a one-third share of the Mansion of Bahjí for one thousand two hundred Liras to Yaḥyá Ṭábúr Áqásí,† that inveterate enemy of the Faith, and used the whole sum in bribes to officials.

* See above, pp. 152–3.
† See above, pp. 188–9, 224.

Majdu'd-Dín arrived back from his mission in a jubilant mood, having secured the Governor's promise of aid. But events now took a different turn. Upon receiving the Governor's report, Sulṭán 'Abdu'l-Ḥamíd became alarmed and ordered that incarceration be re-imposed upon 'Abdu'l-Bahá, His brothers and his followers. Consequently, to the surprise of Majdu'd-Dín, his plans misfired and he himself, as well as his chief, Mírzá Muḥammad-'Alí, together with Mírzá Badí'u'lláh, were incarcerated in the city of 'Akká by the order of the Sultan. The prophecy of 'Abdu'l-Bahá was fulfilled: His brothers were the first to fall into their own trap.

The Master, as always, submitted Himself to the cruelties which his enemies had inflicted upon Him. He accepted the new restrictions in a spirit of radiant acquiescence. The greatest deprivation for Him was His separation from the Shrine of Bahá'u'lláh, which He could not visit during this time. He was also cut off from the building work on Mount Carmel, although He made arrangements for it to continue. For about seven years while this incarceration was in force 'Abdu'l-Bahá continued to direct the affairs of the Bahá'í world in both East and West through the outpouring of His voluminous writings. As the years went by, more pilgrims and visitors were received in His rented house adjacent to the barracks, known as the house of 'Abdu'lláh Pás͟há. On the upper storey of this house He built a small wooden cabin in which He could pray, turning in the direction of the Shrine of Bahá'u'lláh.

As to His brothers: upon being brought to 'Akká where they were ordered to live, Mírzá Muḥammad-'Alí wrote two letters, one after the other, to the Governor of Damascus (whom he had already bribed) desperately seeking assistance for his release. But his letters were left unanswered. However, 'Abdu'l-Bahá met the civil and military authorities and interceded for the release of His brothers, saying that they were not able to endure such restrictions, and secured their freedom. He also secured freedom for the other believers, who were allowed to resume the occupations in which they had been previously engaged, but He assured the authorities that He Himself would remain within the walls of the city.

As to the cause of the restrictions, Mírzá Muḥammad-'Alí: he at first flatly denied having had any communication with the Governor of Damascus and Majdu'd-Dín did likewise. They both alleged that the edict of the Sultan for re-incarceration had been issued as a result of the publication of a book by Mírzá Abu'l-Faḍl, the great Bahá'í scholar, but the truth soon surfaced. Ḥájí 'Alíy-i-Yazdí* has described in his memoirs the circumstances which exposed the treachery

* See above, pp. 184–5.

of Majdu'd-Dín and Mírzá Muḥammad-'Alí. According to Ḥájí 'Alí, Majdu'd-Dín had delivered two petitions personally, one to Náẓim Páshá and the other to Faríq Páshá. The latter was a high-ranking military officer friendly towards 'Abdu'l-Bahá. It appears that the second petition was presented in response to a question raised by Faríq Páshá, who wanted to know the nature of disagreements between 'Abdu'l-Bahá and His brothers.

In order to confuse the issue for Faríq Páshá, who was a Sunní Muslim, Mírzá Muḥammad-'Alí and Majdu'd-Dín forged a document which they attributed to Bahá'u'lláh; they sent this document along with their petition. In this document they composed, in the name of Bahá'u'lláh, certain complimentary passages in praise of 'Umar, the second Caliph of Sunní Islám. In so doing, they made it seem that Bahá'u'lláh was a follower of Sunní Islám. The other document which they sent to the Páshá contained parts of the *Lawḥ-i-Hizár Baytí (Tablet of One Thousand Verses)* in which 'Abdu'l-Bahá condemned 'Umar in strong terms. In their petition they then alleged that 'Abdu'l-Bahá was inciting His followers to arise in enmity against the Sunnís, whereas the rest of Bahá'u'lláh's family were admirers of 'Umar and the Sunní community.

Mírzá Muḥammad-'Alí and Majdu'd-Dín continued to deny having sent any petition to Damascus until Faríq Páshá at last sent it to 'Abdu'l-Bahá, who upon receiving it sent it to the mother of Mírzá Muḥammad-'Alí so that she could see the treachery of her offspring and son-in-law Majdu'd-Dín.

When these preposterous activities came to light, it opened the eyes of some of the Covenant-breakers who had previously been duped into believing that Mírzá Muḥammad-'Alí was a true follower of the Faith of Bahá'u'lláh. These simple-hearted men, who had been for so long deceived by the Arch-breaker of the Covenant, went to 'Abdu'l-Bahá, expressed remorse for their folly and were bountifully forgiven by Him.

As we look back upon these events, we can only be amazed at the craftiness of such a two-faced hypocrite who on the one hand professed to his misguided followers the divine origin of the Revelation of his Father, thereby posing as the most holy and truthful person, worthy of being emulated by all, and on the other, shamelessly announced Bahá'u'lláh and himself to be followers of Sunní Islám. Of course, Mírzá Muḥammad-'Alí knew only too well that Bahá'u'lláh had clearly taught His followers that 'Umar, the second Caliph of Sunní Islám, had broken the unwritten Covenant of Muḥammad and unlawfully usurped the successorship of the Prophet from Imám 'Alí. He also knew that the holy Imáms of the Shí'ah sect of Islám, whose stations Bahá'u'lláh has extolled in His Writings, were the true successors of the Prophet. Despite this there were no limits to which Mírzá Muḥammad-'Alí would not go in order to destroy 'Abdu'l-Bahá. He was a master in the art of falsification, and, as we shall see later in this book, he continued in this vein for years, spreading falsehood and calumnies against the Centre of the Covenant.

When it became public knowledge that the cause of imposing this new incarceration was Majdu'd-Dín's petition, the Covenant-breakers became subdued and chastened for some time. However, once released from the bondage of incarceration within the Prison City, Mírzá Muḥammad-'Alí and his associates became content with their own freedom, and jubilant that the Master, whom they hated so bitterly, was confined within the walls of 'Akká. They therefore considered this a victory, and foolishly thought that the end of 'Abdu'l-Bahá and His leadership was in sight. Little did they know that light cannot be put out by darkness and the power of God cannot be made ineffective through the opposition of the ignoble among men.

CHAPTER TWENTY

Years of Incarceration

DURING the years of His confinement in the city of 'Akká 'Abdu'l-Bahá was engaged in writing numerous Tablets either in His own handwriting or by dictation to His secretaries. Through these He continued to guide the followers of Bahá'u'lláh in their service to the Cause, urging them to remain steadfast in the Covenant and diffuse the divine fragrances with wisdom and perseverance. Though restricted in His movements, the Master was now living in relative peace, directing the construction of the Shrine of the Báb on Mount Carmel, while the emanations of His pen continued to enrapture the souls of the faithful, thus enabling them to scale loftier heights of service in His Cause.

Many significant achievements in the history of the Faith occurred during this time. In 1902, through 'Abdu'l-Bahá's instruction and guidance, the foundation stone of the Mashriqu'l-Adhkár* in 'Ishqábád was laid. This was the first Bahá'í House of Worship in the world.

Another significant development during this period was the breathing of a new spirit of dedication and steadfastness in the Bahá'í community in both the East and the West. This spirit was particularly intensified as a result of the upheaval in the summer of 1903 in Yazd and neighbouring villages, when a great many souls were martyred in the most moving circumstances, shedding through their amazing steadfastness and exemplary heroism an imperishable lustre upon the annals of the Faith.

In the Holy Land, while the Covenant-breakers were rejoicing that 'Abdu'l-Bahá had been made a prisoner, many of the public were moved to sympathize with the Cause. The friendly Governor of 'Akká made several attempts to persuade 'Abdu'l-Bahá not to confine Himself within the city walls, but to go and visit other places outside 'Akká; however, the Master declined the suggestion. Eventually the Governor asked 'Abdu'l-Bahá to accompany him on a visit to the

* Literally, 'Dawning Place of the Mention of God', a Bahá'í House of Worship.

Shrine of Bahá'u'lláh. The Master granted his wish and together they left the city and went to Bahjí. In order to further circumvent the strict edict of the Sultan, the Governor arranged another visit, and this time he invited other high-ranking officials to accompany him, including Faríq Pás͟há mentioned earlier.

When the party arrived at Bahjí, the Covenant-breakers witnessed the majestic figure of 'Abdu'l-Bahá walking at the front of the procession, and the dignitaries walking behind Him as a mark of respect. When Mírzá Muḥammad-'Alí saw the honour and reverence which the Governor and other officials paid to the Master, he became very disheartened, and his hopes that incarceration might diminish 'Abdu'l-Bahá's ascendancy were dashed.

As the year 1902 went by, pilgrims from the East and West were permitted by 'Abdu'l-Bahá to come again. All who attained the presence of the Master became magnetized by the spiritual forces He released and when they returned home they warmed the hearts of the friends through the fire of divine love ignited by the Master in their hearts. As we look back upon those perilous years we note that far from impeding the progress of the Faith, 'Abdu'l-Bahá's incarceration in the city of 'Akká, with all the hardships it entailed, coincided with an upsurge of the activities of the friends and the expansion of the community throughout the world.

Eye-witnesses have testified that during this agitated period in His life he used to pen no less than ninety Tablets per day in His own hand. It was the outpouring of these Tablets in such profusion that was chiefly responsible for the expansion of the Faith and the exhilaration and upliftment of the believers everywhere.

As these developments were taking place in the Bahá'í world, the Covenant-breakers resumed their malicious propaganda against the Master. In 1904 fresh adversities appeared on the horizon. The Covenant-breakers had assiduously plotted until the friendly Governor of 'Akká was replaced by one who was hostile toward 'Abdu'l-Bahá. Mírzá Muḥammad-'Alí took full advantage of this and stirred up mischief among certain elements of the population who had shown their opposition toward the Master. As a result, newspapers in Syria and Egypt wrote disturbing reports about Him, and the partisans of Mírzá Muḥammad-'Alí fanned into flame all the unfounded allegations these articles contained.

These activities culminated in the Arch-breaker of the Covenant finally drawing up an official indictment against the Master. In it he brought false and outrageous accusations against Him, and through bribery gathered a number of signatures from certain inhabitants of 'Akká to support his case. This document was sent to the authorities in Istanbul, the Seat of Sulṭán 'Abdu'l-Ḥamíd, in the hope that the

Sultan, who was a despot, might take measures to destroy 'Abdu'l-Bahá.

As a result of all this, it did not take very long before a Commission of Enquiry arrived in 'Akká. The news spread immediately and agitation seized the inhabitants of the city. Spies were planted in the neighbourhood and the approaches to the house of the Master were watched day and night. For the protection of the Faith and the community, 'Abdu'l-Bahá advised most of the believers to leave 'Akká and seek residence elsewhere. At the same time, pilgrimage by the believers was also temporarily halted.

'Abdu'l-Bahá was summoned by the Commission to face charges brought against Him by the violators of the Covenant. He visited the members of the Commission several times, and ably refuted the false accusations. He disproved each one of these in such a masterly way as to leave no doubt about their spurious nature. His explanations, spoken with majesty and eloquence, were so convincing that the members of the Commission had no choice but to dismiss the case and return home. Once again Mírzá Muḥammad-'Alí and his fellow conspirators were frustrated. Their shameful public encounter with the Master brought no benefit to them; instead it had cost them large sums of money in bribes.

As the year 1904 drew to a close, the Master's situation gradually returned to normal, the believers returned to their homes in 'Akká, and even pilgrimages were resumed. On one occasion, when a few pilgrims were seated in His presence, 'Abdu'l-Bahá described His suffering at the hands of the Covenant-breakers. The stories He recounted were so heart-rending that all who heard Him were deeply distressed. At this point Dr Yúnis Khán asked the Master to tell him how long these Covenant-breakers would continue to oppose Him. 'Abdu'l-Bahá is reported to have said that in four years' time they would become impotent to act against Him. He then stated that whereas in the future some vestige would remain of Mírzá Yaḥyá's followers in the world, no trace would be left of these Covenant-breakers. And indeed, as we shall see in the forthcoming pages, this prophecy of 'Abdu'l-Bahá has been fulfilled.

In one of His talks the Master is reported to have said that God always assisted the Covenant-breakers during His Ministry and enabled them to make every possible breach in the stronghold of the Cause, so that the Master might stop them all, and thus ensure that others in the future would be unable to do likewise.

The years 1905 and 1906 passed without major incident, although 'Abdu'l-Bahá was continually harassed by these enemies of the Faith and had to take appropriate measures to protect the Cause from their various manoeuvres. In the meantime the political situation in the heart of the Ottoman Empire was becoming increasingly unstable, and the Sultan correspondingly alarmed. He was known to be nervous of any popular movement in the country and had shown himself ruthless in dealing with dissidents.

The Covenant-breakers, who had lost hope of carrying out their evil plots, were heartened by the political situation in Istanbul. They now decided to take advantage of the Sultan's weakness and play on his fears and suspicions. All they had to do was to re-open their case against 'Abdu'l-Bahá and send their complaints anew to the court of the Sultan. This they did, but their last major onslaught against the Master proved to be a complete failure.

In their petition, Mírzá Muḥammad-'Alí and his associates re-affirmed their false claim that whereas Bahá'u'lláh was merely a holy man and an admirer of Sunní Islám, 'Abdu'l-Bahá had condemned the Sunní Faith and claimed the station of Prophethood for Himself. They also charged that 'Abdu'l-Bahá had not only acquired vast tracts of land in 'Akká and neighbouring villages, and had gathered a large following in the Holy Land, but that He had also built a mighty fortress on Mount Carmel,* had made a banner of 'Yá Bahá'u'l-Abhá' and raised it among the inhabitants, had received American and other Western military advisers† at His home, and was about to overthrow the government. Such inflammatory claims, made at a time when the government was apprehensive of revolt by some of the Turkish factions, disturbed the mind of the Sultan, who immediately ordered a new Commission of Enquiry to be despatched to 'Akká. This Commission, consisting of four officials, arrived in the winter of 1907. They had in their possession all the papers relating to the previous Commission of Enquiry, which had, ironically enough, found all the allegations against 'Abdu'l-Bahá to be baseless.

The Commission assumed full authority in the administration of the City, dismissed the Governor of 'Akká who was friendly toward 'Abdu'l-Bahá, and even disregarded the orders from the Governor of the Province of Syria who wielded supreme authority over the region. The members of the Commission then established direct contact with Mírzá Muḥammad-'Alí and his associates, and planned their course of action in consort with them. They took as their residence the house of 'Abdu'l-G͟haní Bayḍún, a wealthy and influential man who was living in close proximity to the Mansion of Bahjí and had friendly association with the violators of the Covenant.

Their first act was to again plant a number of spies around the house of 'Abdu'l-Bahá. They then began to obtain testimonies from

* This refers to the building of the Shrine of the Báb.
† This refers to Western pilgrims.

those very enemies who had put their signature to Mírzá Muḥammad-'Alí's original petition to the authorities. With the assistance of the Covenant-breakers, the members of the Commission even sought to bring pressure upon people to testify against the Master. In this way, through intimidation, people were forced to give false testimony while a local grocer who refused to comply was put in jail. Thus the inhabitants of the city were afraid to approach the house of the Master, lest they become incriminated by the authorities. Even the poor of 'Akká, whom 'Abdu'l-Bahá had succoured always, did not dare to come in contact with Him.

At one point the members of the Commission paid a visit to Mount Carmel, examined the six-room building of the Shrine, noted its massive walls, and commented on its extraordinary strength. Later in their report, they confirmed the Covenant-breakers' allegation that 'Abdu'l-Bahá had indeed built a fortress on a strategic location on the mountain! They also endorsed the other charges which had been brought against Him. Soon rumours began to circulate far and wide that the Commission was about to exile the Master to Fizán in Tripolitania, situated in the middle of the desert in North Africa.

During this period the Master remained unperturbed and confident. He continued to write His Tablets to the Bahá'ís of the East and the West, spent some time in planting a few trees in His small garden, and to the astonishment of some notables of 'Akká who considered His banishment to be imminent, was seen to be attending to repairs of His rented house. Their surprise was further intensified when they learned that he had bought and stored fuel for the winter.

The members of the Commission, who were actively engaged in preparing their report in collaboration with the Covenant-breakers, sent one of their agents to 'Abdu'l-Bahá inviting Him to meet with them, but He declined the invitation, saying that the Commission was biased against Him, and as such there was no point in meeting with its members. At the same time He had made it clear, as on previous occasions, that He was ready to submit Himself to whatever decision they made and reminded them that His greatest ambition was to follow in the footsteps of His Lord the Báb and die a martyr's death.

'Abdu'l-Bahá Himself mentioned this episode in a talk to the friends. The following is the gist of what he said:

> Upon their arrival, the Commission of Enquiry invited Me to meet with them, but I declined. They sent a certain official by the name of Ḥikmat Big to persuade Me to call on them. This agent begged Me, and even hypocritically brought tears to his eyes, pleading with Me to meet with

members of the Commission even for a short time. I told him that since they had come to investigate accusations against Me, it would be better that I did not meet them. I told him that they had already sent a report to the capital, and I had sent a letter to Sulṭán 'Abdu'l-Ḥamíd through Shaykh Badru'd-Dín, the gist of which was as follows:

'The members of the Commision have come to 'Akká, but I have not met with them. I understand that they have made a report in which they have levelled several accusations against Me and for this I am grateful. Their main complaints are as follows:

1. That I have rebelled against the government and established my own.
2. That I have built fortifications on Mount Carmel.
3. That with the help of Mírzá Dhikru'lláh* I have hoisted a banner with the inscription of 'Yá Bahá'u'l-Abhá' [O Glory of the Most Glorious] among the inhabitants including the Bedouins.
4. That two-thirds of the land in 'Akká is owned by me.

The reason that I am grateful to the members of the Commission for the above accusations is that by their first complaint, they have, in reality, praised Me and attributed great powers to Me. How can a prisoner and an exile establish a new government? Anyone who could do that deserves to be congratulated.

Similarly, by their second complaint they have also commended Me by ascribing to Me extraordinary capabilities. It would be a miracle for one who is a captive in the hands of the authorities to build fortifications strong enough to be capable of withstanding bombardment by powerful naval ships.

But one is surprised by their third complaint, for how is it that the many government agents posted all over the country have failed to see the banner which has allegedly been hoisted among the inhabitants of these lands? Perhaps, during the last two years these officials have been asleep, or some angels have blinded their eyes.

Concerning the fourth complaint, that I own most of the land in 'Akká and neighbouring villages, I am willing to sell them all for the small sum of one thousand liras.'[1]

That 'Abdu'l-Bahá wrote this letter in such ironic language is indicative of the depravity of those with whom He was dealing. In the meantime, events were moving to a climax in which it was almost certain that 'Abdu'l-Bahá would be exiled or put to death. The atmosphere was becoming more tense with every passing day.

There is an interesting account of an Italian who was Acting Consul for Spain at this time. He was an admirer of the Master and his wife was friendly with the family of 'Abdu'l-Bahá. This man and his relatives were the chief agents of an Italian shipping company. When he was informed that 'Abdu'l-Bahá's life was in danger, he came to the Master in the dead of night and offered to transport Him

* The son of Mírzá Muḥammad-Qulí, the faithful half-brother of Bahá'u'lláh who remained steadfast in the Covenant after the ascension of Bahá'u'lláh.

out of the Holy Land to a safe spot. He even delayed a particular ship's departure for a few days in the hope of rescuing Him. 'Abdu'l-Bahá took the unusual step of inviting some of the elders of the Bahá'í community in 'Akká, including the celebrated Ḥájí Mírzá Ḥaydar-'Alí, to consult together and give their opinion on this offer. It is amusing to see how 'Abdu'l-Bahá wanted to test these people and teach them a lesson. The group unanimously decided to advise the Master to accept the offer of the Italian friend and leave the Holy Land for a place of safety. 'Abdu'l-Bahá looked at them disapprovingly, and reminded them that running away had never been the practice of the Chosen Ones of God. His Lord the Báb had offered up His life, so how could He do otherwise? As a result of this episode, each one of the group recognized his own shortsightedness and lack of understanding of the spirit of the Faith.

Then, one day, late in the afternoon, the members of the Commission of Enquiry boarded their ship in Haifa and headed towards 'Akká. The sun was setting as the ship sailed closer to the prison city. Everyone in Haifa and 'Akká was certain that the ship was on its way to take 'Abdu'l-Bahá on board as a prisoner. In the meantime, 'Abdu'l-Bahá was calmly pacing the yard in His house, and the believers, extremely perturbed, were nervously watching the approaching ship. Suddenly, to their great relief, the ship changed course, headed out to sea and sailed towards Istanbul.

In one of His Tablets 'Abdu'l-Bahá states that at that moment the guns of God went into action, removed the chains from the neck of 'Abdu'l-Bahá and placed them on the neck of 'Abdu'l-Ḥamíd, the Sultan of Turkey. This was a reference to the ultimate fate of the Sultan, who narrowly escaped death when returning from the mosque on a fateful Friday that same year. A bomb which was meant for him exploded, killing and injuring others, and it was this event which prompted the authorities to recall the members of the Commission. Some months later, the 'Young Turk' Revolutionaries demanded from the Sultan the release of all political prisoners. This was done, and in the summer of 1908 'Abdu'l-Bahá was freed. A few months later the tyrannical Sulṭán 'Abdu'l-Ḥamíd was deposed. 'Abdu'l-Bahá's total freedom after forty years of imprisonment thus enabled Him to fulfil one of the most important undertakings of His Ministry, the interment of the remains of the Báb, the Martyr-Prophet of the Faith, in the Shrine built by Him on Mount Carmel.*

In one of His Tablets to the believers in Persia, 'Abdu'l-Bahá describes some of the events in the Holy Land during this period.

* For more detailed information on this see *The Revelation of Bahá'u'lláh*, vol. 3, Appendix I, also vol. 1, p. 268.

O ye the cherished loved ones of 'Abdu'l-Bahá! It is a long time now since my inward ear hath heard any sweet melodies out of certain regions, or my heart been gladdened; and this despite the fact that ye are ever present in my thoughts and standing clearly visible before my sight. Filled to overflowing is the goblet of my heart with the wine of the love I bear you, and my yearning to set eyes upon you streameth like the spirit through my arteries and veins. From this it is clear how great is my affliction. At this time and throughout this tempest of calamities now tossing its waves to high heaven, cruel and incessant darts are being hurled against me from every point of the compass, and at every moment, here in the Holy Land, terrifying news is received, and every day bringeth its quota of horror. The Centre of Sedition had imagined that it needed but his arrogant rebellion to bring down the Covenant and Testament in ruins; it needed but this, so he thought, to turn the righteous away from the Holy Will. Wherefore he sent out far and wide his leaflets of doubt, devising many a secret scheme. Now he would cry out that God's edifice had been subverted and His divine commands annulled, and that accordingly, the Covenant and Testament was abolished. Again he would set himself to sighing and groaning that he was being held a prisoner and was kept hungry and thirsty day and night. Another day he would raise an uproar, saying that the oneness of God had been denied, since another Manifestation had been proclaimed, prior to the expiration of a thousand years.

When he saw that his calumnies had no effect, he gradually formed a plan to incite a disturbance. He began stirring up mischief, and went knocking at every door. He started making false accusations to the officials of the Government. He approached some of the foreigners, made himself their intimate, and together with them prepared a document and presented it to the Seat of the Sultanate, bringing consternation to the authorities. Among the many slanderous charges was this, that this hapless one had raised up a standard of revolt, a flag bearing the words *Yá Bahá'u'l-Abhá*; that I had paraded this throughout the countryside, to every city, town and village, and even among the desert tribes, and had summoned all the inhabitants to unite under this flag.

O my Lord, verily I seek refuge with Thee from the very thought of such an act, which is contrary to all the commandments of Bahá'u'lláh, and which would indeed be a mighty wrong that none but a grievous sinner would ever perpetrate. For Thou hast made it incumbent upon us to obey the rulers and kings.

Another of his slanders was that the Shrine on Mount Carmel was a fortress that I had built strong and impregnable – this when the building under construction compriseth six rooms – and that I had named it Medina the Resplendent, while I had named the Holy Tomb* Mecca the Glorified. Yet another of his calumnies was that I had established an independent sovereignty, and that – God forbid! God forbid! God forbid!

* At Bahjí.

– I had summoned all the believers to join me in this massive wrongdoing. How dire, O my Lord, is his slander!

Yet again, he claimeth that since the Holy Shrine hath become a point visited by pilgrims from all over the world, great damage will accrue to this Government and people. He, the Centre of Sedition, averreth that he himself hath had no hand in all these matters, that he is a Sunní of the Sunnites and a devoted follower of Abú-Bakr and 'Umar, and regardeth Bahá'u'lláh as only a pious man and a mystic; all these things, he saith, were set afoot by this wronged one.

To be brief, a Commission of Investigation was appointed by the Sulṭán, may the glory of his reign endure. The Commission journeyed hither and immediately upon arrival betook themselves to the house of one of the accusers. They then summoned the group who, working with my brother, had prepared the accusatory document and asked them whether it was true. The group explained the contents of the document, stated that everything they had reported therein was nothing but the truth, and added further accusations. Thus they functioned at one and the same time as plaintiffs, witnesses, and judge.

The Commission hath now returned to the seat of the Caliphate, and reports of a most frightful nature are coming in daily from that city. However, praised be God, 'Abdu'l-Bahá remaineth composed and unperturbed. To none do I bear ill will because of this defamation. I have made all my affairs conditioned upon His irresistible Will and I am waiting, indeed in perfect happiness, to offer my life and prepared for whatever dire affliction may be in store. Praise be to God, the loving believers also accept and remain submissive to God's Will, content with it, radiantly acquiescent, offering thanks.

The Centre of Sedition hath imagined that once the blood of this wronged one is spilled out, once I have been cast away on the wide desert sands or drowned in the Mediterranean Sea – nameless, gone without trace, with none to tell of me – then would he at last have a field where he could urge his steed ahead, and with his mallet of lies and doubts, hit hard at the polo ball of his ambitions, and carry off the prize.

Far from it! For even if the sweet musk-scent of faithfulness should pass, and leave no trace behind, who would be drawn by the stench of perfidy? And even if some gazelle of heaven were to be ripped apart by dogs and wolves, who would go running to seek out a ravening wolf? Even should the day of the Mystic Nightingale draw to its close, who would ever lend his ear to the raven's croak, or the cawing of the crow? What an empty supposition is his! What a foolish presumption! 'Their works are like the vapour in a desert which the thirsty dreameth to be water, until when he cometh unto it, he findeth nothing.'*

O ye loved ones of God! Be ye firm of foot, and fixed of heart, and through the power of the Blessed Beauty's help, stand ye committed to your purpose. Serve ye the Cause of God. Face ye all nations of the world with the constancy and the endurance of the people of Bahá, that all men

* *Qur'án* 24:39.

may be astounded and ask how this could be, that your hearts are as well-springs of confidence and faith, and as mines so rich in the love of God. Be ye so, that ye shall neither fail nor falter on account of these tragedies in the Holy Land; let not these dread events make you despondent. And if all the believers be put to the sword, and only one be left, let that one cry out in the name of the Lord and tell the joyous tidings; let that one rise up and confront all the peoples of the earth . . .

O ye loving friends! Strive ye with heart and soul to make this world the mirror-image of the Kingdom, that this nether world may teem with the blessings of the world of God, that the voices of the Company on high may be raised in acclamation, and signs and tokens of the bounties and bestowals of Bahá'u'lláh may encompass all the earth . . .[2]

'Abdu'l-Bahá's dramatic release from confinement was the greatest blow that the Covenant-breakers had ever sustained in their entire period of opposition of the Master. It signalized the approaching end of their satanic endeavours to uproot from within the very foundations of the Cause of God. 'Abdu'l-Bahá's prophecy, uttered in 1904, that in four years' time they would become impotent, was thus fulfilled.

During these turbulent and perilous years of incarceration great dangers had faced the Cause of God, and 'Abdu'l-Bahá had written in many of His Tablets about the sufferings which were inflicted on Him by His faithless brothers in this period. The threat from the Commission of Enquiry was not the only danger. One of the disgraceful accusations made by Mírzá Muḥammad-'Alí against 'Abdu'l-Bahá was that 'Abdu'l-Bahá claimed to be a new Manifestation of God following Bahá'u'lláh. They made a plan to take his life, pointing to the following passage in the *Kitáb-i-Aqdas* as justification:

Whoso layeth claim to a Revelation direct from God, ere the expiration of a full thousand years, such a man is assuredly a lying imposter. We pray God that He may graciously assist him to retract and repudiate such claim. Should he repent, God will, no doubt, forgive him. If, however, he persisteth in his error, God will, assuredly, send down one who will deal mercilessly with him. Terrible, indeed, is God in punishing![3]

'Abdu'l-Bahá's Will and Testament was penned by Him during these fateful years. In the following passage 'Abdu'l-Bahá mentions one of the sons of Mírzá Muḥammad-'Alí, Shu'á'u'lláh, as one who was aware of this plan to take his life:

In like manner, the focal Centre of Hate hath purposed to put 'Abdu'l-Bahá to death and this is supported by the testimony written by Mírzá Shu'á'u'lláh himself and is here enclosed. It is evident and indisputable that they are privily and with the utmost subtlety engaged in conspiring against me. The following are his very words written by him in this letter: 'I curse at every moment him that hath kindled this discord, imprecate in these words "Lord! have no mercy upon him" and I hope ere long God will make manifest the one that shall have no pity on him, who now weareth another garb and about whom I cannot any more explain.' Reference he doth make by these words to the sacred verse that beginneth as follows: 'He that layeth a claim ere the passing of a thousand years . . .' Reflect! How intent they are upon the death of 'Abdu'l-Bahá! Ponder in your hearts upon the phrase 'I cannot any more explain' and realize what schemes they are devising for this purpose. They fear lest, too fully explained, the letter might fall into alien hands and their schemes be foiled and frustrated. The phrase is only foretelling good tidings to come, namely that regarding this all requisite arrangements have been made.[4]

Here too from the Will and Testament are 'Abdu'l-Bahá's words which speak eloquently of the perils threatening His life:

O dearly beloved friends! I am now in very great danger and the hope of even an hour's life is lost to me. I am thus constrained to write these lines for the protection of the Cause of God, the preservation of His Law, the safeguarding of His Word and the safety of His Teachings. By the Ancient Beauty! This wronged one hath in no wise borne nor doth he bear a grudge against any one; towards none doth he entertain any ill-feeling and uttereth no word save for the good of the world. My supreme obligation, however, of necessity, prompteth me to guard and preserve the Cause of God. Thus, with the greatest regret, I counsel you saying: – Guard ye the Cause of God, protect His law and have the utmost fear of discord.[5]

Surrounded thus by enemies within and without, 'Abdu'l-Bahá in the Will and Testament now appointed His grandson Shoghi Effendi, who was then a young child, as the Guardian of the Cause. At this same time He also wrote a Tablet[6] of great significance to Ḥájí Mírzá Muḥammad-Taqí, the Vakílu'd-Dawlih, the cousin of the Báb. He was a distinguished believer who was designated by 'Abdu'l-Bahá as one of the '. . . four and twenty elders which sat before God on their seats . . .' mentioned in the Revelation of St John the Divine.* In this Tablet He intimates to the Vakílu'd-Dawlih the great dangers which have surrounded His person, and urges him to make arrangements, when and if it becomes necessary, for the election of the Universal House of Justice. To bring this about, He directs him to gather the Afnán† and the Hands of the Cause in one place and establish this institution in accordance with the provisions of His Will and Testament.

* *Revelation*, ch. 11. Of the other twenty-three 'elders', only nineteen have been named by 'Abdu'l-Bahá, i.e. the Báb and eighteen Letters of the Living.
† The kinsmen of the Báb and those of His wife.

It is in the same Tablet that He gives the glad-tidings of the progress of the Cause, emphasizes its greatness, foretells the appearance of dire opposition by the nations of the world, and assures its followers of ultimate victory. The following passage is part of this Tablet translated into English by Shoghi Effendi:

> How great, how very great is the Cause! How very fierce the onslaught of all the peoples and kindreds of the earth. Ere long shall the clamour of the multitude throughout Africa, throughout America, the cry of the European and of the Turk, the groaning of India and China, be heard from far and near. One and all, they shall arise with all their power to resist His Cause. Then shall the knights of the Lord, assisted by His grace from on high, strengthened by faith, aided by the power of understanding, and reinforced by the legions of the Covenant, arise and make manifest the truth of the verse: 'Behold the confusion that hath befallen the tribes of the defeated!'[7]

These ominous events, the struggle between the forces of light and darkness, foreshadowed in such clear and unequivocal terms, have not as yet taken place except in the Cradle of the Faith, where the onslaught of the people against the persecuted Bahá'í community has continued from time to time since its birth in 1844. The opposition which, according to the above prophecy is to take place on a universal scale, will have a far greater effect in the promotion of the Cause of Bahá'u'lláh than that which past persecutions have ever produced. The Founders of the Faith and the Guardian of the Cause have, in many of their writings, described the dire opposition which the infant Faith of God will encounter from its enemies, both secular and ecclesiastic, prophesying stupendous victories which will be won as a result of this opposition.

In one of His Tablets Bahá'u'lláh states:

> Behold how in this Dispensation the worthless and foolish have fondly imagined that by such instruments as massacre, plunder and banishment they can extinguish the Lamp which the Hand of Divine power hath lit, or eclipse the Day Star of everlasting splendour. How utterly unaware they seem to be of the truth that such adversity is the oil that feedeth the flame of this Lamp! Such is God's transforming power. He changeth whatsoever He willeth; He verily hath power over all things . . .[8]

The following are the words of 'Abdu'l-Bahá describing the onslaught of the peoples of the world upon the Faith:

> This day the powers of all the leaders of religion are directed towards the dispersion of the congregation of the All-Merciful, and the shattering of the Divine Edifice. The hosts of the world, whether material, cultural or political are from every side launching their assault, for the Cause is

great, very great. Its greatness is, in this day, clear and manifest to men's eyes.[9]

Shoghi Effendi has also foreshadowed in many of his writings the advent of severe opposition to the Cause of God on a universal scale. We cite a few passages:

The resistless march of the Faith of Bahá'u'lláh . . . propelled by the stimulating influences which the unwisdom of its enemies and the force latent within itself, both engender, resolves itself into a series of rhythmic pulsations, precipitated, on the one hand, through the explosive outbursts of its foes, and the vibrations of Divine Power, on the other, which speed it, with ever-increasing momentum, along that predestined course traced for it by the Hand of the Almighty.[10]

We cannot believe that as the Movement grows in strength, in authority and in influence, the perplexities and the sufferings it has had to contend with in the past will correspondingly decrease and vanish. Nay, as it grows from strength to strength, the fanatical defendants of the strongholds of orthodoxy, whatever be their denomination, realizing the penetrating influence of this growing Faith, will arise and strain every nerve to extinguish its light and discredit its name. For has not our beloved 'Abdu'l-Bahá sent forth His glowing prophecy from behind the prison walls of the citadel of 'Akká – words so significant in their forecast of the coming world turmoil, yet so rich in their promise of eventual victory . . .[11]

Nor should a survey of the outstanding features of so blessed and fruitful a ministry omit mention of the prophecies which the unerring pen of the appointed Centre of Bahá'u'lláh's Covenant has recorded! These foreshadow the fierceness of the onslaught that the resistless march of the Faith must provoke in the West, in India and in the Far East when it meets the time-honoured sacerdotal orders of the Christian, the Buddhist and Hindu religions. They foreshadow the turmoil which its emancipation from the fetters of religious orthodoxy will cast in the American, the European, the Asiatic and African continents.[12]

For let every earnest upholder of the Cause of Bahá'u'lláh realize that the storms which this struggling Faith of God must needs encounter, as the process of the disintegration of society advances, shall be fiercer than any which it has already experienced. Let him be aware that so soon as the full measure of the stupendous claim of the Faith of Bahá'u'lláh comes to be recognized by those time-honoured and powerful strongholds of orthodoxy, whose deliberate aim is to maintain their stranglehold over the thoughts and consciences of men, this infant Faith will have to contend with enemies more powerful and more insidious than the cruellest torture-mongers and the most fanatical clerics who have afflicted it in the past. What foes may not in the course of the convulsions that shall seize a dying civilization be brought into existence, who will reinforce the indignities which have already been heaped upon it![13]

Fierce as may seem the onslaught of the forces of darkness that may still afflict this Cause, desperate and prolonged as may be that struggle, severe as may be the disappointments it may still experience, the ascendancy it will eventually obtain will be such as no other Faith has ever in its history achieved . . .[14]

CHAPTER TWENTY-ONE

Covenant-breaking in the West

WE now go back a few years to return to 'Akká at the close of the nineteenth century. As we have seen, the Covenant-breakers were becoming very frustrated, for they found themselves impotent to arrest the progress of the Cause of God. The news of the expansion of the Faith, especially the conversion of a number of souls in the Western world, had caused the fire of jealousy to burn more fiercely within their breasts. In December 1898 the first party of western pilgrims had arrived in the Holy Land and attained the presence of 'Abdu'l-Bahá. For the first time these newly enrolled believers came in contact with the magnetic personality of the Master. They felt the warmth of His genuine love and compassion and saw the light of divine spirit shining from His countenance.

May Bolles Maxwell, who was among them, describes her impressions of meeting 'Abdu'l-Bahá for the first time in these words:

> In a moment I stood on the threshold and dimly saw a room full of people sitting quietly about the walls, and then I beheld my Beloved. I found myself at His feet, and He gently raised me and seated me beside Him, all the while saying some loving words in Persian in a voice that shook my heart. Of that first meeting I can remember neither joy nor pain nor anything that I can name. I had been carried suddenly to too great a height; my soul had come in contact with the Divine Spirit; and this force so pure, so holy, so mighty, had overwhelmed me. He spoke to each one of us in turn of ourselves and our lives and those whom we loved, and although His Words were so few and so simple they breathed the Spirit of Life to our souls . . .
>
> We could not remove our eyes from His glorious face: we heard all He said; we drank tea with Him at His bidding; but existence seemed suspended, and when He arose and suddenly left us we came back with a start to life: but never again, thank God, to the same life on this earth! We had 'beheld the King in His beauty. We had seen the land which is very far off.'[1]

Another disciple of 'Abdu'l-Bahá, Mrs Thornburgh-Cropper, writes:

> Upon arrival* we went to an hotel, where we remained until nightfall as it was too dangerous for us, and for 'Abdu'l-Bahá, . . . for strangers to be seen entering the city of sorrow.
>
> We took a carriage after the night had fallen, and drove along the hard sand by 'way of the sea beyond Jordan', which led us to the gates of the prison city. There our trusted driver arranged for us to enter. Once inside we found the friends who were awaiting us, and we started up the uneven stairs that led to Him. Someone went before us with a small piece of candle, which cast strange shadows on the walls of this silent place.
>
> Suddenly the light caught a form that at first seemed a vision of mist and light. It was the Master which the candle-light had revealed to us. His white robe, and silver, flowing hair, and shining blue eyes gave the impression of a spirit, rather than of a human being. We tried to tell Him how deeply grateful we were at His receiving us. 'No,' He answered, 'you are kind to come . . .'
>
> Then He smiled, and we recognized the Light which He possessed in the radiance which moved over His fine and noble face. It was an amazing experience. We four visitors from the Western world felt that our voyage, with all its accompanying inconvenience, was a small price to pay for such treasure as we received from the spirit and words of the Master, Whom we had crossed mountain and seas and nations to meet. Thus began our work to 'spread the teachings', to 'mention the Name of Bahá'u'lláh, and acquaint the world with the Message'.[2]

During their short visit these pilgrims became galvanized by the soul-stirring words of the Master. They were utterly devoted to Him and longed to serve Him and the Cause He represented with unflinching loyalty and faithfulness. These souls showed such radiance and heavenly joy as a result of meeting 'Abdu'l-Bahá that the Covenant-breakers became inflamed with rage and envy; their gloom and disappointment knew no bounds. They had to find a way to counteract these developments and to devise a plan to impede the progress of the Cause in the West. At last Mírzá Muḥammad-'Alí discovered a means whereby he could attempt to disrupt the unity of the believers in America.

Among the party from the West which came to visit the Master was a man by the name of Ibráhím Khayru'lláh. He was a Lebanese Christian who had embraced the Cause in Egypt during Bahá'u-'lláh's lifetime and had moved to the United States in 1892. Two years later he succeeded in converting Thornton Chase, the first western Christian to embrace the Faith of Bahá'u'lláh, and the Master referred to Khayru'lláh as 'Bahá's Peter'. For a few years Khayru'lláh taught the Faith to several souls in various parts of the United States. He was the only teacher to whom the believers turned for enlightenment in that vast country.

* In Haifa.

During the time that Khayru'lláh was turning to 'Abdu'l-Bahá and was loyal to Him, he had succeeded in converting several people to the Faith. In one of his letters to the Master he expresses profound loyalty to Him and gives the news of the conversion of several souls in America. The following is a translation of this letter, which he wrote in 1897.

> To the sacred court of my Master and the Master of the entire world . . . may my soul be a sacrifice unto the dust of His pathway; After offering obedience and servitude unto the sacred threshold of my Master, I beg to state that the believers in these regions and I greet the morn immersed in the sea of your bounties, and meet the night with the grace of your mercy which encompasses the East and the West of the earth, because you have turned unto them and unto me the glances of your favour. You have revealed of divine verses three Tablets: one for the believers in America, one for Anṭún Effendi Ḥaddád, and the last one for your servant, who forever and ever, lowly and poor, awaits the generous dispensations of his bountiful Lord . . . Enclosed with this petition are seventy-four petitions from those who have recently come into the Faith of God, and shall soon send other petitions. Seekers who wish to hear the Word of God and come into the knowledge of truth arrive in large numbers . . .[3]

But here is an example of how pride and ambition can extinguish the fire of faith which burns in the heart of a believer. There is nothing more vital for a follower of Bahá'u'lláh who becomes successful in teaching the Cause than genuine humility, utter self-effacement and complete servitude toward the loved ones of God. But alas, Khayru'lláh was vain and egotistical. As the years went by and he saw the fruit of his teaching work multiply, he became proud and entertained the thought of dividing the Bahá'í world into two parts, he becoming the leader of the Bahá'ís of the West, and 'Abdu'l-Bahá that of the East!

While nurturing these selfish ambitions in his heart, he arrived in 'Akká and met the Master for the first time. He felt His majesty and authority as well as His love and compassion. For a short while He showed his subordination to 'Abdu'l-Bahá who one day took him to Mount Carmel and there laid the foundation stone of the mausoleum of the Báb on the site purchased by Him and chosen by Bahá'u'lláh Himself.

In the meantime, Mírzá Muḥammad-'Alí had discovered signs of ambition and egotism in Khayru'lláh which he exploited to the full. Soon a clandestine relationship was established between the two and Khayru'lláh became a tool in the hand of Mírzá Muḥammad-'Alí. He joined the infamous band of Covenant-breakers, rose up in opposition against 'Abdu'l-Bahá, disseminated his misgivings among the friends, and published far and wide some of his own ideologies. His defection brought great tests for the believers in the West, but the vast majority of the American Bahá'ís remained faithful to the Cause.

The news of Khayru'lláh's defection brought sorrow to the heart of 'Abdu'l-Bahá, who tried to save him as he was heading toward his spiritual downfall. In 1901 the Master asked 'Abdu'l-Karím-i-Ṭihrání, a merchant from Cairo who had taught the Faith to Khayru'lláh, to go to the United States especially to make this faltering soul realize the error of his ways. When his mission failed, 'Abdu'l-Bahá sent Ḥájí Mírzá Ḥasan-i-Khurásání in that same year for the same purpose. He also could not help. When Ḥájí Mírzá Ḥasan returned, Mírzá Asadu'lláh-i-Iṣfahání was despatched to the United States. He was the one who had previously been commissioned by 'Abdu'l-Bahá to transport the remains of the Báb to the Holy Land, a task which he had carried out with great success. He had a link with the Holy Family since he had married a sister of Munírih Khánum, the wife of 'Abdu'l-Bahá. Although he tried to help Khayru'lláh remain faithful to the Covenant, sadly, a few years later, he himself and his son Dr Faríd (Fareed) likewise became Covenant-breakers.

It is interesting to note that in spite of all Khayru'lláh's attempts to mislead those whom he had earlier helped to embrace the Faith, he did not succeed in bringing about a schism in the community. As in Persia, the believers remained loyal to the Covenant of Bahá'u'lláh, and thereafter refused to associate with their teacher. This can be credited to a great extent to the arrival in the United States of the celebrated Bahá'í scholar Mírzá Abu'l-Faḍl in 1901. The visit of this eminent teacher, which was undertaken at the behest of 'Abdu'l-Bahá, lasted for about two years. During this period, Mírzá Abu'l-Faḍl dedicated himself fully to the task of deepening the believers in verities of the Faith of Bahá'u'lláh. He spent many hours, day and night, discussing various aspects of the Revelation of Bahá'u'lláh, its history, its teachings, its laws and its Covenant, which he pointed out was the guarantor of the unity of the Community. In the course of these discussions he was able to clarify those subjects which had hitherto been obscure to the American Bahá'ís. In this he was assisted by Ali-Kuli Khan, who acted as his interpreter. Thus, as a result of Mírzá Abu'l-Faḍl's teaching work, the believers in America became filled with the spirit of faith and vitality, and many among them were transformed into spiritual giants of this Dispensation.

Khayru'lláh, who craved power and continued to struggle to become the leader of the Bahá'í community in the West, was being continually urged by the Arch-breaker of the Covenant to foment discord and contention among the believers, and the efforts of prominent Bahá'í teachers to purify his heart and mind from the poison of Covenant-breaking failed. 'Abdu'l-Bahá expelled him from the community and commented that as a result of his violation of the Covenant he would be reckoned as dead, and that soon the repugnant odour of his deeds would repel people everywhere. In 1917 Khayru'lláh wrote a letter to Professor Edward Browne of Cambridge which is indicative of his despair:

> The Bahá'í movement in America became slow and dull since the sad dissension reached the West nineteen years ago. I thought then that to call the people to this Great Truth was equivalent to inviting them into a quarrel. But the visit of 'Abbás Efendi 'Abdu'l-Bahá to this country, his false teachings, his misrepresentation of Bahá'ism, his dissimulation, and the knowledge that his end is nigh, aroused me to rise up for helping the work of God, declaring the Truth, and refuting the false attacks of theologians and missionaries. Now I am struggling hard to vivify the Cause of God, after its having received by the visit of 'Abbás Efendi a death-blow.[4]

On the other hand, as the years went by, the Message of Bahá'u-'lláh spread throughout the United States and Canada. It reached the continent of Europe, where a nucleus of Bahá'í communities was established in several countries including Britain, France and Germany. When 'Abdu'l-Bahá was freed from His forty-year confinement He travelled to the West and openly proclaimed the Message of Bahá'u'lláh to the people of Europe and America. So powerful was the influence He exerted on the hearts of the people that great numbers flocked to churches and public halls to gaze upon His countenance and hear Him speak. The believers in the West who came into contact with the person of 'Abdu'l-Bahá were transformed spiritually and magnetized by His all-encompassing love. 'Abdu'l-Bahá laid such a solid foundation, specially in North America, that a few years later he conferred upon that community a measure of primacy in the execution of His Tablets of the Divine Plan.*

Shoghi Effendi describes the significance of 'Abdu'l-Bahá's travels to the West and the power of the Covenant in these words:

> 'Abdu'l-Bahá's historic journeys to the West, and in particular His eight-month tour of the United States of America, may be said to have marked the culmination of His ministry, a ministry whose untold blessings and stupendous achievements only future generations can adequately estimate. As the day-star of Bahá'u'lláh's Revelation had shone forth in its meridian splendour at the hour of the proclamation of His Message to the rulers of the earth in the city of Adrianople, so did the Orb of His Covenant mount its zenith and shed its brightest rays when

* A series of fourteen Tablets addressed to American believers, which constitute a charter for the teaching work throughout the world.

He Who was its appointed Centre arose to blazon the glory and greatness of His Father's Faith among the peoples of the West.

That divinely instituted Covenant had, shortly after its inception, demonstrated beyond the shadow of a doubt its invincible strength through its decisive triumph over the dark forces which its Arch-Breaker had with such determination arrayed against it. Its energizing power had soon after been proclaimed through the signal victories which its torch-bearers had so rapidly and courageously won in the far-off cities of Western Europe and the United States of America. Its high claims had, moreover, been fully vindicated through its ability to safeguard the unity and integrity of the Faith in both the East and the West. It had subsequently given further proof of its indomitable strength by the memorable victory it registered through the downfall of Sulṭán 'Abdu'l-Ḥamíd, and the consequent release of its appointed Centre from a forty-year captivity. It had provided for those still inclined to doubt its Divine origin yet another indisputable testimony to its solidity by enabling 'Abdu'l-Bahá, in the face of formidable obstacles, to effect the transfer and the final entombment of the Báb's remains in a mausoleum on Mt. Carmel. It had manifested also before all mankind, with a force and in a measure hitherto unapproached, its vast potentialities when it empowered Him in Whom its spirit and its purpose were enshrined to embark on a three-year-long mission to the Western world – a mission so momentous that it deserves to rank as the greatest exploit ever to be associated with His ministry.[5]

'Abdu'l-Bahá's success in proclaiming the Cause to multitudes in the West, and the tributes which were paid Him by people of power and influence likewise came as the most paralysing blow to Mírzá Muḥammad-'Alí and his associates. In one of His Tablets written in this period, 'Abdu'l-Bahá refers to the Covenant-breakers, who were on the retreat, as 'blind creatures that dwell beneath the earth'. The following is part of this Tablet:

O ye loved ones of God! Praise be to Him, the bright banner of the Covenant is flying higher every day, while the flag of perfidy hath been reversed, and hangeth at half-mast. The benighted attackers have been shaken to their core; they are now as ruined sepulchres, and even as blind creatures that dwell beneath the earth they creep and crawl about a corner of the tomb, and out of that hole, from time to time, like unto savage beasts, do they jibber and howl. Glory be to God! How can the darkness hope to overcome the light, how can a magician's cords hold fast 'a serpent plain for all to see'? 'Then lo! It swallowed up their lying wonders.'* Alas for them! They have deluded themselves with a fable, and to indulge their appetites they have done away with their own selves. They gave up everlasting glory in exchange for human pride, and they sacrificed greatness in both worlds to the demands of the insistent self.

* *Qur'án* 26:31; 26:44; the reference is to Moses's rod, and the enchanters.

This is that of which We have forewarned you. Ere long shall ye behold the foolish in manifest loss.[6]

In many of His Tablets 'Abdu'l-Bahá assured the believers that in the end the Covenant-breakers who rose up against Him during His Ministry would fail utterly and perish in disgrace. For instance, in a Tablet we find this prophecy:

The case of all of them resembleth the violation of the Covenant by Judas Iscariot and his followers. Consider: hath any result or trace remained after them? Not even a name hath been left by his followers and although a number of Jews sided with him it was as if he had no followers at all. This Judas Iscariot who was the leader of the apostles betrayed Christ for thirty pieces of silver. Take heed, O ye people of perception!

At this time these insignificant violators will surely betray the Centre of the Covenant for the large sum which by every subtle means they have begged. It is now thirty years since Bahá'u'lláh ascended, and in that time these violators have striven with might and main. What have they achieved? Under all conditions those who have remained firm in the Covenant have conquered, while the violators have met defeat, disappointment and dejection. After the ascension of 'Abdu'l-Bahá, no trace of them shall remain. These souls are ignorant of what will happen and are proud of their own fancies.[7]

Shoghi Effendi briefly describes the doom of those few individuals who struggled with all their might to wrest the reins of the Cause from the hands of 'Abdu'l-Bahá, and to subvert the Divine Edifice which the Lord had reared for all mankind.

. . . he [Mírzá Muḥammad-'Alí] who, from the moment the Divine Covenant was born until the end of his life, showed a hatred more unrelenting than that which animated the afore-mentioned adversaries of 'Abdu'l-Bahá, who plotted more energetically than any one of them against Him, and afflicted his Father's Faith with a shame more grievous than any which its external enemies had inflicted upon it – such a man, together with the infamous crew of covenant-breakers whom he had misled and instigated, was condemned to witness, in a growing measure, as had been the case with Mírzá Yaḥyá and his henchmen, the frustration of his evil designs, the evaporation of all his hopes, the exposition of his true motives and the complete extinction of his erstwhile honour and glory. His brother, Mírzá Ḍíyá'u'lláh, died prematurely; Mírzá Áqá Ján, his dupe, followed that same brother, three years later, to the grave; and Mírzá Badí'u'lláh, his chief accomplice, betrayed his cause, published a signed denunciation of his evil acts, but rejoined him again, only to be alienated from him in consequence of the scandalous behaviour of his own daughter. Mírzá Muḥammad-'Alí's half-sister, Furúghíyyih, died of cancer, whilst her husband, Siyyid 'Alí, passed away from a heart attack before his sons could reach him, the eldest being subsequently stricken in the prime of life, by the same malady. Muḥammad-Javád-i-Qazvíní, a notorious Covenant-breaker, perished miserably. Shu'á'u'lláh who, as witnessed by 'Abdu'l-Bahá in His Will, had counted on the murder of the Centre of the Covenant, and who had been despatched to the United States by his father to join forces with Ibráhím Khayru'lláh, returned crestfallen and empty-handed from his inglorious mission. Jamál-i-Burújirdí, Mírzá Muḥammad-'Alí's ablest lieutenant in Persia, fell a prey to a fatal and loathsome disease; Siyyid Mihdíy-i-Dahají, who, betraying 'Abdu'l-Bahá, joined the Covenant-breakers, died in obscurity and poverty, followed by his wife and his two sons; Mírzá Ḥusayn-'Alíy-i-Jahrumí, Mírzá Ḥusayn-i-Shírázíy-i-Khurṭúmí and Ḥájí Muḥammad-Ḥusayn-i-Káshání, who represented the arch-breaker of the Covenant in Persia, India and Egypt, failed utterly in their missions; whilst the greedy and conceited Ibráhím-i-Khayru'lláh, who had chosen to uphold the banner of his rebellion in America for no less than twenty years, and who had the temerity to denounce, in writing, 'Abdu'l-Bahá, His 'false teachings, His misrepresentations of Bahaism, His dissimulation', and to stigmatize His visit to America as 'a death-blow' to the 'Cause of God', met his death soon after he had uttered these denunciations, utterly abandoned and despised by the entire body of the members of a community, whose founders he himself had converted to the Faith, and in the very land that bore witness to the multiplying evidences of the established ascendancy of 'Abdu'l-Bahá, Whose authority he had, in his later years, vowed to uproot.

As to those who had openly espoused the cause of this arch-breaker of Bahá'u'lláh's Covenant, or who had secretly sympathized with him, whilst outwardly supporting 'Abdu'l-Bahá, some eventually repented and were forgiven; others became disillusioned and lost their faith entirely; a few apostatized, whilst the rest dwindled away, leaving him in the end, except for a handful of his relatives, alone and unsupported. Surviving 'Abdu'l-Bahá by almost twenty years, he who had so audaciously affirmed to His face that he had no assurance he might outlive Him, lived long enough to witness the utter bankruptcy of his cause, leading meanwhile a wretched existence within the walls of a Mansion that had once housed a crowd of his supporters; was denied by the civil authorities, as a result of the crisis he had after 'Abdu'l-Bahá's passing foolishly precipitated, the official custody of his Father's Tomb; was compelled, a few years later, to vacate that same Mansion, which, through his flagrant neglect, had fallen into a dilapidated condition; was stricken with paralysis which crippled half his body; lay bedridden in pain for months before he died; and was buried according to Muslim rites, in the immediate vicinity of a local Muslim shrine, his grave remaining until the present day devoid of even a tombstone – a pitiful reminder of the hollowness of the claims he had advanced, of the depths of infamy to which he had sunk, and of the severity of the retribution his acts had so richly merited.[8]

'Abdu'l-Bahá, the Centre of the Covenant

'Abdu'l-Bahá and the Purest Branch

Áqáy-i-Kalím, faithful brother of Bahá'u'lláh

'Abdu'l-Bahá as a young man
A photograph taken in Adrianople

Bahíyyih Khánum,
the Greatest Holy Leaf

Ustád Muḥammad-ʻAlíy-i-Salmaní

Ḥájí Mírzá Ḥaydar-ʻAlí

Dr Habíb Mu'ayyad

Dr Yunis Khán-i-Afrukhtih

Ḥájí 'Alí Yazdí

The House of 'Abdu'lláh Pá<u>sh</u>á
The wooden cabin was added by the Master

The House of Abdu'lláh Pa<u>sh</u>á restored to its original form

The House of 'Abdu'l-Bahá in Haifa

A view of the six rooms of the Shrine of the Báb built by 'Abdu'l-Bahá
See Chapter 19

The superstructure of the Shrine of the Báb illuminated at nightfall

CHAPTER TWENTY-TWO

The Bahá'í Attitude to Covenant-Breaking

COVENANT-BREAKING is a deadly spiritual disease, and never before in the history of religion have its pernicious effects been brought to light. In this Dispensation however, the position of the Covenant-breakers and their spiritual condition have been exposed and fully examined. As we have described in a previous chapter,* Covenant-breaking provokes the wrath of God. Therefore, when a believer breaks the Covenant, his spiritual life-line is cut off. Although he may have great knowledge of the teachings and the history of the Faith, and may have had a brilliant record of service to the Cause, he becomes a lifeless being. Spiritually he turns blind and deaf, and his heart turns cold and bereft of faith. In reality he is not the same person any more. This is the reason why the violators of the Covenant of Bahá'u'lláh acted in the way they did.

We observe in nature that water can only flow from a high level to a lower one. It cannot flow to a point on the same level or on a higher one. Similarly, in order for a believer to receive the bounties of God from on high, he must be positioned at the opposite end of the scale, to be lowly, humble and self-effacing. This the Covenant-breakers were not. They aspired to be equal to the Centre of the Covenant, and thus the spiritual energies released by God could not reach them, and they became deprived of the outpouring of the spirit of faith. Their lives, once guided by the Light of Truth, were now based on falsehood. Deception, intrigue, dishonesty and violence became their way of life. These vices have proved throughout the ages to be the weapons which the ungodly uses against the righteous. But in the end they are obliterated by the power of truth.

These unholy characteristics are not exclusive to the violators at the time of 'Abdu'l-Bahá. The Covenant-breakers who opposed Shoghi Effendi, and those who appeared after his passing, conducted their shameful careers in the same manner.

It is necessary here to distinguish between enemies of the Faith and Covenant-breakers. The former attack the Cause of God mainly

* See above, p. 167.

through ignorance, and perhaps they will be forgiven by God. The latter, however, know where the Source of Truth is, but are unable to turn to it; instead, for their own selfish reasons, they knowingly rise up against it. To inflict harm upon a human being is reprehensible in the sight of God, and perhaps can be forgiven by Him. But to wilfully oppose the Cause of the Almighty and strike at its roots, as the violators of the Covenant do, are grave transgressions which are unforgivable. Christ, for example, describes this as a 'sin against the Holy Ghost'. The subject of Covenant-breaking was frequently broached by the Master according to Dr Yúnis Khán's testimony. In order to protect the community from their poisonous influence, He used to speak about their schemes and intrigues, their plots and conspiracies. He often likened Covenant-breaking to a contagious disease: the only way to prevent it from spreading was to confine the patient and place him in quarantine. He used to explain that physical health is not contagious. The health of one individual has no effect on another individual. But an infectious disease spreads rapidly and can affect a multitude. 'Abdu'l-Bahá often explained that the protection of the believers from the deadly disease of Covenant-breaking was imperative, and could be achieved only by cutting off association with them.

In one of His last messages to the American believers, 'Abdu'l-Bahá warned them of the consequences of association with the Covenant-breakers. He cabled them:

> He who sits with leper catches leprosy. He who is with Christ shuns Pharisees and abhors Judas Iscariot. Certainly shun violators . . .[1]

In many of their Tablets Bahá'u'lláh and 'Abdu'l-Bahá have warned the believers emphatically to avoid associating with the Covenant-breakers. In His Will and Testament, 'Abdu'l-Bahá admonishes them in these words:

> One of the greatest and most fundamental principles of the Cause of God is to shun and avoid entirely the Covenant-breakers, for they will utterly destroy the Cause of God, exterminate His Law and render of no account all efforts exerted in the past.[2]

In answer to a question 'Abdu'l-Bahá wrote:

> Thou hadst asked some questions; that why the blessed and spiritual souls, who are firm and steadfast, shun the company of degenerate persons. This is because, that just as bodily diseases . . . are contagious, likewise the spiritual diseases are also infectious. If a consumptive should associate with a thousand safe and healthy persons, the safety and health of these thousand persons would not affect the consumptive and would not cure him of his consumption. But when this consumptive associates

with those thousand souls, in a short time the disease of consumption will infect a number of those healthy persons. This is a clear and self-evident question.[3]

To check the spread of this spiritual disease, it is necessary not only to shun the Covenant-breakers, but also to expel them from the community in the same way that a cancerous growth is cut out of the body. As has already been stated, the Prophets of old did not establish a firm and explicit Covenant* with their followers, and so the adherents of past religions did not experience a discipline which necessitated the cutting off of one's association with the violators. A look at the history of religions, a history which clearly reveals the many schisms which have taken place, will amply demonstrate the danger. If, in this Dispensation, the Covenant-breakers had not been expelled and had been allowed to associate freely with the believers, certainly after a short period of time the Bahá'í community too would have been divided into sects as in other religions, its unity, which is its distinguishing feature, would have been destroyed forever and its goal of establishing the oneness of mankind on this planet brought to naught.

In order to appreciate this matter, let us examine some of the laws of nature as applied to a human body. The Cause of God may be likened to the body of man. When healthy, the body can withstand manifold external pressures. It can endure extremes of temperature, overcome thirst and hunger, defend itself when confronted with hardship, and preserve its wholesomeness against the effects of disease. Similarly the Cause of Bahá'u'lláh can withstand the onslaught of its external enemies and can resist every opposition from its adversaries. All the persecutions whereby thousands of its followers were martyred have failed to extinguish its light, break up its unity or undermine its rising institutions.

On the other hand, a healthy person can be fatally afflicted if poison is allowed to enter his blood stream and circulate within it. Such an intrusion, if allowed to take place, will undoubtedly end the person's life. Nature has provided certain organs inside the body, an immune system which removes the unwanted poisonous substances from the blood stream and discharges them at intervals, thus cleansing the body from their deadly effects and ensuring its health and well-being.

It is the same with the Cause of God. Bahá'u'lláh has provided an instrument for casting out from the community any individual who, while claiming to be a believer, opposes the Centre of the

* See above, pp. 99, 158.

Cause and tries to remain in the community to disrupt its foundations. When the unwholesome elements, those egotistical personalities who lust for power and are ready to sacrifice the religion of God to their own selfish desires, are expelled from the Faith, the community, cleansed from the poison of Covenant-breaking, acquires a fresh vitality and vigour, and is enabled to maintain its health, and continue its forward march toward ultimate victory.

During the days of Bahá'u'lláh the authority to expel Covenant-breakers was vested in Himself alone. Later it devolved upon 'Abdu'l-Bahá, as the Centre of the Covenant, and then upon Shoghi Effendi, as the Guardian of the Cause. Today this expulsion would take place by decision of the Hands of the Cause of God* residing in the Holy Land, subject to the approval of the Universal House of Justice.

It is important to realize that no one is lightly or hurriedly declared a Covenant-breaker by the Centre of the Cause. Great efforts are made to enlighten the individual and guide him to the path of truth. Only when every possible effort to save him from his spiritual downfall has failed will he be expelled from the community. For example, 'Abdu'l-Bahá made every endeavour during the first few years of His Ministry to change the attitude of His unfaithful brothers; only after they failed to heed His counsels and intensified their rebellion did He announce them as Covenant-breakers and cast them out of the community.

Never before has a Manifestation of God created the instrument whereby the breakers of His Covenant, those who oppose the Centre of the Cause from within the community, are cast out. This is one of the unique features of the Revelation of Bahá'u'lláh, providing a means by which the Cause of God is purged from the impurities which may force their way in from time to time.

In one of His Tablets 'Abdu'l-Bahá describes the Covenant-breakers as dead bodies which the ocean casts out on its shores:

> The tests of every dispensation are in direct proportion to the greatness of the Cause, and as heretofore such a manifest Covenant, written by the Supreme Pen, hath not been entered upon, the tests are proportionately more severe. These trials cause the feeble souls to waver while those who are firm are not affected. These agitations of the violators are no more than the foam of the ocean, which is one of its inseparable features; but the ocean of the Covenant shall surge and shall cast ashore the bodies of the dead, for it cannot retain them. Thus it is seen that the ocean of the

* The functions of the Hands of the Cause, as defined in the *Will and Testament* of 'Abdu'l-Bahá, are mainly the protection and propagation of the Faith. Those now living were appointed by the Guardian, Shoghi Effendi.

Covenant hath surged and surged until it hath thrown out the dead bodies – souls that are deprived of the Spirit of God and are lost in passion and self and are seeking leadership. This foam of the ocean shall not endure and shall soon disperse and vanish, while the ocean of the Covenant shall eternally surge and roar . . .

From the early days of creation down to the present time, throughout all the divine dispensations, such a firm and explicit Covenant hath not been entered upon. In view of this fact is it possible for this foam to remain on the surface of the ocean of the Covenant? No, by God! The violators are trampling upon their own dignity, are uprooting their own foundations and are proud at being upheld by flatterers who exert a great effort to shake the faith of feeble souls. But this action of theirs is of no consequence; it is a mirage and not water, foam and not the sea, mist and not a cloud, illusion and not reality. All this ye shall soon see.[4]

Those who are expelled from the Faith as Covenant-breakers are left to their own devices. The believers will never oppose them in their activities and they are left free to continue their actions against the Cause of God. But the history of the Faith demonstrates that by their very opposition to the Centre of the Faith they sow the seeds of their own extinction, and after a while fade away ignominiously. Their position is like that of a branch once it is cut off from the tree. At first it is green and appears to have some life, but as it has no root, it will inevitably wither and die.

Severing association with Covenant-breakers must not be confused with acts of opposition or hatred toward them. Dr Yúnis Khán recounts a story of 'Abdu'l-Bahá which throws light on this subject. The following is a summary translation of a part of his memoirs:

Sometimes in the course of His talks, 'Abdu'l-Bahá used to explain that Covenant-breaking exerts an evil influence upon the conduct and morals of the public. The seed of sedition which the Covenant-breakers have sown among the people is capable of inclining the world of humanity toward ungodliness and iniquity. Therefore, the believers must manifest righteousness and divine virtues in their lives, so as to remove the foul odour of this rebellion from the world. At the same time they will have to be vigilant and resourceful lest the Covenant-breakers influence public opinion, because whenever their foul breath reaches a certain area, it impairs the spiritual nostrils of the people and obscures their vision. Consequently these people are unable to inhale the sweet savours of holiness, or to behold the effulgence of the divine light . . .

One of the important duties enjoined upon the loved ones of God is to make every endeavour to prevent the Covenant-breakers from infiltrating the Bahá'í community . . .

'Abdu'l-Bahá quoted Bahá'u'lláh as saying that should one who is a follower of Mírzá Yaḥyá be living in a town, the foul odour of his presence will linger for a long time in that town and the progress of the

Cause of God will be impeded there. The Master gave the example of the city of Kirmán* and said that the breath of the Covenant-breakers [Muḥammad-'Alí and his associates], which is none other than the tempting of Satan, is far more deadly than that of the followers of Mírzá Yaḥyá . . .

One day when this servant and two other friends were in 'Abdu'l-Bahá's presence, he was talking in the same vein about Covenant-breakers . . . At one point I remembered an incident which happened in Ṭihrán, and in order to support His arguments, I said: 'A new school has recently been opened in Ṭihrán, and Ḥubbu'lláh, a son of the notorious Jamál-i-Burújirdí [father and son were both Covenant-breakers], was being considered for employment as a teacher. As soon as we heard of this, the Hands of the Cause, two other friends and myself consulted together in a meeting and agreed to do everything in our power to prevent the appointment of Ḥubbu'lláh to this post. We sent a certain individual to persuade the school authorities not to appoint him . . .'

I had not yet finished my sentence, when 'Abdu'l-Bahá interrupted me and instead of praising our action, said: 'Do you mean to say that you consulted together and decided to stop a Covenant-breaker earning a living? This is not the way to serve the Cause of God. In matters connected with one's livelihood there should be no differentiation between a believer and a Covenant-breaker. The loved ones of the Abhá Beauty must be the signs of the bounty of God among the people. They should, like the sun, illumine the world, and like the clouds of the spring season rain down upon everything. They must not look upon the capacity and worthiness of the individual . . .' 'Abdu'l-Bahá spoke in this vein to us for some time and I hung my head in shame![5]

In many of their Tablets Bahá'u'lláh and 'Abdu'l-Bahá exhorted the believers to show the utmost kindness to all, including their enemies, and to pray for them.

In His Will and Testament 'Abdu'l-Bahá counsels His loved ones in these words:

Wherefore, O my loving friends! Consort with all the peoples, kindred and religions of the world with the utmost truthfulness, uprightness, faithfulness, kindliness, good-will and friendliness; that all the world of being may be filled with the holy ecstasy of the grace of Bahá, that ignorance, enmity, hate and rancour may vanish from the world and the darkness of estrangement amidst the peoples and kindreds of the world may give way to the Light of Unity. Should other peoples and nations be unfaithful to you show your fidelity unto them, should they be unjust toward you show justice towards them, should they keep aloof from you attract them to yourself, should they show their enmity be friendly towards them, should they poison your lives, sweeten their souls, should they inflict a wound upon you, be a salve to their sores. Such are the attributes of the sincere! Such are the attributes of the truthful![6]

* A city in Persia where some notorious Azalís (followers of Mírzá Yaḥyá) were living.

Whereas association with the peoples of the world is enjoined on the Bahá'ís, the Covenant-breakers are a legitimate exception. They are cast out of the community and shunned by the believers, but to hate, oppose or confront them is against the teachings of Bahá'u'lláh. The above story by Dr Yúnis Khán demonstrates that Bahá'ís are forbidden to take any measures designed to harm the Covenant-breakers or obstruct their personal work and activities. On the contrary, knowing that these people are misguided and ignorant of the truth, the believers should overlook and forgive their transgressions. Following in the foot-steps of the Master, they are encouraged to feel the utmost compassion toward them in their hearts, for they are aware that unless these misguided souls change their ways, their plight will be disastrous and their end perilous. Since they do not associate with Covenant-breakers, the only way they can help them is to pray that they may be guided to the pathway of truth. Indeed, a number of Covenant-breakers have recognized their folly, repented to the Centre of the Cause, been forgiven and welcomed back into the Bahá'í community. The following prayer of 'Abdu'l-Bahá for the Covenant-breakers, who had inflicted untold sufferings upon Him for almost three decades, demonstrates that although the Bahá'ís shun these sick souls, they do not bear antagonism or hatred toward them in their hearts.

> I call upon Thee, O Lord my God! with my tongue and with all my heart, not to requite them for their cruelty and their wrong-doings, their craft and their mischief, for they are foolish and ignoble and know not what they do. They discern not good from evil, neither do they distinguish right from wrong, nor justice from injustice. They follow their own desires and walk in the footsteps of the most imperfect and foolish amongst them. O my Lord! Have mercy upon them, shield them from all afflictions in these troubled times and grant that all trials and hardships may be the lot of this Thy servant that hath fallen into this darksome pit. Single me out for every woe and make me a sacrifice for all Thy loved ones. O Lord, Most High! May my soul, my life, my being, my spirit, my all be offered up for them. O God, my God! Lowly, suppliant and fallen upon my face, I beseech Thee with all the ardour of my invocation to pardon whosoever hath hurt me, forgive him that conspired against me and offended me, and wash away the misdeeds of them that have wrought injustice upon me. Vouchsafe unto them Thy good gifts, give them joy, relieve them from sorrow, grant them peace and prosperity, give them Thy bliss and pour upon them Thy bounty.
>
> Thou are the Powerful, the Gracious, the Help in Peril, the Self-Subsisting![7]

It is helpful at this juncture to clarify the difference between Covenant-breakers and those who withdraw from the Faith of

Bahá'u'lláh. There are always a small number of individuals who recognize Bahá'u'lláh as the Manifestation of God, embrace His Faith, and even become active members of the community, but later, for some reason, change their minds and withdraw from the Faith. Such individuals are not Covenant-breakers. The Bahá'ís will maintain friendly relationships with such people and respect their decision to withdraw their membership in the Faith. Bahá'u'lláh has enjoined upon His followers to associate with them in a spirit of love and fellowship.

There is another category of believers who become deprived of their administrative rights by the sanction, at the present time, of the National Spiritual Assemblies. This happens when the individual flagrantly breaks certain laws of Bahá'u'lláh which are related to social or administrative activities and by so doing brings disgrace upon the Faith. Although not Bahá'ís in good standing, these people are nevertheless part of the community and may, under certain conditions, regain their administrative rights.

'Abdu'l-Bahá has described Covenant-breaking as a contagious disease and therefore counselled the believers for the sake of their own salvation and the unity of the community, to cut their association from Covenant-breakers and have no personal contact with them. By the same token, the believers are also strongly discouraged from reading their propaganda, for their words also can inject poison into the mind. When Mírzá Muḥammad-'Alí distributed his false propaganda against the Centre of the Covenant, the recipients in Persia who were loyal to the Faith used to return his communications to him sealed and unread. The same is true today.

By their fidelity, courage, and faith, the believers during the Ministries of 'Abdu'l-Bahá and Shoghi Effendi rallied around the Centre of the Cause, guarded the stronghold of the Faith, protected it from the onslaught of the Covenant-breakers, and prevented them from spreading their venom among the believers. Thus they handed down to later generations a world-wide community whose unity is firmly established and the invincibility of its rising institutions fully demonstrated.

CHAPTER TWENTY-THREE

Fostering Steadfastness in the Covenant

One of the most important teachings of Bahá'u'lláh is the unfettered search after truth. By this is meant that the individual is duty bound to search after truth prayerfully and without prejudice until, it is hoped, he is enabled to recognize Bahá'u'lláh as the Manifestation of God for this age, and to embrace His Cause. There is nothing more precious and more vital for a Bahá'í than his faith in Bahá'u'lláh. But faith is a relative term. Its intensity varies in individuals and is dependent upon the extent to which one has recognised the station of Bahá'u'lláh as the Supreme Manifestation of God.

Once a believer embraces the Cause of Bahá'u'lláh, he will have unlimited scope in the investigation of the many truths enshrined in the Revelation; this path of exploration in the teachings can continue until the end of one's life. Shoghi Effendi has made it 'the first obligation' of a believer to deepen his understanding of the Revelation of Bahá'u'lláh. These are his words:

> To strive to obtain a more adequate understanding of the significance of Bahá'u'lláh's stupendous Revelation must, it is my unalterable conviction, remain the first obligation and the object of the constant endeavour of each one of its loyal adherents. An exact and thorough comprehension of so vast a system, so sublime a revelation, so sacred a trust, is for obvious reasons beyond the reach and ken of our finite minds. We can, however, and it is our bounden duty to seek to derive fresh inspiration and added sustenance as we labour for the propagation of His Faith through a clearer apprehension of the truths it enshrines and the principles on which it is based.[1]

When the individual recognizes Bahá'u'lláh as the Manifestation of God, a spark of faith is ignited in his heart. At first a faint glimmer of light, this spark must be allowed to become a fire of ever-growing intensity, for it is then that the believer will fall in love with Bahá'u'lláh. But how can a person who has just embraced this belief draw closer to Bahá'u'lláh, fan into flame the spark of his faith and increase his love for Him day by day?

It is stated in Islám, and Bahá'u'lláh confirms and reiterates this, that 'Knowledge is a light which God casteth into the heart of whomsoever He willeth.' The statement that the heart is the dawning-place of the knowledge of God may sound strange to some, because it is commonly thought that the mind is the vehicle for acquiring knowledge and not the heart. But faith and knowledge of God, like seeds, are planted first in the heart. It is only afterwards that the mind grasps the truth and begins to understand it. In the end it is the interaction of the two – the heart and the mind – which brings confirmation and certitude to the soul.

Although in some cases a believer's faith in Bahá'u'lláh may come to him through an intellectual approach, its intensification and growth day by day cannot continue purely by intellectual pursuits. And if a person's faith does not increase with the passage of time it is like a child which is born but fails to grow. Such a person is very likely to feel a measure of doubt in his innermost heart concerning the Faith, and may experience great conflicts in his mind, especially when he goes through tests. Although intellectually he may accept Bahá'u'lláh as a Manifestation of God and may even be well versed in His Writings, he will not be able to have that absolute certitude which endows a human being with spiritual qualities and confers upon him perpetual contentment, assurance and happiness.

The heart is the focal point of warmth and love. It is characteristic of the heart to fall in love with another party, but it is the individual who finds and chooses that party. If he turns his affections to the material world, his heart will very easily become attached to material things. But if he turns to God and spiritual things, then his heart can fall in love with his Creator, provided he fulfils one condition stated by Bahá'u'lláh:

> *O Son of Being!*
> Thy heart is My home; sanctify it for My descent. Thy spirit is My place of revelation; cleanse it for my Manifestation.[2]

How can one sanctify the heart? In another passage, Bahá'u'lláh explains:

> *O Son of Dust!*
> All that is in heaven and earth I have ordained for thee, except the human heart, which I have made the habitation of My beauty and glory; yet thou didst give My home and dwelling to another than Me; and whenever the manifestation of My holiness sought His own abode, a stranger found He there, and, homeless, hastened unto the sanctuary of the Beloved . . .[3]

and again:

> *O My Friend in Word!*
> Ponder a while. Hast thou ever heard that friend and foe should abide in one heart? Cast out then the stranger, that the Friend may enter His home.[4]

To acquire faith, then, and enable the revelation of God to shine within the heart, one must cast out the 'stranger'. This 'stranger' is man's attachment to this world. The most formidable type of attachment, and the most harmful, is attachment to one's own self. It manifests itself mainly in the form of pride in one's own knowledge and in other accomplishments such as rank and position. It is the love of one's own self that renders the individual opinionated, self-centred, proud and egotistical, and in fact denudes him of spiritual qualities. Such a person has indeed harboured within his heart a great enemy, namely, the 'stranger', referred to by Bahá'u'lláh. Even if he becomes a Bahá'í, he will find it difficult to derive spiritual uplift-ment from the Writings of Bahá'u'lláh because attachment to his own self has become a barrier between him and God.

To read the Writings purely with the eye of intellect, while proudly regarding oneself as a being endowed with great qualities and accomplishments, undoubtedly closes the door to the bounties and confirmations of Bahá'u'lláh, and His words therefore cannot influence the heart. Of course when a person truly recognises Bahá'u'lláh as the Manifestation of God he becomes humble before Him, and this is one of the main prerequisites for driving the 'stranger', step by step, out of one's heart. 'Humble thyself before Me, that I may graciously visit thee . . .' is Bahá'u'lláh's clear admonition to man.

> Blind thine eyes, that thou mayest behold My beauty; stop thine ears, that thou mayest hearken unto the sweet melody of My voice; empty thyself of all learning, that thou mayest partake of My knowledge; and sanctify thyself from riches, that thou mayest obtain a lasting share from the ocean of My eternal wealth . . .[5]

There is a beautiful Persian story in verse which elucidates this point quite vividly. It concerns a drop of rain falling down from the clouds. The drop knew itself to be the water of life, the most precious element that God had created, and so it was proud of itself. Boasting all the way down it suddenly saw that it was falling into an ocean beneath. Suddenly it recognised its own insignificance and exclaimed: 'If this exists then what am I?!' When the ocean heard this expression of humility it attracted the drop to itself and, as a reward, made it a companion of the pearl.

The following is part of one of the obligatory prayers by Bahá'u'lláh. Though very brief, it is reminiscent of the story of the drop and the ocean, and serves as a perfect confession of who we are:

> I bear witness, O my God, that thou has created me to know Thee and to worship Thee. I testify, at this moment, to my powerlessness and to Thy might, to my poverty and to Thy wealth . . .[6]

The daily recital of any of the three obligatory prayers can act as a mighty weapon in the spiritual battle against one's own self, a battle that every believer must fight in order to subdue his greatest enemy and drive the 'stranger' away. The recital of the obligatory prayer, which is enjoined upon every believer by Bahá'u'lláh and constitutes one of the most sacred rites of the Faith, is a major factor in enabling a soul to recognise its own impotence in relation to its Creator and to acknowledge its own shortcomings.

The saying of obligatory prayers, coupled with the daily reciting of the Holy Writings as ordained by Bahá'u'lláh in the *Kitáb-i-Aqdas*, and a deeper study of the Revelation of Bahá'u'lláh, will enable the believer to gain a glimpse of the majesty and grandeur of the Blessed Beauty. Like the drop when it saw the ocean, he will become humble and self-effacing. The 'stranger' will be driven out and the heart filled with the spirit of God's Faith. It is at this stage that the believer will be tested.

Tests are an integral part of life. Even in the physical world there are tests: for example, we note that when there is movement there is also resistance; the faster one moves, the greater the resistance. Therefore, a fast-moving object meets enormous resistance from the air because of its sheer speed.

This is true in a spiritual sense too. When the individual recognizes the station of Bahá'u'lláh and embraces His Cause, he is tested in many ways, often without realizing it. Each time he is successful in passing a test, he will acquire greater spiritual insight and grow stronger in faith. He will then come closer to God and will be elevated to a higher level of service; next time his tests will be more difficult. We are not always able to pass a test, but God in His mercy will provide the opportunity to overcome the barriers on another occasion. But if through attachment to this world the ego dominates, one's faith will be weakened and one may even lose it altogether.

For no matter how strongly an individual may believe in Bahá'u'lláh, and however intense may be his love for Him, his faith will depend upon the extent to which he is willing and eager to obey His laws, teachings and commandments. Indeed, man's part in the Covenant is to first recognize and then wholeheartedly obey the Manifestation of God in every respect.

Many people today frown upon the word 'obedience'. In present-day society, in which all moral and spiritual values are declining, the concept of obedience is usually associated with dictatorship, tyranny, religious fanaticism and narrow-mindedness. Often this view is held by educated men and women who are otherwise open-minded and intelligent. These people come from all walks of life; some belong to religious movements with liberal leanings, others may be humanist, agnostic or atheists. They have keenly observed the terrible consequences which blind obedience to various political regimes or religious hierarchies has engendered, and they are fearful of any movement, whether religious or secular, which demands absolute obedience to its commandments.

Bahá'ís consider these people to be worthy of praise and admiration, fully sympathize with their views and appreciate their apprehension. They are not to be blamed for their attitude towards the subject. The fault lies within religious and political institutions; even a cursory study of the old established religions, now broken up into so many differing sects, indicates that their leaders have strayed far from the path which their Founders originally laid down for them. Many of these leaders have misrepresented the true religion of God, misunderstood its purpose, misinterpreted its teachings, adulterated its verities, compromised its principles, fabricated its dogmas, and, for expediency and selfish benefit, paid only lip service to its spiritual truths. There are today millions of people, followers of the world's major religions, who have fallen into the trap of outdated religious doctrines which they do not comprehend, but who blindly accept and follow their leaders.

No wonder that Bahá'u'lláh has condemned religious leaders in such strong terms as these:

> The source and origin of tyranny have been the divines. Through the sentences pronounced by these haughty and wayward souls the rulers of the earth have wrought that which ye have heard . . . The reins of the heedless masses have been, and are, in the hands of the exponents of idle fancies and vain imaginings. Those decree what they please.[7]

In the *Kitáb-i-Íqán*, He states:

> Leaders of religion, in every age, have hindered their people from attaining the shores of eternal salvation, inasmuch as they held the reins of authority in their mighty grasp. Some for the lust of leadership, others through want of knowledge and understanding, have been the cause of the deprivation of the people.[8]

In another passage in the same book He deplores the state of those who blindly follow their religious leaders:

> And the people also, utterly ignoring God and taking them for their masters, have placed themselves unreservedly under the authority of these pompous and hypocritical leaders, for they have no sight, no hearing, no heart of their own to distinguish truth from falsehood.[9]

The new spirit of the age breathing into the minds and hearts of men in this century has awakened many of them to this tragedy. Religious leaders have so distorted the truth of their religions that their voices, which in olden days inspired multitudes, are now heard by these people with various degrees of indifference or hostility. Consequently, a great many people today have broken the shackles which religious leaders had placed on their minds and succeeded in freeing themselves from this bondage. Many are disillusioned with religion altogether, some are lukewarm followers, while others have swelled the ranks of agnostics and atheists. Most of these people are honest thinkers who have come as a result of their bitter experience to denounce the doctrine of obedience to the teachings of a religion.

It is not only the leaders of the established religions who, by misrepresenting the teachings of their Faiths, have alienated the people. We also come across many a 'false prophet' who, out of love for leadership and personal gain, has appeared in the guise of a 'holy man', announcing himself as a saviour of men and founder of a religious sect, advocating some sensational or corrupt and immoral practice. He then attracts simple-minded or ignorant persons to his cause, exploits them for his own benefit, holds them tight in the clutches of his authority and rules over their minds and souls. It is this kind of blind obedience which is abhorred by every discerning person.

On the other hand, man in his daily life wholeheartedly obeys the directive of individuals or institutions that speak with the voice of truth. He is willing to accept authority which is credible and trustworthy in his view. For instance, a motorist will unhesitatingly follow the sign-post on a road until he reaches his destination. This blind following is due to his faith in the authority of the body which has set up the signposts. Similarly, a patient will willingly allow a surgeon to operate on a cancerous growth because he has faith in his diagnosis.

There will be a similar response if one recognizes the truth of the Cause of God. Once recognized as credible, obedience to the teachings will not be difficult to achieve. Since man's part in the Covenant of God is obedience to His teachings, it is clear that he cannot fulfil his obligation unless he recognizes the truth of His Revelation. It is highly significant that the first subject which Bahá'u'lláh has chosen to expound in the *Kitáb-i-Aqdas* is the part man has to play in this Covenant with his Creator. The following is the opening paragraph of the Most Holy Book:

> The first duty prescribed by God for His servants is the recognition of Him Who is the Dayspring of His Revelation and the Fountain of His laws, Who representeth the Godhead in both the Kingdom of His Cause and the world of creation. Whoso achieveth this duty hath attained unto all good; and whoso is deprived thereof, hath gone astray, though he be the author of every righteous deed. It behoveth every one who reacheth this most sublime station, this summit of transcendent glory, to observe

every ordinance of Him Who is the Desire of the world. These twin duties are inseparable. Neither is acceptable without the other. Thus hath it been decreed by Him Who is the Source of Divine inspiration.[10]

So we see that what is required of man in this Covenant is two-fold: to recognize the Manifestation of God as the source of all good and then to follow His commandments.

As has already been stated, one of the most important commandments of Bahá'u'lláh is to turn to the Centre of His Covenant after Him. This injunction has been revealed in the *Kitáb-i-Aqdas*, the *Kitáb-i-'Ahd*, and other Tablets. In the *Súriy-i-Ghuṣn* Bahá'u'lláh refers to 'Abdu'l-Bahá in these words:

> Render thanks unto God, O people, for His appearance; for verily He is the most great Favour unto you, the most perfect bounty upon you; and through Him every mouldering bone is quickened. Whoso turneth towards Him hath turned towards God, and whoso turneth away from Him hath turned away from My Beauty, hath repudiated My Proof, and transgressed against Me. He is the Trust of God amongst you, His charge within you, His manifestation unto you and His appearance among His favoured servants . . . We have sent Him down in the form of a human temple. Blest and sanctified be God Who createth whatsoever He willeth through His inviolable, His infallible decree. They who deprive themselves of the shadow of the Branch, are lost in the wilderness of error, are consumed by the heat of worldly desires, and are of those who will assuredly perish.[11]

Therefore, to a true Bahá'í who is steadfast in the Covenant, obedience to the utterances of 'Abdu'l-Bahá is obedience to God. Recognition of the station of Bahá'u'lláh and believing in Him, important as they are, will not be a sufficient guarantee of one's faith unless one remains loyal and steadfast in His Covenant. One of the distinguishing features of the Faith of Bahá'u'lláh is that He has not abandoned His followers to their own devices. He has left in their midst a source of divine guidance to which they can turn. He conferred His divine powers and authority upon 'Abdu'l-Bahá and made a firm covenant with the believers to follow and obey Him with absolute devotion and love. This covenant was extended to include Shoghi Effendi and the Universal House of Justice. Therefore faith in Bahá'u'lláh is not a mere acknowledgement of His divine message, but involves, in addition, obedience and faithfulness to those upon whom He has conferred the mantle of infallibility.

It is natural for a human being to accept and follow those teachings with which he is already in agreement. The measure of man's steadfastness in the Covenant, however, may be determined by the individual's response to teachings or statements in Bahá'í Holy Writings which may be contrary to his way of thinking. Should a believer who comes across such a teaching, unhesitatingly and at once acknowledge that he must be wrong in his understanding of the subject, and that the words of Bahá'u'lláh and His teachings are the truth born of the Revelation of God for this age, such a soul is truly firm in the Covenant. Of course, the individual may go through conflicts in his mind resulting from his inability to understand the wisdom of a particular statement; he should not despair, for through prayer and action he may in time recognise the truth of the point that caused him such a problem earlier.

By the time the Ministry of 'Abdu'l-Bahá was drawing to a close, the communities of the East and the West had grown steadily and the believers had been deepened in the subject of the Covenant. Firmness in the Covenant was the most commonly discussed topic among the friends in those days. Indeed, 'Abdu'l-Bahá had bestowed upon them a most precious heritage: a wealth of knowledge and understanding of the Covenant, its significance and its vital link with the faith of the believer.

Those who have reached the pinnacle of faith and recognize the station of Bahá'u'lláh with absolute certitude – that He and no one else is God's Viceregent on earth – cannot but render instant and exact obedience to every one of His commandments. In a spirit of love and devotion, they will also show the same measure of obedience and submissiveness to the words of 'Abdu'l-Bahá and Shoghi Effendi, and to the directives of the Universal House of Justice. The following words of Bahá'u'lláh revealed in the *Kitáb-i-Aqdas* establish for all time the criterion for constancy and firmness in His Covenant:

> Were He to decree as lawful the thing which from time immemorial had been forbidden, and forbid that which had, at all times, been regarded as lawful, to none is given the right to question His authority. Whoso will hesitate, though it be for less than a moment, should be regarded as a transgressor.[12]

Steadfastness in the Covenant is a relative term, and its intensity varies in each individual. The measure of a believer's firmness in the Covenant depends upon the extent to which he will readily acknowledge the truth of the utterances of Bahá'u'lláh or of those upon whom He has conferred infallibility.

Dr Yúnis Khán, that trusted secretary of the Master who was immortalized by the designation 'herald of the Covenant', has, in his precious memoirs, left for posterity some examples of firmness in the Covenant. The following is a summary translation of a story which describes the aftermath of the defection of Mírzá Áqá Ján to the Covenant-breakers, when a great many of his defamatory letters fell into the hands of 'Abdu'l-Bahá.* It is a story which demonstrates the intensity of Dr Yúnis Khán's faith in the Master and his utter submission to His word.

> After the rebellion of Mírzá Áqá Ján, his many letters written in denunciation of the Covenant were scattered all over a table in the reception room of 'Abdu'l-Bahá, and the friends used to read some of them and become aware of the machinations and plots of the trouble-makers and stirrers of mischief . . . In those days when He visited the reception room, 'Abdu'l-Bahá would often say something about these letters. One day, as He was looking at them, His attention was drawn to a certain letter which He picked up and read aloud; he showed its seal and signature to the friends who were present. As I was standing at the far end of the room, He called me to come forward and see the signature for myself. As a gesture of humility I bowed and went a little forward. He again called me to come close and see it. I took one step forward and bowed, meaning that it was not necessary for me to see as I believed that the words of the Master were true. Thereupon for the third time He emphatically ordered me to go forward and see the signature with my own eyes. This time I complied with His command.
>
> After this experience my mind was troubled and I became very concerned. I wanted to know what was the wisdom of the Master in insisting that I must see the signature with my own eyes, because I did not believe in my eyes as much as I believed in the words of the Master. My vision might make mistakes but His words were the truth of God's Revelation. For a long time I was worried that perhaps I did not have enough faith. I used to pray about this, until years later the wisdom of it became clear to me . . .[13]

Dr Yúnis Khán explains that some time later when he returned to Ṭihrán he became aware that some of the believers were confused about Mírzá Áqá Ján. One day Dr Yúnis Khán met a certain Prince who was a believer of wide repute, but who could not understand that Mírzá Áqá Ján had been unfaithful and had written many defamatory letters addressed to various Bahá'ís. Dr Yúnis Khán continues the story:

> I said to the Prince that I had seen the letters myself, indeed I was ordered by the Master to examine Mírzá Áqá Ján's signature and seal. He said 'Did you really see it with your own eyes?' When I answered in the affirmative, he said: 'I trust in your words; you have dispelled my doubts. I am so relieved.' I said to him: 'You don't know how relieved *I* am!' Then I told him the story of the anguish of my heart.[14]

Dr Yúnis Khán then realized that the Master's insistence that he see the signature with his own eyes had not meant that he was not firm in the Covenant, but was rather necessary in order to strengthen the faith of this other believer.

* See above, pp. 187–9.

PART III

THE LESSER COVENANT

2. The Formative Age

CHAPTER TWENTY-FOUR

The Close of the Heroic Age

As we survey the Ministry of 'Abdu'l-Bahá, we are struck by the evidences of unprecedented victories which had been won in both East and West as a direct result of the establishment of the Covenant of Bahá'u'lláh. The overshadowing power of divine authority born of that Covenant and released to the community of the Most Great Name by 'Abdu'l-Bahá over a period of almost three decades, had endowed the believers with a new vitality. That same power had also confounded both the Covenant-breakers and their non-Bahá'í allies. The Centre of the Covenant Himself, though surrounded by a host of unfaithful, cruel and devious relatives and other individuals who had broken the Covenant and were assiduously trying to eliminate Him, had established His ascendancy over His adversaries and demonstrated the invincibility of the Cause. He had built for posterity that solid foundation upon which the unity of the Bahá'í community is now based, and invested the believers with the impregnable armour of the Covenant which Bahá'u'lláh has bequeathed to His followers for the protection of their Faith.

During 'Abdu'l-Bahá's Ministry the message of Bahá'u'lláh had reached the Western world, but adherents of the Cause were few in number in most parts of the globe. Had the violators of the Covenant remained faithful, the Cause of God would have achieved greater victories and vast numbers would have embraced the Faith. The breaking of the Covenant, as we have already stated,* caused the course of history to change. However, because of the greatness of this Revelation which has ushered in the Day of God, the Covenant-breakers did not succeed in changing the character of the Faith, or in altering the course of its progress. Their action has only resulted in slowing down its growth and delaying the spread of its Message.

In one of His Tablets, 'Abdu'l-Bahá confirms that the onward march of the Faith had been slowed down by the action of the Covenant-breakers. These are His words:

* See above, pp. 156–9.

. . . This musk-scented breeze* shall perfume the nostrils of the people of the world, and this spirit shall resuscitate the dead.

The offensive odour of violation hath temporarily arrested the onward movement of the Cause, for otherwise the divine teachings, like unto the rays of the sun, would immediately spread and permeate all regions.[1]

Shoghi Effendi has summarized some of the major achievements of the Cause during the Ministry of the Master in the following passage:

Through Him the Covenant, that '*excellent and priceless Heritage*' bequeathed by the Author of the Bahá'í Revelation, has been proclaimed, championed and vindicated. Through the power which that Divine Instrument had conferred upon Him the light of God's infant Faith had penetrated the West, had diffused itself as far as the Islands of the Pacific, and illumined the fringes of the Australian continent. Through His personal intervention the Message, Whose Bearer had tasted the bitterness of a life-long captivity, had been noised abroad, and its character and purpose disclosed, for the first time in its history, before enthusiastic and representative audiences in the chief cities of Europe and of the North American continent. Through His unrelaxing vigilance the holy remains of the Báb, brought forth at long last from their fifty-year concealment, had been safely transported to the Holy Land and permanently and befittingly enshrined in the very spot which Bahá'u'lláh Himself had designated for them and had blessed with His presence. Through His bold initiative the first Mashriqu'l-Adhkár of the Bahá'í world had been reared in Central Asia, in Russian Turkistán, whilst through His unfailing encouragement a similar enterprise, of still vaster proportions, had been undertaken, and its land dedicated by Himself in the heart of the North American continent. Through the sustaining grace over-shadowing Him since the inception of His ministry His royal adversary had been humbled to the dust, the arch-breaker of His Father's Covenant had been utterly routed, and the danger which, ever since Bahá'u'lláh had been banished to Turkish soil, had been threatening the heart of the Faith, definitely removed. In pursuance of His instructions, and in conformity with the principles enunciated and the laws ordained by His Father, the rudimentary institutions, heralding the formal inauguration of the Administrative Order to be founded after His passing, had taken shape and been established. Through His unremitting labours, as reflected in the treatises He composed, the thousands of Tablets He revealed, the discourses He delivered, the prayers, poems and commentaries He left to posterity, mostly in Persian, some in Arabic and a few in Turkish, the laws and principles, constituting the warp and woof of His Father's Revelation, had been elucidated, its fundamentals restated and interpreted, its tenets given detailed application and the validity and indispensability of its verities fully and publicly demonstrated. Through the warnings He sounded, an unheeding humanity, steeped in materialism and forgetful of

* The Message of Bahá'u'lláh.

its God, had been apprized of the perils threatening to disrupt its ordered life, and made, in consequence of its persistent perversity, to sustain the initial shocks of that world upheaval which continues, until the present day, to rock the foundations of human society. And lastly, through the mandate he had issued to a valiant community, the concerted achievements of whose members had shed so great a lustre on the annals of His own ministry, He had set in motion a Plan which, soon after its formal inauguration, achieved the opening of the Australian continent, which, in a later period, was to be instrumental in winning over the heart of a royal convert to His Father's cause, and which, today, through the irresistible unfoldment of its potentialities, is so marvellously quickening the spiritual life of all the Republics of Latin America as to constitute a befitting conclusion to the records of an entire century.[2]

With the passing of 'Abdu'l-Bahá on 28 November 1921, the most glorious period in the history of the Faith, described by Shoghi Effendi as the 'heroic' or 'Apostolic' age, came to an end. The most precious seed of the community of the Most Great Name, planted in the soil of human society by the hand of the Blessed Beauty and watered by the blood of countless martyrs of the Faith, had germinated; by the time of the ascension of 'Abdu'l-Bahá it had grown sufficiently to attract the allegiance of a number of followers. The stage was now set for the further growth of the Bahá'í community in the succeeding years of the 'Formative Age', destined to flourish in the fullness of time as a world community embracing the peoples and nations of the world in one common Faith. Concerning that consummation in the development of the Bahá'í world community Shoghi Effendi writes:

The Age that had witnessed the birth and rise of the Faith had now closed. The Heroic, the Apostolic Age of the Dispensation of Bahá'u'lláh, that primitive period in which its Founders had lived, in which its life had been generated, in which its greatest heroes had struggled and quaffed the cup of martyrdom, and its pristine foundations been established – a period whose splendours no victories in this or any future age, however brilliant, can rival – had now terminated with the passing of One Whose mission may be regarded as the link binding the Age in which the seed of the newborn Message had been incubating and those which are destined to witness its efflorescence and ultimate fruition.

The Formative Period, the Iron Age, of that Dispensation was now beginning, the Age in which the institutions, local, national and international, of the Faith of Bahá'u'lláh were to take shape, develop and become fully consolidated, in anticipation of the third, the last, the Golden Age destined to witness the emergence of a world-embracing Order enshrining the ultimate fruit of God's latest Revelation to mankind, a fruit whose maturity must signalize the establishment of a world civilization and the formal inauguration of the Kingdom of the Father upon earth as promised by Jesus Christ Himself.[3]

Although the passing of 'Abdu'l-Bahá was a harbinger of a new Age which was to usher in the systematic development and consolidation of the Bahá'í Community, its immediate effect upon the believers was that of a paralysing blow striking them down and plunging them into agony. The loss of the Master was a calamity to the grief-stricken and inconsolable community. Added to this tragic bereavement was a deep sense of anxiety which seized the minds and hearts of the followers of Bahá'u'lláh immediately after 'Abdu'l-Bahá's passing. This bitter ordeal, which lasted for no less than forty days, ended with the announcement by the Greatest Holy Leaf of the appointment of Shoghi Effendi as the Guardian of the Faith, as set out in the Will and Testament of the Master.

During the short period separating the ascension of the Master and the announcement of Shoghi Effendi's appointment, the perturbing thought uppermost in the minds of some of the believers was the position of the Arch-breaker of the Covenant, Mírzá Muḥammad-'Alí. Was he going to succeed 'Abdu'l-Bahá as laid down in the *Kitáb-i-'Ahd*, the Will and Testament of Bahá'u'lláh? Some were confused, wondering how the provisions of this momentous document could be allowed to materialize when the very person who had assiduously tried to undermine the foundation of the Cause of God for almost thirty years was none other than Muḥammad-'Alí himself. But the great majority of the believers knew that because of his deviation from the Faith, his appointment was null and void. We have discussed this particular subject in more detail in Chapter 8 describing the circumstances through which Mírzá Muḥammad-'Alí's appointment by Bahá'u'lláh was not fulfilled.

Soon after 'Abdu'l-Bahá's ascension, Mírzá Muḥammad-'Alí published far and wide his claim that according to the text of the *Kitáb-i-'Ahd* he was now 'Abdu'l-Bahá's successor. Not only did he publish this claim among the Persian Bahá'í community, but he also announced himself as the successor of Bahá'u'lláh in an Egyptian newspaper. The Bahá'ís of Egypt responded to his statement by publishing a refutation of his claims in the same newspaper. The following account by Muḥammad Said Adham, an Egyptian believer, describes the events which took place during those anxiety-filled days:

> The beauty of the Beloved disappeared and the hearts are melted by this great calamity. Our only hope is to raise the banner of the Covenant, and with all righteousness, unity and servitude we serve His sublime threshold.
>
> A few days later the great violator addressed the Bahais through the columns of the Arabic newspapers, calling upon them to follow him, according, as he stated, to the will of BAHA'ULLAH, pretending, in his call, that although he had been separated from his brother by God's destiny,

> yet the filial relationship and hearty sensations were strong in his heart, and he tried outwardly to show sorrow for the passing of Abdul-Baha. One of his only two followers in Alexandria confirmed his call on a page of the same paper, but the House of Spirituality in Cairo replied and contested both statements, stating in effect that this violator is not recognized at all by the Bahais, and since he has violated the Covenant of BAHA'ULLAH for thirty years, he is not considered among the Bahais, and has not the authority to speak in their behalf, for all the affairs of the Bahais are now directed by the Houses of Spirituality, all over the world, whose members are elected and who will come under the control of the House of Justice, and they are the only representatives of the Bahais. And this violator is not a Bahai in the true sense of the word and according to the dictates of BAHA'ULLAH. This reply was given especially for the benefit of the public, to give them correct information and to prove to them that the violators are not Bahais and were cut off thirty years ago by their disobedience to the command of BAHA'ULLAH to turn, after His departure, to the Centre of the Covenant, Abdul-Baha, and by their harmful actions to the Cause.
>
> The reply produced the desired effect and we, individually, spread it among the inquirers and thus enlarged the circle of its influence.[4]

In the United States of America a public statement was issued by Shu'á'u'lláh, that son of the Arch-breaker of the Covenant who had been involved in the conspiracy to put 'Abdu'l-Bahá to death. In it he invited the American Bahá'ís to turn to his father who, he claimed, was the legitimate successor of Bahá'u'lláh after 'Abdu'l-Bahá. His call was utterly ignored by the believers in the West.

In Persia, with the exception of a few Covenant-breakers, the Bahá'í community paid no attention to Muḥammad-'Alí's circular letters claiming successorship of 'Abdu'l-Bahá. The publication of the *Will and Testament* among the believers brought much comfort and consolation to their hearts; they realised that the Master had not abandoned them, but rather had left the custodianship of the Cause of God in the hands of Shoghi Effendi, His eldest grandson, whom He appointed as the Guardian of the Faith and the Interpreter of the Holy Writings.

When 'Abdu'l-Bahá passed away in Haifa, Shoghi Effendi was studying at Oxford University in England. The news of the ascension of 'Abdu'l-Bahá came to him as a shattering blow, so much so that when he was informed of it he collapsed and fell flat on the ground. We read the following account by Rúḥíyyih Khánum in her immortal work *The Priceless Pearl*.

> The address of Major Tudor Pole, in London, was often used as the distributing point for cables and letters to the Bahá'ís. Shoghi Effendi himself, whenever he went up to London, usually called there. On 29 November 1921 at 9.30 in the morning the following cable reached that office:

Cyclometry London
His Holiness 'Abdu'l-Bahá ascended Abhá Kingdom. Inform friends.

Greatest Holy Leaf

In notes he made of this terrible event and its immediate repercussions Tudor Pole records that he immediately notified the friends by wire, telephone and letter. I believe he must have telephoned Shoghi Effendi, asking him to come at once to his office, but not conveying to him at that distance a piece of news which he well knew might prove too much of a shock. However this may be, at about noon Shoghi Effendi reached London, went to 61 St James' Street (off Piccadilly and not far from Buckingham Palace) and was shown into the private office. Tudor Pole was not in the room at the moment but as Shoghi Effendi stood there his eye was caught by the name of 'Abdu'l-Bahá on the open cablegram lying on the desk and he read it. When Tudor Pole entered the room a moment later he found Shoghi Effendi in a state of collapse, dazed and bewildered by this catastrophic news. He was taken to the home of Miss Grand, one of the London believers, and put to bed there for a few days. Shoghi Effendi's sister Rouhangeze (sic) was studying in London and she, Lady Blomfield and others did all they could to comfort the heart-stricken youth.[5]

In a letter to a Bahá'í friend written a few days after the passing of the Master, Shoghi Effendi shares with him his thoughts about 'Abdu'l-Bahá and informs him of his plans:

The terrible news has for some days so overwhelmed my body, my mind and my soul that I was laid for a couple of days in bed almost senseless, absent-minded and greatly agitated. Gradually His power revived me and breathed in me a confidence that I hope will henceforth guide me and inspire me in my humble work of service. The day had to come, but how sudden and unexpected. The fact however that His Cause has created so many and such beautiful souls all over the world is a sure guarantee that it will live and prosper and ere long will compass the world! I am immediately starting for Haifa to receive the instructions He has left and have now made a supreme determination to dedicate my life to His service and by His aid to carry out His instructions all the days of my life.

The friends have insisted on my spending a day or two of rest in this place with Dr. Esslemont after the shock I have sustained and tomorrow I shall start back to London and thence to the Holy Land.

The stir which is now aroused in the Bahá'í world is an impetus to this Cause and will awaken every faithful soul to shoulder the responsibilities which the Master has now placed upon every one of us.

The Holy Land will remain the focal centre of the Bahá'í world; a new era will now come upon it. The Master in His great vision has consolidated His work and His spirit assures me that its results will soon be made manifest.

I am starting with Lady Blomfield for Haifa, and if we are delayed in London for our passage I shall then come and see you and tell you how marvellously the Master has designed His work after Him and what remarkable utterances He has pronounced with regard to the future of the Cause. . . .

With prayer and faith in His Cause, I am your well-wisher in His service,

Shoghi

From Shoghi Effendi's other statements it is clear that although he knew that an envelope addressed to him by the Master was awaiting his return to the Holy Land, he had no prior knowledge at this time that he was appointed by 'Abdu'l-Bahá in His Will and Testament as the Guardian of the Faith, the Interpreter of the Word of God, and the One to whom all were bidden to turn. Such a heavy burden, so suddenly and unexpectedly laid upon his shoulders, came to him as a further shock not less agonizing than the earlier one caused by the news of 'Abdu'l-Bahá's passing.

CHAPTER TWENTY-FIVE

Shoghi Effendi, Guardian of the Faith

SHOGHI Effendi was born on 1 March 1897 into the household of 'Abdu'l-Bahá in the prison city of 'Akká. He was a descendant of both Bahá'u'lláh and the Báb. His mother Ḍíyá'íyyih Khánum was the eldest daughter of 'Abdu'l-Bahá. His father Mírzá Hádí Shírází was an Afnán, a grandson of Ḥájí Mírzá Abu'l-Qásim, who was a cousin of the mother of the Báb and a brother of His wife. Thus 'Abdu'l-Bahá describes Shoghi Effendi as 'the most wondrous, unique and priceless pearl that doth gleam from out the twin surging seas . . . the blest and sacred bough that hath branched out from the twin holy Trees.'[1]

Knowing full well the glorious mission which the Almighty had destined for His first grandson, 'Abdu'l-Bahá extended to him from the time he was born a special measure of care and love, and kept him under the wings of His protection. A few of those who had been admitted to the presence of Bahá'u'lláh and who were endowed with spiritual insight observed that the same relationship which existed between Bahá'u'lláh and 'Abdu'l-Bahá* was also apparent between 'Abdu'l-Bahá and Shoghi Effendi. That deep sense of humility and utter nothingness which 'Abdu'l-Bahá manifested toward His Father and which was reciprocated by Him through an outpouring of bounty and love, was likewise established between the young grandchild and his beloved Master. But in order to avoid creating jealousy in the family, 'Abdu'l-Bahá was cautious of openly showing the intensity of His love for Shoghi Effendi. In spite of this, those believers who were endowed with discernment had noticed this special relationship and had no doubt that the reins of the Cause of God would one day be placed in the hands of Shoghi Effendi.

Ḥájí Mírzá Ḥaydar-'Alí and Dr Yúnis Khán were among these enlightened believers. The famous poet and devoted promoter of the Cause 'Andalíb saw signs of his future glory as Shoghi Effendi lay in his cradle, and he composed a most delightful lullaby, a song of praise and victory for him. 'Abdu'l-Bahá conferred upon his first

* See above, ch. 9.

grandchild the name 'Shoghi' (one who longs), but commanded everyone to add the title 'Effendi'* after his name. He even told the father of Shoghi Effendi not to call him merely 'Shoghi'. The Master Himself called him Shoghi Effendi when he was only a child, and wrote this prayer which reveals His cherished hopes for the future of His first grandchild.

> . . . O God! This is a branch sprung from the tree of Thy mercy. Through Thy grace and bounty enable him to grow and through the showers of Thy generosity cause him to become a verdant, flourishing, blossoming and fruitful branch. Gladden the eyes of his parents, Thou Who giveth to whomsoever Thou willest, and bestow upon him the name Shoghi so that he may yearn for Thy Kingdom and soar into the realms of the unseen![2]

From his early childhood, Shoghi Effendi developed a passionate love for 'Abdu'l-Bahá. Their relationship was unlike that between any other child and his grandfather; it was a spiritual force, a heavenly power which linked Shoghi Effendi with his beloved Master. It was this degree of attachment and humble devotion which was reminiscent of 'Abdu'l-Bahá's own attitude toward Bahá'u'lláh. Mrs Ella Goodall Cooper, one of the distinguished believers of the West who attained the presence of 'Abdu'l-Bahá in 'Akká in 1899, has recounted her impressions of Shoghi Effendi as a child when he came into a room to pay his respects to the Master. This took place in the house of 'Abdu'lláh Páshá.

> One day . . . I had joined the ladies of the Family in the room of the Greatest Holy Leaf for early morning tea, the beloved Master was sitting in His favourite corner of the divan where, through the window on His right, He could look over the ramparts and see the blue Mediterranean beyond. He was busy writing Tablets, and the quiet peace of the room was broken only by the bubble of the samovar, where one of the young maidservants, sitting on the floor before it, was brewing the tea.
>
> Presently the Master looked up from His writing with a smile, and requested Ziyyih Khanum to chant a prayer. As she finished, a small figure appeared in the open doorway, directly opposite 'Abdu'l-Bahá. Having dropped off his shoes he stepped into the room, with his eyes focused on the Master's face. 'Abdu'l-Bahá returned his gaze with such a look of loving welcome it seemed to beckon the small one to approach Him. Shoghi, that beautiful little boy, with his exquisite cameo face and his soulful appealing, dark eyes, walked slowly toward the divan, the Master drawing him as by an invisible thread, until he stood quite close in front of Him. As he paused there a moment 'Abdu'l-Bahá did not offer to embrace him but sat perfectly still, only nodding His head two or three

* 'Effendi' is a title which is given to people as a term of respect.

times, slowly and impressively, as if to say—'You see? This tie connecting us is not just that of a physical grandfather but something far deeper and more significant.' While we breathlessly watched to see what he would do, the little boy reached down and picking up the hem of 'Abdu'l-Bahá's robe he touched it reverently to his forehead, and kissed it, then gently replaced it, while never taking his eyes from the adored Master's face. The next moment he turned away, and scampered off to play, like any normal child . . . At that time he was 'Abdu'l-Bahá's only grandchild . . . and, naturally, he was of immense interest to the pilgrims.[3]

This attitude of humility and profound reverence toward the Master was one of the most outstanding features of the life and personality of Shoghi Effendi till the end of his life.

When Shoghi Effendi was a child, a Persian believer asked 'Abdu'l-Bahá about the future of the Cause after Him. In a Tablet He wrote;

> . . . Know verily that this is a well-guarded secret. It is even as a gem concealed within its shell. That it will be revealed is predestined. The time will come when its light will appear, when its evidences will be made manifest, and its secrets unravelled.[4]

Another believer from America wrote to the Master that from the study of the Bible one gathers that the prophecy of Isaiah 'a little child shall lead them'[5] relates to the time after 'Abdu'l-Bahá, and wanted to know if this referred to a real person who would succeed Him. In answer to this, the following Tablet was written:

> O Maidservant of God!
>
> Verily, that child is born and is alive and from him will appear wondrous things that thou wilt hear of in the future. Thou shalt behold him endowed with the most perfect appearance, supreme capacity, absolute perfection, consummate power and unsurpassed might. His face will shine with a radiance that illumines all the horizons of the world; therefore forget this not as long as thou dost live inasmuch as ages and centuries will bear traces of him.
>
> Upon thee be greetings and praise
> 'Abdu'l-Bahá 'Abbás[6]

Dr Yúnis Khán, who was not aware of this Tablet, once received a letter from an American believer saying that some of the friends had heard that the one who would succeed the Master had been born recently. At first, Dr Yúnis Khán found it very difficult to mention this to 'Abdu'l-Bahá, because he could not bring himself to think of a day when the Master would pass away. After some days, he mentioned the question timorously and in a low voice, whereupon 'Abdu'l-Bahá responded in the affirmative and said: 'The triumph of the Cause of God is in his hands.'

Shoghi Effendi grew up in the household of 'Abdu'l-Bahá under His care and protection, but his childhood years were spent in 'Akká during the time when the Master and His family were incarcerated within the walls of the City and subjected to violent opposition by the Covenant-breakers. Great dangers surrounded the Holy Family. Thus Shoghi Effendi experienced, from the early years of his life, the venomous assaults launched against the Cause by the violators of the Covenant. When at one point the situation in 'Akká became too dangerous and unbearable, 'Abdu'l-Bahá sent Shoghi Effendi to Haifa with his nurse; here he lived until the Master was released from imprisonment and the Holy Family moved there permanently.

Concerning Shoghi Effendi's schooling Rúḥíyyih Khánum writes:

> Shoghi Effendi entered the best school in Haifa, the *Collège des Frères*, conducted by the Jesuits. He told me he had been very unhappy there. Indeed, I gathered from him that he never was really happy in either school or university. In spite of his innately joyous nature, his sensitivity and his background – so different from that of others in every way – could not but set him apart and give rise to many a heart-ache; indeed, he was one of those people whose open and innocent hearts, keen minds and affectionate natures seem to combine to bring upon them more shocks and suffering in life than is the lot of most men. Because of his unhappiness in this school 'Abdu'l-Bahá decided to send him to Beirut where he attended another Catholic school as a boarder, and where he was equally unhappy. Learning of this in Haifa the family sent a trusted Bahá'í woman to rent a home for Shoghi Effendi in Beirut and take care of and wait on him. It was not long before she wrote to his father that he was very unhappy at school, would refuse to go to it sometimes for days, and was getting thin and run down. His father showed this letter to 'Abdu'l-Bahá Who then had arrangements made for Shoghi Effendi to enter the Syrian Protestant College, which had a school as well as a university, later known as the American College in Beirut, and which the Guardian entered when he finished what was then equivalent to the high school. Shoghi Effendi spent his vacations at home in Haifa, in the presence as often as possible of the grandfather he idolized and Whom it was the object of his life to serve. The entire course of Shoghi Effendi's studies was aimed by him at fitting himself to serve the Master, interpret for Him and translate His letters into English.[7]

Shoghi Effendi received his Bachelor of Arts degree from the University of Beirut in 1918. He was then able to return to Haifa and serve the Master, which he did uninterruptedly, day and night, with a devotion that knew no bounds. Not only did he serve Him as secretary and translator of His Tablets into English, he also attended to many other duties which he took upon himself in order to assist the Master in His manifold activities. He did this with characteristic sincerity, promptness, and thoroughness, and brought great joy to the heart of the Master. The following story told by Rúḥíyyih Khánum demonstrates Shoghi Effendi's earnestness and perseverance in his work throughout his life.

> Although the Master's work had now increased to such an extent that many people were engaged in constantly serving and assisting Him, there can be no doubt that no one compared with Shoghi Effendi. I remember the Guardian telling me of how (I believe it must have been in early 1920) one of the old American Bahá'ís had sent a gift to the Master of a Cunningham automobile; notice of its arrival at the quayside in port came just as the weekend commenced and the Master gave Shoghi Effendi instructions to see that it was cleared and delivered to the house. Shoghi Effendi told me that although the next day there were no high officials in the port and it was not a business day, he succeeded in getting the car delivered and when it arrived he went to the Master and informed Him it was outside the door. He said the Master was very surprised and immensely pleased and asked him how he had succeeded in doing this. Shoghi Effendi told Him he had taken the papers and gone to the homes of various officials, asking them to sign the documents and give the necessary orders for the car of Sir 'Abdu'l-Bahá 'Abbás to be delivered to Him at once. This was typical of the way Shoghi Effendi did his work throughout his entire life. He always wanted everything done at once, if not sooner, and everything he had any personal control over progressed at that speed.[8]

For a period of two years, until 1920, Shoghi Effendi was the constant companion of 'Abdu'l-Bahá. He accompanied his grandfather when He visited high ranking government officials or religious dignitaries, and saw how the Master treated His friends and dealt with His enemies. In all these encounters, Shoghi Effendi observed the manner in which 'Abdu'l-Bahá conducted Himself, with that majesty and authority which were characteristic of His Person. This period, which brought Shoghi Effendi so close to the Master and linked his heart with His, were among the most fertile years of his life. But this intimate association, in the course of which 'Abdu'l-Bahá bountifully endowed the future Guardian of the Cause of God with special powers and capacities, irrevocably came to an end when it was decided that Shoghi Effendi should enter Oxford University in England to perfect his English in order to achieve his heart's desire to better translate the Tablets of 'Abdu'l-Bahá and other holy writings.

Shoghi Effendi left the Holy Land in the spring of 1920 and began his studies at Balliol College in the autumn of that year. During his short stay in Oxford – a little over one year – he concentrated all his energies on mastering the English language. But he could not complete his education, for the plan of God cut across his plans in a most painful way when 'Abdu'l-Bahá passed away.

Accompanied by his sister Rúḥangíz and by Lady Blomfield, Shoghi Effendi sailed from England on 16 December and arrived in Haifa on the 29th, one month after the passing of the Master. The agony of bereavement had taken its toll, and Shoghi Effendi was physically a broken man. So frail was he that he had to be assisted up the steps of his home on his arrival. Grief-stricken by the absence of the Master, he then had to be confined to bed for a number of days.

The Will and Testament of 'Abdu'l-Bahá was awaiting the arrival of Shoghi Effendi to be opened. Concerning this, Rúḥíyyih Khánum writes:

> When 'Abdu'l-Bahá so unexpectedly and quietly passed away, after no serious illness, the distracted members of His family searched His papers to see if by chance He had left any instructions as to where He should be buried. Finding none, they entombed Him in the centre of the three rooms adjacent to the inner Shrine of the Báb. They discovered His Will – which consists of three Wills written at different times and forming one document – addressed to Shoghi Effendi. It now became the painful duty of Shoghi Effendi to hear what was in it; a few days after his arrival they read it to him. In order to understand even a little of the effect this had on him we must remember that he himself stated on more than one occasion, not only to me, but to others who were present at the table of the Western Pilgrim House, that he had had no foreknowledge of the existence of the Institution of Guardianship, least of all that he was appointed as Guardian; that the most he had expected was that perhaps, because he was the eldest grandson, 'Abdu'l-Bahá might have left instructions as to how the Universal House of Justice was to be elected and he might have been designated the one to see these were carried out and act as Convenor of the gathering which would elect it.[9]

The belief that the Universal House of Justice would come into being immediately after the passing of 'Abdu'l-Bahá was not uncommon among the Bahá'ís. Many of them thought this would happen, and soon after Shoghi Effendi's appointment a few ambitious individuals such as Ávárih and Ahmad Sohrab* tried to insist that the House of Justice should be formed without delay. It is interesting to note that the Master, when in America, spoke to a few friends about the protection of the Faith and the role of the Universal House of Justice in securing this. Here is a summary translation of His words as recorded by Mírzá Maḥmúd Zarqání, the faithful chronicler of His journeys to the West:

> In the car, on the way to the hotel, 'Abdu'l-Bahá expressed His deep concern about the future of the Cause and said: 'I have endured hardships on this journey in order that no breaches may take place within the Cause of God. But I am not optimistic about the turn of events after Me. If I

* See below, chs. 30 and 31.

were certain that all would be well, I would not have left the Holy Land, I would have stayed there close to the Holy Shrine. After the martyrdom of the Báb, the Cause of God for the first time came under strong attack by Mírzá Yaḥya. Another time after the ascension of Bahá'u'lláh it was severely assailed by the Covenant-breakers. I am now afraid that after me some egotistical persons might make fresh attempts to introduce divisions within the community of the friends. If the time were propitious, the House of Justice could be brought into being and it would protect the Cause.'[10]

The Master knew well that Covenant-breakers old and new would renew their onslaught against the Cause of God. From the way the institutions of the Faith have developed since the ascension of 'Abdu'l-Bahá, it can be seen that it was not timely then to establish the Univesal House of Justice straight away. In His wisdom He knew that the Faith first needed a Guardian, whose purpose would be, on the one hand, to lay the foundation of the Administrative Order for future generations to build upon, and, on the other, to wipe out the evils of Covenant-breaking in the Holy Land.

Although the *Will and Testament* of 'Abdu'l-Bahá was read out to Shoghi Effendi soon after his arrival in Haifa, it had to be formally presented to the members of the Family and others in the Holy Land. On 3 January 1922 in the presence of nine persons, mainly senior members of 'Abdu'l-Bahá's family, and in Shoghi Effendi's absence the *Will and Testament* was read aloud, and its seal, signature and handwriting were shown to them. Later, the Greatest Holy Leaf sent cables to Persia and America – the two major communities at that time – informing them that according to the *Will and Testament* of 'Abdu'l-Bahá, Shoghi Effendi was appointed 'Guardian of the Cause of God'.

A major source of consolation and support for Shoghi Effendi from the time he returned to the Holy land until the end of her earthly life in 1932 was the Greatest Holy Leaf, the adored sister of 'Abdu'l-Bahá. She, the most outstanding woman in the Bahá'í Dispensation, was a tower of strength for everyone. And now that the Master had gone to His heavenly abode, the burden of many responsibilities, and, especially in the early days, the protection of the Guardian from the assaults of the Covenant-breakers, were placed upon her shoulders.

Rúḥíyyih Khánum writes:

Immediately after these events Shoghi Effendi selected eight passages from the Will and circulated them among the Bahá'ís; only one of these referred to himself, was very brief and was quoted as follows: 'O ye the faithful loved ones of 'Abdu'l-Bahá! It is incumbent upon you to take the greatest care of Shoghi Effendi . . . For he is, after 'Abdu'l-Bahá, the

> guardian of the Cause of God, the Afnán, the Hands (pillars) of the Cause and the beloved of the Lord must obey him and turn unto him.' Of all the thundering and tremendous passages in the Will referring to himself, Shoghi Effendi chose the least astounding and provocative to first circulate among the Bahá'ís. Guided and guiding he was from the very beginning.[11]

The Bahá'í world was now embarking upon a new age, but as in those days after the ascension of Bahá'u'lláh when the community had entered a prolonged period of tests and trials, the *Will and Testament* likewise provided the same challenges to the Bahá'ís. We have discussed in some detail the significance of the *Will and Testament* of Bahá'u'lláh, and that of 'Abdu'l-Bahá, and how these two Wills acted as examination papers for the followers of Bahá'u'lláh. Before they were issued, every believer was part of the community of the Most Great Name, and there was no division, but after their contents became known, the unfaithful failed the tests of the Covenant; they were cast out and the community was purged.

The news of Shoghi Effendi's appointment as Guardian of the Cause of God was hailed by the entire Bahá'í world. There were nevertheless some faithless individuals, motivated by their ambition to emerge as leaders of the community, who arose in opposition to Shoghi Effendi and despite all his efforts to save them, proved unrepentant and were expelled from the community. However, it took some time before these egotistical personalities surfaced and launched their attacks.

There was another category of people, who, although they did not openly oppose Shoghi Effendi in those early days, ultimately revealed their lack of faith in him as the Guardian of the Cause of God. These included most of the members of 'Abdu'l-Bahá's family. They failed to see Shoghi Effendi in the light of 'Abdu'l-Bahá's *Will and Testament* in which he is referred to, among other things, as the 'Sign of God', the 'expounder of the Words of God' and the 'Light that . . . shineth from the Dayspring of Divine Guidance'. These people contended that since Shoghi Effendi was only a youth, he ought to establish the House of Justice so that it could assist him in his work. In later years, one by one, the members of the family rose up against Shoghi Effendi, violated the Covenant, and were responsible for the greatest of sufferings which were inflicted upon him during his ministry.

But the immediate opposition came from the old, established Covenant-breakers, especially Mírzá Muḥammad-'Alí, his brother and his associates. These unscrupulous men, who during the latter part of 'Abdu'l-Bahá's Ministry had became demoralized, with no choice but to creep into the limbo of ignominy and defeat, raised their heads once again when they saw a youth of twenty-five years of age at the helm. They thought they could wrest the leadership of the Bahá'í community from him, but soon discovered that they were gravely mistaken.

The Arch-breaker of the Covenant in the Holy Land, and a few of his supporters in America and Persia, actively tried to create division within the Community. Shortly before Shoghi Effendi's arrival in Haifa, the Greatest Holy Leaf sent a cable to the American believers which read: NOW IS PERIOD OF GREAT TESTS. THE FRIENDS SHOULD BE FIRM AND UNITED. NAKESEENS* STARTING ACTIVITIES THROUGH PRESS, OTHER CHANNELS ALL OVER WORLD. SELECT COMMITTEE OF WISE COOL HEADS TO HANDLE PRESS PROPAGANDA IN AMERICA.[12]

At the same time as Mírzá Muḥammad-'Alí was calling on the Bahá'ís to follow him as 'Abdu'l-Bahá's successor, he took ruthless action to take over the custody of the Shrine of Bahá'u'lláh for himself. Rúḥíyyih Khánum describes this:

> Shortly after 'Abdu'l-Bahá's ascension, this disgruntled and perfidious half-brother had filed a claim, based on Islamic law (he who pretended he had still a right to be the successor of Bahá'u'lláh!), for a portion of the estate of 'Abdu'l-Bahá which he now claimed a right to as His brother. He had sent for his son, who had been living in America and agitating his father's claims there, to join him in this new and direct attack on the Master and His family. Not content with this exhibition of his true nature he applied to the civil authorities to turn over the custodianship of Bahá'u'lláh's Shrine to him on the grounds that he was 'Abdu'l-Bahá's lawful successor. The British authorities refused on the grounds that it appeared to be a religious issue; he then appealed to the Muslim religious head and asked the Mufti of Akka to take formal charge of Bahá'u'lláh's Shrine; this dignitary, however, said he did not see how he could do this as the Bahá'í teachings were not in conformity with Shariah law. All other avenues having failed he sent his younger brother, Badiullah, with some of their supporters, to visit the Shrine of Bahá'u'lláh where, on Tuesday, 30 January, they forcibly seized the keys of the Holy Tomb from the Bahá'í caretaker, thus asserting Muḥammad 'Alí's right to be the lawful custodian of his Father's resting-place. This unprincipled act created such a commotion in the Bahá'í Community that the Governor of Akka ordered the keys to be handed over to the authorities, posted guards at the Shrine, but went no further, refusing to return the keys to either party.[13]

Since Shoghi Effendi had arrived in Haifa, the shock of the announcement of his appointment as the Guardian of the Faith, coupled with the terrible ordeal of the passing of the Master, were taking their toll on his health. He was so crushed under the weight of

* Covenant-breakers.

bereavement that he could not even attend a memorial meeting for the Master which was held in His residence forty days after His ascension. Three weeks later, this latest transgression by the Covenant-breakers in laying hands on the sacred Shrine of Bahá'u-'lláh came as a further blow.

Although the seizure of the key of the Shrine by this bitterest enemy brought further shock and sorrow to the tender and sensitive heart of Shoghi Effendi, yet, in spite of his physical weakness, the evidence of divine guidance was apparent in his actions, actions characterised by a resolve and a wisdom which called to mind the wisdom of 'Abdu'l-Bahá and His penetrating foresight. Shoghi Effendi appealed to the government for the return of the key, but his absence from the Holy Land, which lasted about eight months, postponed the issue. He pursued this matter with great diligence until full rights of possession were restored to him by the authorities. Rúḥíyyih Khánum writes in greater detail about this episode:

> The matter which concerned Shoghi Effendi most, however, was the Shrine of Bahá'u'lláh at Bahjí. The keys of the inner Tomb were still held by the authorities; the right of access to other parts of the Shrine was accorded Bahá'ís and Covenant-breakers alike; the Bahá'í custodian looked after it as before, and any decision seemed in a state of abeyance. Shoghi Effendi never rested until, through representations he made to the authorities, backed by insistent pressure from Bahá'ís all over the world, he succeeded in getting the custody of the Holy Tomb back into his own hands. On 7 February 1923 he wrote to Tudor Pole: 'I have had a long talk with Col. Symes and have fully explained to him the exact state of affairs, the unmistakable and overwhelming voice of all the Bahá'í Community and their unshakable determination to stand by the Will and Testament of 'Abdu'l-Bahá. Recently sent a message to Muḥammad 'Alí requiring from him the sum of £108. for the expenses of the policeman, contending that he being the aggressor is liable to this expense. So far he has not complied with this request and I await future developments with deep anxiety.'
>
> The following day Shoghi Effendi received this telegram from his cousin, who was in Jerusalem:
>
> His Eminence Shoghi Effendi Rabbani, Haifa.
> Letter received immediate steps taken the final decision by the High Commissioner is in our favour the key is yours.[14]

As time went on, the pressures from the Covenant-breakers increased. At the same time, there were some whom 'Abdu'l-Bahá had befriended, but who did not take Shoghi Effendi's leadership seriously because they thought he could never manage to govern the affairs of the Faith after 'Abdu'l-Bahá. These people created an uneasy situation within the Family by their negative attitude. For instance, when they noticed that Shoghi Effendi was not following the practice of 'Abdu'l-Bahá in attending the mosque every Friday, and that he wore European clothes, they gradually distanced themselves from the Bahá'í community.

It is important to note at this juncture that although Shoghi Effendi did not find it appropriate in his day, there had been great wisdom in 'Abdu'l-Bahá's attendance at the mosque during His Ministry. At the time of Bahá'u'lláh's arrival, the people of 'Akká considered a man who did not attend a mosque or a church to be an infidel. The Faith had neither formulated its teachings and laws, nor was its true identity known to the inhabitants of the Holy Land. It had been presented to the population as a misguided sect of unbelievers. In these circumstances, refusal to go to the mosque would have stigmatized Bahá'u'lláh and His companions as infidels. By attending the mosque they came to be regarded in the eyes of the public as believers in God. One of the useful by-products of attending the mosque was that 'Abdu'l-Bahá established a marvellous relationship with the people, and in time emerged, in the words of an admirer, as the 'Master of 'Akká'.

Bearing in mind his ill-health and the weight of the custodianship of so mighty a Cause which was so suddenly placed upon his shoulders, the pressures which were building up around Shoghi Effendi were intolerable. Under such circumstances he decided to leave the Holy Land for a temporary period during which he hoped to pray and commune with his Beloved in solitude, to regain his strength and confidence, and return to the duties which were awaiting him at the World Centre. He announced his decision in a letter he wrote in English to the Bahá'ís of the West, and in a similar one in Persian to the Bahá'ís of the East.

> He is God!
>
> This servant, after that grievous event and great calamity – the ascension of His Holiness 'Abdu'l-Bahá to the Abhá Kingdom – has been so stricken with grief and pain and so entangled in the troubles (created) by the enemies of the Cause of God, that I consider my presence here, at such a time and in such an atmosphere, is not in accordance with the fulfillment of my important and sacred duties.
>
> For this reason, unable to do otherwise, I have left for a time the affairs of the Cause, both at home and abroad, under the supervision of the Holy Family and the headship of the Greatest Holy Leaf – may my soul be a sacrifice to her – until, by the Grace of God, having gained health, strength, self-confidence and spiritual energy, and having taken into my hands, in accordance with my aim and desire, entirely and regularly the work of service, I shall attain to my utmost spiritual hope and aspiration.
>
> The servant of His Threshold,
> Shoghi[15]

At so crucial a time in the history of the Faith, the direction of the affairs of the Cause by the Holy Family headed by the Greatest Holy Leaf is yet more evidence of the invincibility of the Covenant of Bahá'u'lláh. As we look back upon those critical days so soon after the passing of the Master, when the Covenant-breakers had embarked upon their relentless campaign of opposition, the departure of Shoghi Effendi from the Holy Land seemed, if we look at it from a human point of view, to provide an opportunity for the Covenant-breakers to manoeuvre divisions within the community. But there were no such ill effects. Although the Guardian had left, the believers remained united and steadfast in the Covenant. They rallied around the Greatest Holy Leaf, that noble figure who bore the weight of so great a responsibility during Shoghi Effendi's absence, and who handed the reins of the Cause back to him on his return. Through her writings she instilled the spirit of confidence into the Bahá'í community and directed the manifold efforts of the believers. These writings, addressed to the Bahá'ís of the East and the West, are inspiring, eloquent and soul-stirring. In their lucidity, profundity and style, they are similar to the Tablets of 'Abdu'l-Bahá. In them the Greatest Holy Leaf urges the Bahá'ís to remain firm in their faith and steadfast in their love for the Guardian of the Cause of God. From the moment the Master passed away until her last breath, the Greatest Holy Leaf poured out upon Shoghi Effendi her loving support and protection. To attempt to recount her noble activities and splendid leadership during this period is beyond the scope of this book; suffice it to say that having rendered devoted services to Bahá'u'lláh and 'Abdu'l-Bahá during the Heroic Age of the Faith, she played a vital role in the Formative Age. She was instrumental in helping to bring about a transition from that former Age into the latter. During Shoghi Effendi's absence from the Holy Land, she prepared the Bahá'í world for the advent of a new day in the fortunes of the Faith, and after his return she continued to support him in the work of the building of Bahá'u'lláh's new World Order.

CHAPTER TWENTY-SIX

Building the Foundations of the Administrative Order

WHEN the *Will and Testament* of 'Abdu'l-Bahá was circulated among the friends, many who studied its provisions reached the conclusion that the formation of the Universal House of Justice had to take place at an early date. Indeed, in January 1922, soon after the announcement of his appointment as the Guardian of the Faith was made, Shoghi Effendi wrote a very inspiring letter to the Bahá'ís of Persia[1] in which he indicated that he would be sending them detailed arrangements for the establishment of the Universal House of Justice.

Shortly before Shoghi Effendi's departure for Europe, a number of prominent Bahá'ís visited the Holy Land at his invitation. They impressed upon him the necessity of bringing into being the House of Justice. This opinion, as we have seen, was shared by most members of 'Abdu'l-Bahá's family as well as some high-ranking government officials. Most likely the government authorities were concerned about Shoghi Effendi's ability to govern the affairs of the Bahá'í world single-handed. This lack of faith by non-Bahá'ís was understandable, but from the members of the family it revealed a sign of weakness in the Covenant.

Apart from his own thoughts, the pressure of public opinion for the establishment of the House of Justice must have exercised Shoghi Effendi's mind for some time, but the guidance of Bahá'u'lláh and His protection, as promised by 'Abdu'l-Bahá, were always vouchsafed to the Guardian, and his decisions were divinely guided. It did not take long before Shoghi Effendi decided that the time was not ripe for the formation of the Universal House of Justice. In retrospect it can be seen that such an august institution needed a solid foundation upon which it could be built. The Local Spiritual Assemblies* which are the foundation of this Supreme Institution

* The Local Spiritual Assembly is a council of nine members elected by the Bahá'ís in a locality. It is the body which has jurisdiction over the affairs of the local Bahá'í community.

were weak and very few in number, and National Spiritual Assemblies,* the pillars upon which it had to be erected, were non-existent.

It must be remembered that towards the end of 'Abdu'l-Bahá's Ministry, there were only a few rudimentary local Bahá'í institutions in America and Persia.† They were loosely organised, and the believers had no conception of the real function of a Local Spiritual Assembly, nor did they have any experience in the art of Bahá'í consultation. In these circumstances, Shoghi Effendi wisely concentrated his attention on the building of the local and national institutions of the Faith which were later to buttress and support the structure of the international institutions. Although he was physically under a great deal of strain and stress, nevertheless Bahá'u'lláh's protection was surrounding him. With the unshakeable resolve and determination which were characteristic of him, and before departing for Europe in April 1922, Shoghi Effendi sent verbal messages to Germany and Britain to form Local Spiritual Assemblies and to arrange for the election of a National Assembly in each country. To the United States he sent a message to transform the body known as 'Executive Board' into a legislative institution. As we look back upon these early days of Shoghi Effendi's ministry, we may see these actions as initial steps towards the erection of the framework of the Administrative Order of Bahá'u'lláh.

On his return to the Holy Land in December 1922, Shoghi Effendi, recovered from his fatigue, refreshed and re-invigorated, took over the reins of the Cause of God and actively dedicated himself to the task of directing the many activities of the Bahá'í communities in the East and the West. From the start he found himself in need of a competent secretariat for English and Persian letters. The only person who responded to his call for such service was the renowned Dr John Esslemont who served the Guardian with the utmost devotion, zeal and enthusiasm until his untimely death in 1925 robbed Shoghi Effendi of one of his ablest assistants. Although he tried to invite others to undertake a similar service, there were no suitable candidates available anywhere in the Bahá'í world.

There were very few believers, if any, who had the vision and the experience needed to work with Shoghi Effendi in his efforts to build the foundations of the institutions of the Faith around the world. Although there were a number of outstanding scholars of the Faith in Persia who had studied all the Holy Writings available to them and were well versed in the history of the Faith as well as in the

* The National Spiritual Assembly is elected by the national community through its delegates; it has jurisdiction over the affairs of the Bahá'í community in a country or region.

† For a detailed account of the formation of the first Spiritual Assembly in the Bahá'í world, see *The Revelation of Bahá'u'lláh*, vol. 4, pp. 290–3.

Scriptures of older religions, it is highly unlikely that any of them had perceived the significance of the institutions of the Faith, the inevitability of their rise and the emergence of the Administrative Order of Bahá'u'lláh, the framework of His World Order for mankind. These learned Bahá'is were fully conscious of the importance of the Spiritual Assemblies, which Bahá'u'lláh and 'Abdu'l-Bahá had emphasized. But probably none of them realized that the Local Spiritual Assembly was destined to become the primary institution of the Administrative Order, of which very little was known at the time. Nor did anyone realize that the institutions of the Faith would become channels for the flow of the spiritual forces latent within the Revelation of Bahá'u'lláh.

It becomes clear now only after the lapse of many decades how little the early Bahá'ís understood the basic principles of Bahá'u'lláh's Administrative Order, whose foundations Shoghi Effendi had begun to build. This is perhaps the main reason why Shoghi Effendi could not find a single believer who sufficiently understood the nature of the work which he had set himself to carry out, and who was free to come to the Holy Land and assist him. In the West, for example, there was Horace Holley, an able administrator who had grasped the significance of what Shoghi Effendi was doing, and would serve him faithfully in the important work of building the local and national institutions of the Faith in America. But because of his work there, he could not be spared to go to the Holy Land to assist Shoghi Effendi.

It is important to realize that whoever was given the privilege to work with the Guardian was never in a position to make a decision for him. It was he and he alone who directed the affairs of the Cause. Unlike world leaders who usually authorize their subordinates to make decisions, 'Abdu'l-Bahá and Shoghi Effendi were the sole decision-makers, because they alone were the recipients of divine guidance and no one else was. Indeed, the writings of 'Abdu'l-Bahá and Shoghi Effendi are all products of that infallible guidance which was conferred upon them by the Author of the Faith Himself.

In order to comprehend the workings and development of the Administrative Order of Bahá'u'lláh, one should study its genesis. It goes back to the Author of the Faith Himself. A distinguishing feature of the Revelation of Bahá'u'lláh is that the Word of God, sent down for the spiritualization and guidance of man, has been preserved in its original purity and freed from every manner of human interference. This vast and glorious Revelation is not subject to man's meddling, for to no one is given the right to tamper with His Word or His teachings.

In a previous chapter* we stated that the revelation of the Word of God may be likened to the rain which falls and creates a pool which in this analogy represents the repository of the Word of God – of the holy scriptures of each religion. In this Dispensation, the outpourings of the words of Bahá'u'lláh have been so copious as to create a veritable ocean of Revelation, and Bahá'u'llah sealed off this ocean from all intruders. During His lifetime, He Himself proferred the Water of Life to the peoples of the world, and after His passing, the outpouring of His Revelation was channelled through the person of 'Abdu'l-Bahá. He it was who was created especially by God to act after the passing of Bahá'u'lláh as a container and reservoir for this great ocean. Bahá'u'lláh did not simply hand over His word and His Revelation free for all to manipulate. Rather, He entrusted them to 'Abdu'l-Bahá and enjoined upon all the believers to turn to Him in order to receive their portion of the bounties of God which were enshrined within His Revelation. To no one did He give the right to interpret His words, to add or take away even a dot from His Writings. Using the above analogy, this mighty ocean was placed within the Person of 'Abdu'l-Bahá, who acted as a wall around it and sealed it off from man's interference. So thoroughly did He embody the Revelation of Bahá'u'lláh within His soul that after the ascension of Bahá'u'lláh, it was only through 'Abdu'l-Bahá that the redeeming power of His Faith and the spiritual energies He had released could flow to mankind.

Despite the many unscrupulous attempts to break through the walls which protected that ocean, despite those several outstanding followers of the Faith who rebelled against the Centre of the Covenant in order to promote their own selfish desires, to introduce their own ideas into the teachings, to divide the Faith of God and consequently to contaminate the heavenly stream of the Word of God, the Covenant of Bahá'u'lláh was based on a firm foundation and the walls around the ocean – the Covenant – were impregnable. This great ocean surged within the soul of 'Abdu'l-Bahá for twenty-nine years, and He bestowed its life-giving waters upon thousands of men and women throughout the East and the West. He left for posterity the unadulterated Word of God free of every trace of distortion or defilement.

God in His everlasting Covenant has bestowed upon mankind two priceless gifts. One is the Revelation of Bahá'u'lláh, which is supreme over all things; the other, His Centre of the Covenant. He has given man both the ocean and the receptacle for it. These two gifts are God's part in His Covenant. Man's part is to draw the life-

* See above, pp. 100–102.

giving waters of His Revelation from this reservoir. But how was it possible for this objective to be achieved after the passing of 'Abdu'l-Bahá? To bring this about, the Master delineated in His *Will and Testament* the outlines of a marvellous scheme: the institutions of the Administrative Order, designed to provide access to this spiritual reservoir.

The believers in the Formative Age had now to play their part, as bidden by 'Abdu'l-Bahá, in the building up of the institutions of the Faith which were to act as channels for carrying the energies released by the Revelation of Bahá'u'lláh to every part of the planet. The raising of these institutions is to be regarded as the role that man has to fulfil in the eternal Covenant which God has made with him in this Dispensation.

Knowing their inadequacy and immaturity, 'Abdu'l-Bahá did not leave the believers alone in this task. He gave them Shoghi Effendi, whom He extolled as a pearl, unique and priceless, the Sign of God on earth, the Guardian of the Cause of God and the Expounder and Interpreter of His Word. The blue-print of the institutions, local, national and international – the channels designed to carry the water of life – had been given by Bahá'u'lláh and 'Abdu'l-Bahá. Shoghi Effendi's task then was that of the builder. In the same way as a city engineer distributes clean water to each home from the reservoir by means of the pumping station and the use of main ducts and local pipes, the world-vitalizing forces of the Faith of Bahá'u'lláh pour out from its World Centre through the institutions of the Guardianship and the Universal House of Justice into the National Spiritual Assemblies and through these to the Local Spiritual Assemblies all over the planet. Thus the water of life, deposited within the ocean of Bahá'u'lláh's Revelation and protected by the institution of the Covenant, is carried to the peoples of the world through the national and local institutions of the Faith without being adulterated by man.

In the course of his thirty-six years of Guardianship, Shoghi Effendi acted, in terms of the above analogy, as the pumping station, connecting the ocean of Bahá'u'lláh's Revelation to the National and Local Assemblies. Today this function is performed by the Universal House of Justice, and the world-vivifying forces of the Faith stream out from this divinely ordained institution into a vast network of Assemblies, bestowing spiritual life upon multitudes in every part of the world. Concerning the significance of these divinely ordained channels, Shoghi Effendi makes this remarkable statement:

> The moment had now arrived* for that undying, that world-vitalizing Spirit that was born in Shíráz, that had been rekindled in Ṭihrán, that had been fanned into flame in Baghdád and Adrianople, that had been carried

* The beginning of the Formative Age.

to the West, and was now illuminating the fringes of five continents, to incarnate itself in institutions designed to canalize its outspreading energies and stimulate its growth.[2]

The 'world-vitalizing spirit' mentioned by Shoghi Effendi is generated by the Revelation of Bahá'u'lláh and is the cause of the quickening of mankind. It is the vivifying energies released by this spirit which penetrate the hearts of men and enable them to recognize the station of Bahá'u'lláh and embrace His Faith.

This statement by Shoghi Effendi conferred a completely new insight upon the followers of Bahá'u'lláh in every land. It became evident to them that whereas in the Heroic Age* this 'world-vitalizing spirit' which bestowed spiritual life upon the believers had been released by Bahá'u'lláh and 'Abdu'l-Bahá Themselves, in the Formative Age this same spirit reaches humanity through the instrumentality of the local, national and international institutions of the Faith. It follows therefore, that in this day, a Local Spiritual Assembly becomes a channel through which the forces of the Revelation of Bahá'u'lláh can reach a locality. Once this institution is established, the believers in that locality can bring this 'world-vitalizing spirit' into contact with the people, thus enabling its life-giving energies to enter their hearts.

The usual process by which an individual is influenced by the Message of Bahá'u'lláh and becomes assured of its truth is through the instrumentality of a Bahá'í teacher, or by reading some literature on the Faith. But in the final analysis, what makes a person a confirmed Bahá'í is the spirit of the Faith which touches his heart. This spirit flows today through the Spiritual Assembly and permeates the locality where this institution is established. The Spiritual Assembly thus plays a vital part in releasing the spiritual energies emanating from the ocean of the Revelation of Bahá'u'lláh in a town, city or village.

Should there be no Spiritual Assembly in a locality, a Bahá'í group† will provide this channel, for it is an institution which is destined to evolve into a Spiritual Asembly. The same is true of a Bahá'í centre‡ when the lone individual acts as a nucleus of an Assembly. It can be seen therefore that the institution of the Spiritual Assembly is the essential element in the propagation of the Faith of Bahá'u'lláh throughout the world. The other element is the individual Bahá'í, who is the means for diffusing 'divine fragrances' among the people. All this demonstrates that the local, national and international institutions of the Faith, the carriers of the 'world-

* The period covering the Ministries of the Báb, Bahá'u'lláh, and 'Abdu'l-Bahá, 1844–1921.
† A Bahá'í group consists of two to eight believers in a locality.
‡ A Bahá'í centre is a locality in which one believer resides.

vitalizing spirit', are an essential means for the propagation of the Faith, its establishment in every land, and its emergence in the fullness of time.

It took several years for the Bahá'ís to appreciate the significance of the Local and National Spiritual Assemblies and their relationship to the institution of the Universal House of Justice. A clear picture emerged when Shoghi Effendi built a monument over the grave of the Greatest Holy Leaf on Mount Carmel. He described this monument as a symbol of the Administrative Order. It consists of a base, symbolic of the Local Spiritual Assemblies, a number of columns placed upon the base, symbolic of the National Spiritual Assemblies, and a dome built upon these representing the Universal House of Justice. The weight of this supreme institution of the Faith of Bahá'u'lláh is placed upon the National Spiritual Assemblies which in turn rest upon the Local Spiritual Assemblies. This interdependence of the institutions of the Administrative Order, which is built from the grass roots upwards (and not from the top down!) demonstrates that, in the absence of Local and National Spiritual Assemblies, it was not possible for Shoghi Effendi to arrange for the election of the Universal House of Justice.

The Administrative Order is the nucleus and the pattern of the promised World Order of Bahá'u'lláh which must come into being in the distant future; this Administrative Order has been developing since the ministry of Shoghi Effendi began in 1921. It is functioning today and is concerned with the affairs of the Bahá'í community, but the writings of Shoghi Effendi make it clear that it is destined in the fullness of time to evolve into that new World Order designed to govern the whole of the human race under one universal Faith. It is important to note that Bahá'u'lláh Himself revealed the principles of His new World Order and ordained the establishment of some of its institutions. 'Abdu'l-Bahá, in His Will and Testament, created further institutions and thus filled the gaps which Bahá'u'lláh had deliberately left open. Like an architect, 'Abdu'l-Bahá, in this important document, delineated the features of the Administrative Order and appointed Shoghi Effendi to be its builder.

Barely two months had passed from the passing of the Master when Shoghi Effendi, grief-stricken and disconsolate, and encompassed by a number of distressing problems including bitter opposition from Mírzá Muḥammad-'Alí and the 'old' Covenant-breakers, turned his attention to the two major communities of the Bahá'í world, Persia and America. In January 1922 He wrote important letters to these two communities in which he urged the believers in tender and moving language to arise in service for the triumph of His Cause. The following excerpts from his first letter to the friends in

North America demonstrate his extraordinary capacity to rise above the intense afflictions which had assailed him from every direction, to entirely detach himself from his other cares and to turn his attention to the vital issues of enthusing the believers and assuring them of the promise of divine assistance.

Dearly beloved brethren and sisters in 'Abdu'l-Bahá:

At this early hour when the morning light is just breaking upon the Holy Land, whilst the gloom of the dear Master's bereavement is still hanging thick upon the hearts, I feel as if my soul turns in yearning love and full of hope to that great company of His loved ones across the seas, who now share with us all the agonies of His separation.

. . . the shock has been too terrible and sudden for us all to recover from in so short a time, but whenever we recall His Sayings and read His Writings, hope springs in our hearts and gives us the peace that no other material comfort can give.

How well I remember when, more than two years ago, the Beloved Master turning to a distinguished visitor of His, who was seated by Him in His garden, suddenly broke the silence and said:– *'My work is now done upon this plane; it is time for me to pass on to the other world.'* Did He not in more than one occasion state clearly and emphatically:– *'Were ye to know what will come to pass after me, surely would ye pray that my end be hastened?'* In a Tablet sent to Persia when the storm raised years ago by that Committee of Investigation was fiercely raging around Him, when the days of His incarceration were at their blackest, He reveals the following:– *'Now in this world of being, the Hand of Divine Power hath firmly laid the foundations of this all-highest Bounty and this wondrous Gift. Gradually whatsoever is latent in the inner-most of this Holy Cycle shall appear and be made manifest, for now is but the beginning of its growth and the dayspring of the revelation of its Signs. Ere the close of this Century and of this Age, it shall be made clear and manifest how wondrous was that Springtide and how heavenly was that Gift!'*

With such assuring Utterances and the unmistakable evidences of His sure and clear knowledge that His end was nigh, is there any reason why the followers of His Faith, the world over, should be perturbed? Are not the prayers He revealed for us sufficient source of inspiration to every worker in His Cause? Have not His instructions paved before us the broad and straight Path of Teaching? Will not His now doubly effective power of Grace sustain us, strengthen us and confirm us in our work for Him? Ours is the duty to strive by day and night to fulfil our own obligations and then trust in His Guidance and never failing Grace. Unity amongst the friends, selflessness in our labours in his Path, detachment from all worldly things, the greatest prudence and caution in every step we take, earnest endeavour to carry out only what is His Holy Will and Pleasure, the constant awareness of His Presence and of the example of His Life, the absolute shunning of whomsoever we feel to be an enemy of the Cause . . . these, and foremost among them is the need for unity, appear to me as our most vital duties, should we dedicate our lives for His service. Should we in this spirit arise to serve Him, what surer and greater promise have we than the one His Glorious Father, Bahá'u'lláh, gives us in His Most Holy Book:– '*Verily, We behold you from Our Realm of Effulgent Glory, and shall graciously aid whosoever ariseth for the triumph of Our Cause with the hosts of the Celestial Concourse and a company of Our chosen angels.*'[3]

Shoghi Effendi thus embarked upon the building of the foundations of the Administrative Order. Issuing his second letter to the friends in America as early as March 1922, a little over three months after the passing of 'Abdu'l-Bahá, he began a programme of education of the believers in the art of Bahá'í administration. In this letter, Shoghi Effendi calls on the American believers to recognize 'the full significance of this Hour of Transition', calls on them to set aside 'minor considerations' and to 'present a solid united front to the world animated by no other desire but to serve and propagate His Cause'. He emphasizes the importance of having Local Spiritual Assemblies 'in every locality where the number of adult declared believers exceeds nine', and advocates the establishment, through indirect election by the believers, of a National Body to administer 'the spiritual activities of the body of the friends in that land'. He quotes the words of Bahá'u'lláh and 'Abdu'l-Bahá describing the duties and functions of the Spiritual Assemblies, the attitude of those who take counsel together, the spirit that must animate them during consultation, and the steps they must take to bring about unity, love and harmony among the members of the Assembly. Indeed, Bahá'í consultation is one of the most important subjects which Shoghi Effendi dwells upon in this letter.

He quotes parts of a celebrated Tablet by 'Abdu'l-Bahá which may be regarded as a charter for the functioning of every Spiritual Assembly in the Bahá'í world:

> The prime requisites for them that take counsel together are purity of motive, radiance of spirit, detachment from all else save God, attraction to His Divine Fragrances, humility and lowliness amongst His loved ones, patience and long-suffering in difficulties and servitude to His exalted Threshold. Should they be graciously aided to acquire these attributes, victory from the unseen Kingdom of Bahá shall be vouchsafed to them. In this day, assemblies of consultation are of the greatest importance and a vital necessity. Obedience unto them is essential and obligatory. The members thereof must take counsel together in such wise that no occasion for ill-feeling or discord may arise. This can be attained when every member expresseth with absolute freedom his own opinion and setteth forth his argument. Should any one oppose, he must on no account feel hurt for not until matters are fully discussed can the right way be revealed. The shining spark of truth cometh forth only after the clash of differing opinions. If after discussion, a decision be carried

unanimously well and good; but if, the Lord forbid, differences of opinion should arise, a majority of voices must prevail.

The first condition is absolute love and harmony amongst the members of the assembly. They must be wholly free from estrangement and must manifest in themselves the Unity of God, for they are the waves of one sea, the drops of one river, the stars of one heaven, the rays of one sun, the trees of one orchard, the flowers of one garden. Should harmony of thought and absolute unity be non-existent, that gathering shall be dispersed and that assembly be brought to naught. The second condition:– They must when coming together turn their faces to the Kingdom on High and ask aid from the Realm of Glory. They must then proceed with the utmost devotion, courtesy, dignity, care and moderation to express their views. They must in every matter search out the truth and not insist upon their own opinion, for stubbornness and persistence in one's views will lead ultimately to discord and wrangling and the truth will remain hidden. The honoured members must with all freedom express their own thoughts, and it is in no wise permissible for one to belittle the thought of another, nay, he must with moderation set forth the truth, and should differences of opinion arise a majority of voices must prevail, and all must obey and submit to the majority. It is again not permitted that any one of the honoured members object to or censure, whether in or out of the meeting, any decision arrived at previously, though that decision be not right, for such criticism would prevent any decision from being enforced. In short, whatsoever thing is arranged in harmony and with love and purity of motive, its result is light, and should the least trace of estrangement prevail the result shall be darkness upon darkness. . . . If this be so regarded, that assembly shall be of God, but otherwise it shall lead to coolness and alienation that proceed from the Evil One. Discussions must all be confined to spiritual matters that pertain to the training of souls, the instruction of children, the relief of the poor, the help of the feeble throughout all classes in the world, kindness to all peoples, the diffusion of the fragrances of God and the exaltation of His Holy Word. Should they endeavour to fulfil these conditions the Grace of the Holy Spirit shall be vouchsafed unto them, and that assembly shall become the centre of the Divine blessings, the hosts of Divine confirmation shall come to their aid, and they shall day by day receive a new effusion of Spirit.[4]

The pattern of the institutions of the Faith was thus to be first built up in North America, which he referred to as 'the Cradle of the Administrative Order'. Later, Bahá'í institutions in other countries were to be fashioned on the same model. This was a noteworthy action, which as the years went by proved to be of vital importance for the development of the institutions of the Faith throughout the world. Shoghi Effendi's directives, embodied in his letters, for the establishment and proper functioning of spiritual assemblies and other agencies of the Faith, were issued in the course of several years and were implemented and put into practice first by the North American community, thus creating a suitable pattern for other communities to adopt.

In the early years of the Guardianship there were two major Bahá'í communities in the world: Persia and North America. Persia was the Cradle of the Faith. The twin Manifestations of God, the Báb and Bahá'u'lláh, had appeared in that country when its people were sunk in the depths of ignorance and perversity, but from within such a corrupt nation God raised up heroes and heroines, men and women who were transformed into spiritual giants and who became immortalized through their sacrificial deeds during the Heroic Age of the Faith. Through this transformation the power of God and the influence of His word could be demonstrated to the peoples of the world.

Now, in the Formative Age, this same process was to be repeated in the West. Shoghi Effendi decided to build up the institutions of the new world order in North America, a continent which despite its spirit of enterprise and benevolence, was 'notorious', he said, for its political and social corruption. Once again God's omnipotence was to be demonstrated, through the building up of the Faith's nascent institutions within such a materialistic society. Concerning this development, Shoghi Effendi writes:

> In the light of this fundamental principle it should always be borne in mind, nor can it be sufficiently emphasized, that the primary reason why the Báb and Bahá'u'lláh chose to appear in Persia, and to make it the first repository of their Revelation, was because, of all the peoples and nations of the civilized world, that race and nation had, as so often depicted by 'Abdu'l-Bahá, sunk to such ignominious depths, and manifested so great a perversity, as to find no parallel among its contemporaries. For no more convincing proof could be adduced demonstrating the regenerating spirit animating the Revelations proclaimed by the Báb and Bahá'u'lláh than their power to transform what can be truly regarded as one of the most backward, the most cowardly, and perverse of peoples into a race of heroes, fit to effect in turn a similar revolution in the life of mankind. To have appeared among a race or nation which by its intrinsic worth and high attainments seemed to warrant the inestimable privilege of being made the receptacle of such a Revelation would in the eyes of an unbelieving world greatly reduce the efficacy of that Message, and to detract from the self-sufficiency of its omnipotent power. The contrast so strikingly presented in the pages of Nabíl's Narrative between the heroism that immortalized the life and deeds of the Dawn-Breakers and the degeneracy and cowardice of their defamers and persecutors is in itself a most impressive testimony to the truth of the Message of Him Who had instilled such a spirit into the breasts of His disciples. For any believer of that race to maintain that the excellence of his country and the innate

nobility of its people were the fundamental reasons for its being singled out as the primary receptacle of the Revelations of the Báb and Bahá'u'lláh would be untenable in the face of the overwhelming evidence afforded so convincingly by that Narrative.

To a lesser degree this principle must of necessity apply to the country which has vindicated its right to be regarded as the cradle of the World Order of Bahá'u'lláh. So great a function, so noble a role, can be regarded as no less inferior to the part played by those immortal souls who, through their sublime renunciation and unparalleled deeds, have been responsible for the birth of the Faith itself. Let not, therefore, those who are to participate so predominantly in the birth of that world civilization, which is the direct offspring of their Faith, imagine for a moment that for some mysterious purpose or by any reason of inherent excellence or special merit Bahá'u'lláh has chosen to confer upon their country and people so great and lasting a distinction. It is precisely by reason of the patent evils which, notwithstanding its other admittedly great characteristics and achievements, an excessive and binding materialism has unfortunately engendered within it that the Author of their Faith and the Centre of His Covenant have singled it out to become the standard-bearer of the New World Order envisaged in their writings. It is by such means as this that Bahá'u'lláh can best demonstrate to a heedless generation His almighty power to raise up from the very midst of a people, immersed in a sea of materialism, a prey to one of the most virulent and long-standing forms of racial prejudice, and notorious for its political corruption, lawlessness and laxity in moral standards, men and women who, as time goes by, will increasingly exemplify those essential virtues of self-renunciation, of moral rectitude, of chastity, of indiscriminating fellowship, of holy discipline, and of spiritual insight that will fit them for the preponderating share they will have in calling into being that World Order and that World Civilization of which their country, no less than the entire human race, stands in desperate need. Theirs will be the duty and privilege, in their capacity first as the establishers of one of the most powerful pillars sustaining the edifice of the Universal House of Justice, and then as the champion-builders of that New World Order of which that House is to be the nucleus and forerunner, to inculcate, demonstrate, and apply those twin and sorely-needed principles of Divine justice and order – principles to which the political corruption and the moral license, increasingly staining the society to which they belong, offer so sad and striking a contrast.

Observations such as these, however distasteful and depressing they may be, should not, in the least, blind us to those virtues and qualities of high intelligence, of youthfulness, of unbounded initiative, and enterprise which the nation as a whole so conspicuously displays, and which are being increasingly reflected by the community of the believers within it. Upon these virtues and qualities, no less than upon the elimination of the evils referred to, must depend, to a very great extent, the ability of that community to lay a firm foundation for the country's future role in ushering in the Golden Age of the Cause of Bahá'u'lláh.[5]

In the first sixteen years of his Guardianship Shoghi Effendi devoted His efforts to teaching the principles of Bahá'í administration patiently and with the utmost love and perseverance to the Bahá'ís of the East and the West. He taught them how to build spiritual assemblies, how to serve on them, and how to reinforce and consolidate their foundations. In the course of innumerable letters which he wrote in English and Persian to individuals as well as to Assemblies during this period, he explained the significance of the Administrative Order, the role of the institutions of the Faith in Bahá'í communities, and their future emergence as the framework of the new World Order of Bahá'u'lláh.

In pursuit of this he elaborated on various aspects of the functioning of these Assemblies, the manner of their election, the election of delegates to the National Convention and their responsibilities in electing the National Spiritual Assembly, the relationship which must bind the Local to the National bodies, the management of the Bahá'í Fund, and other details which ensure, on the one hand, uniformity of practice in the Bahá'í world on matters of principle, and on the other, diversity on issues of a secondary nature.

It is important to state at this juncture that during the thirty-six years of his Guardianship and as a consequence of his building the foundations of the Administrative Order, Shoghi Effendi did not add anything to, or take anything from, the teachings, laws and principles which Bahá'u'lláh and 'Abdu'l-Bahá had promulgated. In his capacity as the authorized Interpreter of the Word of God, and as the Guardian of the Cause appointed by 'Abdu'l-Bahá, he applied those teachings and ordinances to the structuring of the Bahá'í community, and implemented those directives which Bahá'u'lláh and 'Abdu'l-Bahá had either implicitly or explicitly issued in Their Writings for the building up of these institutions. These, he explained, were to be the channels for the flow of the spiritual forces released by the Revelation of Bahá'u'lláh. Indeed, Shoghi Effendi did not make pronouncements or issue explanations or directives on matters which were not already included in the Sacred Text. He referred these to the Universal House of Justice, which is authorized by Bahá'u'lláh to legislate on those subjects which are either obscure, or not mentioned in the Writings.

It did not take very long for the believers in both the East and the West to realize that the day had now dawned for the structuring of the Bahá'í community throughout the world. In the Heroic Age of the Faith, the believers were so enamoured of Bahá'u'lláh that they hardly paid any attention to anything but Him; they were intoxicated by the wine of His presence. Many of the early believers who had come in contact with Bahá'u'lláh and 'Abdu'l-Bahá had become new creations endowed with divine qualities and ablaze with His love. These souls were oblivious of themselves, so wholly were they attracted to Bahá'u'lláh. Most of them did not know much about the laws and the teachings of the Faith, but they were so carried into the realms of the spirit by His all-swaying power that they willingly offered up their lives for their Beloved.

But now in the Formative Age, it was time to put into practice some of the teachings and ordinances of Bahá'u'lláh whose purpose was building the foundations of His new World Order. Through Shoghi Effendi's guidance, new vision and new insight were bestowed upon the believers. They began to appreciate the workings of the Faith, and many souls rendered valuable service in establishing Local and National Spiritual Assemblies in various parts of the world. During these first sixteen years of the Guardianship a growing number of Local Spiritual Assemblies were established in many countries, and no less than eight National Spiritual Assemblies were formed in the five continents.

Among other events which took place during this period, the most grievous was the passing of the Greatest Holy Leaf in July 1932. The anguish her death brought to the heart of Shoghi Effendi is indescribable. She had been the only source of solace, encouragement and real support for him in the family. In the course of a few years after her passing, almost the entire family of 'Abdu'l-Bahá broke the Covenant one after another and rose up against him. Forsaken and betrayed, Shoghi Effendi carried the enormous weight of the responsibilities of the Cause, alone, until, in 1937, he took as his consort Rúḥíyyih K͟hánum, the only daughter of Mr and Mrs Sutherland Maxwell, and she assisted him ably till the end of his life in 1957.

This union brought special joy to the hearts of the American believers. In answer to their message of congratulations, Shoghi Effendi sent the following cable to the National Spiritual Assembly of the Bahá'ís of the United States and Canada.

> Deeply moved by your message. Institution of Guardianship, head cornerstone of the Administrative Order of the Cause of Bahá'u'lláh, already ennobled through its organic connection with the Persons of Twin Founders of the Bahá'í Faith, is now further reinforced through direct association with West and particularly with the American believers, whose spiritual destiny is to usher in the World Order of Bahá'u'lláh. For my part I desire to congratulate community of American believers on acquisition of tie vitally binding them to so weighty an organ of their Faith.[6]

The achievements of the Faith and the important events which took place during these first sixteen years of the Guardianship are numerous. Notable among them was the verdict of the highest ecclesiastical court in Egypt issued on 10 May 1925 declaring the Faith to be heretical in character, and wholly incompatible with Islám. This document was hailed as a victory by the Guardian because it acknowledged that the Faith is an independent religion, and that it is as different from Islám as Islám is from either the Christian or Jewish Faiths.

Another event which created great agitation in the Bahá'í world, occupied much of Shoghi Effendi's time, and brought anxiety to him was the seizure of the House of Bahá'u'lláh in Baghdád by the Shí'ah community there. This resulted in the submission of a petition to the Council of the League of Nations. After a great many deliberations by that body, a resolution upholding the claim of the Bahá'í Community to that House was issued, but was not implemented by the government concerned.

Among the glorious victories in this period were the teaching exploits of Martha Root, who travelled several times around the world and proclaimed the message of Bahá'u'lláh in a spirit of selfless devotion and self-sacrifice to a great many people. This culminated in Queen Marie of Romania's acknowledgement of the truths enshrined in the Revelation of Bahá'u'lláh. In one of her letters to Shoghi Effendi this noble Queen wrote these moving words:

> Indeed a great light came to me with the Message of Bahá'u'lláh and 'Abdu'l-Bahá. It came as all great messages come at an hour of dire grief and inner conflict and distress, so the seed sank deeply . . . We pass on the Message from mouth to mouth and all those we give it to see a light suddenly lighting before them and much that was obscure and perplexing becomes simple, luminous and full of hope as never before . . . With bowed head I recognize that I too am but an instrument in greater Hands and rejoice in the Knowledge . . .[7]

Other significant developments during this period were the growth of organized youth activities; the enlargement of Bahá'í endowments and properties in the Holy Land, the United States and Persia; the acquisition of historic sites connected with the Faith in Persia; the formation of an International Bahá'í Archives, and the implementation of the ordinance of the Nineteen Day Feast as enjoined by Bahá'u'lláh. Although the injunction of the Nineteen Day Feast had been well known to the believers in Persia from the days of the Báb, yet it was not strictly observed. The followers of Bahá'u'lláh in those days used to hold meetings quite frequently at their homes, but these were not organized at nineteen-day intervals. It was Shoghi Effendi who encouraged the regular observance of the Feast, explained its significance as the bedrock of the Bahá'í community and delineated its main features as the spiritual, the administrative and social parts.

CHAPTER TWENTY-SEVEN

The Expounder of the Revelation of Bahá'u'lláh

OF all the work the Guardian did during his ministry, the greatest and the most enduring contribution to the Cause of Bahá'u'lláh may be said to be his writings, which derive their excellence from the Revelation itself. Shoghi Effendi received his inspiration from the utterances of Bahá'u'lláh and 'Abdu'l-Bahá, which are revealed in the greatest majesty and eloquence and have produced a new and wonderful style in both Persian and Arabic literature. They inspired Bahá'í scholars and writers, who were not only uplifted by the profundity of their words but were enchanted with the new style and new terminologies, which they tried to emulate in their own works. But no one was able to achieve this as Shoghi Effendi did. He grew up in the school of Bahá'u'lláh's and 'Abdu'l-Bahá's writings, he imbibed the essence of their words in such wise that his writings possess a special potency, born of the utterances of the Author of the Faith and of the Centre of His Covenant.

The writings of Shoghi Effendi, looking at them from a literary point of view alone, are truly superb. The eloquence and beauty of his compositions in Persian and Arabic are breathtaking. Although English was not his mother tongue, his writings in that language have been acclaimed by scholars to be remarkable in their expressiveness, forcefulness and fluency. The following passages demonstrate the descriptive power of his inspired pen. Recounting the episode of the Báb, he writes:

> We behold, as we survey the episodes of this first act of a sublime drama, the figure of its Master Hero, the Báb, arise meteor-like above the horizon of Shíráz, traverse the sombre sky of Persia from south to north, decline with tragic swiftness, and perish in a blaze of glory. We see His satellites, a galaxy of God-intoxicated heroes, mount above that same horizon, irradiate that same incandescent light, burn themselves out with that self-same swiftness, and impart in their turn an added impetus to the steadily gathering momentum of God's nascent Faith.[1]

On the occasion of the passing of the Greatest Holy Leaf, he writes:

> Whatever betide us, however distressing the vicissitudes which the nascent Faith of God may yet experience, we pledge ourselves, before the mercy-seat of thy glorious Father, to hand on, unimpaired and undivided, to generations yet unborn, the glory of that tradition of which thou hast been its most brilliant exemplar.
>
> In the innermost recesses of our hearts, O thou exalted Leaf of the Abhá Paradise, we have reared for thee a shining mansion that the hand of time can never undermine, a shrine which shall frame eternally the matchless beauty of thy countenance, an altar whereon the fire of thy consuming love shall burn forever.[2]

These passages, so beautifully composed, speak for themselves. Those Bahá'ís who have studied Shoghi Effendi's works realize that he was under the guidance of Bahá'u'lláh, his pen inspired by Him. Thousands of letters to individuals, Spiritual Assemblies, and Bahá'í communities throughout the world poured from that pen, expounding the teachings and laws of the Faith. These letters are a priceless heritage for generations to come, until the end of this Dispensation.

The only work that Shoghi Effendi wrote originally as a book is *God Passes By*. A masterpiece, it is a concise history filled with vivid detail of the significant events of the first Bahá'í century; it covers the ministries of the Báb, Bahá'u'lláh and 'Abdu'l-Bahá, as well as the birth and development of the Administrative Order. In his masterly style, Shoghi Effendi has condensed many volumes of material within the compass of a few hundred pages. Almost every line of this book is laden with information superbly gleaned, without apparent effort, from numerous historical documents and narratives. It is also profusely and delicately laced with quotations from the vast reservoir of the writings of the Central Figures of the Faith.

The importance attached to *God Passes By* is not merely due to the historical detail which it contains. Being the Guardian of the Faith, Shoghi Effendi was more qualified than anyone else to write such a book on Bahá'í history, because the art of writing any history lies not merely in describing events, but in relating them to each other, putting them in their proper context and in interpreting their influence in society.

As the unerring interpreter of Bahá'u'lláh's Writings, Shoghi Effendi was endowed with a unique capacity to understand and appreciate the Revelation of Bahá'u'lláh to an extent that no other human being can ever hope to achieve. Therein lies the unique nature of *God Passes By*. In it he elucidates every major event in the light of the Revelation of Bahá'u'lláh and injects into every subject a measure of the truth of the Faith. In the course of writing the accounts of the lives of the Central Figures of the Cause and their disciples, he explains the true motives behind their actions, comments on the effect of these actions, puts into right perspective the heroism and self-sacrifice of the Bábí and Bahá'í martyrs, enumerates the victories and the crises that the Faith has encountered, recounts the downfall of its enemies, demonstrates the unfoldment of its world-embracing institutions and foreshadows its future destiny.

Shoghi Effendi's matchless translations of the writings of the Báb, Bahá'u'lláh and 'Abdu'l-Bahá, from Persian and Arabic into English, are another priceless gift to the world. There is no doubt for the Bahá'ís that these superb renderings, which have evoked the praise and appreciation of so many outstanding scholars, were not due to Shoghi Effendi's academic attainments alone, but were influenced by the guidance of Bahá'u'lláh which was vouchsafed to him during his ministry. The modes of expression and the composition of sentences in the Persian and Arabic languages are different from those in English. There are also many words in these two languages for which there are no English equivalents. Shoghi Effendi has overcome these difficulties so successfully that, without losing any thought or concept of the original, he conveys the meaning faithfully in elegant English fully comprehensible to the reader, while at the same time retaining the special flavour of their original form. In translating the Holy Writings Shoghi Effendi has left for posterity a priceless, well-endowed model. The words, phrases and sentences he has used to translate the writings of the Central Figures of the Faith are extensively consulted and used by those who, since his passing, have been engaged in the task of rendering the matchless utterances of Bahá'u'lláh, the Báb and 'Abdu'l-Bahá into English.

The major translations by Shoghi Effendi of the writings of Bahá'u'lláh include the *Hidden Words*, the *Kitáb-i-Íqán*, *Gleanings from the Writings of Bahá'u'lláh*, *Prayers and Meditations of Bahá'u'lláh*, *Epistle to the Son of the Wolf* and numerous passages which he quoted in his own writings. Although not holy scripture, *The Dawn-Breakers*, the history of the first few years of the Faith by Nabíl-i-'Aẓam was also masterfully edited and translated by Shoghi Effendi. The publication of this monumental work in 1932 contributed greatly to a deeper understanding of the life and Revelation of the Báb.

The writings of Shoghi Effendi in Persian and English, although not in the same category as the Tablets of Bahá'u'lláh and 'Abdu'l-Bahá, have greatly enriched Bahá'í literature. In expounding and interpreting the revealed Word, as he was empowered to do by

'Abdu'l-Bahá in the Will and Testament, he clarified many of the abstruse and mysterious passages in the Writings of the Central Figures of the Faith. A source of inspiration for the believers, his letters addressed to individuals and Spiritual Assemblies provide a vast reservoir of guidance which will assist and enlighten the Bahá'í community until the end of this Dispensation in its endeavours to build up and maintain the world-embracing institutions of the new Order of Bahá'u'lláh and usher in the Golden Age of His Faith.

In the early days of his ministry, when the believers in East and West were engaged in promoting the Faith and establishing its institutions, Shoghi Effendi turned his attention to the community in Persia in order to initiate the process of the implementation of the laws of the *Kitáb-i-Aqdas*. The friends in that country were subjected to sporadic outbursts of persecution, resulting in the martyrdom of many. Having built up the framework of the Administrative Order throughout many towns and villages where Local Spiritual Assemblies were functioning, he gave the Persian believers this special task of great importance to the Cause.

Shoghi Effendi refers to the *Kitáb-i-Aqdas* as 'the Charter of the future world civilization'. The laws revealed in that Book are one of the pillars upon which the World Order of Bahá'u'lláh rests. The other pillar is the principles of the Faith which were revealed by Bahá'u'lláh in His Tablets and especially elucidated by 'Abdu'l-Bahá in the course of His travels in the West. That the laws and the principles of the Faith are the two basic parts of the World Order is borne out by Shoghi Effendi's statement: 'Behind the walls of the prison fortress of 'Akká the Bearer of God's newborn Revelation had ordained the laws and formulated the principles that were to constitute the warp and woof of His World Order.'[3]

The concept of religious law as the mainstay of a religion is not often fully appreciated by followers of other religions, including Christians. This is perhaps because the Message of Christ was primarily the establishment of spiritual teachings among His followers, and He did not lay down many laws. On the other hand, a great emphasis is placed upon religious law in Islám, as in Judaism. The laws promulgated by the Prophet of Islám play an important role in His religion, and obedience to them is considered by Muslims to be conducive to the good pleasure of God. For over a thousand years the people of Persia were accustomed to observe the laws of Islám, and considered it to be an act of devotion to God.

Because of their Islamic background, the believers in Persia were very well suited to put into practice some of the laws of the *Kitáb-i-Aqdas*. Not only were they accustomed to observing religious law, but they also had access to the *Kitáb-i-Aqdas*, which the believers in the West did not. However, during the Ministries of Bahá'u'lláh and 'Abdu'l-Bahá, the Bahá'ís were so overwhelmed by the outpouring of the Word of God and so oblivious of everything except their Beloved, that it was as if they were not living in this world. Their thoughts were focused on the glory of Bahá'u'lláh's Revelation; they spent their energies in teaching their fellow men. In these circumstances they did not dwell much on the laws and ordinances of the new Dispensation.

In addition, there were the exhortations of Bahá'u'lláh not to exceed the bounds of wisdom if they were to implement any of His laws. For instance, in the *Kitáb-i-Aqdas* Bahá'u'lláh has forbidden His followers to use the public baths of Persia, because in those days they were extremely filthy.* Yet when one of the believers urged the friends to observe this commandment, Bahá'u'lláh stopped him doing this, and advised the friends not to implement this injunction of the *Kitáb-i-Aqdas* at that time, because if they were to keep away from the public baths the enemies of the Faith would become agitated and this would result in increased persecution of the friends. There were other instances where the implementation of the laws of the *Aqdas* was either unwise, untimely or utterly impractical.

For these and other reasons, the Bahá'ís during the Heroic Age of the Faith were not very inclined (with the exception of some spiritual ordinances such as obligatory prayer and fasting) to carry out the laws of Bahá'u'lláh. They lived their lives by following the customs, traditions and laws of older religions. For instance, they married according to the laws of their former religion, depending on their backgrounds. Those who came from a Muslim background followed the laws of Islám and had Islamic marriage ceremonies, while those of Jewish or Zoroastrian origin followed the marriage ceremonies of those religions. In other fields too the believers observed the various religious laws which were practised by the nation.

It was Shoghi Effendi who began the implementation of some of the laws of the *Kitáb-i-Aqdas* in Persia in the early days of his ministry. He directed the Local Spiritual Assemblies in that country to begin to apply certain of these laws. In the course of his ministry, he elaborated a great deal on their application, explained many intricacies connected with them, urged the Spiritual Assemblies never to compromise when enforcing the laws, counselled them to uphold the standard of justice and impartiality in all cases, and advocated the imposition of sanctions in the form of deprivation of

* See above, p. 81, for a note on the public baths.

voting rights on those who flagrantly violated the laws, or who through their misdeeds brought disgrace upon the Faith.

For more than three decades in innumerable letters to the National and Local Spiritual Assemblies as well as to individuals in Persia, Shoghi Effendi elucidated the details of the laws of the *Kitáb-i-Aqdas*. He thus built up in this particular field a great reservoir of knowledge and experience in the application of the laws which will be of great value in the future when the whole Bahá'í world will be in a position to put into practice the laws of this new Dispensation.

As a result of the observance of certain Bahá'í laws, the believers in Persia were able to distance themselves from old religious practices and instead identify themselves with the new World Order. For instance, the Bahá'í marriage ceremony took the place of Islamic, Jewish or Zoroastrian ceremonies. It is interesting to note that since the Bahá'í marriage ceremony was not recognized legally by the government of Persia, and since the Bahá'ís refused to have any other religious ceremony to legalize their marriage, the couple had to face certain deprivations in their lives, and at one time the newly wedded husband had to serve a few months' sentence in prison. In spite of these difficulties, Shoghi Effendi urged the believers to remain steadfast and not to bow to government pressure, for in this way they could demonstrate the independent character of the Faith to the public.

It is important at this juncture to mention that Bahá'ís are enjoined to obey the government on matters which deal with the administration of their Faith or with matters of secondary importance. But on matters of faith and spiritual subjects they prefer to die rather than renounce their beliefs. The observance of the laws of Bahá'u'lláh by the members of the community brought in its wake a vitality, a solidarity and a new identity to the Bahá'í community of Persia.

In certain cases Shoghi Effendi urged the friends of Persia not to compromise on basic principles, even if it meant great hardship. One example is the closure of all Bahá'í schools in various towns in Persia in 1934 by order of the government as a direct result of the refusal by the believers to keep the schools open on Bahá'í holy days. There were Bahá'í schools for boys and separate ones for girls in most major cities and sometimes there were more than two schools in a town. Bahá'í schools, which were owned and controlled by the Bahá'ís, were usually known as the best-run schools in the country and many non-Bahá'í pupils attended them. Their closure came as a blow to Bahá'ís and non-Bahá'ís alike, but a compromise in order to enable the government to re-open the schools was unthinkable to Shoghi Effendi, for it was against the law of Bahá'u'lláh requiring suspension of work on Bahá'í holy days.

The laws of the *Kitáb-i-Aqdas* were not enforced in the West during the earlier part of the ministry of Shoghi Effendi. Later, when the American Bahá'í community began to build up the institutions of the Faith, he introduced a few of the laws of Bahá'u'lláh as basic and essential for the communities in the Western world. Thus in 1935 he wrote, through his secretary, to the National Spiritual Assembly of the United States and Canada:

> He feels it his duty to explain that the Laws revealed by Bahá'u'lláh in the Aqdas are, whenever practicable and not in direct conflict with the Civil Laws of the land, absolutely binding on every believer or Bahá'í institution whether in the East or in the West. Certain laws, such as fasting, obligatory prayers, the consent of the parents before marriage, avoidance of alcoholic drinks, monogamy, should be regarded by all believers as universally and vitally applicable at the present time. Others have been formulated in anticipation of a state of society, destined to emerge from the chaotic conditions that prevail today. When the Aqdas is published this matter will be further explained and elucidated. What has not been formulated in the Aqdas, in addition to matters of detail and of secondary importance arising out of the application of the laws already formulated by Bahá'u'lláh, will have to be enacted by the Universal House of Justice. This body can supplement but never invalidate or modify in the least degree what has already been formulated by Bahá'u'lláh. Nor has the Guardian any right whatsoever to lessen the binding effect, much less to abrogate the provisions of so fundamental and sacred a Book.[4]

CHAPTER TWENTY-EIGHT

The Administrative Order in Action

In North America, the scene of the building of the pattern of the Administrative Order, the institutions of the Faith had grown and developed to such an extent after sixteen years of receiving guidance and direction from the Guardian that in 1937 he was able to launch the first Seven Year Plan of the American Bahá'í Community. This highly significant enterprise opened a fresh chapter in the history of the Formative Age. The main goals of the Plan were 'the permanent establishment of at least one centre in every state of the American Republic and in every Republic of the American Continent' as well as the resumption of work for completion of the exterior ornamentation of the Bahá'í House of Worship at Wilmette, temporarily halted for lack of funds during the recession of the 1930s. This historic Plan entrusted by Shoghi Effendi to the North American Community marks the initial phase of the first Epoch* of the fulfilment of the Tablets of the Divine Plan of 'Abdu'l-Bahá. These Tablets, fourteen in all, written by the Master during the First World War and addressed to the Bahá'ís in various States of America and one to Canada, are the Charter for teaching the Faith of Bahá'u'lláh throughout the world and a mandate conferred by 'Abdu'l-Bahá upon the North American Community.

When Shoghi Effendi called upon the American believers to execute the Seven Year Plan the Bahá'í community was still in the early stages of its development. It might be compared to a child which stands on its own feet for the first time. His mother, excited and proud, holds his hand and encourages him to take a few steps, only to see him fall down. Again she lifts the child up and with much reassurance and love takes his hand and helps him to take another step, until he can at last walk by himself. This is almost what Shoghi Effendi did with the North American Bahá'í Community in the early stages of its development. He gave them a Plan, and for seven years he lovingly held their hands, supported them in their difficulties,

* Not to be confused with 'epochs' of the Formative Age. See below, pp. 373–5.

guided every step they took and poured his encouragement upon them, until in 1944, the Centenary of the birth of the Faith in Persia, the Plan was successfully won.

In this Plan Shoghi Effendi introduced two basic strategies which have been carried out ever since throughout the Bahá'í world for teaching the Cause and building its institutions. One is the dispatch of a believer – a Bahá'í pioneer – to a territory; the pioneer engages in teaching the Cause until enough people embrace the Faith to be able to establish a Local Spiritual Assembly. The other is the systematic formation of Spiritual Assemblies in various localities, so that at the end of a Plan a specific number of Assemblies have been established. The Seven Year Plan served as a model for all the other teaching plans that followed. The two invariable elements of every Plan so far have been the planting of the banner of the Faith in localities where there are no Bahá'ís, and the establishment of a number of Spiritual Assemblies in a country or a region.

It took quite a long time for the Bahá'ís throughout the world to appreciate the significance of the American Seven Year Plan. One reason for this was the lack of an efficient system of communication, especially during the war years. By the time the goals of the Plan were triumphantly won, coinciding with the world-wide celebration on 23 May 1944 of the centenary of the birth of the Faith, the number of Local Spiritual Assemblies in the United States had almost doubled, the number of localities in which Bahá'ís were residing had considerably increased, the nucleus of the institutions of the Administrative Order had been established in every republic of Latin America, and the exterior ornamentation of the only House of Worship in the Western world had been completed.

The news of these victories created excitement throughout the Bahá'í world. It awakened the Bahá'ís of other lands to the significance of these marvellous developments in the Americas, opening their eyes to the pattern of methodical expansion and consolidation of the institutions of the Faith which had taken place as a result of this first teaching Plan devised and initiated by Shoghi Effendi and carried out by the Bahá'í community in the Cradle of the Administrative Order. Such glorious achievements by the American Bahá'ís, who for most of the seven-year period were bitterly handicapped through the formidable difficulties of the war years, inspired the believers in other parts of the world, and created an upsurge of enthusiasm and confidence in their hearts.

The first Bahá'í community to turn to the Guardian was the British, who sent a cable to him during their National Convention of 1944 and asked for a similar plan in the British Isles. To this Shoghi Effendi responded favourably; he gave them a Six Year Plan to end in 1950. Other national plans followed within two to three years. As each National Assembly reached a state of readiness, Shoghi Effendi gave them a plan mainly designed to increase the number and consolidate the foundation of Local Assemblies, to open up virgin territories to the Faith, and to multiply the number of localities in which Bahá'ís resided in that country.

Foremost among these was the second Seven Year Plan of the Bahá'ís of the United States and Canada, whose duration marked the second phase of the first Epoch* of the Divine Plan of 'Abdu'l-Bahá. This teaching Plan began in 1946 and incorporated some major international goals, including the establishment of Local Spiritual Assemblies in ten countries of Western Europe, the formation of three National Spiritual Assemblies in the Western Hemisphere, and the interior ornamentation of the House of Worship in Wilmette. These were successfully accomplished in 1953. Other national plans carried out at the same time were the Indian Four-and-a-Half Year Plan followed by a Nineteen Month Plan, the Persian Forty-Five Month Plan, the Australian Six Year Plan, the 'Iráqi Three Year Plan, the Egyptian Five Year Plan, the German Five Year Plan, and the Canadian Five Year Plan. Each of these Plans either ended in 1950, the hundredth anniversary of the Martyrdom of the Báb, or in 1953, the Holy Year, the centenary of the birth of Bahá'u'lláh's Revelation in the Síyáh-Chál of Ṭihrán.

Prior to the launching of these national plans, the Bahá'ís were mostly active only in their own towns or villages. They taught the Faith to the local people, rendered their services to the Cause locally, were thinking in local terms and involved themselves in local activities. They did not have a sense of a national Bahá'í identity, and were not concerned with Bahá'í activities in other towns within their country. Although there were Bahá'í communities in many localities, there was no proper cohesion between them. The national Bahá'í community as a dynamic unit embracing the whole nation and pulsating with inter-assembly activities had not yet come into being. However, these national plans provided the means for active communication between the communities in each country, and afforded believers the opportunity to take part in Bahá'í activities outside their own local communities. Thus a sense of Bahá'í national identity was gradually created in the minds of the believers and their local outlook changed into a national one. Parallel with this, the means of communication were also improved in most countries during this period, resulting in more effective co-operation and cohesion between local communities. A similar transformation took

* See above, p. 314, and below, p. 319.

place during the Ten Year Crusade* when the national Bahá'í communities found themselves integrated into one international Bahá'í community. Here again the activities which had been carried out on a national level were extended during the Crusade to include the whole world and as a result the Bahá'í international community with all its agencies came into being.

In 1950 the Guardian announced the launching of a Two Year Plan for Africa. This Plan proved to be of special significance in the development of the institutions of the Faith world-wide. The responsibility for its execution was given to the British National Spiritual Assembly with the co-operation of the National Spiritual Assemblies of the United States, Persia, and Egypt. This was the first inter-Assembly co-operation in the Bahá'í world, paving the way for the launching in 1953 of the Ten Year Crusade during which every National Spiritual Assembly in the Bahá'í world took part in a world-encircling Plan. The Two Year Africa Plan was announced to the British Community by the Guardian on the eve of their triumphant conclusion of the Six Year Plan. It was to be launched in 1951, but the British believers began its implementation almost immediately after its announcement in 1950. A year later Shoghi Effendi wrote the National Spiritual Assembly of the British Isles a letter of great import. We quote an excerpt here:

> The magnificent spirit of devotion and the initiative and resourcefulness demonstrated in recent months by a triumphant community, in its eagerness to launch, ahead of the appointed time, the enterprise destined to carry the fame of its members and establish its outposts as far afield as the African Continent, merit the highest praise. By their organising ability, by their zeal in enlisting the collaboration of their sister communities in the African, the American and Asiatic continents for the effective prosecution of this epoch-making enterprise; by the tenacity, sagacity and fidelity which they have displayed in the course of its opening phase; by their utter consecration and their complete reliance on the One Who watches over their destiny, they have set an example worthy of emulation by the members of Bahá'í communities in both the East and the West.
>
> The despatch of the first pioneer to Tanganyika, signalising the inauguration of the African campaign, following so closely upon the successful termination of the Six Year Plan, will be recognised by posterity as the initial move in an undertaking designed to supplement and enrich the record of signal collective services rendered by the members of this community within the confines and throughout the length and breadth of its homeland. On it, however great the support it will receive from its sister communities in the days to come, will devolve the chief responsibility of guiding the destinies, of supplying the

* See below, pp. 318–21.

motive power, and of contributing to the resources of a crusade which, for the first time in Bahá'í history, involves the collaboration, and affects the fortunes, of no less than four National Assemblies, in both Hemispheres and within four continents of the globe.

On the success of this enterprise, unprecedented in its scope, unique in its character and immense in its spiritual potentialities, must depend the initiation, at a later period in the Formative Age of the Faith, of undertakings embracing within their range all National Assemblies functioning throughout the Bahá'í World, undertakings constituting in themselves a prelude to the launching of world-wide enterprises destined to be embarked upon, in future epochs of that same Age, by the Universal House of Justice, that will symbolise the unity and coordinate and unify the activities of these National Assemblies.[2]

These words of Shoghi Effendi were truly prophetic, for they alluded to a time when the Guardian would not be there to launch other teaching plans after the Ten Year Crusade, and to the fact that these would be formulated by the Universal House of Justice. The Africa Plan resulted in spectacular advances for the Faith: the Cause of God was introduced for the first time into several countries of that vast continent, and large numbers of the African peoples embraced the Faith.

At a time when the Guardian was subjected to unbearable pressures due to the unfaithfulness of many of the Master's family, these unprecedented victories in Africa brought great joy to his heart, a joy that remained with him till the end of his life.

The victories won in Africa, together with the triumphant conclusion of all the national plans, endowed the Community of the Most Great Name with enormous potentiality for the expansion and consolidation of the Faith on a world-wide scale. The national communities had by then acquired the vision and the capacity to take part in the first, and greatest ever, international Plan, designated as the Ten Year Crusade, which was launched by the Guardian in 1953. He referred to this Plan as a 'spiritual venture, at once arduous, audacious, challenging, unprecedented in scope and character in the entire field of Bahá'í history'.[3] The concept of the spiritual conquest of the virgin territories on the planet, as well as the formation of forty-eight new National Spiritual Assemblies and many other goals* specified in detail by Shoghi Effendi astonished the Bahá'í world and staggered the imagination of the believers everywhere. The following excerpts from the exhilarating Message announcing the launching of the Ten Year Spiritual Crusade to the Bahá'í world by the Guardian in October 1952 demonstrates his world-embracing vision

* For information about details of the goals of the Ten Year Crusade, see *Messages to the Bahá'í World*.

and dynamism, and the fervour with which he inspired the Bahá'ís of the world to arise and bring victory to the Cause of God:

> Feel hour propitious to proclaim to the entire Bahá'í world the projected launching on the occasion of the convocation of the approaching Intercontinental Conferences on the four continents of the globe the fate-laden, soul-stirring, decade-long, world-embracing Spiritual Crusade involving the simultaneous initiation of twelve national Ten Year Plans and the concerted participation of all National Spiritual Assemblies of the Bahá'í world aiming at the immediate extension of Bahá'u'lláh's spiritual dominion as well as the eventual establishment of the structure of His administrative order in all remaining Sovereign States, Principal Dependencies comprising Principalities, Sultanates, Emirates, Shaykhdoms, Protectorates, Trust Territories, and Crown Colonies scattered over the surface of the entire planet. The entire body of the avowed supporters of Bahá'u'lláh's all-conquering Faith are now summoned to achieve in a single decade feats eclipsing in totality the achievements which in the course of the eleven preceding decades illuminated the annals of Bahá'í pioneering.
>
> The four-fold objectives of the forthcoming Crusade, marking the third and last phase of the initial epoch of the evolution of 'Abdu'l-Bahá's Divine Plan are destined to culminate in the world-wide festivities commemorating the fast-approaching Most Great Jubilee. First, development of the institutions at the World Centre of the Faith in the Holy Land. Second, consolidation, through carefully devised measures on the home front of the twelve territories destined to serve as administrative bases for the operations of the twelve National Plans. Third, consolidation of all territories already opened to the Faith. Fourth, the opening of the remaining chief virgin territories on the planet through specific allotments to each National Assembly functioning in the Bahá'í world.
>
> The projected historic, spiritual venture, at once arduous, audacious, challenging, unprecedented in scope and character in the entire field of Bahá'í history, soon to be set in motion, involves: . . . Adoption of preliminary measures to the construction of Bahá'u'lláh's Sepulchre in the Holy Land.
>
> Doubling the number of countries within the pale of the Faith through planting its banner in the remaining Sovereign States of the planet as well as the remaining virgin Territories mentioned in 'Abdu'l-Bahá's Tablets of the Divine Plan, involving the opening of forty-one countries on the Asiatic, thirty-three on the African, thirty on the European, twenty-seven on the American continents. Over twofold increase in the number of languages into which Bahá'í literature is translated, printed or in process of translation – forty in Asia, thirty-one in Africa, ten each in Europe and America, to be allocated to the American, British, Indian and Australian Bahá'í communities, including for the most part those into which Gospels have been already translated. Doubling the number of Mashriqu'l-Adhkárs, through the initiation of the construction of one on the Asiatic and the other on the European continent. The acquisition of

the site of the future Mashriqu'l-Adhkár on Mount Carmel. The purchase of the land for eleven future Temples, three on the American, three on the African, two on the Asiatic, two on the European, one on the Australian continents. The erection of the first dependency of the Mashriqu'l-Adhkár in Wilmette. The development of the functions of the institution of the Hands of the Cause. The establishment of a Bahá'í Court in the Holy Land, preliminary to the emergence of the Universal House of Justice . . . Extension of international Bahá'í endowments in the Holy Land, on the plain of 'Akká and the slopes of Mount Carmel. Construction of international Bahá'í Archives in the neighbourhood of the Báb's Sepulchre . . . More than quadruple the number of National Spiritual Assemblies – twenty-one on the American, thirteen on the European, ten on the Asiatic, three on the African and one on the Australian continents. Multiply seven-fold national Ḥaẓíratu'l-Quds, their establishment in the capital cities of the chief Sovereign States and chief cities of the principal Dependencies of the planet – twenty-one in America, fifteen in Europe, nine in Asia, three in Africa, one in New Zealand. Framing national Bahá'í constitutions, and establishment of national Bahá'í endowments in same capitals and cities of same States and Dependencies.

More than quintuple the number of incorporated National Assemblies – twenty-one in America, thirteen in Europe, twelve in Asia, three in Africa, one in Australasia. The establishment of six national Bahá'í Publishing Trusts – two in America, two in Asia, one in Africa, one in Europe . . .

Current Bahá'í history must henceforth, as second decade of second Bahá'í century opens, move rapidly and majestically as it has never moved before since the inception of the Faith over a century ago. Earthly symbols of Bahá'u'lláh's unearthly Sovereignty must needs, ere the decade separating the two memorable Jubilees draws to a close, be raised as far north as Franklin beyond the Arctic Circle and as far south as the Falkland Islands, marking the southern extremity of the western hemisphere, amidst the remote, lonely, inhospitable islands of the archipelagos of the South Pacific, the Indian and Atlantic oceans, the mountain fastnesses of Tibet, the jungles of Africa, the deserts of Arabia, the steppes of Russia, the Indian Reservations of North America, the wastelands of Siberia and Mongolia, amongst the Eskimos of Greenland and Alaska, the Negroes of Africa, Buddhist strongholds in the heart of Asia, amongst Lapps of Finland, the Polynesians of the South Sea Islands, Negritos of the archipelagos of the South Pacific Ocean.

The broad outlines of the world-encircling plan were divinely revealed. Its course was chartered by 'Abdu'l-Bahá's infallible Pen. Its shining goals have been set. The requisite administrative machinery has been created. Signal has been given by the Author of the Plan, its Supreme Commander. The Lord of Hosts, the King of Kings has pledged unfailing aid to every crusader battling for His Cause. Invisible battalions are mustered, rank upon rank, ready to pour forth reinforcements from on high. Bahá'u'lláh's army of light is standing on the threshold of the Holy Year. Let them, as they enter it, vow with one voice, one heart, one soul, never to turn back in the entire course of the fateful decade ahead until each and every one will have contributed his share in laying on a world-wide scale an unassailable administrative foundation for Bahá'u'lláh's Christ-promised Kingdom on earth, swelling thereby the chorus of universal jubilation wherein earth and heaven will join as prophesied by Daniel, echoed by 'Abdu'l-Bahá: 'on that day will the faithful rejoice with exceeding gladness.'[4]

CHAPTER TWENTY-NINE

Vital Developments at the World Centre

ONE of the most important developments in the period of Shoghi Effendi's ministry is the appointment in 1951 of the first contingent of the Hands of the Cause of God: twelve in all. This institution was created by Bahá'u'lláh towards the end of His Ministry when He appointed four Hands of the Cause* charged with the responsibility of teaching and promoting the interests of the Faith. 'Abdu'l-Bahá describes the duties of the Hands of the Cause in these words:

> The obligation of the Hands of the Cause of God are to diffuse the Divine Fragrances, to edify the souls of men, to promote learning, to improve the character of all men and to be, at all times and under all conditions, sanctified and detached from earthly things. They must manifest the fear of God by their conduct, their manners, their deeds and their words.[1]

The four Hands appointed by Bahá'u'lláh served during the ministry of 'Abdu'l-Bahá. 'Abdu'l-Bahá did not appoint any Hands; He only conferred this rank upon a few posthumously. However, He authorized Shoghi Effendi to appoint Hands during his ministry. Shoghi Effendi waited thirty years before he implemented the wishes of the Master, although he nominated some posthumously during this period. As we look back upon the early years of the Guardianship, we observe a lack of maturity on the part of the main body of the believers as they strove to build up the institutions of the Faith under the direction of the Guardian himself. But after thirty years of active participation in Bahá'í activities, the Bahá'ís around the world had acquired sufficient capacity to derive benefit from the institution of the Hands, who played a magnificent role in the acceleration of the development of the Administrative Order towards the end of the Guardian's ministry and beyond.

Three of the Hands were invited by Shoghi Effendi to serve at the World Centre while the remainder were to discharge their responsibilities on a continental basis. Later, from time to time, Shoghi Effendi elevated a number of individuals to the rank of Hand of the

* For details of these appointments see *The Revelation of Bahá'u'lláh*, vol. 4, p. 277.

Cause. He appointed altogether thirty-one Hands,[2] twenty-seven of whom were still living at the time of his passing in 1957. The presence of the Hands of the Cause in the Holy Land serving the Guardian during the last six years of his life proved to be a significant development in the unfoldment of the Administrative Order, for it was a prelude to the time when the Hands had to take the responsibility of administering the affairs of the Faith for a short period after the passing of Shoghi Effendi.

Another significant development in the unfoldment of the Administrative Order was the establishment at the World Centre of the Faith of the International Bahá'í Council, whose members were appointed by Shoghi Effendi. It was established in 1951; its membership was increased to eight in 1952 and to nine in 1953. Of this institution Shoghi Effendi writes:

> Hail with thankful, joyous heart at long last the constitution of International Council which history will acclaim as the greatest event shedding lustre upon second Epoch of Formative Age of Bahá'í Dispensation potentially unsurpassed by any enterprise undertaken since inception of Administrative Order of Faith on morrow of 'Abdu'l-Bahá's ascension, ranking second only to glorious immortal events associated with Ministries of the Three Central Figures of Faith . . .[3]

Concerning the functions of the International Council Shoghi Effendi writes:

> Nascent Institution now created is invested with threefold function: first, to forge link with authorities of newly emerged State; second, to assist me to discharge responsibilities involved in erection of mighty superstructure of the Báb's Holy Shrine; third, to conduct negotiations related to matters of personal status with civil authorities.[4]

The International Bahá'í Council, working under the direction of Shoghi Effendi, rendered him valuable services in carrying out some of the important tasks in the Holy Land. This resulted in the further strengthening of the World Centre of the Faith. The manner in which the International Bahá'í Council carried out its duties is described in *The Priceless Pearl* by Rúḥíyyih Khánum:

> . . . In its functions the International Bahá'í Council acted as that Secretariat the Guardian, so many years earlier, had desired to establish; its members received their instructions from him individually, in the informal atmosphere of the dinners at the Pilgrim House table, and not formally as a body; its meetings were infrequent as all its members were kept constantly busy with the many tasks allotted to them by the Guardian himself. Skilfully Shoghi Effendi used this new institution to create in the minds of government and city officials the image of a body of an international character handling the administrative affairs at the

World Centre. It was no concern of the public how much or how little that body had authority; we who were on it knew Shoghi Effendi was everything; the public, however, began to see an image which could evolve later into the Universal House of Justice.[5]

In his writings Shoghi Effendi attached great importance to the International Council, which was to evolve by stages into the Universal House of Justice. The first stage was the Council in its initial form as an appointed body. The second stage was its becoming an elected body. This took place in 1961, during the Custodianship of the Hands of the Cause, when the National Spiritual Assemblies throughout the world elected a nine-member Council. The third stage was for the Council to be transformed into the International Bahá'í Court* in Israel, and the fourth stage was to be the election and the establishment of the Universal House of Justice. The third stage did not materialize because when the Hands of the Cause, after the passing of Shoghi Effend, investigated the matter through legal channels they found that the prerogatives and privileges which could legally be granted to a Bahá'í Court were inadequate or unbefitting the prestige of the Faith. The International Council continued its service until 1963 when it ceased to exist with the election of the Universal House of Justice.

The presence of the Hands of the Cause and members of the International Bahá'í Council in the Holy Land who were engaged in rendering various forms of service to Shoghi Effendi unfortunately did not reduce his work-load. On the contrary, it increased it. Towards the latter part of Shoghi Effendi's ministry the Bahá'í world had grown enormously, the institutions of the Faith, both local and national, had multiplied. The World Centre had also grown. The building of the Shrine of the Báb, the Terraces and the Archives, the work of the beautification of the Gardens in Haifa and Bahjí, as well as the strengthening of ties with the government: all these developments brought in their wake heavier burdens to be borne by Shoghi Effendi during the later part of his ministry. One of his most momentous achievements was the construction of the superstructure of the Shrine of the Báb. This was the culmination of a historic process which, beginning with Bahá'u'lláh's Revelation of the *Lawḥ-i-Karmil*† (Tablet of Carmel) toward the end of His earthly life, was accelerated during the Master's ministry through the construction of the original building on Mount Carmel and the interment of the holy remains of the Báb in one of its chambers. It was fulfilled in 1953 through the building of a majestic mausoleum

* In Islamic countries and in Israel there are religious courts legally recognized to administer legal matters in the context of religious law.
† See *The Revelation of Bahá'u'lláh*, vol. 4.

which enshrines the edifice built by the Master, in whose centre is deposited the sacred dust of the Martyr-Prophet of this Dispensation.

In 1951, halfway through building the superstructure of the Shrine, Shoghi Effendi wrote an illuminating letter to the Bahá'ís of the world about the sacredness of that holy Spot. The following is an excerpt:

> I cannot at this juncture overemphasize the sacredness of that holy dust embosomed in the heart of the Vineyard of God, or overrate the unimaginable potencies of this mighty institution founded sixty years ago, through the operation of the Will of, and the definite selection made by, the Founder of our Faith, on the occasion of His historic visit to that holy mountain, nor can I lay too much stress on the role which this institution, to which the construction of the superstructure of this edifice is bound to lend an unprecedented impetus, is destined to play in the unfoldment of the World Administrative Centre of the Faith of Bahá'u'lláh and in the efflorescence of its highest institutions constituting the embryo of its future World Order.
>
> For, just as in the realm of the spirit, the reality of the Báb has been hailed by the Author of the Bahá'í Revelation as 'The Point round Whom the realities of the Prophets and Messengers revolve', so, on this visible plane, His sacred remains constitute the heart and centre of what may be regarded as nine concentric circles, paralleling thereby, and adding further emphasis to the central position accorded by the Founder of our Faith to One 'from Whom God hath caused to proceed the knowledge of all that was and shall be', 'the Primal Point from which have been generated all created things'.
>
> The outermost circle in this vast system, the visible counterpart of the pivotal position conferred on the Herald of our Faith, is none other than the entire planet. Within the heart of this planet lies the 'Most Holy Land', acclaimed by 'Abdu'l-Bahá as 'the Nest of the Prophets' and which must be regarded as the centre of the world and the Qiblih of the nations. Within this Most Holy Land rises the Mountain of God of immemorial sanctity, the Vineyard of the Lord, the Retreat of Elijah, Whose return the Báb Himself symbolizes. Reposing on the breast of this holy mountain are the extensive properties permanently dedicated to, and constituting the sacred precincts of, the Báb's holy Sepulchre. In the midst of these properties, recognized as the international endowments of the Faith, is situated the most holy court, an enclosure comprising gardens and terraces which at once embellish, and lend a peculiar charm to, these sacred precincts. Embosomed in these lovely and verdant surroundings stands in all its exquisite beauty the mausoleum of the Báb, the shell designed to preserve and adorn the original structure raised by 'Abdu'l-Bahá as the tomb of the Martyr-Herald of our Faith. Within this shell is enshrined that Pearl of Great Price, the holy of holies, those chambers which constitute the tomb itself, and which were constructed

by 'Abdu'l-Bahá. Within the heart of this holy of holies is the tabernacle, the vault wherein reposes the most holy casket. Within the vault rests the alabaster sarcophagus in which is deposited that inestimable jewel, the Báb's holy dust. So precious is this dust that the very earth surrounding the edifice enshrining this dust has been extolled by the Centre of Bahá'u'lláh's Covenant, in one of His Tablets in which He named the five doors belonging to the six chambers which He originally erected after five of the believers associated with the construction of the Shrine, as being endowed with such potency as to have inspired Him in bestowing these names, whilst the tomb itself housing this dust He acclaimed as the spot round which the Concourse on high circle in adoration.[6]

Of the exquisite beauty of this Shrine Shoghi Effendi writes:

> . . . The Queen of Carmel enthroned on God's Mountain, crowned in glowing gold, robed in shimmering white, girdled in emerald green, enchanting every eye from air, sea, plain and hill.[7]

The Shrine of the Báb, referred to in the *Tablet of Carmel* as the 'City of God' and the 'celestial Kaaba', is the spiritual Centre of the Faith of Bahá'u'lláh on Mount Carmel. The administrative Centre is alluded to in the same Tablet as the sailing of 'His Ark'* upon that Mountain. This Ark has been described by the Guardian as the Ark of the Laws of God. The world administrative centre of the Faith was brought into being by Shoghi Effendi in stages. In 1932 the remains of the Greatest Holy Leaf were laid to rest in close proximity to the Shrine of the Báb on Mount Carmel. Later, in 1939 the remains of the Purest Branch and Navváb, his mother, were transferred to that same spot. This momentous event was a prelude to the establishment, around the resting places of these exalted souls, of a series of buildings comprising the world administrative headquarters of the Faith of Bahá'u'lláh. Concerning this Shoghi Effendi wrote:

> The transfer of the sacred remains of the brother and mother of our Lord and Master 'Abdu'l-Bahá to Mount Carmel and their final interment within the hallowed precincts of the Shrine of the Báb, and in the immediate neighbourhood of the resting place of the Greatest Holy Leaf, constitute, apart from their historic associations and the tender sentiments they arouse, events of such capital institutional significance as only future happenings, steadily and mysteriously unfolding at the world centre of our Faith, can adequately demonstrate.[8]

In the following passages Shoghi Effendi describes the nature, the significance and the future glory of the world administrative centre of the Faith. On the occasion of the successful termination of

* Not to be confused with the buildings of the Arc on Mount Carmel around which the edifices of the world administrative centre are to be built.

negotiations for the acquisition of a certain plot of property on Mount Carmel he writes:

> The ownership of this plot will now enable us to locate the site, excavate the foundations, and erect the structure, of the International Bahá'í Archives . . . which will serve as the permanent and befitting repository for the priceless and numerous relics associated with the Twin Founders of the Faith, with the Perfect Exemplar of its teachings and with its heroes, saints and martyrs, and the building of which constitutes one of the foremost objectives of the Ten-Year Plan.
>
> The raising of this Edifice will in turn herald the construction, in the course of successive epochs of the Formative Age of the Faith, of several other structures, which will serve as the administrative seats of such divinely appointed institutions as the Guardianship, the Hands of the Cause, and the Universal House of Justice. These Edifices will, in the shape of a far-flung arc, and following a harmonizing style of architecture, surround the resting-places of the Greatest Holy Leaf, ranking as foremost among the members of her sex in the Bahá'í Dispensation, of her Brother, offered up as a ransom by Bahá'u'lláh for the quickening of the world and its unification, and of their Mother, proclaimed by Him to be His chosen 'consort in all the worlds of God'. The ultimate completion of this stupendous undertaking will mark the culmination of the development of a world-wide divinely-appointed Administrative Order whose beginnings may be traced as far back as the concluding years of the Heroic Age of the Faith.
>
> This vast and irresistible process, unexampled in the spiritual history of mankind, and which will synchronize with two no less significant developments – the establishment of the Lesser Peace and the evolution of Bahá'í national and local institutions – the one outside and the other within the Bahá'í world – will attain its final consummation, in the Golden Age of the Faith, through the raising of the standard of the Most Great Peace, and the emergence, in the plenitude of its power and glory, of the focal Centre of the agencies constituting the World Order of Bahá'u'lláh. The final establishment of this seat of the future Bahá'í World Commonwealth will signalize at once the proclamation of the sovereignty of the Founder of our Faith and the advent of the Kingdom of the Father repeatedly lauded and promised by Jesus Christ.[9]

Shoghi Effendi began the building of the International Archives in 1954 and completed it by 1957. This was another remarkable accomplishment at the World Centre, a building majestically raised at the extreme end of the Arc on Mount Carmel, and enshrining within its walls the most precious relics of the Founders of the Faith as well as other historical materials of great value.

One of the distinguishing features of the Faith of Bahá'u'lláh is that unlike the Islamic or Christian Faiths, its spiritual and administrative centres are located in one area. The Shrine of Bahá'u'lláh and that of the Báb constitute the spiritual centre, and the various buildings around the Arc on Mount Carmel its administrative centre. These two are thus combined together in one spot. In Islám the two centres were separated: the spiritual centre was in Mecca, while the Islamic institutions invested with temporal power were removed from Arabia to other lands. The same was true of Christianity when its main churches, the centres for the administration of the community, were removed from the Holy Land, its spiritual centre.

During the thirty-six years of his ministry Shoghi Effendi created, from the very limited resources which were at his disposal, a befitting World Centre in which the Holy Shrines and other holy places were preserved and in some cases restored in the most dignified way. A special feature of Bahá'í holy places and other institutions at the World Centre is that most are surrounded by gardens, especially laid out to grace and embellish them. This practice takes its origin from Bahá'u'lláh, who was greatly attracted by the beauty of nature. In spite of their meagre resources, the believers of His days tried wherever possible to create simple yet beautiful surroundings for Him. They even brought flowering trees and shrubs from lands as far away as Persia and planted them in the Garden of Riḍván outside 'Akká, that Bahá'u'lláh loved to visit after so many years of incarceration within the walls of the City.

'Abdu'l-Bahá during His Ministry laid out small gardens around the Shrine of Bahá'u'lláh and the Báb. Shoghi Effendi enlarged these and made new and extensive gardens all over Mount Carmel and in Bahjí. He himself designed and created these exquisite formal gardens around the Shrines and other Monuments which are so admired by the public. The Shrine of the Báb and the gardens around it were further enhanced when Shoghi Effendi built nine terraces on the hillside below the Shrine, as 'Abdu'l-Bahá had envisaged.

In spite of these successes in Haifa, Shoghi Effendi experienced great difficulties in his efforts to extend and beautify the gardens surrounding the Shrine of Bahá'u'lláh. The Mansion of Bahjí which 'God hath ordained as the most sublime vision of mankind' and where Bahá'u'lláh had spent the last twelve years of His life, had been occupied by the Covenant-breakers for almost forty years since the passing of Bahá'u'lláh. It had fallen into such a pitiful state of disrepair that the roof had caved in in many places and its rooms were largely abandoned. Mírzá Muḥammad-'Alí, who used it as his personal residence, had no choice but to ask Shoghi Effendi to repair the building. In 1929 the building was vacated and repair work began immediately. Shoghi Effendi restored the Mansion to its original state, furnished it with beautiful carpets, placed in its rooms various photographs and some original items associated with Bahá'u'lláh, as well as bookcases filled with Bahá'í literature in many langauges. He then invited the British High Commissioner to view the Mansion with him. It was on the occasion of that visit that the High Commissioner decided that the Mansion was a holy site for the Bahá'ís and a place of pilgrimage for them. Thus the custody of this sacred place was transferred to Shoghi Effendi, and Mírzá Muḥammad-'Alí was not allowed in the Mansion again.

At the sides of the Mansion and near the Shrine of Bahá'u'lláh there were several houses which had been built by the Covenant-breakers over the years. It was a disgrace to build such houses around such holy precincts, and it had been Shoghi Effendi's aim for many years to demolish and cleanse the area from the pollution of Covenant-breakers. This was achieved in two stages: one in 1952, the other in the last year of Shoghi Effendi's life. Rúḥíyyih Khánum writes in *The Priceless Pearl* as follows:

> I remember how, in spite of the fact that Shoghi Effendi had possession of the Mansion, he was constantly irked, until the very end of his life, by the fact that Covenant-breakers still occupied the adjacent house. The night of the Ascension of Bahá'u'lláh, when the Guardian, at the head of the Bahá'í men, would proceed to His Shrine after visiting the room in the Mansion in which He had passed away, he was obliged to pass in front of the room where the Covenant-breakers were keeping their own vigil and often they would make audible comments on him as he passed, adding to the distress of a night that was already distressing enough in its associations. . . .
>
> From the time, in January 1923, when he had written to the eldest son of Bahá'u'lláh's daughter requesting him to make a definite pronouncement that whatever the legal rights of these Afnans might be the Shrine at Bahjí because of its nature belonged to the Bahá'í Movement, until the end of his life, Shoghi Effendi struggled to place on an unshakeable foundation the legal position of this Sacred Spot, in spite of the opposition of that tainted band of relatives who resisted his every effort for over thirty years. It was due to the mysterious workings of Providence that after the War of Independence, through the mass exodus of the Arabs, including many enemies of the Faith, Shoghi Effendi was able to at last emerge triumphant from this long struggle. In 1952 the long-coveted lands surrounding the Tomb and Mansion of Bahá'u'lláh, amounting to over 145,000 square metres, were obtained. As early as 1931 Shoghi Effendi had endeavoured to get the Government to requisition part of this land – which had originally belonged to the Mansion property but had been usurped by the Muslim friends and supporters of Muḥammad 'Alí – but it had refused to intervene and the asking price was over ten times the market value of the land. The Guardian had to wait over twenty years until the fortunes of war brought it back to its rightful owners. In addition to this both the Pilgrim House, which had been under the control of 'Abdu'l-Bahá since the ascension of Bahá'u'lláh, and

a building known as the Tea House of the Master, where He often entertained the believers – including the first group of pilgrims from the West – were acquired by the Guardian during the last years of his life.[10]

One of the Covenant-breakers had built a blacksmith's shop next to the eastern wall of the Holy Tomb. There were also stables which had been built between the Mansion and the Shrine. Shoghi Effendi removed these unsightly buildings. He created an inner court between the block of buildings in which the Holy Tomb is situated, and the wall of the Mansion Garden. Toward the south of the Shrine of Bahá'u'lláh, there was a small one-storey building with five rooms which was in ruins. It had been in Bahá'í possession during the days of Bahá'u'lláh and 'Abdu'l-Bahá. When Shoghi Effendi began to demolish this building, the Covenant-breakers served the custodian of the Shrine with a stay order from the Haifa Court on the grounds that they had a small share in the property.

The bitterness of the Covenant-breakers was motivated by Majdu'd-Dín, then a few years short of a hundred and paralyzed, who was living in one of the houses in close proximity to the Mansion. A struggle ensued led by the notorious Sáḍíjih,* a daughter of Badí'u'lláh. This lasted for a long time, the legal action initiated by the Covenant-breakers took its course, until they had the temerity to summon the Head of the Faith himself as a witness in court. It was at this point that as a result of Shoghi Effendi's appeal to the Government stating that the matter was a religious issue, the case was lifted from the civil court, and orders were issued in 1952 directly from the Government in favour of Shoghi Effendi.

Within forty-eight hours of the receipt of the official order, the half-demolished building was razed to the ground. The following statement by the International Bahá'í Council in Haifa describes the amazing transformation which took place in the vicinity of the Shrines:

> . . . Servants, Arab labourers and Bahá'í pilgrims had scattered the stones of the building in a blast of joy.
>
> One week later the Guardian of the Cause, who went over to Bahjí himself to supervise the work, had created, in time for the night of the Ascension of Bahá'u'lláh a beautiful entrance, into what is now called the Holy Court leading to the Shrine. In front of the Mansion, and in the very spot where the ruined house had stood, a wide expanse of garden sprung from the dust, marble vases, carved white Carrara marble ornaments, lamp posts, cypress trees, borders, pebbled walks – lo! like a dream they spread before the eyes of the Bahá'ís. Indeed the Arab labourers would quote to each other the old saying: 'The ring of Solomon

* See below, p. 365.

has been found!', which stems from a tradition that the king lost his ring, and that whoever found it and turned it on his finger – whatever he wished for would materialize instantly.

Without the innocent remark thrown out by the Guardian one day as he left Bahjí after visiting the Holy Tomb to the keeper: 'Bring labourers and destroy these ruins,' and which he made because he could no longer tolerate this dilapidation so near the Holy Shrine, and because he desired to build a befitting entrance at the end of the Garden adjacent to the Shrine, which had never had, for sixty years, any entrance, befitting or otherwise, the Covenant-breakers would not have once again been routed, suffered defeat and lost many of the privileges they enjoyed for sixty years in respect to visiting the Holy Shrine.

The final stage in securing the government order for the demolition of the rest of the houses situated in close proximity to the Mansion and occupied by the few remaining Covenant-breakers took place in 1957. This will be described later in this book.

Outside 'Akká stands the Mansion of Mazra'ih, which served as Bahá'u'lláh's residence after His release from the Prison City. This building was a religious endowment, and after much effort Shoghi Effendi secured, in 1950, the sanction of the highest government authority to lease* it to the Bahá'í Community as a Holy Place. Shoghi Effendi furnished the Mansion befittingly, beautified the gardens around it and opened it for pilgrims to visit. The work of restoration and furnishing of the Holy Places and other institutions, as well as the extension and beautification of gardens in Haifa and Bahjí, occupied a great part of Shoghi Effendi's time and effort, and is one of his most outstanding achievements during the thirty-six years of his Guardianship. To describe all these labours in detail is beyond the scope of this book. Rúḥíyyih Khánum writes:

The development of the World Centre of the Faith under the aegis of the Guardian represents one of the major achievements of his life and can only be compared in importance to the spread and consolidation of the Cause itself throughout the entire globe. Of the unique significance of this Centre Shoghi Effendi wrote that it was: '. . . the Holy Land – the Qiblih of a world community, the heart from which the energizing influences of a vivifying Faith continually stream, and the seat and centre around which the diversified activities of a divinely appointed Administrative Order revolve'.[11]

* The Mansion is now owned by the Bahá'í World Centre.

CHAPTER THIRTY

Rebellion in the East against the Guardian

THE ministry of Shoghi Effendi was characterized on the one hand by the release of the enormous spiritual forces which resulted in the building of the institutions of the Administrative Order and the achievement of momentous victories unprecedented in the annals of the Faith, and on the other hand by the anguish, tribulation and untold suffering which he endured at the hands of the enemies of the Faith, both from within and without, throughout the thirty-six years of the Guardianship. These two contrasting aspects of his ministry – one the superb achievements of the Cause, the other, the cruel pains he underwent – are inseparable parts of his life, and thus portray the enormous pressures which were brought to bear upon him during each and every day of his ministry.

One of the titles of Bahá'u'lláh is the Wronged One of the World, and this title could well be applied to Shoghi Effendi too, for he suffered in silence the torments inflicted on him by those who were closest to him. Whereas Bahá'u'lláh's main enemies had been the divines of Islám and the despotic monarchs of Persia and Turkey, the main adversaries of 'Abdu'l-Bahá and Shoghi Effendi were the Covenant-breakers. 'Abdu'l-Bahá, unlike Shoghi Effendi, did not always remain silent when sufferings were heaped upon him. In His writings and public appearances He disclosed the evil-doings of the Covenant-breakers and thus frustrated their wicked schemes to some extent. But Shoghi Effendi acted differently; he did not follow 'Abdu'l-Bahá's pattern of life as a public figure. He concentrated on his work of directing the affairs of the Cause and building the institutions of the Faith mainly through correspondence. In so doing, he privately endured the onslaught of the enemies from within with resignation and forbearance.

We recall that towards the end of 'Abdu'l-Bahá's ministry, the band of old Covenant-breakers had to curtail their ignoble activities and retire into their dens as a result of the unprecedented progress of the Faith in the east and the west as well as the magnetic personality of the Master which had subdued their vigour. But when the Master was succeeded by Shoghi Effendi, they re-appeared on the scene and took advantage of the intense shock of the passing of 'Abdu'l-Bahá which caused the Guardian's illness and necessitated his temporary departure from the Holy Land. With renewed energy, these unfaithful men and women unleashed their attacks on the Cause of God and its youthful leader.

We have already seen how in the early days of Shoghi Effendi's ministry, this infamous band of old Covenant-breakers, led by Mírzá Muḥammad-'Alí, made a fierce assault on the sacred institutions of the Faith including the seizure, by Mírzá Badí'u'lláh, of the keys of the Shrine of Bahá'u'lláh from its faithful custodian. As the years went by, they intensified their opposition to Shoghi Effendi and were subsequently strengthened when most members of 'Abdu'l-Bahá's family joined them. Hand in hand, they rose up against the Guardian of the Cause of God and fought him with all their venom and hatred until the end of his life.

The opposition to the Guardian was not limited to Covenant-breakers residing in the Holy Land. Several believers raised their heads in violation of the Covenant in other parts of the world and began their onslaught against him from the early days of his ministry. One of the age-old factors which led certain believers to violate the Covenant of Bahá'u'lláh was their ambition and pride in wanting to become leaders of the community and obtain important positions in the Cause. The truth, however, is that the Bahá'í community has no leaders as such, and those who are elected or appointed to an administrative office are expected to be servants of the Cause – those who will manifest the qualities of self-effacement, humility and detachment from the things of this world. An inherent characteristic of the Faith of Bahá'u'lláh is that it does not harbour egotistical personalities. Its watchword is the servitude which was so exemplified by 'Abdu'l-Bahá in His life. His supplication to God was to give Him 'to drink from the chalice of selflessness' and to make Him as 'dust' in the pathway of the loved ones of God.

Considering the exalted attribute of 'servitude' which must govern the activities of the friends, as exemplified by 'Abdu'l-Bahá, it is not surprising to witness the eventual downfall of those who, either through their folly or their ambition and pride, tried with all their power to introduce into the Faith of Bahá'u'lláh the concepts of leadership and dominance, and to create the cult of personality within its ranks. These people in their struggle for power brought about severe crises in the community; they violated the Covenant, rose up against Shoghi Effendi and, in the end, tragically destroyed themselves.

Soon after Shoghi Effendi assumed the office of the Guardianship, and while there was widespread expectation among the the Bahá'ís of the immediate establishment of the Universal House of Justice, some egotistical personalities longed to become members of that august institution. One such person in the East was 'Abdu'l-Ḥusayn, entitled by 'Abdu'l-Bahá as Ávárih (Wanderer). In the West it was Ahmad Sohrab. Both men were prominent teachers of the Faith in Persia and North America respectively, and both had one thing in common: a passionate love of leadership.

Ávárih was a native of the village of Taft in the Province of Yazd. Before he embraced the Faith he was a Muslim clergyman. Soon after becoming a follower of Bahá'u'lláh he was recognized by the believers to be a man of learning and knowledge, and not long after that he became renowned as one of the erudite teachers of the Faith. For several years, he travelled around Persia, 'Iráq and Egypt, and became one of the most respected and famous Bahá'ís of the East as he employed his talents in teaching and writing for the Faith. 'Abdu'l-Bahá, who was fully aware of the vices and corrupt practices of this man, did not prevent him from serving the Cause, and as long as he acted faithfully in relation to the Faith, He encouraged him, praised his work, and wrote several Tablets in his honour.

However, from the beginning of his Bahá'í involvement, he displayed a pride and vanity which puzzled those Bahá'ís who were in close contact with him. They could not reconcile the quality and goodness of his service to the Cause with his egotistical behaviour, and were surprised when they came across some of his despicable habits such as smoking opium in secret, a practice that Bahá'u'lláh had strictly forbidden. However, the rank and file of the believers were drawn to him, and during the time when he was actively teaching the Faith and promoting its interests he became renowned among the Bahá'ís as the foremost teacher of the Cause in the community and the outstanding personality within its ranks.

Shortly after the passing of 'Abdu'l-Bahá, a number of prominent Bahá'ís from several countries were invited to go to the Holy Land in order that Shoghi Effendi might discuss the affairs of the Cause with them. Ávárih was one of them, but he arrived late and so missed the discussions. However, he did have the opportunity to talk about various matters with Shoghi Effendi. One of the dreams entertained by Ávárih was to become a member of the Universal House of Justice. He knew that if there were to be an election of this body, he would most likely be elected, as he was one of the foremost teachers of the Faith in Persia and well-known even in some communities in the West.

Ávárih was an outright hypocrite who had endeared himself to the friends. This he did by writing letters, full of loving exhortation couched in moving language, which he used to disseminate among the believers in both the East and the West. He wrote one such letter in April 1923 addressed to the annual Convention of the Bahá'ís of the United States of America. Although he had no faith in Shoghi Effendi and was about to undermine his position as the Guardian of the Faith, yet he used to write to Bahá'í communities extolling his station in superlative terms and urged the friends to turn to him and remain steadfast in the Covenant.

Considering himself to be an erudite and knowledgeable Bahá'í, and regarding Shoghi Effendi as young and inexperienced, Ávárih advised him in Haifa to arrange for the establishment of the Universal House of Justice at an early stage. Shoghi Effendi clearly explained to him that the election of that body had to wait until such time as local and national Spiritual Assemblies could be formed in various countries and were fully functioning. But Ávárih was not satisfied with this explanation and was still determined to press his point of view.

After Ávárih's short stay in the Holy Land, Shoghi Effendi advised him to proceed to England where he was to help the believers deepen their knowledge of the Faith. He arrived there some time in January 1923, and after a short stay he went to Egypt where he succeeded in publishing two volumes of the book* he had written on the history of the Faith. He achieved this aim with the help of certain believers early in September 1923.

During the few months that he remained in Cairo, he created dissension and disunity among the believers to such an extent that the Spiritual Assembly of Cairo complained to Shoghi Effendi. Thus he was again invited to go to the Holy Land. Ávárih questioned the authenticity of the *Will and Testament* of 'Abdu'l-Bahá but was satisfied with it when he was shown the original copy in 'Abdu'l-Bahá's handwriting. He then met with the Greatest Holy Leaf and reiterated to her his opinion that Shoghi Effendi should be advised to call for the election of the Universal House of Justice. He is reported to have uttered a veiled threat that if his demand were not acted upon, he would have no choice but to arouse the Bahá'ís of Persia to rebel against the Guardian.

In the meantime, he wrote letters to the believers expressing his dissatisfaction with the way the affairs of the Cause were being

* *Kawákib'ud-Durríyyih* (Brilliant Stars).

conducted. When he arrived in Persia, he began propagating his misconceived ideas aimed at creating division among the friends there. In May 1924 the Spiritual Assembly of Ṭihrań sought guidance from the Guardian as to how to deal with Ávárih. The response was that the friends must be protected from his misguided intentions, and a few days later the Greatest Holy Leaf sent the following message to the Trustee of the Ḥuqúqu'lláh, Ḥájí Abu'l-Ḥasan entitled Amín.

> The question of Ávárih has surely come to your attention. In spite of the fact that last year, the first time that he visited this sacred Spot, he was shown the greatest kindness and love, and he was the object of every consideration and care, and everything was done to help him in every way; that when he left for Europe, as the reason for his visit was to teach the Faith, and he was favoured and praised by the Guardian, the friends in England showed him reverence to what was really an exaggerated degree, and received him with the warmest hospitality – that is, no one failed in showing him the utmost regard – still, when he returned to Cairo and busied himself with publishing his book, as it became apparent later on, he put the Assembly and the friends at odds, stirred up the mischief himself and then secretly wrote here and there that there was trouble in Cairo, and presented the situation so as to further his own ends.
>
> The beloved Guardian at once laid hold of every possible means to quiet the dissension in Cairo, but it proved impossible because Ávárih, using all kinds of devices, prevented the reconciliation of the Assembly and the friends in that city. When the Guardian could endure this no longer and there was nothing more that he could do, with deep regret he left the Holy Land. His letter clearly shows how heavy was his heart.
>
> Later, Ávárih left Egypt and came again to the Holy Land, and the interesting thing is that the moment he left, the misunderstandings among the friends in Cairo disappeared, and Bahá'í affairs went forward again in proper fashion, so that it became perfectly clear that he had been the cause of the disruption.
>
> From here, too, he began to send out letters, and it would only grieve you to tell of the falsehoods and calumnies they contained. In Beirut, too, his talks and his actions were the same, and he spread the word that, God forbid, there is dissension everywhere. Accordingly, in order to protect the Cause of God, a telegram was sent to Baghdád, citing these words of the Ancient Beauty – exalted be His glory: 'Place not your trust in every new arrival, and believe not every speaker.' As a result, when he reached Baghdád, and wished to stir up mischief there, the friends, with great dignity and firmness, restrained him, and avoided his company.
>
> The point is that although such talk and such behaviour have no effect and no importance whatsoever, and do not merit our attention, still this disloyalty of his in these days of trial and sorrow is such that, unable to

> bear the situation any longer, this grieved and helpless one has felt obliged to set down a brief account of what actually took place.[1]

This clear violation of the Covenant isolated Ávárih from the believers. Even his wife left him and refused to associate with him. Soon he changed his tactics and wrote a series of letters to various members of 'Abdu'l-Bahá's family saying that there had been misunderstandings and suggested that if Shoghi Effendi was willing to arrange an annual income for him, he would be willing to alter his attitude and stop his activities against the Covenant of Bahá'u'lláh.

Covenant-breaking is a spiritual disease and those who are affected by it are victims of their own selfish ambitions. It is only through a real awakening of the soul and recognizing one's transgressions against God that a Covenant-breaker can find the urge to repent, and when the repentant is sincere, God will forgive his past and restore his spiritual health. Indeed, there were a number of Covenant-breakers who were forgiven in this way by 'Abdu'l-Bahá and Shoghi Effendi.

However, in the several letters Ávárih wrote asking for reinstatement there was no expression of repentance. When there was no positive response to his letters, he unveiled his satanic nature and wrote most abusive letters to Shoghi Effendi in which he used rude and offensive language and vowed to destroy the Faith of Bahá'u'lláh altogether. There was never among the Covenant-breakers during Shoghi Effendi's ministry a man so vile and hypocritical as he.

Covenant-breakers usually oppose the Centre of the Faith, but most of them have claimed to be believers in Bahá'u'lláh. However, in this case Ávárih rebelled against the Faith itself. This he did despite the fact that he had spent more than two decades teaching the Cause of Bahá'u'lláh and had published voluminous writings declaring its truth and testifying to the authenticity of the message of its Founder. He joined hands with the Muslim clergy and Christian missionaries in attacking the Faith in Persia. He disseminated far and wide a series of his despicable publications against the Faith. In foul language, he attacked every aspect of the Faith, misrepresented its aims, and uttered slanders about its Central Figures whom he attacked in most distasteful terms. 'The volumes', Shoghi Effendi writes, 'which a shameless apostate composed and disseminated . . . in his brazen efforts not only to disrupt that Order [Administrative Order] but to undermine the very Faith which had conceived it proved . . . abortive.'[2]

In one of his letters to the Bahá'ís of Persia who had completely ignored the activities of this ignoble man, Shoghi Effendi referred to Ávárih as a dead body which the surging ocean of the Cause of God had cast upon its shores and thus cleansed itself from its pollution. A few years later, Shoghi Effendi introduced the episode of Ávárih to the Bahá'ís of the West in these words:

To the Honoured Members of the Bahá'í National Spiritual Assemblies throughout the West.

My dear fellow-workers:

With feelings of burning indignation I find myself impelled to acquaint you with various events that have recently transpired in Persia. Though in their immediate effect these happenings may prove gravely disquieting to the followers of the Faith in Persia and elsewhere, yet they cannot but eventually contribute to the strengthening and purification of the Cause we steadfastly love and serve.

I refer to the treacherous conduct of a professed adherent of the teaching of Bahá'u'lláh, by the name of 'Abdu'l-Husayn Avarih, hitherto regarded as a respected teacher of the Cause, and not unknown by a few of its followers in Europe. Of a nature and character whom those who have learned to know him well have never ceased to despise, even in the brightest days of his public career in the Cause, he has of late been driven by the force of circumstances which his shortsightedness has gravely miscalculated to throw off the mask which for so many years hid his hideous self.

The sudden removal of the commanding personality of our beloved 'Abdu'l-Bahá; the confused consternation that seized His followers in the years immediately succeeding His passing; the reputation which to superficial eyes he had acquired by his travels in Europe; the success attending his voluminous compilation of the history of the Cause – these and other circumstances emboldened him to launch a campaign of insinuation and fraud aiming at the eventual overthrow of the institutions expressly provided by Bahá'u'lláh. He saw clearly his chance in the complete disruption of the Cause to capture the allegiance if not of the whole world-wide Bahá'í community of at least a considerable section of its followers in the East.

No sooner had his evil whisperings reached the ears of the loyal and vigilant followers of Bahá'u'lláh, than they arose with overwhelming force and unhesitating determination to denounce him as a dangerous enemy seeking to undermine the faith and sap the loyalty of the adherents of the Cause of God. Shunned by the entire body of the believers, abandoned by his life-long and most intimate friends, deserted by his wife, separated from his only child, refused admittance into even his own home, denied of the profit he hoped to derive from the sale and circulation of his book, he found to his utter amazement and remorse his best hopes irretrievably shattered.

Forsaken and bankrupt, and in desperate rage, he now with startling audacity sought to expose to friend and foe, the futility and hollowness which he attributed to the Cause, thereby revealing the depths of his own degradation and folly. He has with bitter hatred conspired with the fanatical clergy and the orthodox members of foreign Missions in Ṭihrán, allied himself with every hostile element in the Capital, directed with fiendish subtlety his appeal to the highest dignitaries of the State and sought by every method to secure financial assistance for the furtherance of his aim.

Not content with an infamous denunciation of the originality and efficacy of the teachings and principles of the Cause, not satisfied with a rejection of the authenticity of the Will and Testament of 'Abdu'l-Bahá, he has dared to attack the exalted person of the Author and Founder of the Faith, and to impute to its Forerunner and true Exemplar the vilest motives and most incredible intentions.

He has most malignantly striven to revive the not unfamiliar accusation of representing the true lovers of Persia as the sworn enemies of every form of established authority in that land, the unrelenting disturbers of its peace, the chief obstacles to its unity and the determined wreckers of the venerated faith of Islám. By every artifice which a sordid and treacherous mind can devise he has sought in the pages of his book to strike terror in the heart of the confident believer, to sow the seeds of doubt in the mind of the well-disposed and friendly, to poison the thoughts of the indifferent and to reinforce the power of the assaulting weapon of the adversary.

But, alas! he has laboured in vain, oblivious of the fact that all the pomp and powers of royalty, all the concerted efforts of the mightiest potentates of Islám, all the ingenious devices to which the cruellest torture-mongers of a cruel race have for well-nigh a century resorted, have proved one and all impotent to stem the tide of the beloved Faith or to extinguish its flame. Surely, if we read the history of this Cause aright, we cannot fail to observe that the East has already witnessed not a few of its sons, of wider experience, of a higher standing, of a greater influence, apostatize their faith, find themselves to their utter consternation lose whatsoever talent they possessed, recede swiftly into the shadows of oblivion and be heard of no more.[3]

Owing to his political activities, Ávárih at one time fell into public disgrace, and at an advanced age was exiled by order of the government to the city of Yazd where he lived an ignominious life. Shoghi Effendi predicted that Ávárih would live to a very old age in order to witness with his own eyes the progress of the Faith throughout the world. Indeed he lived to be about one hundred years of age, and witnessed the rising prestige of the Faith, the inauguration of the Holy Year in 1953, the completion of the superstructure of the Shrine of the Báb, the launching of the Ten Year Crusade and the convocation of several international conferences at which a host of teachers and pioneers arose to bring the Message of Bahá'u'lláh to many virgin territories and establish the institutions of His Faith all over the globe.

After Ávárih died, Shoghi Effendi sent the following cable on 16 December 1953 to the Bahá'í world:

> Following the successive blows which fell with dramatic swiftness two years ago upon the ring-leaders of the fast dwindling band of old Covenant-breakers at the World Centre of the Faith, God's avenging hand struck down in the last two months, Avarih, Fareed and Falah, within the cradle of the Faith, North America and Turkey, who demonstrated in varying degrees, in the course of over thirty years, their faithlessness to 'Abdu'l-Bahá.
>
> The first of the above named will be condemned by posterity as being the most shameless, vicious, relentless apostate in the annals of the Faith, who, through ceaseless vitriolic attacks recorded in voluminous writings and close alliance with its traditional enemies, assiduously schemed to blacken its name and subvert the foundations of its institutions.
>
> The second, history will recognize as one of the most perfidious among the kinsmen and the interpreters of the Centre of the Covenant, who, driven by ungovernable cupidity, committed acts causing agonies of grief and distress to the beloved Master and culminating in open association with breakers of Bahá'u'lláh's Covenant in the Holy Land.
>
> The third will be chiefly remembered for his pride, obstinacy and insatiable ambition impelling him to violate the spiritual and administrative precepts of the Faith.
>
> All three, however blinded by perversity, could not have failed to perceive, as their infamous careers approached their end, the futility of their opposition, the measure of their own loss and the degree of progress and consolidation of the triumphant administrative order so magnificently celebrated in the course of the festivities of the recently concluded Holy Year.[4]

'Ringleaders' mentioned in the above cable is a reference to Badí'u'lláh, Shu'á'u'lláh and Músá, the youngest brother and the two sons of the Arch-breaker of the Covenant respectively. Badí'u'lláh died in 1950, following which Shoghi Effendi sent the following cable to the National Spiritual Assembly of the Bahá'ís of the United States about him and his two nephews.

> Badí'u'lláh, brother and chief lieutenant of archbreaker of divine Covenant, has miserably perished after sixty years' ceaseless, fruitless efforts to undermine the divinely-appointed Order, having witnessed within the last five months the deaths of his nephews Shoa and Musa, notorious standard-bearers of the rebellion associated with the name of their perfidious father.[5]

As to Fareed and Falah, whose names are included along with that of Ávárih: they are two long-standing Covenant-breakers. Falah was a resident of Iskandarún, Turkey, a proud and arrogant man who misled a number of his relatives in that city, and remained unrepentant till the end of his life.

Dr Amin Fareed was related to the Holy Family. His mother was the sister of Munírih Khánum, the wife of 'Abdu'l-Bahá. His father, Mírzá Asadu'lláh, a native of Iṣfahán, was charged by 'Abdu'l-Bahá with bringing the remains of the Báb to the Holy Land, a task which he performed successfully. Fareed's career consisted of a series of acts of treachery and despicable conduct. Although 'Abdu'l-Bahá paid every attention to his education and sent him to America where he studied at the University of Chicago and qualified as a medical doctor, he did not remain faithful to the Centre of the Covenant. He accompanied 'Abdu'l-Bahá to the United States, where he acted as His interpreter, but secretly he was engaged in activities which brought disgrace to the Faith. Knowing that 'Abdu'l-Bahá's policy in the West was that of not accepting financial contributions from the believers, he began to solicit funds clandestinely in the name of the Master and having stolen His seal, he used to issue receipts which carried the stamp of 'Abdu'l-Bahá on them. This, and other dishonourable conduct by Fareed, brought great sorrow to the heart of 'Abdu'l-Bahá in such wise that at times His body would be visibly trembling with rage. The Master eventually expelled Fareed from the community. He joined hands with the Covenant-breakers, and in the end destroyed his spiritual life and that of his father who, in spite of much service to the Cause, allied himself with his ignoble son.

Ávárih, like all the other Covenant-breakers, utterly failed in his endeavours to arrest the progress of the Faith or dampen the zeal of its adherents. The only beneficial outcome of his rebellion was that a few unscrupulous and corrupted persons, who claimed allegiance to the Faith, gravitated around him. They too rebelled against the Covenant and were cast out of the Community of the Most Great Name, thereby cleansing it from the pollution of their evil influence.

One such person was the evil-minded Ḥasan-i-Níkú, a close friend of Ávárih. He was a teacher of the Faith who had spent some time in India and who visited Shoghi Effendi in Haifa at the end of 1923. He was an ambitious man who looked for leadership in the Bahá'í community, and when he did not find it he followed the same path as Ávárih. He published three volumes in which he attacked the Faith most viciously, attributed appalling things to the Founders of the Faith, totally misrepresenting its tenets in a language full of bitterness, hate and falsehood. He was ignored by the believers, and his hopes of discrediting the Faith and breaking up the solidarity of its adherents were frustrated.

Another notorious Covenant-breaker in Persia who became a close associate of Ávárih was Fayḍu'lláh Ṣubḥí who for a number of years served the Master as His secretary. He was a vacillating person who on more than one occasion rebelled against the institutions of the Faith and each time repented, only to resume his opposition to the Cause again. Although he was brought up in a Bahá'í family, he fell victim to the influence of Ávárih. His father tried hard to save him from his spiritual extinction, but he remained adamant and continued in his odious activities against the Cause. He sustained a prolonged campaign of shameful vilification not only against the Guardian but also against Bahá'u'lláh and 'Abdu'l-Bahá. At the height of his rebellion, he wrote a letter to Áyatu'lláh Burújirdí, a high-ranking Muslim cleric, in which he repented of having taken part in Bahá'í activities in his earlier days. He used very offensive language against Shoghi Effendi and the Universal House of Justice in this letter which demonstrated the depraved character of this man, who remained in the abyss of ignominy and godlessness till the end of his life. All he left behind is the memory of his vile language and despicable conduct.

The defection of Ávárih in Persia resulted in the expulsion from the Faith of a handful of unfaithful persons who were influenced by his propaganda. In the same way that all impurities are discharged at intervals from the body of man to keep it healthy, the process of expulsion of the Covenant-breakers had a cleansing effect upon the Bahá'ís of Persia. It invigorated the community and gave it the extra stimulus necessary to expand and consolidate the institutions of its divinely-ordained Administrative Order.

Another notorious Covenant-breaker who caused agitation among the Egyptian Bahá'ís was an Armenian by the name of Fá'iq who rebelled against Shoghi Effendi and tried to create an alternative organisation to the Administrative Order. He conceived the idea of establishing a 'Scientific Society' – an experiment which ended in utter failure. The friends dissociated themselves from him. He was left to his own devices, and thus deprived himself of the bounty of faith and died a Covenant-breaker.

CHAPTER THIRTY-ONE

Rebellion in the West

WHILE this handful of Covenant-breakers in Persia was agitating in the early days of Shoghi Effendi's ministry to arrest the onward march of the Faith and dishonour its Founders, a similar situation was brought about in the West. It started as soon as the contents of the *Will and Testament* of 'Abdu'l-Bahá became known to the community. The first person to react was Ahmad Sohrab, who had served for some time as the Master's secretary and interpreter. One of the believers, Mrs Nellie French, has recounted the reaction of Ahmad Sohrab when she communicated to him the contents of the *Will*. He was intensely agitated. His face turned black and pacing back and forth, he exclaimed: 'This cannot be. Shoghi Effendi knows nothing about the Cause. He was never with 'Abdu'l-Bahá as I have been. I am the one who should have been appointed.'

When Mírzá Abu'l-Faḍl was in the United States of America, he used to live alone in his apartment, and the friends were concerned about his health. Ali-Kuli Khan* has described the circumstances which led to the despatch of Ahmad Sohrab to America in order to act as a servant to Mírzá Abu'l-Faḍl. He writes:

> That is how it was. Mírzá sick from not eating, and unable to adjust to American food and American life. He would not let me serve him in any way. If we went shopping, he would not even let me carry the packages. Finally I wrote to the Master, because the responsibility for his life and work was more than I could bear, and I told of the difficulty of expediting Mírzá's book and described everything just as it was. Then I added that it might be a Persian attendant, who could prepare food for Mírzá and look after his needs, would solve the problem. When I had come through Port Sa'íd on my way to America, there was a boy around fifteen who worked in Aḥmad Yazdí's store there. His name was Aḥmad-i-Iṣfahání (later he took the name of Sohrab). This boy had begged me to request the Master to send him to America. I now suggested that he come here to look after Mírzá. The Master sent him here, to serve Mírzá and return with him to

* An eminent Bahá'í teacher; see Gail, *Summon Up Remembrance*.

the East. However, when Mírzá sailed for home in 1904 – with the MacNutts, Mrs. Julia Grundy, and the Woodcocks and their daughter – Aḥmad-i-Iṣfáhání did not accompany him. He remained in the United States until 1912, when the Master Himself took him back to the East, although he seemed loath to go.[1]

While in America, Ahmad became proficient in English and, when the Master went to the United States, he served Him as interpreter. However, from the beginning, Ahmad showed signs of insincerity and faithlessness. Many a time his behaviour brought deep sorrow to the heart of 'Abdu'l-Bahá. But he remained with Him throughout the journey, and later when he went to Haifa, he continued to serve Him as a secretary. The Master knew that Ahmad would rebel against the Centre of the Cause after Him and had intimated this to one or two persons who were close to Him.

At the time of 'Abdu'l-Bahá's passing, Ahmad had become well-known among the believers of the West. Having emerged as a prominent Bahá'í, he, like Ávárih, wanted the establishment of the Universal House of Justice immediately after the passing of 'Abdu'l-Bahá. And as Shoghi Effendi began to create local and national Spiritual Assemblies instead, Ahmad opposed the move. With the help of a certain wealthy woman, Mrs Lewis Stuyvesant (Julie) Chanler, he formed an organisation known as 'The New History Society', and made a great deal of propaganda to recruit members. He used the name and teachings of the Faith to attract people to his cause, clearly denouncing Shoghi Effendi's directives for the building of the Administrative Order. He also created the 'Caravan of East and West', the chief activity of which was international correspondence.

Ahmad Sohrab, who was referred to by the believers as 'Ávárih of the West', tried to create a new sect of his own based on the teachings of Bahá'u'lláh. He did not question the authenticity of the *Will and Testament* of 'Abdu'l-Bahá, but maintained that Shoghi Effendi had erred in his function as the Guardian of the Faith. He made great efforts to penetrate the American Bahá'í community in order to undermine the foundation of the local and national Spiritual Assemblies and to establish himself in place of Shoghi Effendi, but he utterly failed. The Bahá'ís remained faithful to the Covenant; they shunned him entirely, and with the passage of time his hopes were dashed and his plans and activities bore no fruit whatsoever. At the height of his endeavours, Shoghi Effendi wrote the following to the American National Spiritual Assembly through his secretary:

> In regard to the activities of Ahmad Sohrab, Shoghi Effendi has already stated that such attacks, however perfidious, do not justify the friends

replying or taking any direct action against them. The attitude of the National Spiritual Assembly should be to ignore them entirely . . .[2]

A common pattern of behaviour of most Covenant-breakers is that at first they claim to be devoted and sincere Bahá'ís but later they demonstrate by their actions that they are not. For instance, those who broke the Covenant during Shoghi Effendi's Ministry declared their faith in Bahá'u'lláh and 'Abdu'l-Bahá in the early stages but as time went on and they foresaw the bankruptcy of their position they compromised and progressively distanced themselves from their earlier practices and assertions. In almost every case the new Covenant-breakers joined hands with the old ones whom they had previously denounced. For example, Ahmad Sohrab at first did not have anything to do with Mírzá Muḥammad-'Alí and his associates, whom he regarded as enemies of 'Abdu'l-Bahá. But at a later time, when he noticed the ascendancy of the Cause of God, he forged links of friendship and co-operation with them. He even went further and denounced 'Abdu'l-Bahá, whom he used to regard in the early days of his rebellion as the Centre of the Covenant of Bahá'u'lláh and whose writings he used to quote in his public pronouncements.

In 1954, the year that witnessed the extraordinary expansion of the Faith when hundreds of Bahá'í pioneers had settled in virgin territories of the globe, Ahmad Sohrab, incensed by the growth and consolidation of the institutions of the Cause world-wide, visited the Holy Land, went to the home of some of the old Covenant-breakers, held meetings there and gave them his support and encouragement. He publicly announced that Bahá'u'lláh had appointed two successors, 'Abdu'l-Bahá and Mírzá Muḥammad-'Alí, and charged that 'Abdu'l-Bahá had disobeyed the Will of Bahá'u'lláh, taken charge of the affairs of the Cause and eliminated Muḥammad-'Alí.

At a press conference in Haifa he told the reporters that 'Abdu'l-Bahá was a Muslim. And when they questioned this, he reiterated his statement, and asserted that he was indeed a Muslim. Such a statement by one who used to preach that Bahá'u'lláh was the new Manifestation of God and 'Abdu'l-Bahá His successor, reveals the extent of his hypocrisy and falsehood.

In another interview in Tel Aviv, Ahmad introduced himself as the secretary of 'Abdu'l-Bahá and His leading disciple. One of the reporters reminded him that 'Abdu'l-Bahá had left a Will, and asked, if Ahmad was sincere in his devotion to 'Abdu'l-Bahá, how was it that he was not working with the present world Bahá'í community? Ahmad acknowledged the authenticity of the Will of the Master and accepted the fact that 'Abdu'l-Bahá had appointed Shoghi Effendi as the Guardian of the Faith. But he said that while the Master apparently thought Shoghi Effendi would make a good Guardian of the Faith, this had not been the case, and the problem was now how to get rid of Shoghi Effendi.

Having failed to make an impression upon the public in the Holy Land, Ahmad's hopes of weakening the position of Shoghi Effendi were dashed. Frustrated and embittered, he and his associates sought by every means to exploit some of the contentious claims which surfaced from time to time against the Guardian from the Covenant-breakers in the Holy Land. For instance, when Shoghi Effendi in 1956 demolished one of the houses situated in close proximity to the Shrine of Bahá'u'lláh, Mrs Chanler sent a petition to the President of Israel in which she supported the claim of one of the Covenant-breakers to the property and introduced the latter as the representative in the Holy Land of a group of people whom she described as 'free Bahá'í'.

Activities such as this continued until the end of Shoghi Effendi's Ministry, but they produced no positive results for Ahmad. On the contrary, toward the end of his life, the movement which he had created and spent so much effort in promoting was near extinction. It completely disintegrated after his death in 1958. All endeavours which this misguided man exerted over several decades to undermine the Cause of God brought forth quite the opposite effect of stimulating its growth. The Message of Bahá'u'lláh had reached the furthest corners of the earth, and by then the institutions of His Faith were established in most countries and territories of the globe.

In 1941, when Ahmad was at the height of his rebellion, Shoghi Effendi wrote of him in these words:

> And now more particularly concerning the prime mover of this latest agitation, which, whatever its immediate consequences, will sooner or later come to be regarded as merely one more of those ugly and abortive attempts designed to undermine the foundation, and obscure the purpose, of the Administrative order of the Faith of Bahá'u'lláh. Obscure in his origin, ambitious of leadership, untaught by the lesson of such as have erred before him, odious in the hopes he nurses, contemptible in the methods he pursues, shameless in his deliberate distortions of truths he has long since ceased to believe in, ludicrous in his present isolation and helplessness, wounded and exasperated by the downfall which his own folly has precipitated, he, the latest protagonist of a spurious cause, cannot but in the end be subjected, as remorselessly as his infamous predecessors, to the fate which they invariably have suffered.
>
> Generated by the propelling and purifying forces of a mysterious Faith, born of delusion or malice, winning a fleeting notoriety derived from the precarious advantages of wealth, fame or fortune, these movements sponsored by deluded, self-seeking adventurers find themselves, sooner

> or later, enmeshed in the machinations of their authors, are buried in shame, and sink eventually into complete oblivion.
>
> The schism which their foolish leaders had contrived so sedulously to produce within the Faith, will soon, to their utter amazement, come to be regarded as a process of purification, a cleansing agency, which, far from decimating the ranks of its followers, reinforces its indestructible unity, and proclaims anew to a world, sceptical or indifferent, the cohesive strength of the institutions of that Faith, the incorruptibility of its purposes and principles, and the recuperative powers inherent in its community life.[3]

After his death, the Hands of the Cause in the Holy Land, who were acting as custodians of the Faith prior to the establishment of the Universal House of Justice, sent the following telegram to the Bahá'í world on 28 April 1958.

> Sohrab, relentless enemy faith after witnessing for third of a century the irresistible spread of the Holy Cause, in forty-five hundred centres under guidance beloved Guardian, died the first of Riḍván, every hope frustrated, every plan extinguished, every ambition thwarted. This striking evidence of God's avenging wrath on the one hand and on the other the unfailing protection of the community and institutions reared by the beloved Guardian inspires believers to arise and serve with renewed courage and dedication to insure the complete success of the crusade.[4]

Another person who rose up in opposition to Shoghi Effendi and to the establishment of the institutions of the Faith was Mrs Ruth White in the United States; she was an old believer and had visited 'Abdu'l-Bahá in the Holy Land in 1920. She claimed that the *Will and Testament* of 'Abdu'l-Bahá was not authentic, and she created much agitation in the community by attacking the National Spiritual Assembly whose establishment she considered to be against the teachings and wishes of 'Abdu'l-Bahá. For several years Mrs White persevered in her determination to prevent the establishment of the institutions of the Faith. She wrote a letter to the United States Postmaster General and asked him, among other things, to prohibit the National Spiritual Assembly from 'using the United States Mails to spread the falsehood that Shoghi Effendi is the successor of 'Abdu'l-Bahá and the Guardian of the Cause'.

Mrs White wrote many letters to the National Spiritual Assembly of the Bahá'ís of the United States and Canada, as well as to some believers. In these she vehemently objected to the directives of Shoghi Effendi and the administration of the Cause through the local and national institutions. One of Mrs White's converts was Dr Herrigel, a founder member of the German Bahá'í community. He too rejected the authority of the *Will and Testament* and became numbered among the Covenant-breakers.

Mrs White also wrote a letter to the High Commissioner for Palestine in which she completely misrepresented the position of Shoghi Effendi. But the authorities in the Holy Land were well aware of the facts and did not heed her appeals.

It is interesting to note that no one who has studied the *Will and Testament* of 'Abdu'l-Bahá, with the exception of Mrs White and a few others whom she influenced, has ever questioned its authenticity. Even other Covenant-breakers who rose up against Shoghi Effendi did not agree with her. Ahmad Sohrab and Ṣubḥí had both served 'Abdu'l-Bahá as His secretary. They never questioned the authenticity of the Will. Neither did Muḥammad-'Alí or Badí'u'lláh, or other enemies who were looking for any flaws they could find with which to attack the Guardian of the Faith.

It must be remembered that the *Will and Testament* was written in 'Abdu'l-Bahá's handwriting and bore His seal. The *Will and Testament* was very familiar to the Persian believers. This is because 'Abdu'l-Bahá had written innumerable Tablets in His own hand and almost every Bahá'í family in Persia had been the recipient of these Tablets. When the photostat text of the *Will and Testament* was sent to Persia and elsewhere, it was easily acknowledged by everyone to be in the handwriting of 'Abdu'l-Bahá.

Another criterion for its authenticity is 'Abdu'l-Bahá's unique style and mode of expression which is familiar to the Persian friends. Indeed, anyone who is versed in the Writings of the Faith in the original language can easily tell the difference between the writings of Bahá'u'lláh, 'Abdu'l-Bahá or Shoghi Effendi, as each has its own special tone and style. The Universal House of Justice has made the following statements:

> The second aspect, the literary style of the Will, can only be properly judged by one who is familiar with the Persian language because most of the Master's Tablets that are published in English are in early translations that leave great room for improvement. 'Abdu'l-Bahá had a very characteristic, inimitable style and there is no doubt at all in the minds of the Persian Bahá'ís (who, until the time of Shoghi Effendi's passing, composed the majority of the followers of Bahá'u'lláh) that the Will and Testament is written in that style.
>
> Thirdly, as regards the handwriting of the Will, you should know that Shoghi Effendi sent out photostatic copies of the Will not only to National Spiritual Assemblies, but also for distribution among individual believers in Persia. You should also remember that the members of the Master's family, including his half-brother, Muḥammad-'Alí, who is so strongly condemned in the Will, as well as the thousands of Persian

believers who had received or studied Tablets from Him, were thoroughly familiar with the handwriting of 'Abdu'l-Bahá, and the Will is so obviously in that handwriting that no one who was qualified to judge – even those who could profit by claiming that the Will was invalid – has ever questioned its authenticity. Even believers who became bitter enemies of Shoghi Effendi after the passing of the Master, . . . did not question the validity of the Will. The only challenge came from Mrs. White, an American ignorant of Persian, who had the ulterior motive of trying to discredit an administration which she personally opposed. The handwriting expert whose opinion she quoted in support of her argument was also a westerner and himself stated that he could not give a final opinion without seeing the writing in the original.

Mrs. White went as far as appealing to the civil authorities of Palestine to take legal action in the matter, a request which the British Authorities curtly refused. When, several months later, Badí'u'lláh, the brother and lieutenant of the deceased arch-breaker of Bahá'u'lláh's Covenant, approached these same authorities claiming the right to oppose the projected transfer of the remains of the Mother and Brother of 'Abdu'l-Bahá from 'Akká to Haifa, they categorically upheld the authority of Shoghi Effendi as the Successor of 'Abdu'l-Bahá on the basis of their scrutiny of the Will and Testament, the validity of which Badí'u'lláh did not dispute.

'Abdu'l-Bahá's Will was written in three parts at three different times in His life. All three parts are in His handwriting and are signed by Him. All three, comprising twelve pages in all, were in an envelope under lock and key in His safe when He died. The face of the envelope was addressed to Shoghi Effendi in the Master's handwriting and signed by Him. On the back it bears three more signatures of 'Abdu'l-Bahá across the flap where it was stuck down. Shoghi Effendi was in England when the Master died and therefore His Will was taken from His safe at that time by some members of His family and opened to see if He had given any instructions about His burial.[5]

Although the violators of the Covenant in the East and the West during Shoghi Effendi's ministry were few in numbers yet the relentless attacks which they launched against the Faith during the entire period of Shoghi Effendi's ministry were fierce. In spite of their persistent efforts to make a breach within the Bahá'í community, they did not succeed. The vast majority of believers remained firm in the Covenant, turned to Shoghi Effendi with great devotion and laboured in the promotion of the Faith and the establishment of its divinely-ordained institutions throughout the world. Nevertheless the Guardian, being the Centre of the Cause of God, was the target of all the assaults which the Covenant-breakers inflicted upon him. The sufferings that he endured as a result of their rebellion are truly heart-rending. However, at the same time that Shoghi Effendi sustained the attacks which they had directed against him and the

Cause of which he was the Guardian, he exhorted the believers to shun the Covenant-breakers and completely ignore their odious propaganda. In this way, each one of them was severed from the community, and, like a branch of a tree which is cut off, withered away and perished in time.

CHAPTER THIRTY-TWO

The Faithless Relatives of Shoghi Effendi

THE pain and suffering which were inflicted upon Shoghi Effendi by the members of 'Abdu'l-Bahá's family who broke the Covenant and bitterly opposed him were far more distressing than all the attacks which the enemies of the Faith and the Covenant-breakers outside the Holy Land had mounted against the Cause and its Guardian.

The rebellion of most members of 'Abdu'l-Bahá's family against Shoghi Effendi is reminiscent of the rebellion of Bahá'u'lláh's family after His ascension. We have given some reasons for this in previous chapters,* and explained that it is usually those who are closest to the Manifestation of God or to His Chosen Ones who are in greatest danger of becoming Covenant-breakers. Only those who are true servants of God, and are the embodiments of humility and utter nothingness, can survive spiritually and remain faithful in that holy and rarified atmosphere of the presence of 'Abdu'l-Bahá or Shoghi Effendi. Any trace of ambition or self-glorification which a believer may have in his personality can be fatal if he comes in frequent contact with the Source of divine Revelation, because in that holy presence He shall 'accept naught but absolute virtue and deeds of stainless purity'.[1]

The history of the Faith has shown that many of those who were closest to Bahá'u'lláh fell from grace because of their insincerity and selfish interests. These people, however, could have remained faithful believers if they were not serving in His presence. A proud and egotistical person who serves the Cause of Bahá'u'lláh in his local community, may create many unpleasant problems for himself and the other believers, but these difficulties will not necessarily be the cause of the extinction of his faith. To give an analogy: A man who falls on the ground may hurt himself, whereas if a person is flying high above the ground, his fall will be fatal.

Most members of the family of 'Abdu'l-Bahá were devoid of those spiritual qualities which distinguish a man of God from the ungodly. Materialism had eaten into the core of their beings, and 'Abdu'l-Bahá

* For an explanation of this particular phenomenon which relates to special tests surrounding the members of the family of Bahá'u'lláh or 'Abdu'l-Bahá, see above, pp. 168–9.

knew it. The high esteem in which they were held by the believers, and the tokens of respect shown to them by Bahá'ís and non-Bahá'ís alike, instead of making them humble and lowly as it would true believers, made them haughty and vain. 'Abdu'l-Bahá was not pleased with the spiritual development of His family, and He used to make remarks about it. For instance, Rúḥíyyih Khánum tells this story:

> The Guardian told me once the Master came to him in the drawing room, where he was working, and stood and looked out of the window into the garden, His back to Shoghi Effendi; the laughing and chattering voices of the family could be heard in another room. 'Abdu'l-Bahá turned to Shoghi Effendi and said, 'I do not want you to be like them – worldly.'[2]

When Shoghi Effendi became the Guardian of the Faith, it was expected of the family of the Master to turn to him devotedly in a spirit of lowliness and humility as true believers did. But of course this was not easy for his brothers and sisters and cousins to do. After all, Shoghi Effendi had grown up with them and they were his peers and next of kin. Although they acknowledged his appointment and outwardly showed their submissiveness to him, it was obvious from the very beginning that they were not sincere in their hearts. We notice the contrast in the case of the Greatest Holy Leaf. Although she was the most venerable member of the Holy Family and the most outstanding woman in the Bahá'í era, and one who had seen Shoghi Effendi grow up in the household of 'Abdu'l-Bahá, yet she turned to him in a spirit of devotion and humility. This is because she believed in the words of 'Abdu'l-Bahá that Shoghi Effendi was the Guardian of the Cause and the 'Sign of God' on earth.

In the first few years of the ministry of Shoghi Effendi the family remained outwardly loyal, but the seed of rebellion and Covenant-breaking was planted in their hearts from the very beginning. It only needed time to germinate and bring forth the fruit of sedition and opposition later. In His *Will and Testament* 'Abdu'l-Bahá exhorts the believers 'to show their obedience, submissiveness and subordination unto the Guardian of the Cause of God, to turn unto him and be lowly before him'. Whereas the followers of Bahá'u'lláh turned devotedly to Shoghi Effendi in the spirit of the Master's exhortation, Shoghi Effendi's attitude toward them was that of absolute love and humility. Unlike some of the world leaders who show an air of superiority and project themselves as authoritarian in relation to their subjects, Shoghi Effendi extended to all the believers, and, especially to his relatives, the hand of fellowship and brotherhood. To the western Bahá'ís he often signed himself, 'Your true brother, Shoghi', and in his Persian letters, 'The servant of His ['Abdu'l-

Bahá's] Threshold, Shoghi'. A few months after the ascension of 'Abdu'l-Bahá, Shoghi Effendi wrote this postscript to a letter to the American friends:

> May I also express my heartfelt desire that the friends of God in every land regard me in no other light but that of a true brother, united with them in our common servitude to the Master's Sacred Threshold, and refer to me in their letters and verbal addresses always as Shoghi Effendi, for I desire to be known by no other name save the one our Beloved Master was wont to utter, a name which of all other designations is the most conducive to my spiritual growth and advancement.[3]

Yet in spite of his meekness and magnanimity, Shoghi Effendi's relatives did not respond with sincerity and faithfulness. Knowing very well that most members of 'Abdu'l-Bahá's family were not able to turn to him as befitted the station of the Guardian, Shoghi Effendi turned a blind eye to their aloofness, and instead showed extra warmth and encouragement to them. For instance, we are told that when he returned to the Holy Land after the passing of 'Abdu'l-Bahá, he stayed with one of his aunts instead of his mother. This was to show his attachment and unity with his close relatives. He wanted them to feel his love and affection for them so that they could feel at ease in his presence and cooperate with him in the arduous task which the Master had placed upon his shoulders. But alas, he could see their insincerity from the very start, and although he looked upon them with a sin-covering eye, as a result, he suffered immensely. This suffering did not stem from the fact that they did not obey him personally, but because the *Will and Testament* enjoined them to be obedient to the Guardian, and he knew that as Guardian he would have to expel them from the Faith if they continued in this way.

For several years, Shoghi Effendi called on the services of his close relatives in the work of the Faith in the Holy Land. His younger brother Ḥusayn and some of his cousins served him as secretaries. He bore with resignation and forbearance their deceitful and faithless actions, their disobedience to him as Guardian, while they were working with him, enduring in silence the unfaithfulness of these relatives who were serving him in various capacities.

In the earlier years of the Guardianship, through the influence of the Greatest Holy Leaf everyone in the household of 'Abdu'l-Bahá, even though insincere, rallied around Shoghi Effendi. The only people who were publicly opposing the Cause and the person of the Guardian were the old Covenant-breakers – from Mírzá Muḥammad-'Alí down to some old enemies of the Faith. The Greatest Holy Leaf acted as a shield for 'Abdu'l-Bahá's family, all of whom stood firm against the company of the old Covenant-breakers. Every member of the family of the Master knew well that the old Covenant-breakers were all deadly enemies of the Master and of the Faith and were to be shunned as He had directed. They had not associated with them during the lifetime of 'Abdu'l-Bahá and they did not do so in the early years of Shoghi Effendi's ministry. It did not take very long, however, before secret ties were established between the old Covenant-breakers and certain members of the Master's family. As if a virus had attacked it, the disease of Covenant-breaking spread and eventually infected every surviving member of that noble family, sparing no one. This grievous downfall happened because of disobedience to the commandment to shun the Covenant-breakers. How clearly 'Abdu'l-Bahá admonishes the believers to avoid associating with them! In His *Will and Testament*, He thus enjoins:

> And now, one of the greatest and most fundamental principles of the Cause of God is to shun and avoid entirely the Covenant-breakers, for they will utterly destroy the Cause of God, exterminate His Law and render of no account all efforts exerted in the past.

And in another passage He repeats the same injunction:

> Hence, the beloved of the Lord must entirely shun them, avoid them, foil their machinations and evil whisperings, guard the Law of God and His religion, engage one and all in diffusing widely the sweet savours of God and to the best of their endeavour proclaim His Teachings.

The most obvious reason that the members of His family failed to obey the Master was their lack of faith in Him and in His words. 'Abdu'l-Bahá wanted them to turn to Shoghi Effendi in a spirit of devotion and servitude, but they did otherwise. These are the words of the Master and in His *Will and Testament*:

> O my loving friends! After the passing away of this wronged one, it is incumbent upon the Aghṣán (Branches), the Afnán (Twigs) of the Sacred Lote-Tree, the Hands (pillars) of the Cause of God and the loved ones of the Abhá Beauty to turn unto Shoghi Effendi – the youthful branch branched from the two hallowed and sacred Lote-Trees and the fruit grown from the union of the two offshoots of the Tree of Holiness, – as he is the sign of God, the chosen branch, the guardian of the Cause of God, he unto whom all the Aghṣán, the Afnán, the Hands of the Cause of God and His loved ones must turn. He is the expounder of the words of God and after him will succeed the first-born of his lineal descendents.
>
> The sacred and youthful branch, the guardian of the Cause of God as well as the Universal House of Justice, to be universally elected and established, are both under the care and protection of the Abhá Beauty, under the shelter and unerring guidance of His Holiness, the Exalted One

(may my life be offered up for them both). Whatsoever they decide is of God. Whoso obeyeth him not, neither obeyeth them, hath not obeyed God; whoso rebelleth against him and against them hath rebelled against God; whoso opposeth him hath opposed God; whoso contendeth with them hath contended with God; whoso disputeth with him hath disputed with God; whoso denieth him hath denied God; whoso disbelieveth in him hath disbelieved in God; whoso deviateth, separateth himself and turneth aside from him hath in truth deviated, separated himself and turned aside from God. May the wrath, the fierce indignation, the vengeance of God rest upon him! The mighty stronghold shall remain impregnable and safe through obedience to him who is the guardian of the Cause of God. It is incumbent upon the members of the House of Justice, upon all the Aghsán, the Afnán, the Hands of the Cause of God to show their obedience, submissiveness and subordination unto the guardian of the Cause of God, to turn unto him and be lowly before him. He that opposeth him hath opposed the True One, will make a breach in the Cause of God, will subvert His Word and will become a manifestation of the Centre of Sedition.

The tragic spiritual extinction of the family of 'Abdu'l-Bahá, as one by one of its members fell a victim to the devouring flames of Covenant-breaking, left Shoghi Effendi entirely on his own. Over the years, his brothers and sisters, his several cousins, his aunts and other relatives were cut off from the tree of the Cause. As each one rebelled against the Guardian, he tried his utmost to save them. He even refrained from disclosing their rebellion to the community for a considerable period of time. Instead he ignored their insults and endured in silence their despicable conduct until, at the end, he was left with no choice but to announce them as Covenant-breakers.

We will not review every detail of the activities of the Covenant-breakers in the Holy Land during Shoghi Effendi's ministry. Enough has been said in this book about the evil doings of Mírzá Muḥammad-'Alí, the Arch-breaker of the Covenant of Bahá'u'lláh. He outlived the Master by sixteen years, during which he did everything in his power to extinguish the light of the Faith, but he failed miserably. In 1937, Shoghi Effendi sent the following cable to Bahá'í world after his death;

> The Hand of Omnipotence has removed the archbreaker of Bahá'u'lláh's Covenant, his hopes shattered, his plottings frustrated, the society of his fellow-conspirators extinguished. God's triumphant Faith forges on, its unity unimpaired, its purpose unsullied, its stability unshaken. Such a death calls for neither exultation nor recrimination, but evokes overwhelming pity at so tragic a downfall unparalleled in religious history.[4]

The next in command, Mírzá Badí'u'lláh, the youngest son of Bahá'u'lláh, the account of whose despicable deeds has been given in previous chapters, died in 1950. He left behind bitter memories of acts of treachery, deceit and arrogance which he perpetrated for almost six decades, staining thereby the annals of the glorious Faith which his own Father had founded.

Another unrepentant Covenant-breaker was the notorious Majdu'd-Dín, son of the faithful brother of Bahá'u'lláh, Áqáy-i-Kalím. He was an inveterate enemy of the Master, and later of Shoghi Effendi. He lived to an old age and was one of those who succeeded in spreading the poison of Covenant-breaking among the family of 'Abdu'l-Bahá. He and his accomplice, Badí'u'lláh, caused a great deal of trouble. The following cable sent by Shoghi Effendi to the Bahá'í world after his death in 1955 is clearly indicative of Majdu'd-Dín's diabolical misdeeds against the Centre of the Covenant and the Guardian of the Faith.

> Announce to National Assemblies that Majdu'd-Dín, the most redoubtable adversary of 'Abdu'l-Bahá, denounced by Him as the incarnation of Satan and who played a predominant part in kindling the hostility of 'Abdu'l-Ḥamíd and Jamál Pá<u>sh</u>á, and who was the chief instigator of Covenant-breaking and archbreaker of Bahá'u'lláh's Covenant, and who above sixty years labored with fiendish ingenuity and guile to undermine its foundations, miserably perished struck with paralysis affecting his limbs and tongue. Dispensation of Providence prolonged the span of his infamous life to a hundred years, enabling him to witness the extinction of his cherished hopes and the disintegration with dramatic rapidity of the infernal crew he unceasingly incited and zealously directed, and the triumphant progress and glorious termination of 'Abdu'l-Bahá's thirty-year ministry as well as evidences of the rise and establishment in all continents of the globe of the administrative order, child of the divinely-appointed Covenant and harbinger of the world-encircling order.[5]

Another veteran Covenant-breaker was Ḥájí Siyyid 'Alí Afnán. He was a son of the venerable Ḥájí Mírzá Siyyid Ḥasan,* entitled Afnán-i-Kabír (Great Afnán), brother of the wife of the Báb. Siyyid 'Alí joined hands with the Arch-breaker of the Covenant and became one of 'Abdu'l-Bahá's great enemies. He had risen to eminence through the efforts of the wife of the Báb, who sent a special message to Bahá'u'lláh through Munírih <u>Kh</u>ánum, the wife of 'Abdu'l-Bahá, when she visited her in <u>Sh</u>íráz. Munírih <u>Kh</u>ánum has written the following account:

> . . . The wife of the Báb said: 'Please supplicate the Blessed Perfection to grant two wishes of mine. One, that one of the exalted Leaves† of the blessed Family may be permitted to join in wedlock with a member of the

* For an account of his illustrious life see *The Revelation of Bahá'u'lláh*, vol. 4.

† Bahá'u'lláh has referred to His male descendants as A<u>gh</u>ṣán (Branches) and the female descendants as Varaqát (Leaves).

family of the Báb, so that the two holy Trees may be outwardly knit together. The other, to grant me permission to attend His presence.' I conveyed this message when I attained the presence of Bahá'u'lláh; He readily assented to both her requests.[6]

The person whom the wife of the Báb had in mind was Ḥájí Siyyid 'Alí. Bahá'u'lláh granted her wish, and he was joined in wedlock with Furúghíyyih, a daughter of Bahá'u'lláh. As a token of his appreciation, Siyyid 'Alí promised his aunt, the wife of the Báb, that he would accompany her to the Holy Land if Bahá'u'lláh accepted the proposal for his marriage. However, when the time arrived he left for 'Akká alone. Thus he broke his promise and with it the heart of that noble lady. Being unable to travel on her own, she was sorrowful and disconsolate. It is reported that as a result of this cruel treatment, which came to her as a serious blow, she was grief-stricken. Soon her health was impaired and a few months later she passed away.

After the ascension of Bahá'u'lláh, Siyyid 'Alí and his wife Furúghíyyih sided with Mírzá Muḥammad-'Alí and rose up in opposition to 'Abdu'l-Bahá. After inflicting much pain upon the Centre of the Covenant for several years, Siyyid 'Alí repented of his iniquitous deeds and the Master forgave him. But his repentance was short-lived; he returned to his den again and resumed his odious activities against the Master. During Shoghi Effendi's ministry, as we shall see, it was the members of his family who were chiefly responsible for delivering the most painful blows upon the person of Shoghi Effendi. They caused havoc in the family of the Master and tore it apart altogether.

'Abdu'l-Bahá was survived by His sister, the Greatest Holy Leaf; His wife Munírih Khánum; his four daughters and their families.

The Greatest Holy Leaf, the most distinguished member of the Holy Family and the most outstanding woman in the Dispensation of Bahá'u'lláh, passed away in 1932. In previous chapters reference has been made to her glorious life of exemplary service to the Cause of Bahá'u'lláh, and as we have already stated, her passing brought untold sorrow to Shoghi Effendi and broke his heart forever. He built a befitting monument over her resting place in the vicinity of the Shrine of the Báb on Mount Carmel.

Munírih Khánum, the consort of 'Abdu'l-Bahá, came from a noble family* in Persia. Their marriage took place in 1872 in 'Akká at the command of Bahá'u'lláh. Munírih Khánum served the Master with great devotion, and has paid the following tribute to His memory:

* For more information see *The Revelation of Bahá'u'lláh*, vol. 2, pp. 206–9, 384, 386.

If I were to write the details of the fifty years of my association with the beloved of the world, of His love, His mercy and bounty, I would need fifty years more of time and opportunity in order to write it; yet, if the seas of the world were turned into ink and the leaves of the forest into paper, I would not render adequate justice to the subject.[7]

Munírih Khánum passed away in 1938. Her resting place is in close proximity to that of the Greatest Holy Leaf. Shoghi Effendi sent the following cable to the Bahá'í world following her death:

Holy Mother Munírih Khánum ascended Abhá Kingdom. With sorrowful hearts Bahá'ís world over recall divers phases her rich eventful life marked by unique services darkest days 'Abdu'l-Bahá's life. All Riḍván festivities suspended. Advise Convention delegates devote special session her memory hold befitting gathering Auditorium Mashriqu'l-Adhkár.

'Abdu'l-Bahá had four surviving daughters; they were all married and between them had fourteen children. Shoghi Effendi was the eldest grandchild of the Master. The remaining thirteen, one by one, rebelled against Shoghi Effendi and were expelled from the Faith. The other members of the family were likewise disobedient to Shoghi Effendi; in some cases, he announced them as Covenant-breakers, in others he remained silent about their status.

The eldest daughter of 'Abdu'l-Bahá was Ḍíyá'i'yyih Khánum who married Mirzá Hadí, an Afnán and a grandson of Ḥájí Mírzá Abu'l-Qásim, the other brother of the wife of the Báb.* This marriage brought forth three sons: Shoghi Effendi, Ḥusayn and Riáz; and two daughters: Rúḥangíz and Mehrangíz. Their family name was Rabbáni, a name given them by 'Abdu'l-Bahá.

Ṭubá Khánum married Mírzá Muḥsin, an Afnán, a son of Ḥájí Mírzá Siyyid Ḥasan (the Great Afnán), the brother of the wife of the Báb. They had three sons: Ruḥí, Suhayl, and Fu'ád, and one daughter, Thurayyá. Their family name was Afnán.

Rúḥá Khánum married Mirzá Jalál, the son of the 'King of the Martyrs'.† They had two sons: Muníb and Ḥasan; and three daughters: Maryam and Zahrá. Their family name was Shahíd (Martyr).

Munavvar Khánum married Aḥmad Yazdí, the youngest son of Hájí 'Abdu'r-Raḥím-i-Qannád.‡ They were without issue.

It is beyond the scope of this book to go into all the details of the activities of Shoghi Effendi's brothers, sisters, cousins, aunts and uncles, or to describe some of their reprehensible conduct.

* See Shoghi Effendi, 'Genealogy of the Báb, showing Connection with Bahá'u'lláh's Descendants', a chart in his own hand published in *The Dawn-Breakers*, p. lviii.
† For a detailed account of his sacrificial life, see *The Revelation of Bahá'u'lláh*, vol. 4, ch. 5.
‡ For an account of his life see *The Revelation of Bahá'u'lláh*, vol. 4, p. 23.

We cannot estimate the measure of the agony Shoghi Effendi must have undergone when he had to expel his brothers, sisters and aunts from the Faith.

Among those instrumental in instilling the spirit of Covenant-breaking which had lain dormant within the hearts of most members of 'Abdu'l-Bahá's family during the early years of Shoghi Effendi's ministry, were the family of Siyyid 'Alí Afnán whom we have mentioned earlier (see p. 356). He had been an inveterate adversary of 'Abdu'l-Bahá. Now his sons, the grandchildren of Bahá'u'lláh, all Covenant-breakers, inflicted the greatest injury upon the person of Shoghi Effendi.

Although Bahá'ís do not associate with Covenant-breakers, Rúḥangíz, the eldest sister of Shoghi Effendi, married one. He was Nayyir Afnán, the second son of Siyyid 'Alí. Nayyir proved to be the greatest enemy of Shoghi Effendi throughout his ministry. This marriage created an unprecedented convulsion in the family, and was followed by two similar marriages, one between the Covenant-breaker Ḥasan, another son of Siyyid 'Alí, and Mehrangíz, the younger sister of Shoghi Effendi; and the other, between another son, Fayḍí, and Thurayyá, Shoghi Effendi's cousin.

These inroads made by the old Covenant-breakers into the family of 'Abdu'l-Bahá were fatal, and soon most of its members became Covenant-breakers. Shoghi Effendi usually delayed announcing to the Bahá'í world the misdeeds committed by his relatives. He patiently endured their despicable behaviour and tried to rescue them from their tragic downfall, but eventually he had no choice but to expel them from the community and cut his relationship from them. To describe their fate we can do no better than to review some of Shoghi Effendi's messages.

On 2 November 1941 Shoghi Effendi sent the following two cables to the National Spiritual Assembly of the United States and Canada:

> Rúḥí's sister married Covenant-breaker Fayḍí whose mother joined and supported arch-enemy Muḥammad-'Alí and whose father 'Abdu'l-Bahá denounced openly and repeatedly as His deadly enemy. Rúḥí's family concurred. Inform all believers all manner communication excommunicated family forbidden.

and

> Flagrant disloyalty Rúḥí's family compels me disclose information so long patiently withheld American believers concerning his failure obtain my approval his second visit America. His subsequent conduct regarding his marriage which I refrained from revealing anyone except your Assembly, as well as Fu'ád's departure England without my knowledge,

should now be made known believers. Confident unshakable steadfastness exemplary American Bahá'í community.[9]

These cables concern the family of Mírzá Muḥsin Afnán and Ṭúbá Khánum, daughter of 'Abdu'l-Bahá. Several years before this episode, Mírzá Muḥsin had passed away in 1927, and Shoghi Effendi described him as the 'beloved son-in-law' of the Master and 'distinguished servant of His Cause'.[10] The rest of the family, who were now expelled from the Cause, included Ṭúbá Khánum, her sons, Rúḥí, Suhayl and Fu'ád and daughter Thurayyá. It was the latter who married Covenant-breaker Fayḍí Afnán, a brother of Nayyir mentioned above.

Rúḥí Afnán, Shoghi Effendi's cousin, had served him as secretary for some years, and so his name was known to the North American believers who received these cables and were now asked to cut off all association with him and his family. We recall that Fayḍí's mother, referred to in the first cable, was Furúghíyyih, a daughter of Bahá'u'lláh and the wife of Ḥájí Siyyid 'Alí Afnán, the enemy of the Master. Rúḥí Afnán himself married his cousin Zahrá Shahíd (see above, p. 358). Fu'ád was Rúḥí's youngest brother.

In another cable dated October 1941, to the Bahá'ís of 'Iráq, Shoghi Effendi confirmed the status of Nayyir's brothers:

> Nayyir's brothers Fayḍí and Ḥasan have been still are Covenant-breakers warn all believers association with them forbidden under all circumstances.

In the same year, the following cable was sent by Shoghi Effendi to the National Spiritual Assembly of the Bahá'ís of the British Isles:

> Sister Mehrangis [Mehrangíz] followed example Ruhi's [Rúḥí] sister Justice demands announce believers her expulsion.[11]

Mehrangíz was the youngest sister of Shoghi Effendi, and had married the Covenant-breaker Ḥasan Afnán. We have already stated that Rúḥí's sister, Thurayyá, married Fayḍí. No one can ever imagine the enormity of Shoghi Effendi's pain and anguish as he observed his two sisters and a cousin renounce their faith and join in wedlock with three Covenant-breakers, sons of Siyyid 'Alí, whom 'Abdu'l-Bahá had condemned as His 'deadly enemy'. Not content with this, Ruḥangíz, Shoghi Effendi's eldest sister, did not rest until she arranged another marriage between her cousin, Ḥasan Shahid, and the granddaughter of the notorious Siyyid 'Alí. But in order not to degrade the family of the Master in public by announcing them all as Covenant-breakers, Shoghi Effendi acted with great patience and concealed their acts of infamy and unfaithfulness as long as he could. We see therefore long gaps between his announcements expelling certain members of the family from the Faith. For example, although the family of Mirzá Jalál Shahíd (the son-in-law of the Master), including his wife, had been in close association with the Covenant-breakers, and had shown defiance to Shoghi Effendi, he did not disclose their defection until years later. Only when Muníb, the son of Mírzá Jalál, with the approval of his parents, married the daughter of one of the enemies of the Faith, did Shoghi Effendi send the following cable to the Bahá'í world in November 1944. It must be noted that Mírzá Jalál was the son of the most illustrious of Bahá'u'lláh's apostles, the King of Martyrs.*

> Moníb Shahíd, grandson of both 'Abdu'l-Bahá and the King of Martyrs, married according to the Moslem rites the daughter of a political exile who is nephew of the Grand Mufti of Jerusalem. This treacherous act of alliance with enemies of the Faith merits condemnation of entire Bahá'í world.[12]

In response to a cable by the American National Spiritual Assembly expressing their loyalty to him, Shoghi Effendi sent the following message:

> Comforted, strengthened, by assurance of sympathy and loyalty of American believers in the deplorable, delicate situation created by dishonorable alliances made by members of my family, first with Covenant-breakers and now with external enemies of the Faith.
>
> The marvellous, rapid, sound evolution of the institutions of the Faith in five continents, particularly in the Western Hemisphere, constitutes best monition, most effective counteraction to the detrimental influence of those whose acts proclaim their severance from the Holy Tree and their forfeiture of their sacred birthright.
>
> The occasion demands that you direct special attention to passages in *God Passes By*† indicating the gravity of the past crises precipitated since the inception of the Faith by kinsmen both of the Manifestation and Centre of His Covenant, demonstrating the pitiful futility of their nefarious activities and the sad fate overtaking defectors and betrayers.
>
> The present hour calls for unrelaxing vigilance, continued heroism, redoubled efforts, renewed dedication by rank and file of the community enjoying preponderating share alike in the erection, the defence, and the consolidation of the worldwide Administrative Order of the Faith of Bahá'u'lláh since the passing of the Centre of His Covenant.[13]

Next to Shoghi Effendi in age, his brother Ḥusayn acted as his secretary for some years, but he too was affected by the spirit of Covenant-breaking. The following account by Rúḥíyyih Khanum is indicative of Shoghi Effendi's patience and long-suffering in dealing with his brother.

* For an account of his life and martyrdom, see *The Revelation of Bahá'u'lláh*, vol. 5.
† See *God Passes By*, chs. X and XV.

> The patience of Shoghi Effendi in handling these terrible situations that arose in his own family is shown by the fact that on one occasion he held for eight months a cable excommunicating his brother while he tried – vainly – to remedy the situation and obviate the necessity of sending a message that was so heart-breaking to him.[14]

In April 1945 he sent this cable for the Bahá'í world:

> My faithless brother Ḥusayn, after long period of dishonourable conduct, has abandoned the Master's home to consort with his sister and other Covenant-breakers.[15]

The 'sister' mentioned above is Rúḥangíz, who had married the Covenant-breaker Nayyir. Ḥusayn's association with her was sufficient ground for him to be denounced as a Covenant-breaker. Now, of Shoghi Effendi's brothers and sisters, only Riáz was left.

In December 1949, Shoghi Effendi sent the following cable to the Bahá'í world.

> Faithless brother Hussein [Ḥusayn], already abased through dishonourable conduct over period of years followed by association with Covenant-breakers in Holy Land and efforts to undermine Guardian's position, recently further demeaned himself through marriage under obscure circumstances with low-born Christian girl in Europe. This disgraceful alliance, following four successive marriages by sisters and cousins with three sons of Covenant-breaker denounced repeatedly by 'Abdu'l-Bahá as His enemy, and daughter of notorious political agitator, brands them with infamy greater than any associated with marriages contracted by old Covenant-breakers whether belonging to family of Muḥammad-'Alí or Badí'u'lláh.[16]

We have already mentioned the marriages by Rúḥangíz and Mehrangíz, the two sisters of Shoghi Effendi and by his cousin Thurayyá. The fourth one was that of Ḥasan Shahíd. The 'three sons of Covenant-breaker' are Nayyir, Ḥasan and Fayḍí, sons of Siyyid 'Alí Afnán. 'Daughter of notorious political agitator' is a reference to the marriage of Muníb Shahíd with the daughter of Jamál Husseini, nephew of the Mufti of Jerusalem.

The term 'low-born Christian girl' prompted the National Spiritual Assembly of the Bahá'ís of the British Isles to seek further clarification from Shoghi Effendi. In answer to them he wrote through his secretary:

> Regarding his cable concerning Hussein: he has been very surprised to note that the terms 'low-born Christian girl' and 'disgraceful alliance' should arouse any question: it seems to him that the friends should realise it is not befitting for the Guardian's own brother, the grandchild of the Master, an Afnán and Aghsán mentioned in the Will and Testament of the Master, and of whom so much was expected because of his relation to

the Family of the Prophet, to marry an unknown girl, according to goodness knows what rite, who is not a believer at all. Surely, every Bahá'í must realise that the terms low-born and Christian are definitions of a situation and in no way imply any condemnation of a person's birth or the religion they belong to as such. We have no snobbery and no religious prejudice in our Faith. But the members of the Master's family have contracted marriages which cannot be considered in any other light than disgraceful, in view of what 'Abdu'l-Bahá wished for them.[17]

In the year 1948 a fierce political upheaval erupted in the Holy Land. The State of Israel was founded, which resulted in the ending of the British Mandate. War broke out between Arabs and Jews and a great many Arabs fled the country. During this period Shoghi Effendi remained in Haifa and in the face of great dangers and severe difficulties carried on his work as usual, including the building of the superstructure of the Shrine of the Báb. But the rest of the family who were Covenant-breakers allied themselves with the Arab community and fled the land. Among them were the family of Mírzá Jalál Shahíd, which included Rúḥá Khánum, the daughter of 'Abdu'l-Bahá; Ṭúbá Khánum and her son Rúḥí, his wife Zahrá and his brother; three cousins of Dr Faríd; Nayyir Afnán, his wife Rúḥangíz (sister of Shoghi Effendi) and their children. Others who fled to the Lebanon were Badí'u'lláh (next in command to the Arch-breaker of the Covenant) and his relatives, together with those Bahá'ís who were disloyal to Shoghi Effendi. As time went on these people, who were already cut off from the Holy Family by virtue of their association with the enemies of the Faith, integrated themselves into the Islamic society.

In 1950 Shoghi Effendi sent yet another cable to the Bahá'í world denouncing the activities of Rúḥí Afnán.

> Inform friends that Rúḥí, his mother, with Rúḥá, his aunt, and their families, not content with years of disobedience and unworthy conduct, are now showing open defiance. Confident that exemplary loyalty of American believers will sustain me in carrying overwhelming burden of cares afflicting me.[18]

Thus the families of the second and third daughters of 'Abdu'l-Bahá were now openly defiant to the Guardian. The fourth daughter, Munavvar, was also among the Covenant-breakers. The two families mentioned in the above cable included eight cousins of Shoghi Effendi.

Another announcement about Rúḥí Afnán was made in 1953 on the morrow of the launching of the Ten Year Crusade.

> Treacherous Rúḥí Afnán, not content with previous disobedience, correspondence with Ahmad Sohrab, contact with old Covenant-

breakers, sale, in conjunction with other members of family, of sacred property purchased by Founder of Faith, and allowing his sister to marry son of 'Abdu'l-Bahá's enemy, is now openly lecturing on Bahá'í movement, claiming to be its exponent and is misrepresenting the teachings and deliberately causing confusion in minds of authorities and the local population. Inform National Assemblies.[19]

In December 1951 Shoghi Effendi sent the following cable in which he discloses, among other things, the unfaithfulness and treachery of his youngest brother Riáz.

With feeling profound concern, grief, indignation, am compelled disclose Bahá'í world recent developments Holy land furnishing further incontestable proof relationship established old and new Covenant-breakers demonstrating increasing boldness, marked, tragic decline in character and spiritual condition grandchildren 'Abdu'l-Bahá. Their shameful attitude and conduct receiving approbation their elders. Evidences multiplying attesting Ruhi's increasing rebelliousness, efforts exerted my eldest sister pave way fourth alliance members family Siyyid 'Ali involving marriage his granddaughter with Ruha's son and personal contact recently established my own treacherous, despicable brother Riaz with Majdi'd-Dín, redoubtable enemy Faith, former henchman Muhammad-'Ali, Archbreaker Bahá'u'lláh's Covenant. Convey information all National Assemblies.[20]

Nayyir, the son of 'Abdu'l-Bahá's great enemy, and the man who had married Shoghi Effendi's eldest sister, died in 1952. Shoghi Effendi's cable announcing his death summed up the heart-breaking events of the previous years. The cable was addressed to the National Spiritual Assembly of the United States for the Bahá'ís of the world:

Inform National Assemblies that God's avenging wrath having afflicted in rapid succession during recent years two sons brother and sister-in-law of Archbreaker of Bahá'u'lláh's Covenant, has now struck down second son of Siyyid 'Alí, Nayer [Nayyir] Afnán, pivot of machinations, connecting link between old and new Covenant-breakers. Time alone will reveal extent of havoc wreaked by this virus of violation injected, fostered over two decades in 'Abdu'l-Bahá's family. History will brand him [Nayyir] one whose grandmother, wife of Bahá'u'lláh, joined breakers of His Covenant on morrow of His passing, whose parents lent her undivided support, whose father openly accused 'Abdu'l-Bahá as one deserving capital punishment, who broke his promise to the Báb's wife to escort her to Holy Land, precipitating thereby her death, who was repeatedly denounced by Centre of the Covenant as His chief enemy, whose eldest brother through deliberate misrepresentation of facts inflicted humiliation upon defenders of the House of Bahá'u'lláh in Baghdád, whose sister-in-law is championing the cause of declared enemies of Faith, whose brothers supported him attributing to 'Abdu'l-

Bahá responsibility for fatal disease which afflicted their mother, who himself [Nayyir] in retaliation first succeeded in winning over through marriage my eldest sister, subsequently paved way for marriage of his brothers to two other grandchildren of the Master, who was planning a fourth marriage between his daughter and grandson of 'Abdu'l-Bahá, thereby involving in shameful marriages three branches of His family, who over twenty years schemed to undermine the position of the Centre of the Faith through association with representatives of traditional enemies of Faith in Persia, Muslim Arab communities, notables and civil authorities in Holy Land, who lately was scheduled to appear as star witness on behalf of daughter of Badí'u'lláh in recent lawsuit challenging the authority conferred upon Guardian of Faith in 'Abdu'l-Bahá's Testament.[21]

The following notes may be helpful in identifying the various individuals and events referred to in this cable:

'two sons'	Shu'á'u'lláh and Músá, the two sons of Mírzá Muḥammad-'Alí. See pp. 277, 340 above.
'brother'	a reference to Badí'u'lláh.
'Archbreaker'	Mírzá Muḥammad-'Alí.
'Siyyid 'Ali'	Ḥájí Siyyid 'Alí Afnán, who married Furúghíyyih, daughter of Bahá'u'lláh. See pp. 356 above.
'grandmother'	Gawhar Khánum, the third wife of Bahá'u'lláh and the mother of Furúghíyyih. See above, pp. 117–18.
'father'	Ḥájí Siyyid 'Alí Afnán.
'promise'	see above, p. 357.
'eldest brother'	Ḥusayn Afnán
'brothers'	Ḥasan Afnán and Fayḍí Afnán, sons of Siyyid 'Alí. Ḥasan married Mehrangíz, the second sister of Shoghi Effendi, and Fayḍí married Thurayyá, grand-daughter of 'Abdu'l-Bahá. See below.
'mother'	Furúghíyyih, a daughter of Bahá'u'lláh.
'my eldest sister'	Rúḥangíz, who married Nayyir.
'two other grandchildren'	Mehrangíz and Thurayyá, as above.
'his daughter'	Bahíyyih
'grandson of 'Abdu'l-Bahá'	Ḥasan Shahíd. See above, p. 358.
'daughter of Badi'u'llah'	Sádhíjih, a notorious woman with a criminal record. She was a political agitator, in prison because of her complicity in unlawful plots against the authorities.
'lawsuit'	refers to a case brought against Shoghi Effendi in 1952 in connection with the demolition of a house in the vicinity of the Shrine of Bahá'u'lláh. The case resulted in victory for Shoghi Effendi. See above, pp. 329–331.

Thus ended the life of Nayyir, who with the help of his relatives was instrumental in corrupting and destroying the Master's family and in inflicting the most unbearable suffering upon Shoghi Effendi.

Every one of these messages sent by Shoghi Effendi to the Bahá'í world at different times during his ministry was the result of many agonizing episodes of Covenant-breaking, of acts of opposition, betrayal and open defiance by the members of the family of the Master. But their defection and that of some of the outstanding Bahá'ís who broke the Covenant, far from weakening the fabric of the Bahá'í community, strengthened and invigorated it. This is a cleansing process by which the impurities are thrown out of the body of the Cause. Concerning the effect of rebellion by the Covenant-breakers, Shoghi Effendi wrote:

> We should also view as a blessing in disguise every storm of mischief with which they who apostatize their faith or claim to be its faithful exponents assail it from time to time. Instead of undermining the Faith, such assaults, both from within and from without, reinforce its foundations, and excite the intensity of its flame. Designed to becloud its radiance, they proclaim to all the world the exalted character of its precepts, the completeness of its unity, the uniqueness of its position, and the pervasiveness of its influence.[22]

Rúḥíyyih Khánum writes the following about the effect of the Covenant-breaking in the household of the Master;

> But the tale of defections such as these does not convey the true picture of what Covenant-breaking signified in the ministry of Shoghi Effendi. To understand that one must understand the old story of Cain and Abel, the story of family jealousies which, like a sombre thread in the fabric of history, runs through all its epochs and can be traced in all its events. Ever since the opposition of the younger brother of Bahá'u'lláh, Mírzá Yaḥyá, the poison of Covenant-breaking, which is opposition to the Centre of the Covenant, entered the Faith and remained. It is difficult for those who have neither experienced what this disease is, nor devoted any consideration to the subject, to grasp the reality of the power for destruction it possesses. All the members of the family of Bahá'u'lláh grew up in the shadow of Covenant-breaking. The storms, separations, reconciliations, final sundering of ties, which are involved when a close, distinguished and often dear relative is dying spiritually of a spiritual disease, are inconceivable to one who has not experienced them . . .
>
> It looks simple on paper. But when year after year a house is torn by heart-breaking emotions, shaken by scenes that leave one's brain numb, one's nerves decimated and one's feelings in a turmoil, it is not simple, it is just plain hell. Before a patient lies on the operating table and the offending part is removed there is a long process of delay, of therapeutic effort to remedy the disease, of hope for recovery. So it is with Covenant-breaking; the taint is detected; warning, remonstrance, advice

follow; it seems better; it breaks out again, worse than before; convulsive situations arise – repentance, forgiveness follow – and then all over again, the same thing, worse than before, recommences. With infinite variations this is what took place in the lifetimes of Bahá'u'lláh, 'Abdu'l-Bahá and Shoghi Effendi.[23]

Although the Cause of God benefits from the expulsion of unfaithful individuals who break the Covenant, the Centre of the Faith is the one who suffers most. This suffering is deepened, in the case of Shoghi Effendi, by the fact that he was duty bound, by virtue of his position as Guardian of the Faith, to expel his closest loved ones. Concerning this Rúḥíyyih Khánum writes:

> Whereas we ordinary human beings react in one way, these extraordinary human beings react in an entirely different way. They are, in such matters – however great the difference in their own stations – entirely different from us. I used to wonder, in the early years of my life with the Guardian, why he got so terribly upset by these happenings, why he reacted so violently to them, why he would be prostrated from evidences of Covenant-breaking. Gradually I came to understand that such beings, so different from us, have some sort of mysterious built-in scales in their very souls; automatically they register the spiritual state of others, just as one side of a scale goes down instantly if you put something in it because of the imbalance this creates. We individual Bahá'ís are like the fish in the sea of the Cause, but these beings are like the sea itself, any alien element in the sea of the Cause, so to speak, with which, because of their nature, they are wholly identified, produces an automatic reaction on their part; the sea casts out its dead.[24]

The Covenant-breakers struggled continually to hurt Shoghi Effendi in whatever way they could. They attacked him from every direction and inflicted on him unbearable pain; while he resisted their onslaught until they were vanquished one by one in different ways. In 1957, a few months before he passed away, he accomplished the task of removing once and for all the last traces of the Covenant-breakers' evil influence from the Holy Land. This he did when he attempted to develop the gardens around the Mansion of Bahjí, while there were still a few houses of Covenant-breakers around the Shrine of Bahá'u'lláh. Shoghi Effendi continued in his efforts until he secured from the government orders for demolition of these houses. The following is part of the cable Shoghi Effendi sent in June 1957 to the Bahá'í world on this occasion:

> With feelings of profound joy, exultation and thankfulness, announce on morrow of sixty-fifth Anniversary of Ascension of Bahá'u'lláh, signal, epoch-making victory won over the ignoble band of breakers of His Covenant which, in the course of over six decades, has entrenched itself

in the precincts of the Most Holy Shrine of the Bahá'í world, provoking through acts of overt hostility and ingenious machinations, in alliance with external enemies under three successive regimes, the wrath of the Lord of the Covenant Himself, incurring the malediction of the Concourse on high, and filling with inexpressible anguish the heart of 'Abdu'l-Bahá.

The expropriation order issued by the Israeli government, mentioned in the recent Convention Message, related to the entire property owned by Covenant-breakers within the Ḥaram-i-Aqdas, recently contested by these same enemies through appeal to Israel's Supreme Court, now confirmed through adverse decision just announced by same Court, enabling the civil authorities to enforce the original decision and proceed with the eviction of the wretched remnants of the once redoubtable adversaries who, both within the Holy land and beyond its confines, laboured so long and so assiduously to disrupt the foundations of the Faith, sap their loyalty and cause a permanent cleavage in the ranks of its supporters.

The implementation of this order will, at long last, cleanse the Outer Sanctuary of the Qiblih of the Bahá'í world of the pollution staining the fair name of the Faith and pave the way for the adoption and execution of preliminary measures designed to herald the construction in future decades of the stately, befitting Mausoleum designed to enshrine the holiest dust the earth ever received into its bosom.[25]

Rúḥíyyih Khánum recounts the following:

Finally, in 1957, again through the cooperation of the State authorities, Shoghi Effendi was able to secure an expropriation order, on the grounds of their nearness to a sacred place of pilgrimage, for the houses occupied by what he termed the 'wretched remnants' of the Covenant-breakers and thus at long last bring about what he described as the cleansing of the Ḥaram-i-Aqdas of this spiritual defilement. So hotly was this expropriation order, which involved their eviction from Bahjí, contested by the Covenant-breakers that they took it before the Supreme Court of Israel, lost their case and were obliged to leave once and for all.

It had been the expressed desire of the Guardian himself to supervise the demolition of these houses that abutted on the Mansion and were right next to the Shrine, but he never returned to the Holy Land. When, in fulfilment of his own plan, they were pulled down, a few months after his passing, it was found that the large formal garden he had made in front of them was so accurately measured out and planned that it could be continued – I am tempted to say rolled out like a carpet – with complete accuracy right over the place where they stood and up to the very wall of the Mansion.[26]

The obtaining of this expropriation order was the last act in uprooting the nests of corruption and hatred which had plagued the holiest Shrine of the Bahá'í world for over six decades. During this time countless schemes had been devised against 'Abdu'l-Bahá and Shoghi Effendi by the Arch-breaker of the Covenant, his kinsmen and associates, and by enemies of the Faith. Today no trace of any of them remains in the areas surrounding the Shrine.

CHAPTER THIRTY-THREE

The Onward March of the Faith

THESE are the words of 'Abdu'l-Bahá testifying to the power of the Covenant of Bahá'u'lláh:

> Today, the Lord of Hosts is the defender of the Covenant, the forces of the Kingdom protect it, heavenly souls tender their services, and heavenly angels promulgate and spread it broadcast. If it is considered with insight, it will be seen that all the forces of the universe, in the last analysis serve the Covenant. In the future it shall be made evident and manifest. In view of this fact, what can these weak and feeble souls achieve? Hardy plants that are destitute of roots and are deprived of the outpourings of the cloud of mercy will not last. What then may be expected from feeble weeds?[1]

Opposition from outside enemies contributes to the growth of the body of the Cause; while opposition from within cleanses it from impure elements. Far from destroying the Cause of God, opposition has enhanced its prestige and added vitality to its inner spirit, as history demonstrates. The contrast between the progressive advancement of the Faith on the one hand, and the decline in the fortunes of the Covenant-breakers on the other, has never been so obvious as in the period of Shoghi Effendi's ministry. It was during this time that the Cause of Bahá'u'lláh encircled the globe and the institutions of the Administrative Order took firm root throughout the world. In the earlier part of his ministry, Shoghi Effendi wrote these words:

> From the record of its tumultuous history, almost every page of which portrays a fresh crisis, is laden with the description of a new calamity, recounts the tale of a base betrayal, and is stained with the account of unspeakable atrocities, there emerges, clear and incontrovertible, the supreme truth that with every fresh outbreak of hostility to the Faith, whether from within or from without, a corresponding measure of outpouring grace, sustaining its defenders and confounding its adversaries, has been providentially released, communicating a fresh impulse to the onward march of the Faith, while this impetus, in its turn, would through its manifestations, provoke fresh hostility in quarters heretofore unaware of its challenging implications – this increased hostility being accompanied by a still more arresting revelation of Divine Power and a

> more abundant effusion of celestial grace, which, by enabling the upholders of that Faith to register still more brilliant victories, would thereby generate issues of still more vital import and raise up still more formidable enemies against a Cause that cannot but, in the end, resolve those issues and crush the resistance of those enemies, through a still more glorious unfoldment of its inherent power.
>
> The resistless march of the Faith of Bahá'u'lláh, viewed in this light, and propelled by the stimulating influences which the unwisdom of its enemies and the force latent within itself, both engender, resolves itself into a series of rhythmic pulsations, precipitated, on the one hand, through the explosive outbursts of its foes, and the vibrations of Divine Power, on the other, which speed it, with ever-increasing momentum, along that predestined course traced for it by the Hand of the Almighty.[2]

As one surveys the progress of the Faith during the ministry of Shoghi Effendi, it becomes apparent that one of his great achievements was to bring about unity between the various elements which constituted the Bahá'í community in the early years of the Formative Age. When 'Abdu'l-Bahá passed away there was very little Bahá'í literature available in the West and the teachings of the Faith had not fully penetrated the hearts of the believers there. Consequently, one could find some very strange ideas about the Faith circulating among the believers in that part of the world. In Persia, the Cradle of the Faith, the Bahá'ís were still identified with their old religions. They were even referred to as Bahá'ís from the Muslim, the Jewish or Zoroastrian backgrounds. Although there was unity of belief and thought concerning the station of Bahá'u'lláh among the various sections of the community, the differences in their background, culture and social habits were discernible to all. For instance, Jewish Bahá'ís had their own meetings, distinct from the meetings held by Muslim Bahá'ís. The same was true of Zoroastrian Bahá'ís. Of course, there were occasions when the whole community worked together and whenever circumstances permitted held large gatherings – such as on Bahá'í holy days, when Bahá'ís of different religious backgrounds met together in a spirit of joy and unity. Nevertheless there were social barriers between these three groups of Bahá'ís in Persia. One of the great achievements of Shoghi Effendi was to transform these differences into unity. Then, towards the end of his ministry, he brought together the Bahá'ís of the East and the West in a world-embracing fellowship – the international Bahá'í community.

By the time the Ten Year Crusade was launched in 1953, all the Bahá'ís were working together in a spirit of absolute unity and love under the guidance and leadership of Shoghi Effendi. Indeed, one of the Guardian's feats was the formation of a community spread throughout the world, consisting of peoples of every colour and former creed, of diversified backgrounds, young and old, educated and unlettered, tribal people and citizens of various cultures, speaking different languages and dialects, yet all united in one Faith, practising the same religious teachings, building the same Administrative Order, and having one common purpose – the establishment of the oneness of mankind on this planet. Each local community with its Local Spiritual Assembly was linked to a National Assembly and through that institution to the World Centre of the Faith, described by Shoghi Effendi as the heart of the Bahá'í world. From this mighty heart, the vivifying forces of the Revelation of Bahá'u'lláh flowed through the national and local institutions of the Faith to every believer in five continents of the globe, uniting and harmonizing their activities in the building of Bahá'u'lláh's embryonic institutions everywhere on the surface of the earth.

Another outstanding step taken during the Guardian's ministry was the vast extension in the range of Bahá'í literature, which had been limited to only a few languages during the lifetime of 'Abdu'l-Bahá. This was raised to about two hundred and forty languages and dialects,* thus enabling the words of Bahá'u'lláh and His teachings to be widely disseminated among the diversified nations and peoples of the world.

The utterances of Bahá'u'lláh and 'Abdu'l-Bahá enshrine the truths of God's Revelation for this age. To use an analogy, each one of Bahá'u'lláh's teachings and ordinances resembles a piece of a colossal jigsaw puzzle. Each piece has a unique place in the overall scheme which, when assembled, produces a certain image intended by the makers. A player may be familiar with each piece, but not until the whole set is assembled can he see the full picture emerge before his eyes. The same is true of the Revelation of Bahá'u'lláh. The scholars of the Faith and those who were well-versed in the Holy Writings and the history of the Cause had full knowledge of the teachings and were able to appreciate the significance of His utterances as well as some of the events which were associated with them. But they did not have the vision to fully grasp the overall features of the Faith. At the close of 'Abdu'l-Bahá's Ministry, the Bahá'ís were enamoured of Bahá'u'lláh, but at the same time, many had their own crude ideas about the Faith and its true status.

It was the Guardian who through his writings constructed, as in the above analogy, a full image of the Faith for the Bahá'ís to see. He put together all the elements of truth enshrined in the utterances of Bahá'u'lláh, related them to each other, defined the verities of the

* At the time of writing this book, this number has increased to over eight hundred.

Faith, explained their significance, clarified the station of its Herald, its Author, and the Centre of its Covenant, described the glorious destiny of its Administrative Order and portrayed the splendours of the Golden Age during which the sovereignty of Bahá'u'lláh will be established on the surface of the earth and His grandeur acclaimed by the generality of mankind. Thus, the Guardian presented the Faith of Bahá'u'lláh to the Bahá'í community in its true perspective. This is one of his greatest gifts to this generation and to future generations yet unborn.

Shoghi Effendi has explained in his writings that during the Formative Age, the Faith of Bahá'u'lláh will pass through distinct epochs in the course of its development. The Cause of God has an organic pattern of growth and like any other living organism, develops and attains specific conditions at certain points in its life. The Cause of God too passes through progressive stages in a single evolutionary process.

The First Epoch of the Formative Age began with the ministry of Shoghi Effendi in 1921. As stated in Chapter 26, in the first sixteen years the Guardian concentrated on teaching the believers how to build Spiritual Assemblies and the Bahá'í administration. He explained the function, scope and ultimate purpose of local and national institutions. After this period, the first Seven Year Plan of the American believers was launched by the Guardian in 1937. We have already made a brief reference* to the significance of this Plan, an enterprise of great significance in the prosecution of the divine mandate conferred on the American believers by 'Abdu'l-Bahá, and which marks an important development in the history of the Administrative Order of the Faith. By 1946, twenty-five years had passed from the inception of the Administrative Order; Shoghi Effendi designated this entire period as the First Epoch of the Formative Age, and from his other writings we gather that this First Epoch ended between 1944 and 1946. In his message dated June 1947 to the North American community, he describes the main features of this First Epoch in these words:

> The first epoch witnessed the birth and the primary stages in the erection of the framework of the Administrative Order of the Faith – the nucleus and pattern of its World Order – according to the precepts laid down in 'Abdu'l-Bahá's Will and Testament, as well as the launching of the initial phase of the world-encompassing Plan bequeathed by Him to the American Bahá'í Community. That epoch was characterized by a two-fold process aiming at the consolidation of the administrative structure of the Faith and the extension of the range of its institutions. It

* See above, p. 314–15.

witnessed, on the one hand, the emergence and the laying of the groundwork of that embryonic World Order . . . It was marked on the other hand by the launching, in the Western Hemisphere, of the first stage of a Plan whose . . . Charter was revealed by the Centre of His Covenant in the evening of His life.[3]

The scope of the progress of the Cause and the expansion of its institutions during this period may be realized from the following statement by the beloved Guardian:

> The subsequent quarter of a century [1921–1946] constituting the first Epoch of the Formative Age of the Bahá'í Dispensation, witnessed the planting of the banner of the Faith in over forty territories of the globe, raising the number of countries included within its pale, on the eve of the Centenary Celebrations of the Declaration of the Báb's Mission to seventy-eight.[4]

Apart from the expansion of the Faith, other important events took place in the First Epoch; we have referred to them previously.*

The Second Epoch of the Formative Age began in 1946 when the Guardian gave the North American believers the second Seven Year Plan, of far greater consequence than the first. Of this Epoch Shoghi Effendi wrote in 1947:

> The Epoch we have now entered is destined to impart a great impetus to this historic, this two-fold process. It must witness, on the one hand, the consummation of a laboriously constructed Administrative Order, and, on the other, the unfoldment of successive stages in the development of 'Abdu'l-Bahá's Plan beyond the confines of the Western Hemisphere and of the continent of Europe.[5]

We note that the main feature of the Second Epoch was the two-fold process of building the institutions of the Faith and extending their range through the operation of the teaching plans. In his cable (December 1951) to the Bahá'í world, the Guardian outlines some of the main features of the First and Second Epochs of the Faith in these words:

> Quarter century constituting opening epoch this Age signalized successively by erection consolidation over period no less than sixteen years of local, national institutions of Bahá'í Administrative Order in five continents of globe in conformity with provisions of the Will of Centre of Covenant, and initiation of first Seven Year Plan by American Bahá'í Community . . . opening years of the second epoch of the Formative Age now witnessing at long last commencement of third vast majestic fate-laden process following two above-mentioned developments destined

* See above, pp. 304–6.

through gradual emergence of the manifold institutions in World Centre of the Faith as crown of the administrative structure of Bahá'u'lláh's embryonic World Order.[6]

The expansion of the Faith in the Second Epoch was prodigious, a phenomenal growth of the Cause mainly due to the formulation by the Guardian of first the series of national Plans and later the launching of the Ten Year World Crusade. As a result of these almost two hundred and sixty countries, territories and islands were opened to the Faith and the number of localities in which Bahá'ís resided increased to over eleven thousand.* Some of the other achievements of the Second Epoch have already been described. The establishment of the Universal House of Justice in the Second Epoch had also been implied in the message. The Universal House of Justice did come into being during this epoch, and, as we shall see later, a few months after its formation it announced to the Bahá'í world the opening of the Third Epoch of the Formative Age.†

It is appropriate at this juncture to refer to the *Tablets of the Divine Plan of 'Abdu'l-Bahá*. This series of fourteen Tablets addressed to the North American Bahá'ís, and revealed during the First World War, constitute the Charter for teaching the Faith of Bahá'u'lláh throughout the World. Shoghi Effendi has stated that the process of teaching the Faith would also go through different epochs. These are distinct from the epochs of the Formative Age and should not be confused with them. The First Epoch of the Tablets of the Divine Plan began in 1937 with the first American Seven Year Plan and ended with the launching of the Ten Year Crusade in 1953 when the Second Epoch began, continuing until the present time in the year 1991. But whenever the Universal House of Justice perceives that teaching work has assumed new dimensions, it may usher in a new epoch of the Tablets of the Divine Plan.

It is important to bear in mind these epochs, like those of the Formative Age, are not merely divisions created to satisfy the statistical aspect of the Faith. Rather, they are distinct stages in the unfoldment of the Cause of God. They resemble the growth of the embryo in the womb where, at different times, it develops certain limbs and organs, each one contributing to its progressive evolution. As one studies the progress of the Faith during the first two epochs of the Tablets of the Divine Plan, it becomes apparent that teaching opportunities in the First Epoch were far less than those during the Second. No doubt future epochs will witness far greater victories for the Cause of God on a global scale.

* In the year 1991, this number has reached over 108,000. The Faith is growing so rapidly that any statistical figure will be out of date within days.

† The Fourth Epoch of the Formative Age began in 1986.

Any unbiased observer who looks back upon the ministry of Shoghi Effendi will be astonished at the range of his stupendous achievements, which can only be described as miraculous. Every major accomplishment during this period took place because of the Guardian's encouragement and guidance to the Bahá'ís of the world. Had it not been for him, the Formative Age of the Faith would never have unfolded itself, and the institutions of the Faith, destined to be channels for the flow of the spiritual forces released by the Revelation of Bahá'u'lláh, would have remained unbuilt. Indeed, it is impossible to imagine how the Faith of Bahá'u'lláh could have survived in the world had it not been for the institution of the Guardianship. Shoghi Effendi was appointed by 'Abdu'l-Bahá, the divine Architect, to build the foundations of His world-embracing institutions for mankind. It was he who fashioned the Adminstrative Order, devised the plans, and spurred on the Bahá'ís to implement them. He laid down the base and erected the pillars which, today, sustain and buttress the mighty edifice of the Universal House of Justice. It was he who through his masterly translations and his own original writings expounded the true nature of the Faith of Bahá'u'lláh for the public in general and Bahá'ís in particular.

And it was he who accomplished the most momentous feat of welding and organising the loosely-knit, struggling and heterogenous groups and elements which composed the Bahá'í world of the time of 'Abdu'l-Bahá into a united and harmoniously-functioning, world-encircling community which is unique in the annals of religion, and which is destined to be the glory, the promise and the harbinger of that Kingdom of God on earth foretold by the Prophets of the past and whose establishment in future centuries is to be the main outcome of the Revelation of Bahá'u'lláh.

CHAPTER THIRTY-FOUR

The Chief Stewards

SHOGHI Effendi passed away in the sixtieth year of his life on 4 November 1957 in London, half-way through the Ten Year Crusade. His death, caused by a sudden heart attack in his sleep, came as a cruel blow to the Bahá'ís of the world and another test of the Covenant. This unexpected tragedy plunged the Bahá'í world into a state of utter grief and sorrow, and shook the community of the Most Great Name to its foundations. The news flashed around the world in the following cable:

> Shoghi Effendi beloved of all hearts sacred trust given believers by Master passed away sudden heart attack in sleep following Asiatic flu. Urge believers remain steadfast cling institution Hands lovingly reared recently reinforced emphasized by beloved Guardian. Only oneness heart oneness purpose can befittingly testify loyalty all National Assemblies believers departed Guardian who sacrificed self utterly for service Faith.
>
> Rúḥíyyih[1]

Later, the news of the funeral was cabled to the Bahá'í world:

> Beloved all hearts precious Guardian Cause God passed peacefully away yesterday after Asiatic flu. Appeal Hands National Assemblies Auxiliary Boards shelter believers assist meet heartrending supreme test. Funeral our beloved Guardian Saturday London Hands Assembly Board members invited attend any press release should state meeting Hands shortly Haifa will make arrangement to Bahá'í world regarding future plans. Urge hold memorial meetings Saturday.
>
> Rúḥíyyih[2]

These two cables were sent to the Bahá'í communities from the city of Haifa, based on a policy that all communications to the Bahá'í world should be issued from its World Centre.

The information that the Hands of the Cause were to meet in Haifa to 'arrange future plans' was welcomed by the Bahá'ís, because the Hands were appointed by the Guardian for the protection and propagation of the Faith. They were its highest dignitaries. There were twenty-seven Hands when Shoghi Effendi passed away; no body was more suited to advise the believers of the future development of the Cause and to consider the question of a successor to Shoghi Effendi. Almost the entire Bahá'í community expected that the Will and Testament of Shoghi Effendi would announce the appointment of a successor to himself, as the Wills of Bahá'u'lláh and 'Abdu'l-Bahá had done. For almost a month, the Bahá'ís of the world waited anxiously for news of this from the beloved and trusted Hands of the Cause, but when the news finally came, it was that the Guardian had left no Will.

Bahá'u'lláh had appointed 'Abdu'l-Bahá in the *Kitáb-i-'Ahd* as the Centre of His Covenant; 'Abdu'l-Bahá in His turn had appointed Shoghi Effendi in the *Will and Testament* as Guardian of the Faith: in both cases, the faithful knew where to turn. But Shoghi Effendi did not leave a Will, and this caused some to become perplexed. Indeed, the Bahá'ís all over the world had taken it for granted that he would follow the same practice as Bahá'u'lláh and 'Abdu'l-Bahá and appoint his successor.

That Shoghi Effendi did not write a Will was due to the circumstances of his ministry and of his life. It must be realized that he was a most meticulous person who never left anything to chance, especially in the case of such a vital issue as writing his Will and Testament to appoint a successor to himself. Only through reflection will a believer come to appreciate the wisdom and inevitability of Shoghi Effendi remaining silent on this question.

One of Bahá'u'lláh's injunctions in the *Kitáb-i-Aqdas* is that every Bahá'í should write a Will and Testament, and that foremost in it he should bear witness to the oneness of God in the Dayspring of His Revelation, Bahá'u'lláh. This confession of faith is to be a testimony for him in both this world and the next. A Will also directs the distribution of wealth among one's heirs. As to the first requirement, Shoghi Effendi's letter entitled *The Dispensation of Bahá'u'lláh* is one of the finest declarations of faith ever written. No believer has written such an outstanding confession of his religious beliefs as Shoghi Effendi did in this remarkable document. As to the second part of a Will, which is the bequeathing of a person's wealth to his inheritors, Shoghi Effendi did not have any worldly possessions and therefore had no need to distribute them. Thus, it can be said that he carried out the commandment of Bahá'u'lláh with regard to the writing of a Will.

As to the appointment of a successor, the Master had stated in His *Will and Testament* that should the 'first-born' of the Guardian not inherit his spiritual qualities, he should appoint another *Ghuṣn* (Branch). The word *Ghuṣn* has been used by Bahá'u'lláh to signify His male descendants exclusively. 'Abdu'l-Bahá was designated as

Ghuṣn-i-A'ẓam (The Most Great Branch) and Shoghi Effendi as Ghuṣn-i-Mumtáz (The Chosen Branch). Shoghi Effendi was not in a position to appoint a successor to himself because he had no son and there was not a single Ghuṣn who was faithful to the Cause of God. Every one of the descendants of 'Abdu'l-Bahá had been declared a Covenant-breaker.

Not only was Shoghi Effendi unable to appoint a successor to himself, but his hands were also tied in making a pronouncement about it. This is because Shoghi Effendi was the Interpreter of the Word of God. This allowed him to explain everything which was in the Writings of Bahá'u'lláh and 'Abdu'l-Bahá and apply their teachings and commandments within the framework of the exigencies of the time. However, what Shoghi Effendi could not do was to pronounce on subjects which were not recorded in the Holy Writings. These fell within the purview of the Universal House of Justice, which alone has the authority to legislate on matters which are not revealed by the Pen of Bahá'u'lláh or 'Abdu'l-Bahá. Since the *Will and Testament* of 'Abdu'l-Bahá did not indicate the course to be taken should there be no Ghuṣn (Branch) to succeed Shoghi Effendi, the resolution of this question did not fall within the domain of the Guardianship; it was the prerogative of the Universal House of Justice to find a solution. This is probably the main reason why Shoghi Effendi did not make any statement about his successor.

After the ascension of Bahá'u'lláh, the Bahá'í community was engulfed in a furious tempest of Covenant-breaking, a tempest which continued to rage throughout the ministry of 'Abdu'l-Bahá. The faith of every believer was severely tested, and many a faint-hearted individual was thrown out of the Ark of salvation – the Covenant of Bahá'u'lláh. There was a similar situation after the ascension of 'Abdu'l-Bahá. The provisions of His *Will and Testament* were violated and tests encompassed the community.

After the passing of Shoghi Effendi, however, the circumstances were different. The tests which faced the believers were, in some respects, far greater than those which had descended upon the earlier believers as a result of the passing of Bahá'u'lláh or 'Abdu'l-Bahá. This is because this time there was no Will and Testament; Shoghi Effendi had gone, and left the believers on their own. In spite of this, the institutions of the Administrative Order, born of the Covenant, had been strengthened to such a point that practically the whole Bahá'í community over the entire surface of the globe remained loyal to the Cause and its institutions. The believers of every land remained united as one soul in many bodies, and for two years after the passing of Shoghi Effendi there was no voice of dissent anywhere. All the believers turned to the Hands of the Cause of God, and every national and local Spiritual Assembly declared their loyalty to that body. There was never in the history of the Faith a time when the believers demonstrated such unity and solidarity in spite of the uncertainty created by the circumstances resulting from the passing of Shoghi Effendi. This is indeed the best proof of the indestructibility of the Covenant of Bahá'u'lláh.

It is very significant that five months before he passed away, Shoghi Effendi sent a cablegram to the Bahá'í world in which he conferred upon the Hands of the Cause the responsibility of protecting the Bahá'í community. In another message one month before his passing, he referred to the Hands as 'the Chief Stewards of Bahá'u'lláh's embryonic World Commonwealth'. These two messages by Shoghi Effendi contained strong indications for the future destiny of the Cause and led the Bahá'í community to rally around the Hands after his passing. The first message was sent on 4 June 1957; here are some excerpts:

> Divinely appointed Institution of the Hands of the Cause, invested by virtue of the authority conferred by the Testament of the Centre of the Covenant with the twin functions of protecting and propagating the Faith of Bahá'u'lláh, now entering new phase in the process of the unfoldment of its sacred mission. To its newly assured responsibility to assist National Spiritual Assemblies of the Bahá'í world in the specific purpose of effectively prosecuting the World Spiritual Crusade, the primary obligation to watch over and insure protection to the Bahá'í world community, in close collaboration with these same National Assemblies, is now added . . .
>
> Evidences of increasing hostility without, persistent machinations within, foreshadowing dire contests destined to range the Army of Light against the forces of darkness, both secular and religious, predicted in unequivocal language by 'Abdu'l-Bahá, necessitate in this crucial hour closer association of the Hands of the five continents and the bodies of the elected representatives of the national Bahá'í communities the world over for joint investigation of the nefarious activities of internal enemies and the adoption of wise, effective measures to counteract their treacherous schemes, protect the mass of the believers, and arrest the spread of their evil influence.
>
> Call upon Hands and National Assemblies, each continent separately, to establish henceforth direct contact and deliberate, whenever feasible, as frequently as possible, to exchange reports to be submitted by their respective Auxiliary Boards and national committees, to exercise unrelaxing vigilance and carry out unflinchingly their sacred, inescapable duties. The security of our precious Faith, the preservation of the spiritual health of the Bahá'í communities, the vitality of the faith of its individual members, the proper functioning of its laboriously erected institutions, the fruition of its worldwide enterprises, the fulfilment of its ultimate destiny, all are directly dependent upon the befitting discharge of the

weighty responsibilities now resting upon the members of these two institutions, occupying, with the Universal House of Justice, next to the Institution of the Guardianship, foremost rank in the divinely ordained administrative hierarchy of the World Order of Bahá'u'lláh.[3]

The second letter was written in October 1957. The following passage is relevant to this subject.

So marvellous a progress, embracing so vast a field, achieved in so short a time, by so small a band of heroic souls, well deserves, at this juncture in the evolution of a decade-long Crusade, to be signalized by, and indeed necessitates, the announcement of yet another step in the progressive unfoldment of one of the cardinal and pivotal institutions ordained by Bahá'u'lláh, and confirmed in the Will and Testament of 'Abdu'l-Bahá, involving the designation of yet another contingent* of the Hands of the Cause of God, raising thereby to thrice nine the total number of the Chief Stewards of Bahá'u'lláh's embryonic World Commonwealth, who have been invested by the unerring Pen of the Centre of His Covenant with the dual function of guarding over the security, and of ensuring the propagation, of His Father's Faith.[4]

The Manifestation of God gives birth to the religion of God as a mother gives birth to her child. One may observe that if the mother of a child becomes aware that she is going to die, she will entrust her infant to the care of a trustworthy nurse or other reliable person, to look after and protect him until he becomes older and able to stand on his own feet and become self-supporting. This is what Bahá'u'lláh did when He wrote the *Kitáb-i-'Ahd* and appointed 'Abdu'l-Bahá to assume responsibility for the Cause of God which, in the terms of the above analogy, was passing through the stages of infancy and childhood, and needed to be nurtured and cared for. Had it not been for the divine protection vouchsafed to it in the person of 'Abdu'l-Bahá, the Faith of Bahá'u'lláh, left on its own, would have been like an orphaned infant without a nurse, and it would have suffered the same fate as older religions did when schisms occurred and the followers divided it into many sects.

Under the guidance and loving care of 'Abdu'l-Bahá, the infant Faith of Bahá'u'lláh grew up protected from the onslaught of the Covenant-breakers and acquired greater strength and vitality. The message of Bahá'u'lláh reached the peoples of the East and West and, although not fully integrated, small Bahá'í communities sprung up in several countries of the world. Yet the Faith was still very young; it continued to need further protection after 'Abdu'l-Bahá. The child needed yet another nurse. Again the measures which had been taken

* The last contingent consisted of eight Hands of the Cause, appointed by Shoghi Effendi in this same October message.

by Bahá'u'lláh were adopted by 'Abdu'l-Bahá when He appointed Shoghi Effendi as the Guardian to nurture the tender and flourishing faith which was still vulnerable to attacks from within and without the community.

During the thirty-six years of the Guardianship, Shoghi Effendi built up the foundations of the institutions of the Administrative Order of Bahá'u'lláh which were to act as channels for the outpouring of the spiritual energies latent in His Revelation. These institutions, which derive their authority from the *Kitáb-i-Aqdas* and from the *Will and Testament* of 'Abdu'l-Bahá, became bastions of protection for the Bahá'ís of the world. When Shoghi Effendi passed away, the Administrative Order was well-established. By virtue of these institutions the Faith of Bahá'u'lláh had become impregnable and the body of the believers was united and harmonized everywhere. The forces of negation which had attacked the Faith from within after the ascension of Bahá'u'lláh and 'Abdu'l-Bahá, and which had posed severe threats to its unity, were now impotent to penetrate the mighty stronghold of the Administrative Order which Shoghi Effendi had built up with meticulous care and with so much suffering to himself. In the terms of the above analogy, the child, though still very young, was at last able to stand on its own feet. The mother had suddenly gone without any warning, but she knew that after the preliminary shock the child would gather himself together and take the reins of affairs into his own hands. This is exactly what happened after the sudden passing of Shoghi Effendi. The Bahá'í community, having learned from the Hands of the Cause that Shoghi Effendi had left no Will, was at first shaken and dismayed, but soon it recovered and organised itself to carry on the work without a Guardian. The following are excerpts from the first letter by the Hands of the Cause addressed to the Bahá'ís of the world on this issue:

> Beloved Friends:
>
> Nine days had not yet elapsed after the interment of the sacred remains of our beloved Guardian, Shoghi Effendi, in London, when the Hands of the Cause, to the number of twenty-six, assembled at the World Center of the Faith, in our capacity as 'Chief Stewards of the Embryonic World Commonwealth of Bahá'u'lláh', to consult together on the most tragic situation facing the Bahá'ís since the Ascension of 'Abdu'l-Bahá, and to take all necessary and appropriate measures to safeguard the highest interests of our Faith.
>
> On November 18th the Hands conducted a Memorial Meeting at Bahjí, in the Ḥaram-i-Aqdas surrounding the most sacred Shrine in the Bahá'í world, afterward entering the Holy Tomb itself and prostrating ourselves in utter humility at the Sacred Threshold.

On the following morning, November 19th, nine Hands of the Cause, selected from the Holy Land and the several continents of East and West, with Amatu'l-Bahá Rúḥíyyih Khánum, broke the seals placed upon the beloved Guardian's safe and desk and made careful examination of their precious contents. These same Hands, rejoining the other Hands assembled in the Mansion of Bahá'u'lláh at Bahjí, certified that Shoghi Effendi had left no Will and Testament. It was likewise certified that the beloved Guardian had left no heir. The Aghṣán (branches) one and all are either dead or have been declared violators of the Covenant by the Guardian for their faithlessness to the Master's Will and Testament and their hostility to him named first Guardian in that sacred document.

The first effect of the realization that no successor to Shoghi Effendi could have been appointed by him was to plunge the Hands of the Cause into the very abyss of despair. What must happen to the world community of his devoted followers if the Leader, the Inspirer, the Planner of all Bahá'í activities in all countries and islands of the seas could no longer fulfil his unique mission?

From this dark abyss, however, contemplation of the Guardian's own life of complete sacrifice and his peerless services gradually redeemed our anguished hearts. Shoghi Effendi himself, we know, would have been the first to remind the Hands and the widespread body of the believers, that the Dispensation of Bahá'u'lláh has quickened those powers and resources of faith within mankind which will achieve the unity of the peoples and the triumph of His World Order. In this new light of understanding the company of the Hands could perceive with heightened gratitude the existence of those innumerable blessings which Shoghi Effendi had created and left as his true legacy to all Bahá'ís.

Has not the World Centre, with its sacred Shrines and institutions, been firmly established? Has not the Message been established in 254 countries and dependencies? Have not the National and Regional Spiritual Assemblies, forerunners of the Universal House of Justice, been implanted in twenty-six great areas of all continents? Has not the Guardian left us not only his incomparable translations, for English-reading Bahá'ís, of the Bahá'í Sacred Literature but also his own master works of interpretation which disclose to us the unshatterable edifice of evolving Bahá'í Order and world community? Has not the Guardian, building upon the enduring foundation of the Master's Tablets of the Divine Plan, created the World Crusade to guide our work until 1963? . . .

Such reflections could but, in such a world-shattering experience as all Bahá'ís have this month endured, reveal to us how strongly Shoghi Effendi has laid the foundations of the world order of Bahá'u'lláh through the appointments of Hands of the Cause and likewise the appointment of the International Bahá'í Council, the institution destined to evolve into the Universal House of Justice.

In our capacity of Chief Stewards of the Embryonic World Commonwealth of Bahá'u'lláh, we Hands of the Cause have constituted a body of nine Hands to serve at the Bahá'í World Centre. This body of nine Hands will energetically deal with the protection of the Faith whenever attacks, whether from within or outside the Bahá'í community, are reported by Hands from their areas or by National or Regional Assemblies, or whether they arise within the Holy Land. Correspondence will likewise be maintained with the Hands of the Cause working in the several continents. This same body will correspond with National Assemblies on matters connected with the prosecution of the objectives of the Ten Year Plan. On matters involving administrative questions this same body will assist National Assemblies by citing those passages of the Bahá'í Sacred Literature which direct the Assemblies to a sound solution.

As to the International Bahá'í Council, appointed by the Guardian and heralded in his communications to the Bahá'í world, that body will in the course of time finally fulfil its purpose through the formation of the Universal House of Justice, that supreme body upon which infallibility, as the Master's Testament assures us, is divinely conferred: 'The source of all good and freed from all error' . . .

Meanwhile the entire body of the Hands assembled by the nine Hands of the World Centre will decide when and how the International Bahá'í Council is to evolve through the successive stages outlined by the Guardian, culminating in the call to election of the Universal House of Justice by the membership of all National Spiritual Assemblies.

When that divinely ordained body comes into existence, all the conditions of the Faith can be examined anew and the measures necessary for its future operation determined on consultation with the Hands of the Cause . . .[5]

The believers faithfully rallied around the Hands of the Cause, who now assumed the function of guiding the Bahá'í world. All National Spiritual Assemblies declared their loyalty to the Hands and turned to that institution with devotion. The nine Hands appointed to serve at the World Centre were referred to as Custodians of the Faith. From the outset, the Hands made it clear to the Bahá'ís that, unlike the Guardian and the Universal House of Justice, they were not promised infallible guidance. The only way that they could carry out their responsibilities satisfactorily was to follow faithfully the provisions of the Ten Year Plan as delineated by the Guardian. In this way, there was no danger of misguiding the community.

The greatest achievement of the Hands in this period is that they did not deviate a hair's breadth from the teachings and guidance of Shoghi Effendi. For more than five years they held the reins of the Cause in their hands. This period may be regarded as the most critical stage in the history of the Faith of Bahá'u'lláh. From the day the Faith was born until the passing of Shoghi Effendi, divine protection had been vouchsafed to the community. For one hundred and thirteen years, the infant Faith of Bahá'u'lláh had been nurtured by the infallible guidance of its Central Figures* and its Guardian. But now it was entrusted to the care of a number of religious leaders, the Hands of the Cause, who did not have this promise of divine guidance.

It was a period fraught with dangers. Similar to subjecting a newly-built airplane to a series of rigorous tests in order to be sure that it works properly, the Covenant of Bahá'u'lláh was severely tested during these six years and found to be absolutely impregnable. The Custodianship of the Hands was itself a proof of the invincibility of the Covenant, in that, unlike the leaders of former religions who introduced many man-made practices into the teachings of their Prophets, the Hands of the Cause added not even a single dot to the Cause, nor did they introduce any innovation into the workings of its institutions. They guided the Bahá'í community strictly in accordance with the Holy Text and the writings of the Guardian. Their responses to questions from the National Spiritual Assemblies or individuals were based on the Holy Writings, and if they could not find the answer in the Tablets of Bahá'u'lláh or 'Abdu'l-Bahá or letters of Shoghi Effendi, they strictly refrained from making any pronouncement. Such questions were left for the future to be determined by the Universal House of Justice.

The Hands acted with such loyalty that when they handed over the Cause of God, pure and unadulterated, to the elected body of the Universal House of Justice in 1963 the whole Bahá'í world acclaimed their devotion. This generation and generations yet unborn owe the Hands of the Cause an immeasurable debt of gratitude. Through their faithfulness they took charge of the Ark of the Covenant from the hands of the Guardian, steered it for over five years through treacherous waters, brought it safely to the shores of salvation and humbly delivered it into the hands of the Universal House of Justice.

This period witnessed the emergence of a new brand of Covenant-breakers, headed by Mason Remey, who had himself been appointed a Hand of the Cause of God by Shoghi Effendi and was one of the signatories of the first declaration of the Hands issued after the passing of Shoghi Effendi. In order to appreciate the genesis of this rebellion against the Covenant, we must look back at the Bahá'í community as it was then. At that time there were some believers who thought that the Faith must always have a Guardian. This belief was partly due to the following statement by Shoghi Effendi in *The Dispensation of Bahá'u'lláh*:

> An attempt, I feel, should at the present juncture be made to explain the character and functions of the twin pillars that support this almighty

* The Báb, Bahá'u'lláh and 'Abdu'l-Bahá.

Administrative Structure – the institutions of the Guardianship and of the Universal House of Justice . . .

It should be stated, at the very outset, in clear and unambiguous language, that these twin institutions of the Administrative Order of Bahá'u'lláh should be regarded as divine in origin, essential in their functions and complementary in their aim and purpose. Their common, their fundamental object is to insure the continuity of that divinely-appointed authority which flows from the Source of our Faith, to safeguard the unity of its followers and to maintain the integrity and flexibility of its teachings. Acting in conjunction with each other these two inseparable institutions administer its affairs, co-ordinate its activities, promote its interests, execute its laws and defend its subsidiary institutions. Severally, each operates within a clearly defined sphere of jurisdiction; each is equipped with its own attendant institutions – instruments designed for the effective discharge of its particular responsibilities and duties. Each exercises, within the limitations imposed upon it, its powers, its authority, its rights and prerogatives. These are neither contradictory, nor detract in the slightest degree from the position which each of these institutions occupies. Far from being incompatible or mutually destructive, they supplement each other's authority and functions, and are permanently and fundamentally united in their aims.

Divorced from the institution of the Guardianship the World Order of Bahá'u'lláh would be mutilated and permanently deprived of that hereditary principle which, as 'Abdu'l-Bahá had written, has been invariably upheld by the Law of God. '*In all the Divine Dispensations*', He states, in a Tablet addressed to a follower of the Faith in Persia, '*the eldest son hath been given extraordinary distinctions. Even the station of prophethood hath been his birthright*'. Without such an institution the integrity of the Faith would be imperilled, and the stability of the entire fabric would be gravely endangered, Its prestige would suffer, the means required to enable it to take a long, an uninterrupted view over a series of generations would be completely lacking, and the necessary guidance to define the sphere of the legislative action of its elected representatives would be totally withdrawn.

Severed from the no less essential institution of the Universal House of Justice this same System of the Will of 'Abdu'l-Bahá would be paralyzed in its action and would be powerless to fill in those gaps which the Author of the Kitáb-i-Aqdas has deliberately left in the body of His legislative and administrative ordinances.[6]

When it became clear that Shoghi Effendi had not appointed a successor to himself, some Bahá'ís failed to appreciate the true significance of the above statement by Shoghi Effendi. Because they had not understood the spirit of the Covenant of Bahá'u'lláh, they insisted that a second Guardian must be created. Mason Remey, an ambitious individual, became the candidate, and with constant encouragement by a few equally ambitious men he claimed in 1960 that he was the successor of Shoghi Effendi. Sadly however, this was like trying to make a flower from paper and pretend that it was real.

'Abdu'l-Bahá in His *Will and Testament* extolled Shoghi Effendi as the 'Sign of God', the 'Chosen Branch', the 'blest and sacred bough that hath branched out from the Twin Holy Trees', 'the most wondrous, unique and priceless pearl that doth gleam from out the Twin surging seas'. Such a being was created by God especially to become the Guardian of the Cause, and his appointment was made by the Centre of the Covenant Himself. He was a descendant both of Bahá'u'lláh and of the family of the Báb. How could a few individuals who looked for leadership and sought power for their own selfish interests raise up a lesser man to the station of the Guardianship? In His *Will and Testament*, 'Abdu'l-Bahá has laid down the conditions that Shoghi Effendi's successor must be either the 'first-born' of the Guardian or another Ghuṣn (male descendant of Bahá'u'lláh), and that the Hands of the Cause must give their assent to his choice. How could Mason Remey fulfil these conditions? It is interesting to note that, in a Tablet to the Hand of the Cause of God, Mullá 'Alí-Akbar, 'Abdu'l-Bahá makes this important statement.

> . . . for 'Abdu'l-Bahá is in a tempest of dangers and infinitely abhors differences of opinion . . . Praise be to God, there are no grounds for differences.
>
> The Báb, the Exalted One, is the Morn of Truth, the splendour of Whose light shineth through all regions. He is also the Harbinger of the Most Great Light, the Abhá Luminary. The Blessed Beauty is the One promised by the sacred books of the past, the revelation of the Source of light that shone upon Mount Sinai, Whose fire glowed in the midst of the Burning Bush. We are one and all, servants of Their threshold, and stand each as a lowly keeper at Their door . . .
>
> My purpose is this, that ere the expiration of a thousand years, no one has the right to utter a single word, even to claim the station of Guardianship. The most Holy Book is the Book to which all peoples shall refer, and in it the Laws of God have been revealed. Laws not mentioned in the Book should be referred to the decision of the Universal House of Justice. There will be no grounds for difference . . . Beware, beware lest anyone create a rift or stir up sedition.[7]

After Mason Remey made his absurd claim, the Hands of the Cause in the Holy Land tried their utmost to bring him to his senses. But in his delusion, he persisted on his errant course and consequently he and those few who followed him were announced as Covenant-breakers.* The Bahá'í community was once again purged by this process; the impurities which would have imposed dire

* See Appendix 2.

afflictions upon the Faith had they been allowed to remain within the fold, were cast out, resulting in revitalization of the body of the Cause of God.

This episode of Covenant-breaking by Mason Remey was one of the flimsiest of all rebellions in the history of the Faith. It did not take very long until a number of those who had been misled by him realized their mistake, repented and returned to the community or withdrew from the Faith altogether. Mason Remey's efforts to form a following for himself failed miserably. After his death, serious rivalries broke out between his lieutenants who claimed to be his successors. The divinely-ordained instruments serving the Covenant of Bahá'u'lláh have been so strengthened today that the efforts of this group of Covenant-breakers have become null and void, and the power of the Covenant has driven them into oblivion.

Concerning the statement by Shoghi Effendi quoted above: 'Divorced from the institution of the Guardianship, the World Order of Bahá'u'lláh would be mutilated', it must be emphasized that although there are no more Guardians after Shoghi Effendi, the institution of the Guardianship will always exist. Consider for example, that when the Prophet leaves this world, the position He occupies within His religion is not lost. For instance, Bahá'u'lláh is the Author of the Faith. Access to Him during His ministry was mainly through His Writings. It is the same after His ascension; He will always be the Author of the Faith, and the way to approach Him is through His Writings. Likewise, 'Abdu'l-Bahá will always be the centre of the Covenant of Bahá'u'lláh. The fact that He has ascended to the next world does not alter His position in the Faith. In order to turn to Him, one must turn to His Writings.

It is the same with the institution of the Guardianship. Shoghi Effendi is the Guardian of the Faith. During his ministry the believers received guidance through his writings and continue to do so after his passing. The institution of the Guardianship will always serve as a pillar supporting the mighty structure of the Administrative Order, regardless of whether the Guardian is living or not. The writings of Shoghi Effendi will continue to guide and sustain the ever-advancing community of the Most Great Name. Today, the Universal House of Justice, before taking decisions on various matters whether in the field of legislation or administration, consults the writings of Shoghi Effendi and is guided by the vast body of his letters, in which he has elucidated almost every conceivable subject. Thus, far from being divorced from the World Order of Bahá'u'lláh, the institution of the Guardianship plays a preponderating role now and for ever, in conjunction with the institution of the Universal House of Justice, in guiding and directing the Bahá'í community toward its ultimate goal – the establishment of the oneness of mankind on this planet.

In their search to find an alternative solution to fill the vacancy after Shoghi Effendi, a few believers came up with the erroneous theory that the institution of the Hands of the Cause of God was part of the institution of the Guardianship and therefore the Hands would carry forward the function of the Guardianship. This concept is entirely baseless; there is nothing in the Holy Text or the writings of Shoghi Effendi to support it. The relationship that the Hands had with the Guardian was that they were appointed by him for the purpose of serving the Cause under his direction. The mere fact that the Hands were appointed by Shoghi Effendi does not entitle them to become part of the institution of the Guardianship. Otherwise, the members of the International Bahá'í Council, who were also appointed by Shoghi Effendi, should similarly become part of that institution. Nowhere do we find any authoritative text to support such an idea. Indeed, the Hands of the Cause served under the Guardian during his lifetime and continue today to serve under the direction of the present-day Head of the Faith, the Universal House of Justice.

Only a lack of proper comprehension of the verities of the Faith, coupled with insatiable ambition, could have led Mason Remey to claim that Shoghi Effendi's statement about mutilation of the World Order of Bahá'u'lláh implied that the line of Guardians must not be broken. A more profound understanding of the workings of religion in general, and a deeper study of the Faith of Bahá'u'lláh in particular, reveals a different view altogether. The appearance of the Manifestation of God is similar to the advent of the springtime in nature which infuses new life into all living organisms. The Founder of a religion releases spiritual forces which are capable of quickening the souls of men. But every springtime has a limited duration. In nature the four seasons inevitably follow one another; spring is followed by summer, when the fruit appears. The spring season does not last for ever; if it did, it would become counterproductive. Likewise, the outpouring of divine revelation continues for a relatively short period in each Dispensation. It then ceases, and for the rest of that Dispensation man responds of his own volition to these spiritual forces and develops the powers which are latent within him. For instance, the springtime of Christianity was about three years, during which Christ preached His mission. Divine guidance ceased with His crucifixion, and there was no guidance coming from on high until the advent of the Prophet of Islám. The ministry of Muḥammad lasted for twenty-three years, following which eleven Imáms were the channels of guidance until the year 260 AH. After that the nation of Islám was left without divine guidance until the coming of the Báb one thousand lunar years later in 1260 AH (1844 AD). The history of religion shows that there has always been a break in divine guidance amounting to hundreds of years until the next Manifestation of God appears.

That 'Abdu'l-Bahá in His Will and Testament makes provision for a successor to Shoghi Effendi does not necessarily mean that there will be one. The Will is a comprehensive document which must be capable of dealing with all eventualities. In it, 'Abdu'l-Bahá makes a covenant with the believers, and therefore, some of its provisions may not be realized. For there are two parties to a covenant, in this case, 'Abdu'l-Bahá and the believers. The fulfilment of the terms of this covenant therefore depends on the actions and attitudes of the followers and on the circumstances relating to the Cause. In this connection, the Universal House of Justice states:

> Future Guardians are clearly envisaged and referred to in the Writings, but there is nowhere any promise or guarantee that the line of Guardians would endure forever; on the contrary there are clear indications that the line could be broken. Yet, in spite of this, there is a repeated insistance in the Writings on the indestructibility of the Covenant and the immutability of God's Purpose for this Day.
>
> One of the most striking passages which envisage the possibility of such a break in the line of Guardians is in the Kitáb-i-Aqdas itself:
>
> > The endowments dedicated to charity revert to God, the Revealer of Signs. No one has the right to lay hold on them without leave from the Dawning-Place of Revelation. After Him the decision rests with the Aghsán (Branches), and after them with the House of Justice – should it be established in the world by then – so that they may use these endowments for the benefit of the Sites exalted in this Cause, and for that which they have been commanded by God, the Almighty, the All-Powerful. Otherwise the endowments should be referred to the people of Bahá, who speak not without His leave and who pass no judgment but in accordance with that which God has ordained in this Tablet, they who are the champions of victory betwixt heaven and earth, so that they may spend them on that which has been decreed in the Holy Book by God, the Mighty, the Bountiful.
>
> The passing of Shoghi Effendi in 1957 precipated the very situation provided for in this passage, in that the line of Aghsán ended before the House of Justice had been elected. Although, as is seen, the ending of the line of Aghsán at some stage was provided for, we must never underestimate the grievous loss that the Faith has suffered. God's purpose for mankind remains unchanged, however, and the mighty Covenant of Bahá'u'lláh remains impregnable.[8]

The above passage in the *Kitáb-i-Aqdas* was prophetic, in that a period of over five years separated the passing of Shoghi Effendi from the establishement of the Universal House of Justice, and the Hands of the Cause during this period – 'the people of Bahá who speak not without His leave' – fulfilled the last provision stated in the above text.

Those few who gathered around Mason Remey and others who in recent times have taken his place, have tried to justify their rebellion against the Covenant. They misled themselves by interpreting the word 'branch' mentioned in the *Will and Testament* of 'Abdu'l-Bahá concerning a successor to Shoghi Effendi. They claimed that since Bahá'u'lláh referred to human beings as 'the fruits of one tree and the leaves of one branch', therefore any believer was a branch who could succeed Shoghi Effendi. This assumption was made either through self-deception, or was due to ignorance, or maybe both. The fact of the matter is that the word *Ghuṣn* (branch) which has been used by Bahá'u'lláh exclusively to refer to his male descendants, is Arabic, while the other is Persian, and is another word entirely. Both are translated as 'branch'. Furthermore, in neither language are there capital letters.*

Before Mason Remey's preposterous claim, the wisdom of the words of 'Abdu'l-Bahá in His *Will and Testament* that the Hands of the Cause 'must give their assent to the choice of the one whom the Guardian of the Cause of God hath chosen as his successor' was not clear to many. But after Remey's defection, it became clear that this requirement was a means for the protection of the Cause of God. If there was to be a successor to Shoghi Effendi, he needed the approval of the Hands, and Mason Remey did not have this.

Propelled by the forces of the Covenant, the Faith of Bahá'u'lláh during the custodianship of the Hands of the Cause of God, advanced to such an extent as to eclipse the victories which had been won in preceding decades. The teaching work in five continents of the globe was intensified as the believers exerted themselves to win the goals of the Ten Year Crusade which the Guardian had formulated. Great numbers entered the Faith, especially in Africa, Latin America and Asia. In the sub-continent of India, tens of thousands swelled the number of believers when large-scale entry by troops was experienced by the Bahá'í community there. The number of local Spiritual Assemblies, the bedrock upon which the National Spiritual Assemblies were established, increased enormously throughout the world. More National Spiritual Assemblies were also formed during the remaining years of the Ten Year Crusade.

In 1961 the Hands of the Cause arranged for the election of the International Bahá'í Council, the forerunner of the Universal House

* For more information see Appendix 2.

of Justice. The electors were members of the National Spiritual Assemblies which were functioning at the time in the five continents of the globe. The International Bahá'í Council, whose members had been appointed by the Guardian was now transformed into an elected body.

The call for the election of the Universal House of Justice was made by the Hands of the Cause in their message of 5 November 1961 to the Bahá'í world. The following are excerpts from this message:

> With the erection in 1962 of twelve more future pillars* of that supreme legislative Body of the Bahá'í World, a firm foundation will have been laid for the election of 'that Universal House of Justice which', Shoghi Effendi stated, 'as its title implies, is to be the exponent and guardian of the Divine Justice which can alone insure the security of, and establish the reign of law and order in a strangely disordered world.'
>
> We are now able to envisage the steps that must still be taken before that 'Ark' referred to in Bahá'u'lláh's prophetic Tablet of Carmel shall come into being, an ark whose dwellers, the Guardian told us, 'are the men of the Supreme House of Justice which, in conformity with the exact provisions of the Will and Testament of the Centre of the mighty Covenant, is the Body which should legislate on laws not explicitly revealed in the text. In this Dispensation these laws are destined to flow from this holy Mountain, even as in the Mosaic Dispensation the law of God was promulgated from Zion.'
>
> The Chief Stewards of the Faith are therefore calling a convention in the Holy Land for the election of the Universal House of Justice on the first, second and third days of Riḍván, 1963. The members of all National and Regional Spiritual Assemblies elected by the Bahá'ís in Riḍván, 1962, will, in conformity with the teachings, constitute the electoral body empowered to vote for this crowning unit of the embryonic World Order of Bahá'u'lláh, upon whose deliberations the unique bounty of receiving divine inspiration has been bestowed, and whose decisions are infallibly guided by both the Báb and Bahá'u'lláh.
>
> After long and conscientious consideration of the needs of the present hour and the writings of our dearly-loved Guardian, the following decision has been reached: All male voting members throughout the Bahá'í World are eligible for election to the Universal House of Justice. The Hands of the Cause do not limit the freedom of the electors. However, as they have been given the explicit duties of guarding over the security and insuring the propagation of the Faith, they ask the electors to leave them free at this time to discharge their duties. When that supreme infallible Body has been elected it will decide on all matters concerning its own membership.

* National Spiritual Assemblies. These twelve National Spiritual Assemblies (11 in Europe, 1 in Ceylon) brought the number of National Spiritual Assemblies in the world up to 56.

On 21 April 1963, exactly one hundred years after the declaration of Bahá'u'lláh in the Garden of Riḍván in Baghdád, the members of fifty-six National Spiritual Assemblies throughout the world took part in the election of the Universal House of Justice. The voting took place in the home of 'Abdu'l-Bahá in Haifa, in a profoundly spiritual atmosphere. Thus the sailing of the Ark upon Mount Carmel, prophesied by Bahá'u'lláh, took place and the House of Justice came into being. It was a moment of relief and supreme joy for the members of the National Spiritual Assemblies and the Hands of the Cause to witness the birth of an institution which was to be the source of divine guidance until the end of this Dispensation. On the occasion of this momentous day the Hands of the Cause, on 22 April 1963, sent the following message to the Bahá'í communities throughout the world.

> Occasion worldwide celebrations Most Great Jubilee commemorating centenary ascension Bahá'u'lláh throne His sovereignty with hearts overflowing gratitude His unfailing protection overflowing bounties joyously announce friends East West election supreme legislative body ordained by Him in His Most Holy Book promised by Him receive His infallible guidance. Members first historic House Justice duly elected by delegates comprising members fifty six National Assemblies are Charles Wolcott Ali Nakhjavani Borrah Kavelin Ian Semple Lotfullah Hakim David Hofman Hugh Chance Amoz Gibson Hushmand Fath-i-'Aẓam.
>
> To jubilation entire Bahá'í world victorious completion beloved Guardian's unique Crusade now added humble gratitude profound thanksgiving followers Bahá'u'lláh for erection Universal House Justice august body to whom all believers must turn whose destiny is to guide unfoldment His embryonic World Order through administrative institutions prescribed by Bahá'u'lláh elaborated by 'Abdu'l-Bahá laboriously erected by Shoghi Effendi and ensure early dawn golden age Faith when the Word of the Lord will cover the earth as the waters cover the sea (signed) Handsfaith. April 22nd, 1963.

CHAPTER THIRTY-FIVE

The Universal House of Justice

WITH the coming into being of the Universal House of Justice a new era opened in the history of the Bahá'í Faith. Divine guidance had been vouchsafed to the community for almost one hundred and thirteen years, first through the persons of the Manifestations of God, then through the chosen Centre of the Cause and the authorized interpreter of His words. But now, with the passing of Shoghi Effendi and the establishment of the Universal House of Justice, the vehicle of that guidance was changed from a personal channel, organically linked to the Manifestation of God, to an elected body whose members are fallible individuals, yet whose collective resolutions are guided by Bahá'u'lláh since He conferred infallibility upon their decisions.

This provision of the continuity of divine guidance on matters which are within the prerogative of the House of Justice, and which are clearly defined to exclude any changes to the laws, the teachings and other provisions revealed in the Bahá'í scriptures, is unique in the history of religion. Never before has a Manifestation of God given authority to a council elected by universal suffrage to enact laws and administer the affairs of His religion in the assurance that it will be guided by God in its decisions. In this Dispensation, the Covenant of Bahá'u'lláh has provided mankind with the continuity of divine guidance on all problems which have caused difference, questions that are obscure, and matters that are not expressly recorded in the Book.

The Universal House of Justice was instituted when in 1963 members of the National Spiritual Assemblies, in a prayerful attitude and in an atmosphere of intense spirituality and profound devotion, elected nine souls from among the Bahá'ís of the world as members of this supreme institution. The occasion is considered by the Bahá'ís to be, next to the appointment of Shoghi Effendi as the Guardian of the Faith, the most momentous event in the history of the Formative Age of the Faith. Even the manner of the election itself was befitting that institution described as the 'sole refuge of a tottering civilization'. The election of the Universal House of Justice now takes place every five years in the same spirit of atmosphere of spirituality and dedication.

Bahá'í elections are unlike any of the other forms of election currently practised in the various parts of the world. For a Bahá'í, it is an act of devotion to God to elect members of Bahá'í institutions. There are no candidates, no propaganda and no canvassing of any kind, and the elections are conducted in a spirit of prayer and meditation. It is a sacred responsibility of the electorate to vote for those 'who can best combine the necessary qualities of unquestioned loyalty, of selfless devotion, of a well-trained mind, of recognized ability and mature experience'.[1] The act of voting in Bahá'í elections is free and secret; even the closest of relatives or friends do not consult together on their choice. To do so would be tantamount to breaking one of God's sacred spiritual commandments.

Every religion has spiritual and moral teachings. The Sermon on the Mount, for example, epitomizing the spiritual and moral teachings of Christ, has made a deep and abiding impression upon the followers of Jesus. Other religions have similar spiritual teachings. The passage of time has not usually affected the reverence with which the adherents of each religion view these teachings; for example, Muslims conscientiously carry out the law of daily prayer because they consider this teaching to be God's commandment and regard its violation as a sinful act.

Not until the advent of the Bahá'í Dispensation did a Manifestation of God include administrative principles among His spiritual teachings. This is an entirely new dimension which Bahá'u'lláh has introduced; He has placed the spiritual and administrative principles on a par with each other. A violation of an administrative principle, such as electioneering, is as grave a betrayal of the Cause of Bahá'u'lláh as breaking a spiritual law. Through this the purity, the integrity and incorruptibility of Bahá'í institutions are preserved, and the institutions themselves are protected from malpractice.

The Universal House of Justice has been ordained by Bahá'u'lláh as a channel of divine guidance, and is not to be considered as merely the international administrative body of the Faith. It is endowed with infallibility which the Founder of the Faith has conferred upon it.

We have already discussed the question of infallibility.* The Manifestations of God – in this day, the Báb and Bahá'u'lláh – are possessed of supreme infallibility; this is something inherent within them. It is similar to the sun, which produces its own heat and light, and is thus independent of other sources of energy. But 'Abdu'l-Bahá and Shoghi Effendi and the Universal House of Justice are under the

* See above, p. 103.

protection of Bahá'u'lláh by virtue of the fact that He has conferred infallibility upon Them. This resembles the light of the moon, which is not inherent but cast upon it by the sun. This infallibility is validated in the Writings of Bahá'u'lláh and 'Abdu'l-Bahá, and specifically in Bahá'u'lláh's *Kitáb-i-'Ahd* (The Book of the Covenant) and the *Will and Testament* of 'Abdu'l-Bahá. The following are the words of 'Abdu'l-Bahá in this connection.

> To epitomize: essential infallibility belongs especially to the supreme Manifestations, and acquired infallibility is granted to every holy soul. For instance, the Universal House of Justice, if it be established under the necessary conditions – with members elected from all the people – that House of Justice will be under the protection and the unerring guidance of God. If that House of Justice shall decide unanimously, or by a majority, upon any question not mentioned in the Book, that decision and command will be guarded from mistake. Now the members of the House of Justice have not, individually, essential infallibility; but the body of the House of Justice is under the protection and the unerring guidance of God: this is called conferred infallibility.[2]

The Universal House of Justice derives its authority and infallibility from Bahá'u'lláh Himself. In the *Tablet of Bishárát*, Bahá'u'lláh in unmistakable terms confers upon the House of Justice the authority to rule, and assures it of His unfailing guidance.

> The men of God's House of Justice have been charged with the affairs of the people. They, in truth, are the Trustees of God among His servants and the daysprings of authority in His countries.
>
> O people of God! That which traineth the world is Justice, for it is upheld by two pillars, reward and punishment. These two pillars are the sources of life to the world. Inasmuch as for each day there is a new problem and for every problem an expedient solution, such affairs should be referred to the Ministers of the House of Justice that they may act according to the needs and requirements of the time. They that, for the sake of God, arise to serve His Cause, are the recipients of divine inspiration from the unseen kingdom. It is incumbent upon all to be obedient unto them. All matters of State should be referred to the House of Justice, but acts of worship must be observed according to that which God hath revealed in His Book.[3]

And in another Tablet, *Kalimát-i-Firdawsíyyih*, Bahá'u'lláh reveals:

> It is incumbent upon the Trustees of the House of Justice to take counsel together regarding those things which have not outwardly been revealed in the Book, and to enforce that which is agreeable to them. God will verily inspire them with whatsoever He willeth, and He, verily, is the Provider, the Omniscient.[4]

'Abdu'l-Bahá confirms the authority of the Universal House of Justice and asserts its infallibility. In His *Will and Testament* He writes:

> The sacred and youthful branch, the Guardian of the Cause of God, as well as the Universal House of Justice, to be universally elected and established, are both under the care and protection of the Abhá Beauty, under the shelter and unerring guidance of His Holiness, the Exalted One (may my life be offered up for them both). Whatsoever they decide is of God. Whoso obeyeth him not, neither obeyeth them, hath not obeyed God, whoso rebelleth against him and against them hath rebelled against God, whoso opposeth him hath opposed God, whoso contendeth with them hath contended with God; whoso disputeth with him hath disputed with God, whoso denieth him hath denied God, whoso disbelieveth in him hath disbelieved in God, whoso deviateth, separateth himself and turneth aside from him hath in truth deviated, separated himself and turned aside from God. May the wrath, the fierce indignation, the vengeance of God rest upon him!

And again:

> . . . This is the foundation of the belief of the people of Bahá (may my life be offered up for them): 'His Holiness, the Exalted One (the Báb), is the Manifestation of the Unity and Oneness of God and the Forerunner of the Ancient Beauty. His Holiness the Abhá Beauty (may my life be a sacrifice for His steadfast friends) is the Supreme Manifestation of God and the Dayspring of His Most Divine Essence. All others are servants unto Him and do His bidding.' Unto the most Holy Book everyone must turn, and all that is not expressly recorded therein must be referred to the Universal House of Justice. That which this body, whether unanimously or by a majority doth carry, that is verily the truth and the purpose of God Himself. Whoso doth deviate therefrom is verily of them that love discord, hath shown forth malice, and turned away from the Lord of the Covenant. By this House is meant that Universal House of Justice which is to be elected from all countries, that is from those parts in the East and West where the loved ones are to be found, after the manner of the customary elections in Western countries such as those of England.

Furthermore, in a Tablet 'Abdu'l-Bahá states:

> Let it not be imagined that the House of Justice will take any decision according to its own concepts and opinions. God forbid! The Supreme House of Justice will take decisions and establish laws through the inspiration and confirmation of the Holy Spirit, because it is in the safekeeping and under the shelter and protection of the Ancient Beauty, and obedience to its decisions is a bounden and essential duty and an absolute obligation, and there is no escape for anyone.
>
> Say, O People: Verily the Supreme House of Justice is under the wings of your Lord, the Compassionate, the All-Merciful, that is under His

> protection, His care, and His shelter, for He has commanded the firm believers to obey that blessed, sanctified and all subduing body, whose sovereignty is divinely ordained and of the Kingdom of Heaven and whose laws are inspired and spiritual.[5]

From the study of the above Writings, it becomes clear that it is an article of faith for a Bahá'í to believe in the authority and infallibility of the Universal House of Justice. An individual embraces the Faith of Bahá'u'lláh when he recognizes Him to be the Manifestation of God for this age. But this is only the beginning of the process of becoming a Bahá'í. The recognition of Bahá'u'lláh must be followed by an acknowledgment of the station of 'Abdu'l-Bahá as the Centre of the Covenant and Shoghi Effendi as the Guardian of the Faith, and a belief that their words and their interpretations of the Holy Writings are divinely guided and infallible. Similarly, a Bahá'í must believe that the Universal House of Justice is now the Head of the Faith and its supreme institution, and that its pronouncements, legislations and general instructions are all derived from the unerring guidance of Bahá'u'lláh and the Báb, and in the words of 'Abdu'l-Bahá: 'That which this body, whether unanimously or by a majority doth carry, that is verily the truth and the purpose of God Himself.'

It does not seem possible for a person who is not a Bahá'í to accept the House of Justice as 'the source of all good and freed from all error', nor is it possible to prove this statement to him scientifically. The only way that the individual can become convinced of the authority and infallibility of the Universal House of Justice is to recognize Bahá'u'lláh as God's Messenger for this age. Then, as a matter of faith, he will be able to accept His assurances in this regard and become convinced of the truths which are enshrined in His words. As the believer grows in his faith and acquires greater depth in his understanding of the teachings of Bahá'u'lláh, he becomes progressively assured that the Blessed Beauty 'shall guard it [the Universal House of Justice] from error and will protect it under the wing of His sanctity and infallibility'.

Even a cursory review of the workings of the House of Justice since its establishment in 1963 makes it clear to a believer that every directive issued by that body has been divinely inspired, that every plan it devised and every act it carried out has been blessed by Providence. Its achievements and victories, both at the World Centre of the Faith and around the world, and the progress it has made during the last three decades despite its modest resources, have been miraculous. In circumstances of crisis as well as of triumph, the House of Justice has been enabled to steer the Bahá'í community on the course set for it by the hand of the Almighty. All these accomplishments are entirely due to the assistance and confirmations of Bahá'u'lláh which have reached it continuously at all times, and guided every step it has taken in the execution of God's plan for mankind.

It is natural that the members of the House of Justice are always conscious of that outpouring of divine assistance; they know only too well that the decisions of the House are guided by Bahá'u'lláh. They have openly declared before their electors their sense of unworthiness to serve on that august institution, but have confidently taken on the burden of such immense responsibility in the assurance of the protection, guidance and confirmations of Bahá'u'lláh which reach them during their deliberations.

One of the most important decisions which the Universal House of Justice made soon after its election was the question of the Guardianship. Since Shoghi Effendi could not have appointed a successor to himself, the decision regarding this important matter had to be taken by this body, as there was nothing in the *Will and Testament* of 'Abdu'l-Bahá to show how to resolve a situation where there was no one to succeed Shoghi Effendi.* The following statement was issued by the House of Justice on this vital matter:

> After prayerful and careful study of the Holy Texts bearing upon the question of the appointment of the successor to Shoghi Effendi as Guardian of the Cause of God, and after prolonged consultation which included consideration of the views of the Hands of the Cause of God residing in the Holy Land, the Universal House of Justice finds that there is no way to appoint or legislate to make it possible to appoint a second Guardian to succeed Shoghi Effendi.[6]

A similar statement was issued by the House of Justice concerning the Hands of the Cause of God:

> There is no way to appoint, or to legislate to make it possible to appoint, Hands of the Cause of God.
>
> Responsibility for decisions of matters of general policy affecting the institution of the Hands of the Cause, which was formerly exercised by the beloved Guardian, now devolves upon the Universal House of Justice as the supreme and central institution of the Faith to which all must turn.[7]

We have already stated that in the absence of the Guardian, the Universal House of Justice, apart from turning to the Holy Text, consults the writings of Shoghi Effendi when it begins the process of legislation, or prepares its general communications, or makes decisions on various subjects. In this way, it ensures that its pronouncements are not in conflict with the meaning of the Holy

* See above, pp. 378–9.

Text and do not depart from the spirit of Bahá'u'lláh's revealed utterances. In the absence of the Guardian who was to have been its permanent head, the Universal House of Justice has no officers, all members having equal responsibility in consultation and other functions. This is one of its outstanding features.

Membership of the Universal House of Justice is confined to men. This guideline is taken from the explicit Writings of Bahá'u'lláh and therefore is not subject to being changed through legislation of the House of Justice. The fact that the members of the House of Justice are to be men should not be regarded as a negation of the principle of equality of men and women proclaimed by Bahá'u'lláh in His teachings. Concerning the equality of men and women, 'Abdu'l-Bahá states:

> And among the teachings of Bahá'u'lláh is the equality of women and men. The world of humanity has two wings – one is women and the other men. Not until both wings are equally developed can the bird fly. Should one wing remain weak, flight is impossible. Not until the world of women becomes equal to the world of men in the acquisition of virtues and perfections, can success and prosperity be attained as they ought to be.[8]

To appreciate this apparent contradiction, one should look at different aspects of equality. First, there is the equality of the spirit. We are told that although God has created men and women physically different, there is no difference between the soul of a man and the soul of a woman. Both have the same attributes of God and are created in His image, and this is the most important aspect of equality. 'Abdu'l-Bahá states:

> Know though, O handmaid, that in the sight of Bahá, women are accounted the same as men, and God hath created all humankind in His own image, and after His own likeness. That is, men and women alike are the revealers of His names and attributes, and from the spiritual viewpoint there is no difference between them. Whosoever draweth nearer to God, that one is the most favoured, whether man or woman. How many a handmaid, ardent and devoted, hath, within the sheltering shade of Bahá, proved superior to the men, and surpassed the famous of the earth.[9]

Another aspect of equality is that of rights and privileges. Here again 'Abdu'l-Bahá is unequivocal:

> In this Revelation of Bahá'u'lláh, the women go neck and neck with the men. In no movement will they be left behind. Their rights with men are equal in degree. They will enter all the administrative branches of politics. They will attain in all such a degree as will be considered the very highest station of the world of humanity and will take part in all affairs. Rest ye assured.[10]

But we should not confuse equality with identity of functions. For women and men to perform identical functions, as sought by many people today, is not possible in all cases. While in many functions men and women can perform equally well, there are some areas of work for which men are better suited than women, and others where women excel men. This difference of function comes more into focus when we realize that there are certain areas in which it is impossible for one sex to carry out the functions of the other; for instance, it is not possible for a male to give birth to a child.

Bahá'u'lláh, in creating the institution of the Universal House of Justice, has envisaged men to be more suited for its membership. The wisdom of this is not apparent today, because we are too close to this nascent institution. 'Abdu'l-Bahá has promised that the wisdom of this commandment of Bahá'u'lláh will become clear in the future:

> The House of Justice, however, according to the explicit text of the Law of God, is confined to men; this for a wisdom of the Lord God's, which will ere long be made manifest as clearly as the sun at high noon.[11]

The Guardian commented on this:

> The Bahá'ís should accept this statement of the Master in a spirit of deep faith, confident that there is a divine guidance and wisdom behind it which will be gradually unfolded to the eyes of the world.[12]

The Universal House of Justice has made the point that

> To the general premise that women and men have equality in the Faith, this, as often explained by 'Abdu'l-Bahá, is a fundamental principle deriving from Bahá'u'lláh and therefore His mention of the 'Men of Justice' in the *Kitáb-i-Aqdas* should be considered in light of that principle.[13]

The Seat of the Universal House of Justice is on Mount Carmel in Haifa. This was foretold by Bahá'u'lláh in the *Tablet of Carmel*, the charter for the building of the World Centre of the Faith. We have already discussed the creation of this Centre by Shoghi Effendi.* In one of his letters to the Bahá'ís of the East, he elucidates some of the significances of the Tablet of Carmel and, in particular, the passage: 'Ere long will God sail His Ark upon Thee, and will manifest the people of Bahá who have been mentioned in the Book of Names.'[14]

> In this great Tablet [of Carmel] which unveils divine mysteries and heralds the establishment of two mighty, majestic and momentous undertakings – one of which is spiritual and the other administrative, both at the World Centre of the Faith – Bahá'u'lláh refers to an 'Ark', whose dwellers are the men of the Supreme House of Justice, which, in conformity with the exact provisions of the Will and Testament of the

* See above, pp. 326–7.

Centre of the Mighty Covenant is the body which should lay down laws not explicitly revealed in the Text. In this Dispensation, these laws are destined to flow from this holy mountain, even as in the Mosaic Dispensation the law of God was promulgated from Zion. The 'sailing of the Ark' of His laws is a reference to the establishment of the Universal House of Justice, which is indeed the Seat of Legislation, one of the branches of the World Administrative Centre of the Bahá'ís on this holy mountain . . .[15]

Bahá'u'lláh and 'Abdu'l-Bahá in their Writings have counselled the Universal House of Justice to promote the best interests of mankind and to work for the betterment of the affairs of the world. In the *Kitáb-i-Aqdas*, Bahá'u'lláh thus reveals:

O ye Men of Justice! Be ye in the realm of God shepherds unto His sheep and guard them from the ravening wolves that have appeared in disguise, even as ye would guard your own sons. Thus exhorteth you the Counsellor, the Faithful.[16]

In a Tablet, the *Kalimát-i-Firdawsíyyih*, He addresses the members of the Universal House of Justice in these words:

We exhort the men of the House of Justice and command them to ensure the protection and safeguarding of men, women and children. It is incumbent upon them to have the utmost regard for the interests of the people at all times and under all conditions. Blessed is the ruler who succoureth the captive, and the rich one who careth for the poor, and the just one who secureth from the wrong doer the rights of the downtrodden, and happy the trustee who observeth that which the Ordainer, the Ancient of Days hath prescribed unto him.[17]

And in the *Tablet of Ishráqát* He reveals:

The progress of the world, the development of nations, the tranquillity of peoples, and the peace of all who dwell on earth are among the principles and ordinances of God. Religion bestoweth upon man the most precious of all gifts, offereth the cup of prosperity, imparteth eternal life, and showereth imperishable benefits upon mankind. It behoveth the chiefs and rulers of the world, and in particular the Trustees of God's House of Justice, to endeavour to the utmost of their power to safeguard its position, promote its interests and exalt its station in the eyes of the world. In like manner it is incumbent upon them to enquire into the conditions of their subjects and to acquaint themselves with the affairs and activities of the divers communities in their dominions.[18]

In His *Will and Testament*, 'Abdu'l-Bahá makes the following statement:

It is incumbent upon these members (of the Universal House of Justice) to gather in a certain place and deliberate upon all problems which have caused difference, questions that are obscure and matters that are not expressly recorded in the Book. Whatsoever they decide has the same effect as the Text itself. And inasmuch as this House of Justice hath power to enact laws that are not expressly recorded in the Book and bear upon daily transactions, so also it hath power to repeal the same. Thus, for example, the House of Justice enacteth today a certain law and enforceth it, and a hundred years hence, circumstances having profoundly changed and the conditions having altered, another House of Justice will then have power, according to the exigencies of the time, to alter that law. This it can do because that law formeth no part of the Divine Explicit Text. The House of Justice is both the initiator and the abrogator of its own laws. . . . All must seek guidance and turn unto the Centre of the Cause and the House of Justice. And he that turneth unto whatsoever else is indeed in grievous error.

He also outlines the manner of the election of the House of Justice in His *Will and Testament*.

And now, concerning the House of Justice which God hath ordained as the source of all good and freed from all error, it must be elected by universal suffrage, that is, by the believers. Its members must be manifestations of the fear of God and daysprings of knowledge and understanding, must be steadfast in God's faith and the well-wishers of all mankind. By this House is meant the Universal House of Justice, that is, in all countries a secondary House of Justice* must be instituted, and these secondary Houses of Justice must elect the members of the Universal one. Unto this body all things must be referred. It enacteth all ordinances and regulations that are not to be found in the explicit Holy Text. By this body all the difficult problems are to be resolved and the Guardian of the Cause of God is its sacred head† and the distinguished member for life of that body. Should he not attend in person its deliberations, he must appoint one to represent him. Should any of the members commit a sin, injurious to the common weal, the Guardian of the Cause of God hath at his own discretion the right to expel him,‡ whereupon the people must elect another one in his stead. This House of Justice enacteth the laws and the Government enforceth them. The legislative body must reinforce the executive, and the executive must aid and assist the legislative body so that through the close union and harmony of these two forces, the foundation of fairness and justice may become firm and strong, that all the regions of the world may become even as Paradise itself.

From the above statements made by Bahá'u'lláh and 'Abdu'l-Bahá, it is clear that the Universal House of Justice is the protector of the Covenant of Bahá'u'lláh, and the channel through which the forces of the Revelation of Bahá'u'lláh will flow to mankind. Through this august institution, the unity of the Bahá'í community and the

* National Spiritual Assembly.
† In the absence of the Guardian, the House of Justice has no officers.
‡ This function now falls upon the Universal House of Justice itself.

integrity of the Faith will be preserved. One of the causes of disunity in former Dispensations has been that the leaders of religion and men of learning have differed in their interpretations of the teachings of their faith, and through their conflicting views have created divisions within the community. But in this Dispensation the door for such controversies to take place is completely closed. Bahá'ís will give credence to the interpretations of 'Abdu'l-Bahá and Shoghi Effendi, and consider these as authentic and infallible, while any statement made by an individual which is contrary to the spirit and form of the authorized interpretations of the Word of God will not be acceptable. Furthermore, no pronouncements by the learned on various aspects of the Faith will be considered valid unless sanctioned by the Universal House of Justice. The following Text is from the pen of 'Abdu'l-Bahá:

> Briefly, this is the wisdom of referring the laws of society to the House of Justice. In the religion of Islám, similarly, not every ordinance was explicitly revealed; nay not a tenth part of a tenth part was included in the Text; although all matters of major importance were specifically referred to, there were undoubtedly thousands of laws which were unspecified. These were devised by the divines of a later age according to the laws of Islamic jurisprudence, and individual divines made conflicting deductions from the original revealed ordinances. All these were enforced. Today this process of deduction is the right of the body of the House of Justice, and the deductions and conclusions of individual learned men have no authority, unless they are endorsed by the House of Justice. The difference is precisely this, that from the conclusions and endorsements of the body of the House of Justice whose members are elected by and known to the worldwide Bahá'í community, no differences will arise; whereas the conclusions of individual divines and scholars would definitely lead to differences, and result in schism, division, and dispersion. The oneness of the Word would be destroyed, the unity of the Faith would disappear, and the edifice of the Faith of God would be shaken.[19]

The above statement must not lead the reader to think that the hands of Bahá'í scholars are tied, and that they are unable to make their own research and reach their own conclusions on matters connected with the Faith. On the contrary, every believer is free to read the Writings and make his own interpretation, as long as he makes it clear that his views are his own and are not authentic. The Universal House of Justice has clarified this subject as follows.

> A clear distinction is made in our Faith between authoritative interpretation and the interpretation or understanding that each individual arrives at for himself from his study of its teachings. While the former is confined to the Guardian, the latter, according to the guidance given to us by the Guardian himself, should by no means be suppressed. In fact such individual interpretation is considered the fruit of man's rational power

and conducive to a better understanding of the teachings, provided that no disputes or arguments arise among the friends and the individual himself understands and makes it clear that his views are merely his own. Individual interpretations continually change as one grows in comprehension of the teachings. As Shoghi Effendi wrote: 'To deepen in the Cause means to read the writings of Bahá'u'lláh and the Master so thoroughly as to be able to give it to others in its pure form. There are many who have some superficial idea of what the Cause stands for. They, therefore, present it together with all sorts of ideas that are their own. As the Cause is still in its early days we must be most careful lest we fall into this error and injure the Movement we so much adore. There is no limit to the study of the Cause. The more we read the Writings, the more truths we can find in them, the more we will see that our previous notions were erroneous.' So, although individual insights can be enlightening and helpful, they can also be misleading. The friends must therefore learn to listen to the views of others without being overawed or allowing their faith to be shaken, and to express their own views without pressing them on their fellow Bahá'ís.[20]

In every Dispensation, the Manifestation of God has promulgated a number of teachings and ordinances which may be described as the framework of that religion. These teachings have been designed by God to bring about the advancement of people who have embraced them. They are always adapted to suit the condition of the people, and are given in accordance with their capacity. As a result of the application of these teachings in their lives, the members of a religious community grow and acquire higher levels of understanding and development. In the course of their progress they eventually reach a position where the teachings of their religion no longer adequately satisfy their spiritual and mental needs. When the teachings and laws of a religion become outdated, when they are no longer practicable in a new age, the followers have arrogated to themselves the right to amend or alter these teachings so as to make them conform with new conditions prevailing at the time. But man has no right to interfere with the revealed teachings of God. Only a new Manifestation of God can abrogate the laws of a previous Dispensation and bring new laws for a new age. Otherwise, man's interference will cause the teachings of a religion to become adulterated.

Bahá'u'lláh has envisaged, and this has already become evident, that in His Dispensation man will advance and progress at an unprecedented rate, needing new laws at every stage of his development. Therefore, He has empowered the Universal House of Justice to enact secondary laws that conform with the circumstances of the time, laws which can be changed at a later time as conditions change. It must be noted, however, that the teachings, laws and ordinances which are revealed by Bahá'u'lláh Himself are unalterable until the advent of a future Manifestation of God who has the right to abrogate them. 'Abdu'l-Bahá states:

> Those matters of major importance which constitute the foundation of the Law of God are explicitly recorded in the Text, but subsidiary laws are left to the House of Justice. The wisdom of this is that the times never remain the same, for change is a necessary quality and an essential attribute of this world, and of time and place. Therefore the House of Justice will take action accordingly.[21]

We have discussed in previous chapters the gradual unfoldment of the Administrative Order and its stages of development. The first two epochs of the Formative Age during the ministry of Shoghi Effendi witnessed the laying of the foundations of the institutions of the Faith first in North America, and later during the Ten Year Crusade in almost every country of the world. With the establishment of the Universal House of Justice, the Cause of Bahá'u'lláh entered the Third Epoch of the Formative Age; this was announced in October 1963. A major achievement and special feature of this epoch was the public proclamation of the Faith in most countries of the world. The Universal House of Justice published Bahá'u'lláh's summons to the kings and rulers of the world, shared them with contemporary heads of states in 1967, and invited them to heed His warnings and exhortations. Some years later this process of proclamation was further intensified with the publication in 1985 of the message *The Promise of World Peace* addressed to the peoples of the world.

Another noteworthy development during the Third Epoch was the consolidation of the local and national institutions of the Cause, and the establishment of five Continental Boards of Counsellors whose members were to carry into the future the twin functions of the Hands of the Cause of God, namely, the protection and propagation of the Faith of Bahá'u'lláh.

A new stage in the unfoldment of the Faith was ushered in when the Universal House of Justice announced in 1986 that the Formative Age had entered its Fourth Epoch. At present the duration of this epoch is unknown, but within the short space of time since its inception, unprecedented victories have been won by Bahá'í communities in many parts of the world. To enumerate the achievements of the Faith in this short period is beyond the scope of this book. Suffice it to say that at no time in the history of the Formative Age has the Cause of Bahá'u'lláh made such remarkable progress as in these years. The marvellous advancement in the fortunes of the Faith augurs well for the future years of this epoch. Through the guidance of the Universal House of Justice, the onward march of the Faith of Bahá'u'lláh will continue, His followers believe, until such time as it will be universally recognized and its new world order firmly established throughout the world.

Envisioning the mighty victories of the future, Shoghi Effendi foretells in his letters to Persian believers that through the guidance of the Universal House of Justice, the Cause of God will be exalted and the sovereignty of Bahá'u'lláh made manifest to the peoples of the world. The following are translations of some of these letters:

> The National Spiritual Assemblies, like unto pillars will be gradually and firmly established in every country on the strong and fortified foundations of the Local Assemblies. On these pillars, the mighty Edifice, the Universal House of Justice, will be erected, raising high its noble frame above the world of existence. The unity of the followers of Bahá'u'lláh will thus be realized and fulfilled from one end of the earth to the other . . . and the living waters of everlasting life will stream forth from that fountain-head of God's World Order upon all the warring nations and peoples of the world, to wash away the evils and iniquities of the realm of dust, and heal man's age-old ills and ailments.
>
> . . . Then will the throne of Bahá'u'lláh's sovereignty be founded in the promised land and the scales of justice be raised on high. Then will the banner of the independence of the Faith be unfurled, and His Most Great Law be unveiled and rivers of laws and ordinances stream forth from this snow-white spot with all-conquering power and awe-inspiring majesty, the like of which past ages have never seen. Then will appear the truth of what was revealed by the Tongue of Grandeur: 'Call out to Zion, O Carmel, and announce the joyful tidings: He that was hidden from mortal eyes is come! His all-conquering sovereignty is manifest; His all-encompassing splendour is revealed . . . O Carmel . . . Well is it with him that circleth around thee, that proclaimeth the revelation of thy glory, and recounteth that which the bounty of the Lord, thy God, hath showered upon thee . . . Ere long will God sail His Ark upon thee, and will manifest the people of Bahá who have been mentioned in the Book of Names.' . . . Through it the pillars of the Faith on this earth will be firmly established and its hidden powers be revealed, its signs shine forth, its banners be unfurled and its light be shed upon all peoples.[22]

CHAPTER THIRTY-SIX

The Unfoldment of the Covenant

THE Covenant of Bahá'u'lláh is a growing organism, which has existed since the very beginning of Bahá'u'lláh's Revelation. In one of His Tablets 'Abdu'l-Bahá states that the Sun of Truth [Bahá'u'lláh] shone forth and its effulgent rays illumined the world of being, and that the first ray that shed its light was that of the Covenant.[1] There are several passages revealed by Bahá'u'lláh in the *Hidden Words* in the early years of His Ministry which refer to the Covenant, a Covenant which was made explicit years later through the revelation of the *Kitáb-i-'Ahd*. One such passage is the following:

> *O My Friends!*
> Call ye to mind that covenant ye have entered into with Me upon Mount Paran, situate within the hallowed precincts of Zaman. I have taken to witness the concourse on high and the dwellers in the city of eternity, yet now none do I find faithful unto the covenant. Of a certainty pride and rebellion have effaced it from the hearts, in such wise that no trace thereof remaineth. Yet knowing this, I waited and disclosed it not.[2]

'Abdu'l-Bahá states in a Tablet[3] that the Covenant upon Mount Pa'rán refers to the Covenant of Bahá'u'lláh written by the Exalted Pen in the Holy Land, and announced there after His ascension. Another passage which alludes to the Covenant of Bahá'u'lláh is the following:

> *O My Friends!*
> Have ye forgotten that true and radiant morn, when in those hallowed and blessed surroundings ye were all gathered in My presence beneath the shade of the tree of life, which is planted in the all-glorious paradise? Awe-struck ye listened as I gave utterance to these three most holy words: O friends! Prefer not your will to Mine, never desire that which I have not desired for you, and approach Me not with lifeless hearts, defiled with worldly desires and cravings. Would ye but sanctify your souls, ye would at this present hour recall that place and those surroundings, and the truth of My utterance should be made evident unto all of you.[4]

In one of His Tablets 'Abdu'l-Bahá states:

The Lord, the All-Glorified, hath, beneath the shade of the Tree of Anísa [tree of life] made a new Covenant and established a great Testament.[5]

From the above statements we may deduce that the unfoldment of the Covenant of Bahá'u'lláh was a continuing process during the forty years of Bahá'u'lláh's ministry. 'Abdu'l-Bahá, the Centre of the Covenant, was nurtured by the hand of Bahá'u'lláh who progressively bestowed upon Him the powers inherent within that Covenant. The exalted titles He conferred upon 'Abdu'l-Bahá while He was in His early teens, the Tablets in which He glorified His station, the clear allusions He made to Him in the *Kitáb-i-Aqdas* as the Centre of His Covenant and the Interpreter of His teachings, all indicate that during Bahá'u'lláh's lifetime His Covenant was progressively developing in its embryonic form; it was born when the *Kitáb-i-'Ahd* was read and its contents became known.

As we have stated in previous chapters, the appointment of 'Abdu'l-Bahá as the Centre of the Covenant opened a new chapter in the history of the Faith and ushered in the third and last epoch of the Heroic or Apostolic Age of the dispensation of Bahá'u'lláh. This period witnessed the gradual unfoldment of the institution of the Covenant, despite the most relentless onslaught by a treacherous group of Covenant-breakers who did everything in their power to destroy that most precious heritage which Bahá'u'lláh had bequeathed to His followers.

After the passing of 'Abdu'l-Bahá, the Covenant-breakers continued their ruthless attacks against the Guardian of the Cause. But while he suffered immensely, the Covenant of Bahá'u'lláh triumphed and gave birth to the institutions of the Administrative Order – channels through which the forces of the Revelation of Bahá'u'lláh flow to mankind, and a shell within whose core His most precious Faith will be for all times protected. Indeed, it has been through the rising institutions of the Administrative Order, acting as a shield safeguarding the unity of the Bahá'í community, that the fortunes of the Covenant-breakers since the establishment of the Universal House of Justice have steadily declined.

Gone the days when after the ascension of Bahá'u'lláh an ignoble band of faithless men and women, including most members of His family, headed by no less a person than Bahá'u'lláh's son, Mírzá Muḥammad-'Alí, rose up against the Master with all their power and prestige and tried to wrest from Him the reins of the Cause of God which had been entrusted to Him by His heavenly Father.

Gone the days that some of the most erudite and outstanding teachers of the Faith, together with a number of influential men who ranked foremost in the community, rebelled against 'Abdu'l-Bahá, most viciously attacked that newly born institution of the Covenant, and caused grievous convulsions within the community of the Most Great Name.

Gone the days when falsehoods and outrageous misrepresentations against the Centre of the Covenant by Mírzá Muḥammad-'Alí gained credibility among the people, both within and without this small and seemingly fragile community.

Gone the days when the Master was maliciously accused in public by His unfaithful brothers of the most heinous crimes, causing thereby alarm and apprehension within government circles in the Holy Land, and further afield in the heart and centre of the Ottoman Empire.

Gone the days that, through his persistent machinations and intrigues, the Arch-breaker of the Covenant succeeded at last in poisoning the mind of the Sultan of Turkey to such an extent that he ordered 'Abdu'l-Bahá's incarceration within the walls of the Prison City, an ordeal which He endured for eight years.

And gone the days when the youthful Guardian of the Cause was subjected to untold sufferings at the hands of the members of 'Abdu'l-Bahá's family and the old Covenant-breakers, who, assisted by a number of erstwhile outstanding teachers of the Faith – then violators of the Covenant – opposed him for over three decades.

Now, with the establishment of the Universal House of Justice, the situation is changed, and the precious institution of the Covenant bequeathed by Bahá'u'lláh to His followers has been greatly fortified. Although there may always be a few souls from among the followers who will, from time to time, rebel against the Cause of God and will arise to break the Covenant, yet they will never be able to divide the Faith into sects and break up the unity of its community. The truth of this may be evidenced in the history of the Faith. For almost one hundred years, desperate endeavours were made by various groups of Covenant-breakers who launched fierce onslaughts against the Cause of Bahá'u'lláh in order to bring about schism within its world-wide community, and yet their efforts were in vain and they miserably failed in their objectives. Bahá'u'lláh has thus clearly proven that 'this is a day that shall not be followed by night'.

Today, the activities of a small number of misguided individuals, mostly residing in North America, who follow in the footsteps of Mason Remey and who are trying to disrupt the unity of the Bahá'í community, have proved to be an utter failure and of no significance whatsoever. Their case is truly pathetic, their argument most feeble and their influence in the Bahá'í community almost non-existent. A major cause of their ineffectiveness is the progressive unfoldment of the Covenant of Bahá'u'lláh, and the organic growth and strengthening of its world-wide institutions culminating in the establishment of the Universal House of Justice.

'Abdu'l-Bahá has likened the activities of the Covenant-breakers to the movements of a tiny ant, as compared with the irresistible onward march of the Faith motivated by the power of the Covenant, a power which has, as testified by 'Abdu'l-Bahá, encompassed the world. This Covenant has given birth to an Administrative Order which may be regarded as the embryo of the new world order to be established in the fullness of time when the generality of mankind will have recognized Bahá'u'lláh and, by turning to Him, will have achieved the unity of the human race on this planet.

The Administrative Order was conceived by the generating influence of the Revelation of Bahá'u'lláh. It is growing at the present time in the womb of this turbulent age. The institutions of the Faith – the organs of this Administrative Order – are today embryonic in nature. Today the generality of mankind is unaware that human society is in a state of pregnancy, bearing this precious child of the new world order within its womb. Whenever the time comes that it is destined to lay down its burden, the institutions of the Faith will emerge from obscurity and a new era will begin, signalizing the birth of a new order.

Such a process will also bring in its wake the pangs of birth which humanity must sooner or later experience with all the sufferings they entail. In the following passage written in 1957, Shoghi Effendi foreshadows dire afflictions which will envelop humanity as it is led to its ultimate salvation:

> Against the background of these afflictive disturbances – the turmoil and tribulations of a travailing age – we may well ponder the portentous prophecies uttered well-nigh fourscore years ago, by the Author of our faith, as well as the dire predictions made by Him Who is the unerring Interpreter of His teachings, all foreshadowing a universal commotion, of a scope and intensity unparalleled in the annals of mankind.
>
> The violent derangement of the world's equilibrium; the trembling that will seize the limbs of mankind; the radical transformation of human society; the rolling up of the present-day Order; the fundamental changes affecting the structure of government; the weakening of the pillars of religion; the rise of dictatorships; the spread of tyranny; the fall of monarchies; the decline of ecclesiastical institutions; the increase of anarchy and chaos; the extension and consolidation of the Movement of the Left; the fanning into flame of the smouldering fire of racial strife; the development of infernal engines of war; the burning of cities; the contamination of the atmosphere of the earth – these stand out as the signs and portents that must either herald or accompany the retributive calamity which, as decreed by Him Who is the Judge and Redeemer of

> mankind, must, sooner or later, afflict a society which, for the most part, and for over a century, has turned a deaf ear to the Voice of God's Messenger in this day – a calamity which must purge the human race of the dross of its age-long corruptions, and weld its component parts into a firmly-knit world-embracing Fellowship – a Fellowship destined, in the fullness of time, to be incorporated in the framework, and to be galvanized by the spiritualizing influences, of a mysteriously expanding, divinely appointed Order, and to flower, in the course of future Dispensations, into a Civilization, the like of which mankind has, at no stage in its evolution, witnessed.[6]

At the present time the local and national institutions of the Faith – the organs of the embryonic new world order – are in obscurity. Although the Faith itself has been proclaimed in many countries, these institutions by virtue of their embryonic state are not yet known to the public, who are unaware of the major role these institutions will play in the future, and of their transformation in the fullness of time into Houses of Justice when they will direct the affairs of humanity in conformity with the teachings of Bahá'u-'lláh.

The Administrative Order of Bahá'u'lláh has been developing since the inception of the Formative Age in 1921. It has now acquired many of its organs, the local, national and international institutions widely spread throughout the world. Today, the embryonic nature of these institutions is reflected in the immaturity and weakness of the local and national Spiritual Assemblies. Although these have deficiencies and imperfections at the present time, they are pulsating with a new life and contain within them the promise of the future, when they will evolve into rising institutions of Bahá'u'lláh's new world order for mankind.

No one knows when this embryonic order may pass from the obscurity of the womb-world and emerge as a new-born instrument destined to grow and mature into a world order in that distant future when the unity of mankind will have been achieved and the Most Great Peace established. We note that in nature a child is born some time after all its limbs and organs are formed in the womb of its mother. If this principle is applicable to the development of the Administrative Order, we may deduce that its birth will take place when all the institutions of the Faith have been formed in their embryonic condition.

Today, in the Fourth Epoch of the Formative Age, almost all the necessary institutions of the Faith have been created. A vast network of local Spiritual Assemblies covers the surface of the planet. Likewise, National Spiritual Assemblies have also been formed in almost every country of the world, and in all continents of the globe.

Shoghi Effendi, Guardian of the Cause of God

The Shrine of Bahá'u'lláh and the Mansion of Bahjí
surrounded by the unsightly residences of the Covenant-breakers
At the extreme right is the Bahjí Pilgrim House

The Pilgrim House at Bahjí

Views of the Mansion of Bahjí in ruins

The Mansion of Bahjí restored to its original condition

A view of the formal gardens surrounding the Shrine of Bahá'u'lláh

The Shrine of Bahá'u'lláh

Entrance to the Shrine of Bahá'u'lláh

The Mansion of Mazra'ih in olden times

The Mansion of Mazra'ih after restoration

The International Archives Building

The resting-places of the Purest Branch and Navváb situated in the Monument Gardens

The Hands of the Cause of God assembled in the Holy Land in 1959

The resting-place of the Greatest Holy Leaf
In the background is the Seat of the Universal House of Justice

The international institutions of the Faith are also functioning effectively. But there is one remaining organ of the Administrative Order which is not yet fully established, namely, the world's administrative Centre of the Faith on Mount Carmel. Not until this vital agency of the Faith ordained by Bahá'u'lláh in the *Tablet of Carmel* comes into being can we say that all the component parts of the Administrative Order of Bahá'u'lláh have been created. Shoghi Effendi confirms this view in one of his most illuminating letters in which he portrays a few glimpses of the future glory of the world order of Bahá'u'lláh:

> The raising of this Edifice* will in turn herald the construction, in the course of successive epochs of the Formative Age of the Faith, of several other structures, which will serve as the administrative seats of such divinely appointed institutions as the Guardianship, the Hands of the Cause, and the Universal House of Justice. These Edifices will, in the shape of a far-flung arc, and following a harmonizing style of architecture, surround the resting-places of the Greatest Holy Leaf, ranking as foremost among the members of her sex in the Bahá'í Dispensation, of her Brother, offered up as a ransom by Bahá'u'lláh for the quickening of the world and its unification, and of their Mother, proclaimed by Him to be His chosen 'consort in all the worlds of God'. The ultimate completion of this stupendous undertaking will mark the culmination of the development of a world-wide divinely-appointed Administrative Order whose beginnings may be traced as far back as the concluding years of the Heroic Age of the Faith.[7]

The stage at which the culmination of the development of the Administrative Order, coinciding with the completion of the buildings on the Arc, takes place, resembles the stage at which a child in the womb of his mother has acquired all the limbs and organs he needs, and is ready to be born.

Having described the relationship between the completion of the buildings of the World Administrative Centre on Mount Carmel and the development of the Administrative Order, Shoghi Effendi in this same letter further links this process with the evolution of local and national institutions of the Faith. He continues:

> This vast and irresistible process, unexampled in the spiritual history of mankind . . . will synchronize with two no less significant developments – the establishment of the Lesser Peace† and the evolution of Bahá'í national and local institutions – the one outside and the other within the Bahá'í world . . .[8]

* A reference to the International Archives building which was being constructed by Shoghi Effendi. It is situated at one end of the Arc on Mount Carmel.

† See above, p. 327.

Could this evolution mentioned by Shoghi Effendi be the same process, referred to in the preceding pages, as the stage at which the institutions of the Faith will emerge from obscurity and progressively assume greater involvement in human society? It is of great significance that he associates this stage of evolution with the founding of the Lesser Peace, which 'Abdu'l-Bahá states will be established in the twentieth century. The evolution of the institutions of the Faith and their greater involvement in human affairs, a process which is destined to take place in the near future, must not be confused with the establishment of the World Order of Bahá'u'lláh in the distant future. This process, Shoghi Effendi explains, 'will attain its final consummation in the Golden Age of the Faith, through the raising of the standard of the Most Great Peace and the emergence, in the plenitude of its power and glory, of the focal Centre of the agencies constituting the World Order of Bahá'u'lláh'.[9]

The Revelation of Bahá'u'lláh vouchsafed by the Almighty to the human race is preserved within the sanctuary of His Covenant. This mighty instrument, acting as a shield, protects the Cause of Bahá'u'lláh and all its institutions, enabling them to grow and develop. It is the begetter of the unity of the Faith, the upholder of its integrity, the promoter of its teachings, and the guarantor of its incorruptibility.

Shoghi Effendi, in the masterly style of his writings, describes the potentialities of the Covenant of Bahá'u'lláh and the unique nature of the Administrative Order in these words:

> The Covenant of Bahá'u'lláh had been instituted solely through the direct operation of His Will and purpose. The Will and Testament of 'Abdu'l-Bahá, on the other hand, may be regarded as the offspring resulting from that mystic intercourse between Him Who had generated the forces of a God-given Faith and the One Who had been made its sole Interpreter and was recognized as its perfect Exemplar. The creative energies unleashed by the Originator of the Law of God in this age gave birth, through their impact upon the mind of Him Who had been chosen as its unerring Expounder, to that Instrument, the vast implications of which the present generation, even after the lapse of twenty-three years, is still incapable of fully apprehending. This Instrument can, if we would correctly appraise it, no more be divorced from the One Who provided the motivating impulse for its creation than from Him Who directly conceived it. The purpose of the Author of the Bahá'í Revelation had, as already observed, been so thoroughly infused into the mind of 'Abdu'l-Bahá, and His Spirit had so profoundly impregnated His being, and their aims and motives been so completely blended, that to dissociate the doctrine laid down by the former from the supreme act associated with the mission of the latter would be tantamount to a repudiation of one of the most fundamental verities of the Faith.

The Administrative Order which this historic Document has established, it should be noted, is, by virtue of its origin and character, unique in the annals of the world's religious systems. No Prophet before Bahá'u'lláh, it can be confidently asserted, not even Muḥammad Whose Book clearly lays down the laws and ordinances of the Islamic Dispensation, has established, authoritatively and in writing, anything comparable to the Administrative Order which the authorized Interpreter of Bahá'u'lláh's teachings has instituted, an Order which, by virtue of the administrative principles which its Author has formulated, the institutions He has established, and the right of interpretation with which He has invested its Guardian, must and will, in a manner unparalleled in any previous religion, safeguard from schism the Faith from which it has sprung. Nor is the principle governing its operation similar to that which underlies any system, whether theocratic or otherwise, which the minds of men have devised for the government of human institutions. Neither in theory nor in practice can the Administrative Order of the Faith of Bahá'u'lláh be said to conform to any type of democratic government, to any system of autocracy, to any purely aristocratic order, or to any of the various theocracies, whether Jewish, Christian or Islamic which mankind has witnessed in the past. It incorporates within its structure certain elements which are to be found in each of the three recognized forms of secular government, is devoid of the defects which each of them inherently possesses, and blends the salutary truths which each undoubtedly contains without vitiating in any way the integrity of the Divine verities on which it is essentially founded. The hereditary authority which the Guardian of the Administrative Order is called upon to exercise, and the right of the interpretation of the Holy Writ solely conferred upon him; the powers and prerogatives of the Universal House of Justice, possessing the exclusive right to legislate on matters not explicitly revealed in the Most Holy Book; the ordinance exempting its members from any responsibility to those whom they represent, and from the obligation to conform to their views, convictions or sentiments; the specific provisions requiring the free and democratic election by the mass of the faithful of the Body that constitutes the sole legislative organ in the world-wide Bahá'í community – these are among the features which combine to set apart the Order identified with the Revelation of Bahá'u'lláh from any of the existing systems of human government.[10]

APPENDIX I

The Will and Testament of 'Abdu'l-Bahá

ALL-PRAISE to Him Who, by the Shield of His Covenant, hath guarded the Temple of His Cause from the darts of doubtfulness, Who by the Hosts of His Testament hath preserved the Sanctuary of His most Beneficent Law and protected His Straight and Luminous Path, staying thereby the onslaught of the company of Covenant-breakers, that have threatened to subvert His Divine Edifice; Who hath watched over His Mighty Stronghold and All-Glorious Faith, through the aid of men whom the slander of the slanderer affect not, whom no earthly calling, glory and power can turn aside from the Covenant of God and His Testament, established firmly by His clear and manifest words, writ and revealed by His All-Glorious Pen and recorded in the Preserved Tablet.

Salutation and praise, blessing and glory rest upon that primal branch of the Divine and Sacred Lote-Tree, grown out, blest, tender, verdant and flourishing from the Twin Holy Trees; the most wondrous, unique and priceless pearl that doth gleam from out the Twin surging seas; upon the offshoots of the Tree of Holiness, the twigs of the Celestial Tree, they that in the Day of the Great Dividing have stood fast and firm in the Covenant; upon the Hands (pillars) of the Cause of God that have diffused widely the Divine Fragrances, declared His Proofs, proclaimed His Faith, published abroad His Law, detached themselves from all things but Him, stood for righteousness in this world, and kindled the Fire of the Love of God in the very hearts and souls of His servants; upon them that have believed, rested assured, stood steadfast in His Covenant and followed the Light that after my passing shineth from the Dayspring of Divine Guidance – for behold! he is the blest and sacred bough that hath branched out from the Twin Holy Trees. Well is it with him that seeketh the shelter of his shade that shadoweth all mankind.

O ye beloved of the Lord! The greatest of all things is the protection of the True Faith of God, the preservation of His Law, the safeguarding of His Cause and service unto His Word. Ten thousand souls have shed streams of their sacred blood in this path, their precious lives they offered in sacrifice unto Him, hastened wrapt in holy ecstasy unto the glorious field of martyrdom, upraised the Standard of God's Faith and writ with their life-blood upon the Tablet of the world the verses of His Divine Unity. The sacred breast of His Holiness, the Exalted One (may my life be a sacrifice unto Him), was made a target to many a dart of woe, and in Mázindarán, the blessed feet of the Abhá Beauty (may my life be offered up for His loved ones) were so grievously scourged as to bleed and be sore wounded. His neck also was put into captive chains and His feet made fast in the stocks. In every hour, for a period of fifty years, a new trial and calamity befell Him and fresh afflictions and cares beset Him. One of them: after having suffered intense vicissitudes, He was made homeless and a wanderer and fell a victim to still new vexations and troubles. In 'Iráq, the Day-Star of the world was so exposed to the wiles of the people of malice as to be eclipsed in splendour. Later on He was sent an exile to the Great City

(Constantinople) and thence to the Land of Mystery (Adrianople), whence grievously wronged, He was eventually transferred to the Most Great Prison ('Akká). He Whom the world hath wronged (may my life be offered up for His loved ones) was four times banished from city to city, till at last, condemned to perpetual confinement, He was incarcerated in this prison, the prison of highway robbers, of brigands and of man-slayers. All this is but one of the trials that have afflicted the Blessed Beauty, the rest being even as grievous as this.

And still another of His trials was the hostility, the flagrant injustice, the iniquity and rebellion of Mírzá Yaḥyá. Although that Wronged One, that Prisoner, had through His loving-kindness nurtured him in His own bosom ever since his early years, had showered at every moment His tender care upon him, exalted his name, shielded him from every misfortune, endeared him to them of this world and the next, and despite the firm exhortations and counsels of His Holiness, the Exalted One (the Báb) and His clear and conclusive warning; – 'Beware, beware, lest the Nineteen Letters of the Living and that which hath been revealed in the Bayán veil thee!' yet notwithstanding this, Mírzá Yaḥyá denied Him, dealt falsely with Him, believed Him not, sowed the seeds of doubt, closed his eyes to His manifest verses and turned aside therefrom. Would that he had been content therewith! Nay, he even attempted to shed the sacred blood (of Bahá'u'lláh) and then raised a great clamour and tumult around him, attributing unto Bahá'u'lláh malevolence and cruelty towards himself. What sedition he stirred up and what a storm of mischief he raised whilst in the Land of Mystery (Adrianople)! At last, he wrought that which caused the Day-Star of the world to be sent an exile to this, the Most Great Prison, and sorely wronged, and in the West of this Great Prison He did set.

O ye that stand fast and firm in the Covenant! The Centre of Sedition, the Prime Mover of mischief, Mírzá Muḥammad-'Alí, hath passed out from under the shadow of the Cause, hath broken the Covenant, hath falsified the Holy Text, hath inflicted a grievous loss upon the true Faith of God, hath scattered His people, hath with bitter rancour endeavoured to hurt 'Abdu'l-Bahá and hath assailed with the utmost enmity this servant of the Sacred Threshold. Every dart he seized and hurled to pierce the breast of this wronged servant, no wound did he neglect to grievously inflict upon me, no venom did he spare but he poisoned therewith the life of this hapless one. I swear by the most holy Abhá Beauty and by the Light shining from His Holiness, the Exalted One (may my soul be a sacrifice for Their lowly servants), that because of this iniquity the dwellers in the Pavilion of the Abhá Kingdom have bewailed, the Celestial Concourse is lamenting, the Immortal Maids of Heaven in the All-Highest Paradise have raised their plaintive cries and the angelic company sighed and uttered their moanings. So grievous the deeds of this iniquitous person became that he struck with his axe at the root of the Blessed Tree, dealt a heavy blow at the Temple of the Cause of God, deluged with tears of blood the eyes of the loved ones of the Blessed Beauty, cheered and encouraged the enemies of the One True God, by his repudiation of the Covenant turned many a seeker after Truth aside from the Cause of God, revived the blighted hopes of Yaḥyá's following, made himself detested, caused the enemies of the Greatest Name to become audacious and arrogant, put aside the firm and conclusive verses and sowed the seeds of doubt. Had not the promised aid of the Ancient Beauty been graciously vouchsafed at every moment to this one, unworthy though he be, he surely would have destroyed, nay exterminated the Cause of God and utterly subverted the Divine Edifice. But, praised be the Lord, the triumphant assistance of the Abhá Kingdom was received, the hosts of the Realm above hastened to bestow victory. The Cause of God was promoted far and wide, the call of the True One was noised abroad, ears in all regions were inclined to the Word of God, His standard was unfurled, the ensigns of

Holiness gloriously waved aloft and the verses celebrating His Divine Unity were chanted. Now, that the true Faith of God may be shielded and protected, His Law guarded and preserved and His Cause remain safe and secure, it is incumbent upon everyone to hold fast unto the Text of the clear and firmly established blessed verse, revealed about him. None other transgression greater than his can be ever imagined. He (Bahá'u'lláh) sayeth, glorious and holy is His Word:– 'My foolish loved ones have regarded him even as my partner, have kindled sedition in the land and they verily are the mischief-makers.' Consider, how foolish are the people! They that have been in His (Bahá'u'lláh's) Presence and beheld His Countenance, have nevertheless noised abroad such idle talk, until, exalted be His explicit words, He said:– 'Should he for a moment pass out from under the shadow of the Cause, he surely shall be brought to naught.' Reflect! What stress He layeth upon one moment's deviation: that is, were he to incline a hair's breadth to the right or to the left, his deviation would be clearly established and his utter nothingness made manifest. And now ye are witnessing how the wrath of God hath from all sides afflicted him and how day by day he is speeding towards destruction. Ere long will ye behold him and his associates, outwardly and inwardly, condemned to utter ruin.

What deviation can be greater than breaking the Covenant of God! What deviation can be greater than interpolating and falsifying the words and verses of the Sacred Text, even as testified and declared by Mírzá Badí'u'lláh! What deviation can be greater than calumniating the Centre of the Covenant himself! What deviation can be more glaring than spreading broadcast false and foolish reports touching the Temple of God's Testament! What deviation can be more grievous than decreeing the death of the Centre of the Covenant, supported by the holy verse:– 'He that layeth a claim ere the passing of a thousand years . . .', whilst he (Muḥammad-'Alí) without shame in the days of the Blessed Beauty had advanced such a claim as this and been confuted by Him in the aforementioned manner, the text of his claim being still extant in his own handwriting and bearing his own seal. What deviation can be more complete than falsely accusing the loved ones of God! What deviation can be more evil than causing their imprisonment and incarceration! What deviation can be more severe than delivering into the hands of the government the Holy Writings and Epistles, that haply they (the government) might arise intent upon the death of this wronged one! What deviation can be more violent than threatening the ruin of the Cause of God, forging and slanderously falsifying letters and documents so that this might perturb and alarm the government and lead to the shedding of the blood of this wronged one, – such letters and documents being now in the possession of the government! What deviation can be more odious than his iniquity and rebellion! What deviation can be more shameful than dispersing the gathering of the people of salvation! What deviation can be more infamous than the vain and feeble interpretations of the people of doubt! What deviation can be more wicked than joining hands with strangers and with the enemies of God!

A few months ago, in concert with others, he that hath broken the Covenant, hath prepared a document teeming with calumny and slander wherein, the Lord forbid, among many similar slanderous charges, 'Abdu'l-Bahá is deemed a deadly enemy, the ill-wisher of the Crown. They so perturbed the minds of the members of the Imperial Government that at last a Committee of Investigation was sent from the seat of His Majesty's Government which, violating every rule of justice and equity that befit His Imperial Majesty, nay, with the most glaring injustice, proceeded with its investigations. The ill-wishers of the One True God surrounded them on every side and explained and excessively enlarged upon the text of the document whilst they (the members of the Committee) in their turn blindly acquiesced. One of their many calumnies was that this servant had raised aloft a banner in this city, had summoned the people together under it, had established a new sovereignty for himself, had erected upon Mount Carmel a mighty stronghold, had rallied around him all the peoples of the land and made them obedient to him, had caused disruption in the Faith if Islám, had covenanted with the following of Christ and, God forbid, had purposed to cause the gravest breach in the mighty power of the Crown. May the Lord protect us from such atrocious falsehoods!

According to the direct and sacred command of God we are forbidden to utter slander, are commanded to show forth peace and amity, are exhorted to rectitude of conduct, straightforwardness and harmony with all the kindreds and peoples of the world. We must obey and be the well-wishers of the governments of the land, regard disloyalty unto a just king as disloyalty to God Himself and wishing evil to the government a transgression of the Cause of God. With these final and decisive words, how can it be that these imprisoned ones should indulge in such vain fancies; incarcerated, how could they show forth such disloyalty! But alas! The Committee of Investigation hath approved and confirmed these calumnies of my brother and ill-wishers and submitted them to the presence of His Majesty the Sovereign. Now at this moment a fierce storm is raging around this prisoner who awaiteth, be it favourable or unfavourable, the gracious will of His Majesty, may the Lord aid him by His grace to be just. In whatsoever condition he may be, with absolute calm and quietness, 'Abdu'l-Bahá is ready for self-sacrifice and is wholly resigned and submitted to His Will. What transgression can be more abominable, more odious, more wicked than this!

In like manner, the focal Centre of Hate, hath purposed to put 'Abdu'l-Bahá to death and this is supported by the testimony written by Mírzá Shu'á'u'lláh himself and is here enclosed. It is evident and indisputable that they are privily and with the utmost subtlety engaged in conspiring against me. The following are his very words written him in this letter:– 'I curse at every moment him that hath kindled this discord, imprecate in these words "Lord! have no mercy upon him" and I hope ere long God will make manifest the one that shall have no pity on him, who now weareth another garb and about whom I cannot any more explain.' Reference he doth make by these words to the sacred verse that beginneth as follows:– 'He that layeth a claim ere the passing of a thousand years . . . ' Reflect! How intent they are upon the death of 'Abdu'l-Bahá! Ponder in your hearts upon the phrase 'I cannot any more explain' and realize what schemes they are devising for this purpose. They fear lest, too fully explained, the letter might fall into alien hands and their schemes be foiled and frustrated. The phrase is only foretelling good tidings to come, namely that regarding this all requisite arrangements have been made.

O God, my God! Thou seest this wronged servant of Thine, held fast in the talons of ferocious lions, of ravening wolves, of bloodthirsty beasts. Graciously assist me, through my love for Thee, that I may drink deep of the chalice that brimmeth over with faithfulness to Thee and is filled with Thy bountiful Grace; so that, fallen upon the dust, I may sink prostrate and senseless whilst my vesture is dyed crimson with my blood. This is my wish, my heart's desire, my hope, my pride, my glory. Grant, O Lord my God, and my Refuge, that in my last hour, my end may even as musk shed its fragrance of glory! Is there a bounty greater than this? Nay, by Thy Glory! I call Thee to witness that no day passeth but that I quaff my fill from this cup, so grievous are the misdeeds wrought by them that have broken the Covenant, kindled discord, showed their malice, stirred sedition in the land and dishonoured Thee amidst Thy servants. Lord! Shield Thou from these Covenant-breakers the mighty Stronghold of Thy Faith and protect Thy secret Sanctuary from the onslaught of the ungodly. Thou art in truth the Mighty, the Powerful, the Gracious, the Strong.

In short, O ye beloved of the Lord! The Centre of Sedition, Mírzá Muḥammad-'Alí, in accordance with the decisive words of God and by reason of his boundless transgression, hath grievously fallen and been cut off from the Holy Tree. Verily, we wronged them not, but they have wronged themselves!

O God, my God! Shield Thy trusted servants from the evils of self and passion, protect them with the watchful eye of Thy loving kindness from all rancour, hate and envy, shelter them in the impregnable stronghold of Thy care and, safe from the darts of doubtfulness, make them the manifestations of Thy glorious Signs, illumine their faces with the effulgent rays shed from the Dayspring of Thy Divine Unity, gladden their hearts with the verses revealed from Thy Holy Kingdom, strengthen their loins by Thy all-swaying power that cometh from Thy Realm of Glory. Thou art the All-Bountiful, the Protector, the Almighty, the Gracious!

O ye that stand fast in the Covenant! When the hour cometh that this wronged and broken-winged bird will have taken its flight unto the celestial Concourse, when it will have hastened to the Realm of the Unseen and its mortal frame will have been either lost or hidden neath the dust, it is incumbent upon the Afnán, that are steadfast in the Covenant of God, and have branched from the Tree of Holiness; the Hands, (pillars) of the Cause of God (the glory of the Lord rest upon them), and all the friends and loved ones, one and all to bestir themselves and arise with heart and soul and in one accord, to diffuse the sweet savours of God, to teach His Cause and promote His Faith. It behooveth them not to rest for a moment, neither to seek repose. They must disperse themselves in every land, pass by every clime and travel throughout all regions. Bestirred, without rest and steadfast to the end they must raise in every land the triumphal cry 'O Thou the Glory of Glories!' (Yá Bahá'u'l-Abhá), must achieve renown in the world wherever they go, must burn brightly even as a candle in every meeting and must kindle the flame of Divine love in every assembly; that the light of truth may rise resplendent in the midmost heart of the world, that throughout the East and throughout the West a vast concourse may gather under the shadow of the Word of God, that the sweet savours of holiness may be diffused, that faces may shine radiantly, hearts be filled with the Divine spirit and souls be made heavenly.

In these days, the most important of all things is the guidance of the nations and peoples of the world. Teaching the Cause is of utmost importance for it is the head corner-stone of the foundation itself. This wronged servant has spent his days and nights in promoting the Cause and urging the peoples to service. He rested not a moment, till the fame of the Cause of God was noised abroad in the world and the celestial strains from the Abhá Kingdom roused the East and the West. The beloved of God must also follow the same example. This is the secret of faithfulness, this is the requirement of servitude to the Threshold of Bahá!

The disciples of Christ forgot themselves and all earthly things, forsook all their cares and belongings, purged themselves of self and passion and with absolute detachment scattered far and wide and engaged in calling the peoples of the world to the Divine Guidance, till at last they made the world another world, illumined the surface of the earth and even to their last hour proved self-sacrificing in the pathway of that Beloved One of God. Finally in various lands they suffered glorious martyrdom. Let them that are men of action follow in their footsteps!

O my loving friends! After the passing away of this wronged one, it is incumbent upon the Aghṣán (Branches), the Afnán (Twigs) of the Sacred Lote-Tree, the Hands (pillars) of the Cause of God and the loved ones of the Abhá Beauty to turn unto Shoghi Effendi – the youthful branch branched from the two hallowed and sacred Lote-Trees and the fruit grown from the union of the two offshoots of the Tree of Holiness, – as he is the sign of God, the chosen branch, the guardian of the Cause of

God, he unto whom all the Aghṣán, the Afnán, the Hands of the Cause of God and His loved ones must turn. He is the expounder of the words of God and after him will succeed the first-born of his lineal descendents.

The sacred and youthful branch, the guardian of the Cause of God as well as the Universal House of Justice, to be universally elected and established, are both under the care and protection of the Abhá Beauty, under the shelter and unerring guidance of His Holiness, the Exalted One (may my life be offered up for them both). Whatsoever they decide is of God. Whoso obeyeth him not, neither obeyeth them, hath not obeyed God; whoso rebelleth against him and against them hath rebelled against God; whoso opposeth him hath opposed God; whoso contendeth with them hath contended with God; whoso disputeth with him hath disputed with God; whoso denieth him hath denied God; whoso disbelieveth in him hath disbelieved in God; whoso deviateth, separateth himself and turneth aside from him hath in truth deviated, separated himself and turned aside from God. May the wrath, the fierce indignation, the vengeance of God rest upon him! The mighty stronghold shall remain impregnable and safe through obedience to him who is the guardian of the Cause of God. It is incumbent upon the members of the House of Justice, upon all the Aghṣán, the Afnán, the Hands of the Cause of God to show their obedience, submissiveness and subordination unto the guardian of the Cause of God, to turn unto him and be lowly before him. He that opposeth him hath opposed the True One, will make a breach in the Cause of God, will subvert His Word and will become a manifestation of the Centre of Sedition. Beware, beware, lest the days after the ascension (of Bahá'u'lláh) be repeated when the Centre of Sedition waxed haughty and rebellious and with Divine Unity for his excuse deprived himself and perturbed and poisoned others. No doubt every vain-glorious one that purposeth dissension and discord will not openly declare his evil purposes, nay rather, even as impure gold, would he seize upon divers measures and various pretexts that he may separate the gathering of the people of Bahá. My object is to show that the Hands of the Cause of God must be ever watchful and so soon as they find anyone beginning to oppose and protest against the guardian of the Cause of God, cast him out from the congregation of the people of Bahá and in no wise accept any excuse from him. How often hath grievous error been disguised in the garb of truth, that it might sow the seeds of doubt in the hearts of men!

O ye beloved of the Lord! It is incumbent upon the guardian of the Cause of God to appoint in his own life-time him that shall become his successor, that differences may not arise after his passing. He that is appointed must manifest in himself detachment from all worldly things, must be the essence of purity, must show in himself the fear of God, knowledge, wisdom and learning. Thus, should the first-born of the guardian of the Cause of God not manifest in himself the truth of the words:– 'The child is the secret essence of its sire,' that is, should he not inherit of the spiritual within him (the guardian of the Cause of God) and his glorious lineage not be matched with a goodly character, then must he, (the guardian of the Cause of God) choose another branch to succeed him.

The Hands of the Cause of God must elect from their own number nine persons that shall at all times be occupied in the important services in the work of the guardian of the Cause of God. The election of these nine must be carried either unanimously or by majority from the company of the Hands of the Cause of God and these, whether unanimously or by a majority vote, must give their assent to the choice of the one whom the guardian of the Cause of God hath chosen as his successor. This assent must be given in such wise as the assenting and dissenting voices may not be distinguised (i.e., secret ballot).

O friends! The Hands of the Cause of God must be nominated and appointed by the guardian of the Cause of God. All must be under his shadow and obey his command. Should any, within or without the company of the Hands of the Cause of God disobey and seek division, the wrath of God and His vengeance will be upon him, for he will have caused a breach in the true Faith of God.

The obligations of the Hands of the Cause of God are to diffuse the Divine Fragrances, to edify the souls of men, to promote learning, to improve the character of all men and to be, at all times and under all conditions, sanctified and detached from earthly things. They must manifest the fear of God by their conduct, their manners, their deeds and their words.

This body of the Hands of the Cause of God is under the direction of the guardian of the Cause of God. He must continually urge them to strive and endeavour to the utmost of their ability to diffuse the sweet savours of God, and to guide all the peoples of the world, for it is the light of Divine Guidance that causeth all the universe to be illumined. To disregard, though it be for a moment, this absolute command which is binding upon everyone, is in no wise permitted, that the existent world may become even as the Abhá Paradise, that the surface of the earth may become heavenly, that contention and conflict amidst peoples, kindreds, nations and governments may disappear, that all the dwellers on earth may become one people and one race, that the world may become even as one home. Should differences arise they shall be amicably and conclusively settled by the Supreme Tribunal, that shall include members from all the governments and peoples of the world.

O ye beloved of the Lord! In this sacred Dispensation, conflict and contention are in no wise permitted. Every aggressor deprives himself of God's grace. It is incumbent upon everyone to show the utmost love, rectitude of conduct, straightforwardness and sincere kindliness unto all the peoples and kindreds of the world, be they friends or strangers. So intense must be the spirit of love and loving kindness, that the stranger may find himself a friend, the enemy a true brother, no difference whatsoever existing between them. For universality is of God and all limitations earthly. Thus man must strive that his reality may manifest virtues and perfections, the light whereof may shine upon everyone. The light of the sun shineth upon all the world and the merciful showers of Divine Providence fall upon all peoples. The vivifying breeze reviveth every living creature and all beings endued with life obtain their share and portion at His heavenly board. In like manner, the affections and loving kindness of the servants of the One True God must be bountifully and universally extended to all mankind. Regarding this, restrictions and limitations are in no wise permitted.

Wherefore, O my loving friends! Consort with all the peoples, kindreds and religions of the world with the utmost truthfulness, uprightness, faithfulness, kindliness, good-will and friendliness, that all the world of being may be filled with the holy ecstasy of the grace of Bahá, that ignorance, enmity, hate and rancour may vanish from the world and the darkness of estrangement amidst the peoples and kindreds of the world may give way to the Light of Unity. Should other peoples and nations be unfaithful to you show your fidelity unto them, should they be unjust toward you show justice towards them, should they keep aloof from you attract them to yourself, should they show their enmity be friendly towards them, should they poison your lives, sweeten their souls, should they inflict a wound upon you, be a salve to their sores. Such are the attributes of the sincere! Such are the attributes of the truthful.

And now, concerning the House of Justice which God hath ordained as the source of all good and freed from all error, it must be elected by universal suffrage, that is, by the believers. Its members must be manifestations of the fear of God and daysprings of knowledge and understanding, must be steadfast in God's faith and the well-wishers of all mankind. By this House is meant the Universal House of Justice, that is, in all countries a secondary House of Justice must be instituted, and these secondary Houses of Justice must elect the members of the Universal one. Unto this body all things must be referred. It enacteth all ordinances and regulations that are not to be found in the explicit Holy Text. By this body all the difficult problems are to be resolved and the guardian of the Cause of God is its sacred head and the distinguished member for life of that body. Should he not attend in person its deliberations, he must appoint one to represent him. Should any of the members commit a sin, injurious to the common weal, the guardian of the Cause of God hath at his own discretion the right to expel him, whereupon the people must elect another one in his stead. This House of Justice enacteth the laws and the government enforceth them. The legislative body must reinforce the executive, the executive must aid and assist the legislative body so that through the close union and harmony of these two forces, the foundation of fairness and justice may become firm and strong, that all the regions of the world may become even as Paradise itself.

O Lord, my God! Assist Thy loved ones to be firm in Thy Faith, to walk in Thy ways, to be steadfast in Thy Cause. Give them Thy grace to withstand the onslaught of self and passion, to follow the light of Divine Guidance. Thou art the Powerful, the Gracious, the Self-Subsisting, the Bestower, the Compassionate, the Almighty, the All-Bountiful.

O friends of 'Abdu'l-Bahá! The Lord, as a sign of His infinite bounties, hath graciously favoured His servants by providing for a fixed money offering (Huqúq), to be dutifully presented unto Him, though He, the True One and His servants have been at all times independent of all created things, and God verily is the All-Possessing, exalted above the need of any gift from His creatures. This fixed money offering, however, causeth the people to become firm and steadfast and draweth Divine increase upon them. It is to be offered through the guardian of the Cause of God, that it may be expended for the diffusion of the Fragrances of God and the exaltation of His Word, for benevolent pursuits and for the common weal.

O ye beloved of the Lord! It is incumbent upon you to be submissive to all monarchs that are just and to show your fidelity to every righteous king. Serve ye the sovereigns of the world with utmost truthfulness and loyalty. Show obedience unto them and be their well-wishers. Without their leave and permission do not meddle with political affairs, for disloyalty to the just sovereign is disloyalty to God Himself.

This is my counsel and the commandment of God unto you. Well is it with them that act accordingly.

Note: (This written paper hath for a long time been preserved under ground, damp having affected it. When brought forth to the light it was observed that certain parts of it were injured by the damp, and the Holy Land being sorely agitated it was left untouched.)

PART TWO

He Is God

O My Lord, my heart's Desire, Thou Whom I ever invoke, Thou Who art my Aider and my Shelter, my Helper and my Refuge! Thou seest me submerged in an ocean of calamities that overwhelm the soul, of afflictions that oppress the heart, of woes that disperse Thy gathering, of ills and pains that scatter Thy flock. Sore trials have compassed me round and perils have from all sides beset me. Thou seest me immersed in a sea of unsurpassed tribulation, sunk into a fathomless abyss, afflicted by mine enemies and consumed with the flame of their hate, enkindled by my kinsmen with whom Thou didst make Thy strong Covenant and Thy firm Testament, wherein Thou biddest them turn their hearts to this wronged one, to keep away from me the foolish, the unjust, and refer unto this lonely one all that about which they differ in thy Holy Book, so that the Truth may be revealed unto them, their doubts may be dispelled and Thy manifest Signs be spread abroad.

Yet now Thou seest them, O Lord, my God! with Thine eye that sleepeth not, how that they have broken Thy Covenant and turned their backs thereon, how with hate and rebelliousness they have erred from Thy Testament and have arisen intent upon malice.

Adversities have waxed still more severe as they rose with unbearable cruelty to overpower and crush me, as they scattered far and wide their scrolls of doubt and in utter falsehood hurled their calumnies upon me. Not content with this, their chief, O my God, hath dared to interpolate Thy Book, to fraudulently alter Thy decisive Holy Text and falsify that which hath been revealed by Thy All-Glorious Pen. He did also maliciously insert that which Thou didst reveal for the one that hath wrought the most glaring cruelty upon Thee, disbelieved in Thee and denied Thy wondrous Signs, into what Thou didst reveal for this servant of Thine that hath been wronged in this world. All this he did that he might beguile the souls of men and breathe his evil whisperings into the hearts of Thy devoted ones. Thereunto did their second chief testify, confessing it in his own handwriting, setting thereupon his seal and spreading it throughout all regions. O my God! Could there be a more grievous injustice than this? And still they rested not, but further strove with stubbornness, falsehood and slander, with scorn and calumny to stir up sedition in the midst of the government of this land and elsewhere, causing them to deem me a sower of sedition and filling the minds with things that the ear abhorreth to hear. The government was thus alarmed, fear fell upon the sovereign, and the suspicion of the nobility was aroused. Minds were troubled, affairs were upset, souls were perturbed, the fire of anguish and sorrow was kindled within the breasts, the Holy Leaves (of the Household) were convulsed and shaken, their eyes rained with tears, their sighs and lamentations were raised and their hearts burned within them as they bewailed this wronged servant of Thine, fallen a victim into the hands of these, his kindred, nay, his very enemies!

Lord! Thou seest all things weeping me and my kindred rejoicing in my woes. By Thy Glory, O my God! Even amongst mine enemies, some have lamented my troubles and my distress, and of the envious ones a number have shed tears because of my cares, my exile and my afflictions. They did this because they found naught in me but affection and care and witnessed naught but kindliness and mercy. As they saw me swept into the flood of tribulation and adversity and exposed even as a target to the arrows of fate, their hearts were moved with compassion, tears came to their eyes and they testified declaring:– 'The Lord is our witness; naught have we seen from him but faithfulness, generosity and extreme compassion.' The Covenant-breakers, foreboders of evil, however, waxed fiercer in their rancour, rejoiced as I fell a victim to the most grievous ordeal, bestirred themselves against me and made merry over the heartrending happenings around me.

I call upon Thee, O Lord my God! with my tongue and with all my heart, not to requite them for their cruelty and their wrong-doings, their craft and their mischief, for they are foolish and ignoble and know not what they do. They discern not good from evil, neither do they distinguish right from wrong, nor justice from injustice. They follow their own desires and walk in the footsteps of the most imperfect and foolish amongst them. O my Lord! Have mercy upon them, shield them from all afflictions in these troubled times and grant that all trials and hardships may be the lot of this Thy servant that hath fallen into this darksome pit. Single me out for every woe and make me a sacrifice for all Thy loved ones. O Lord, Most High! May my soul, my life, my being, my spirit, my all be offered up for them. O God, my God! Lowly, suppliant and fallen upon my face, I beseech Thee with all the ardour of my invocation to pardon whosoever hath hurt me, forgive him that hath conspired against me and offended me, and wash away the misdeeds of them that have wrought injustice upon me. Vouchsafe unto them Thy goodly gifts, give them joy, relieve them from sorrow, grant them peace and prosperity, give them Thy bliss and pour upon them Thy bounty.

Thou art the Powerful, the Gracious, the Help in Peril, the Self-Subsisting!

O dearly beloved friends! I am now in very great danger and the hope of even an hour's life is lost to me. I am thus constrained to write these lines for the protection of the Cause of God, the preservation of His Law, the safeguarding of His Word and the safety of His Teachings. By the Ancient Beauty! This wronged one hath in no wise borne nor doth he bear a grudge against any one; towards none doth he entertain any ill-feeling and uttereth no word save for the good of the world. My supreme obligation, however, of necessity, prompteth me to guard and preserve the Cause of God. Thus, with the greatest regret, I counsel you saying:– Guard ye the Cause of God, protect His law and have the utmost fear of discord. This is the foundation of the belief of the people of Bahá (may my life be offered up for them): 'His Holiness, the Exalted One (the Báb), is the Manifestation of the Unity and Oneness of God and the Forerunner of the Ancient Beauty. His Holiness the Abhá Beauty (may my life be a sacrifice for His steadfast friends) is the Supreme Manifestation of God and the Dayspring of His Most Divine Essence. All others are servants unto Him and do his bidding.' Unto the Most Holy Book every one must turn and all that is not expressly recorded therein must be referred to the Universal House of Justice. That which this body, whether unanimously or by a majority doth carry, that is verily the Truth and the Purpose of God Himself. Whoso doth deviate therefrom is verily of them that love discord, hath shown forth malice and turned away from the Lord of the Covenant. By this House is meant that Universal House of Justice which is to be elected from all countries, that is from those parts in the East and West where the loved ones are to be found, after the manner of the customary elections in Western countries such as those of England.

It is incumbent upon these members (of the Universal House of Justice) to gather in a certain place and deliberate upon all problems which have caused difference, questions that are obscure and matters that are not expressly recorded in the Book. Whatsoever they decide has the same effect as the Text itself. And inasmuch as this House of Justice hath power to enact laws that are not expressly recorded in the Book and bear upon daily transactions, so also it hath power to repeal the same. Thus for example, the House of Justice enacteth today a certain law and enforceth it, and a hundred years hence, circumstances having profoundly changed and the conditions having altered, another House of Justice will then have power, according to the exigencies of the time, to alter that law. This it can do because that law formeth no part of the Divine Explicit Text. The House of Justice is both the initiator and the abrogator of its own laws.

And now, one of the greatest and most fundamental principles of the Cause of God is to shun and avoid entirely the Covenant-breakers, for they will utterly destroy the Cause of God, exterminate His Law and render of no account all efforts exerted in the past. O friends! It behooveth you to call to mind with tenderness the trials of His Holiness, the Exalted One, and show your fidelity to the Ever-Blest Beauty. The utmost endeavour must be exerted lest all these woes, trials and afflictions, all this pure and sacred blood that hath been shed so profusely in the Path of God, may prove to be in vain. Ye know well what the hands of the Centre of Sedition, Mírzá Muḥammad-'Alí, and his associates have wrought. Among his doings, one of them is the corruption of the Sacred Text whereof ye are all aware, the Lord be praised, and know that it is evident, proven and confirmed by the testimony of his brother, Mírzá Badí'u'lláh, whose confession is written in his own handwriting, beareth his seal, is printed and spread abroad. This is but one of his misdeeds. Can a transgression be imagined more glaring than this, the interpolation of the Holy Text? Nay, by the righteousness of the Lord! His transgressions are writ and recorded in a leaflet by itself. Please God, ye will peruse it.

In short, according to the explicit Divine Text the least transgression shall make of this man a fallen creature, and what transgression is more grievous than attempting to destroy the Divine Edifice, breaking the Covenant, erring from the Testament, falsifying the Holy Text, sowing the seeds of doubt, calumniating 'Abdu'l-Bahá, advancing claims for which God hath sent down no warrant, kindling mischief and striving to shed the very blood of 'Abdu'l-Bahá, and many other things whereof ye are all aware! It is thus evident that should this man succeed in bringing disruption into the Cause of God, he will utterly destroy and exterminate it. Beware lest ye approach this man, for to approach him is worse than approaching fire!

Gracious God! After Mírzá Badí'u'lláh had declared in his own handwriting that this man (Muḥammad-'Alí) had broken the Covenant and had proclaimed his falsification of the Holy Text, he realized that to return to the True Faith and pay allegiance to the Covenant and Testament would in no wise promote his selfish desires. He thus repented and regretted the thing he had done and attempted privily to gather in his printed confessions, plotted darkly with the Centre of Sedition against me and informed him daily of all the happenings within my household. He has even taken a leading part in the mischievous deeds that have of late been committed. Praise be to God affairs recovered their former stability and the loved ones obtained partial peace. But ever since the day he entered again into our midst, he began afresh to sow the seeds of sore sedition. Some of his machinations and intrigues will be recorded in a separate leaflet.

My purpose is, however, to show that it is incumbent upon the friends that are fast and firm in the Covenant and Testament to be ever wakeful lest after this wronged one is gone this alert and active worker of mischief may cause disruption, privily sow the seeds of doubt and sedition and utterly root out the Cause of God. A thousand times shun his company. Take heed and be on your guard. Watch and examine; should anyone, openly or privily, have the least connection with him, cast him out from your midst, for he will surely cause disruption and mischief.

O ye beloved of the Lord! Strive with all your heart to shield the Cause of God from the onslaught of the insincere, for souls such as these cause the straight to become crooked and all benevolent efforts to produce contrary results.

O God, my God! I call Thee, Thy Prophets and Thy Messengers, Thy Saints and Thy Holy Ones, to witness that I have declared conclusively Thy Proofs unto Thy loved ones and set forth clearly all things unto them, that they may watch over Thy Faith, guard Thy Straight Path and protect Thy Resplendent Law. Thou art, verily, the All-Knowing, the All-Wise!

PART THREE

He Is the Witness, the All-Sufficing

O My God! my Beloved, my heart's Desire! Thou knowest, Thou seest that which hath befallen this servant of Thine, that hath humbled himself at Thy Door, and

Thou knowest the sins committed against him by the people of malice, they that have broken Thy Covenant and turned their backs on Thy Testament. In the day-time they afflicted me with the arrows of hate and in the night-season they privily conspired to hurt me. At dawn they committed that which the Celestial Concourse did lament and at eventide they unsheathed against me the sword of tyranny and hurled in the presence of the ungodly their darts of calumny upon me. Notwithstanding their misdeeds, this lowly servant of Thine was patient and did endure every affliction and trial at their hands, though by Thy power and might he could have destroyed their words, quenched their fire and stayed the flame of their rebelliousness.

Thou seest, O my God! how my long-suffering, my forbearance and silence have increased their cruelty, their arrogance and their pride. By Thy Glory, O Beloved One! They have misbelieved in Thee and rebelled against Thee in such wise that they left me not a moment of rest and quiet, that I might arise as it is meet and seemly, to exalt Thy Word amidst mankind, and might serve at Thy Threshold of Holiness with a heart that overfloweth with the joy of the dwellers of the Abhá Kingdom.

Lord! My cup of woe runneth over, and from all sides blows are fiercely raging upon me. The darts of affliction have compassed me round and the arrows of distress have rained upon me. Thus tribulation overwhelmed me and my strength, because of the onslaught of the foemen, became weakness within me, while I stood alone and forsaken in the midst of my woes. Lord! Have mercy upon me, lift me up unto Thyself and make me to drink from the Chalice of Martyrdom, for the wide world with all its vastness can no longer contain me.

Thou art, verily, the Merciful, the Compassionate, the Gracious, the All-Bountiful!

O ye the true, the sincere, the faithful friends of this wronged one! Everyone knoweth and believeth what calamities and afflictions have befallen this wronged one, this prisoner, at the hands of those who have broken the Covenant at the time when, after the setting of the Day-Star of the world, his heart was consumed with the flame of His bereavement.

When, in all parts of the earth, the enemies of God profiting by the passing of the Sun of Truth, suddenly and with all their might launched their attack; at such a time and in the midst of so great a calamity, the Covenant-breakers arose with the utmost cruelty, intent upon harm and the stirring up of the spirit of enmity. At every moment a misdeed they did commit and bestirred themselves to sow the seeds of grievous sedition, and to ruin the edifice of the Covenant. But this wronged one, this prisoner, did his utmost to hide and veil their doings, that haply they might regret and repent. His long-suffering and forbearance of these evil deeds, however, made the rebellious ones still more arrogant and daring; until, through leaflets written with their own hands, they sowed the seeds of doubt, printing these leaflets and scattering them broadcast throughout the world, believing that such foolish doings would bring to naught the Covenant and the Testament.

Thereupon the loved ones of the Lord arose, inspired with the greatest confidence and constancy and aided by the power of the Kingdom, by Divine Strength, by heavenly Grace, by the unfailing help and Celestial Bounty, they withstood the enemies of the Covenant in well-nigh three score and ten treatises and supported by conclusive proofs, unmistakable evidences and clear texts from the Holy Writ, they refuted their scrolls of doubt and mischief-kindling leaflets. The Centre of Sedition was thus confounded in his craftiness, afflicted by the wrath of God, sunk unto a degradation and infamy that shall be lasting until the Day of Doom. Base and wretched is the plight of the people of evil deeds, they that are in grievous loss!

And as they lost their cause, grew hopeless in their efforts against the loved ones of God, saw the Standard of His Testament waving throughout all regions and witnessed the power of the Covenant of the Merciful One, the flame of envy so blazed within them as to be beyond recounting. With the utmost vigour, exertion, rancour and enmity, they followed another path, walked in another way, devised another plan: that of kindling the flame of sedition in the heart of the very government itself, and thus caused this wronged one, this prisoner to appear as a mover of strife, inimical to the government and a hater and opponent of the Crown. Perchance 'Abdu'l-Bahá may be put to death and his name be made to perish whereby an arena may be opened unto the enemies of the Covenant wherein they may advance and spur on their charger, inflict a grievous loss upon everyone and subvert the very foundations of the edifice of the Cause of God. For so grievous is the conduct and behaviour of this false people that they are become even as an axe striking at the very root of the Blessed Tree. Should they be suffered to continue they would, in but a few days' time, exterminate the Cause of God, His Word, and themselves.

Hence, the beloved of the Lord must entirely shun them, avoid them, foil their machinations and evil whisperings, guard the Law of God and His religion, engage one and all in diffusing widely the sweet savours of God and to the best of their endeavour proclaim His Teachings.

Whosever and whatsoever meeting becometh a hindrance to the diffusion of the Light of Faith, let the loved ones give them counsel and say: 'Of all the gifts of God the greatest is the gift of Teaching. It draweth unto us the Grace of God and is our first obligation. Of such a gift how can we deprive ourselves? Nay, our lives, our goods, our comforts, our rest, we offer them all as a sacrifice for the Abhá Beauty and teach the Cause of God.' Caution and prudence, however, must be observed even as recorded in the Book. The veil must in no wise be suddenly rent asunder. The Glory of Glories rest upon you.

O ye the faithful loved ones of 'Abdu'l-Bahá! It is incumbent upon you to take the greatest care of Shoghi Effendi, the twig that hath branched from and the fruit given forth by the two hallowed and Divine Lote-Trees, that no dust of despondency and sorrow may stain his radiant nature, that day by day he may wax greater in happiness, in joy and spirituality, and may grow to become even as a fruitful tree.

For he is, after 'Abdu'l-Bahá, the guardian of the Cause of God, the Afnán, the Hands (pillars) of the Cause and the beloved of the Lord must obey him and turn unto him. He that obeyeth him not, hath not obeyed God; he that turneth away from him, hath turned away from God and he that denieth him, hath denied the True One. Beware lest anyone falsely interpret these words, and like unto them that have broken the Covenant after the Day of Ascension (of Bahá'u'lláh) advance a pretext, raise the standard of revolt, wax stubborn and open wide the door of false interpretation. To none is given the right to put forth his own opinion or express his particular conviction. All must seek guidance and turn unto the Centre of the Cause and the House of Justice. And he that turneth unto whatsoever else is indeed in grievous error.

The Glory of Glories rest upon you!

APPENDIX 2

Letter from the Hands of the Cause in the Holy Land

Haifa, Israel
15 October, 1960

To all National Spiritual Assemblies
Dear Bahá'í friends,

In view of the proclamation issued by Mason Remey in which he claims to be the second guardian of the Faith of Bahá'u'lláh, and the present circulation of what he calls encyclical letters, as well as various letters being written by his misguided supporters, the Hands of the Cause feel it imperative to place before the believers certain facts and passages from the sacred Writings of our Faith in refutation of these spurious and highly misleading statements.

Mason Remey has had the temerity to assert that the beloved Guardian of the Cause appointed him during his own lifetime as his successor. He builds up his claim by saying that because he was appointed President of the first International Bahá'í Council, he becomes automatically the President of the elected International Bahá'í Council, and later, on its election, Chairman of the Universal House of Justice. To quote his own argument:

> 'He who is President of the Universal House of Justice is the Guardian of the Faith for he who is that Guardian of the Faith is President of the Universal House of Justice. These two offices are one and the same. Therefore, when the beloved Guardian Shoghi Effendi appointed me President of the Bahá'í International Council, that he explained was the forerunner of the Universal House of Justice that was the Embrionic Universal House of Justice that would eventually develop into the Universal House of Justice, I or one of my successors in Guardianship would be President of this divinely instituted infallible body, the Universal House of Justice; therefore the Guardianship of the Bahá'í Faith and the Presidency of the Universal House of Justice are one and the same position in the Faith.'

This contention requires a careful study of the Words of 'Abdu'l-Bahá in the Will and Testament, because this sacred document sets forth the conditions requisite for Guardianship in no uncertain terms. We must never forget for a moment that it was the Master Who established the Station of the Guardianship; and in fact appointed the successor of Shoghi Effendi, as between Shoghi Effendi's first-born, or another branch (Ghuṣn).

In the Will He clearly states:

> 'He is the expounder of the Words of God and after him will succeed the first-born of his lineal descendants . . .
>
> 'It is incumbent upon the guardian of the Cause of God to appoint in his own lifetime him that shall become his successor, that differences may not arise after

his passing. He that is appointed must manifest in himself detachment from all worldly things, must be the essence of purity, must show in himself the fear of God, knowledge, wisdom and learning. Thus, should the first-born of the guardian of the Cause of God not manifest in himself the truth of the words: 'the child is the secret essence of its sire', that is, should he not inherit of the spiritual within him (the guardian of the Cause of God) and his glorious lineage not be matched with a goodly character, then must he (the guardian of the Cause of God) choose another branch to succeed him.'

It has become clear during the past months that lack of knowledge of the meaning of the word 'branch' as used in the Master's Will and Testament has led to great confusion in certain quarters in the West.

The word 'Ghuṣn' (plural Aghṣán) is an Arabic word, meaning branch.

Bahá'u'lláh used this word specifically to designate His own male descendants. It does not apply to any other category of people. He gave the title to 'Abdu'l-Bahá of 'The Most Great Branch'. His second son, Muhammad Ali, was known as 'the Greater Branch'; His third son, Mehdi, 'the Purest Branch', etc. The Guardian himself is designated in the Master's Will as 'the Chosen Branch'.

All the male relatives of the Báb are invariably referred to as 'Afnán', which means 'twigs'.

These two designations are not interchangeable.

Over and over in Bahá'u'lláh's Tablets these terms 'Aghṣán' and 'Afnán' are specifically used in this sense.

For instance, in the Tablet of the branch, the original word is 'Ghuṣn' (i.e. branch), referring to 'Abdu'l-Bahá.

The ordinary English usage of the word 'branch' has caused a great deal of confusion, whereas there is not a shadow of ambiguity in the Persian and Arabic texts.

Because of ignorance of the Arabic and Persian languages and the use of these two terms in our sacred texts, spurious arguments have been put forth by those making the false claim that Shoghi Effendi could have appointed a successor other than a blood descendant of Bahá'u'lláh.

It should likewise be pointed out that neither in Persian nor Arabic are there ever any capital letters, so that it is impossible to deduce any arguments from a capitalisation or lack of capitalisation in the English texts.

We direct attention to the first Proclamation issued by the Hands of the Bahá'í world from Bahji, 25 November 1957 (including Mason Remey).

'The same Hands (one of whom was Mason Remey), rejoining the other Hands assembled in the Mansion of Bahá'u'lláh at Bahji, certified that Shoghi Effendi had left no Will and Testament. It was likewise certified that the beloved Guardian had left no heir. The Aghṣán (branches) one and all are either dead, or have been declared violators of the Covenant by the Guardian for their faithlessness to the Master's Will and Testament and their hostility to him named first Guardian in that Sacred document . . .'

Thus it is clear that no one but a blood descendant of Bahá'u'lláh could possibly have been appointed by Shoghi Effendi as the Guardian of the Faith.

Bahá'u'lláh, in writing, in unambiguous terms established the Master as the Centre of His Covenant. 'Abdu'l-Bahá in His turn, in His own handwriting created the beloved Guardian, Shoghi Effendi, as the Centre of His Covenant and specified the conditions of future Guardianship.

Without one written word from the Guardian, Mason Remey claims that because he was the President of the International Bahá'í Council, and because this body is the embryonic International Institution, it automatically makes him the President of that future body, and hence, Guardian of the Faith.

If the President of the International Bahá'í Council is *ipso facto* the Guardian of the Bahá'í Faith, then the beloved Guardian, himself, Shoghi Effendi, would have had to be the President of the International Bahá'í Council.

If the presidency of the first International Bahá'í Council, which was not an elected body but appointed by Shoghi Effendi, was a permanent thing, why did the beloved Guardian himself call for an elected International Bahá'í Council in the future as part of the evolution of this institution and its eventual efflorescence into the Universal House of Justice?

We have not even an intimation in any writing of Shoghi Effendi that the officers of the first appointed International Bahá'í Council would be carried forward into the elected International Bahá'í Council.

There is nothing to indicate anywhere in the Teachings that the officers of the elected International Bahá'í Council would not be elected according to the pattern of election of every other Bahá'í elected body.

The manner of the election of the Universal House of Justice has been laid down by 'Abdu'l-Bahá Himself.

There is no possible reason for concluding that Mason Remey or any other Council member would automatically be carried forward into membership in that body.

If the presidency of either an appointed or an elected International Bahá'í Council were synonymous with the presidency of the Universal House of Justice, then it follows the beloved Guardian himself would have assumed this position.

Mason Remey signed the first communication sent out by 26 Hands of the Faith, from Bahji in November 1957, in which it was stated that as the beloved Guardian had left no Will and no successor, the Hands of the Faith, designated by Shoghi Effendi as the Chief Stewards of Bahá'u'lláh's embryonic World Commonwealth, would carry on the work of the Crusade until the formation of that infallible body, the Universal House of Justice.

Although Mason Remey, himself a Hand of the Cause, acted as one of the nine Hands in the Holy Land until the end of October 1959, he never intimated his claim to be the second Guardian to any individual Hand, to the group of Hands serving at the World Centre, or to the body of the Hands gathered in Bahji at their Conclaves.

The first intimation any of us received of this astounding claim was when he mailed us a copy of his proclamation, at a time when it was already in the mail to National Assemblies and individuals.

How can Mason Remey reconcile his assertion that he was appointed by Shoghi Effendi as his successor during his lifetime with the provisions in the Will and Testament of 'Abdu'l-Bahá that during the lifetime of the Guardian, nine of the Hands of the Cause of God must be elected by their fellow-Hands, and give their assent to the choice made by him of his successor? If the Guardian appointed Mason Remey why did he go against provisions of the Will in this important respect? Such an implication is a flagrant attack on Shoghi Effendi himself.

The terrible dangers of accepting so manifestly false a claim as that which Mason Remey has made are thus clear for all to see.

In addition to having set aside the provisions of 'Abdu'l-Bahá's Will in making this claim, in addition to not having one single written word in evidence that the beloved Guardian intended to make him his successor, Mason Remey has written that he will appoint his own successor to the Guardianship.

Every believer, into whose mind has crept for even a second, a shadow of a doubt as regards the personal status of Mason Remey may see for himself to what a degree he has entirely brushed aside every single foundation laid by 'Abdu'l-Bahá in His Will for the Guardianship.

The glorious Báb forbade association with Covenant Breakers, Bahá'u'lláh strictly forbade association with the Covenant Breakers, and even warned the friends against entering if possible a city where Covenant Breakers resided as their poison polluted the entire area. 'Abdu'l-Bahá's teaching with regard to shunning and having no contact whatsoever with the Covenant Breakers is contained in hundreds of Tablets. The beloved Guardian forbade all association with Covenant Breakers and warned that their poison was so deadly, that it was not permissible to have even their literature in one's possession.

The Chief Stewards of the Faith, mindful of their paramount responsibility to protect the believers, have taken action to expel from the Faith Mason Remey and his supporters because of the Covenant-breaking activities and to forbid all association with them.

The beloved Master, in His Will and Testament, issued this clear warning to all the friends:

> 'Beware, beware, lest the days after the ascension (of Bahá'u'lláh) be repeated, when the Centre of Sedition waxed haughty and rebellious and with Divine Unity for his excuse deprived himself and perturbed and poisoned others.' . . . 'O God, my God! I call Thee, Thy Prophets and Thy Messengers, Thy Saints and Thy Holy Ones, to witness that I have declared conclusively Thy Proofs unto Thy loved ones and set forth clearly all things unto them, that they may watch over Thy Faith, guard Thy Straight Path and protect Thy Resplendent Law. Thou art, verily, the All-Knowing, the All-Wise!'

With warm Bahá'í love
In the service of the beloved Guardian,
HANDS OF THE CAUSE IN THE HOLY LAND

APPENDIX 3

The Guardianship and the Universal House of Justice

Passages from letters written in response to questions asked by individual believers.

27 May 1966

. . . You query the timing of the election of the Universal House of Justice in view of the Guardian's statement: '. . . given favourable circumstances under which the Bahá'ís of Persia and the adjoining countries under Soviet rule may be enabled to elect their national representatives . . . the only remaining obstacle in the way of the definite formation of the International House of Justice will have been removed.' On April 19, 1947 the Guardian, in a letter written on his behalf by his secretary, replied to the inquiry of an individual believer about this passage: 'At the time he referred to Russia there were Bahá'ís there. Now the community has practically ceased to exist; therefore the formation of the International House of Justice cannot depend on a Russian national spiritual assembly, but other strong national spiritual assemblies will have to be built up before it can be established.'

You suggest the possibility that, for the good of the Cause, certain information concerning the succession to Shoghi Effendi is being withheld from the believers. We assure you that nothing whatsoever is being withheld from the friends for whatever reason. There is no doubt at all that in the Will and Testament of 'Abdu'l-Bahá, Shoghi Effendi was the authority designated to appoint his successor; but he had no children and all the surviving Aghsán had broken the Covenant. Thus, as the Hands of the Cause stated in 1957, it is clear that there was no one he could have appointed in accordance with the provisions of the Will. To have made an appointment outside the clear and specific provisions of the Master's Will and Testament would obviously have been an impossible and unthinkable course of action for the Guardian, the divinely appointed upholder and defender of the Covenant. Moreover, that same Will had provided a clear means for the confirmation of the Guardian's appointment of his successor, as you are aware. The nine Hands to be elected by the body of the Hands were to give their assent by secret ballot to the Guardian's choice. In 1957 the entire body of the Hands, after fully investigating the matter, announced that Shoghi Effendi had appointed no successor and left no will. This is documented and established.

The fact that Shoghi Effendi did not leave a will cannot be adduced as evidence of his failure to obey Bahá'u'lláh – rather should we acknowledge that in his very silence there is a wisdom and a sign of his infallible guidance. We should ponder deeply the writings that we have, and seek to understand the multitudinous significances that they contain. Do not forget that Shoghi Effendi said two things were necessary for a growing understanding of the World Order of Bahá'u'lláh: the passage of time and the guidance of the Universal House of Justice.

The infallibility of the Universal House of Justice, operating within its ordained sphere, has not been made dependent upon the presence in its membership of the Guardian of the Cause. Although in the realm of interpretation the Guardian's pronouncements are always binding, in the area of the Guardian's participation in legislation it is always the decision of the House itself which must prevail. This is supported by the words of the Guardian: 'The interpretation of the Guardian, functioning within his own sphere, is as authoritative and binding as the enactments of the International House of Justice, whose exclusive right and prerogative is to pronounce upon and deliver the final judgment on such laws and ordinances as Bahá'u'lláh has not expressly revealed. Neither can, nor will ever, infringe upon the sacred and prescribed domain of the other. Neither will seek to curtail the specific and undoubted authority with which both have been divinely invested.

'Though the Guardian of the Faith has been made the permanent head of so august a body he can never, even temporarily, assume the right of exclusive legislation. He cannot override the decision of the majority of his fellow members, but is bound to insist upon a reconsideration by them of any enactment he conscientiously believes to conflict with the meaning and to depart from the spirit of Bahá'u'lláh's revealed utterances.'

However, quite apart from his function as a member and sacred head for life of the Universal House of Justice, the Guardian, functioning within his own sphere, had the right and duty 'to define the sphere of the legislative action' of the Universal House of Justice. In other words, he had the authority to state whether a matter was or was not already covered by the Sacred Texts and therefore whether it was within the authority of the Universal House of Justice to legislate upon it. No other person, apart from the Guardian, has the right or authority to make such definitions. The question therefore arises: In the absence of the Guardian, is the Universal House of Justice in danger of straying outside its proper sphere and thus falling into error? Here we must remember three things: First, Shoghi Effendi, during the thirty-six years of his Guardianship, has already made innumerable such definitions, supplementing those made by 'Abdu'l-Bahá and by Bahá'u'lláh Himself. As already announced to the friends, a careful study of the Writings and interpretations on any subject on which the Universal House of Justice proposes to legislate always precedes its act of legislation. Second, the Universal House of Justice, itself assured of Divine guidance, is well aware of the absence of the Guardian and will approach all matters of legislation only when certain of its sphere of jurisdiction, a sphere which the Guardian has confidently described as 'clearly defined.' Third, we must not forget the Guardian's written statement about these two institutions: 'Neither can, nor will ever infringe upon the sacred and prescribed domain of the other.'

As regards the need to have deductions made from the Writings to help in the formulation of the enactments of the House of Justice, there is the following text from the pen of 'Abdu'l-Bahá:

> 'Those matters of major importance which constitute the foundation of the Law of God are explicitly recorded in the Text, but subsidiary laws are left to the House of Justice. The wisdom of this is that the times never remain the same, for change is a necessary quality and an essential attribute of this world, and of time and place. Therefore the House of Justice will take action accordingly.
>
> 'Let it not be imagined that the House of Justice will take any decision according to its own concepts and opinions. God forbid! The Supreme House of Justice will take decisions and establish laws through the inspiration and confirmation of the Holy Spirit, because it is in the safekeeping and under the shelter and protection of the Ancient Beauty, and obedience to its decisions is a bounden and essential duty and an absolute obligation, and there is no escape for anyone.

'Say, O People: Verily the Supreme House of Justice is under the wings of your Lord, the Compassionate, the All-Merciful, that is under His protection, His care, and His shelter; for He has commanded the firm believers to obey that blessed, sanctified, and all-subduing body, whose sovereignty is divinely ordained and of the Kingdom of Heaven and whose laws are inspired and spiritual.

'Briefly, this is the wisdom of referring the laws of society to the House of Justice. In the religion of Islám, similarly, not every ordinance was explicitly revealed; nay not a tenth part of a tenth part was included in the Text; although all matters of major importance were specifically referred to, there were undoubtedly thousands of laws which were unspecified. These were devised by the divines of a later age according to the laws of Islamic jurisprudence, and individual divines made conflicting deductions from the original revealed ordinances. All these were enforced. Today this process of deduction is the right of the body of the House of Justice, and the deductions and conclusions of individual learned men have no authority, unless they are endorsed by the House of Justice. The difference is precisely this, that from the conclusions and endorsements of the body of the House of Justice whose members are elected by and known to the worldwide Bahá'í community, no differences will arise; whereas the conclusions of individual divines and scholars would definitely lead to differences, and result in schism, division and dispersion. The oneness of the Word would be destroyed, the unity of the Faith would disappear, and the edifice of the Faith of God would be shaken.'

In the Order of Bahá'u'lláh there are certain functions which are reserved to certain institutions, and others which are shared in common, even though they may be more in the special province of one or the other. For example, although the Hands of the Cause of God have the specific functions of protection and propagation, and are specialized for these functions, it is also the duty of the Universal House of Justice and the spiritual assemblies to protect and teach the Cause – indeed teaching is a sacred obligation placed upon every believer by Bahá'u'lláh. Similarly, although after the Master authoritative interpretation was exclusively vested in the Guardian, and although legislation is exclusively the function of the Universal House of Justice, these two institutions are, in Shoghi Effendi's words, 'complementary in their aim and purpose'. 'Their common, their fundamental object is to ensure the continuity of that divinely appointed authority which flows from the Source of our Faith, to safeguard the unity of its followers, and to maintain the integrity and flexibility of its teachings.' Whereas the Universal House of Justice cannot undertake any function which exclusively appertained to the Guardian, it must continue to pursue the object which it shares in common with the Guardianship.

As you point out with many quotations, Shoghi Effendi repeatedly stressed the inseparability of these two institutions. Whereas he obviously envisaged their functioning together, it cannot logically be deduced from this that one is unable to function in the absence of the other. During the whole thirty-six years of his Guardianship Shoghi Effendi functioned without the Universal House of Justice. Now the Universal House of Justice must function without the Guardian, but the principle of inseparability remains. The Guardianship does not lose its significance nor position in the Order of Bahá'u'lláh merely because there is no living Guardian. We must guard against two extremes: one is to argue that because there is no Guardian all that was written about the Guardianship and its position in the Bahá'í World Order is a dead letter and was unimportant; the other is to be so overwhelmed by the significance of the Guardianship as to underestimate the strength of the Covenant, or to be tempted to compromise with the clear Texts in order to find somehow, in some way, a 'Guardian'.

Service to the Cause of God requires absolute fidelity and integrity and unwavering faith in Him. No good but only evil can come from taking the responsibility for the future of God's Cause into our own hands and trying to force it into ways that we wish it to go regardless of the clear texts and our own limitations. It is His Cause. He has promised that its light will not fail. Our part is to cling tenaciously to the revealed Word and to the institutions that He has created to preserve His Covenant.

It is precisely in this connection that the believers must recognize the importance of intellectual honesty and humility. In past dispensations many errors arose because the believers in God's Revelation were overanxious to encompass the Divine Message within the framework of their limited understanding, to define doctrines where definition was beyond their power, to explain mysteries which only the wisdom and experience of a later age would make comprehensible, to argue that something was true because it appeared desirable and necessary. Such compromises with essential truth, such intellectual pride, we must scrupulously avoid.

If some of the statements of the Universal House of Justice are not detailed the friends should realize that the cause of this is not secretiveness, but rather the determination of this body to refrain from interpreting the teachings and to preserve the truth of the Guardian's statement that 'Leaders of religion, exponents of political theories, governors of human institutions . . . need have no doubt or anxiety regarding the nature, the origin, or validity of the institutions which the adherents of the Faith are building up throughout the world. For these lie embedded in the Teachings themselves, unadulterated and unobscured by unwarranted inferences or unauthorized interpretations of His Word.'

A clear distinction is made in our Faith between authoritative interpretation and the interpretation or understanding that each individual arrives at for himself from his study of its teachings. While the former is confined to the Guardian, the latter, according to the guidance given to us by the Guardian himself, should by no means be suppressed. In fact such individual interpretation is considered the fruit of man's rational power and conducive to a better understanding of the teachings, provided that no disputes or arguments arise among the friends and the individual himself understands and makes it clear that his views are merely his own. Individual interpretations continually change as one grows in comprehension of the teachings. As Shoghi Effendi wrote: 'To deepen in the Cause means to read the writings of Bahá'u'lláh and the Master so thoroughly as to be able to give it to others in its pure form. There are many who have some superficial idea of what the Cause stands for. They, therefore, present it together with all sorts of ideas that are their own. As the Cause is still in its early days we must be most careful lest we fall into this error and injure the Movement we so much adore. There is no limit to the study of the Cause. The more we read the Writings, the more truths we can find in them, the more we will see that our previous notions were erroneous.' So, although individual insights can be enlightening and helpful, they can also be misleading. The friends must therefore learn to listen to the views of others without being overawed or allowing their faith to be shaken, and to express their own views without pressing them on their fellow Bahá'ís.

The Cause of God is organic, growing and developing like a living being. Time and again it has faced crises which have perplexed the believers, but each time the Cause, impelled by the immutable purpose of God, overcame the crisis and went on to greater heights.

However great may be our inability to understand the mystery and the implications of the passing of Shoghi Effendi, the strong cord to which all must cling with assurance is the Covenant. The emphatic and vigorous language of

'Abdu'l-Bahá's Will and Testament is at this time, as at the time of His own passing the safeguard of the Cause:

> 'Unto the Most Holy Book every one must turn and all that is not expressly recorded therein must be referred to the Universal House of Justice. That which this body, whether unanimously or by a majority doth carry, that is verily the truth and the purpose of God Himself. Whoso doth deviate therefrom is verily of them that love discord, hath shown forth malice, and turned away from the Lord of the Covenant.' And again: 'All must seek guidance and turn unto the Centre of the Cause and the House of Justice. And he that turneth unto whatsoever else is indeed in grievous error.'

The Universal House of Justice, which the Guardian said would be regarded by posterity as 'the last refuge of a tottering civilization', is now, in the absence of the Guardian, the sole infallibly guided institution in the world to which all must turn, and on it rests the responsibility for ensuring the unity and progress of the Cause of God in accordance with the revealed Word. There are statements from the Master and the Guardian indicating that the Universal House of Justice, in addition to being the highest legislative body of the Faith, is also the body to which all must turn, and is the 'apex' of the Bahá'í Administrative Order, as well as the 'supreme organ of the Bahá'í Commonwealth'. The Guardian has in his writings specified for the House of Justice such fundamental functions as the formulation of future worldwide teaching plans, the conduct of the administrative affairs of the Faith, and the guidance, organization, and unification of the affairs of the Cause throughout the world. Furthermore in *God Passes By* the Guardian makes the following statement: 'The Kitáb-i-Aqdas . . . not only preserves for posterity the basic laws and ordinances on which the fabric of His future World Order must rest, but ordains, in addition to the function of interpretation which it confers upon His successor, the necessary institutions through which the integrity and unity of His Faith can alone be safeguarded.' He has also, in 'The Dispensation of Bahá'u'lláh,' written that the members of the Universal House of Justice 'and not the body of those who either directly or indirectly elect them, have thus been made the recipients of the Divine guidance which is at once the lifeblood and ultimate safeguard of this Revelation.'

As the Universal House of Justice has already announced, it cannot legislate to make possible the appointment of a successor to Shoghi Effendi, nor can it legislate to make possible the appointment of any more Hands of the Cause, but it must do everything within its power to ensure the performance of all those functions which it shares with these two mighty institutions. It must make provision for the proper discharge in future of the functions of protection and propagation, which the administrative bodies share with the Guardianship and the Hands of the Cause; it must, in the absence of the Guardian, receive and disburse the Ḥuqúqu'lláh, in accordance with the following statement of 'Abdu'l-Bahá: 'Disposition of the Ḥuqúq, wholly or partly is permissible, but this should be done by permission of the authority in the Cause to whom all must turn.' It must make provision in its constitution for the removal of any of its members who commits a sin 'injurious to the common weal'. Above all, it must, with perfect faith in Bahá'u'lláh, proclaim His Cause and enforce His law so that the Most Great Peace shall be firmly established in this world and the foundation of the Kingdom of God on earth shall be accomplished.[1]

7 December 1969

Your recent letter, in which you share with us the questions that have occurred to some of the youth in studying 'The Dispensation of Bahá'u'lláh,' has been carefully considered, and we feel that we should comment both on the particular passage you mention and on a related passage in the same work, because both bear on the relationship between the Guardianship and the Universal House of Justice.

The first passage concerns the Guardian's duty to insist upon a reconsideration by his fellow-members in the Universal House of Justice of any enactment which he believes conflicts with the meaning and departs from the spirit of the Sacred Writings. The second passage concerns the infallibility of the Universal House of Justice without the Guardian, namely Shoghi Effendi's statement that 'Without such an institition [the Guardianship] . . . the necessary guidance to define the sphere of the legislative action of its elected representatives would be totally withdrawn.'

Some of the youth, you indicate, were puzzled as to how to reconcile the former of these two passages with such statements as that in the Will of 'Abdu'l-Bahá which affirms that the Universal House of Justice is 'freed from all error'.

Just as the Will and Testament of 'Abdu'l-Bahá does not in any way contradict the Kitáb-i-Aqdas but, in the Guardian's words, 'confirms, supplements, and correlates the provisions of the Aqdas', so the writings of the Guardian contradict neither the revealed Word nor the interpretations of the Master. In attempting to understand the Writings, therefore, one must first realize that there is and can be no real contradiction in them, and in the light of this we can confidently seek the unity of meaning which they contain.

The Guardian and the Universal House of Justice have certain duties and functions in common; each also operates within a separate and distinct sphere. As Shoghi Effendi explained, '. . . it is made indubitably clear and evident that the Guardian of the Faith has been made the Interpreter of the Word and that the Universal House of Justice has been invested with the function of legislating on matters not expressly revealed in the teachings. The interpretation of the Guardian, functioning within his own sphere, is as authoritative and binding as the enactments of the International House of Justice, whose exclusive right and prerogative is to pronounce upon and deliver the final judgment on such laws and ordinances as Bahá'u'lláh has not expressly revealed.' He goes on to affirm, 'Neither can, nor will ever, infringe upon the sacred and prescribed domain of the other. Neither will seek to curtail the specific and undoubted authority with which both have been divinely invested.' It is impossible to conceive that two centres of authority, which the Master has stated 'are both under the care and protection of the Abhá Beauty, under the shelter and unerring guidance of His Holiness the Exalted One,' could conflict with one another, because both are vehicles of the same Divine Guidance.

The Universal House of Justice, beyond its function as the enactor of legislation, has been invested with the more general functions of protecting and administering the Cause, solving obscure questions and deciding upon matters that have caused difference. Nowhere is it stated that the infallibility of the Universal House of Justice is by virtue of the Guardian's membership or presence on that body. Indeed, 'Abdu'l-Bahá in His Will and Shoghi Effendi in his 'Dispensation of Bahá'u'lláh' have both explicitly stated that the elected members of the Universal House of Justice in consultation are recipients of unfailing Divine Guidance. Furthermore the Guardian himself in 'The World Order of Bahá'u'lláh' asserted that 'It must be also clearly understood by every believer that the institution of Guardianship does not under any circumstances abrogate, or even in the slightest degree detract from, the powers granted to the Universal House of Justice by Bahá'u'lláh in the Kitáb-i-Aqdas, and repeatedly and solemnly confirmed by 'Abdu'l-Bahá in His Will. It does not constitute in any manner a contradiction to the Will and Writings of Bahá'u'lláh, nor does it nullify any of His revealed instructions.'

While the specific responsibility of the Guardian is the interpretation of the Word, he is also invested with all the powers and prerogatives necessary to discharge his function as Guardian of the Cause, its Head and supreme protector. He is, furthermore, made the irremovable head and member for life of the supreme legislative body of the Faith. It is as the head of the Universal House of Justice, and as a member of that body, that the Guardian takes part in the process of legislation. If the following passage, which gave rise to your query, is considered as referring to this last relationship, you will see that there is no contradiction between it and the other texts: 'Though the Guardian of the Faith has been made the permanent head of so august a body he can never, even temporarily, assume the right of exclusive legislation. He cannot override the decision of the majority of his fellow-members, but is bound to insist upon a reconsideration by them of any enactment he conscientiously believes to conflict with the meaning and to depart from the spirit of Bahá'u'lláh's revealed utterances.'

Although the Guardian, in relation to his fellow-members within the Universal House of Justice, cannot override the decision of the majority, it is inconceivable that the other members would ignore any objection he raised in the course of consultation or pass legislation contrary to what he expressed as being in harmony with the spirit of the Cause. It is, after all, the final act of judgment delivered by the Universal House of Justice that is vouchsafed infallibility, not any views expressed in the course of the process of enactment.

It can be seen, therefore, that there is no conflict between the Master's statements concerning the unfailing divine guidance conferred upon the Universal House of Justice and the above passage from 'The Dispensation of Bahá'u'lláh'.

It may help the friends to understand this relationship if they are aware of some of the processes that the Universal House of Justice follows when legislating. First, of course, it observes the greatest care in studying the Sacred texts and the interpretations of the Guardian as well as considering the views of all the members. After long consultation the process of drafting a pronouncement is put into effect. During this process the whole matter may well be reconsidered. As a result of such reconsideration the final judgment may be significantly different from the conclusion earlier favored, or possibly it may be decided not to legislate at all on that subject at that time. One can understand how great would be the attention paid to the views of the Guardian during the above process were he alive.

In considering the second passage we must once more hold fast to the principle that the teachings do not contradict themselves.

Future Guardians are clearly envisaged and referred to in the Writings, but there is nowhere any promise or guarantee that the line of Guardians would endure forever; on the contrary there are clear indications that the line could be broken. Yet, in spite of this, there is a repeated insistence in the Writings on the indestructiblity of the Covenant and the immutability of God's Purpose for this Day.

One of the most striking passages which envisage the possibility of such a break in the line of Guardians is in the Kitáb-i-Aqdas itself:

> The endowments dedicated to charity revert to God, the Revealer of Signs. No one has the right to lay hold on them without leave from the Dawning-Place of Revelation. After Him the decision rests with the Aghṣán (Branches), and after them with the House of Justice – should it be established in the world by then – so that they may use these endowments for the benefit of the Sites exalted in this Cause, and for that which they have been commanded by God, the Almighty, the All-Powerful. Otherwise the endowments should be referred to the people of Bahá, who speak not without His leave and who pass no judgment but in accordance with that which God has ordained in this Tablet, they who are the

champions of victory betwixt heaven and earth, so that they may spend them on that which has been decreed in the Holy Book by God, the Mighty, the Bountiful.

The passing of Shoghi Effendi in 1957 precipitated the very situation provided for in this passage, in that the line of Aghṣán ended before the House of Justice had been elected. Although, as is seen, the ending of the line of Aghṣán at some stage was provided for, we must never underestimate the grievous loss that the Faith has suffered. God's purpose for mankind remains unchanged, however, and the mighty Covenant of Bahá'u'lláh remains impregnable. Has not Bahá'u'lláh stated categorically, 'The Hand of Omnipotence hath established His Revelation upon an unassailable, an enduring foundation.' While 'Abdu'l-Bahá confirms: 'Verily, God effecteth that which He pleaseth; naught can annul His Covenant; naught can obstruct His favor nor oppose His Cause!' 'Everything is subject to corruption; but the Covenant of thy Lord shall continue to pervade all regions.' 'The tests of every dispensation are in direct proportion to the greatness of the Cause and as heretofore such a manifest Covenant, written by the Supreme Pen, has not been entered upon, the tests are proportionately severe . . . These agitations of the violators are no more than the foam of the ocean, . . . this froth of the ocean shall not endure and shall soon disappear and vanish, while on the other hand the ocean of the Covenant shall eternally surge and roar.' And Shoghi Effendi has clearly stated: 'The bedrock on which this Administrative Order is founded is God's immutable Purpose for mankind in this day.' '. . . this priceless gem of Divine Revelation, now still in its embryonic state, shall evolve within the shell of His Law, and shall forge ahead, undivided and unimpaired, till it embraces the whole of mankind.'

In the Bahá'í Faith there are two authoritative centres appointed to which the believers must turn, for in reality the Interpreter of the Word is an extension of that centre which is the Word itself. The Book is the record of the utterance of Bahá'u'lláh, while the divinely inspired Interpreter is the living Mouth of that Book – it is he and he alone who can authoritatively state what the Book means. Thus one centre is the Book with its Interpreter, and the other is the Universal House of Justice guided by God to decide on whatever is not explicitly revealed in the Book. This pattern of centres and their relationships is apparent at every stage in the unfoldment of the Cause. In the Kitáb-i-Aqdas Bahá'u'lláh tells the believers to refer after His passing to the Book, and to 'Him Whom God hath purposed, Who hath branched from this Ancient Root.' In the Kitáb-i-Ahdí (the Book of Bahá'u'lláh's Covenant), He makes it clear that this reference is to 'Abdu'l-Bahá. In the Aqdas Bahá'u'lláh also ordains the institution of the Universal House of Justice, and confers upon it the powers necessary for it to discharge its ordained functions. The Master in His Will and Testament explicitly institutes the Guardianship, which Shoghi Effendi states was clearly anticipated in the verses of the Kitáb-i-Aqdas, reaffirms and elucidates the authority of the Universal House of Justice, and refers the believers once again to the Book: 'Unto the Most Holy Book everyone must turn and all that is not expressly recorded therein must be referred to the Universal House of Justice,' and at the very end of the Will He says: 'All must seek guidance and turn unto the Centre of the Cause and the House of Justice. And he that turneth unto whatsoever else is indeed in grievous error.'

As the sphere of jurisdiction of the Universal House of Justice in matters of legislation extends to whatever is not explicitly revealed in the Sacred Text, it is clear that the Book itself is the highest authority and delimits the sphere of action of the House of Justice. Likewise, the Interpreter of the Book must also have the authority to define the sphere of the legislative action of the elected representatives of the Cause. The writings of the Guardian and the advice given by him over the thirty-six years of his Guardianship show the way in which he exercised this function in relation to the Universal House of Justice as well as to National and Local Spiritual Assemblies.

The fact that the Guardian has the authority to define the sphere of the legislative action of the Universal House of Justice does not carry with it the corollary that without such guidance the Universal House of Justice might stray beyond the limits of its proper authority; such a deduction would conflict with all the other texts referring to its infallibility, and specifically with the Guardian's own clear assertion that the Universal House of Justice never can or will infringe on the sacred and prescribed domain of the Guardianship. It should be remembered, however, that although National and Local Spiritual Assemblies can receive divine guidance if they consult in the manner and spirit described by 'Abdu'l-Bahá, they do not share in the explicit guarantees of infallibility conferred upon the Universal House of Justice. Any careful student of the Cause can see with what care the Guardian, after the passing of 'Abdu'l-Bahá, guided these elected representatives of the believers in the painstaking erection of the Administrative Order and in the formulation of Local and National Bahá'í Constitutions.

We hope that these elucidations will assist the friends in understanding these relationships more clearly, but we must all remember that we stand too close to the beginnings of the System ordained by Bahá'u'lláh to be able fully to understand its potentialities or the interrelationships of its component parts. As Shoghi Effendi's secretary wrote on his behalf to an individual believer on 25 March 1930. 'The contents of the Will of the Master are far too much for the present generation to comprehend. It needs at least a century of actual working before the treasures of wisdom hidden in it can be revealed . . .'

With loving Bahá'í greetings,
THE UNIVERSAL HOUSE OF JUSTICE[2]

Bibliography

'ABDU'L-BAHÁ. *Foundations of World Unity*. Wilmette, Illinois: Bahá'í Publishing Trust, 1979.
—— *Paris Talks: Addresses Given by 'Abdu'l-Bahá in Paris in 1911–12*. London: Bahá'í Publishing Trust, 1951.
—— *Selections from the Writings of 'Abdu'l-Bahá*. Compiled by the Research Department of the Universal House of Justice; translated by a Committee at the Bahá'í World Centre and by Marzieh Gail. Haifa: Bahá'í World Centre, 1978.
—— *Some Answered Questions*. Compiled by Laura Clifford Barney. Wilmette, Illinois: rev. edn 1981.
—— *A Traveller's Narrative written to illustrate the episode of the Báb*. Translated by E.G. Browne. 1930, RP Amsterdam: Philo Press 1975.
—— *Will and Testament of 'Abdu'l-Bahá*. Wilmette, Illinois: Bahá'í Publishing Committee, 1944.
AFRÚKHTIH, DR YÚNIS KHÁN. *Kháṭirát-i-Nuh-Sáliy-i-'Akká* (Memories of Nine Years in 'Akká). Written in the year BE 99 (AD 1942). Ṭihrán, undated.
BÁB, THE. *Selections from the Writings of the Báb*. Compiled by the Research Department of the Universal House of Justice and translated by Habib Taherzadeh with the assistance of a Committee at the Bahá'í World Centre. Haifa: Bahá'í World Centre, 1976.
Bahá'í News. no. 1 (Dec. 1924). Wilmette, Illinois: National Spiritual Assembly of the Bahá'í of the United States.
Bahá'í World, The. An International Record. Vol. VIII. 1938–40. Wilmette, Illinois: Bahá'í Publishing Committee, 1942. Vol. IX. 1940–44. Wilmette, Illinois: Bahá'í Publishing Committee, 1945. Vol. XVIII. 1979–1983. Haifa: Bahá'í World Centre, 1986.
BAHÁ'U'LLÁH. *Áthár-i-Qalam-i-A'lá* (The Traces of the Supreme Pen). A compilation of the Writings of Bahá'u'lláh. Ṭihrán: Bahá'í Publishing Trust. Vol. 1, BE 120 (AD 1963); Vol. 4, BE 125 (AD 1968).
—— *Epistle to the Son of the Wolf*. Trans. by Shoghi Effendi. Wilmette, Illinois: Bahá'í Publishing Trust, rev. edn. 1953.
—— *Gleanings from the Writings of Bahá'u'lláh*. Trans. by Shoghi Effendi. Wilmette, Illinois: Bahá'í Publishing Trust, 1935; rev. edn 1952. London: Bahá'í Publishing Trust, 1949.
—— *The Hidden Words*. Trans. by Shoghi Effendi with the assistance of some English friends. First published in England 1932. London: Bahá'í Publishing Trust, 1949. Wilmette, Illinois: Bahá'í Publishing Trust, rev. edn 1954.
—— *Iqtidárát*. A compilation of the Tablets of Bahá'u'lláh. AH 1310 (AD 1892–3).
—— *Ishráqát*. A compilation of the Tablets of Baha'u'llah. India: AH 1310 (AD 1892–3).
—— *Kitáb-i-Aqdas*. Extracts translated by Shoghi Effendi in *Synopsis and Codification*

of the Kitáb-i-Aqdas, the Most Holy Book of Bahá'u'lláh. Haifa: Bahá'í World Centre, 1973.

—— *Kitáb-i-Íqán. The Book of Certitude*. Translated by Shoghi Effendi. Wilmette, Illinois: Bahá'í Publishing Trust, rev. edn 1974.

—— *Prayers and Meditations by Bahá'u'lláh*. Translated by Shoghi Effendi. Wilmette, Illinois: Bahá'í Publishing Trust, 6th RP 1974.

—— *The Proclamation of Bahá'u'lláh to the Kings and Leaders of the World*. Haifa: Bahá'í World Centre, 1967.

—— *Tablets of Bahá'u'lláh revealed after the Kitáb-i-Aqdas*. Compiled by the Research Department of the Universal House of Justice and translated by Habib Taherzadeh with the assistance of a Committee at the Bahá'í World Centre. Haifa: Bahá'í World Centre, 1978.

Bahíyyih Khánum, the Greatest Holy Leaf. Haifa: Bahá'í World Centre, 1982.

Balyuzi, H.M. *'Abdu'l-Bahá, the Centre of the Covenant of Bahá'u'lláh*. Oxford: George Ronald, 1971.

—— *Bahá'u'lláh, the King of Glory*. Oxford: George Ronald, 1980.

Blomfield, Lady (Sitárih Khánum). *The Chosen Highway*. London: Bahá'í Publishing Trust, 1940. Wilmette, Illinois: Bahá'í Publishing Trust, 1967.

Browne, E.G. *Materials for the Study of the Bábí Religion*. Cambridge: Cambridge University Press, 1918.

Fáḍil-i-Mázindarání, Asadu'lláh, Mírzá. *Amr Va Khalq* (Revelation and Creation). Ṭihrán: Bahá'í Publishing Trust. Vol. 1, BE 122 (AD 1965); Vol. 3, BE 128 (AD 1971); Vol. 4, BE 131 (AD 1974).

—— *Asráru'l-Áthár*. A glossary of Bahá'í terms. Ṭihrán: Bahá'í Publishing Trust, 5 Vols., BE 124–9 (AD 1967–72).

Fáḍil-i-Yazdí. *Mináhiju'l-Aḥkám*. Vol. 2. Unpublished compilation, National Archives Committee of Persia.

Furútan, A.A. *Stories of Bahá'u'lláh*. Oxford: George Ronald, 1986.

Gail, Marzieh. *Summon Up Remembrance*. Oxford: George Ronald, 1987.

Ḥaydar-'Alí, Ḥájí Mírzá. *Bihjatu'ṣ-Ṣudúr*. Reminiscences and autobiography. Bombay: 1913.

Holley, Horace. *Religion for Mankind*. Oxford: George Ronald, 1976.

Ishráq Khávarí, 'Abdu'l-Ḥamíd. *Raḥíq-i-Makhtúm*. A commentary on a letter of Shoghi Effendi. 2 vols. Ṭihrán, Bahá'í Publishing Trust, BE 103 (AD 1946).

—— *Risáliy-i-Ayyám-i-Tis'ih*. The history of the nine Bahá'í Holy Days together with a compilation of relevant Tablets. Ṭihrán: Bahá'í Publishing Trust, BE 103 (AD 1946); 3rd RP BE 121 (AD 1964).

Ives, Howard Colby. *Portals to Freedom*. London: George Ronald, 1967.

Koran, The. Translated by George Sale. London: Frederick Warne & Co., undated.

Má'idiy-i-Ásamání. A compilation of Bahá'í Writings. Compiled by 'Abdu'l-Ḥamíd Ishráq Khávarí. 9 vols. and one index volume. Ṭihrán: Bahá'í Publishing Trust, BE 129 (AD 1972).

Maxwell, May. *An Early Pilgrimage*. Oxford: George Ronald, 1969.

Mu'ayyad, Dr Ḥabíb. *Kháṭirát-i-Ḥabíb* (Memoirs of Ḥabíb). Ṭihrán: 1961.

Nabíl-i-A'ẓam (Muḥammad-i-Zarandí). *The Dawn-Breakers*. Nabíl's Narrative of the Early Days of the Bahá'í Revelation. Wilmette. Illinois: Bahá'í Publishing Trust, 1932.

Owen, Rosamond Dale. *My Perilous Life in Palestine*. London: George Allen & Unwin, 1928.

Rabbani, Ruḥíyyih. *The Passing of Shoghi Effendi*. London: Bahá'í Publishing Trust, 1958.

—— *The Priceless Pearl*. London: Bahá'í Publishing Trust, 1969.
SHOGHI EFFENDI. *The Advent of Divine Justice*. First published 1939. Wilmette, Illinois: Bahá'í Publishing Trust, rev. edn 1963.
—— *Bahá'í Administration*. 5th rev. edn. Wilmette, Illinois: Bahá'í Publishing Trust, 1968.
—— *Citadel of Faith: Messages to America* 1947–1957. Wilmette, Illinois: Bahá'í Publishing Trust, RP 1980.
—— *God Passes By*. Wilmette, Illinois: Bahá'í Publishing Trust, 1944.
—— *High Endeavours: Messages to Alaska*. National Spiritual Assembly of the Bahá'ís of Alaska, 1976.
—— *Messages to America*. Selected Letters and Cablegrams Addressed to the Bahá'ís of North America 1932–1946. Wilmette, Illinois: Bahá'í Publishing Committee, 1947.
—— *Messages to the Bahá'í World:* 1950–1957. Wilmette, Illinois: Bahá'í Publishing Trust, 1971.
—— *The Promised Day Is Come*. First published 1941. Wilmette, Illinois: Bahá'í Publishing Trust, rev. edn 1961.
—— *The Unfolding Destiny of the British Bahá'í Community*. London: Bahá'í Publishing Trust, 1981.
—— *The World Order of Bahá'u'lláh*. First published 1938. Wilmette, Illinois: Bahá'í Publishing Trust, rev. edn 1955.
Star of the West. v.1, no. 1 (1910) – v.25. no. 12 (1935). Chicago: Bahá'í News Service. 8 vols. Reprinted. Oxford: George Ronald, 1978.
SULAYMÁNÍ, 'AZÍZU'LLÁH. *Maṣábiḥ-i-Hidáyat*. Biography of some of the early Bahá'ís. Ṭihrán: Bahá'í Publishing Trust, Vol. 7, BE 129 (AD 1972).
TOWNSHEND, G. *The Covenant, An Analysis*. Manchester: Bahá'í Publishing Trust, 1950.
TUDOR-POLE, WELLESLEY. *Writing on the Ground*. London: Neville Spearman, 1968.
THE UNIVERSAL HOUSE OF JUSTICE. *Messages from The Universal House of Justice* 1968–1973. Wilmette, Illinois: Bahá'í Publishing Trust, 1976.
—— *Wellspring of Guidance: Messages* 1963–1968. Wilmette, Illinois: Bahá'í Publishing Trust, 1969.
The Universal House of Justice. Extracts from the Writings of Bahá'u'lláh, 'Abdu'l-Bahá and Shoghi Effendi. Compiled by the Research Department of the Universal House of Justice. London: Bahá'í Publishing Trust, 1984.
Women. Extracts from the Writings of Bahá'u'lláh, 'Abdu'l-Bahá, Shoghi Effendi and the Universal House of Justice. Compiled by the Research Department of the Universal House of Justice. London, Wilmette: Bahá'í Publishing Trust, 1986.
ZARQÁNÍ, MÍRZÁ MAḤMÚD-I-. *Kitáb-i-Badáyi'u'l-Á<u>th</u>ár*. Diary of 'Abdu'l-Bahá's travels in Europe and America, written by His secretary. Bombay: Vol. I, 1914: Vol. II, 1921.

References

Full details of authors and titles are given in the Bibliography.

INTRODUCTION

1. *Hidden Words*, Persian no. 29.
2. Townshend, *The Covenant, An Analysis*.

PROLOGUE: THE COVENANT AND THE HUMAN SOUL

1. *Hidden Words*, Arabic no. 5.
2. *Gleanings*, LXXXIII, para. 4.
3. John 16: 12–13.
4. *Qur'án* 17:89.
5. *Gleanings*, LXXXII, paras. 1 and 6.
6. *Messages to Alaska*, p. 71.
7. *Gleanings*, LXXXII, para. 8.
8. *Selections from the Writings of 'Abdu'l-Bahá*, pp. 152–3.
9. *Má'idiy-i-Ásamání*, vol. 7, pp. 119–25.
10. *Gleanings*, LXXVII.
11. *Gleanings*, LXXX, para. 2.
12. *Má'idiy-i-Ásamání*, vol. 4, p. 20.
13. *Gleanings*, LXXXI.
14. *ibid.* LXXXII, para. 7.
15. *Foundations of World Unity*, p. 77.
16. *Gleanings*, LXXXII, para. 1.
17. *ibid.* LXXXVI, paras. 1, 2, 3.
18. *Some Answered Questions*, ch. 62.
19. *ibid.*
20. Short Obligatory Prayer, in most Bahá'í prayer books.
21. Quoted by Shoghi Effendi, *The Advent of Divine Justice*, p. 64.
22. *Gleanings*, VI, paras. 1 and 3.
23. *Iqtidárát*, p. 151.
24. *Gleanings*, LXXXI.
25. *Má'idiy-i-Ásamání*, vol. IV, p. 26.
26. *ibid.* CLIII, para. 6.
27. *The Proclamation of Bahá'u'lláh*, p. 95.
28. *Hidden Words*, Persian no. 27.
29. Quoted by Shoghi Effendi, *The Advent of Divine Justice*, p. 28.
30. *Má'idiy-i-Ásamání*, vol. 8, p. 29.
31. *Hidden Words*, Persian no. 69.
32. *Synopsis and Codification*, p. 12.
33. Quoted by Shoghi Effendi in *The World Order of Bahá'u'lláh*, p. 139.

CHAPTER 1: THE COVENANT OF THE BÁB

1. Shoghi Effendi, *God Passes By*, p. 57.

2. *The World Order of Bahá'u'lláh*, p. 123.
3. *Má'idiy-i-Ásamání*, vol. 4, p. 154.
4. *Ishráqát*, p. 221.
5. *Selections from the Writings of the Báb*, p. 149.
6. *The Dawn-Breakers*, p. 96.
7. *ibid.* pp. 104–8.
8. *ibid.* pp. 126–8.
9. *Selections from the Writings of the Báb*, p. 104.
10. Quoted by Shoghi Effendi in *The World Order of Bahá'u'lláh*, p. 10.
11. *ibid.* p. 113.
12. *Prayers and Meditations*, no. 176.
13. *Messages to America*, p. 100.
14. Quoted by Shoghi Effendi in *The World Order of Bahá'u'lláh*, pp. 109.
15. Letter to an individual believer, 23 July 1936.
16. Quoted by Shoghi Effendi in *The Advent of Divine Justice*, p. 64.
17. *ibid.* p. 65.
18. *ibid.*
19. *ibid.*
20. Quoted by Shoghi Effendi, in *The World Order of Bahá'u'lláh*, pp. 106–7.
21. *ibid.* p. 104.
22. *ibid.* p. 109.
23. *ibid.* p. 100.
24. *ibid.* p. 101.
25. *ibid.* p. 101.
26. *Selections from the Writings of the Báb*, p. 3.
27. Quoted by Bahá'u'lláh in *Epistle to the Son of the Wolf*, p. 171.
28. *ibid.* p. 154.
29. *ibid.*
30. *The World Order of Bahá'u'lláh*, p. 112.
31. *Selections from the Writings of the Báb*, p. 98.
32. Quoted by Bahá'u'lláh in *Epistle to the Son of the Wolf*, p. 142.
33. *Selections from the Writings of the Báb*, pp. 156–7.
34. *ibid.* p. 86.
35. Quoted by Bahá'u'lláh in *Epistle to the Son of the Wolf*, p. 155.
36. *Selections from the Writings of the Báb*, p. 131.
37. *ibid.* p. 155.
38. *Persian Bayán* III:7.
39. *ibid.* III:15.
40. Quoted by Shoghi Effendi in *God Passes By*, p. 25.
41. *Kitáb-i-Panj-Sha'n* III, III:16.
42. Quoted by Bahá'u'lláh in *Epistle to the Son of the Wolf*, pp. 154–5.
43. *ibid.* p. 152.
44. *ibid.* p. 174.
45. *Selections from the Writings of the Báb*, p. 104.
46. *ibid.* p. 100.
47. Quoted by Bahá'u'lláh in *Epistle to the Son of the Wolf*, p. 151.
48. *Persian Bayán* III:2.
49. *Selections from the Writings of the Báb*, p. 85.
50. Quoted by Bahá'u'lláh in *Epistle to the Son of the Wolf*, p. 158.
51. *ibid.* p. 153.
52. *Selections from the Writings of the Báb*, pp. 132–3.
53. *ibid.* p. 144.

54. Quoted by Bahá'u'lláh in *Epistle to the Son of the Wolf*, p. 159.
55. *ibid.* p. 172.
56. *Selections from the Writings of the Báb*, p. 148.
57. Quoted by Bahá'u'lláh in *Epistle to the Son of the Wolf*, p. 141.
58. *ibid.* p. 152.
59. Quoted by Shoghi Effendi in *God Passes By*, p. 29.
60. Quoted by Bahá'u'lláh in *Epistle to the Son of the Wolf*, p. 174.
61. *ibid.* p. 41.
62. Quoted by Shoghi Effendi in *God Passes By*, p. 29.
63. *Selections from the Writings of the Báb*, p. 7.
64. Quoted by Shoghi Effendi in *God Passes By*, pp. 29–30.
65. *Selections from the Writings of the Báb*, pp. 129–30.
66. *ibid.* p. 134.
67. *ibid.* p. 144.
68. Quoted by Bahá'u'lláh in *Epistle to the Son of the Wolf*, p. 165.
69. *Selections from the Writings of the Báb*, p. 144.
70. *ibid.* p. 101.
71. *ibid.* p. 164.

CHAPTER 2: THE FULFILMENT OF THE COVENANT OF THE BÁB

1. *God Passes By*, pp. 93–99.
2. Quoted by Blomfield, *Chosen Highway*, p. 45.
3. *Má'idiy-i-Ásamání*, vol. 7, p. 98.
4. *Asráru'l-Á<u>th</u>ár*, vol. 2, pp. 7–18.
5. *The Dawn-Breakers*, pp. 32–3.

CHAPTER 3: MÍRZÁ YAḤYÁ, THE NOMINEE OF THE BÁB

1. *The Dawn-Breakers*, p. 443.
2. *ibid.* p. 583.

CHAPTER 4: THE BREAKING OF THE BÁB'S COVENANT

1. *God Passes By*, pp. 112–13.
2. In Sulaymání, *Maṣábiḥ-i-Hidáyat*, vol. 2, pp. 504–6.
3. *God Passes By*, p. 117.
4. *Synopsis and Codification*, p. 11.
5. *Persian Bayán* VI:14.
6. Quoted by Shoghi Effendi, *God Passes By*, p. 113.
7. *ibid.* p. 3.
8. *ibid.* p. 115.
9. *Kitáb-i-Íqán*, pp. 250–51.
10. Quoted by Blomfield, *Chosen Highway*, pp. 50–52.
11. *Epistle to the Son of the Wolf*, pp. 176–7.
12. *ibid.* p. 173.
13. *ibid.* p. 23.
14. Quoted by Shoghi Effendi, *God Passes By*, p. 133.
15. *Bihjatu'ṣ-Ṣudúr*, pp. 22–4.
16. *ibid.* pp. 24–6.
17. Quoted by Balyuzi, *Bahá'u'lláh, the King of Glory*, pp. 183–4.
18. *Epistle to the Son of the Wolf*, p. 168.
19. *God Passes By*, pp. 165–6.
20. Translated by the author.
21. *ibid.*
22. Quoted by Shoghi Effendi, *God Passes By*, p. 167.
23. *ibid.*

24. *Bihjatu'ṣ-Ṣudúr*, p. 76.
25. *God Passes By*, pp. 167–8.

CHAPTER 5: THE TRIUMPH OF THE COVENANT OF THE BÁB

1. *God Passes By*, pp. 168–9.
2. *Bihjatu'ṣ-Ṣudúr*, pp. 77–9.
3. *II Thessalonians* 2: 3,4,8; stated by Shoghi Effendi in a letter to Isfandíyar-i-Majzúb, 17 November 1935.
4. *God Passes By*, pp. 170–71.
5. *Má'idiy-i-Ásamání*, vol. 4, p. 259.
6. *God Passes By*, pp. 183–4.
7. *Raḥíq-i-Makhtúm*, vol. 2.
8. *God Passes By*, p. 233.

CHAPTER 6: 'ABDU'L-BAHÁ, THE CENTRE OF THE COVENANT

1. Quoted by Shoghi Effendi, *The World Order of Bahá'u'lláh*, p. 135.
2. *ibid.* p. 139.
3. *A Traveller's Narrative*, introduction, p. xxxvi.
4. *Writing on the Ground*, pp. 142–6.
5. *Religion for Mankind*, p. 232–3.
6. *Portals to Freedom*, pp. 30–33.
7. *Kitáb-i-Badí'*, pp. 176–7.

CHAPTER 7: THE FAMILY OF BAHÁ'U'LLÁH

1. Quoted by Shoghi Effendi, *The Promised Day Is Come*, pp. 40–41.
2. See Balyuzi, *Bahá'u'lláh the King of Glory*; Furútan, *Stories of Bahá'u'lláh*.
3. *The Dawn-Breakers*, pp. 294–5.
4. Quoted by Blomfield, *Chosen Highway*, pp. 39–40.
5. Quoted by Shoghi Effendi, *Messages to America*, pp. 34–5.
6. *Isaiah* 54: 1–13.
7. Quoted by Shoghi Effendi, *Messages to America*, pp. 35–6.
8. *Bahíyyih Khánum*, pp. 3–4.
9. *ibid.* p. 4.
10. *ibid.* pp. 7–8.
11. *ibid.* pp. 42–5 passim.
12. *Messages to America*, p. 34.
13. Quoted by Shoghi Effendi, *ibid.* pp. 33–4.

CHAPTER 8: THE ARCH-BREAKER OF BAHÁ'U'LLÁH'S COVENANT

1. *Raḥíq-i-Makhtúm*, vol. 2, p. 850.
2. Quoted by Shoghi Effendi, *God Passes By*, p. 242.
3. *Raḥíq-i-Makhtúm*, vol. 1, p. 551.
4. Quoted by Shoghi Effendi, *God Passes By*, p. 251.
5. *Tablets of Bahá'u'lláh*, p. 222.
6. Quoted by Shoghi Effendi, *God Passes By*, p. 251.
7. *ibid.* p. 249.
8. *Gleanings*, LXXIV.

CHAPTER 9: THE RELATIONSHIP OF BAHÁ'U'LLÁH AND 'ABDU'L-BAHÁ

1. Quoted by Shoghi Effendi, *The World Order of Bahá'u'lláh*, p. 135.
2. *ibid.*
3. *ibid.*
4. *ibid.* pp. 135–6.
5. *Tablets of Bahá'u'lláh*, pp. 227–8.
6. *Bihjatu'ṣ-Ṣudúr*, pp. 251–2.

CHAPTER 10: THE APPOINTMENT OF 'ABDU'L-BAHÁ

1. *Synopsis and Codification*, p. 24.
2. *ibid.* p. 27.
3. Cited by Fáḍil-i-Yazdí, *Mináhiju'l-Aḥkám*, vol. 2, p. 657.
4. *Tablets of Bahá'u'lláh*, pp. 219–223.

CHAPTER 11: THE BREAKING OF BAHÁ'U'LLÁH'S COVENANT

1. Printed in Egypt, no date. Translation by the author.

CHAPTER 12: THE DAY THAT SHALL NOT BE FOLLOWED BY NIGHT

1. *God Passes By*, pp. 237–8.
2. *Kitáb-i-Íqán*, p. 144.
3. *Gleanings*, XXII, para. 2.
4. Quoted by Shoghi Effendi, *The World Order of Bahá'u'lláh*, p. 119.
5. *Synopsis and Codification*, p. 24.

CHAPTER 13: PRINCIPAL COVENANT-BREAKERS DURING THE MINISTRY OF 'ABDU'L-BAHÁ

1. Bahá'u'lláh, *Hidden Words*, Arabic No. 4.

CHAPTER 14: CLANDESTINE OPPOSITION TO THE COVENANT

1. *Bihjatu'ṣ-Ṣudúr*, p. 323.
2. *ibid.* pp. 326–31.
3. *ibid.* pp. 337–8.
4. *Kh͟áṭirát-i-Nuh-Sáliy-i-'Akká*, pp. 51–2.
5. *Bijhatu'ṣ-Ṣudúr*, pp. 334–5.
6. *Kh͟áṭirát-i-Nuh-Sálih*, p. 216.

CHAPTER 15: MÍRZÁ ÁQÁ JÁN

1. *Matthew* 5:5.
2. *Qur'án* 28:5.
3. *Kh͟áṭirát-i-Nuh-Sálih*, pp. 54–6.
4. *ibid.* p. 80.
5. *ibid.* pp. 90–91
6. *ibid.* p. 84.
7. *ibid.*
8. *Bihjatu'ṣ-Ṣudúr*, p. 479.

CHAPTER 16: DISCREDITING THE CENTRE OF THE COVENANT

1. *Kh͟áṭirát-i-Nuh-Sálih*, pp. 250–56.
2. *My Perilous Life in Palestine*, pp. 230–35.

CHAPTER 17: 'ABDU'L-BAHÁ IN ACTION

1. *Kh͟áṭirát-i-Nuh-Sálih*, pp. 63–6.
2. *ibid.* pp. 570–73.
3. *ibid.* pp. 259–65.

CHAPTER 18: COVENANT-BREAKING IN PERSIA

1. *Synopsis and Codification*, p. 27.
2. *Iqtidárát*, pp. 294–5.
3. *Gleanings*, CXLII, paras. 1–3.
4. *Raḥíq-i-Mak͟htúm*, vol. 1, p. 317.
5. Unpublished memoirs.
6. *Má'idiy-i-Ásamání*, vol. 5, pp. 98–9.
7. Quoted by Shoghi Effendi, *The World Order of Bahá'u'lláh*, p. 133.
8. *ibid.* p. 138.
9. *Kh͟áṭirát-i-Nuh-Sálih*, pp. 331–6.

CHAPTER 19: BUILDING THE SHRINE OF THE BÁB

1. *Kháṭirát-i-Nuh-Sálih*, pp. 145–7.
2. Quoted by Shoghi Effendi, *God Passes By*, p. 275.
3. *Kháṭirát-i-Ḥabíb*, vol. 1, p. 81.
4. *ibid.* p. 449.

CHAPTER 20: YEARS OF INCARCERATION

1. Recorded by Fáḍil-i-Mázandaráni, *Asráru'l-Áthár*, vol. 4, pp. 361–3.
2. *Selections from the Writings of 'Abdu'l-Bahá*, pp. 216–221.
3. *Synopsis and Codification*, p. 14.
4. See Appendix I.
5. *ibid.*
6. *Khánidán-i-Afnán*, p. 117.
7. *The World Order of Bahá'u'lláh*, p. 17.
8. *Gleanings*, XXIX, para. 5.
9. Quoted by Shoghi Effendi, *The Advent of Divine Justice*, p. 5.
10. *Messages to America*, p. 51.
11. *Bahá'í Administration*, p. 123.
12. *God Passes By*, p. 315.
13. *The World Order of Bahá'u'lláh*, p. 17.
14. Shoghi Effendi, in *The Dawn-Breakers*, p. 667.

CHAPTER 21: COVENANT-BREAKING IN THE WEST

1. *An Early Pilgrimage*, pp. 12–13.
2. Quoted by Blomfield, *Chosen Highway*, pp. 235–6.
3. Balyuzi, *'Abdu'l-Bahá*, pp. 271–2.
4. Quoted by Browne, *Materials*, p. 171.
5. *God Passes By*, p. 295.
6. *Selections from the Writings of 'Abdu'l-Bahá*, pp. 258–9.
7. *ibid.* p. 212.
8. *God Passes By*, pp. 319–20.

CHAPTER 22: THE BAHÁ'Í ATTITUDE TO COVENANT-BREAKING

1. Quoted by Rúḥíyyih Rabbání, *Priceless Pearl*, p. 49.
2. *Will and Testament*, see Appendix I.
3. *Star of the West*, vol. XII, p. 233.
4. *Selections from the Writings of 'Abdu'l-Bahá*, pp. 210–11.
5. *Kháṭirát-i-Nuh-Sálih*, pp. 357–8.
6. *Will and Testament*, see Appendix I.
7. *ibid.*

CHAPTER 23: FOSTERING STEADFASTNESS IN THE COVENANT

1. *The World Order of Bahá'u'lláh*, p. 100.
2. *Hidden Words*, Arabic no. 59.
3. *ibid.* Persian no. 27.
4. *ibid.* Persian no. 26.
5. *ibid.* Persian no. 11.
6. Short Obligatory Prayer, in most Bahá'í prayer books.
7. Quoted by Shoghi Effendi, *The Promised Day Is Come*, p. 82.
8. *Kitáb-i-Íqán*, p. 15.
9. *ibid.*
10. *Synopsis and Codification*, p. 11.
11. Quoted by Shoghi Effendi, *The World Order of Bahá'u'lláh*, p. 135.
12. *Synopsis and Codification*, pp. 25–6.

13. *Khátirát-i-Nuh-Sálih*, p. 99.
14. *ibid.* p. 123.

CHAPTER 24: THE CLOSE OF THE HEROIC AGE

1. *Tablets*, p. 224.
2. *God Passes By*, pp. 314–15.
3. *ibid.* p. 324.
4. *Star of the West*, 2 March 1922, pp. 294–5.
5. *The Priceless Pearl*, p. 39.
6. *ibid.* pp. 40–41.

CHAPTER 25: SHOGHI EFFENDI, GUARDIAN OF THE FAITH

1. *Will and Testament*, see Appendix I.
2. Quoted by Ruhíyyih Rabbání, *Priceless Pearl*, p. 5.
3. *ibid.* pp. 5–6.
4. *ibid.* p. 1.
5. *Isaiah* 15:16.
6. Quoted in *The Priceless Pearl*, p. 2.
7. *ibid.* p. 17.
8. *ibid.* p. 29.
9. *ibid.* pp. 42–3.
10. Zarqání, *Kitáb-i-Badayi'u'l-Áthár*, vol. 2, p. 250.
11. *The Priceless Pearl*, p. 48.
12. *ibid.* p. 49.
13. *ibid.* pp. 53–4.
14. *ibid.* pp. 70–71.
15. *ibid.* p. 57.

CHAPTER 26: BUILDING THE FOUNDATIONS OF THE ADMINISTRATIVE ORDER

1. *Tawqí'át-i-Mubárikih*, Bahá'í Publishing Trust, Ṭihrán, 129 BE.
2. *God Passes By*, p. 324.
3. *Bahá'í Administration*, pp. 15–16.
4. *ibid.* pp. 21–23.
5. *The Advent of Divine Justice*, pp. 15–17.
6. *Messages to America*, pp. 8–9.
7. Quoted by Rabbani, *The Priceless Pearl*, p. 108.

CHAPTER 27: THE EXPOUNDER OF THE REVELATION OF BAHÁ'U'LLÁH

1. *God Passes By*, p. 3.
2. *Bahá'í Administration*, p. 196.
3. *God Passes By*, p. 323.
4. *Bahá'í News*, no. 258.

CHAPTER 28: THE ADMINISTRATIVE ORDER IN ACTION

1. Shoghi Effendi, *Messages to America*, p. 7.
2. *Unfolding Destiny*, pp. 260–61.
3. *Messages to the Bahá'í World*, p. 42.
4. *ibid.* pp. 40–44.

CHAPTER 29: VITAL DEVELOPMENTS AT THE WORLD CENTRE

1. *Will and Testament*.
2. See *The Bahá'í World*, vol. 18, pp. 473–5, 516–27.
3. *Messages to the Bahá'í World*, p. 8.
4. *ibid.* p. 7.
5. *The Priceless Pearl*, p. 253.

6. *Citadel of Faith*, pp. 95–6.
7. *Messages to the Bahá'í World*, p. 169.
8. *Messages to America*, p. 31.
9. *Messages to the Bahá'í World*, pp. 74–5.
10. *The Priceless Pearl*, pp. 232–3.
11. *ibid.* pp. 228–9.

CHAPTER 30: REBELLION IN THE EAST AGAINST THE GUARDIAN

1. *Bahíyyih Khánum*, pp. 218–19.
2. *God Passes By*, p. 327.
3. *Bahá'í Administration*, pp. 137–9.
4. *Messages to the Bahá'í World*, pp. 53–4.
5. *Citadel of Faith*, p. 89.

CHAPTER 31: REBELLION IN THE WEST

1. *The Bahá'í World*, vol. IX, p. 858.
2. *Bahá'í News*, May 1934.
3. *Messages to America*, pp. 49–50.
4. Published in *Bahá'í News*.
5. Letter to an individual believer, 2 October 1974.

CHAPTER 32: THE FAITHLESS RELATIVES OF SHOGHI EFFENDI

1. *Hidden Words*, Persian no. 69.
2. *The Priceless Pearl*, pp. 13–14.
3. *Bahá'í Administration*, p. 25.
4. *Messages to America*, p. 11.
5. *Messages to the Bahá'í World*, pp. 87–8.
6. *Kháṭirát-i-Afnán*, pp. 165–6.
7. *The Bahá'í World*, vol. VIII, p. 262.
8. *ibid.* p. 260.
9. *Bahá'í News*, no. 149.
10. *ibid.* no. 16.
11. *Unfolding Destiny*, p. 149.
12. *Bahá'í News*, no. 172.
13. *Messages to America*, p. 75.
14. *The Priceless Pearl*, p. 124.
15. *Bahá'í News*, no. 174.
16. *Citadel of Faith*, pp. 78–9.
17. *Unfolding Destiny*, p. 248.
18. *Citadel of Faith*, p. 87.
19. *Messages to the Bahá'í World*, p. 48.
20. *ibid.* p. 16.
21. *ibid.* pp. 24–5.
22. *The Priceless Pearl*, p. 120.
23. *ibid.* pp. 121–2.
24. *ibid.* pp. 122–3.
25. *Messages to the Bahá'í World*, pp. 120–21.
26. *The Priceless Pearl*, p. 234.

CHAPTER 33: THE ONWARD MARCH OF THE FAITH

1. *Selections*, p. 228.
2. *Messages to America*, p. 51.
3. *Citadel of Faith*, p. 5.
4. *Messages to the Bahá'í World*, p. 61.

5. *Citadel of Faith*, p. 6.
6. *Messages to the Bahá'í World*, p. 19.

CHAPTER 34: THE CHIEF STEWARDS

1. *The Passing of Shoghi Effendi*, p. 12.
2. *ibid.* p. 14.
3. *Messages to the Bahá'í World*, pp. 122–3.
4. *ibid.* p. 127.
5. *Bahá'í News*, no. 323.
6. In *The World Order of Bahá'u'lláh*, pp. 147–8.
7. *Wellspring of Guidance*, p. 47.
8. *Messages*, pp. 40–41.

CHAPTER 35: THE UNIVERSAL HOUSE OF JUSTICE

1. Shoghi Effendi, *Bahá'í Administration*, p. 88.
2. *Some Answered Questions*, pp. 172–3.
3. *Tablets of Bahá'u'lláh*, pp. 26–7.
4. *ibid.* p. 68.
5. Quoted in *Wellspring of Guidance*, pp. 84–5.
6. *ibid.* p. 11.
7. *ibid.* p. 41.
8. *Selections*, p. 302.
9. *ibid.* pp. 79–80.
10. *Paris Talks*, p. 182.
11. *Selections*, p. 80.
12. Letter of 28 July 1936, quoted in *Women*, p. 12.
13. *Women*, p. 14.
14. Bahá'u'lláh, *Tablets*, p. 5.
15. Letter to the Persian Bahá'ís, Naw-Ruz, 111.
16. *Synopsis and Codification*, p. 16.
17. *Tablets*, pp. 69–70.
18. *ibid.* pp. 129–30.
19. Quoted in *The Universal House of Justice* (comp.), p. 48.
20. *ibid.* p. 51.
21. Quoted in *Wellspring of Guidance*, p. 84.
22. Letter to the Persian Bahá'ís, 27 November 1929.

CHAPTER 36: THE UNFOLDMENT OF THE COVENANT

1. *Raḥíq-i-Ma<u>kh</u>túm*, vol. 2, p. 632.
2. *Hidden Words*, Persian no. 71.
3. *Asráru'l-Á<u>th</u>ár*, vol. 5, p. 39.
4. *Hidden Words*, Persian No. 19.
5. *God Passes By*, p. 238.
6. *Messages to the Bahá'í World*, p. 103.
7. *ibid.* p. 74.
8. *ibid.*
9. *ibid.*
10. *God Passes By*, pp. 325–7.

APPENDIX 3: THE GUARDIANSHIP AND THE UNIVERSAL HOUSE OF JUSTICE

1. *Wellspring of Guidance*, pp. 89–91.
2. *Messages from the Universal House of Justice*, pp. 37–44.

INDEX

Entries are alphabetized word by word: component parts of hyphenated names are treated as separate words, but the connective -i- is ignored. Thus, 'Alíy-i- is treated as if it were spelt 'Alí.

'Abbás Effendi, *see* 'Abdu'l-Bahá
'Abbás-i-Núrí, Mírzá, *see* Buzurg, Mírzá
'Abdu'l-'Azíz, Sulṭán, 86
  Edict of, 94
'Abdu'l-Bahá, 117, 125, 127, 130, 304, 372
  achievements of, 274–5
  actions of, in face of opposition, 201–7
  advises Salmání, 83
  appoints Shoghi Effendi Guardian, 133, 145, 241, 276, 277, 279, 286, 376, 378, 381
  attempts on life of, 224, 277
  attempts to contain Covenant-breaking, 150–1, 170, 171-4, 178, 427
  attempts to discredit, 193–200, 410, 428
  attended mosque, 290
  attributes of, 104–6
  authority to expel Covenant-breakers, 256
  birth of, 110
  Browne's account of meeting, 105
  builds the Shrine of the Báb, 223–30, 231, 325, 326
  carriages of, 189
  carries water to flower-beds at Shrine of Bahá'u'lláh, 191
  Centre of the Covenant, 104–10, 111, 121, 134, 135, 141, 409
    declares position as, in open court, 199
  characteristics of, 201–2
  Commission of Enquiry investigates, 233, 234–40, 299, 418
  court case against, 199–200
  Covenant of, 4
  Covenant-breakers during Ministry of, 111, 148–54, 162, 170–80, 226–30, 411, 416–28
  daughters of, 358
  demonstrated detachment, 25
  describes events after passing of Bahá'u'lláh, 148–9
  description of, by May Bolles Maxwell, 245
  description of, by Mrs Thornburgh-Cropper, 245–6
  designated 'the Master' by Bahá'u'lláh, 104
  detachment of, 201
    from earthly possessions, 179
  devotion of Persian Bahá'ís to, 218–19
  did not accept financial contributions from believers, 341
  did not live at Bahjí, 175
  divine powers conferred on, 267
  effect of presence of, 204–5
  enemies of, 332
  exemplary life of, 201
  expels Jamál from Faith, 215
  explanation of Manifestation, 9
  explanation of soul, 6, 11, 13
  family of, *see* Family of Bahá'u'lláh and 'Abdu'l-Bahá
  forgives Covenant-breakers, 229, 337
  freed by revolution of 'Young Turks', 237, 240, 249, 250
  Ghuṣn-i-A'ẓam, 379, 430
  glances of, 204–5
  grandchildren of, 358
    see also Shoghi Effendi
  Hands of the Cause during ministry of, 322
  handwriting of, 348–9
  'Him Whom God hath purposed', 139, 141, 143, 162, 440
  His successor, *see* Shoghi Effendi
  Horace Holley's description of, 107–8
  incident with Mírzá Áqá Ján at the Shrine of Bahá'u'lláh, 183–90
  indictment against, 198–200, 232–3
  infallibility conferred upon, by Bahá'u'lláh, 103, 294, 395–6, 404
  innate knowledge of, 106
  inters remains of the Báb, 226, 237, 250
  Interpreter of the Writings of Bahá'u'lláh, 102, 135, 219, 220, 435
  Ives's account of meeting, 108–10
  life of, in danger, 187, 236–7, 240–1
  likened Covenant-breaking to a contagious disease, 254
  literary style of, 348–9

lived life of austerity, 193
love and encouragement of believers, 202
makes gardens at Shrine of Bahá'u'lláh, 191, 328
the Master, 138–9
ministry of, 97–269, 273
Mírzá Áqá Ján and, 184, 186
misrepresented by Covenant-breakers in 'Akká, 224, 227, 234
Munírih Khánum's tribute to, 358
'Mystery of God', 104
not a Manifestation, 103, 104, 173n
obedience to, is obedience to God, 267
passing of, 275, 276, 285, 298, 299, 344, 349, 379
photograph of, 25
prayed for hardships, 203
prayers of, 420, 423
 for Covenant-breakers, 259
 for Shoghi Effendi, 281
promotion of Cause, 202
prophecies of
 concerning Covenant-breakers, 226, 228, 233, 234, 251
 concerning future of the Cause, 242, 243
 concerning Haifa, 203, 225–6
 concerning Majdu'd-Dín, 164
 concerning the Shrine of the Báb, 225–6
quotations from Writings and statements of
 counselling Majdu'd-Dín, 180
 describing events in the Holy Land, 238–40
 on Bahá'u'lláh's exile to the Holy Land, 95
 on Bahá'u'lláh's revival of the Bábí community in 'Iráq, 74
 on being photographed, 25
 on building the Shrine of the Báb, 224
 on Commission of Enquiry, 235–6
 on consultation, requisites for, 300–1, 354
 on the Covenant, 409
 on Covenant-breakers, 250–1, 256–7
 on the effect of Covenant-breaking, 274
 on equality of men and women, 400
 on the future of the Cause, 242, 282, 285–6, 299
 on the Greatest Holy Leaf, 122
 on the greatness of Bahá'u'lláh's Revelation, 55
 on Guardianship, 387, 397
 on His own passing, 299
 on His station, 26, 104, 219, 220
 on human perfection, 16
 on infallibility, 396
 on kindness to enemies, 258
 on Mírzá Yaḥyá's arrival at Mosul, 79
 on need to shun Covenant-breakers, 254–5
 on opposition to the Cause, 242–3
 on power of the Covenant, 370
 on praying for one's departed parents, 17
 on Shoghi Effendi, 282, 355
 on the soul, 7
 on the sufferings of Navváb, 121
 on the Universal House of Justice, 285–6, 397–8, 401, 402–3, 404, 434–5
 prayer for Shoghi Effendi, 281
 to the Covenant-breakers, 174
received Revelation of Bahá'u'lláh on behalf of mankind, 102
recognized station of Bahá'u'lláh while still a child, 55–6, 102
refers to Mírzá Muḥammad-'Alí as a Covenant-breaker, 178
refutes claims of brothers, 200
re-incarceration of, 227–8, 231–44, 410
relationship of Bahá'u'lláh and, 135–40, 280, 281
relationship of Shoghi Effendi and, 280–4
remains in 'Akká, 135–6
reputation of, in 'Akká, 193–4
safeguarded the Faith, 110
schooling of, 105–6
seals of, stolen by Fareed, 341
secures freedom for family, 228
service of, 102–3, 110
servitude of, 219–20, 333
states that Isaiah 54 refers to Navváb, 120
station of, 26, 104–5, 130, 136, 139, 141, 156, 177, 219–21
successor to Bahá'u'lláh, 141–7, 295, 378, 381
suffering of, 202, 424, 427
supports family of Bahá'u'lláh, 179–80, 193–4, 196–7, 223–4
Tablets of the Divine Plan, 249, 314, 319, 375, 383
Tablets of, revelation of, 205–7, 231, 232, 348–9
 see also Tablets of 'Abdu'l-Bahá
Tablets of Bahá'u'lláh about, 104, 130, 136–7
Tea House of, 330
titles of, 25–6, 218, 220, 409
transcribes verses of Bahá'u'lláh, 94
travels to the West, 249–50, 344
Tudor-Pole's description of, 107
urges steadfastness in the Covenant, 178
utterances of, inspired Shoghi Effendi, 307
visits Shrine of Bahá'u'lláh, 186–7, 189–92
Western pilgrims describe, 245–6
Will and Testament of, *see* Will and Testament of 'Abdu'l-Bahá
Writings of, 107, 228, 274, 309, 388, 396
'Abdu'l-Ḥamíd, Sulṭán, 227, 228, 232, 234, 236, 237, 250, 356, 410
'Abdu'l-Ḥusayn, *see* Avárih
'Abdu'l-Karím, Mullá, of Qazvín (Mírzá Aḥmad), 61
'Abdu'l-Karím-Ṭihrání, 248
'Abdu'l-Kháliq-i-Iṣfahání 116
'Abdu'lláh, Mírzá, 127
'Abdu'lláh Páshá, house of, 228, 281

'Abdu'llah-i-Qazvíní, 62
'Abdu'r-Raḥím-i-Iṣfahání, Áqá Siyyid, 77
'Abdu'r-Raḥím-i-Qannád, Ḥájí, 358
'Abdu'r-Razzáq, Tablet to, 6–7, 11, 13
Abel, 366
Abraham, 54
Abú Bakr, 156–7, 239
Abu'l-Faḍl, Mírzá, 177, 218, 228, 248, 343–4
Abu'l-Ḥasan-i-Amín, Ḥájí (Ḥájí Amín), 218, 336–7
Abu'l-Qásim (intermediary between Mírzá Yaḥyá and believers), 67
Abu'l-Qásim, Ḥájí Mírzá, 280, 358
Abyssinia, 77
Adam, 3, 32
Á<u>dh</u>irbáyján, 158, 215, 216
Administrative Centre, *see* World Centre
Administrative Order, 286, 293-306, 327, 331, 342, 346, 374, 409, 411, 414–15
  in action, 314–21
  built and strengthened by Shoghi Effendi, 164, 286, 292–306, 376, 379, 382, 406
  child of the Covenant, 164, 356, 379
  consolidation of, 373
  Cradle of, 301
  development of, in North America, 314
  embryonic institutions of, 412
  establishment of, 274, 356, 370, 373
  institutions of, *see* Assemblies *and* Universal House of Justice
  genesis of, 294, 296
  principles of, 395
  symbol of, 298
  twin pillars of, 385–6
  Universal House of Justice is apex of, 437
  will evolve into new World Order, 298
Administrative rights, withdrawal of, 260, 311–12
Adrianople, 126, 138, 165, 211, 417
  Bahá'u'lláh's stay in, 79–96
Afnán, the, 19, 130, 143, 144, 150, 176, 199, 241, 280, 329, 354, 355, 362, 420, 421, 428, 430
Afnán, 'Alí, 356–7, 358, 358, 359, 360, 362, 364, 365
Afnán, Bahíyyih, 365
Afnán, Fayḍí, 359, 360, 362, 364, 365
Afnán, Fu'ád, 358, 359, 360
Afnán, Ḥasan, 359, 360, 364, 365
Afnán, Ḥusayn, 364, 365
Afnán, Mírzá Muḥsin, 358, 360
Afnán, Nayyir, 359, 360, 361, 362, 363, 364–6
Afnán, Rúḥí, 358, 359–60, 363–4
Afnán, Suhayl, 358, 360
Afnán, <u>Th</u>urayyá, 358, 359, 360, 362, 365
Afnán, Ṭúbá <u>Kh</u>ánum, 358, 360, 363
Afnán-i-Kabír, 356, 358
Africa, 317–18, 319, 320, 391
Ages of Bahá'í Faith, 273, 275, 327
A<u>gh</u>ṣán, the, 143, 144, 150, 171, 176, 184–5, 199, 213, 354, 355, 362, 383, 390, 420, 421, 430, 433, 439
Agnostics, 265, 266
Aḥmad-i-Az<u>gh</u>andí, Mírzá, 37
Aḥmad-i-Ká<u>sh</u>ání, Ḥájí Mírzá, 80, 82
Aḥmad-i-Rúḥí, <u>Sh</u>ay<u>kh</u>, 105
Aḥmad Yazdí, 343
'Akká, 138
  Bahá'u'lláh banished to, 94, 290, 417
  friendly Governor of, 231–2
Alaska, 320
Alcohol, 313
'Alí, Áqá, 127, 128
'Alí, Ḥájí, 129
'Alí, Imám, *see* 'Alí-Ibn-i-Abú Tálib
'Alí, Siyyid, 251
'Alí Afnán, Ḥájí Siyyid, 356–7, 358, 359, 360, 362, 364, 365
'Alí-Akbar, Mírzá (cousin of the Báb), 72, 73
'Alí-Akbar, Mírzá (son of Mi<u>sh</u>kín-Qalam), 188
'Alí-Akbar, Mullá, 387
'Alí-Akbar-i-Qú<u>ch</u>ání, <u>Sh</u>ay<u>kh</u>, 205
'Alí-Ibn-i-Abú Ṭálib, Imám 'Alí, 99–100, 156, 158, 160, 229
'Alíy-i-Kirmán<u>sh</u>áhí (name taken by Mírzá Yaḥyá), 79, 91
Ali-Kuli Khan, 248, 342–3
'Alíy-i-Lás Furú<u>sh</u> (name taken by Mírzá Yaḥyá), 65
'Alí-Muḥammad-i-Varqá, Mírzá, 128, 141
'Álí Pá<u>sh</u>á, 86n
'Alí-Riḍá, 152
'Alí Shawkat Pá<u>sh</u>á, 106
'Alíy-i-Tabrízí, Mírzá, 72
'Alíy-i-Yazdí, Ḥájí, 184–5, 196–7, 228–9
Amatu'l-Bahá Rúḥíyyih <u>Kh</u>ánum, *see* Rúḥíyyih <u>Kh</u>ánum
America, *see* United States, North America *and* West, the
American College in Beirut, 283
American Indians, 320
Amín Ḥájí (Ḥájí Abu'l-Ḥasan), 218, 336–7
Amos, 96
Amru'lláh, house of, 84, 91
'Andalíb, 280
'Angel of Carmel', *see* Ḥaydar-'Alí, Ḥájí Mírzá
Anísa, Tree of, 409
Antichrist of the Bahá'í Revelation, *see* Muḥammad-i-Iṣfahání, Siyyid
Apostolic Age, 275, 409
Áqá Ján, Mírzá (<u>Kh</u>ádim, <u>Kh</u>ádimu'lláh, amanuensis of Bahá'u'lláh), 32, 63, 80, 82, 84, 94, 95, 128, 129
  Covenant-breaking of, 165, 181–92, 198
  estate of, used to raise money, 227
  fate of, 251
  lived at the Shrine of Bahá'u'lláh, 189, 191
  Mírzá Muḥammad-'Alí plots to take life of, 183–4
  'revelation writing' of, 182, 187
Áqá <u>Kh</u>án, Mírzá, 62
Áqáy-i-Kalím, *see* Músá, Mírzá
Arabia, 320, 328
Arabs, in the Holy Land, 329, 363
Arc, 326n, 327, 328, 413

Arch-breaker of the Covenant of Bahá'u'lláh, *see* Muḥammad-'Alí, Mírzá
Archives, International Bahá'í, 306, 320, 324, 327, 413
Aristocracy, 415
Ark, 326, 392, 402, 407
Asadu'lláh, Mírzá (Dayyán), 72
Asadu'lláh-i-Iṣfahání, Mírzá, 248, 341
Ascension of Bahá'u'lláh, 26, 111, 145, 148–9, 286, 295, 329, 330, 379
Ashraf, Mírzá, 96
Asia, 317, 319, 320, 391
Ásíyih Khánum, *see* Navváb
Assemblies, 277, 293–4, 296–8, 301–2, 304, 305, 308, 310, 335, 372, 373, 383, 441
  consolidation of, 316, 317, 406
  duties of, 435
  embryonic, 412
  evolution of, 327, 413
  formation of, 315, 316, 344
  House of Spirituality, Cairo, 276
  Local Spiritual, 292–3, 296, 300, 305, 391, 407, 412
  National Spiritual, 260, 293, 296, 300, 304, 305, 403, 433
    collaboration among, 317–18
    elect Universal House of Justice, 384, 392, 394
    and Hands of the Cause, 380–1
    increase in number of, 320, 391, 407, 412
    loyalty of, after passing of Shoghi Effendi, 377, 380, 384
    of the British Isles, 317–18
    of the United States and Canada, 305, 313
    Plans given to, 316
  numbers of, in United States doubled, 315
  Persian, 214, 310–12
  requisites for consultation on, 300–1
  significance of, 298
  Spiritual Assembly of Ṭihrán, 214
Atheists, 265, 266
Attachment, 20–4
  to Kingdom of Names, 25, 26
Attributes
  acquisitions of divine, 1, 3, 10–11, 14, 17–18, 27
  God in His essence exalted above, 24–5
  good things of world are manifestations of, of God, 22–3
  revealed by God, 24–5
Australia, 274, 275, 316, 319, 320
Autocracy, 415
Auxiliary Boards, 380
Ávárih, 285, 334–42, 344
Azalís, 88, 258n
  in Qazvín, 126
'Azíz Páshá, 86

Báb, the, 307
  advises followers concerning 'Him Whom God shall make manifest', 45–6, 48–51, 61
  appeared in Persia, 302–3
  appointment of Mírzá Yaḥyá as successor, 59–64
  Covenant of, 4, 29–51
    breaking of, 65–88
    fulfilment of, 52–9
    triumph of, 89–96
  declaration of Mission of, 110, 374
  followers of, *see* Bábís
  historic relics of, sent to Mírzá Yaḥyá, 85
  infallibility of, 395
  laws of, 33–4
  martyrdom of, 34, 58, 61, 77, 158, 286, 316
  Mission of, 31–2
  quotations from the Writings of,
    on Bahá'u'lláh, 40–3
    on the *Bayán*, 44–6
    on 'Him Whom God shall make manifest', 40–51
    on His acknowledgement of the Cause of Bahá'u'lláh, 41
    on not engaging in disputation, 49
    on purpose of the *Bayán*, 37
    on purpose of His laws
  refers to Bahá'u'lláh by name, 44
  refers to 'Him Whom God shall make manifest', 32, 33–4, 40–51, 52, 55, 76, 146
  relationship to Bahá'u'lláh, 32, 37–8
  remains of
    interment of, 226, 237, 250, 324
    transferred to Holy Land, 248, 250, 274, 341
  Revelation of, dependent on 'Him Whom God shall make manifest', 41
  sense of humour of, 51
  Shrine of, *see* Shrine of the Báb
  spiritual link between Bahá'u'lláh and, 37
  states Revelation of a Manifestation requires a first believer, 110
  station of, 31
  symbolizes return of Elijah, 325
  wife of, 356–7, 364
  Writings of, 33, 37, 42, 45, 77, 309
    see also Bayán
Bábí Faith
  Bahá'u'lláh revives, in 'Iráq, 74
  decline in fortunes of, 67, 69, 70, 74
  sects of, 68
Bábís,
  become followers of Bahá'u'lláh, 87–8
  followers of Azal become Azalís
  in 'Iráq, 66–7, 70
  persecution of, 58, 62
  some recognize station of Bahá'u'lláh, 56, 64, 67
  remain faithful to Bahá'u'lláh, 86
Badasht, Conference of, 44, 56, 68, 77, 115
Badí, 13n
Badí'u'lláh, 117, 129, 149, 363, 364, 365, 418
  Covenant-breaking of, 152–4, 165, 197–8

death of, 355–6
did not question authenticity of Will of 'Abdu'l-Bahá, 348, 349
incarceration of, 228
fate of, 251, 340
'letter of confession', 227, 426
seizes keys to Shrine of Bahá'u'lláh, 288, 333

Badru'-Dín, Shaykh, 236

Baghdád, 5, 138, 165, 336

Bahá, people of, 401, 407

Bahá'í Faith, 23
'Abdu'l-Bahá's promotion of, 202
achievements of, 231, 274–5, 406–7
Administrative Order, *see* Administrative Order *and* Assemblies
Centenary of birth of, 315, 316, 374
Covenant a unique feature of, 256
crisis in, created by Mírzá Muḥammad-'Alí, 164
development of world community, 275, 371–2, 376
does not harbour egotistical personalities, 333
effect of Covenant-breakers on, 273–4
emergence from obscurity, 412, 413–14
enemies of, different from Covenant-breakers, 253–4
epochs in development of, 318, 323, 373–5
events during Guardianship, 304–6
expansion of, 232, 275
'free Bahá'ís', 346
future of, 202–3, 233, 282, 309, 378, 407, 411–12
goal of, is establishing oneness of mankind, 255, 389
history of, written by Shoghi Effendi, 308–9
independent religion, 306
institutions of, *see* Administrative Order, Assemblies *and* Universal House of Justice
literature of, 309–10, 319, 329, 371, 372
number of adherents to, 273
onward march of, 370–6
opposition to, 242–4, 370
from members of Bahá'u'lláh's family, 111
pattern of crisis and victory characteristic of growth of, 111
persecution of, in Persia, 310
proclamation of, 406
progress of, 406–7
propagation of, 297–8, 406
protected by the Covenant, 295
protection of, 406
purpose of, 143, 372
rites of, 264
scholars of, 293–4, 307, 372
teachers of, 218, 247
teaching, 203–4, 297–8, 299, 311, 314, 375
temporary breach in ranks of supporters of, 93
unity of, 260, 347, 371, 376, 403–4, 407, 410
distinguishing feature, 255
protected by Covenant, 156, 248, 250, 409
withdrawal from, 259–60
World Centre of, *see* World Centre

Bahá'í Publishing Trusts, 320

Bahá'í World Commonwealth, 327, 380, 381, 382, 383, 431, 437

Bahá'ís, 162–3, 297
'Abdu'l-Bahá's love and encouragement of, 202
American, 300
attitude of, to Covenant-breakers, 253–60, 350
birthdays of, 16
conduct when walking with 'Abdu'l-Bahá, Bahá'u'lláh or Shoghi Effendi, 92n
discouraged from reading Covenant-breakers' propaganda, 260
do not oppose Covenant-breakers, 257
during 'Most Great Separation', 84–5
forbidden to associate with Covenant-breakers, 254–5, 259, 260
growth of individual, through tests, 264
loyalty of, after passing of Shoghi Effendi. 379–80
martyrs, 231, 309
obligation of, to deepen, 261
persecution of, 310
Persian, 85–6, 87–8, 89, 90, 93, 310–12
process of becoming a Bahá'í, 398
should pray for Covenant-breakers, 258, 259
steadfastness of, 231
unity of, 15, 246
withdrawal of administrative rights of, 260
youth, 306

Bahá'u'lláh
acknowledgement of the Báb's Message, 34–8
appeared in Persia, 302–3
arrival in 'Akká, 290
Ascension of, 26, 111, 145, 148–9, 286, 295, 329, 330, 379
asked 'Abdu'l-Bahá to build Shrine of the Báb, 224
assumed title of 'Bahá' at Conference of Badasht, 44
attitude to Imáms, 156
authority to expel Covenant-breakers, 256
the Báb refers to, by name, 44
birth of, 113
cares for Mírzá Yaḥyá, 60–3, 417
characteristics of, 201–2
childhood of, 113–14
children of, 114, 117
the 'Concealer', 209
conferred divine powers on 'Abdu'l-Bahá, 267
Covenant of,

arch-breaker of, *see* Muḥammad-'Alí, Mírzá
regarding 'Abdu'l-Bahá, 4
Covenant-breakers in the time of, 165–6
creative power of, 131–2
declaration of, 47, 83, 113, 393
detachment of, from earthly possessions, 179
education of, 113–14
enemies of, 332, 365
exile of, to Holy Land, 95–6
explanation of Manifestation, 9
explanation of soul, 6, 11
family of, *see* Family of Bahá'u'lláh and 'Abdu'l-Bahá
followers of, *see* Bahá'ís
formally declares Himself to Mírzá Yaḥyá, 83–4
had knowledge of His own station from childhood, 57
'Him Whom God shall make manifest'
Bahá'u'lláh recognized as, by Bábís, 56
see also 'Him Whom God shall make manifest'
House of, in Baghdád, 306
identification with attributes, not Essence, of God, 42, 52
infallibility of, 395
love of, 18
loved nature, 328
Manifestation of God for this day, 261
marriages of, 114, 117
Mírzá Yaḥyá attempts to take life of, 80–3, 417
the 'Most Great Spirit of God', 39, 52
Mullá Ḥusayn traces, 34–6
passing of, *see* Ascension of
personal life of, 111–14
possessions of, 200
prayer beads of, 200
prayers of, 18
'Primal Will' of God, 39, 44
proclamation to kings and rulers, 93–4, 406
quotations from Writings of
about 'Abdu'l-Bahá, 104, 130, 136–7, 267
calling monks to come out of their seclusion, 21–2
condemning religious leaders, 265
deploring those who blindly follow religious leaders, 265
from an obligatory prayer, 263
on the Covenant, 100, 161, 162, 168, 408
on creation of man, 2–3, 10, 167
on creation of world for man, 22
on the creative power of the words of Bahá'u'lláh, 131–2
on deeds, pure and goodly, 24
on detachment, 21, 22
on dishonour to the Báb caused by Mírzá Yaḥyá, 73
on divine assistance, 300
on God as an unknowable Essence, 38
on the Greatest Holy Leaf, 121–2
on greatness of His Revelation, 39–40, 55
on His concealment of sins, 209–10
on His experience in the Síyáh-Chál, 114
on His retirement to Kurdistán, 69–70
on His revival of the Bábí community in 'Iráq, 74
on His station, 90, 127
on His successor, 141
on humility, 263
on knowing and worshipping God, 24
on love between God and man, 5
on miracles, 92
on Mírzá Yaḥyá, 73, 79
on morality, 68
on Muḥammad-'Alí, 128
on Navváb, 119–20
on the next world, 12
on obeying God, 24
on opposition to the Cause, 242
on the proclamation of His Mission, 62
on the Purest Branch, 123–4
on the revelation of verses whilst in Adrianople, 94
on the soul, 5, 6–7, 11, 13, 14, 15, 19–20
on the station of Muḥammad-'Alí, 130, 131
on Universal House of Justice, 396, 402
on volition, 10
text of *Kitáb-i-Ahd*, 142–4
warning of tests to come, 69
Qur'án belonging to, 200
refused government allowance, 87
relationship of 'Abdu'l-Bahá and, 135–40, 280, 281
relationship to the Báb, 32, 37–8
retirement to mountains of Kurdistán, 69–71, 84, 181–2
reveals principles of World Order, 298
Revelation of, 3, 38, 372
distinguishing features of, 101–2
greatness of, 40–3, 55
preservation of purity of, 101–2
written down, 101
seals of, 150
sends historic relics of the Báb to Mírzá Yaḥyá, 85
Shrine of, *see* Shrine of Bahá'u'lláh
in the Síyáh-Chál, 46, 52, 55, 56, 57, 58, 62, 105
spiritual link between the Báb and, 37
split between, and Mírzá Yaḥyá, 84–9
station of, 26, 33, 38–9, 53, 135, 199
described by Shoghi Effendi, 53–5
recognition of, by believers, 162, 261, 267, 398
recognized by 'Abdu'l-Bahá, 55–6
recognized by Bábís, 56, 64, 67
recognized by Shaykh Ḥasan-i-Zunúzí, 57–8
successor to, 141–7, 378, 381
sufferings of, 142, 202, 416–17
Supreme Manifestation, 33, 38, 163, 261

Tablets of, *see* Tablets of Bahá'u'lláh
teaches the Cause of the Báb, 61
teachings of, *see* Teachings
titles of, 53–5
utterances of, inspired Shoghi Effendi, 307
Will and Testament of, *see Kitáb-i-'Ahd*
wins respect of dignitaries of Adrianople, 79
wives of, 114, 117–18
World Order of, *see* World Order
Writings of, *see* Bahá'u'lláh, quotations from Writings of *and* Writings, of Bahá'u'lláh
Bahíyyih Khánum, *see* Greatest Holy Leaf
Bahjí, Mansion of, 135–6, 138, 148, 165, 174, 175, 232, 234, 383
'Abdu'l-Bahá and His family did not live at, 175
cleansed by Shoghi Effendi, 176, 329–31
gardens at, 324, 328, 331, 367
life of Bahá'u'lláh's family at, 179–80
memorial meeting for Shoghi Effendi at, 382
occupied by Covenant-breakers, 175–6, 223, 252, 328–31
restored by Shoghi Effendi. 328–9
share of, sold by Covenant-breakers, 227
Bákú, 171
Balliol College, Oxford, 284
Báqir, Mullá, 47
Báqir-i-Shírází, Mírzá, 94
Baths, public, 81, 311
Bayán, the, 33, 41, 44–6, 49, 58, 64, 68, 417
Arabic, 33
interpretation of, 45
Persian, 33, 37, 42, 44, 50, 55, 68, 75, 94
Bayánís, 68
Baydún, 'Abdu'l-Ghaní, house of, 234
Beg, Ḥikmat, 235–6
Beirut, 137, 171, 283, 336
Believer
faith of, undermined and weakened by Covenant-breakers, 177
growth of, through tests, 264
proper attitude of, towards Manifestation, 167, 169
true, 12, 19, 151, 163
see also Bábís *and* Bahá'ís
Bible, 282
Bihjatu's-Sudúr, 87
Birthdays, celebration of, 16
Blomfield, Lady, 278, 285
Body
relationship to soul, 7
Bombay, 175, 185
Branch, explanation of use of term in Writings, 430
Britain, 249, 277, 293, 319
letter of Shoghi Effendi to, 317–18
National Spiritual Assembly of, 360, 362
Six Year Plan, 315–16, 317
Two Year Plan for Africa, 317
Browne, Professor Edward G., 105, 249
Buddha, 54
Buddhism, 320
Burújirdí, Ayatu'lláh, 342
Buzurg, Mírzá (Mírzá 'Abbás), 54, 113

Cain, 366
Cairo, 276, 335, 336
Calamity, 411–12
Caliphs, 157
Calligraphy, 113
Canada, 249, 305, 313, 314, 316, 347
Caravan of East and West, 344
Carmel, Mount, 95, 96, 223, 225–6, 231, 234, 247, 298, 320, 324, 325, 326, 327, 328, 357, 401, 407, 413, 419
Carmel, Tablet of, 324, 326, 392, 401, 407, 413
Cause of God, *see* Bahá'í Faith
Centenary, of birth of Bahá'í Faith, 315, 316
Centre of the Covenant, 4, 104–10, 111, 121, 134, 135
'Abdu'l-Bahá appointed as, in *Kitáb-i-Ahd*, 142, 161, 409
'Abdu'l-Bahá declares Himself, in court, 199
attacks against, 161–2
discrediting of, 193–200
identity of, kept secret, 145
'turning toward', pivot of the Covenant, 162–3, 267
see also 'Abdu'l-Bahá
Centre of Sedition, *see* Muḥammad-'Alí, Mírzá
Centres, Bahá'í, 297
Certitude, 26
Chance, Hugh, 393
Chanler, Mrs Lewis Stuyvesant (Julie), 344, 346
Charity, 16
Chase, Thornton, 246
Chicago, 341
Children, 7, 17
Christ, 6, 16, 38, 40, 54, 68, 104, 226, 254, 275, 310, 321, 327, 420
bestowed gift of faith, 18
betrayal of, 251
did not impose a Covenant on followers, 160
did not marry, 112
lived as Israelites of the time did, 113
Sermon on the Mount, 395
successor to, 99
Christianity, 68, 99, 160, 197–8, 202, 306, 310, 327, 328, 389, 415
Chúpán, Dr, 80
Civilization, 412
Clergy, Islamic, 208–9, 212n
Collége des Fréres, 283
Commission of Enquiry, 233, 234–40, 299, 418, 419
Commonwealth, Bahá'í World, 327, 380, 381, 382, 383, 431, 437
Communication, means of, 315, 316
Community of the Most Great Name, *see* Bahá'ís *and* Bahá'í Faith
Concourse on high, 13
Conflict, forbidden, 143

Consolidation, 319, 406
  of Local Assemblies, 316
Constantinople, 416–17
Consultation, 293
  requisites for, 300–1
Continental Boards of Counsellors, 406
Convention, National, 304
Cooper, Mrs Ella Goodall, 281–2
Counsellors, Continental Boards of, 406
Court
  Bahá'í, 320, 324
  case against 'Abdu'l-Bahá, 200
  case concerning Ḥaram-i-Aqdas, 368
  Egyptian, declaring Faith independent, 306
  Shoghi Effendi summoned to, 330, 365
Covenant
  'Abdu'l-Bahá urges steadfastness in, 178, 203
  arch-breaker of the Covenant of Bahá'u'lláh, *see* Muḥammad-'Alí, Siyyid
  of the Báb, *see* Báb, the, Covenant of
  Bahá'í Faith protected by, 295, 414
  of Bahá'u'lláh concerning 'Abdu'l-Bahá, 4
  breaking of, of Bahá'u'lláh, 148–54
  Centre of the, *see* Centre of the Covenant
  clandestine opposition to, 170–80
  definition of, 1
  faithfulness to, 159, 215, 216, 267
  features of, 131–2
  forms of, 3–4
  fortified, 410
  fostering steadfastness in, 261–9
  Greater, *see* Greater Covenant
  a growing organism, 408
  Lesser, *see* Lesser Covenant
  man enjoined to recognize Manifestation of God, *see* Greater Covenant
  man's fulfilment of the, 26
    is in obedience, 266
  man's soul governed by laws of, 1,
  nature of, 1–2, 131–3
  obedience to, 27
  of past Dispensations, 158–9
  power of, 370, 440
  safeguards unity of Faith, 156, 248, 250, 414
  soul and the, 4–27
  a source of tests for believers, 146
  steadfastness in, *see* Covenant, faithfulness to strength of, 380
  theme of *Tablet of the Holy Mariner*, 167–8
  unfoldment of, 408–15
Covenant-breakers, 146–7, 150–1, 163, 409–11, 416, 424–8
  after passing of 'Abdu'l-Bahá, 286, 379, 409
  ambition of, 167, 333
  announced their own rebellion, 170–1, 199
  arch-breaker of the Covenant of Bahá'u'lláh, *see* Muḥammad-'Alí, Mírzá
  association with, forbidden, 254–5, 259, 260, 350, 354, 425–6, 427, 432
  attempts of, on life of 'Abdu'l-Bahá, 224
  attempts to discredit 'Abdu'l-Bahá, 193–200, 232
  authority to expel, 152, 256
  Bahá'í attitude to, 253–60
  Bahá'ís discouraged from reading propaganda of, 260
  Bahá'ís should pray for, 258, 259
  behaviour of, 345
  believers do not oppose, 257
  characteristics of, 199
  decline in fortunes of, 409–10
  definition of, 151–2, 168
  description of, 256–7
  different from enemies of the Faith, 253–4
  during the custodianship of the Hands of the Cause, 385–91
  during ministry of 'Abdu'l-Bahá, 111, 148–54, 162, 170–80, 226–30, 411
  during ministry of Shoghi Effendi, 111, 253, 287–91, 298, 305, 332–50, 409
  effect of, 218, 220–2, 273–4
  expulsion of, from community, 255–7, 341, 342, 359–67
    need for, 255
  factors turning believers into, 167
  failure of, to destroy Cause, 156
  family of Bahá'u'lláh, *see* Family of Bahá'u'lláh
  fate of, 251–2
  forgiven by 'Abdu'l-Bahá, 229, 337
  foundations of, laid, 150
  misrepresent 'Abdu'l-Bahá's motives for building Shrine of the Báb, 224, 227
  not cast out during life of Bahá'u'lláh, 166–7
  occupy Bahjí, 175–6, 223, 252, 328–31
  old and new, join hands, 345, 354, 363–4
  opposed to Shoghi Effendi, 253, 287–91
  in Persia, 165–6, 208–22, 332–42
  powerlessness of, 161–2
  praise teachers of Faith as a trick, 177
  prayer for, 259
  principal, during Ministry of 'Abdu'l-Bahá, 164–9
  prophecies of 'Abdu'l-Bahá concerning, 226, 228, 233, 234, 251
  rebellion of, not disclosed for four years, 150–1, 170, 171–4, 178, 199
  undermine faith of believers, 177
  use Mírzá Áqá Ján, 184–9
  in the West, 245–52, 343–50
Covenant-breaking
  Bahá'í attitude to, 253–60
  described by Ḥájí Mírzá Ḥaydar-'Alí, 171–5
  description of, 167, 168, 253, 426
  differs from withdrawal from Faith, 259–60
  evils of, 158, 418
  likened by 'Abdu'l-Bahá to a contagious disease, 254, 260
  nature of, 253–4, 366
  in Persia, 165–6, 208–22. 332–42
  a spiritual disease, 253, 337
  in the West, 245–52, 343-50

Cradle of the Administrative Order, 301, 303
Cradle of the Faith, 302
Creation
act of, 2
kingdoms of, 3, 14, 15
one entity, 8
purpose of, 2
spiritual, 7, 8
worlds of, *see* Worlds, of God
'Crimson Book', *see* *Kitáb-i-Ahd*
'Crisis and victory', 111
Crusade, Ten Year, 317, 318–21, 339, 347, 363, 371, 375, 377, 380, 381, 383, 384, 391, 393, 406, 431
Custodianship of the Hands, 324, 347, 377–93
'Cycle of Fulfilment', 33
Cycles, religious, 32–3, 38
universal, 38, 53
Cyprus, 94–6

Dahaj, 216
Damascus, 227, 229
Daniel, 321
David, 54, 95
Dawn-Breakers, 302
Dawn-Breakers The, 309
Day of God, 33
Dayyán (Mírzá Asadu'lláh of Khuy, 72–3
Death, life after, *see* Life after death
Deepening, 26, 203, 218, 405, 436
in understanding of Revelation of Bahá'u'lláh, 261
Delegates, 304
Democracy, 415
Detachment, 8, 21–4, 333
'Abdu'l-Bahá demonstrated, 25
Dhabíḥ (Siyyid Ismá'íl of Zavárih), 12
Dhikru'lláh, Mírzá, 236
Dictatorship, 264
Dispensation
of Bahá'u'lláh, 6
of Muḥammad, 6
Dispensation of Bahá'u'lláh, The, 378, 385–6, 437, 439
Divine Plan, 316
Tablets of the, 249, 314, 319, 375, 383
Divines, condemned, 265–6
Díyá'íyyih Khánum, 280, 358
Díyá'u'lláh, son of Bahá'u'lláh, 117, 129, 165, 178, 185n, 223, 251

Ego, 23, 25, 264
Egypt, 174, 246, 276, 306, 316, 317, 334, 335, 336, 342
Elections, Bahá'í, 395, 421, 431
of Assemblies, 304
of Universal House of Justice, 392–3, 394, 397, 403, 431
Elijah, 325
Embryo, human
compared to soul, 9–10
Enemies, 253–4, 348
England, 277, 284, 285, 335, 336, 349, 397, 425
Environment, 3
Epistle to the Son of the Wolf, 73, 79, 142, 162, 309
Epochs
of Formative Age, 318, 323, 373–5, 406
of fulfilment of Tablets of the Divine Plan, 314, 316, 319, 375
Equality, of men and women, 400–1
Eskimos, 320
Esslemont, Dr John E., 278, 293
Ethiopia, 77
Europe, 249, 274, 293, 319, 320, 338, 374
establishment of Assemblies in, 316
Evil, 13
absence of good, 13–14
'Executive Board', 293
Existence, absolute and contingent, 20

Fáḍil-i-Shírází, 205
Fáiq, 342
Faith, 18, 26, 163, 261–2, 312
confession of, 378
spirit of, 18–19
Faithfulness
to Covenant, 3, 159
Falah, 340
Falkland Islands, 320
Famagusta, 96
Family of Bahá'u'lláh and 'Abdu'l-Bahá, 111–25, 135, 162, 164–5, 171, 176–7, 351, 366
accusations of, against 'Abdu'l-Bahá
arrest of, in 'Akká, 227
Avárih writes to, 337
freedom of, secured by 'Abdu'l-Bahá, 228
life of, at Bahjí, 179–80
members of, expelled from Faith, 353, 359–67
opposed Shoghi Effendi, 287–92, 305, 333, 351–69, 410
supported by 'Abdu'l-Bahá, 179–80, 193–4, 196–7, 223–4
why, defected, 168–9, 351
Fanaticism, religious, 264
Faraju'lláh, Áqá, 179
Faríd (Fareed), Dr Amín, 248, 340–1, 363
Faríq Páshá, 229, 232
Fasting, ordinance of, 311, 313
Fatḥ-i-'Aẓam, Hushmand, 393
Fátimih, daughter of Bahá'u'lláh, *see* Greatest Holy Leaf
Fátimih, daughter of Muḥammad, 115f
Fátimih, second wife of the Báb, 73
Fátimih Khánum, second wife of Bahá'u'lláh, *see* Mahd-i-Ulyá
Finland, 320
Five Year Plan, Canadian, 316
Five Year Plan, Egyptian, 316
Five Year Plan, German, 316
Formative Age, 271–415
epochs of, 318, 323, 373–5
Forty-Five Month Plan, Persian, 316
Four-and-a-Half Year Plan, Indian, 316
France, 249
Franklin, Canada, 320
'Free Bahá'ís', 346

Free will, 1, 8, 112, 133
French, Mrs Nellie, 343
Fulfilment, cycle of, 33
Furúghíyyih, daughter of Bahá'u'lláh, 118, 251, 357, 360, 365
Future, the, 202–3, 233, 282, 309, 407, 411–12

Ganjih, 171
Garden of Riḍván ('Akká), 328
Garden of Riḍván (Baghdád)
  Bahá'u'lláh's declaration in, 47, 83, 113, 393
Gardens, at World Centre, 191, 324, 328, 331, 367
Gawhar Khánum, third wife of Bahá'u'lláh, 117–18, 364, 365
Generosity, 25
Germany, 249, 293, 316, 347
Ghadír-i-Khumm, 99, 157
Ghuṣn-i-Akbar, *see* Muḥammad-'Alí, Mírzá
Gibson, Amoz, 393
Gleanings from the Writings of Bahá'u'lláh, 309
God, 167, 422
  attributes of, 24–5, 26
  barriers between, and man, 20–1
  bounty of, 14, 16
  Covenant of, with man, 1–2
  created man in own image, 1
  Day of, *see* Day of God
  Essence of, 20n, 24, 38
    station of Bahá'u'lláh not to be confused with, 42, 52
    unknowable, 38, 42, 44
  exalted above attributes, 24–5
  gifts of, 295
  Kingdom of, on earth, 275, 321, 327, 376
  knowledge of, 21, 24, 26
  love of, 262
  man's response to, 1
  Messengers of, *see* Manifestations
  partnership with, 173
  provides for man's well-being, 2–3
  purpose of man is to know, 24
  Reality of, 20n
  relationship to man, 1–3
  soul manifests signs of, 19
  station of, 103
  will of, 3
  Word of, 18
    creative power of, 131–2
    interpretation of, 100–1
God Passes By, 308–9, 361
  quotations from, 31, 437
Golden Age, 275, 303, 327, 373, 414
Gospels, the, 38, 99, 100, 183, 319
Government, 415
  obedience to, 312, 419, 423
Grand, Miss, 278
Greater Branch, *see* Muḥammad-'Alí, Mírzá
Greater Covenant, 4, 18
Greatest Holy Leaf (Bahíyyih Khánum), 56, 117, 121, 125, 276, 277, 281, 288, 357
  account of life during Bahá'u'lláh's absence in Kurdistán, 70–1
  description of Navváb, 118–19
  detachment of, from earthly possessions, 179
  directed Faith in absence of Shoghi Effendi, 290–1
  monument to, 298, 326, 327, 357, 358, 413
  passing of, 305, 308
  relationship with Bahá'u'lláh, 135
  response to Avárih, 335–7
  Shoghi Effendi's account of, 122–3
  support to Shoghi Effendi, 286, 291, 305, 352, 353
  Tablets to, 121–2
Greenland, 320
Groups, Bahá'í, 297
Grundy, Mrs Julia, 344
Guardian, *see* Shoghi Effendi
Guardianship, institution of, 285, 305, 327, 376, 381, 385–6, 388–9, 403, 413, 415
  future Guardians, 390, 399, 439–40
  second, 429–32

Habíbiu'lláh-i-Afnán, Ḥájí Mírzá, 139–40
Haddád, Antún, 247
Hádíy-i-Dawlat-Abádí, 73, 96
Hádíy-i-Qazvíní, Mullá, (Letter of the Living), Tablet to, 5
Hádí Shírází, Mírzá, 280, 358
Haifa, 224, 328, 345, 401
  'Abdu'l-Bahá in, 223, 225
  'Abdu'l-Bahá's prophecies concerning, 203, 225–6
  gardens at, 324, 331
Hakim, Lotfullah, 393
Hands, kissing of, forbidden, 208, 212n
Hands of the Cause of God, 152, 218, 241, 258, 322–4, 327, 399, 413, 420, 421–2, 428, 433
  appointment of, 322, 381, 399
  are to teach the Cause, 420, 422
  authority to expel Covenant-breakers, 256
  'Chief Stewards', 380, 381, 382, 431
  Custodianship of, 323, 324, 347, 377–93
  first letter of, 382–3
  functions of, 256n, 320, 377, 380, 406, 422, 435, 437
  Horace Holley appointed, 107
  letter from, about Mason Remey, 429–32
  loyalty to, after passing of Shoghi Effendi, 384
  and National Spiritual Assemblies, 380–1, 384
  opposed by Jamál, 213, 214
  to turn to Shoghi Effendi, 354, 355
Ḥaram-i-Aqdas, 368, 382
Ḥasan, Ḥájí, 127, 128
Ḥasan, Ḥájí Mírzá Siyyid (Afnán-i-Kabír), 356, 358
Ḥasan-i-Khurásání, Ḥájí Mírzá, 248
Ḥasan-i-Níkú, 341
Ḥasan-i-Zunúzí, Shaykh, 57–8
Ḥaydar-'Alí, Ḥájí Mírzá, 75–7, 86–7, 91–2, 137–8, 170–6, 191, 213, 214, 216–17, 218, 237, 280

describes Covenant-breaking of Mírzá Muḥammad-'Alí, 172–5
description of life of Bahá'u'lláh's family after His passing, 179–80
interview with Mírzá Muḥammad-'Alí, 176
recounts story of Mírzá Áqá Ján at Shrine of Bahá'u'lláh, 191–2
Tablet of 'Abdu'l-Bahá to, 219
Ḥazíratu'l-Quds, 320
Heart, dawning-place of mention of God, 261–3
'Heavenly Father', 38
Heroic Age, 273–9, 291, 297, 302, 304, 311, 327, 409, 413
Herrigel, Dr, 347–8
Hidden Words, The, 309
quotations from, 2–3, 5, 22, 24, 408
High Commissioner, British, 329, 348
Hikmat Beg, 235–6
'Him Whom God hath purposed', 139, 141, 143, 156, 162, 440
see also 'Abdu'l-Bahá
'Him Whom God shall make manifest', 4, 32, 33, 34, 44–51, 61, 75, 76, 77, 146
Bahá'u'lláh declares Himself to be, to Mírzá Yaḥyá, 83–4
Mírzá Áqá Ján first to believe in Bahá'u'lláh as, 181
Mírzá Yaḥyá claims to be, 84
see also Bahá'u'lláh
History, of Bahá'í Faith, 308–9
Hofman, David, 393
Holley, Horace, 107–8, 294
Holy Days, 371
suspension of work on, 312
visits to the Shrine of Bahá'u'lláh on, 190
Holy Land, 325
Bahá'í properties in, 306, 327, 386
Covenant-breaking in, 164–5
fulfilment of prophecies concerning, 95–6
political upheaval in, 363
Holy Mariner, Tablet of the, 167–8
Holy Spirit, 38–40
Holy Year, 320, 339, 340
House of Bahá'u'lláh in Baghdád, 306
House of Justice, Secondary, 423
see also Assemblies, National
Houses of Spirituality, *see* Assemblies
Houses of Worship, 226, 319, 320, 358
in 'Ishqábád, 231, 274
in North America, 274, 314, 315, 316
Ḥubbu'lláh, 258
Humanists, 265
Humanity, *see* Man
Humans, *see* Man
Humility, 25, 26, 159, 167, 263–4, 333
of learned, 209
teachers of Cause need, 247
Humour, the Báb's sense of, 51
Ḥuqúqu'lláh, 179, 194, 336, 423, 437
Ḥusayn, brother of Shoghi Effendi, 353, 361
Ḥusayn, Imám, 158
Ḥusayn, Mullá, 34–7, 56, 110
Ḥusayn-i-Jahrumí, Mullá (Mírzá Ḥusayn-'Alíy-i-Jahrumí), 185, 252
Ḥusayn-i-Shírází-i-Khurtúmí, Mírzá, 252
Husseini, Jamál

Ibn-i-Asdaq, 213
Ibráhim, Siyyid, 72
Imáms, 157–8, 389
Immortality, 7
India, 77, 316, 319, 391
Infallibility, 103, 267, 294, 404
Most Great, 173
of Universal House of Justice, 384, 394, 395–8, 421, 422, 434, 438, 441
Infidels, 15
Intercontinental Conferences, 319
International Bahá'í Archives, 306, 320, 324, 327, 413
International Bahá'í Council, 323–4, 330–1, 383–4, 389, 429, 430–1
election of, 391–2
International Bahá'í Court, 320, 324
Interpretation, 404–5, 435–6, 440
of the *Bayán*, 45
of the Word of God, 100–2
Interpreter, *see* 'Abdu'l-Bahá *and* Shoghi Effendi
'Iráq, 175, 181, 334, 360
Bábís in, 66–7
Bahá'u'lláh's exile to, 66–7, 416
Three Year Plan, 316
Iron Age, 275
Isaiah, 54, 95
verse 54 refers to Navváb, 120–1, 124
Iṣfahán, 341
Ishqábád, 171
Ishráqát, Tablet of, 166, 215
Iskandarún, 340
Islám, 6, 24, 31, 33, 156–8, 160–1, 202, 324, 327, 371, 389–90, 415
centres of, 328
clergy, 208–9, 212n
customs of, 208–9, 212n
no firm Covenant provided in, 160
laws of, 310, 311, 312, 404, 435
Shí'ah, 57n, 99–100, 156, 229
successorship in, 99–100
Sunní, 99–100, 156, 229, 234, 239
Isle of Satan (Cyprus), 95, 96
Ismá'il, Siyyid, of Savarih (Dhabih), 12
Ismá'il-i-Vázír, 117
Ismu'lláhu'l-Jamál, 166, 210
Ismu'lláhu'l-Javád, 165
Ismu'lláhu'l-Mihdí, 166, 216
Israel, State of, 323, 324, 346, 368
War of Independence, 329, 363
Istanbul, Bahá'u'lláh's departure for, 77
Ives, Howard Colby, 108–10

Jaláli'd-Dín-i-Rúmí, 92
Jalíl-i-Khú'í, 158, 166, 215–16
Jamál-i-Burújirdí, 166, 167, 171, 172, 178, 208–16, 252, 258
Jamál Páshá, 356
Jammál, Garden of, 174
Javád-i-Karbilá'í, Ḥájí Siyyid, 66, 106

Jerusalem, Mufti of, 361, 362
Jesse, 54
Jesuits, 283
Jubilee, Most Great, 319, 320
Judaism, 306, 310, 311, 312, 371, 415
Judas Iscariot, 251, 254
Junayih, Garden of, 139
Justice, 112, 311, 396, 422

Kalimát-i-Firdawsíyyih, 396, 402
Karbilá, 181
Katurah, 54
Kavelin, Borrah
Kawákib'ud-Durríyyih (Avárih), 335n, 336, 338
Kázim-i-Rashtí Siyyid, 66, 67, 115
Kázim-i-Samandar, Shaykh, 127, 185n
Khadíjih Bagum, 113
Khádim, Khádimu'lláh, *see* Áqá Ján, Mírzá
Khalífs, 157
Khalíl, Ḥájí (Ḥájí Muḥammad-Ibráhim), 10, 127
Khávar, Ḥájí, 139
Khayru'lláh, Ibráhim, 246–9, 252
Khurásán, 19, 213
Khurshíd Páshá, 86
Kindness, 258
King of Martyrs, 358, 360
Kingdom of God on earth, 275, 321, 327, 376
Kingdom of Names, 20, 24–5
Kingdoms, natural, 3, 14, 15
Kings, 225, 226, 423
  Bahá'u'lláh's proclamation to, 93–4, 406
Kirmán, 258
Kissing, of hands, forbidden, 208, 212n
Kitáb-i-'Ahd, 99, 130, 131, 132, 133, 142, 146, 149–50, 161–2, 175, 176, 218, 219, 267, 276, 378, 381, 408, 409
  'Crimson Book', 142, 162
  described by Shoghi Effendi, 155–6
  read by 'Abdu'l-Bahá at court, 199–200
  read to family and believers, 150, 155, 164
  removed letter of negation, 161
  text of, 142–4
  violation of, 158, 166, 167
Kitáb-i-Aqdas, 24, 68, 99, 141, 143, 155–6, 175, 176, 212, 218, 219, 240, 267, 378, 382, 386, 390, 396, 401, 402, 409, 438, 439–40
  daily reciting of Writings ordained in, 264
  implementation of laws of, 310–13
  opening paragraph of, 266–7
Kitáb-i-Asmá, 34
Kitáb-i-Íqán, 55, 69, 75–6, 201
  condemns religious leaders, 265
  revealed in a few hours, 101
  translated by Shoghi Effendi, 309
Kitáb-i-Mubín, 130
Kitáb-i-Panj-Sha'n, 44
Knowledge, 25, 261–2
  of self, 21
Krishna, 54
Kurdistán, Bahá'u'lláh's withdrawal to, 69–71, 84, 181–2

Languages, 319, 372
Lapps, 320
Latin America, 275, 314, 315, 319, 320, 391
Lawḥ-i-Hizár Baytí (Tablet of One Thousand Verses), 148–9, 157, 158, 215–16, 229
Lawḥ-i-Karmíl, 324
Lawḥ-i-Khalíl, 127–8
Lawḥ-i-Mubáhilih, 93
Laws, 305
  abrogation of, 31, 405
  breaking, of Bahá'u'lláh, 260
  of Islam, 310, 311, 312, 404, 435
  of *Kitáb-i-Aqdas*, 310–13
  of nature, 1, 8–9
  spiritual, 8–9
  Universal House of Justice can enact, 403, 405–6, 415, 425, 434–5
Leaders, religious, 265–6
League of Nations, 306
Learned, 209, 218, 404
  and rulers, 143
Lebanon, 363
Legislation, role of Universal House of Justice, 304, 313, 403, 405, 415, 425, 434, 438, 439
Lesser Covenant, 4, 97–415
  characteristics of, delineated by Bahá'u'lláh, 100
  definition of, 99
Lesser Peace, 327, 413, 414
'Letter of negation', 160
Letters of the Living, 417
Life after death, 12, 15, 16
  Tablet of Bahá'u'lláh on, 19–20
Literature, Bahá'í, 309–10, 319, 329, 371, 372
Local Spiritual Assemblies, *see* Assemblies
London, 377, 382
Love, 22, 262, 422
  between God and man, 5, 167, 262
  requisite for consultation, 301
Loyalty, 24, 159

MacNutts, 344
Mahd-i-'Ulyá, second wife of Bahá'u'lláh, 117, 118, 125, 136, 229
Maḥmúd-i-Káshání, Mírzá, 138–9, 173, 188, 191
Maḥmúd-i-Zarghání, Mírzá, 216
Maḥmúd Zarqání, Mírzá, 285–6
Maids of Heaven, 20
Majdu'd-Dín, son of Mírzá Músá, 148, 150, 152, 164, 180, 185, 187, 227–30, 330, 356, 364
Man
  attachment to world, 263
  attributes of, 167
  barriers between God and, 20–1
  ego of, *see* Ego
  first duty of, is recognition of Manifestation, 266–7
  free will of, 1, 8, 112
  life after death of, *see* Life after death

maturity of, 159
nature of, 1, 23
perfection of, 16
progress of, 12, 13
purpose of, is to know God, 24
recognition of Manifestation, 18
relationship to Covenant, 2, 26, 27
relationship to God, 1–3
response of, to God, 1
rules nature, 15
stages of humanity, 3
station of, 26, 103, 142–3
is knowledge of own self, 21
is servitude, 167
virtues of, 25, 26
well-being of, 2–3
world created for, 22
Manifestations, 2, 38–40, 159, 389
'Abdu'l-Bahá not a Manifestation, 103, 104
appear to be ordinary people, 111–13
barriers to recognition of, 112
bestow gift of faith, 18–19
earlier, did not make Covenants with followers, 159, 255, 257
enables man to acquire spiritual attributes, 14
for this day is Bahá'u'lláh, 261
God reveals Himself through, 3
have no access to the Inner Reality of God, 38, 43
Holy Spirit associated with, 38–9
impart knowledge to man, 6
infallibility of, 395, 396
Manifestation of God is always a Manifestation, 57
marriage of, 112–13
persecution of, 4
personal lives of, 111–13
proper attitude of a believer towards, 167, 169
purpose of, 20, 145
recognition of, 18
station of, 103, 112
Supreme, *see* Bahá'u'lláh
teachings of, *see*Teachings of Manifestations
Mankind, oneness of, 255, 372, 389
see also Man
Marie, Queen, of Romania, 306
Marriage
arranged, 116–17
Bahá'í, 312, 313
of early Bahá'ís, 311
of Bahá'u'lláh, 117
of Manifestations, 112–113
Martyrs, 231, 275, 309, 310, 416
Mashriqu'l-Adhkár, 226, 319, 320, 358
in 'Ishqábád, 231, 274
in North America, 274, 314, 315, 316
Master, the, *see* 'Abdu'l-Bahá
Materialism, 18, 21, 274, 302, 303, 351
Mathnaví, 92, 219
Mawlaví (Jaláli'd-Dín-i-Rúmí), 92
Mawlavís, 92
Maxwell, May Bolles, 234, 305
Maxwell, Sutherland, 305
Mázindarán, 214, 215, 416
Mazra'ih, 135–6, 138, 331
Mecca, 328
Memorial meetings, 16–17
Men,
equality with women, 400–401
service of, on Universal House of Justice, 400
Messengers, divine, *see* Manifestations
Mihdí, Mírzá, *see* Purest Branch
Mihdíy-i-Dahajı, Mírzá, 166, 216–17, 252
Mihdíy-i-Káshání, Mírzá, 118
Mirrors of the Bábí Dispensation, 66
Mishkín-Qalam, 188
Monasticism, 21–2
Mongolia, 320
Monks, 21–2
Monogamy, 313
Monuments, at World Centre, 328
Morality, 68
Moses, 38, 40, 91
Most Exalted Leaf, *see* Navváb
Most Great Branch, *see* 'Abdu'l-Bahá
Most Great Infallibility, 103
Most Great Jubilee, 319
Most Great Law, 407
Most Great Peace, 327, 412, 414, 437
Most Great Prison, 138, 153, 417
Most Great Separation, 84–7
Most Great Spirit of God, 38–40, 43, 52
Most Mighty Branch, *see* 'Abdu'l-Bahá
Mosul, 78–9, 118
Motive, purity of, 24
Mount Carmel, *see*, Carmel, Mount
Mu'ayyad, Dr Habib, 191, 225–6
Mubáhilih, 89–92
Muḥammad, 6, 31, 33, 40, 54, 68, 99–100, 101, 310, 389, 415
Covenant of, 156–61, 229
Muḥammad, Hájí Siyyid, 75, 76
Muḥammad-'Alí, son of Bahá'u'lláh and arch-breaker of His Covenant, 117, 125–34, 139, 156, 232, 250, 258, 345, 357, 359, 362, 364, 365, 409–10, 421, 426, 427
accepted authenticity of *Kitáb-i-'Ahd*, 164, 178
allies of, 164–9, 215, 217, 426
attempts to discredit 'Abdu'l-Bahá, 193–200, 227, 230, 234–5, 238–9, 240, 410
attempts to overthrow 'Abdu'l-Bahá, 148–54, 168, 171, 409
Bahjí the personal residence of, 328–9
claimed successorship to 'Abdu'l-Bahá, 131, 276–7
death of, 355
declared a Covenant-breaker, 417–18, 420
defeated, 274
did not question authenticity of Will of 'Abdu'l-Bahá, 348–9
fate of, 251, 252, 355
fate of followers of, 252
financially supported by 'Abdu'l-Bahá, 179–80, 193–4, 196–7

Greater Branch, 430
Ḥájí Mírzá Ḥaydar-'Alí describes rebellion of, 172–5
incarceration of, 228
indictment against 'Abdu'l-Bahá, 198–200, 232–3
ignoble works of, revealed by Badí'u'lláh, 152–4
influence of, 162
among teachers in Persia, 208
influences Jamál, 208, 213
influences Mírzá Áqá Ján, 181
interpolates Writings of Bahá'u'lláh, 153–4, 164, 172, 216, 424
interview with Ḥájí Mírzá Ḥaydar-'Alí, 176
jealousy of and opposition to 'Abdu'l-Bahá, 129, 134, 136, 164, 172
Khayru'lláh in league with, 246–8
misrepresentations to Náẓim Páshá, 227, 228–9
opposition to 'Abdu'l-Bahá, 150–4, 164, 168–9, 170–80, 215, 230
not revealed by 'Abdu'l-Bahá, 150–1, 170, 171–4, 178, 214
opposition to Shoghi Effendi, 287–9, 298, 353
plans to take life of 'Abdu'l-Bahá, 240–1
plots to take life of Mírzá Áqá Ján, 183
position of, after passing of 'Abdu'l-Bahá, 276–7
power of utterance conferred upon him, 126, 128
pretends family is on verge of starvation, 193–4
propaganda of, 178, 193, 215, 238, 260, 276–7
seizure of keys to Shrine of Bahá'u'lláh, 288–9, 333
Muḥammad-'Alíy-i-'Aṭṭár, Mír, 76
Muḥammad-'Alíy-i-Salmání, Ustád, 81–3, 211–12
Muḥammad-'Alíy-i-Tambákú-Furúsh, 75
Muḥammad-Ḥusayn-i-Káshání, Ḥájí, 252
Muḥammad-Ibrahím-i-Káshání, Áqá, 129
Muḥammad-Ibráhím-i-Khalíl, Ḥájí, 127
Tablet in honour of, 10, 127
Muḥammad-i-Iṣfáhání, Siyyid (Antichrist of the Bahá'í Revelation), 65–70, 76, 82, 89
'Abdu'l-Bahá reveals Covenant-breaking of, 178
activities of, aimed at discrediting Bahá'u'lláh, 89–91
allies himself to Mírzá Yaḥyá, 67, 72, 75
arranges Mubáhilih between Bahá'u'lláh and Mírzá Yaḥyá, 89–90
expelled from community, 87
inspires Mírzá Yaḥyá's rebellion against Bahá'u'lláh, 80
jealousy of Bahá'u'lláh, 66–7
letter-writing campaign against Bahá'u'lláh, 85–6
travels with Bahá'u'lláh to Istanbul, 78–9
Muḥammad-Javád-i-Qazvíní, 165, 170–1, 172, 185, 251–2
Muḥammad-Karím, Áqá, 74
Muḥammad-Káẓim, Ḥájí, 78
Muḥammad-i-Mázindarání, Mírzá, 72, 73
Muḥammad Mu'allim, Mullá, 35
Muḥammad-i-Mukárí, Mír, 90, 91
Muḥammad-Muṣṭafáy-i-Baghdádí, Áqá, 171
Muḥammad-Qulí, Mírzá, 236n
Muḥammad-Riḍáy-i-Shírází, Áqá, 173
Muḥammad Said Adham, 276–7
Muḥammad Sháh, 61
Muḥammad-i-Tabrízí, Mullá, 91
Muḥammad Ṭáhir-i-Málmírí, Ḥájí, 129–30
Muḥammad-Taqí, Ḥájí Mírzá, 241
Munavvar Khánum, daughter of 'Abdu'l-Bahá, 358, 363
Muníb, 86
Munírih Khánum, 248, 341, 356–8
Músá, son of Mírzá Muḥammad-'Alí, 340, 364, 365
Músá, Mírzá (Áqáy-i-Kalím), 35, 61, 62–3, 78–9, 80, 83, 84–5, 129, 148, 164, 356
Muslims, 158, 160, 395
Mustayqiz, 72
My Perilous Life in Palestine (Rosamond Dale Owen Oliphant), 197–8

Nabíl-i-A'ẓam, 90–1, 129–300, 309
account of Conference of Badasht, 115–16
accounts of events by, 34, 36, 57, 60, 62, 94
champions Cause of Bahá'u'lláh, 86
Nabíl's Narrative, 302–3
Na'ím, Mírzá, 82
Nakhjaván, 171
Nakhjavání, Ali, 393
Names, Kingdom of, 20, 24–6
Napoleon III, Tablet to, 21–2
Násirí company, 130
Násiri'd-Dín-Sháh, attempt on the life of, 62
National Spiritual Assemblies, *see* Assemblies
Nature,
counterpart in spiritual realm, 9
kingdoms of, *see* Kingdoms, natural
laws of, 1, 8–9, 11
learning from, 7–8, 11
man to work in harmony with, 22
ruled by man, 15
Navváb, 117, 118–21, 123–4, 125, 326, 327, 413
description of, 118–19
detachment of, from earthly possessions, 179
suffering of, 121
Tablets of Bahá'u'lláh to, 119–20
Náẓim Páshá, 227, 228–9
Negritos, 320
Negroes, 320
New History Society, 344
New Zealand, 320
'Next' world, 11–12, 13, 14, 20
Nineteen Day Feast, 306
Nineteen Month Plan, Indian, 316

North America, 249, 274, 298–300, 302, 319, 373
corruption of, 302
Covenant-breaking in, 334, 340, 410
Cradle of Administrative Order, 301, 302
development of Faith in, 314–15, 406
Tablets of the Divine Plan addressed to Bahá'ís of, 375
see also Canada, United States *and* West
Núru'd-Dín (Áqá Mírzá Áqá), 139, 206

Obedience, 14, 21, 26–7, 163, 169, 264–5, 266–7
to government, 312
Oliphant, Laurence, 197
Oliphant, Rosamond Dale Owen, 197–8
Opium, 334
Opposition, 111, 242–4
effect of, 370
Ottoman Empire, 234
Oxford University, 277, 284

Pacific, islands of, 274
Paran, Mount, 408
Parents, 7, 17
Peace, 327
People of Bahá, 88
see also Bahá'ís
Perfection of, 16
Persecution, 23, 242, 310, 311
Persia, 277, 298, 310, 328, 371, 433
Assemblies in, 214, 293, 310–12
Covenant-breaking in, 165–6, 208–22, 334–42
Cradle of the Faith, 302
Forty-Five Month Plan, 316
Two Year Plan for Africa, 317
why Manifestations of God appeared in, 302–3
Pharaoh, 91
Pharisees, 254
Pilgrimage, 329
Pilgrims, 205, 223, 224, 225, 226, 228, 232, 233, 330, 331
Western, 232, 245–6
described as military advisors by Covenant-breakers, 227, 234
Pioneering, 23, 315, 339, 345
Plans, teaching, 275
British Six Year Plan, 315–16
Divine Plan, 316, 375
first Seven Year Plan, 314–15, 373, 374, 375
second Seven Year Plan, 316, 374
strategies of, 315
Ten Year Crusade, 317, 318–21, 339, 347, 363, 371, 375, 377, 380, 381, 383, 384, 391, 393, 396, 431
Two Year Plan for Africa, 317
various national, 316
see also Tablets of the Divine Plan
Pleasure, 22
Polygamy, 113, 114, 117
Polynesians, 320
Port Sa'íd, 343
Prayer, 16
of 'Abdu'l-Bahá, 259, 281, 420, 423
of Bahá'u'lláh, 18
for Covenant-breakers, 259
Muslim, 395
obligatory, 263–4, 311, 313
short obligatory, 24, 263
Prayers and Meditations of Bahá'u'lláh, 309
Priceless Pearl, The (Rúhíyyih Rabbání), 277–8, 329–30
Pride, 263
Priesthood, abolished, 167
Principles, 395
Privileges, 400
Proclamation, 406
Promise of World Peace, The (The Universal House of Justice), 406
Properties, Bahá'í, 306, 327, 368
Prophecies,
of 'Abdu'l-Bahá, 164, 203, 225–6, 228, 233, 240, 242, 243, 251
fulfilment of, 95, 120, 124
Prophetic cycle, 32–3
Prophets, false, 266
Publishing Trusts, Bahá'í, 320
Punishment and reward, 112
Purest Branch (Mírzá Mihdí), 117, 123–4, 125, 135, 212, 326, 327, 413, 430
Purity, 24

Qá'im, 158
Qayyumu'l-Asmá, 41
Qazvín, 10, 126, 214, 215
Qiblih, 325, 331, 368
not fixed by the Báb, 45
Quchan, 19
Quddús, 36–7, 56, 68, 77, 115–16
Queen of Carmel, *see* Shrine of the Báb
Queen Marie of Romania, 306
Questions, freedom to ask, 50
Qur'án, 6, 100, 101, 113, 142, 157, 158, 160, 183
belonging to Bahá'u'lláh, 200

Rabbání, Ḥusayn, 353, 358, 361–2
Rabbání, Mehrangíz, 358, 359, 360, 362, 365
Rabbání, Riáz, 358, 362, 364
Rabbání, Rúḥangíz, 278, 358, 359, 360, 361, 363, 365
Rabbání, Rúḥíyyih, *see* Rúḥíyyih Khánum
Rabbání, Shoghi Effendi, *see* Shoghi Effendi
Rajab-'Alí, Mullá, 76
Rashh-i-'Ama, 52–3
Reality,
spiritual, 6, 7
Religion, 402, 405
divided into sects, 159, 255, 265, 381, 404
law a mainstay of, 310
leaders of, condemned, 265–6
spiritual teachings of, 395
Remey, Charles Mason, 385–91, 410, 429–32
Revelation, 2, 18, 145
of Bahá'u'lláh, *see* Bahá'u'lláh, Revelation of

mysteries of, 40
'Revelation writing', 182, 187
Reward and punishment, 112,
Riḍá Big, House of, Bahá'u'lláh's retirement to the, 84, 85
Riḍáy-i-Qannád, Áqá, 150, 196, 225
Riḍván, Garden of ('Akká), 328
Riḍván, Garden of (Baghdád), 139
Bahá'u'lláh's declaration in, 47, 83, 113
Rights, 400
Rites, 264
Romania, Queen Marie of, 306
Root, Martha, 306
Rose-water, 186, 189
Rúḥá Khánum, daughter of 'Abdu'l-Bahá, 358, 363, 364
Rúḥangíz, sister of Shoghi Effendi, 278, 358, 359, 360, 361, 363
Rúḥíyyih Khánum, 277–8, 283, 284, 285, 286–7, 288, 289, 329–30, 331, 352, 361–2, 368
description of Covenant-breaking, 366–7
marriage of, 305
Rulers and kings, Bahá'u'lláh's proclamation to, 93–4, 406
Rulers and learned, 143
Russia, 320, 433

Sacrifice, 23, 25
Sádhíjih, daughter of Badí'u'lláh, 365
Sádijíh, 330
Sádiq-i-Khurásání, Mullá, 93
Sadratu'l-Muntahá, 136
St Paul, 93
St Peter, 99
Salmán, Shaykh, 63–4
Samadíyyih, daughter of Bahá'u'lláh, 117, 164
Samandar, daughter of Shaykh Kázim, 185
Sayyah, 60
Schism, 4, 159, 160, 255, 381, 404, 410, 415, 435
Scholars, 293–4, 307, 372, 404–5
Schools, Bahá'í, 312
Scientific Society, 342
Seal of the Prophets, 33
see also Muḥammad
'second birth', 18
Sects, 159, 160, 255, 265, 381, 404, 410
Self, battle against, 263–4
Self-effacement, 25, 167, 169, 264, 333
of learned, 209
teachers of Cause need, 247
Semple, Ian, 393
Sermon on the Mount, 395
Service, 24, 25
to Cause of God, 26
prized by 'Abdu'l-Bahá, 26
work rendered in spirit of, is worship, 22
Servitude, 102–3, 167, 169, 217, 333
of 'Abdu'l-Bahá, 219–20
teachers of Cause need, 247
Seven Year Plan, first, 314–15, 373, 374, 375
Seven Year Plan, second, 316, 374
Shahíd, Ḥasan, 358, 360, 362, 365
Shahíd, Mírzá Jalál, 358, 361, 363
Shahíd, Maryam, 358
Shahíd, Muníb, 358, 360, 362
Shahíd, Rúḥá, 358, 363, 364
Shahíd, Zahrá, 358, 360, 363
Shamsí Big, 79
Shaykh Effendi (name given to Bahá'u'lláh by believers), 91, 92
Shaykhís, 66
Shí'ahs, 57n, 99–100, 156, 229, 306
Shíráz, 356
Shíshmán, Dr, 80
Shoghi Effendi, 151, 163, 267, 280–91, 296, 433
achievements of, 331, 332, 371–3, 376
Administrative Order built and strengthened by, 164, 286, 292-306, 376, 382
Ahmad Sohrab attacks, 343–7
appointed Guardian, 133, 145, 241, 276, 277, 279, 286, 287, 345, 376, 387, 394, 420–21, 428, 429
attitude to family, 353
authority to expel Covenant-breakers, 256
Avárih advises Shoghi Effendi, 334–5
Badí'u'lláh's opposition to, 165
birth of, 280
childhood of, 281–3
constructs Shrine of Bahá'u'lláh, 319
constructs superstructure of Shrine of the Báb, 324, 363
Covenant-breakers during ministry of, 111, 253, 287–91, 298, 305, 332–67, 410
decisions divinely guided, 292, 3
develops World Centre, 322–31
did not attend mosque, 290
education of, 283–4
encouraged holding of Nineteen Day Feasts, 306
enemies of, 332
establishment of Universal House of Justice, 287, 292–3, 298, 304
expounder of the Revelation of Bahá'u'lláh, 307–13
faithless relatives of, 351–69
family of, *see* Family of Bahá'u'lláh and 'Abdu'l-Bahá
forgives Covenant-breakers, 337
functions of, 438
Ghuṣn-i-Mumtáz, 379
God Passes By only book written by, 308
Hands of the Cause appointed by, 256n
head of Universal House of Justice, 403, 434, 439
infallibility of, 294, 394, 395, 404, 421, 438
Interpreter of Holy Writings, 277, 279, 304, 308, 310, 379, 415, 435, 438–9
left no heir, 378–9, 382–4, 430, 433
left no Will, 378–9, 382–4, 430, 433
letters of, consulted by Universal House of Justice, 388, 399
marriage of, 305

naming of, 280–1, 353
parents of, 280
passing of, 147, 368, 377, 379, 382, 394, 440
and passing of 'Abdu'l-Bahá, 277–9
and passing of Greatest Holy Leaf, 305
Plans initiated by, 314–21
prayer of 'Abdu'l-Bahá for, 281
quotations from works of,
ages of the Bahá'í Faith, 275
announcing Ten Year Crusade, 318–21
cable to America upon his marriage, 305
cable announcing passing of Majdu'd-Dín, 356
cable announcing passing of Mírzá Muḥammad-'Alí, 355
cable announcing passing of Munírih Khánum, 358
cables about Covenant-breakers, 359–66
describing effect on him of 'Abdu'l-Bahá's passing, 278–9
examples of his descriptive power, 307–8
letter to National Assembly of British Isles, 317–18
letters to North Amercian Bahá'ís, 299–300, 313
on achievements of Faith, 274–5
on administrative centre of Faith, 326–7
on Administrative Order, 296–7, 414–15
on Ahmad Sohrab, 344–5, 346–7
on the Arc, 413
on the Ark, 401–2
on Avárih, 337, 338–9
on Bahá'u'lláh's proclamation to the kings and rulers, 93–4
on cleansing of Bahjí, 367–8
on Covenant-breaking, 366
on deepening, 261, 405, 436
on distress caused to Bahá'u'lláh by Mírzá Yaḥyá, 87
on epochs of the Formative Age, 373–5
on evolution of Assemblies, 412
on exile of Bahá'u'lláh to the Holy Land, 95–6
on fate of Covenant-breakers, 251–2, 340
on fate of Mírzá Yaḥyá, 96, 251
on the future, 407, 411–12
on the Greatest Holy Leaf, 122–3
on Hands of the Cause, 380–1
on interment of Navváb and Purest Branch, 326
on International Bahá'í council, 323
on the *Kitáb-i-Ahd*, 155–6
on laws of the *Aqdas*, 313
on Mírzá Muḥammad-'Alí, 131
on the nature of the soul, 7
on onward march of the Faith, 370–1
on opposition to the Cause, 243–4, 370–1
on passing of Greatest Holy Leaf, 308
on Persia and North America, 302–3
on the poisoning of Bahá'u'lláh by Mírzá Yaḥyá, 80
on the proposed confrontation between Bahá'u'lláh and Mírzá Yaḥyá, 90–1
on the rise and fall of the Bábí religion, 69
on the sacredness of the Shrine of the Báb, 325–6
on service of women on the Universal House of Justice, 401
on significance of 'Abdu'l-Bahá's travels to West, 249–50
on Siyyid Muḥammad-i-Iṣfáhání, 65, 67
on the station of 'Abdu'l-Bahá, 104
on the station of Bahá'u'lláh, 42, 53–5
on the station and Mission of the Báb, 31, 32
on the twin pillars of the Administrative Order, 385–6
on the use of his name, 353
on World Order of Bahá'u'lláh, 310
rebellion against, 332–50
referred matters to Universal House of Justice, 304, 313
relationship of 'Abdu'l-Bahá and, 280–4
relationship to Universal House of Justice, 399–400, 433–41
restoration and furnishing of Holy Places, 331
sent to Haifa to live, 283
successor to, 133, 378–9
successor to 'Abdu'l-Bahá, 145
suffering of, 332
temporary retirement, 290–1, 333
translations of, 309, 376, 383
work of, 283–4
writings of, 307–13, 376, 388, 434
examples of descriptive power of, 307–8
Shrine of the Báb, 237, 250, 320, 357
'Abdu'l-Bahá builds, 223–30, 231
'Abdu'l-Bahá buried in, 285
claimed to be a fortress by Covenant-breakers, 227, 234n, 235, 236, 238
construction of superstructure of, 324, 339, 363
gardens at, 328
Queen of Carmel, 326
sacredness of, 325–6
spiritual centre of Faith, 327–8
Shrine of Bahá'u'lláh, 174, 179, 185–6, 188, 206, 226, 228, 346, 368, 382
'Abdu'l-Bahá makes gardens at, 191
'Abdu'l-Bahá's visits to, 186–7, 189–92
believers not permitted to enter, during residency of Mírzá Áqá Ján, 189, 191
construction of, 319
Covenant-breakers live in vicinity of, 328–31, 367–9
Covenant-breakers plan to take possession of, 188
gardens at, 191, 328, 367
incident at, instigated by Mírzá Áqá Ján, 183–90
seizure of keys to, 288–9, 333

spiritual centre of Faith, 327–8
superstructure of, 323
visits to, on Holy Days, 190
Shu'á'u'lláh, 153, 176, 240–1, 252, 277, 340, 364, 365, 419
Siberia, 320
Sidr-'Alí, Darvísh, 85
Six Year Plan, Australian, 316
Six Year Plan, British, 315–16. 317
Síyáh-Chál, 46, 52, 55, 56, 57, 58, 316
Bahá'u'lláh's imprisonment in, 62, 105
Slander, forbidden to utter, 419
Sohrab, Ahmad, 285, 334, 343–7, 348, 363
Solomon, 330–1
Soul, the, 1, 2, 163, 262
advancement of, 3, 27
characteristics of, 6, 9–10
comes into existence at conception, 7, 18
counterpart of, in physical world is human embryo, 9–10
detachment of, 8
endowed with spirit of faith, 19
essence of, 5, 6
grading of souls, 14–15
grandeur of, 11
immortality of, 7
influence of holy souls, 13
'mighty sign of God', 6
nature of, 4–27
purpose of creation of, 18
progress of, 11, 14, 15, 16, 19
quotations from Bahá'u'lláh on, 5, 6–7, 11, 13, 14
spiritual qualities acquired by, 17–18
stations of different souls, 14, 15, 19
South Pacific Ocean, 320
South Sea Islands, 320
Soviet Union, 433
Spiritual Assemblies, *see* Assemblies
Steadfastness, 19, 24, 143, 159, 203, 215
fostering, in the Covenant, 261–9
Stewards, chief, *see* Hands of the Cause
Subḥ-i-Azal, *see* Yaḥyá, Mírzá
Subḥi, Faidu'lláh, 341–2, 348
Successorship, 3–4, 99, 141–7, 378–9
in Islám, 156–8
Sugar, 36
Sulṭán, Shaykh, 78
Sunnís, 99–100, 156, 229, 234, 239
Supreme Tribunal, 422
Súriy-i-Amr (Súrih of Command), 84
Súriy-i-Ghuṣn (Súrih of the Branch), 104, 136, 219, 267, 430
Súriy-i-Ḥaykal, 38–9, 130
Symes, Col., 289
Syrian Protestant College, 283

Tablets of 'Abdu'l-Bahá
Lawḥ-i-Hizár Baytí, 148–9, 157, 158, 229
of the Divine Plan, 249, 314, 319, 375, 383
of Visitation, 220
to Ḥájí Mírzá Muḥammad-Taqí, 241–2
to Hand of the Cause Mullá 'Alí-Akbar, 387
to Jamál, 215
Tablets of Bahá'u'lláh, 32n
condemning actions of Jamál, 213
in honour of 'Abdu'l-Vahháb, 19–20
in honour of Áqá Muḥammad- 'Alíy-i-Tambákú-Furúsh, 75
in honour of Ḥájí Muḥammad-Ibrahím-i-Khalíl, 10, 127
Kalimát-i-Firdawsíyyih, 396, 402
Lawḥ-i-Karmil (Tablet of Carmel), 324, 326, 401
Lawḥ-i-Khalíl, 10, 127–8
Lawḥ-i-Mubáhilih, 93
Mathnaví, 92, 219
Súriy-i-Amr, 84
Súriy-i-Ghuṣn (Tablet of the Branch), 104, 136, 219, 267, 430
Súriy-i-Ḥaykal, 38–9
Tablet of Bishárát, 396
Tablet of the Holy Mariner, 167–8
Tablet of Ishráqát, 166, 215, 402
Tablet of Qullu't-Ta'ám, 69
Tablet of Salmán, 160, 161
Tablet of Visitation, 186, 189, 190, 191, 206
to 'Abdu'r-Razzaq, 6–7, 11, 13
to Ḥájí Mírzá Ahmad, 82
to Mullá Hadíy-i-Qazvíní, 5
to Mullá Sádiq-i-Khurásání, 93
to Napoleon III, 21–2
to Násiri'd-Dín Sháh, 114
Shaykh Kázim-i-Samandar, 32
to Shaykh Salmán, 87
to Varqá, 32, 141
to Zayn'ul'Muqarrabin, 15, 75
Tablets of the Divine Plan, 249, 214, 383
Tabríz, 158, 216
Taft, 334
Ṭáhirih, 56, 68, 77, 115–16
Tanganyika, 317
Taqíy-i-Manshádí, Ḥájí Siyyid, 223
Tbilisi, 171
Tea, 36
Tea House of the Master, 330
Teachers, need for humility and self-effacement, 247
Teaching, 203–4, 297–8, 299, 311, 314, 420
Tablets of the Divine Plan charter for, 375
Teachings,
of Bahá'u'lláh, 26–7, 261, 305
of Manifestation, 14, 100, 405
Tel Aviv, 345
Ten Year Crusade, 317, 318–21, 339, 347, 363, 371, 375, 377, 380, 381, 383, 384, 391, 393, 406, 431
Terraces, at World Centre, 324, 328
Tests, 146–7, 262, 264
Theocracy, 415
Thornburgh-Cropper, Mrs, 245–6
Three Year Plan, 'Iráqí, 316
Tiberias, 227
Tibet, 320
Tiflís, 171
Ṭihrán, 175, 339
Mullá Ḥusayn sent to, 34–7
Spiritual Assembly of, 214, 336

Townshend, George, 3–4
Translations, 319
 made by Shoghi Effendi, 309, 376, 383
Truth, 266
 unfettered search after, 261
Ṭúbá Khánum, daughter of 'Abdu'l-Bahá, 358, 360, 363
Tudor-Pole, Major Wellesley, 107, 277–8, 289
Turkey, 340
Turkistan, 274
Two Year Plan for Africa, 317
Tyranny, 264

Umar, 156–8, 216, 229, 239
United States, 249, 277, 298–9, 305, 313, 316, 335, 340, 361,
 Assemblies in, 293
 Covenant-breaking in, 246–8, 343-50
 goals of first Seven Year Plan for, 314
 Two Year Plan for Africa, 317
 visit of 'Abdu'l-Bahá to, 249–50
 see also West, the
Unity, 143, 248, 422
 among believers, 299
 of Bahá'í Faith, 255, 260, 347, 371, 376, 403–4, 407, 410
  distinguishing feature, 255
  protected by Covenant, 156, 248, 250, 409
Universal House of Justice, 145, 151, 152, 163, 241, 267, 277, 296, 303, 342, 383, 394–407, 410–11, 413, 425, 428, 429, 433, 437
 accomplishments of, 398–9
 authorized to legislate, 304, 313, 403, 405, 415, 425, 434, 438
 consults writings of Shoghi Effendi, 388, 399, 434, 439
 Covenant-breakers since election of, 409–10
 decision on Guardianship, 399
 election of, in 1963, 392–3, 394, 403, 421, 422–3, 433
 establishment of, 285, 286, 287, 292–3, 298, 320, 324, 334, 335, 344, 347, 375, 376, 384, 390, 391, 406, 431
 functions of, 435, 437, 438
 Guardian sacred head of, 403, 434, 439
 infallibility of, 384, 394, 395–8, 421, 422, 434, 438, 441
 International Bahá'í Council forerunner of, 324, 383–4, 391–2
 interpretation not a function of, 435–6, 438
 membership of, 392, 399
  confined to men, 400–1
 must approve expulsion of Covenant-breakers, 256
 new epochs ushered in by, 375
 no officers of, 400, 403
 one pillar of Administrative Order, 386
 Plans initiated by, 318
 process of legislation, 439
 pronounces on subjects not in Writings, 379, 385, 387, 415, 425, 434
 protector of the Covenant, 403
 rank of, 381
 relationship to Guardian, 399–400, 403, 433–41
 responsibilities of, 402–3
 seat of, on arc, 327, 401–2
 Shoghi Effendi referred matters to, 304
 statements of
  on authenticity of the Will of 'Abdu'l-Bahá, 348–9
  on equality of men and women, 401
  on Guardianship, 390
   and the Universal House of Justice, 433–41
  on interpretation, 404–5
 under care and protection of Abhá Beauty, 354–5
Universe, 11
University of Beirut, 283
University of Chicago, 341
University of Oxford, 277, 284
'Uthmán, 156

Vakílu'd-Dawlih, the, 241
Values, decline of moral and spiritual, 264
Varaqát (Leaves), 356n
Varqá (Mírzá 'Alí-Muḥammad-i-Varqá), 128, 203, 205, 213
 Tablet to, 32, 140
Virtues, *see* Attributes
Visitation, Tablet of (of 'Abdu'l-Bahá), 220
Voting rights, withdrawal of, 260, 310–11

War of Independence, 329
Wealth, distribution of, 378
West, the, 305
 Covenant-breaking in, 245–52, 343–50
 establishment of Faith in, 274
 laws of *Kitáb-i-Aqdas* in, 313
 visit of 'Abdu'l-Bahá to, 249–50, 344
White, Mrs Ruth, 347–9
Will and Testament of 'Abdu'l-Bahá, 133, 240–1, 252, 256n, 276, 277, 279, 287, 298, 310, 352, 354–5, 362, 364, 373, 374, 378, 379, 382, 387, 390, 396, 399, 401, 403, 414, 429–30, 432, 433, 437, 438, 441
 authenticity of, 344, 345, 348
  questioned, 335, 339, 347–9
 counsels kindness to enemies, 258
 literary style of, 348–9
 reaction to, 343
 reading of, 285, 286
 states Bahá'ís must avoid Covenant-breakers, 254
 text of, 416–28
Will and Testament of Bahá'u'lláh, *see* *Kitáb-i-'Ahd*
Wills, writing of, 378
Wilmette, Illinois, 314, 316, 320
Wolcott, Charles, 393
Women
 equality with men, 400–1
 in nineteenth-century Middle East, 114–15, 118
Woodcocks, 344

Word of God, 18, 295
interpretation of, 100–1
Work, rendered in the spirit of service is worship, 22
World, created for man, 22
World Centre, 296, 372, 383, 401
communications to Bahá'í world issued from, 377
development of institutions at, 319, 322–31, 375, 413
gardens at, 328, 367
Hands serving at, 384
World Commonwealth, Bahá'í, 327, 380, 381, 382, 383, 431, 437
World Crusade, *see* Ten Year Crusade
World Order, 294, 373–4, 381, 383, 393, 412, 414
Administrative Order nucleus of, 298
Assemblies in, 304
distinguishing features of, 26
laws of Faith basic part of, 310
new, 22, 146, 291, 411
World Spiritual Crusade, *see* Ten Year Crusade
Worlds, of God
counterpart of physical creation in, 9, 10
limitless, 11
the 'next' world, *see* 'Next' world
one entity, 8–9
physical, 1, 3, 7–9, 11, 4
spiritual, 1, 8–9, 11, 12
soul emanates from, 6–7
Worship, work rendered in spirit of service is, 22
Writers, 307
Writings, of Bahá'u'lláh, 7, 101, 263, 304, 388, 396
clarification of, 145–6
daily reciting of, 264
interpolation of, by Muḥammad-'Alí, 130, 153
need to read, 7, 8, 405
translated by Shoghi Effendi, 309
see also Bahá'u'lláh, quotations from Writings of *and* Tablets of Bahá'u'lláh

'Yá Bahá'u'l-Abhá', 234, 236, 238
Yaḥyá, Mírzá, 5, 58, 77–8, 103, 153, 211, 233, 257, 286, 366, 417
attempts to take Bahá'u'lláh's life, 80–3, 417
Bábí sect associated with, 68
Bahá'u'lláh declares Himself to, 83–4
banished to Cyprus, 94–6
breaks the Covenant of the Báb, 61
children of, 96
claims to be 'Him Whom God shall make manifest', 84, 168
concealment of, 61–5, 67, 78–80
emerges from, 80
conduct during Bahá'u'lláh's absence in Kurdistán, 70–4
discredited in Adrianople, 93
discredits Bahá'u'lláh, 67
downfall of, foretold by St Paul, 93
fate of, described by Shoghi Effendi, 96, 251
historic relics of the Báb sent to, by Bahá'u'lláh, 85
letter-writing campaign against Bahá'u'lláh, 85–6, 89
murders perpetrated by, 72–3
nominated by the Báb, 59–64
poisons Bahá'u'lláh, 80–1
rebellion against Bahá'u'lláh, 89, 148
rumour circulated that *Kitáb-i-Íqán* was written by, 75–7
sends Mírzá Áqá Ján to assassinate the Shah, 181–2
Siyyid Muḥammad-i-Iṣfahání allies himself to, 67
son of, becomes a Bahá'í, 96
sows seeds of doubt in believers' minds, 67, 75
split between, and Bahá'u'lláh, 84–9
takes name Ḥáji 'Alíy-i-Las-Furush, 65
travels with Bahá'u'lláh to Istanbul, 77–9
wives of, 73, 79, 87, 96
writings of, 94
Yaḥyá Ṭábúr Áqásí, 188, 189, 198, 224, 227
Yazd, 216, 334, 339
upheaval in 1903, 231
Yazdi, Ahmad, 358, 363
Yazdi, Munavvar Khánum, 358, 363
Yazdigard, 54
'Year nine', 46–7, 48, 52
'Year nineteen', 47, 48
'Young Turk' Revolutionaries, 237
Youth, 306, 437–8
Yúnis Khán-i-Afrúkhtih, Dr, 178, 180, 259, 280
describes 'Abdu'l-Bahá's visits to the Shrine of Bahá'u'lláh, 186–7, 189–90
describes state of affairs in Haifa, 223–4, 225
notes concerning Mírzá Áqá Ján, 183–4, 186–8
recounts story of 'destitution' of Mírzá Muḥammad-'Alí, 194–6
reminiscences of 'Abdu'l-Bahá, 202–3, 204–7, 219–22, 233, 254, 257–8, 282

Zaman
Zayn'ul-Muqarrabin, Tablet to, 15, 75
Zion, 392, 402, 407
Zoroaster, 54
Zoroastrians, 311, 312, 371

www.ingramcontent.com/pod-product-compliance
Lightning Source LLC
Chambersburg PA
CBHW021752230426
43669CB00006B/57
* 9 7 8 0 8 5 3 9 8 3 4 4 6 *